INVESTMENT SCIENCE

INVESTMENT SCIENCE

DAVID G. LUENBERGER

STANFORD UNIVERSITY

New York   Oxford
OXFORD UNIVERSITY PRESS
1998

OXFORD UNIVERSITY PRESS

Oxford   New York
Athens   Auckland   Bangkok   Bogotá   Bombay   Buenos Aires
Calcutta   Cape Town   Dar es Salaam   Delhi
Florence   Hong Kong   Istanbul   Karachi
Kuala Lumpur   Madras   Madrid   Melbourne
Mexico City   Nairobi   Paris   Singapore
Taipei   Tokyo   Toronto

and associated companies in

Berlin   Ibadan

Published by Oxford University Press, Inc.,
198 Madison Avenue, New York, New York 10016

Oxford is a registered trademark of Oxford University Press

Library of Congress Cataloging-in-Publication Data
Luenberger, David G., 1937–
    Investment science   /   David G. Luenberger.
        p.   cm.
    Includes bibliographical references.
    ISBN 13 978-0-19-510809-5
    ISBN 0–19–510809–4
    1. Investments—Mathematical models. 2. Investment analysis–
–Mathematical models.   3. Cash flow—Mathematical models.
4. Interest rates—Mathematical models.   5. Derivative securities–
–Mathematical models.   I. Title.
HG4515.2.L84   1997   96–41158
                                                              CIP

17 19 20 18 16

Printed in the United States of America
on acid-free paper

To my students:
past, present, and future

CONTENTS

Part III   DERIVATIVE SECURITIES

Part IV GENERAL CASH FLOW STREAMS

PREFACE

Investment theory currently commands a high level of intellectual attention—fueled in part by some extraordinary theoretical developments in finance, by an explosive growth of information and computing technology, and by the global expansion of investment activity. Recent developments in investment theory are being infused into university classrooms, into financial service organizations, into business ventures, and into the awareness of many individual investors. This book is intended to be one instrument in that dissemination process.

The book endeavors to emphasize fundamental principles and to illustrate how these principles can be mastered and transformed into sound and practical solutions of actual investment problems. The book's organizational structure reflects this approach: the material covered in the chapters progresses from the simplest in concept to the more advanced. Particular financial products and investment problems are treated, for the most part, in the order that they fall along this line of conceptual progression, their analyses serving to illustrate concepts as well as to describe particular features of the investment environment.

The book is designed for individuals who have a technical background roughly equivalent to a bachelor's degree in engineering, mathematics, or science; or who have some familiarity with basic mathematics. The language of investment science is largely mathematical, and some aspects of the subject can be expressed only in mathematical terms. The mathematics used in this book, however, is not complex—for example, only elementary portions of calculus are required—but the reader must be comfortable with the use of mathematics as a method of deduction and problem solving. Such readers will be able to leverage their technical backgrounds to accelerate and deepen their study.

Actually, the book can be read at several levels, requiring different degrees of mathematical sophistication and having different scopes of study. A simple road map to these different levels is coded into the typography of the text. Some section and subsection titles are set with an ending star as, for example, "2.6 Applications and Extensions.*" The star indicates that the section or subsection is special: the material may be somewhat tangential or of higher mathematical level than elsewhere and can be skipped at first reading. This coding scheme is only approximate; the text itself often explains what is ahead in each section and gives guidelines on how the reader may wish to proceed.

The end-of-chapter exercises are an important part of the text, and readers should attempt several exercises in each chapter. The exercises are also coded: an exercise marked ◇ is mathematically more difficult than the average exercise; an exercise marked ⊕ requires numerical computation (usually with a spreadsheet program).

This text was influenced significantly by the existence of computer spreadsheet packages. Almost all the essential ideas of investment science—such as present value, portfolio immunization, cash matching, project optimization, factor models, risk-neutral valuation with binomial lattices, and simulation—can be illustrated easily with a spreadsheet package. This makes it possible to provide a variety of examples in the text that are state-of-the-art in terms of conceptual content. Furthermore, students can formulate and solve realistic and challenging investment problems using readily available software. This process deepens understanding by fully engaging the student in all aspects of the problem. Many students who have taken this course have said that they learned the most when completing the course projects (which are the more ambitious of the exercises marked ⊕).

It has been fun to write this book, partly because I received so much encouragement and help from colleagues and students. I especially wish to thank Graydon Barz, Kian Esteghamat, Charles Feinstein, Marius Holtan, Blake Johnson, Robert Maxfield, Paul McEntire, James Smith, Lucie Tepla, and Lauren Wang who all read substantial portions of the evolving manuscript and suggested improvements. The final version was improved by the insightful reviews of several individuals, including Joseph Cherian, Boston University; Phillip Daves, University of Tennessee; Jaime Cuevas Dermody, University of Strathclyde; Myron Gordon, University of Toronto; Robert Heinkel, University of British Columbia; James Hodder, University of Wisconsin; Raymond Kan, University of Toronto; Chris Lamoureux, University of Arizona; Duane Seppi, Carnegie Mellon University; Suresh Sethi, University of Toronto; Costas Skiadas, Northwestern University, and Jack Treynor, Treynor Capital Management, Inc.

I also wish to thank my wife Nancy for her encouragement and understanding of hours lost to my word processor. Finally, I wish to thank the many enthusiastic students who, by their classroom questions and dilligent work on the exercises and projects, provided important feedback as the manuscript took shape.

DAVID G. LUENBERGER
April 1997

1 INTRODUCTION

Traditionally, investment is defined as the current commitment of resources in order to achieve later benefits. If resources and benefits take the form of money, investment is the present commitment of money for the purpose of receiving (hopefully more) money later. In some cases, such as the purchase of a bank certificate of deposit, the amount of money to be obtained later is known exactly. However, in most situations the amount of money to be obtained later is uncertain.

There is also a broader viewpoint of investment—based on the idea of flows of expenditures and receipts spanning a period of time. From this viewpoint, the objective of investment is to tailor the pattern of these flows over time to be as desirable as possible. When expenditures and receipts are denominated in cash, the net receipts at any time period are termed **cash flow,** and the series of flows over several periods is termed a **cash flow stream.** The investment objective is that of tailoring this cash flow stream to be more desirable than it would be otherwise. For example, by taking out a loan, it may be possible to exchange a large negative cash flow next month for a series of smaller negative cash flows over several months, and this alternative cash flow stream may be preferred to the original one. Often future cash flows have a degree of uncertainty, and part of the design, or tailoring, of a cash flow stream may be concerned with controlling that uncertainty, perhaps reducing the level of risk. This broader definition of investment, as tailoring a pattern of cash flows, encompasses the wide assortment of financial activities more fully than the traditional view. It is this broader interpretation that guides the presentation of this book.

Investment science is the application of scientific tools to investments. The scientific tools used are primarily mathematical, but only a modest level of mathematics is required to understand the primary concepts discussed in this book. The purpose of this book is to convey both the principles of investment science and an understanding of how these principles can be used in practice to make calculations that lead to good investment decisions.

There is also an art to investment. Part of this art is knowing what to analyze and how to go about it. This part of the art can be enhanced by studying the material in this

1

book. However, there is also an intuitive art of being able to evaluate an investment from an assortment of qualitative information, such as the personality characteristics of the people involved (the principals), whether a proposed new product will sell well, and so forth. This part of the art is not treated explicitly in this book, although the reader will gain some appreciation for just what this art entails.

1.1 CASH FLOWS

According to the broad interpretation, an investment is defined in terms of its resulting cash flow sequence—the amounts of money that will flow to and from an investor over time. Usually these cash flows (either positive or negative) occur at known specific dates, such as at the end of each quarter of a year or at the end of each year. The stream can then be described by listing the flow at each of these times. This is simplest if the flows are known deterministically, as in bank interest receipts or mortgage payments. In such cases the stream can be described by a series of numbers. For example, if the basic time period is taken as one year, one possible stream over a year, from beginning to end, is $(-1, 1.2)$, corresponding to an initial payment (the investment) of $1 at the beginning of the year and the receipt of $1.20 a year later. An investment over four years might be $(-1, .10, .10, .10, 1.10)$, where an initial investment of $1 leads to payment of $.10 at the end of each year for three years and then a final payment of $1.10. Note that for a span of one year, two cash flow numbers are specified—one at the beginning and one at the end. Likewise, the four-year example involves five cash flow numbers.

Cash flow streams can also be represented in diagram form, as illustrated in Figure 1.1. In such a figure a time axis is drawn and a cash flow at a particular time is indicated by a vertical line at that time, the length of the line being proportional to the magnitude of the flow.

If the magnitudes of some future cash flows are uncertain (as is frequently the case), a more complex representation of a cash flow stream must be employed. There are a few different techniques for doing this, and they are presented later in the book. But whether or not uncertainty is present, investments are described in terms of cash flow streams.

A diversity of investment issues can be stated in terms of cash flow streams, such as the following: Which of two cash flow streams is most preferable? How much would I be willing to pay to own a given stream? Are two streams together worth more to me than the sum of their individual values? If I can purchase a share of a stream, how much should I purchase? Given a collection of available cash flow streams, what is the most favorable combination of them?

Time

FIGURE 1.1   Cash flow stream. The cash flow stream of an investment can be represented by a diagram. In the example shown, the cash flows occur periodically. The first of these flows is negative, representing a cash outlay, and the subsequent flows are all positive.

Other more complex questions also arise. For example, sometimes the timing of all cash flows is not fixed, but can be influenced by the investor. If I purchase stock in a company, I have a negative cash flow initially, corresponding to my purchase payment; while I hold the stock, I perhaps receive dividends (relatively small positive cash flows) on a regular basis; finally, when I sell the stock, I obtain a major cash flow. However, the time of the last cash flow is not predetermined; I am free to choose it. Indeed, investments sometimes can be actively managed to influence both the amounts and the timing of all cash flows. For example, if I purchase a gold mine as an investment, I can decide how to mine it and thereby influence the cash flow every year. Determination of suitable management strategies is also part of investment science.

The view of investment science as the tailoring of cash flow streams gives the subject wide application. For individuals it applies to personal investment decisions, such as deciding on a home mortgage or planning for retirement. It also applies to business decisions, such as whether to invest in product development, whether to build a new manufacturing plant, and how to manage cash resources. Finally, it applies to government decisions, such as whether to build a dam or change the tax rate. Investment science guides us in the process of combining stocks, bonds, and other investment products into an overall package that has desirable properties. This process enhances total productivity by converting projects that in isolation may be too risky into members of attractive combinations.

1.2 INVESTMENTS AND MARKETS

At its root, investment analysis is a process of examining alternatives and deciding which alternative is most preferable. In this respect investment analysis is similar to the analysis of other decisions—operating a production facility, designing a building, planning a trip, or formulating an advertising campaign. Indeed, much of investment science relies on the same general tools used for analysis of these other decisions.

Investment problems differ from other decision problems in an important respect, however: most investments are carried out within the framework of a financial market, and these markets provide alternatives not found in other decision situations. This structure is what makes investment analysis unique and unusually powerful.

The Comparison Principle

Financial markets simplify decision making through a concept that we term the **comparison principle.** To introduce this principle, consider the following hypothetical situation.

Your uncle offers you a special investment. If you give him $100 now, he will repay you $110 in one year. His repayment is fully guaranteed by a trust fund of U.S. Treasury securities, and hence there is virtually no risk to the investment. Also, there is no moral or personal obligation to make this investment. You can either accept the offer or not. What should you do?

To analyze this situation, you would certainly note that the investment offers 10% interest, and you could compare this rate with the prevailing rate of interest that can be obtained elsewhere, say, at your local bank or from the U.S. Government through, for example, a Treasury bill. If the prevailing interest rate were only 7%, you would probably invest in this special offer by your uncle (assuming you have the cash to invest). If on the other hand the prevailing interest rate were 12%, you would surely decline the offer. From a pure investment viewpoint you can evaluate this opportunity very easily without engaging in deep reflection or mathematical analysis. If the investment offers a rate above normal, you accept; if it offers a rate below normal, you decline.

This analysis is an example of the comparison principle. You evaluate the investment by comparing it with other investments available in the financial market. The financial market provides a basis for comparison.

If, on the other hand, your uncle offers to sell you a family portrait whose value is largely sentimental, an outside comparison is not available. You must decide whether, to you, the portrait is worth his asking price.

Arbitrage

When two similar investment alternatives are both available in the market, conclusions stronger than the comparison principle hold. For example, consider (idealized) banks that offer to loan money or accept deposits at the same rate of interest. Suppose that the rate used at one bank for loans and deposits is 10% and at another bank the rate is 12%. You could go to the first bank and borrow, say, $10,000 at 10% and then deposit that $10,000 in the second bank at 12%. In one year you would earn 2% of $10,000, which is $200, without investing any cash of your own. This is a form of **arbitrage**—earning money without investing anything. Presumably, you could even make more money by running your scheme at a higher level. It should be clear that this kind of thing does not occur—at least not very often. The interest rates in the two banks would soon equalize.

The example of the two banks assumed that the interest rate for loans and the interest rate paid for deposits were equal within any one bank. Generally, of course, there is a difference in these rates. However, in markets of high volume, such as the markets for U.S. Treasury securities, the difference between the buying price and the selling price is small. Therefore two different securities with identical properties must have approximately the same price—otherwise there would be an arbitrage opportunity.

Often it is assumed, for purposes of analysis, that no arbitrage opportunity exists. This is the **no-arbitrage** assumption.

Ruling out the possibility of arbitrage is a simple idea, but it has profound consequences. We shall find that the principle of no arbitrage implies that pricing relations are linear, that stock prices must satisfy certain relations, and that the prices of derivative securities, such as options and futures, can be determined analytically.

This one principle, based on the existence of well-developed markets, permeates a good portion of modern investment science.

Dynamics

Another important feature of financial markets is that they are dynamic, in the sense that the same or similar financial instruments are traded on a continuing basis. This means that the future price of an asset is not regarded as a single number, but rather as a process moving in time and subject to uncertainty. An important part of the analysis of an investment situation is the characterization of this process.

There are a few standard frameworks that are used to represent price processes. These include binomial lattice models, difference equation models, and differential equation models, all of which are discussed in this text. Typically, a record of the past prices and other information are used to specify the parameters of such a model.

Because markets are dynamic, investment is itself dynamic—the value of an investment changes with time, and the composition of good portfolios may change. Once this dynamic character is understood and formalized, it is possible to structure investments to take advantage of their dynamic nature so that the overall portfolio value increases rapidly.

Risk Aversion

Another principle of investment science is **risk aversion.** Suppose two possible investments have the same cost, and both are expected to return the same amount (somewhat greater than the initial cost), where the term *expected* is defined in a probabilistic sense (explained in Chapter 6). However, the return is certain for one of these investments and uncertain for the other. Individuals seeking investment rather than outright speculation will elect the first (certain) alternative over the second (risky) alternative. This is the risk aversion principle.

Another way to state this principle is in terms of market rates of return. Suppose one investment will pay a fixed return with certainty—say 10%—as obtained perhaps from a government-guaranteed bank certificate of deposit. A second investment, say the stock in a corporation, has an uncertain return. Then the expected rate of return on that stock must be greater than 10%; otherwise investors will not purchase the stock. In general, we accept more risk only if we expect to get greater expected (or average) return.

This risk aversion principle can be formalized (and made analytical) in a few different ways, which are discussed in later chapters. Once a formalism is established, the risk aversion principle can be used to help analyze many investment alternatives.

One way that the risk aversion principle is formalized is through **mean–variance analysis.** In this approach, the uncertainty of the return on an asset is characterized by just two quantities: the mean value of the return and the variance of the return. The risk aversion principle then says that if several investment opportunities have the same mean but different variances, a rational (risk-averse) investor will select the one that has the smallest variance.

This mean–variance method of formalizing risk is the basis for the most well-known method of quantitative portfolio analysis, which was pioneered by Harry Markowitz (who won the Nobel prize in economics for his work). This approach leads to a comprehensive theory of investment and is widely considered to be the foundation for modern portfolio theory. We discuss this important theory in Chapter 6.

A more general way to formalize the risk aversion principle is through the introduction of individual **utility functions.** This approach is presented in Chapter 9.

Later, in Chapter 15, we find that risk aversion takes on a new character when investments are made repeatedly over time. In fact, short-term variance will be found to be *good,* not bad. This is one of the surprising conclusions of the comprehensive view of investment represented by investment science.

1.3 TYPICAL INVESTMENT PROBLEMS

Every investment problem has unique features, but many fit into a few broad categories or types. We briefly outline some of the most important problem types here. Fuller descriptions of these general types and more specific examples appear in the relevant chapters.

Pricing

Let us go back to our very first example of an investment situation, the first offer from your uncle, but now let us turn it around. Imagine that there is an investment opportunity that will pay exactly $110 at the end of one year. We ask: How much is this investment worth today? In other words, what is the appropriate price of this investment, given the overall financial environment?

If the current interest rate for one-year investments is 10%, then this investment should have a price of exactly $100. In that case, the $110 paid at the end of the year would correspond to a rate of return of 10%. If the current interest rate for one-year investments is less than 10%, then the price of this investment would be somewhat greater than $100. In general, if the interest rate is r (expressed as a decimal, such as $r = .10$), then the price of an investment that pays X after one year should be $X/(1 + r)$.

We determined the price by a simple application of the comparison principle. This investment can be directly compared with one of investing money in a one-year certificate of deposit (or one-year Treasury bill), and hence it must bear the same effective interest rate.

This interest rate example is a simple example of the general pricing problem: Given an investment with known payoff characteristics (which may be random), what is the reasonable price; or, equivalently, what price is consistent with the other securities that are available? We shall encounter this problem in many contexts. For example, early in our study we shall determine the appropriate price of a bond. Later we shall compute the appropriate price of a share of stock with random return characteristics. Still later we shall compute suitable prices of more complicated securities, such as futures and options. Indeed, the pricing problem is one of the basic problems of modern investment science and has obvious practical applications.

As in the simple interest rate example, the pricing problem is usually solved by use of the comparison principle. In most instances, however, the application of that principle is not as simple and obvious as in this example. Clever arguments have been devised to show how a complex investment can be separated into parts, each of which can be compared with other investments whose prices are known. Nevertheless, whether by a simple or a complex argument, comparison is the basis for the solution of many pricing problems.

Hedging

Hedging is the process of reducing the financial risks that either arise in the course of normal business operations or are associated with investments. Hedging is one of the most important uses of financial markets, and is an essential part of modern industrial activity. One form of hedging is **insurance** where, by paying a fixed amount (a **premium**), you can protect yourself against certain specified possible losses—such as losses due to fire, theft, or even adverse price changes—by arranging to be paid compensation for the losses you incur. More general hedging can arise in the following way. Imagine a large bakery. This bakery will purchase flour (made from wheat) and other ingredients and transform these ingredients into baked goods, such as bread. Suppose the bakery wins a contract to supply a large quantity of bread to another company over the next year at a fixed price. The bakery is happy to win the contract, but now faces risk with respect to flour prices. The bakery will not immediately purchase all the flour needed to satisfy the contract, but will instead purchase flour as needed during the year. Therefore, if the price of flour should increase part way during the year, the bakery will be forced to pay more to satisfy the needs of the contract and, hence, will have a lower profit. In a sense the bakery is at the mercy of the flour market. If the flour price goes up, the bakery will make less profit, perhaps even losing money on the contract. If the flour price goes down, the bakery will make even more money than anticipated.

The bakery is in the baking business, not in the flour speculation business. It wants to eliminate the risk associated with flour costs and concentrate on baking. It can do this by obtaining an appropriate number of wheat futures contracts in the futures market. Such a contract has small initial cash outlay and at a set future date gives a profit (or loss) equal to the amount that wheat prices have changed since entering the contract. The price of flour is closely tied to the price of wheat, so if the price of flour should go up, the value of a wheat futures contract will go up by a somewhat comparable amount. Hence the net effect to the bakery—the profit from the wheat futures contracts together with the change in the cost of flour—is nearly zero.

There are many other examples of business risks that can be reduced by hedging. And there are many ways that hedging can be carried out: through futures contracts, options, and other special arrangements. Indeed, the major use, by far, of these financial instruments is for hedging—not for speculation.

Pure Investment

Pure investment refers to the objective of obtaining increased future return for present allocation of capital. This is the motivation underlying most individual investments in the stock market, for example. The investment problem arising from this motivation is referred to as the **portfolio selection problem,** since the real issue is to determine where to invest available capital.

Most approaches to the pure investment problem rely on the risk aversion principle, for in this problem one must carefully assess one's preferences, deciding how to balance risk and expected reward. There is not a unique solution. Judgment and taste are important, which is evidenced by the vast amount of literature and advice directed each year to helping individuals find solutions to this problem.

The pure investment problem also characterizes the activities of a profit-seeking firm which, after all, takes existing capital and transforms it, through investment—in equipment, people, and operations—into profit. Hence the methods developed for analyzing pure investment problems can be used to analyze potential projects within firms, the overall financial structure of a firm, and even mergers of firms.

Other Problems

Investment problems do not always take the special shapes outlined in the preceding categories. A hedging problem may contain an element of pure investment, and conversely an investment may be tempered with a degree of hedging. Fortunately, the same principles of analysis are applicable to such combinations.

One type of problem that occurs frequently is a combined consumption–investment problem. For example, a married couple at retirement, living off the income from their investments, will most likely invest differently than a young couple investing for growth of capital. The requirement for income changes the nature of the investment problem. Likewise, the management of an endowment for a public enterprise, such as a university must consider growth objectives as well as consumptionlike objectives associated with the current operations of the enterprise.

We shall also find that the framework of an investment problem is shaped by the formal methods used to treat it. Once we have logical methods for representing investment issues, new problems suggest themselves. As we progress through the book we shall uncover additional problems and obtain a deeper appreciation for the simple outlines given here.

1.4 ORGANIZATION OF THE BOOK

The organization of this book reflects the notion that investment science is the study of how to tailor cash flow streams. Indeed, the cash flow viewpoint leads to a natural partition of the subject into four main parts, as follows.

Deterministic Cash Flow Streams

The simplest cash flow streams are those that are deterministic (that is, not random, but definite). The first part of the book treats these. Such cash flows can be represented by sequences such as $(-1, 0, 3)$, as discussed earlier. Investments of this type, either with one or with several periods, are analyzed mainly with various concepts of interest rate. Accordingly, interest rate theory is emphasized in this first part of the book. This theory provides a basis for a fairly deep understanding of investment and a framework for addressing a wide variety of important and interesting problems.

Single-Period Random Cash Flow Streams

The second level of complexity in cash flow streams is associated with streams having only a single period, with beginning and ending flows, but with the magnitude of the second flow being uncertain. Such a situation occurs when a stock is purchased at the beginning of the year and sold at the end of the year. The amount received at the end of the year is not known in advance and, hence, must be considered uncertain. This level of complexity captures the essence of many investment situations.

In order to analyze cash flows of this kind, one must have a formal description of **uncertain returns.** There are several such descriptions (all based on probability theory), and we shall study the main ones, the simplest being the **mean–variance** description. One must also have a formal description of how individuals assess uncertain returns. We shall consider such assessment methods, starting with mean–variance analysis. These single-period uncertain cash flow situations are the subject of the second part of the book.

Derivative Assets

The third level of complexity in cash flow streams involves streams that have random flows at each of several time points, but where the asset producing a stream is functionally related to another asset whose price characteristics are known.

An asset whose cash flow values depend functionally on another asset is termed a **derivative asset.** A good example is a stock option. To describe such an option, suppose that I own 100 shares of stock in company A. This asset, the 100 shares, is a **basic asset.** Now suppose that I have granted you the right (but not the obligation) to buy, at say $54 per share, all 100 of my shares in three months. This right is a call option on 100 shares of stock in company A. This option is an asset; it has value, and that value may change with time. It is, however, a derivative of the stock of company A because the value of the option depends on the price of the stock. If the stock price goes up, the option value also goes up. Other derivative assets include futures contracts, other kinds of options, and various other financial contracts. One example seen by many home buyers is the adjustable-rate mortgage, which periodically adjusts interest payments according to an interest rate index. Such a mortgage is a derivative of the securities that determine the interest rate index.

The third part of the book is devoted to these derivative assets. Analysis of these assets is often simpler than that for assets with general multiperiod uncertain cash flows because properties of a derivative can be traced back to the underlying basic asset. The study of derivative assets, however, is an important and lively aspect of investment science, one for which strong theoretical results can be derived and important numerical quantities, such as implied prices, can be obtained.

General Cash Flow Streams

Finally, the fourth part of the book is devoted to cash flow streams with uncertain cash flows at many different times—flows that are not functionally related to other assets. As can be expected, this final level of complexity is the most difficult part of the subject, but also the one that is the most important. The cash flow streams encountered in most investments have this general form.

The methods of this part of the book build on those of earlier parts, but new concepts are added. The fact that the mix of investments—the portfolio structure—can be changed as time progresses, depending on what has happened to that point, leads to new phenomena and new opportunities. For example, the growth rate of a portfolio can be enhanced by employing suitable reinvestment strategies. This part of the book represents some of the newest aspects of the field.

Investment science is a practical science; and because its main core is built on a few simple principles, it can be easily learned and fruitfully applied to interesting and important problems. It is also an evolving science, which is expanding rapidly. Perhaps the reader, armed with a basic understanding of the field, will contribute to this evolution through either theory or application.

PART I

DETERMINISTIC CASH FLOW STREAMS

2 THE BASIC THEORY OF INTEREST

Interest is frequently called *the time value of money,* and the next few chapters explore the structure and implications of this value. In this first chapter on the subject, we outline the basic elements of interest rate theory, showing that the theory can be translated into analytic form and thus used as a basis for making intelligent investment decisions.

2.1 PRINCIPAL AND INTEREST

The basic idea of interest is quite familiar. If you invest $1.00 in a bank account that pays 8% interest per year, then at the end of 1 year you will have in your account the **principal** (your original amount) of $1.00 plus **interest** of $.08 for a total of $1.08. If you invest a larger amount, say A dollars, then at the end of the year your account will have grown to $A \times 1.08$ dollars. In general, if the interest rate is r, expressed as a decimal, then your initial investment would be multiplied by $(1 + r)$ after 1 year.

Simple Interest

Under a **simple interest** rule, money invested for a period different from 1 year accumulates interest proportional to the total time of the investment. So after 2 years, the total interest due is $2r$ times the original investment, and so forth. In other words, the investment produces interest equal to r times the original investment every year. Usually partial years are treated in a proportional manner; that is, after a fraction f of 1 year, interest of rf times the original investment is earned.

The general rule for simple interest is that if an amount A is left in an account at simple interest r, the total value after n years is

$$V = (1 + rn)A.$$

If the proportional rule holds for fractional years, then after any time t (measured in years), the account value is

$$V = (1 + rt)A.$$

13

The account grows **linearly** with time. As shown in the preceding formula, the account value at any time is just the sum of the original amount (the principal) and the accumulated interest, which is proportional to time.

Compound Interest

Most bank accounts and loans employ some form of compounding—producing compound interest. Again, consider an account that pays interest at a rate of r per year. If interest is compounded yearly, then after 1 year, the first year's interest is added to the original principal to define a larger principal base for the second year. Thus during the second year, the account earns *interest on interest*. This is the compounding effect, which is continued year after year.

Under yearly compounding, money left in an account is multiplied by $(1 + r)$ after 1 year. After the second year, it grows by another factor of $(1 + r)$ to $(1 + r)^2$. After n years, such an account will grow to $(1 + r)^n$ times its original value, and this is the analytic expression for the account growth under **compound interest.** This expression is said to exhibit **geometric growth** because of its nth-power form.

As n increases, the growth due to compounding can be substantial. For example, Figure 2.1 shows a graph of a $100 investment over time when it earns 10% interest under simple and compound interest rules. The figure shows the characteristic shapes of linear growth for simple interest and of accelerated upward growth for compound interest. Note that under compounding, the value doubles in about 7 years.

There is a cute little rule that can be used to estimate the effect of interest compounding.

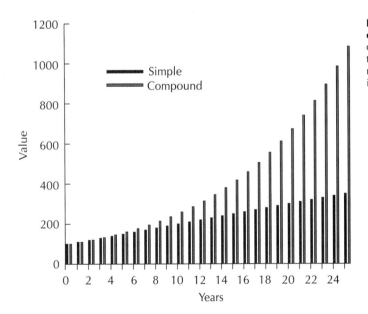

FIGURE 2.1   Simple and compound interest. Simple interest leads to linear growth over time, whereas compound interest leads to an accelerated increase defined by geometric growth. The figure shows both cases for an interest rate of 10%.

The seven–ten rule *Money invested at 7% per year doubles in approximately 10 years. Also, money invested at 10% per year doubles in approximately 7 years.*

(More exactly, at 7% and 10 years, an account increases by a factor of 1.97, whereas at 10% and 7 years it increases by a factor of 1.95.) The rule can be generalized, and slightly improved, to state that, for interest rates less than about 20%, the doubling time is approximately $72/i$, where i is the interest rate expressed as a percentage (that is, 10% interest corresponds to $i = 10$). (See Exercise 2.)

Compounding at Various Intervals

In the preceding discussion, interest was calculated at the end of each year and paid to the account at that time. Most banks now calculate and pay interest more frequently—quarterly, monthly, or in some cases daily. This more frequent compounding raises the effective yearly rate. In this situation, it is traditional to still quote the interest rate on a yearly basis, but then apply the appropriate proportion of that interest rate over each compounding period. For example, consider quarterly compounding. Quarterly compounding at an interest rate of r per year means that an interest rate of $r/4$ is applied every quarter. Hence money left in the bank for 1 quarter will grow by a factor of $1 + (r/4)$ during that quarter. If the money is left in for another quarter, then that new amount will grow by another factor of $1 + (r/4)$. After 1 year the account will have grown by the compound factor of $[1 + (r/4)]^4$. For any $r > 0$, it holds that $[1 + (r/4)]^4 > 1 + r$. Hence at the same annual rate, the amount in the bank account after 4 quarters of compounding is greater than the amount after 1 year without compounding.

The effect of compounding on yearly growth is highlighted by stating an **effective interest rate,** which is the equivalent yearly interest rate that would produce the same result after 1 year without compounding. For example, an annual rate of 8% compounded quarterly will produce an increase of $(1.02)^4 = 1.0824$; hence the effective interest rate is 8.24%. The basic yearly rate (8% in this example) is termed the **nominal rate.**

Compounding can be carried out with any frequency. The general method is that a year is divided into a fixed number of equally spaced periods—say m periods. (In the case of monthly compounding the periods are not quite equal, but we shall ignore that here and regard monthly compounding as simply setting $m = 12$.) The interest rate for each of the m periods is thus r/m, where r is the nominal annual rate. The account grows by $1 + (r/m)$ during 1 period. After k periods, the growth is $[1 + (r/m)]^k$, and hence after a full year of m periods it is $[1 + (r/m)]^m$. The effective interest rate is the number r' that satisfies $1 + r' = [1 + (r/m)]^m$.

Continuous Compounding

We can imagine dividing the year into smaller and smaller periods, and thereby apply compounding monthly, weekly, daily, or even every minute or second. This leads

TABLE 2.1
Continuous Compounding

	Interest rate (%)							
Nominal	1.00	5.00	10.00	20.00	30.00	50.00	75.00	100.00
Effective	1.01	5.13	10.52	22.14	34.99	64.87	111.70	171.83

The nominal interest rates in the top row correspond, under continuous compounding, to the effective rates shown in the second row. The increase due to compounding is quite dramatic at large nominal rates.

to the idea of continuous compounding. We can determine the effect of continuous compounding by considering the limit of ordinary compounding as the number m of periods in a year goes to infinity. To determine the yearly effect of this continuous compounding we use the fact that

$$\lim_{m \to \infty} [1 + (r/m)]^m = e^r$$

where $e = 2.7818...$ is the base of the natural logarithm. The effective rate of interest r' is the value satisfying $1 + r' = e^r$. If the nominal interest rate is 8% per year, then with continuous compounding the growth would be $e^{.08} = 1.0833$, and hence the effective interest rate is 8.33%. (Recall that quarterly compounding produces an effective rate of 8.24%.) Table 2.1 shows the effect of continuous compounding for various nominal rates. Note that as the nominal rate increases, the compounding effect becomes more dramatic.

We can also calculate how much an account will have grown after any arbitrary length of time. We denote time by the variable t, measured in years. Thus $t = 1$ corresponds to 1 year, and $t = .25$ corresponds to 3 months. Select a time t and divide the year into a (large) number m of small periods, each of length $1/m$. Then $t \simeq k/m$ for some k, meaning that k periods approximately coincides with the time t. If m is very large, this approximation can be made very accurate. Therefore $k \approx mt$. Using the general formula for compounding, we know that the growth factor for k periods is

$$[1 + (r/m)]^k = [1 + (r/m)]^{mt} = \left\{[1 + (r/m)]^m\right\}^t \to e^{rt}$$

where that last expression is valid in the limit as m goes to infinity, corresponding to continuous compounding. Hence continuous compounding leads to the familiar **exponential growth** curve. Such a curve is shown in Figure 2.2 for a 10% nominal interest rate.

Debt

We have examined how a single investment (say a bank deposit) grows over time due to interest compounding. It should be clear that exactly the same thing happens to debt. If I *borrow* money from the bank at an interest rate r and make no payments to the bank, then my debt increases according to the same formulas. Specifically, if my debt is compounded monthly, then after k months my debt will have grown by a factor of $[1 + (r/12)]^k$.

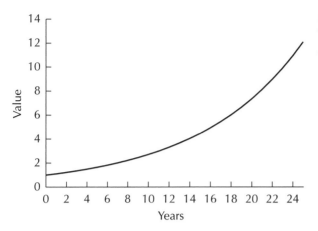

FIGURE 2.2 Exponential growth curve; continuous compound growth. Under continuous compounding at 10%, the value of $1 doubles in about 7 years. In 20 years it grows by a factor of about 8.

Money Markets

Although we have treated interest as a given known value, in reality there are many different rates each day. Different rates apply to different circumstances, different user classes, and different periods. Most rates are established by the forces of supply and demand in broad markets to which they apply. These rates are published widely; a sampling for one day is shown in Table 2.2. Many of these market rates are discussed

TABLE 2.2
Market Interest Rates

Interest rates (August 9, 1995)	
U.S. Treasury bills and notes	
3-month bill	5.39
6-month bill	5.39
1-year bill	5.36
3-year note (% yield)	6.05
10-year note (% yield)	6.49
30-year bond (% yield)	6.92
Fed funds rate	5.6875
Discount rate	5.26
Prime rate	8.75
Commercial paper	5.84
Certificates of deposit	
1 month	5.17
2 months	5.24
1 year	5.28
Banker's acceptances (30 days)	5.68
London late Eurodollars (1 month)	5.75
London Interbank offered rate (1 month)	5.88
Federal Home Loan Mortgage Corp. (Freddie Mae) (30 years)	7.94

Many different rates apply on any given day. This is a sampling.

more fully in Chapters 3 and 4. Not all interest rates are broad market rates. There may be private rates negotiated by two private parties. Or in the context of a firm, special rates may be established for internal transactions or for the purpose of evaluating projects, as discussed later in this chapter.

2.2 PRESENT VALUE

The theme of the previous section is that money invested today leads to increased value in the future as a result of interest. The formulas of the previous section show how to determine this future value.

That whole set of concepts and formulas can be reversed in time to calculate the value that should be assigned now, in the present, to money that is to be received at a later time. This reversal is the essence of the extremely important concept of **present value.**

To introduce this concept, consider two situations: (1) you will receive $110 in 1 year, (2) you receive $100 now and deposit it in a bank account for 1 year at 10% interest. Clearly these situations are identical after 1 year—you will receive $110. We can restate this equivalence by saying that $110 received in 1 year is equivalent to the receipt of $100 now when the interest rate is 10%. Or we say that the $110 to be received in 1 year has a **present value** of $100. In general, $1 to be received a year in the future has a present value of $1/(1+r)$, where r is the interest rate.

A similar transformation applies to future obligations such as the repayment of debt. Suppose that, for some reason, you have an obligation to pay someone $100 in exactly 1 year. This obligation can be regarded as a negative cash flow that occurs at the end of the year. To calculate the present value of this obligation, you determine how much money you would need *now* in order to cover the obligation. This is easy to determine. If the current yearly interest rate is r, you need $100/(1+r)$. If that amount of money is deposited in the bank now, it will grow to $100 at the end of the year. You can then fully meet the obligation. The present value of the obligation is therefore $100/(1+r)$.

The process of evaluating future obligations as an equivalent present value is alternatively referred to as **discounting.** The present value of a future monetary amount is less than the face value of that amount, so the future value must be discounted to obtain the present value. The factor by which the future value must be discounted is called the **discount factor.** The 1-year discount factor is $d_1 = 1/(1+r)$, where r is the 1-year interest rate. So if an amount A is to be received in 1 year, the present value is the discounted amount $d_1 A$.

The formula for present value depends on the interest rate that is available from a bank or other source. If that source quotes rates with compounding, then such a compound interest rate should be used in the calculation of present value. As an example, suppose that the annual interest rate r is compounded at the end of each of m equal periods each year; and suppose that a cash payment of amount A will be received at the end of the kth period. Then the appropriate discount factor is

$$d_k = \frac{1}{[1 + (r/m)]^k} \, .$$

The present value of a payment of A to be received k periods in the future is $d_k A$.

2.3 PRESENT AND FUTURE VALUES OF STREAMS

The previous section studied the impact of interest on a single cash deposit or loan; that is, on a single cash flow. We now extend that discussion to the case where cash flows occur at several time periods, and hence constitute a cash flow stream or sequence. First we require a new concept.

The Ideal Bank

When discussing cash flow streams, it is useful to define the notion of an **ideal bank.** An ideal bank applies the same rate of interest to both deposits and loans, and it has no service charges or transactions fees. Its interest rate applies equally to any size of principal, from 1 cent (or fraction thereof) to $1 million (or even more). Furthermore, separate transactions in an account are completely additive in their effect on future balances.

Note that the definition of an ideal bank does *not* imply that interest rates for all transactions are identical. For example, a 2-year certificate of deposit (CD) might offer a higher rate than a 1-year CD. However, the 2-year CD must offer the same rate as a loan that is payable in 2 years.

If an ideal bank has an interest rate that is independent of the length of time for which it applies, and that interest is compounded according to normal rules, it is said to be a **constant ideal bank.** In the rest of this chapter, we always assume that interest rates are indeed constant.

The constant ideal bank is the reference point used to describe the outside financial market—the public market for money.

Future Value

Now we return to the study of cash flow streams. Let us decide on a fixed time cycle for compounding (for example, yearly) and let a period be the length of this cycle. We assume that cash flows occur at the end of each period (although some flows might be zero). We shall take each cash flow and deposit it in a constant ideal bank as it arrives. (If the flow is negative, we cover it by taking out a loan.) Under the terms of a constant ideal bank, the final balance in our account can be found by combining the results of the individual flows. Explicitly, consider the cash flow stream $(x_0, x_1, \ldots, x_n)$. At the end of n periods the initial cash flow x_0 will have grown to $x_0(1+r)^n$, where r is the interest rate *per period* (which is the yearly rate divided by the number of periods per year). The next cash flow, x_1, received after the first period, will at the final time have been in the account for only $n-1$ periods, and hence it will have a value of $x_1(1+r)^{n-1}$. Likewise, the next flow x_2 will collect interest during $n-2$ periods and have value $x_2(1+r)^{n-2}$. The final flow x_n will not collect any interest, so will remain x_n. The total value at the end of n periods is therefore $FV = x_0(1+r)^n + x_1(1+r)^{n-1} + \cdots + x_n$. To summarize:

Future value of a stream   *Given a cash flow stream $(x_0, x_1, \ldots, x_n)$ and interest rate r each period, the future value of the stream is*

$$FV = x_0(1+r)^n + x_1(1+r)^{n-1} + \cdots + x_n .$$

Example 2.1 (A short stream)   Consider the cash flow stream $(-2, 1, 1, 1)$ when the periods are years and the interest rate is 10%. The future value is

$$FV = -2 \times (1.1)^3 + 1 \times (1.1)^2 + 1 \times 1.1 + 1 = .648 . \tag{2.1}$$

This formula for future value always uses the interest rate per period and assumes that interest rates are compounded each period.

Present Value

The present value of a general cash flow stream—like the future value—can also be calculated by considering each flow element separately. Again consider the stream $(x_0, x_1, \ldots, x_n)$. The present value of the first element x_0 is just that value itself since no discounting is necessary. The present value of the flow x_1 is $x_1/(1+r)$, because that flow must be discounted by one period. (Again the interest rate r is the per-period rate.) Continuing in this way, we find that the present value of the entire stream is $PV = x_0 + x_1/(1+r) + x_2/(1+r)^2 + \cdots + x_n/(1+r)^n$. We summarize this important result as follows.

Present value of a stream   *Given a cash flow stream $(x_0, x_1, \ldots, x_n)$ and an interest rate r per period, the present value of this cash flow stream is*

$$PV = x_0 + \frac{x_1}{1+r} + \frac{x_2}{(1+r)^2} + \cdots + \frac{x_n}{(1+r)^n} . \tag{2.2}$$

Example 2.2   Again consider the cash flow stream $(-2, 1, 1, 1)$. Using an interest rate of 10% we have

$$PV = -2 + \frac{1}{1.1} + \frac{1}{(1.1)^2} + \frac{1}{(1.1)^3} = .487 .$$

The present value of a cash flow stream can be regarded as the present payment amount that is equivalent to the entire stream. Thus we can think of the entire stream as being replaced by a single flow at the initial time.

There is another way to interpret the formula for present value that is based on transforming the formula for future value. Future value is the amount of future payment that is equivalent to the entire stream. We can think of the stream as being transformed into that single cash flow at period n. The present value of this single equivalent flow is obtained by discounting it by $(1+r)^n$. That is, the present value and the future value are related by

$$PV = \frac{FV}{(1+r)^n}.$$

In the previous examples for the cash flow stream $(-2, 1, 1, 1)$ we have $.487 = PV = FV/(1.1)^3 = .648/1.331 = .487$.

Frequent and Continuous Compounding

Suppose that r is the nominal annual interest rate and interest is compounded at m equally spaced periods per year. Suppose that cash flows occur initially and at the end of each period for a total of n periods, forming a stream $(x_0, x_1, \ldots, x_n)$. Then according to the preceding we have

$$PV = \sum_{k=0}^{n} \frac{x_k}{[1 + (r/m)]^k}.$$

Suppose now that the nominal interest rate r is compounded continuously and cash flows occur at times $t_0, t_1, \ldots, t_n$. (We have $t_k = k/m$ for the stream in the previous paragraph; but the more general situation is allowed here.) We denote the cash flow at time t_k by $x(t_k)$. In that case,

$$PV = \sum_{k=0}^{n} x(t_k)e^{-rt_k}.$$

This is the continuous compounding formula for present value.

Present Value and an Ideal Bank

We know that an ideal bank can be used to change the pattern of a cash flow stream. For example, a 10% bank can change the stream $(1, 0, 0)$ into the stream $(0, 0, 1.21)$ by receiving a deposit of $1 now and paying principal and interest of $1.21 in 2 years. The bank can also work in a reverse fashion and transform the second stream into the first by issuing a loan for $1 now.

In general, if an ideal bank can transform the stream $(x_0, x_1, \ldots, x_n)$ into the stream $(y_0, y_1, \ldots, y_n)$, it can also transform in the reverse direction. Two streams that can be transformed into each other are said to be **equivalent streams.**

How can we tell whether two given streams are equivalent? The answer to this is the main theorem on present value.

Main theorem on present value *The cash flow streams* $\mathbf{x} = (x_0, x_1, \ldots, x_n)$ *and* $\mathbf{y} = (y_0, y_1, \ldots, y_n)$ *are equivalent for a constant ideal bank with interest rate* r *if and only if the present values of the two streams, evaluated at the bank's interest rate, are equal.*

> ***Proof:*** Let $v_\mathbf{x}$ and $v_\mathbf{y}$ be the present values of the $\mathbf{x}$ and $\mathbf{y}$ streams, respectively. Then the $\mathbf{x}$ stream is equivalent to the stream $(v_\mathbf{x}, 0, 0, \ldots, 0)$ and the $\mathbf{y}$ stream is equivalent to the stream $(v_\mathbf{y}, 0, 0, \ldots, 0)$.
>
> It is clear that these two streams are equivalent if and only if $v_\mathbf{x} = v_\mathbf{y}$. Hence the original streams are equivalent if and only if $v_\mathbf{x} = v_\mathbf{y}$. ∎

This result is important because it implies that present value is the only number needed to characterize a cash flow stream when an ideal bank is available. The stream can be transformed in a variety of ways by the bank, but the present value remains the same. So if someone offers you a cash flow stream, you only need to evaluate its corresponding present value, because you can then use the bank to tailor the stream with that present value to any shape you desire.

2.4 INTERNAL RATE OF RETURN

Internal rate of return is another important concept of cash flow analysis. It pertains specifically to the entire cash flow stream associated with an investment, not to a partial stream such as a cash flow at a single period. The streams to which this concept is applied typically have both negative and positive elements: the negative flows correspond to the payments that must be made; the positive flows to payments received. A simple example is the process of investing in a certificate of deposit for a fixed period of 1 year. Here there are two cash flow elements: the initial deposit or payment (a negative flow) and the final redemption (a positive flow).

Given a cash flow stream $(x_0, x_1, \ldots, x_n)$ associated with an investment, we write the present value formula

$$\mathrm{PV} = \sum_{k=0}^{n} \frac{x_k}{(1+r)^k}.$$

If the investment that corresponds to this stream is constructed from a series of deposits and withdrawals from a constant ideal bank at interest rate r, then from the main theorem on present value of the previous section, PV would be zero. The idea behind internal rate of return is to turn the procedure around. Given a cash flow stream, we write the expression for present value and then find the value of r that renders this present value equal to zero. That value is called the internal rate of return because it is the interest rate implied by the internal structure of the cash flow stream. The idea can be applied to any series of cash flows.

The preliminary formal definition of the internal rate of return (IRR) is as follows:

Internal rate of return   *Let $(x_0, x_1, x_2, \ldots, x_n)$ be a cash flow stream. Then the internal rate of return of this stream is a number r satisfying the equation*

$$0 = x_0 + \frac{x_1}{1+r} + \frac{x_2}{(1+r)^2} + \cdots + \frac{x_n}{(1+r)^n}. \tag{2.3}$$

Equivalently, it is a number r satisfying $1/(1+r) = c$ [that is, $r = (1/c) - 1$], where c satisfies the polynomial equation

$$0 = x_0 + x_1 c + x_2 c^2 + \cdots + x_n c^n. \tag{2.4}$$

We call this a preliminary definition because there may be ambiguity in the solution of the polynomial equation of degree n. We discuss this point shortly. First, however, let us illustrate the computation of the internal rate of return.

Example 2.3 (The old stream)   Consider again the cash flow sequence $(-2, 1, 1, 1)$ discussed earlier. The internal rate of return is found by solving the equation

$$0 = -2 + c + c^2 + c^3.$$

The solution can be found (by trial and error) to be $c = .81$, and thus IRR $= (1/c) - 1 = .23$.

Notice that the internal rate of return is defined without reference to a prevailing interest rate. It is determined entirely by the cash flows of the stream. This is the reason why it is called the *internal* rate of return; it is defined internally without reference to the external financial world. It is the rate that an ideal bank would have to apply to generate the given stream from an initial balance of zero.

As pointed out, equation (2.4) for the internal rate of return is a polynomial equation in c of degree n, which does not, in general, have an analytic solution. However, it is almost always easy to solve the equation with a computer. From algebraic theory it is known that such an equation always has at least one root, and may have as many as n roots, but some or all of these roots may be complex numbers. Fortunately the most common form of investment, where there is an initial cash outlay followed by several positive flows, leads to a unique positive solution. Hence the internal rate of return is then well defined and relatively easy to calculate. (See Exercise 4.) The formal statement of the existence of the positive root embodies the main result concerning the internal rate of return.

What nonsense!

Main theorem of internal rate of return   *Suppose the cash flow stream $(x_0, x_1, \ldots, x_n)$ has $x_0 < 0$ and $x_k \geq 0$ for all k, $k = 1, 2, \ldots, n$, with at least one term being*

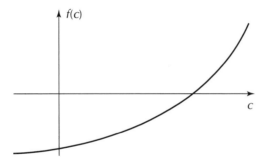

FIGURE 2.3   Function for proof. If $x_0 < 0$ and $x_k \geq 0$ for all k, $1 \leq k \leq n$, with at least one term being strictly positive, then the function $f(c)$ will start below the horizontal axis and increase monotonically as c increases. Therefore there must be a unique positive solution c satisfying $f(c) = 0$.

strictly positive. Then there is a unique positive root to the equation

$$0 = x_0 + x_1 c + x_2 c^2 + \cdots + x_n c^n .$$

Furthermore, if $\sum_{k=0}^{n} x_k > 0$ (meaning that the total amount returned exceeds the initial investment), then the corresponding internal rate of return $r = (1/c) - 1$ is positive.

Proof: We plot the function $f(c) = x_0 + x_1 c + x_2 c^2 + \cdots + x_n c^n$, as shown in Figure 2.3. Note that $f(0) < 0$. However, as c increases, the value of $f(c)$ also increases, since at least one of the cash flow terms is strictly positive. Indeed, it increases without limit as c increases to infinity. Since the function is continuous, it must cross the axis at some value of c. It cannot cross more than once, because it is strictly increasing. Hence there is a unique real value c_0, which is positive, for which $f(c_0) = 0$.

If $\sum_{k=0}^{n} x_k > 0$, which means that there is a net positive (nondiscounted) cash flow, then $f(1) > 0$. This means that the solution c_0 satisfying $f(c_0) = 0$ must be less than 1. Therefore $r_0 = (1/c_0) - 1 > 0$, where r_0 is the internal rate of return. ∎

If some (or all) solutions to the equation for internal rate of return are complex, the interpretation of these values is not simple. In general it is reasonable to select the solution that has the largest real part and use that real part to determine the internal rate of return. In practice, however, this is not often a serious issue, since suitable real roots typically exist.

2.5 EVALUATION CRITERIA

The essence of investment is selection from a number of alternative cash flow streams. In order to do this intelligently, the alternative cash flow streams must be evaluated according to a logical and standard criterion. Several different criteria are used in practice, but the two most important methods are those based on present value and on internal rate of return.

Net Present Value

Present value evaluates alternatives by simply ranking them according to their present values—the higher the present value, the more desirable the alternative. When one uses present value this way, one must include *all* cash flows associated with the investment, both positive and negative. To emphasize that, the expression **net present value** (NPV) is frequently used. Net present value is the present value of the benefits minus the present value of the costs. Often, to emphasize this partition of benefits and costs, the terms **present worth of benefits** and **present worth of costs** are used, both of which are just present values. Net present value is the difference between these two terms. To be worthy of consideration, the cash flow stream associated with an investment must have a positive net present value.

Example 2.4 (When to cut a tree) Suppose that you have the opportunity to plant trees that later can be sold for lumber. This project requires an initial outlay of money in order to purchase and plant the seedlings. No other cash flow occurs until the trees are harvested. However, you have a choice as to when to harvest: after 1 year or after 2 years. If you harvest after 1 year, you get your return quickly; but if you wait an additional year, the trees will have additional growth and the revenue generated from the sale of the trees will be greater.

We assume that the cash flow streams associated with these two alternatives are

(a) $(-1, 2)$ cut early

(b) $(-1, 0, 3)$ cut later.

We also assume that the prevailing interest rate is 10%. Then the associated net present values are

(a) NPV $= -1 + 2/1.1 = .82$

(b) NPV $= -1 + 3/(1.1)^2 = 1.48$.

Hence according to the net present value criterion, it is best to cut later.

The net present value criterion is quite compelling, and indeed it is generally regarded as the single best measure of an investment's merit. It has the special advantage that the present values of different investments can be added together to obtain a meaningful composite. This is because the present value of a sum of cash flow streams is equal to the sum of the present values of the corresponding cash flows. Note, for example, that we were able to compare the two investment alternatives associated with tree farming even though the cash flows were at different times. In general, an investor can compute the present value of individual investments and also the present value of an entire portfolio.

Internal Rate of Return

Internal rate of return can also be used to rank alternative cash flow streams. The rule is simply this: the higher the internal rate of return, the more desirable the investment. However, a potential investment, or project, is presumably not worth considering unless its internal rate of return is greater than the prevailing interest rate. If the internal rate of return is greater than the prevailing interest rate, the investment is considered better than what is available externally in the financial market.

Example 2.5 (When to cut a tree, continued)   Let us use the internal rate of return method to evaluate the two tree harvesting proposals considered in Example 2.4. The equations for the internal rate of return in the two cases are

(a) $-1 + 2c = 0$

(b) $-1 + 3c^2 = 0.$

As usual, $c = 1/(1 + r)$. These have the following solutions:

(a) $c = \dfrac{1}{2} = \dfrac{1}{1+r};$ $r = 1.0$

(b) $c = \dfrac{\sqrt{3}}{3} = \dfrac{1}{1+r};$ $r = \sqrt{3} - 1 \approx .7.$

In other words, for (a), cut early, the internal rate of return is 100%, whereas for (b) it is about 70%. Hence under the internal rate of return criterion, the best alternative is (a). Note that this is opposite to the conclusion obtained from the net present value criterion.

Discussion of the Criteria

There is considerable debate as to which of the two criteria, net present value or internal rate of return, is the most appropriate for investment evaluation. Both have attractive features, and both have limitations. (As shown, they can even give conflicting recommendations.) Net present value is simplest to compute; it does not have the ambiguity associated with the several possible roots of the internal rate of return equation. Also net present value can be broken into component pieces, unlike internal rate of return. However, internal rate of return has the advantage that it depends only on the properties of the cash flow stream, and not on the prevailing interest rate (which in practice may not be easily defined). In fact, the two methods both have appropriate roles, but in different situations.

The primary difference between the two criteria can be explained in terms of the "when to cut a tree" example. We must look beyond the single cycle of tree farming to a series of cycles. Suppose that the proceeds of the first harvest are used to plant additional trees, starting a long series of expansion in the tree farming business. Under plan (*a*), cut early, the business can be doubled every year because the revenue received at the end of the year is twice that required at the beginning. In plan (*b*), cut later, the business can be tripled every 2 years by the same reasoning. Tripling every 2 years is equivalent, in the long run, to increasing by a factor of $\sqrt{3}$ every year. The yearly growth rates of these two plans, factors of 2 and $\sqrt{3}$, respectively, are each equal to 1 plus the internal rates of return of the plans—and this equality is true in general. So in this kind of situation, where the proceeds of the investment can be repeatedly reinvested in the same type of project but scaled in size, it makes sense to select the project with the largest internal rate of return—in order to get the greatest growth of capital.

On the other hand, suppose that this investment is a one-time opportunity and cannot be repeated. Here the net present value method is the appropriate criterion, since it compares the investment with what could be obtained through normal channels (which offer the prevailing rate of interest).

It is widely agreed (by theorists, but not necessarily by practitioners) that, overall, the best criterion is that based on net present value. If used intelligently, it will provide consistency and rationality. In the case of cutting the trees, for example, an enlightened present value analysis will agree with the result obtained by the internal rate of return criterion. If the two possible futures are developed fully, corresponding to the two cutting policies, the present value criterion, applied to the long series of expanding cash flows, would also direct that plan (*a*) be adopted.

There are many other factors that influence a good present value analysis—and perhaps make such an analysis more complex than suggested by the direct formal statement of the criterion. One significant issue is the selection of the interest rate to be used in the calculation. In practice, there are several different "risk-free" rates of interest in the financial market: the rate paid by bank certificates of deposit, the 3-month U.S. Treasury bill rate, and the rate paid by the highest grade commercial bonds are examples. Furthermore, the rates for borrowing are typically slightly higher than those for lending. The difference between all these choices can be several percentage points. In business decisions it is common to use a figure called the **cost of capital** as the baseline rate. This figure is the rate of return that the company must offer to potential investors in the company; that is, it is the cost the company must pay to get additional funds. Or sometimes it is taken to be the rate of return expected on alternative desirable projects. However, some of these cost of capital figures are derived from uncertain cash flow streams and are not really appropriate measures of a risk-free interest rate. For present value calculations it is best to use rates that represent true interest rates, since we assume that the cash flows are certain. Some of the apparent differences in these rates are explained and justified in Chapter 4, but still there is room for judgment.

Another factor to consider is that present value by itself does not reveal much about the rate of return. Two alternative investments might each have a net present value of $100, but one might require an investment of $100 whereas the other requires $1,000,000. Clearly these two alternatives should be viewed differently. Net present value is not the whole story (but we never said it was). It forms a solid starting point, but one must supplement its use with additional structure.

2.6 APPLICATIONS AND EXTENSIONS*

This section illustrates how the concepts of this chapter can be used to evaluate real investment opportunities and projects. Often creative thinking is required to capture the essence of a situation in a form that is suitable for analysis.

Not all of these applications need be read during the first pass through this chapter; but as one returns to the chapter, these examples should help clarify the underlying concepts.

Net Flows

In conducting a cash flow analysis using either net present value or internal rate of return, it is essential that the net of income minus expense (that is, net profit) be used as the cash flow each period. The net profit usually can be found in a straightforward manner, but the process can be subtle in complex situations. In particular, taxes often introduce complexity because certain tax-accounting costs and profits are not always equal to actual cash outflows or inflows. Taxes are considered in a later subsection.

Here we use a relatively simple example involving a gold mine to illustrate net present value analysis. Various gold mine examples are used throughout the book to illustrate how, as we extend our conceptual understanding, we can develop deeper analyses of the same kind of investment. The Simplico gold mine is the simplest of the series.

Example 2.6 (Simplico gold mine)   The Simplico gold mine has a great deal of remaining gold deposits, and you are part of a team that is considering leasing the mine from its owners for a period of 10 years. Gold can be extracted from this mine at a rate of up to 10,000 ounces per year at a cost of $200 per ounce. This cost is the total operating cost of mining and refining, exclusive of the cost of the lease. Currently the market price of gold is $400 per ounce. The interest rate is 10%. Assuming that the price of gold, the operating cost, and the interest rate remain constant over the 10-year period, what is the present value of the lease?

This is fairly straightforward. We ignore the lease expense and just find the present value of the operating profits. It is clear that the mine should be operated at full capacity every year, giving a profit of $10,000 \times (\$400 - \$200) = \$2$ million per year. We assume that these cash flows occur at the end of each year.

The cash flow stream therefore consists of 10 individual flows of $2M (that is, $2 million) at the end of each year. The present value is accordingly

$$PV = \sum_{k=1}^{10} \frac{\$2M}{(1.1)^k}.$$

---

*Sections marked by stars may be skipped at first reading.

This can be evaluated either by direct summation or by using the formula for the sum of a geometric series. The result is

$$PV = \$2M \left[1 - \left(\frac{1}{1.1} \right)^{10} \right] \times 10 = \$12.29M$$

and this is the value of the lease.

Cycle Problems

When using interest rate theory to evaluate ongoing (repeatable) activities, it is essential that alternatives be compared over the same time horizon. The difficulties that can arise from not doing this are illustrated in the tree cutting example. The two alternatives in that example have different cycle lengths, but the nature of the possible repetition of the cycles was not clearly spelled out originally.

We illustrate here two ways to account properly for different cycle lengths. The first is to repeat each alternative until both terminate at the same time. For example, if a first alternative lasts 2 years and a second lasts 4 years, then two cycles of the first alternative are comparable to one of the second. The other method for comparing alternatives with different cycle lengths is to assume that an alternative will be repeated indefinitely. Then a simple equation can be written for the value of the entire infinite-length stream.

Example 2.7 (Automobile purchase) You are contemplating the purchase of an automobile and have narrowed the field down to two choices. Car A costs $20,000, is expected to have a low maintenance cost of $1,000 per year (payable at the beginning of each year after the first year), but has a useful mileage life that for you translates into 4 years. Car B costs $30,000 and has an expected maintenance cost of $2,000 per year (after the first year) and a useful life of 6 years. Neither car has a salvage value. The interest rate is 10%. Which car should you buy?

We analyze this choice by assuming that similar alternatives will be available in the future—we are ignoring inflation—so this purchase is one of a sequence of car purchases. To equalize the time horizon, we assume a planning period of 12 years, corresponding to three cycles of car A and two of car B.

We analyze simple cycles and combined cycles as follows.
Car A:

$$\text{One cycle} \quad PV_A = 20,000 + 1,000 \sum_{k=1}^{3} \frac{1}{(1.1)^k}$$
$$= \$22,487$$
$$\text{Three cycles} \quad PV_{A3} = PV_A \left[1 + \frac{1}{(1.1)^4} + \frac{1}{(1.1)^8} \right]$$
$$= \$48,336$$

Car B:

$$\text{One cycle} \quad PV_B = 30,000 + 2,000 \sum_{k=1}^{5} \frac{1}{(1.1)^k}$$
$$= \$37,582$$

$$\text{Two cycles} \quad PV_{B2} = PV_B \left[1 + \frac{1}{(1.1)^6} \right]$$
$$= \$58,795.$$

Hence car A should be selected because its cost has the lower present value over the common time horizon.

Example 2.8 (Machine replacement) A specialized machine essential for a company's operations costs $10,000 and has operating costs of $2,000 the first year. The operating cost increases by $1,000 each year thereafter. We assume that these operating costs occur at the end of each year. The interest rate is 10%. How long should the machine be kept until it is replaced by a new identical machine? Assume that due to its specialized nature the machine has no salvage value.

This is an example where the cash flow stream is not fixed in advance because of the unknown replacement time. We must also account for the cash flows of the replacement machines. This can be done by writing an equation having PV on *both* sides. For example, suppose that the machine is replaced every year. Then the cash flow (in thousands) is $(-10, -2)$ followed by $(0, -10, -2)$ and then $(0, 0, -10, -2)$, and so forth. However, we can write the total PV of the costs compactly as

$$PV = 10 + 2/1.1 + PV/1.1$$

because after the first machine is replaced, the stream from that point looks identical to the original one, except that this continuing stream starts 1 year later and hence must be discounted by the effect of 1 year's interest. The solution to this equation is $PV = 130$ or, in our original units, $130,000.

We may do the same thing assuming 2-year replacement, then 3 years, and so forth. The general approach is based on the equation

$$PV_{\text{total}} = PV_{1 \text{ cycle}} + \left(\frac{1}{1.1} \right)^k PV_{\text{total}}$$

where k is the length of the basic cycle. This leads easily to Table 2.3.

From the table we see that the smallest present value of cost occurs when the machine is replaced after 5 years. Hence that is the best replacement policy.

Taxes

Taxes can complicate a cash flow value analysis. No new conceptual issues arise; it is just that taxes can obscure the true definition of cash flow. If a uniform tax rate were applied to all revenues and expenses as taxes and credits, respectively, then recommendations from before-tax and after-tax analyses would be identical. The

TABLE 2.3
Machine Replacement

Replacement year	Present value
1	130,000
2	82,381
3	69,577
4	65,358
5	64,481
6	65,196

The total present value is found for various replacement frequencies. The best policy corresponds to the frequency having the smallest total present value.

present value figures from the latter analysis would merely all be scaled by the same factor; that is, all would be multiplied by 1 minus the tax rate. The internal rate of return figures would be identical. Hence rankings using either net present value or internal rate of return would remain the same as those without taxes. For this reason taxes are ignored in many of our examples. Sometimes, however, the cash flows required to be reported to the government on tax forms are *not* true cash flows. This is why firms often must keep two sets of accounts—one for tax purposes and one for decision-making purposes. There is nothing illegal about this practice; it is a reality introduced by the tax code.

A tax-induced distortion of cash flows frequently accompanies the treatment of property depreciation. Depreciation is treated as a negative cash flow by the government, but the timing of these flows, as reported for tax purposes, rarely coincides with actual cash outlays. The following is a simple example illustrating this discrepancy.

Example 2.9 (Depreciation)   Suppose a firm purchases a machine for $10,000. This machine has a useful life of 4 years and its use generates a cash flow of $3,000 each year. The machine has a salvage value of $2,000 at the end of 4 years.

The government does not allow the full cost of the machine to be reported as an expense the first year, but instead requires that the cost of the machine be depreciated over its useful life. There are several depreciation methods, each applicable under various circumstances, but for simplicity we shall assume the straight-line method. In this method a fixed portion of the cost is reported as depreciation each year. Hence corresponding to a 4-year life, one-fourth of the cost (minus the estimated salvage value) is reported as an expense deductible from revenue each year.

If we assume a combined federal and state tax rate of 43%, we obtain the cash flows, before and after tax, shown in Table 2.4. The salvage value is not taxed (since it was not depreciated). The present values for the two cash flows (at 10%) are also shown. Note that in this example tax rules convert an otherwise profitable operation into an unprofitable one.

TABLE 2.4
Cash Flows Before and After Tax

Year	Before-tax cash flow	Depreciation	Taxable income	Tax	After-tax cash flow
0	−10,000				−10,000
1	3,000	2,000	1,000	430	2,570
2	3,000	2,000	1,000	430	2,570
3	3,000	2,000	1,000	430	2,570
4	5,000	2,000	1,000	430	4,570
PV	876				−487

From a present value viewpoint, tax rules for treatment of depreciation can convert a potentially profitable venture into an unprofitable one.

Inflation

Inflation is another factor that often causes confusion, arising from the choice between using actual dollar values to describe cash flows and using values expressed in purchasing power, determined by reducing inflated future dollar values back to a nominal level.

Inflation is characterized by an increase in general prices with time. Inflation can be described quantitatively in terms of an **inflation rate** f. Prices 1 year from now will on average be equal to today's prices multiplied by $(1 + f)$. Inflation compounds much like interest does, so after k years of inflation at rate f, prices will be $(1 + f)^k$ times their original values. Of course, inflation rates do not remain constant, but in planning studies future rates are usually estimated as constant.

Another way to look at inflation is that it erodes the purchasing power of money. A dollar today does not purchase as much bread or milk, for example, as a dollar did 10 years ago. In other words, we can think of prices increasing or, alternatively, of the value of money decreasing. If the inflation rate is f, then the value of a dollar next year in terms of the purchasing power of today's dollar is $1/(1 + f)$.

It is sometimes useful to think explicitly in terms of the same kind of dollars, eliminating the influence of inflation. Thus we consider **constant dollars** or, alternatively, **real dollars,** defined relative to a given reference year. These are the (hypothetical) dollars that continue to have the same purchasing power as dollars did in the reference year. These dollars are defined in contrast to the **actual** or **nominal dollars** that we really use in transactions.

This leads us to define a new interest rate, termed the **real interest rate,** which is the rate at which real dollars increase if left in a bank that pays the nominal rate. To understand the meaning of the real interest rate, imagine depositing money in the bank at time zero, then withdrawing it 1 year later. The purchasing power of the bank balance has probably increased in spite of inflation, and this increase measures the real rate of interest.

If one goes through that thinking, when r is the nominal interest rate and f is the inflation rate, it is easy to see that

$$1 + r_0 = \frac{1+r}{1+f}$$

where r_0 denotes the real rate of interest. This equation expresses the fact that money in the bank increases (nominally) by $1 + r$, but its purchasing power is deflated by $1/(1 + f)$. We can solve for r_0 as

$$r_0 = \frac{r - f}{1 + f}. \tag{2.5}$$

Note that for small levels of inflation the real rate of interest is approximately equal to the nominal rate of interest minus the inflation rate.

A cash flow analysis can be carried out using either actual (nominal) dollars or real dollars, but the danger is that a mixture of the two might be used inadvertently. Such a mixture sometimes occurs in the planning studies in large corporations. The operating divisions, which are primarily concerned with physical inputs and outputs, may extrapolate real cash flows into the future. But corporate headquarters, being primarily concerned with the financial market and tax rules, may find the use of nominal (that is, actual) cash flows more convenient and hence may discount at the nominal rate. The result can be an undervaluation by headquarters of project proposals submitted by the divisions relative to valuations that would be obtained if inflation were treated consistently.

We illustrate now how an analysis can be carried out consistently by using either real or nominal cash flows.

Example 2.10 (Inflation)   Suppose that inflation is 4%, the nominal interest rate is 10%, and we have a cash flow of real (or constant) dollars as shown in the second column of Table 2.5. (It is common to estimate cash flows in constant dollars, relative to the present, because "ordinary" price increases can then be neglected in a simple estimation of cash flows.) To determine the present value in real terms we must use the real rate of interest, which from (2.5) is $r_0 = (.10 - .04)/1.04 = 5.77\%$.

TABLE 2.5
Inflation

Year	Real cash flow	PV @5.77%	Nominal cash flow	PV @10%
0	−10,000	−10,000	−10,000	−10,000
1	5,000	4,727	5,200	4,727
2	5,000	4,469	5,408	4,469
3	5,000	4,226	5,624	4,226
4	3,000	2,397	3,510	2,397
Total		5,819		5,819

The projected real cash flows of the second column have the present values, at the real rate of interest, shown in the third column. The fourth column lists the cash flows that would occur under 4% inflation, and their present values at the 10% nominal rate of interest are given in the fifth column.

Alternatively, we may convert the cash flow to actual (nominal) terms by inflating the figures using the appropriate inflation factors. Then we determine the present value using the nominal interest rate of 10%. Both methods produce the same result.

2.7 SUMMARY

The time value of money is expressed concretely as an interest rate. The 1-year interest rate is the price paid (expressed as a percentage of principal) for borrowing money for 1 year. In simple interest, the interest payment when borrowing money in subsequent years is identical in magnitude to that of the first year. Hence, for example, the bank balance resulting from a single deposit would grow linearly year by year. In compound interest, the interest payment in subsequent years is based on the balance at the beginning of that year. Hence the bank balance resulting from a single deposit would grow geometrically year by year.

A useful approximation is that the number of years required for a deposit to double in value when compounded yearly is $72/i$, where i is the interest rate expressed as a percentage. For example, at 10%, money doubles in about 7 years.

Interest can be compounded at any frequency, not just yearly. It is even possible to compound continuously, which leads to bank balances that grow exponentially with time. When interest is compounded more frequently than yearly, it is useful to define both a nominal rate and an effective annual rate of interest. The nominal rate is the rate used for a single period divided by the length (in years) of a period. The effective rate is the rate that, if applied without compounding, would give the same total balance for money deposited for one full year. The effective rate is larger than the nominal rate. For example, an 8% nominal annual rate corresponds to an 8.24% effective annual rate under quarterly compounding.

Money received in the future is worth less than the same amount of money received in the present because money received in the present can be loaned out to earn interest. Money to be received at a future date must be discounted by dividing its magnitude by the factor by which present money would grow if loaned out to that future date. There is, accordingly, a discount factor for each future date.

The present value of a cash flow stream is the sum of the discounted magnitudes of the individual cash flows of the stream. An ideal bank can transform a cash flow stream into any other with the same present value.

The internal rate of return of a cash flow stream is an interest rate that, if used to evaluate the present value of the stream, would cause that present value to be zero. In general, this rate is not well defined. However, when the cash flow stream has an initial negative flow followed by positive flows, the internal rate of return is well defined.

Present value and internal rate of return are the two main methods used to evaluate proposed investment projects that generate deterministic cash flow streams. Under the present value framework, if there are several competing alternatives, then the one with the highest present value should be selected. Under the internal rate of return criterion, the alternative with the largest internal rate of return should be selected.

Analyses using these methods are not always straightforward. In particular, consideration of various cycle lengths, taxes, and inflation each require careful attention.

EXERCISES

1. (A nice inheritance) Suppose $1 were invested in 1776 at 3.3% interest compounded yearly.

   (a) Approximately how much would that investment be worth today: $1,000, $10,000, $100,000, or $1,000,000?
   (b) What if the interest rate were 6.6%?

2. (The 72 rule) The number of years n required for an investment at interest rate r to double in value must satisfy $(1+r)^n = 2$. Using $\ln 2 = .69$ and the approximation $\ln(1+r) \approx r$ valid for small r, show that $n \approx 69/i$, where i is the interest rate percentage (that is, $i = 100r$). Using the better approximation $\ln(1+r) \approx r - \frac{1}{2}r^2$, show that for $r \approx .08$ there holds $n \approx 72/i$.

3. (Effective rates) Find the corresponding effective rates for:

   (a) 3% compounded monthly.
   (b) 18% compounded monthly.
   (c) 18% compounded quarterly.

4. (Newton's method$\diamond$) The IRR is generally calculated using an iterative procedure. Suppose that we define $f(\lambda) = -a_0 + a_1\lambda + a_2\lambda^2 + \cdots + a_n\lambda^n$, where all a_i's are positive and $n > 1$. Here is an iterative technique that generates a sequence $\lambda_0, \lambda_1, \lambda_2, \ldots, \lambda_k, \ldots$ of estimates that converges to the root $\bar{\lambda} > 0$, solving $f(\bar{\lambda}) = 0$. Start with any $\lambda_0 > 0$ close to the solution. Assuming λ_k has been calculated, evaluate

$$f'(\lambda_k) = a_1 + 2a_2\lambda_k + 3a_3\lambda_k^2 + \cdots + na_n\lambda_k^{n-1}$$

and define

$$\lambda_{k+1} = \lambda_k - \frac{f(\lambda_k)}{f'(\lambda_k)}.$$

This is Newton's method. It is based on approximating the function f by a line tangent to its graph at λ_k, as shown in Figure 2.4. Try the procedure on $f(\lambda) = -1 + \lambda + \lambda^2$. Start with $\lambda_0 = 1$ and compute four additional estimates.

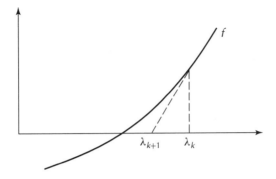

FIGURE 2.4   Newton's method.

$^\diamond$Exercises followed by $\diamond$ are mathematically more difficult than average.

5. (A prize)   A major lottery advertises that it pays the winner $10 million. However, this prize money is paid at the rate of $500,000 each year (with the first payment being immediate) for a total of 20 payments. What is the present value of this prize at 10% interest?

6. (Sunk costs)   A young couple has made a nonrefundable deposit of the first month's rent (equal to $1,000) on a 6-month apartment lease. The next day they find a different apartment that they like just as well, but its monthly rent is only $900. They plan to be in the apartment only 6 months. Should they switch to the new apartment? What if they plan to stay 1 year? Assume an interest rate of 12%.

7. (Shortcut)   Gavin Jones is inquisitive and determined to learn both the theory and the application of investment theory. He pressed the tree farmer for additional information and learned that it was possible to delay cutting the trees of Example 2.4 for another year. The farmer said that, from a present value perspective, it was not worthwhile to do so. Gavin instantly deduced that the revenue obtained must be less than x. What is x?

8. (Copy machines ⊕)   Two copy machines are available. Both have useful lives of 5 years. One machine can be either leased or purchased outright; the other must be purchased. Hence there are a total of three options: A, B, and C. The details are shown in Table 2.6. (The first year's maintenance is included in the initial cost. There are then four additional maintenance payments, occurring at the beginning of each year, followed by revenues from resale.) The present values of the expenses of these three options using a 10% interest rate are also indicated in the table. According to a present value analysis, the machine of least cost, as measured by the present value, should be selected; that is, option B.

TABLE 2.6
Copy Machine Options

	Option		
	A	B	C
Initial outlay	6,000	30,000	35,000
Yearly expense	8,000	2,000	1,600
Resale value	0	10,000	12,000
Present value (@10%)	31,359	30,131	32,621

Option A is a lease; options B and C are purchases of two alternative machines. All have 5-year lives.

It is not possible to compute the IRR for any of these alternatives, because all cash flows are negative (except for the resale values). However, it is possible to calculate the IRR on an incremental basis. Find the IRR corresponding to a change from A to B. Is a change from A to B justified on the basis of the IRR?

9. (An appraisal)   You are considering the purchase of a nice home. It is in every way perfect for you and in excellent condition, except for the roof. The roof has only 5 years of life

---

⊕Exercises followed by ⊕ require numerical computation.

remaining. A new roof would last 20 years, but would cost $20,000. The house is expected to last forever. Assuming that costs will remain constant and that the interest rate is 5%, what value would you assign to the existing roof?

10. (Oil depletion allowance ⊕)   A wealthy investor spends $1 million to drill and develop an oil well that has estimated reserves of 200,000 barrels. The well is to be operated over 5 years, producing the estimated quantities shown in the second column of Table 2.7. It is estimated that the oil will be sold for $20 per barrel. The net income is also shown.

TABLE 2.7
Oil Investment Details

Year	Barrels produced	Gross revenue	Net income	Option 1	Option 2	Depletion allowance	Taxable income	Tax	After-tax income
1	80,000	1,600,000	1,200,000	352,000	400,000	400,000	800,000	360,000	840,000
2	70,000	1,400,000	1,000,000						
3	50,000	1,000,000	500,000						
4	30,000	600,000	200,000						
5	10,000	200,000	50,000						

A depletion allowance, for tax purposes, can be computed in either of two ways each year: 22% of gross revenue up to 50% of net income before such deduction (option 1), or the investment cost of the product, equal in this case to the unit cost of the reserves, $5 per barrel (option 2). The allowance is deducted from the net income to determine the taxable income. The investor is in the 45% tax bracket.

(a) Complete Table 2.7 and show that the total depletion allowance exceeds the original investment.
(b) Calculate the PV and the IRR for this investment. Assume an interest rate of 20%.

11. (Conflicting recommendations ⊕)   Consider the two projects whose cash flows are shown in Table 2.8. Find the IRRs of the two projects and the NPVs at 5%. Show that the IRR and NPV figures yield different recommendations. Can you explain this?

TABLE 2.8

	Years					
	0	1	2	3	4	5
Project 1	−100	30	30	30	30	30
Project 2	−150	42	42	42	42	42

12. (Domination)   Suppose two competing projects have cash flows of the form $(-A_1, B_1, B_1, \ldots, B_1)$ and $(-A_2, B_2, B_2, \ldots, B_2)$, both with the same length and A_1, A_2, B_1, B_2 all positive. Suppose $B_1/A_1 > B_2/A_2$. Show that project 1 will have a higher IRR than project 2.

13. (Crossing ◇)   In general, we say that two projects with cash flows x_i and y_i, $i = 0, 1, 2, \ldots,$ n, *cross* if $x_0 < y_0$ and $\sum_{i=0}^{n} x_i > \sum_{i=0}^{n} y_i$. Let $P_x(d)$ and $P_y(d)$ denote the present values of these two projects when the discount factor is d.

(*a*) Show that there is a crossover value $c > 0$ such that $P_x(c) = P_y(c)$.

(*b*) For Exercise 11, calculate the crossover value c.

14. (Depreciation choice)   In the United States the accelerated cost recovery system (ACRS) must be used for depreciation of assets placed into service after December 1980. In this system, assets are classified into categories specifying the effective tax life. The classification of "3-year property," for example, includes automobiles, tractors for hauling highway trailers, light trucks, and certain manufacturing tools. The percentages of the cost for 3-year property that can be deducted for each of the first 3 years after purchase (including the year of purchase) are 25%, 38%, and 37%, respectively. The tax code also allows the alternate ACRS method, which for 3-year property means that the straight-line percentage of $33\frac{1}{3}\%$ can be used for 3 years.

　　Which of these methods is preferred by an individual who wishes to maximize the present value of depreciation? How does the choice depend on the assumed rate of interest?

15. (An erroneous analysis)   A division of ABBOX Corporation has developed the concept of a new product. Production of the product would require $10 million in initial capital expenditure. It is anticipated that 1 million units would be sold each year for 5 years, and then the product would be obsolete and production would cease. Each year's production would require 10,000 hours of labor and 100 tons of raw material. Currently the average wage rate is $30 per hour and the cost of the raw material is $100 per ton. The product would sell for $3.30 per unit, and this price is expected to be maintained (in real terms). ABBOX management likes to use a 12% discount rate for projects of this type and faces a 34% tax rate on profit. The initial capital expenditure can be depreciated in a straight-line fashion over 5 years. In its first analysis of this project, management did not apply inflation factors to the extrapolated revenues and operating costs. What present value did they obtain? How would the answer change if an inflation rate of 4% were applied?

REFERENCES

The theory of interest, compounding, present value, and internal rate of return is covered extensively in many excellent textbooks. A few investment-oriented texts which discuss general notions of interest are [1–5]. The use of the concepts of NPV and IRR for ranking investment alternatives is developed in detail in the field of engineering economy. Excellent texts in that field include [6–9]. A more advanced study of interest is [10], which contains a continuous-time version of the "when to cut a tree" example, which inspired the example given in Section 2.5. Exercise 10 is a modification of an example in [6].

1. Alexander, G. J., W. F. Sharpe, and V. J. Bailey (1993), *Fundamentals of Investment*, 2nd ed., Prentice Hall, Englewood Cliffs, NJ.
2. Bodie, H. M., A. Kane, and A. J. Marcus (1993), *Investments*, 2nd ed., Irwin, Homewood, IL.
3. Brealey, R., and S. Meyers (1981), *Principles of Corporate Finance,* McGraw-Hill, New York.

4. Francis, J. C. (1991), *Investments: Analysis and Management*, 5th ed., McGraw-Hill, New York.

5. Haugen, R. A. (1993), *Modern Investment Theory*, 3rd ed., Prentice Hall, Englewood Cliffs, NJ.

6. DeGarmo, E. P., W. G. Sullivan, and J. A. Bontadelli (1988), *Engineering Economy*, 8th ed., Macmillan, New York.

7. Grant, E. L., W. G. Ireson, and R. S. Leavensworth (1982), *Principles of Engineering Economy*, 7th ed., Wiley, New York.

8. Steiner, H. M. (1992), *Engineering Economy,* McGraw-Hill, New York.

9. Thuesen, G. J., and W. J. Fabrycky (1989), *Engineering Economy*, 7th ed., Prentice Hall, Englewood Cliffs, NJ.

10. Hirshleifer, J. (1970), *Investment, Interest, and Capital,* Prentice Hall, Englewood Cliffs.

3

FIXED-INCOME SECURITIES

An interest rate is a price, or rent, for the most popular of all traded commodities—money. The one-year interest rate, for example, is just the price that must be paid for borrowing money for one year. Markets for money are well developed, and the corresponding basic market price—interest—is monitored by everyone who has a serious concern about financial activity.

As shown in the previous chapter, the market interest rate provides a ready comparison for investment alternatives that produce cash flows. This comparison can be used to evaluate any cash flow stream: whether arising from transactions between individuals, associated with business projects, or generated by investments in securities.

However, the overall market associated with interest rates is more complex than the simple bank accounts discussed in the last chapter. Vast assortments of bills, notes, bonds, annuities, futures contracts, and mortgages are part of the well-developed markets for money. These market items are not real goods (or hard assets) in the sense of having intrinsic value—such as potatoes or gold—but instead are traded only as pieces of paper, or as entries in a computer database. These items, in general, are referred to as **financial instruments.** Their values are derived from the promises they represent. If there is a well-developed market for an instrument, so that it can be traded freely and easily, then that instrument is termed a **security.** There are many financial instruments and securities that are directly related to interest rates and, therefore, provide access to income—at a price defined by the appropriate interest rate or rates.

Fixed-income securities are financial instruments that are traded in well-developed markets and promise a fixed (that is, definite) income to the holder over a span of time. In our terminology, they represent the ownership of a definite cash flow stream.

Fixed-income securities are important to an investor because they define the market for money, and most investors participate in this market. These securities are also important as additional comparison points when conducting analyses of investment opportunities that are not traded in markets, such as a firm's research projects, oil leases, and royalty rights. A comprehensive study of financial instruments most naturally starts with a study of fixed-income securities.

3.1 THE MARKET FOR FUTURE CASH

The classification of a security as being a fixed-income security is actually a bit vague. Originally this classification meant, as previously stated, that the security pays a fixed, well-defined cash flow stream to the owner. The only uncertainties about the promised stream were associated with whether the issuer of the security might **default** (by, say, going bankrupt), in which case the income would be discontinued or delayed. Now, however, some "fixed-income" securities promise cash flows whose magnitudes are tied to various contingencies or fluctuating indices. For example, payment levels on an adjustable-rate mortgage may be tied to an interest rate index, or corporate bond payments may in part be governed by a stock price. But in common parlance, such variations are allowed within a broader definition of fixed-income securities. The general idea is that a fixed-income security has a cash flow stream that is fixed except for variations due to well-defined contingent circumstances.

There are many different kinds of fixed-income securities, and we cannot provide a comprehensive survey of them here. However, we shall mention some of the principal types of fixed-income securities in order to indicate the general scope of such securities.

Savings Deposits

Probably the most familiar fixed-income instrument is an interest-bearing bank deposit. These are offered by commercial banks, savings and loan institutions, and credit unions. In the United States most such deposits are guaranteed by agencies of the federal government. The simplest **demand deposit** pays a rate of interest that varies with market conditions. Over an extended period of time, such a deposit is not strictly of a fixed-income type; nevertheless, we place it in the fixed-income category. The interest *is* guaranteed in a **time deposit account,** where the deposit must be maintained for a given length of time (such as 6 months), or else a penalty for early withdrawal is assessed. A similar instrument is a **certificate of deposit** (CD), which is issued in standard denominations such as $10,000. Large-denomination CDs can be sold in a market, and hence they qualify as securities.

Money Market Instruments

The term **money market** refers to the market for short-term (1 year or less) loans by corporations and financial intermediaries, including, for example, banks. It is a well-organized market designed for large amounts of money, but it is not of great importance to long-term investors because of its short-term and specialized nature. Within this market **commercial paper** is the term used to describe unsecured loans (that is, loans without collateral) to corporations. The larger denominations of CDs mentioned earlier are also part of this market.

A **banker's acceptance** is a more involved money market instrument. If company A sells goods to company B, company B might send a written promise to company A that it will pay for the goods within a fixed time, such as 3 months. Some bank *accepts* the promise by promising to pay the bill on behalf of company B. Company A can then sell the banker's acceptance to someone else at a discount before the time has expired.

Eurodollar deposits are deposits denominated in dollars but held in a bank outside the United States. Likewise **Eurodollar CDs** are CDs denominated in dollars and issued by banks outside the United States. A distinction between these Eurodollars and regular dollars is due to differences in banking regulations and insurance.

U.S. Government Securities

The U.S. Government obtains loans by issuing various types of fixed-income securities. These securities are considered to be of the highest credit quality since they are backed by the government itself. The most important government securities are sketched here.

U.S. Treasury bills are issued in denominations of $10,000 or more with fixed terms to maturity of 13, 26, and 52 weeks. They are sold on a discount basis. Thus a bill with a face value of $10,000 may sell for $9,500, the difference between the price and the face value providing the interest. A bill can be redeemed for the full face value at the maturity date. New bills are offered each week and are sold at auction. They are highly **liquid** (that is, there is a ready market for them); hence they can be easily sold prior to the maturity date.

U.S. Treasury notes have maturities of 1 to 10 years and are sold in denominations as small as $1,000. The owner of such a note receives a **coupon payment** every 6 months until maturity. This coupon payment represents an interest payment and its magnitude is fixed throughout the life of the note. At maturity the note holder receives the last coupon payment and the face value of the note. Like Treasury bills, these notes are sold at auction.

U.S. Treasury bonds are issued with maturities of more than 10 years. They are similar to Treasury notes in that they make coupon payments. However, some Treasury bonds are **callable,** meaning that at some scheduled coupon payment date the Treasury can force the bond holder to redeem the bond at that time for its face (par) value.

U.S. Treasury strips are bonds that the U.S. Treasury issues in stripped form. Here each of the coupons is issued separately, as is the principal. So a 10-year bond when stripped will consist of 20 semiannual coupon securities (each with a separate CUSIP[1]) and an additional principal security. Each of these securities generates a

---

[1] The Committee on Uniform Securities Identification Procedures (CUSIP) assigns identifying CUSIP numbers and codes to all securities.

single cash flow, with no intermediate coupon payments. Such a security is termed a **zero-coupon bond.**

Other Bonds

Bonds are issued by agencies of the federal government, by state and local governments, and by corporations.

Municipal bonds are issued by agencies of state and local governments. There are two main types: **general obligation bonds,** which are backed by a governing body such as the state; and **revenue bonds,** which are backed either by the revenue to be generated by the project that will initially be funded by the bond issue or by the agency responsible for the project.

The interest income associated with municipal bonds is exempt from federal income tax and from state and local taxes in the issuing state. This feature means that investors are willing to accept lower interest rates on these bonds compared to other securities of similar quality.

Corporate bonds are issued by corporations for the purpose of raising capital for operations and new ventures. They vary in quality depending on the strength of the issuing corporation and on certain features of the bond itself.

Some corporate bonds are traded on an exchange, but most are traded over-the-counter in a network of bond dealers. These over-the-counter bonds are less liquid in the sense that there may be only a few trades per day of a particular issue.

A bond carries with it an **indenture,** which is a contract of terms. Some features that might be included are:

Callable bonds   A bond is callable if the issuer has the right to repurchase the bond at a specified price. Usually this call price falls with time, and often there is an initial call protection period wherein the bond cannot be called.

Sinking funds   Rather than incur the obligation to pay the entire face value of a bond issue at maturity, the issuer may establish a sinking fund to spread this obligation out over time. Under such an arrangement the issuer may repurchase a certain fraction of the outstanding bonds each year at a specified price.

Debt Subordination   To protect bond holders, limits may be set on the amount of additional borrowing by the issuer. Also the bondholders may be guaranteed that in the event of bankruptcy, payment to them takes priority over payments of other debt—the other debt being subordinated.

Mortgages

To a typical homeowner, a mortgage looks like the opposite of a bond. A future homeowner usually will *sell* a home mortgage to generate immediate cash to pay for a home, obligating him- or herself to make periodic payments to the mortgage holder. The standard mortgage is structured so that equal monthly payments are made throughout its term, which contrasts to most bonds, which have a final payment equal to the face value at maturity. Most standard mortgages allow for early repayment of the balance. Hence from the mortgage holder's viewpoint the income stream generated is not completely fixed, since it may be terminated with an appropriate lump-sum payment at the discretion of the homeowner.

There are many variations on the standard mortgage. There may be modest-sized periodic payments for several years followed by a final **balloon payment** that completes the contract. **Adjustable-rate mortgages** adjust the effective interest rate periodically according to an interest rate index, and hence these mortgages do not really generate fixed income in the strict sense.

Mortgages are not usually thought of as securities, since they are written as contracts between two parties, for example, a homeowner and a bank. However, mortgages are typically "bundled" into large packages and traded among financial institutions. These **mortgage-backed securities** are quite liquid.

Annuities

An **annuity** is a contract that pays the holder (the **annuitant**) money periodically, according to a predetermined schedule or formula, over a period of time. Pension benefits often take the form of annuities. Sometimes annuities are structured to provide a fixed payment every year for as long as the annuitant is alive, in which case the price of the annuity is based on the age of the annuitant when the annuity is purchased and on the number of years until payments are initiated.

There are numerous variations. Sometimes the level of the annuity payments is tied to the earnings of a large pool of funds from which the annuity is paid, sometimes the payments vary with time, and so forth.

Annuities are not really securities, since they are not traded. (The issuer certainly would not allow a change in annuitant if payments are tied to the life of the owner; likewise, an annuitant would not allow the annuity company to transfer their obligation to another company which might be less solvent.) Annuities are, however, considered to be investment opportunities that are available at standardized rates. Hence from an investor's viewpoint, they serve the same role as other fixed-income instruments.

3.2 VALUE FORMULAS

Many fixed-income instruments include an obligation to pay a stream of equal periodic cash flows. This is characteristic of standard coupon bonds that pay the holder a fixed sum on a regular basis; it also is characteristic of standard mortgages, of many annuities, of standard automobile loans, and of other consumer loans. It is therefore useful to recognize that the present value of such a constant stream can be determined by a compact formula. This formula is difficult to evaluate by hand, and hence professionals working each day with such financial instruments typically have available appropriate tables, handheld calculators, or computer programs that relate present value to the magnitude and term of periodic payments. There are, for example, extensive sets of mortgage tables, bond tables, annuity rate tables, and so forth. We shall develop the basic formula here and illustrate its use.

Perpetual Annuities

As a step toward the development of the formula we consider an interesting and conceptually useful fixed-income instrument termed a **perpetual annuity,** or **perpetuity,** which pays a fixed sum periodically *forever.* For example, it might pay $1,000 every January 1 forever. Such annuities are quite rare (although such instruments actually do exist in Great Britain, where they are called **consols**).

The present value of a perpetual annuity can be easily derived. Suppose an amount A is paid at the end of each period, starting at the end of the first period, and suppose the *per-period* interest rate is r. Then the present value is

$$P = \sum_{k=1}^{\infty} \frac{A}{(1+r)^k} .$$

The terms in the summand represent a geometric series, and this series can be summed easily using a standard formula. Alternatively, if you have forgotten the standard formula, we can derive it by noting that

$$P = \sum_{k=1}^{\infty} \frac{A}{(1+r)^k} = \frac{A}{1+r} + \sum_{k=2}^{\infty} \frac{A}{(1+r)^k} = \frac{A}{1+r} + \frac{P}{1+r}.$$

We can solve this equation to find $P = A/r$. Hence we have the following basic result:

Perpetual annuity formula   *The present value P of a perpetual annuity that pays an amount A every period, beginning one period from the present, is*

$$P = \frac{A}{r}$$

where r is the one-period interest rate.

Example 3.1 (Perpetual annuity)   Consider a perpetual annuity of $1,000 each year. At 10% interest its present value is

$$P = \frac{1,000}{.10} = \$10,000.$$

Finite-Life Streams

Of more practical importance is the case where the payment stream has a finite lifetime. Suppose that the stream consists of n periodic payments of amount A, starting at the end of the current period and ending at period n. The pattern of periodic cash flows together with the time indexing system is shown in Figure 3.1.

The present value of the finite stream relative to the interest rate r per period is

$$P = \sum_{k=1}^{n} \frac{A}{(1+r)^k} .$$

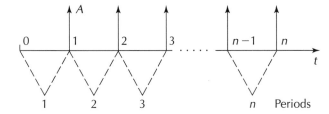

FIGURE 3.1   Time indexing. Time is indexed from 0 to n. A period is a span between time points, with the first period being the time from 0 to 1. A standard annuity has a constant cash flow at the end of each period.

This is the sum of a finite geometric series. If you do not recall the formula for this sum, we can derive it easily by a simple trick. The value can be found by considering two perpetual annuities. Both pay an amount A each year, but one starts at time 1 and the other starts at time $n + 1$. We *subtract* the second from the first. The result is the same as the original stream of finite life. This combination is illustrated in Figure 3.2 for the case of a stream of length 3.

The value of the delayed annuity is found by discounting that annuity by the factor $(1 + r)^{-n}$ because it is delayed n periods. Hence we may write

$$P = \frac{A}{r} - \frac{A}{r(1+r)^n} = \frac{A}{r}\left[1 - \frac{1}{(1+r)^n}\right].$$

We now highlight this important result:

Annuity formulas   *Consider an annuity that begins payment one period from the present, paying an amount A each period for a total of n periods. The present value P, the one-period annuity amount A, the one-period interest rate r, and the number of periods n of the annuity are related by*

$$P = \frac{A}{r}\left[1 - \frac{1}{(1+r)^n}\right]$$

or, equivalently,

$$A = \frac{r(1+r)^n P}{(1+r)^n - 1}.$$

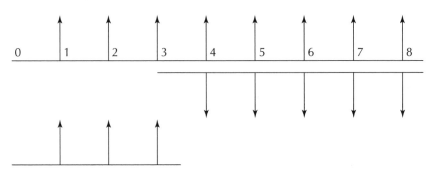

FIGURE 3.2   Finite stream from two perpetual annuities. The top line shows a perpetuity starting at time 1, the second a negative perpetuity starting at time 4. The sum of these two is a finite-life annuity with payments starting at time 1 and ending at time 3.

Although these formulas are simple in concept and quite easy to derive, they are sufficiently complex that they cannot be evaluated easily by hand. It is for this reason that financial tables and financial calculators are commonly available. Professional tables of this type occupy several pages and typically give P/A as a function of r and n. For some purposes A/P (just the reciprocal) is more convenient, and there are tables written both ways.

It is important to note that in the formulas of this section, r is expressed as a per-period interest rate. If the period length is not equal to 1 year, this r will *not* be equal to the yearly rate; so care must be exercised.

The annuity formula is frequently used in the reverse direction; that is, A as a function of P. This determines the periodic payment that is equivalent (under the assumed interest rate) to an initial payment of P. This process of substituting periodic payments for a current obligation is referred to as **amortization.** Hence one may **amortize** the cost of an automobile over 5 years by taking out a 5-year loan.

Example 3.2 (Loan calculation)   Suppose you have borrowed $1,000 from a credit union. The terms of the loan are that the yearly interest is 12% compounded monthly. You are to make equal monthly payments of such magnitude as to repay (amortize) this loan over 5 years. How much are the monthly payments?

Five years is 60 months, and 12% a year compounded monthly is 1% per month. Hence we use the formula for $n = 60$, $r = 1\%$, and $P = \$1,000$. We find that the payments A are $22.20 per month.

Example 3.3 (APR)   A typical advertisement from a mortgage broker is shown in Table 3.1. In addition to the interest rate, term of the loan, and maximum amount, there are listed points and the annual percentage rate (APR), which describe fees and expenses. **Points** is the percentage of the loan amount that is charged for providing the mortgage. Typically, there are additional expenses as well. All of these fees and

TABLE 3.1
Mortgage Broker Advertisement

Rate	Pts	Term	Max amt	APR
7.625	1.00	30 yr	$203,150	7.883
7.875	.50	30 yr	$203,150	8.083
8.125	2.25	30 yr	$600,000	8.399
7.000	1.00	15 yr	$203,150	7.429
7.500	1.00	15 yr	$600,000	7.859

Call 555-1213
Real Estate Broker, CA Dept. of Real Estate,
Mortgage Masters, Inc.
Current Fixed Rates

APR is the rate of interest that implicitly includes the fees associated with a mortgage.

expenses are added to the loan balance, and the sum is amortized at the stated rate over the stated period. This results in a fixed monthly payment amount A.

The **APR** is the rate of interest that, if applied to the loan amount without fees and expenses, would result in a monthly payment of A, exactly as before.

As a concrete example, suppose you took out a mortgage corresponding to the first listing in Table 3.1. Let us calculate the total fees and expenses. Using the APR of 7.883%, a loan amount of $203,150, and a 30-year term, we find a monthly payment of $A = \$1,474$.

Now using an interest rate of 7.625% and the monthly payment calculated, we find a total initial balance of $208,267. The total of fees and expenses is therefore $\$208,267 - \$203,150 = \$5,117$. The loan fee itself is 1 point, or $2,032. Hence other expenses are $\$5,117 - \$2,032 = \$3,085$.

Running Amortization*

The formulas for amortization can be looked at in another way, linked directly to common accounting practice. Consider the loan of $1,000 discussed in Example 3.2, which you will repay over 5 years at 12% interest (compounded monthly). Suppose you took out the loan on January 1, and the first payment is due February 1. The repayment process can be viewed as credits to a running monthly account. The account has an initial balance equal to the value of the loan—the original principal. Each month this balance is increased by an interest charge of 1% and then reduced by the payment amount. Assuming that you make payments as scheduled, the balance will decrease each month, reaching zero after 60 months. On July 1 you might receive a 6-month accounting statement such as that shown in Table 3.2, which illustrates how the balance decreases as payments are made.

It is common to regard each payment as consisting of two parts. The first part is the current interest; the second is a partial repayment of the principal. The running balance account procedure is consistent with reamortizing the loan each month. Specifically, assuming all payments to date were made on schedule and of the proper amount, the payment level predicted by the formula to amortize the current balance over the months remaining in the original contract will always be $22.20. For exam-

TABLE 3.2
Statement of Account Transactions

	Previous balance	Current interest	Payment received	New balance
January 1				1,000.00
February 1	1,000.00	10.00	22.20	987.80
March 1	987.80	9.88	22.20	975.48
April 1	975.48	9.75	22.20	963.03
May 1	963.03	9.63	22.20	950.46
June 1	950.46	9.50	22.20	937.76

Each month the previous balance accumulates interest and is reduced by the current payment. The balance will be zero at the end of the loan term.

ple, based on the July statement, one can amortize the balance of $937.76 at 12% on June 1 (after making the June 1 payment) over a period of 55 months. The monthly payment required by this amortization would be $22.20.

Annual Worth*

The annuity framework provides an alternative method for expressing a net present value analysis. This **annual worth** method has the advantage that it expresses its results in terms of a constant level of cash flow and thus is easily understood.

Suppose a project has an associated cash flow stream $(x_0, x_1, \ldots, x_n)$ over n years. A present value analysis uses a (fictitious) constant ideal bank with interest rate r to transform this stream hypothetically into an equivalent one of the form $(v, 0, 0, \ldots, 0)$, where v is the net present value of the stream.

An annual worth analysis uses the same ideal bank to hypothetically transform the sequence to one of the form $(0, A, A, A, \ldots, A)$. The value A is the annual worth (over n years) of the project. It is the equivalent net amount that is generated by the project if all amounts are converted to a fixed n-year annuity starting the first year.

Clearly $A > 0$ exactly when $v > 0$, so the condition for acceptance of the project based on whether $A > 0$ coincides with the net present value criterion.

Example 3.4 (A capital cost)   The purchase of a new machine for $100,000 (at time zero) is expected to generate additional revenues of $25,000 for the next 10 years starting at year 1. If the discount rate is 16%, is this a profitable investment?

We simply need to determine how to amortize the initial cost uniformly over 10 years; that is, we need to find the annual payments at 16% that are equivalent to the original cost. Using the annuity formula, we find that this corresponds to $20,690 per year. Hence the annual worth of the project is $25,000 − $20,690 = $4,310, which is positive; thus the investment is profitable. Note that if the purchase of the machine were financed at 16% over 10 years, the *actual* yearly net cash flows would correspond exactly to the annual worth.

3.3 BOND DETAILS

Bonds represent by far the greatest monetary value of fixed-income securities and are, as a class, the most liquid of these securities. We devote special attention to bonds, both because of their practical importance as investment vehicles and because of their theoretical value, which will be exploited heavily in Chapter 4. We describe the general structure and trading mechanics of bonds in this section and then discuss in the following few sections some methods by which bonds are analyzed. Our description is intended to be an overview. Specific details are quite involved, and one must refer to specialized literature or to a brokerage firm for the exact features of any particular bond issue.

A **bond** is an obligation by the bond issuer to pay money to the bond holder according to rules specified at the time the bond is issued. Generally, a bond pays a specific amount, its **face value** or, equivalently, its **par value** at the date of maturity. Bonds generally have par values of even amounts, such as $1,000 or $10,000. In addition, most bonds pay periodic **coupon payments.** The term *coupon* is due to the fact that in the past actual coupons were attached to bond certificates. The bond holder would mail these to the agent of the issuer (usually a bank) one at a time, at specified dates, and the appropriate coupon payment would then be sent by return mail. These physical coupons are rare today, but the name remains. The last coupon date corresponds to the maturity date, so the last payment is equal to the face value plus the coupon value.

The coupon amount is described as a percentage of the face value. For example, a 9% coupon bond with a face value of $1,000 will have a coupon of $90 per year. However, the period between coupons may be less than a year. In the United States, coupon payments are generally made every 6 months, paying one-half of the coupon amount. This would be $45 in our example.

The issuer of a bond initially sells the bonds to raise capital immediately, and then is obligated to make the prescribed payments. Usually bonds are issued with coupon rates close to the prevailing general rate of interest so that they will sell at close to their face value. However, as time passes, bonds frequently trade at prices different from their face values. While any two parties can agree on a price and execute a trade, the vast majority of bonds are sold either at auction (when originally issued) or through an exchange organization. The price is therefore determined by a market and thus may vary minute by minute.

An example of publicly available bond quotes (for U.S. Treasury bonds and notes) is shown in Table 3.3. Here the indicated coupon rate is the annual rate (one-

TABLE 3.3
U.S. Treasury Bills, Notes, and Bonds

Rate	Maturity Mo/Yr	Bid	Asked	Chg.	Ask Yld.	Rate	Maturity Mo/Yr	Bid	Asked	Chg.	Ask Yld.
						$5\frac{7}{8}$	Feb 04n	97:28	97:29	+ 9	6.25
$4\frac{3}{4}$	Feb 97n	99:31	100:00	.....	4.64	$7\frac{1}{4}$	May 04n	105:20	105:22	+11	6.26
$6\frac{3}{4}$	Feb 97n	100:00	100:02	− 1	4.98	$12\frac{3}{8}$	May 04	135:03	135:09	+18	6.24
$6\frac{7}{8}$	Feb 97n	100:00	100:02	− 1	5.09	$7\frac{1}{4}$	Aug 04n	105:21	105:25	+13	6.27
$6\frac{5}{8}$	Mar 97n	100:04	100:06	.....	4.97	$13\frac{3}{4}$	Aug 04	144:04	144:10	+20	6.26
$6\frac{7}{8}$	Mar 97n	100:05	100:07	.....	4.97	$7\frac{7}{8}$	Nov 04n	109:20	109:22	+16	6.27
$8\frac{1}{2}$	Apr 97n	100:15	100:17	− 1	5.10	$11\frac{5}{8}$	Nov 04	132:08	132:14	+19	6.27
$6\frac{1}{2}$	Apr 97n	100:07	100:09	.....	5.03	$7\frac{1}{2}$	Feb 05n	107:09	107:12	+11	6.31
$6\frac{7}{8}$	Apr 97n	100:09	100:11	.....	5.10	$6\frac{1}{2}$	May 05n	101:08	101:10	+17	6.29
$6\frac{1}{2}$	May 97n	100:08	100:10	.....	5.14	$8\frac{1}{4}$	May 00-05	105:24	105:26	+ 6	6.24
$8\frac{1}{2}$	May 97n	100:24	100:26	.....	5.08	12	May 05	136:00	136:06	+20	6.30
$6\frac{1}{8}$	May 97n	100:06	100:08	+ 1	5.19	$6\frac{1}{2}$	Aug 05n	101:08	101:10	+18	6.30
$6\frac{3}{4}$	May 97n	100:11	100:13	.....	5.26	$10\frac{3}{4}$	Aug 05	128:20	128:26	+20	6.32
$5\frac{5}{8}$	Jun 97n	100:03	100:05	.....	5.16	$5\frac{7}{8}$	Nov 05n	97:01	97:03	+18	6.31
$6\frac{3}{8}$	Jun 97n	100:12	100:14	.....	5.15	$5\frac{5}{8}$	Feb 06n	95:08	95:10	+18	6.32
$8\frac{1}{2}$	Jul 97n	101:09	101:11	.....	5.17	$9\frac{3}{8}$	Feb 06	120:25	120:31	+21	6.29
$5\frac{1}{2}$	Jul 97n	100:02	100:04	+ 1	5.21	$6\frac{7}{8}$	May 06n	103:21	103:23	+19	6.34

GOVT. BONDS & NOTES

Coupon rate   Maturity date   Denotes note   Price   Change in asked price   Yield to maturity

Prices are quoted as a percentage of face value, with the fractional part expressed in 32nd's. Accrued interest must be added to the quoted price.

Source: *The Wall Street Journal,* February 14, 1997.

half being paid every 6 months in this case). The maturity month is given; the precise maturity date varies with the issue, but it is often the fifteenth of the month of maturity for U.S. Treasury bonds and notes. Prices are quoted as a percentage of face value, so if the face value is $1,000, a price of 100 is equivalent to $1,000. The **bid price** is the price dealers are willing to pay for the bond, and hence the price at which the bond can be sold immediately; whereas the **ask price** is the price at which dealers are willing to sell the bond, and hence the price at which it can be bought immediately. A special and cumbersome feature is that prices are quoted in 32nd's of a point. The bid price for the last bond shown in Table 3.3 is 103 21/32, which for a $1,000 face value translates into $1,036.56. The yield shown is based on the ask price in a manner described in the following section.

Bond quotations ignore **accrued interest,** which must be added to the price quoted in order to obtain the actual amount that must be paid for the bond. Suppose that a bond makes coupon payments every 6 months. If you purchase the bond midway through the coupon period, you will receive your first coupon payment after only 3 months. You are getting extra interest—interest that was, in theory, earned by the previous owner. So you must pay the first 3 months' interest to the previous owner. This interest payment is made at the time of the sale, not when the next coupon payment is made, so this extra payment acts like an addition to the price. The accrued interest that must be paid to the previous owner is determined by a straight-line interpolation based on days. Specifically, the accrued interest (AI) is

$$AI = \frac{\text{number of days since last coupon}}{\text{number of days in current coupon period}} \times \text{coupon amount}.$$

Example 3.5 (Accrued interest calculation)   Suppose we purchase on May 8 a U.S. Treasury bond that matures on August 15 in some distant year. The coupon rate is 9%. Coupon payments are made every February 15 and August 15. The accrued interest is computed by noting that there have been 83 days since the last coupon (in a leap year) and 99 days until the next coupon payment. Hence,

$$AI = \frac{83}{83 + 99} \times 4.50 = 2.05.$$

This 2.05 would be added to the quoted price, expressed as a percentage of the face value. For example, $20.50 would be added to the bond if its face value were $1,000.

Quality Ratings

Although bonds offer a supposedly fixed-income stream, they are subject to default if the issuer has financial difficulties or falls into bankruptcy. To characterize the nature of this risk, bonds are rated by rating organizations. The two primary rating classifications are issued and published by Moody's and Standard & Poor's. Their classification schemes are shown in Table 3.4. U.S. Treasury securities are not rated, since they are considered to be essentially free of default risk.

TABLE 3.4
Rating Classifications

	Moody's	Standard & Poor's
High grade	Aaa	AAA
	Aa	AA
Medium grade	A	A
	Baa	BBB
Speculative grade	Ba	BB
	B	B
Default danger	Caa	CCC
	Ca	CC
	C	C
		D

Ratings reflect a judgment of the likelihood that bond payments will be made as scheduled. Bonds with low ratings usually sell at lower prices than comparable bonds with high ratings.

Bonds that are either high or medium grade are considered to be **investment grade.** Bonds that are in or below the speculative category are often termed **junk bonds.** Historically, the frequency of default has correlated well with the assigned ratings.

The assignment of a rating class by a rating organization is largely based on the issuer's financial status as measured by various financial ratios. For example, the ratio of debt to equity, the ratio of current assets to current liabilities, the ratio of cash flow to outstanding debt, as well as several others are used. The trend in these ratios is also considered important.

A bond with a low rating will have a lower price than a comparable bond with a high rating. Hence some people have argued that junk bonds may occasionally offer good value if the default risk can be diversified. A careful analysis of this approach requires explicit consideration of uncertainty, however.

3.4 YIELD

A bond's yield is the interest rate implied by the payment structure. Specifically, it is the interest rate at which the present value of the stream of payments (consisting of the coupon payments and the final face-value redemption payment) is exactly equal to the current price. This value is termed more properly the **yield to maturity** (YTM) to distinguish it from other yield numbers that are sometimes used. Yields are always quoted on an annual basis.

It should be clear that the yield to maturity is just the internal rate of return of the bond at the current price. But when discussing bonds, the term *yield* is generally used instead.

Suppose that a bond with face value F makes m coupon payments of C/m each year and there are n periods remaining. The coupon payments sum to C within a year.

Suppose also that the current price of the bond is P. Then the yield to maturity is the value of λ such that

$$P = \frac{F}{[1 + (\lambda/m)]^n} + \sum_{k=1}^{n} \frac{C/m}{[1 + (\lambda/m)]^k} . \tag{3.1}$$

This value of λ, the yield to maturity, is the interest rate implied by the bond when interest is compounded m times per year. Note that the first term in (3.1) is the present value of the face-value payment. The kth term in the summation is the present value of the kth coupon payment C/m. The sum of the present values, based on a nominal interest rate of λ, is set equal to the bond's price.

The summation in (3.1) can be collapsed by use of the general value formula for annuities in the previous section, since this sum represents the present value of the equal coupon payments of C/m. The collapsed form is highlighted here:

Bond price formula   *The price of a bond, having exactly n coupon periods remaining to maturity and a yield to maturity of λ, satisfies*

$$P = \frac{F}{[1 + (\lambda/m)]^n} + \frac{C}{\lambda}\left\{1 - \frac{1}{[1 + (\lambda/m)]^n}\right\} \tag{3.2}$$

where F is the face value of the bond, C is the yearly coupon payment, and m is the number of coupon payments per year.

Equation (3.2) must be solved for λ to determine the yield. This cannot be done by hand except for very simple cases. It should be clear that the terms in (3.2) are the familiar terms giving the present value of a single future payment and of an annuity. However, to determine λ one must do more than just evaluate these expressions. One must adjust λ so that (3.2) is satisfied. As in any calculation of internal rate of return, this generally requires an iterative procedure, easily carried out by a computer. There are, however, specialized calculators and bond tables devised for this purpose, which are used by bond dealers and other professionals. Spreadsheet packages also typically have built-in bond formulas.

The formulas discussed here assume that there is an exact number of coupon periods remaining to the maturity date. The price–yield formula requires adjustment for dates between coupon payment dates.

Qualitative Nature of Price–Yield Curves

Although the bond equation is complex, it is easy to obtain a qualitative understanding of the relationship between price, yield, coupon, and time to maturity. This qualitative understanding helps motivate the ideas underlying bond portfolio construction and, specifically, leads to an understanding of the interest rate risk properties of bonds. The following examples should be studied with an eye toward obtaining this kind of understanding.

As a general rule, the yields of various bonds track one another and the prevailing interest rates of other fixed-income securities quite closely. After all, most people would not buy a bond with a yield of 6% when bank CDs are offering 10%. The general interest rate environment exerts a force on every bond, urging its yield to conform to that of other bonds. However, the only way that the yield of a bond can change is for the bond's price to change. So as yields move, prices move correspondingly. But the price change required to match a yield change varies with the structure of the bond (its coupon rate and its maturity). So as the yields of various bonds move more or less in harmony, their prices move by different amounts. To understand bonds, it is important to understand this relation between the price and the yield. For a given bond, this relationship is shown pictorially by the **price–yield curve.**

Examples of price–yield curves are shown in Figure 3.3. Here the price, as a percentage of par, is shown as a function of YTM expressed in percentage terms. Let us focus on the bond labeled 10%. This bond has a 10% coupon (which means 10% of the face value is paid each year, or 5% every 6 months), and it has 30 years to maturity. The price–yield curve shows how yield and price are related.

The first obvious feature of the curve is that it has negative slope; that is, price and yield have an inverse relation. If yield goes up, price goes down. If I am to obtain a higher yield on a fixed stream of received payments, the price I pay for this stream must be lower. This is a fundamental feature of bond markets. When people say "the bond market went down," they mean that interest rates went up.

Some points on the curve can be calculated by inspection. First, suppose that YTM $= 0$. This means that the bond is priced as if it offered no interest. Within the framework of this bond, money in the future is not discounted. In that case, the present value of the bond is just equal to the sum of all payments: here coupon payments of 10 points each year for 30 years, giving 300, plus the 100% of par value received at maturity, for a total of 400. This is the value of the bond at zero yield. Second, suppose that YTM $= 10\%$. Then the value of the bond is equal to the par value. The reason for this is that each year the coupon payment just equals the 10% yield expected on the

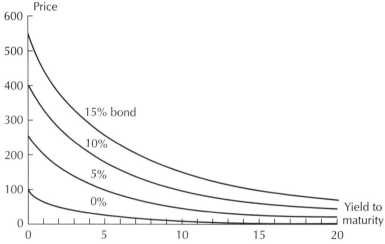

FIGURE 3.3   Price–yield curves and coupon rate. All bonds shown have a maturity of 30 years and the coupon rates indicated on the respective curves. Prices are expressed as a percentage of par.

investment. The value remains at 100 every year. The bond is like a loan where the interest on the principal is paid each year and hence the principal remains constant. In this situation, where the yield is exactly equal to the coupon rate, the bond is termed a **par bond.** In addition to these two specific points on the price–yield curve, we can deduce that the price of the bond must tend toward zero as the yield increases—large yields imply heavy discounting, so even the nearest coupon payment has little present value. Overall, the shape of the curve is **convex** since it bends toward the origin and out toward the horizontal axis. Just given the two points and this rough knowledge of shape, it is possible to sketch a reasonable approximation to the true curve.

Let us briefly examine another one of the curves, say, the 15% bond. The price at YTM $= 0$ is $15 \times 30 + 100 = 550$, and the par point of 100 is at 15%. We see that with a fixed maturity date, the price–yield curve rises as the coupon rate increases.

Now let us consider the influence of the time to maturity. Figure 3.4 shows the price–yield curves for three different bonds. Each of these bonds has a 10% coupon rate, but they have different maturities: 30 years, 10 years, and 3 years. All of these bonds are at par when the yield is 10%; hence the three curves all pass through the common par point. However, the curves pivot upward around that point by various amounts, depending on the maturity. The values at YTM $= 0$ can be found easily, as before, by simply summing the total payments. The main feature is that as the maturity is increased, the price–yield curve becomes steeper, essentially pivoting about the par point. This increased steepness is an indication that longer maturities imply greater sensitivity of price to yield.

The price–yield curve is important because it describes the interest rate risk associated with a bond. For example, suppose that you purchased the 10% bond illustrated in Figure 3.3 at par (when the yield was 10%). It is likely that all bonds of maturity approximately equal to 30 years would have yields of 10%, even though some might not be at par. Then 10% would represent the market rate for such bonds.

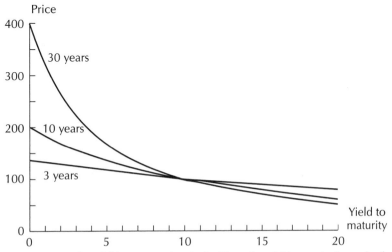

FIGURE 3.4 Price–yield curves and maturity. The price–yield curve is shown for three maturities. All bonds have a 10% coupon.

TABLE 3.5
Prices of 9% Coupon Bonds

Time to maturity	Yield				
	5%	8%	9%	10%	15%
1 year	103.85	100.94	100.00	99.07	94.61
5 years	117.50	104.06	100.00	96.14	79.41
10 years	131.18	106.80	100.00	93.77	69.42
20 years	150.21	109.90	100.00	91.42	62.22
30 years	161.82	111.31	100.00	90.54	60.52

The prices of long-maturity bonds are more sensitive to yield changes than are the prices of bonds of short maturity.

Now suppose that market conditions change and the yield on your bond increases to 11%. The price of your bond will drop to 91.28. This represents an 8.72% change in the value of your bond. It is good to consider the possibility of such a change when purchasing this bond. For example, with a 3-year 10% par bond, if the yield rose to 11%, the price would drop only to 97.50, and hence the interest rate risk is lower with this bond. Of course if yields *decreased*, you would *profit* by similar amounts.

Bond holders are subject to yield risk in the sense described: if yields change, bond prices also change. This is an immediate risk, affecting the near-term value of the bond. You may, of course, continue to hold the bond and thereby continue to receive the promised coupon payments and the face value at maturity. This cash flow stream is not affected by interest rates. (That is after all why the bond is classified as a fixed-income security.) But if you plan to sell the bond before maturity, the price will be governed by the price–yield curve.

Table 3.5 displays the price–yield relation in tabular form for bonds with a 9% coupon rate. It is easy to see that the bond with 30-year maturity is much more sensitive to yield changes than the bond with 1-year maturity.

It is the quantification of this risk that underlies the importance of the price–yield relation. Our rough qualitative understanding is important. The next sections develop additional tools for studying this risk.

Other Yield Measures

Other measures of yield, aside from yield to maturity, are used to gain additional insight into a bond's properties. For example, one important yield measure is **current yield** (CY), which is defined as

$$CY = \frac{\text{annual coupon payment}}{\text{bond price}} \times 100.$$

The current yield gives a measure of the annual return of the bond. For instance, consider a 10%, 30-year bond. If it is selling at par (that is, at 100), then the current yield is 10, which is identical to the coupon rate and to the yield to maturity. If the same bond were selling for 90, then CY = 10/90 = 11.11 while YTM = 11.16.

Another measure, used if the bond is callable after some number of years, is the **yield to call** (YTC), which is defined as the internal rate of return calculated assuming that the bond is in fact called at the earliest possible date.

There are several other yield measures that account for sinking funds, principal payments, and other features.

3.5 DURATION

Everything else being equal, bonds with long maturities have steeper price–yield curves than bonds with short maturities. Hence the prices of **long bonds** are more sensitive to interest rate changes than those of **short bonds.** This is shown clearly in Table 3.5. However, this is only a rough rule of thumb. Maturity itself does not give a complete quantitative measure of interest rate sensitivity.

Another measure of time length termed **duration** *does* give a direct measure of interest rate sensitivity. This section describes this measure.

The duration of a fixed-income instrument is a weighted average of the times that payments (cash flows) are made. The weighting coefficients are the present values of the individual cash flows.

We can write out this definition more explicitly. Suppose that cash flows are received at times $t_0, t_1, t_2, \ldots, t_n$. Then the duration of this stream is

$$D = \frac{\mathrm{PV}(t_0)t_0 + \mathrm{PV}(t_1)t_1 + \mathrm{PV}(t_2)t_2 + \cdots + \mathrm{PV}(t_n)t_n}{\mathrm{PV}}.$$

In this formula the expression $\mathrm{PV}(t_k)$ denotes the present value of the cash flow that occurs at time t_k. The term PV in the denominator is the total present value, which is the sum of the individual $\mathrm{PV}(t_k)$ values.

The expression for D is indeed a weighted average of the cash flow times. Hence D itself has units of time. When the cash flows are all nonnegative, as they are for a bond already owned (so that the purchase is not included in the cash flow), then it is clear that $t_0 \leq D \leq t_n$. Duration is a time intermediate between the first and last cash flows.

Clearly, a zero-coupon bond, which makes only a final payment at maturity, has a duration equal to its maturity date. Nonzero-coupon bonds have durations strictly less than their maturity dates. This shows that duration can be viewed as a generalized maturity measure. It is an average of the maturities of all the individual payments.

Macaulay Duration

The preceding definition is (intentionally) a bit vague about how the present value is calculated; that is, what interest rate to use. For a bond it is natural to base those calculations on the bond's yield. If indeed the yield is used, the general duration formula becomes the Macaulay duration.

Specifically, suppose a financial instrument makes payments m times per year, with the payment in period k being c_k, and there are n periods remaining. The

A	B	C	D	E	F
		Discount factor	Present value of payment	Weight	
Year	Payment	(@ 8%)	($B \times C$)	(D/Price)	$A \times E$
.5	3.5	.962	3.365	.035	.017
1	3.5	.925	3.236	.033	.033
1.5	3.5	.889	3.111	.032	.048
2	3.5	.855	2.992	.031	.061
2.5	3.5	.822	2.877	.030	.074
3	103.5	.790	81.798	.840	2.520
Sum			97.379 Price	1.000	2.753 Duration

FIGURE 3.5 Layout for calculating duration. Present values of payments are calculated in column D. Dividing these by the total present value gives the weights shown in column E. The duration is obtained using this weighted average of the payment times.

Macaulay duration D is defined as

$$D = \frac{\sum_{k=1}^{n} (k/m)c_k/[1 + (\lambda/m)]^k}{\text{PV}}$$

where λ is the yield to maturity and

$$\text{PV} = \sum_{k=1}^{n} \frac{c_k}{[1 + (\lambda/m)]^k}.$$

Note that the factor k/m in the numerator of the formula for D is time, measured in years. In this chapter we always use the Macaulay duration (or a slight modification of it), and hence we do not give it a special symbol, but denote it by D, the same as in the general definition of duration.

Example 3.6 (A short bond)   Consider a 7% bond with 3 years to maturity. Assume that the bond is selling at 8% yield. We can find the value and the Macaulay duration by the simple spreadsheet layout shown in Figure 3.5. The duration is 2.753 years.

Explicit Formula*

In the case where all coupon payments are identical (which is the normal case for bonds) there is an explicit formula for the sum of the series that appears in the numerator of the expression for the Macaulay duration. We skip the algebra here and just give the result.

 Macaulay duration formula   *The Macaulay duration for a bond with a coupon rate c per period, yield y per period, m periods per year, and exactly n periods remaining, is*

$$D = \frac{1 + y}{my} - \frac{1 + y + n(c - y)}{mc[(1 + y)^n - 1] + my}. \tag{3.3}$$

Example 3.7 (Duration of a 30-year par bond) Consider the 10%, 30-year bond represented in Figure 3.3. Let us assume that it is at par; that is, the yield is 10%. At par, $c = y$, and (3.3) reduces to

$$D = \frac{1+y}{my}\left[1 - \frac{1}{(1+y)^n}\right].$$

Hence,

$$D = \frac{1.05}{.1}\left[1 - \frac{1}{(1.05)^{60}}\right] = 9.938.$$

Qualitative Properties of Duration*

The duration of a coupon-paying bond is always less than its maturity, but often it is surprisingly short. An appreciation for the relation between a bond's duration and other parameters of the bond can be obtained by examination of Table 3.6. In this table the yield is held fixed at 5%, but various maturities and coupon rates are considered. This procedure approximates the situation of looking through a list of available bonds at a time when all yields hover near 5%. Within a given class (say, government securities) the available bonds then differ mainly by these two parameters.

One striking feature of this table is that as the time to maturity increases to infinity, the durations do *not* also increase to infinity, but instead tend to a finite limit that is independent of the coupon rate. (See Exercise 14.) Another feature of the table is that the durations do not vary rapidly with respect to the coupon rate. The fact that the yield is held constant tends to cancel out the influence of the coupons.

A general conclusion is that very long durations (of, say, 20 years or more) are achieved only by bonds that have both very long maturities and very low coupon rates.

TABLE 3.6
Duration of a Bond Yielding 5%
as Function of Maturity and Coupon Rate

Years to maturity	Coupon rate			
	1%	2%	5%	10%
1	.997	.995	.988	.977
2	1.984	1.969	1.928	1.868
5	4.875	4.763	4.485	4.156
10	9.416	8.950	7.989	7.107
25	20.164	17.715	14.536	12.754
50	26.666	22.284	18.765	17.384
100	22.572	21.200	20.363	20.067
∞	20.500	20.500	20.500	20.500

Duration does not increase appreciably with maturity. In fact, with fixed yield, duration increases only to a finite limit as maturity is increased.

Duration and Sensitivity

Duration is useful because it measures directly the sensitivity of price to changes in yield. This follows from a simple expression for the derivative of the present value expression.

In the case where payments are made m times per year and yield is based on those same periods, we have

$$PV_k = \frac{c_k}{[1 + (\lambda/m)]^k}.$$

The derivative with respect to λ is

$$\frac{d\,PV_k}{d\lambda} = \frac{-(k/m)c_k}{[1 + (\lambda/m)]^{k+1}} = -\frac{k/m}{1 + (\lambda/m)}PV_k.$$

We now apply this to the expression for price,

$$P = \sum_{k=1}^{n} PV_k.$$

Here we have used the fact that the price is equal to the total present value at the yield (by definition of yield). We find that

$$\frac{dP}{d\lambda} = \sum_{k=1}^{n} \frac{d\,PV_k}{d\lambda} = -\sum_{k=1}^{n} \frac{(k/m)PV_k}{1 + (\lambda/m)} = -\frac{1}{1 + (\lambda/m)}DP \equiv -D_M P. \qquad (3.4)$$

The value D_M is called the **modified duration.** It is the usual duration modified by the extra term in the denominator. Note that $D_M \approx D$ for large values of m or small values of λ. We highlight this important sensitivity relation:

Price sensitivity formula   *The derivative of price P with respect to yield λ of a fixed-income security is*

$$\frac{dP}{d\lambda} = -D_M P \qquad (3.5)$$

where $D_M = D/[1 + (\lambda/m)]$ is the modified duration.

It is perhaps most revealing to write (3.5) as

$$\frac{1}{P}\frac{dP}{d\lambda} = -D_M.$$

The left side is then the relative change in price (or the fractional change). Hence D_M measures the relative change in a bond's price directly as λ changes.

By using the approximation $dP/d\lambda \approx \Delta P/\Delta\lambda$, Equation (3.5) can be used to estimate the change in price due to a small change in yield (or vice versa). Specifically, we would write

$$\Delta P \approx -D_M P\,\Delta\lambda.$$

This gives explicit values for the impact of yield variations.

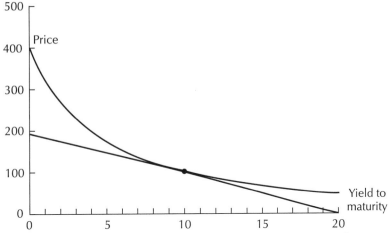

FIGURE 3.6   Price–yield curve and slope. The slope of the line tangent to the curve at P is $-D_M P$.

Example 3.8 (A 10% bond)   The price–yield curve for a 30-year, 10% coupon bond is shown in Figure 3.6. As computed earlier, the duration of this bond at the par point (where price = 100) is $D = 9.94$. Hence $D_M = 9.94/1.05 = 9.47$. The slope of the price–yield curve at that point is, according to (3.3), equal to $dP/d\lambda = -947$. A line with this slope can be placed tangent to the price–yield curve at the point where the duration was calculated, as shown in Figure 3.6. This line provides a straight-line approximation to the curve for nearby points. For example, if the yield changes to 11%, we can estimate the change in price as

$$\Delta P = -D_M 100 \, \Delta\lambda = -947 \times .01 = -9.47 \,.$$

Hence $P \approx 90.53$.

Example 3.9 (A zero-coupon bond)   Consider a 30-year zero-coupon bond. Suppose its current yield is 10%. Then we have $D = 30$ and $D_M \approx 27$. Suppose that yields increase to 11%. According to (3.5), the relative price change is approximately equal to 27%. This is a very large loss in value. Because of their long durations, zero-coupon bonds have very high interest rate risk.

Duration of a Portfolio

Suppose that a portfolio of several bonds of different maturities is assembled. This portfolio acts like a master fixed-income security: it receives periodic payments, but due to the different maturities, the payments may not be of equal magnitude. What can we say about the duration of this portfolio?

First, suppose that all the bonds have the same yield. (This is usually approximately true, since yields tend to track each other closely, if not exactly.) The duration of the portfolio is then just a weighted sum of the durations of the individual bonds—with weighting coefficients proportional to individual bond prices. We can easily verify this for a portfolio that is the sum of two bonds A and B. The durations are

$$D^A = \frac{\sum_{k=0}^{n} t_k PV_k^A}{P^A}$$

$$D^B = \frac{\sum_{k=0}^{n} t_k PV_k^B}{P^B}.$$

Hence,

$$P^A D^A + P^B D^B = \sum_{k=0}^{n} t_k \left(PV_k^A + PV_k^B \right)$$

which gives, upon division by $P = P^A + P^B$,

$$D = \frac{P^A D^A}{P} + \frac{P^B D^B}{P}$$

as the duration of the portfolio. Therefore D is a weighted average of the durations of the individual bonds, with the weight of a bond's duration being proportional to that bond's price. The result easily extends to a portfolio containing several bonds.

Duration of a portfolio   *Suppose there are m fixed-income securities with prices and durations of P_i and D_i, respectively, $i = 1, 2, \ldots, m$, all computed at a common yield. The portfolio consisting of the aggregate of these securities has price P and duration D, given by*

$$P = P_1 + P_2 + \cdots + P_m$$

$$D = w_1 D_1 + w_2 D_2 + \cdots + w_m D_m$$

where $w_i = P_i/P$, $i = 1, 2, \ldots, m$.

The duration of a portfolio measures the interest rate sensitivity of that portfolio, just as normal duration measures it for a single bond. That is, if the yield changes by a small amount, the total value of the portfolio will change approximately by the amount predicted by the equation relating prices to (modified) duration.

If the bonds composing a portfolio have different yields, the composite duration as defined can still be used as an approximation. In this case a single yield must be chosen—perhaps the average. Then present values can be calculated with respect to this single yield value, although these present values will not be exactly equal to the prices of the bonds. The weighted average duration, calculated as shown, will give the sensitivity of the overall present value to a change in the yield figure that is used.

3.6 IMMUNIZATION

We now have the concepts and tools necessary to solve a problem of major practical value, namely, the structuring of a bond portfolio to protect against interest rate risk.

This procedure is termed **immunization** because it "immunizes" the portfolio value against interest rate changes. The procedure, as well as its refinements, is in fact one of the most (if not *the* most) widely used analytical techniques of investment science, shaping portfolios consisting of billions of dollars of fixed-income securities held by pension funds, insurance companies, and other financial institutions.

Before describing the procedure, let us more fully consider its purpose. A portfolio cannot be structured meaningfully without a statement of its purpose. The purpose helps define the character of risk one is willing to assume. For example, suppose that you wish to invest money now that will be used next year for a major household expense. If you invest in 1-year Treasury bills, you know exactly how much money these bills will be worth in a year, and hence there is little risk relative to your purpose. If, on the other hand, you invested in a 10-year zero-coupon bond, the value of this bond a year from now would be quite variable, depending on what happens to interest rates during the year. This investment has high risk relative to your purpose. The situation would be reversed if you were saving the money to pay off an obligation that was due in 10 years. Then the 10-year zero-coupon bond would provide completely predictable results, but the 1-year Treasury bill would impose **reinvestment risk** since the proceeds would have to be reinvested after 1 year at the then prevailing rate (which could be considerably lower than the current rate).

Suppose now that you face a series of cash obligations and you wish to acquire a portfolio that you will use to pay these obligations as they arise. (This is the sort of problem faced by life insurance companies.) One way to do this is to purchase a set of zero-coupon bonds that have maturities and face values exactly matching the separate obligations. However, this simple technique may not be feasible if corporate bonds are used, since there are few corporate zero-coupon bonds. (You may wish to use corporate bonds because they offer higher yields than U.S. Treasury bonds.) If perfect matching is not possible, you may instead acquire a portfolio having a value equal to the present value of the stream of obligations. You can sell some of your portfolio whenever cash is needed to meet a particular obligation; or if your portfolio delivers more cash than needed at a given time (from coupon or face value payments), you can buy more bonds. If the yield does not change, the value of your portfolio will, throughout this process, continue to match the present value of the remaining obligations. Hence you will meet the obligations exactly.

A problem with this present-value-matching technique arises if the yields change. The value of your portfolio and the present value of the obligation stream will both change in response, but probably by amounts that differ from one another. Your portfolio will no longer be matched.

Immunization solves this problem—at least approximately—by matching durations as well as present values. If the duration of the portfolio matches that of the obligation stream, then the cash value of the portfolio and the present value of the obligation stream will respond identically (to first order) to a change in yield. Specifically, if yields increase, the present value of the asset portfolio will decrease, but the present value of the obligation will decrease by approximately the same amount; so the value of the portfolio will still be adequate to cover the obligation. The process is best explained through an example.

Example 3.10 (The X Corporation)   The X Corporation has an obligation to pay $1 million in 10 years. It wishes to invest money now that will be sufficient to meet this obligation.

The purchase of a single zero-coupon bond would provide one solution; but such zeros are not always available in the required maturities. We assume that none are available for this example. Instead the X Corporation is planning to select from the three corporate bonds shown in Table 3.7. (Note that in this table, and throughout this example, prices are expressed in ordinary decimal form, not in 32nd's.)

These bonds all have the same yield of 9%, and this rate is used in all calculations. The X Corporation first considers using bonds 2 and 3 to construct its portfolio. As a first step it calculates the durations and finds $D_2 = 6.54$ and $D_3 = 9.61$, respectively. This is a serious problem! The duration of the obligation is obviously 10 years, and there is no way to attain that with a weighted average of D_2 and D_3 using positive weights. A bond with a longer duration is required. Therefore the X Corporation decides to use bonds 1 and 2. It is found that $D_1 = 11.44$. (Note that, consistent with the discussion on the qualitative nature of durations, it is quite difficult to obtain a long duration when the yield is 9%—a long maturity and a low coupon are required.) Fortunately $D_1 > 10$, and hence bonds 1 and 2 will work.

Next the present value of the obligation is computed at 9% interest. This is PV = $414,643. The immunized portfolio is found by solving the two equations

$$V_1 + V_2 = \text{PV}$$

$$D_1 V_1 + D_2 V_2 = 10\,\text{PV}$$

for the amounts of money V_1 and V_2 to be invested in the two bonds. The first equation states that the total value of the portfolio must equal the total present value of the obligation. The second states that the duration of the portfolio must equal the duration (10 years) of the obligation. (This relation is best seen by dividing through by PV.) The solution to these equations is $V_1 = \$292,788.73$ and $V_2 = \$121,854.27$. The number of bonds to be purchased is then found by dividing each value by the respective bond price. (We assume a face value of $100.) These numbers are then rounded to integers to define the portfolio.

The results are shown in Table 3.8. Note that, except for rounding error, the present value of the portfolio does indeed equal that of the obligation. Furthermore, at different yields (8% and 10% are shown) the value of the portfolio is still approximately equal to that of the obligation. In fact, due to the structure of the price–yield

TABLE 3.7
Bond Choices

	Rate	Maturity	Price	Yield
Bond 1	6%	30 yr	69.04	9.00%
Bond 2	11%	10 yr	113.01	9.00%
Bond 3	9%	20 yr	100.00	9.00%

Three bonds are considered for the X Corporation's immunized portfolio.

TABLE 3.8
Immunization Results

	Percent yield		
	9.0	**8.0**	**10.0**
Bond 1			
Price	69.04	77.38	62.14
Shares	4,241.00	4,241.00	4,241.00
Value	292,798.64	328,168.58	263,535.74
Bond 2			
Price	113.01	120.39	106.23
Shares	1,078.00	1,078.00	1,078.00
Value	121,824.78	129,780.42	114,515.94
Obligation			
Value	414,642.86	456,386.95	376,889.48
Surplus	−19.44	1,562.05	1,162.20

The net surplus of portfolio value minus obligation value remains approximately equal to zero even if yields change.

curve, the portfolio value will always exceed the value of the obligation in both cases. (See Exercise 16.)

Immunization provides protection against changes in yield. If the yield changes immediately after purchase of the portfolio, the new value of the portfolio will, in theory, still approximately match the new value of the future obligation. However, once the yield does change, the new portfolio will not be immunized at the new rate. It is therefore desirable to **rebalance,** or reimmunize, the portfolio from time to time. Also, in practice more than two bonds would be used, partly to diversify default risk if the bonds included are not U.S. Treasury bonds.

Immunization is a clever idea, but it suffers some shortcomings, at least in this simple form. The method assumes that all yields are equal, whereas in fact they usually are not. Indeed it is quite unrealistic to assume that both long- and short-duration bonds can be found with identical yields. Usually long bonds have somewhat higher yields than short bonds. Furthermore, when yields change, it is unlikely that the yields on all bonds will change by the same amount; hence rebalancing would be difficult. We shall consider some important extensions of immunization in the next chapter, and in Chapter 5 we shall consider other approaches to bond portfolio construction. Overall, however, the technique given here is surprisingly practical.

3.7 CONVEXITY*

Modified duration measures the relative slope of the price–yield curve at a given point. As we have seen, this leads to a straight-line approximation to the price–yield curve that is useful both as a means of assessing risk and as a procedure for controlling it.

An even better approximation can be obtained by including a second-order (or quadratic) term. This second-order term is based on **convexity,** which is the relative curvature at a given point on the price–yield curve. Specifically, convexity is the value of C defined as

$$C = \frac{1}{P} \frac{d^2 P}{d\lambda^2}$$

which can be expressed in terms of the cash flow stream as

$$C = \frac{1}{P} \sum_{k=1}^{n} \frac{d^2 PV_k}{d\lambda^2}.$$

Assuming m coupons (and m compounding periods) per year, we have

$$C = \frac{1}{P[1 + (\lambda/m)]^2} \sum_{k=1}^{n} \frac{k(k+1)}{m^2} \frac{c_k}{[1 + (\lambda/m)]^k}.$$

Note that convexity has units of time squared. Convexity is the weighted average of $t_k t_{k+1}$ where, like for duration, the weights are proportional to the present values of the corresponding cash flows. Then the result is *modified* by the factor $1/[1 + (\lambda/m)]^2$. An explicit formula can be derived for the case of equal-valued coupon payments.

Suppose that at a price P and a corresponding yield λ, the modified duration D_M and the convexity C are calculated. Then if $\Delta\lambda$ is a small change in λ and ΔP is the corresponding change in P, we have

$$\Delta P \approx -D_M P \, \Delta\lambda + \frac{PC}{2}(\Delta\lambda)^2.$$

This is the second-order approximation to the price–yield curve. Convexity can be used to improve immunization in the sense that, compared to ordinary immunization, a closer match of asset portfolio value and obligation value is maintained as yields vary. To account for convexity in immunization, one structures a portfolio of bonds such that its present value, its duration, and its convexity match those of the obligation. Generally, at least three bonds are required for this purpose.

3.8 SUMMARY

Fixed-income securities are fundamental investment instruments, which are part of essentially every investment portfolio, and which reflect the market conditions for interest rates directly.

There are numerous kinds of fixed-income securities, designed for various investment and business purposes. However, the vast bulk of money in fixed-income securities is committed to mortgages and bonds.

Many fixed-income securities make periodic payments to the owner of the security. This is true, in particular, for mortgages, loans, annuities, and bonds. In the case of bonds, these payments are usually made every 6 months and are termed coupon payments.

Usually the periodic payments associated with a fixed-income security are of equal magnitude, and there is an important formula relating the payment amount A, the principal value of the security P, the single-period interest rate r, and the number of payment periods n:

$$P = \frac{A}{r}\left[1 - \frac{1}{(1+r)^n}\right].$$

This single formula can be used to evaluate most annuities, mortgages, and bonds, and it can be used to amortize capital expenses over time.

Bonds are the most important type of fixed-income security for general investment purposes. Important reference bonds are U.S. Treasury securities—bills, notes, and bonds—of various maturities and coupon values. These bonds are considered to be default free and thus carry prices that are somewhat higher than corporate securities with similar coupon rates and maturities.

There are many variations to the generic coupon bond—call features, sinking fund bonds, bonds whose coupon rates are tied to economic indices, and so forth. In addition, municipal bonds receive special tax treatment.

A special feature of bonds is that the buyer must usually pay accrued interest in addition to the quoted price. This accrued interest is compensation to the previous owner for the coupon interest that has been earned since the last coupon payment.

Bonds are frequently analyzed by computing the yield to maturity. This is the annual interest rate that is implied by the current price. It is the interest rate that makes the present value of the promised bond payments equal to the current bond price. This calculation of yield can be turned around: the price of a bond can be found as a function of the yield. This is the price–yield relation which, when plotted, produces the price–yield curve.

The slope of the price–yield curve is a measure of the sensitivity of the price to changes in yield. Since yields tend to track the prevailing interest rate, the slope of the price–yield curve is therefore a measure of the interest rate risk associated with a particular bond. As a general rule, long bonds have greater slope than short bonds, and thus long bonds have greater interest rate risk. A normalized version of the slope—the slope divided by the current bond price—is given by the (modified) duration of the bond. Hence duration (or, more exactly, modified duration) is a convenient measure of interest rate risk.

Immunization is the process of constructing a portfolio that has, to first order, no interest rate risk. The process is frequently applied by institutions, such as insurance companies and pension funds, that have large future payment obligations. They wish to prepare for these obligations by making appropriate investments in fixed-income securities. A portfolio is immunized if its present value is equal to that of the stream of obligations and if its duration matches that of the obligation. In other words, the net portfolio, consisting of the obligation stream and the fixed-income assets, has zero present value and zero duration.

EXERCISES

1. (Amortization)   A debt of $25,000 is to be amortized over 7 years at 7% interest. What value of monthly payments will achieve this?

2. (Cycles and annual worth ◇)   Given a cash flow stream $X = (x_0, x_1, x_2, \ldots, x_n)$, a new stream X_∞ of infinite length is made by successively repeating the corresponding finite stream. The interest rate is r. Let P and A be the present value and the annual worth, respectively, of stream X. Finally, let P_∞ be the present value of stream X_∞. Find A in terms of P_∞ and conclude that A can be used as well as P_∞ for evaluation purposes.

3. (Uncertain annuity ◇)   Gavin's grandfather, Mr. Jones, has just turned 90 years old and is applying for a lifetime annuity that will pay $10,000 per year, starting 1 year from now, until he dies. He asks Gavin to analyze it for him. Gavin finds that according to statistical summaries, the chance (probability) that Mr. Jones will die at any particular age is as follows:

age	90	91	92	93	94	95	96	97	98	99	100	101
probability	.07	.08	.09	.10	.10	.10	.10	.10	.10	.07	.05	.04

Then Gavin (and you) answer the following questions:

(a) What is the life expectancy of Mr. Jones?
(b) What is the present value of an annuity at 8% interest that has a lifetime equal to Mr. Jones's life expectancy? (For an annuity of a nonintegral number of years, use an averaging method.)
(c) What is the expected present value of the annuity?

4. (APR)   For the mortgage listed second in Table 3.1 what are the total fees?

5. (Callable bond)   The Z Corporation issues a 10%, 20-year bond at a time when yields are 10%. The bond has a call provision that allows the corporation to force a bond holder to redeem his or her bond at face value plus 5%. After 5 years the corporation finds that exercise of this call provision is advantageous. What can you deduce about the yield at that time? (Assume one coupon payment per year.)

6. (The biweekly mortgage ⊕)   Here is a proposal that has been advanced as a way for homeowners to save thousands of dollars on mortgage payments: pay biweekly instead of monthly. Specifically, if monthly payments are x, it is suggested that one instead pay $x/2$ every two weeks (for a total of 26 payments per year). This will pay down the mortgage faster, saving interest. The savings are surprisingly dramatic for this seemingly minor modification—often cutting the total interest payment by over one-third. Assume a loan amount of $100,000 for 30 years at 10% interest, compounded monthly.

(a) Under a monthly payment program, what are the monthly payments and the total interest paid over the course of the 30 years?
(b) Using the biweekly program, when will the loan be completely repaid, and what are the savings in total interest paid over the monthly program? (You may assume biweekly compounding for this part.)

7. (Annual worth)   One advantage of the annual worth method is that it simplifies the comparison of investment projects that are repetitive but have different cycle times. Consider the automobile purchase problem of Example 2.7. Find the annual worths of the two (single-cycle) options, and determine directly which is preferable.

8. (Variable-rate mortgage ⊕)   The Smith family just took out a variable-rate mortgage on their new home. The mortgage value is $100,000, the term is 30 years, and initially the interest rate is 8%. The interest rate is guaranteed for 5 years, after which time the rate will be adjusted according to prevailing rates. The new rate can be applied to their loan either by changing the payment amount or by changing the length of the mortgage.

   (a) What is the original yearly mortgage payment? (Assume payments are yearly.)
   (b) What will be the mortgage balance after 5 years?
   (c) If the interest rate on the mortgage changes to 9% after 5 years, what will be the new yearly payment that keeps the termination time the same?
   (d) Under the interest change in (c), what will be the new term if the payments remain the same?

9. (Bond price)   An 8% bond with 18 years to maturity has a yield of 9%. What is the price of this bond?

10. (Duration)   Find the price and duration of a 10-year, 8% bond that is trading at a yield of 10%.

11. (Annuity duration ◇)   Find the duration D and the modified duration D_M of a perpetual annuity that pays an amount A at the beginning of each year, with the first such payment being 1 year from now. Assume a constant interest rate r compounded yearly. [*Hint:* It is not necessary to evaluate any new summations.]

12. (Bond selection)   Consider the four bonds having annual payments as shown in Table 3.9. They are traded to produce a 15% yield.

   (a) Determine the price of each bond.
   (b) Determine the duration of each bond (*not* the modified duration).
   (c) Which bond is most sensitive to a change in yield?
   (d) Suppose you owe $2,000 at the end of 2 years. Concern about interest rate risk suggests that a portfolio consisting of the bonds and the obligation should be immunized. If V_A, V_B, V_C, and V_D are the total values of bonds purchased of types A, B, C, and D, respectively, what are the necessary constraints to implement the immunization? [*Hint:* There are two equations. (Do not solve.)]

TABLE 3.9

End of year payments	Bond A	Bond B	Bond C	Bond D
Year 1	100	50	0	0 + 1000
Year 2	100	50	0	0
Year 3	100 + 1000	50 + 1000	0 + 1000	0

(e) In order to immunize the portfolio, you decide to use bond C and one other bond. Which other bond should you choose? Find the amounts (in total value) of each of these to purchase.

(f) You decided in (e) to use bond C in the immunization. Would other choices, including perhaps a combination of bonds, lead to lower total cost?

13. (Continuous compounding ◇)   Under continuous compounding the Macaulay duration becomes

$$D = \frac{\sum_{k=0}^{n} t_k e^{-\lambda t_k} c_k}{P}$$

where λ is the yield and

$$P = \sum_{k=0}^{n} e^{-\lambda t_k} c_k.$$

Find $dP/d\lambda$ in terms of D and P.

14. (Duration limit)   Show that the limiting value of duration as maturity is increased to infinity is

$$D \to \frac{1 + (\lambda/m)}{\lambda}.$$

For the bonds in Table 3.6 (where $\lambda = .05$ and $m = 2$) we obtain $D \to 20.5$. Note that for large λ this limiting value approaches $1/m$, and hence the duration for large yields tends to be relatively short.

15. (Convexity value)   Find the convexity of a zero-coupon bond maturing at time T under continuous compounding (that is, when $m \to \infty$).

16. (Convexity theorem ◇)   Suppose that an obligation occurring at a single time period is immunized against interest rate changes with bonds that have only nonnegative cash flows (as in the X Corporation example). Let $P(\lambda)$ be the value of the resulting portfolio, including the obligation, when the interest rate is $r + \lambda$ and r is the current interest rate. By construction $P(0) = 0$ and $P'(0) = 0$. In this exercise we show that $P(0)$ is a local minimum; that is, $P''(0) \geq 0$. (This property is exhibited by Example 3.10.)

Assume a yearly compounding convention. The discount factor for time t is $d_t(\lambda) = (1 + r + \lambda)^{-t}$. Let $d_t = d_t(0)$. For convenience assume that the obligation has magnitude 1 and is due at time $\bar{t}$. The conditions for immunization are then

$$P(0) = \sum_t c_t d_t - d_{\bar{t}} = 0$$

$$P'(0)(1 + r) = \sum_t t c_t d_t - \bar{t} d_{\bar{t}} = 0.$$

(a) Show that for all values of α and β there holds

$$P''(0)(1 + r)^2 = \sum_t (t^2 + \alpha t + \beta) c_t d_t - (\bar{t}^2 + \alpha \bar{t} + \beta) d_{\bar{t}}.$$

(b) Show that α and β can be selected so that the function $t^2 + \alpha t + \beta$ has a minimum at $\bar{t}$ and has a value of 1 there. Use these values to conclude that $P''(0) \geq 0$.

REFERENCES

The money market is vast and consists of numerous financial instruments and institutions. Detailed descriptions are available from many sources. Some good starting points are [1–5]. For comprehensive treatments of yield curve analysis, see [5–7]. The concept of duration was invented by Macaulay and by Redington, see [8, 9]. For history and details on the elaboration of this concept into a full methodology for immunization, see [10–13]. The result of Exercise 16 is a version of the Fisher–Weil theorem [13].

1. Cook, T. Q., and T. D. Rowe (1986), *Instruments of the Money Market*, Federal Reserve Bank, Richmond, VA.
2. Fabozzi, F. J., and F. Modigliani (1992), *Capital Markets: Institutions and Instruments*, Prentice Hall, Englewood Cliffs, NJ.
3. *Handbook of U.S. Government and Federal Agency Securities and Related Money Market Instruments, "The Pink Book,"* 34th ed. (1990), The First Boston Corporation, Boston, MA.
4. Wann, P. (1989), *Inside the U$ Treasury Market*, Quorum Books, New York.
5. Livingston, G. D. (1988), *Yield Curve Analysis*, New York Institute of Finance, New York.
6. Fabozzi, F. J., and T. D. Fabozzi (1989), *Bond Markets, Analysis and Strategies*, Prentice Hall, Englewood Cliffs, NJ.
7. Van Horne, J. C. (1990), *Financial Market Rates and Flows*, Prentice Hall, Englewood Cliffs, NJ.
8. Macaulay, F. R. (1938), *Some Theoretical Problems Suggested by the Movement of Interest Rates, Bond Yield, and Stock Prices in the United States since 1856*, National Bureau of Economic Research, New York.
9. Redington, F. M. (October 1971), "Review of the Principles of Life-Office Valuations," *Journal of the Institute of Actuaries*, **78**, no. 3, 286–315.
10. Bierwag, G. O., and G. G. Kaufman (July 1977), "Coping with the Risk of Interest-Rate Fluctuations: A Note," *Journal of Business*, **50**, no. 3, 364–370.
11. Bierwag, G. O., G. G. Kaufman, and A. Toevs (July–August 1983), "Duration: Its Development and Use in Bond Portfolio Management," *Financial Analysts Journal*, **39**, no. 4, 15–35.
12. Bierwag, G. O. (1987), *Duration Analysis*, Ballinger Publishing, Cambridge, MA.
13. Fisher, L., and R. L. Weil (1971), "Coping with the Risk of Interest-Rate Fluctuations: Returns to Bondholders from Naïve and Optimal Strategies," *Journal of Business*, **44**, 408–431.

4 THE TERM STRUCTURE OF INTEREST RATES

A richer theory of interest rates is explored in this chapter, as compared to that in previous chapters. The enriched theory allows for a whole family of interest rates at any one time—a different rate for each maturity time—providing a clearer understanding of the interest rate market and a foundation for more sophisticated investment analysis techniques.

4.1 THE YIELD CURVE

The yield to maturity of any bond is strongly tied to general conditions in the fixed-income securities market. All yields tend to move together in this market. However, all bond yields are not exactly the same.

The variation in yields across bonds is explained in part by the fact that bonds have various quality ratings. A strong AAA-rated bond is likely to cost more (and hence have lower yield) than a bond with an identical promised income stream but having a B-quality rating. It is only natural that high quality is more expensive than low quality. However, quality alone does not fully explain the observed variations in bond yields.

Another factor that partially explains the differences in the yields of various bonds is the time to maturity. As a general rule, "long" bonds (bonds with very distant maturity dates) tend to offer higher yields than "short" bonds of the same quality. The situation is depicted in Figure 4.1. The curve featured in this figure is an example of a **yield curve.** It displays yield as a function of time to maturity. The curve is constructed by plotting the yields of various available bonds of a given quality class. Figure 4.1 shows the yields for various government securities as a function of the maturity date. Note that the yields trace out an essentially smooth curve, which rises gradually as the time to maturity increases. A rising curve is a "normally shaped" yield curve; this shape occurs most often. However, the yield curve undulates around in time, somewhat like a branch in the wind, and can assume various other shapes. If long bonds happen to have *lower* yields than short bonds, the result is said to be an **inverted yield curve.** The inverted shape tends to occur when short-term rates

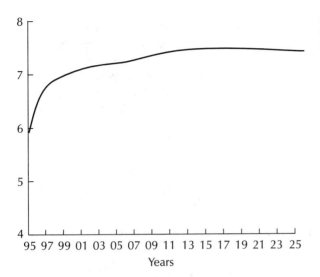

FIGURE 4.1   Yield curve. Yields are plotted as a function of maturity date. The curve shown here is typical and has a normal upward slope.   Source: *Treasury Bulletin*, June 1995.

increase rapidly, and investors believe that the rise is temporary, so that long-term rates remain near their previous levels.

When studying a particular bond, it is useful to determine its yield and maturity date and place it as a point on the yield curve for bonds in its risk class. This will give a general indication of how it is priced relative to the overall market. If it is far from the curve, there is probably a reason, related to special situations or special features (such as call features of the bond or news affecting the potential solvency of the issuer).

The yield curve is helpful, but because it is a bit arbitrary, it does not provide a completely satisfactory explanation of yield differences. Why, for example, should the maturity date be used as the horizontal axis of the curve rather than, say, duration? A more basic theory is required, and such a theory is introduced in the next section.

4.2 THE TERM STRUCTURE

Term structure theory puts aside the notion of yield and instead focuses on pure interest rates. The theory is based on the observation that, in general, the interest rate charged (or paid) for money depends on the length of time that the money is held. Your local bank, for example, is likely to offer you a higher rate of interest for deposits committed for 3 years than for demand deposits (which can be withdrawn at any time). This basic fact, that the interest rate charged depends on the length of time that the funds are held, is the basis of term structure theory. This chapter works out the details and implications of that fact.

Spot Rates

Spot rates are the basic interest rates defining the term structure. The spot rate s_t is the rate of interest, expressed in yearly terms, charged for money held from the present time $(t = 0)$ until time t. Both the interest and the original principal are paid at time t. Hence, in particular, s_1 is the 1-year interest rate; that is, it is the rate paid for money held 1 year. Similarly, the rate s_2 represents the rate that is paid for money held 2 years; however, it is expressed on an annualized basis. Thus if your bank promises to pay a rate of s_2 for a 2-year deposit of an amount A compounded yearly, it will actually repay $(1 + s_2)^2 A$ at the end of 2 years; your money grows by a factor of $(1 + s_2)^2$.

The definition of spot rates implicitly assumes a compounding convention, and this convention might vary with the purpose at hand. The preceding discussion assumed a 1-year compounding convention. It is common to use m periods per year, or continuous compounding, as well. In all cases the rates are usually still quoted as yearly rates. For completeness, we list the various possibilities:

(a) **Yearly**   Under the yearly compounding convention, the spot rate s_t is defined such that

$$(1 + s_t)^t$$

is the factor by which a deposit held t years will grow. (Here t must be an integer, or an adjustment must be made.)

(b) m **periods per year**   Under a convention of compounding m periods per year, the spot rate s_t is defined so that

$$(1 + s_t/m)^{mt}$$

is the corresponding factor. (Here mt must be an integer, so t must be an integral multiple of $1/m$.)

(c) **Continuous**   Under a continuous compounding convention, the spot rate s_t is defined so that $e^{s_t t}$ is the corresponding growth factor. This formula applies directly to all values of t.

For theoretical purposes, continuous compounding is "neater" since the formulas apply without change to all values of t. The other methods require an adjustment for values of t between compounding dates. However, the yearly compounding convention is the most convenient, and it is the convention mainly used in this chapter.

Spot rates can, in theory, be measured by recording the yields of zero-coupon bonds. (In order to eliminate the influence of default risk, it would be best to consider only Treasury securities for this purpose.) Since a zero-coupon bond promises to pay a fixed amount at a fixed date in the future, the ratio of the payment amount to the current price defines the spot rate for the maturity date of the bond. By this measurement process we can develop a **spot rate curve,** which is analogous to the yield curve. Such a curve and a chart of the corresponding data are shown in Figure 4.2.

Discount Factors and Present Value

Once the spot rates have been determined, it is natural to define the corresponding **discount factors** d_t for each time point. These are the factors by which future cash flows

Years	Spot Rate
1	5.571
2	6.088
3	6.555
4	6.978
5	7.361
6	7.707
7	8.020
8	8.304
9	8.561
10	8.793
11	9.003
12	9.193
13	9.365
14	9.520
15	9.661
16	9.789
17	9.904
18	10.008
19	10.103
20	10.188

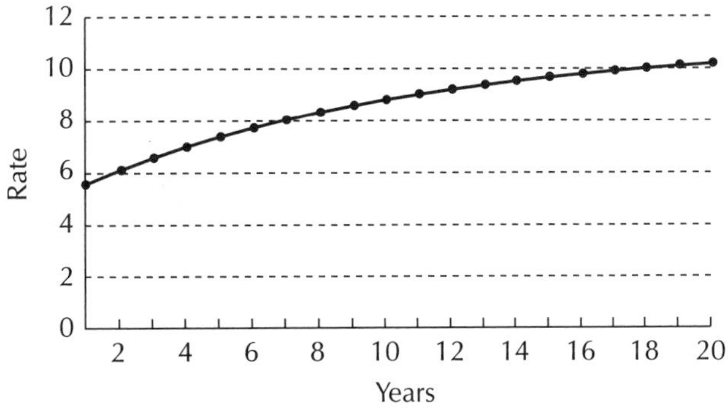

FIGURE 4.2   Spot rate curve. The yearly rate of interest depends on the length of time funds are held.

must be multiplied to obtain an equivalent present value. For the various compounding conventions, they are defined as follows:

(*a*) **Yearly**   For yearly compounding,

$$d_k = \frac{1}{(1+s_k)^k} .$$

(*b*) *m* **periods per year**   For compounding *m* periods per year,

$$d_k = \frac{1}{(1+s_k/m)^{mk}} .$$

(*c*) **Continuous**   For continuous compounding,

$$d_t = e^{-s_t t} .$$

The discount factors transform future cash flows directly into an equivalent present value. Hence given any cash flow stream $(x_0, x_1, x_2, \ldots, x_n)$, the present value, relative to the prevailing spot rates, is

$$PV = x_0 + d_1 x_1 + d_2 x_2 + \cdots + d_n x_n .$$

The discount factor d_k acts like a *price* for cash received at time k. We determine the value of a stream by adding up "price times quantity" for all the cash components of the stream.

TABLE 4.1
Bond Evaluation

Year	1	2	3	4	5	6	7	8	9	10	Total PV
Discount	.947	.889	.827	.764	.701	.641	.583	.528	.477	.431	
Cash flow	8	8	8	8	8	8	8	8	8	108	
PV	7.58	7.11	6.61	6.11	5.61	5.12	4.66	4.22	3.82	46.50	97.34

Each cash flow is discounted by the discount factor for its time.

Example 4.1 (Price of a 10-year bond)   Using the spot rate curve of Figure 4.2, let us find the value of an 8% bond maturing in 10 years.

Normally, for bonds we would use the rates and formulas for 6-month compounding; but for this example let us assume that coupons are paid only at the end of each year, starting a year from now, and that 1-year compounding is consistent with our general evaluation method. We write the cash flows together with the discount factors, take their products, and then sum, as shown in Table 4.1. The value of the bond is found to be 97.34.

Example 4.2 (Simplico gold mine)   Consider the lease of the Simplico gold mine discussed in Chapter 2, Example 2.6, but now let us assume that interest rates follow the term structure pattern of Figure 4.2. We shall find the present value of the lease.

The cash flow stream is identical to that of the earlier example; namely, $2M each year for 10 years. The present value is therefore just the sum of the first 10 discount figures multiplied by $2M, for a total of $13.58M.

Determining the Spot Rate

The obvious way to determine a spot rate curve is to find the prices of a series of zero-coupon bonds with various maturity dates. Unfortunately the set of available zero-coupon bonds is typically rather sparse, and, indeed, until recently there were essentially no "zeros" available with long maturities. Thus it is not always practical to determine a complete set of spot rates this way. However, the existence of zero-coupon bonds is not necessary for the concept of spot rates to be useful, nor are they needed as data to determine the spot rate value.

The spot rate curve can be determined from the prices of coupon-bearing bonds by beginning with short maturities and working forward toward longer maturities. We illustrate the process for the 1-year compounding convention (and assuming coupons are paid only once a year). First determine s_1 by direct observation of the 1-year interest rate—as determined, for example, by the 1-year Treasury bill rate. Next consider a 2-year bond. Suppose that bond has price P, makes coupon payments of amount C at the end of both years, and has a face value F. The price should equal the discounted value of the cash flow stream, so we can write

$$P = \frac{C}{1 + s_1} + \frac{C + F}{(1 + s_2)^2} \, .$$

Since s_1 is already known, we can solve this equation for s_2. Working forward this way, by next considering 3-year bonds, then 4-year bonds, and so forth, we can determine $s_3, s_4, \ldots$, step by step.

    Spot rates can also be determined by a subtraction process. Two bonds of different coupon rates but identical maturity dates can be used to construct the equivalent of a zero-coupon bond. The following example illustrates the method.

Example 4.3 (Construction of a zero)   Bond A is a 10-year bond with a 10% coupon. Its price is $P_A = 98.72$. Bond B is a 10-year bond with an 8% coupon. Its price is $P_B = 85.89$. Both bonds have the same face value, normalized to 100.

    Consider a portfolio with $-.8$ unit of bond A and 1 unit of bond B. This portfolio will have a face value of 20 and a price of $P = P_B - .8P_A = 6.914$. The coupon payments cancel, so this is a zero-coupon portfolio. The 10-year spot rate s_{10} must satisfy $(1 + s_{10})^{10} P = 20$. Thus $s_{10} = 11.2\%$.

    In practice, since spot rates are an idealization, and the spot rates implied by different bonds may differ slightly from one another, it is advisable to modify these procedures to incorporate an averaging method when estimating the spot rates. (See Exercise 4.)

4.3 FORWARD RATES

An elegant and useful concept emerges directly from the definition of spot rates; namely, the concept of forward rates. **Forward rates** are interest rates for money to be borrowed between two dates in the future, *but under terms agreed upon today.*

    It is easiest to explain the concept for a 2-year situation. Suppose that s_1 and s_2 are known. If we leave \$1 in a 2-year account it will, by definition, grow to $\$(1 + s_2)^2$ at the end of the 2 years. Alternatively, we might place the \$1 in a 1-year account and simultaneously make arrangements that the proceeds, which will be $\$(1 + s_1)$, will be lent for 1 year starting a year from now. That loan will accrue interest at a prearranged rate (agreed upon now) of say f. The rate f is the forward rate for money to be lent in this way. The final amount of money we receive at the end of 2 years under this compound plan is $\$(1 + s_1)(1 + f)$.

    We now invoke the comparison principle. We have two alternative methods for investing \$1 for 2 years. The first returns $(1 + s_2)^2$ and the second returns $(1 + s_1)(1 + f)$.

These two should be equal, since both are available.[1] Thus we have

$$(1 + s_2)^2 = (1 + s_1)(1 + f)$$

or

$$f = \frac{(1 + s_2)^2}{1 + s_1} - 1.$$

Hence the forward rate is determined by the two spot rates.

We can justify the use of the comparison principle here through an **arbitrage argument.** If these two methods of investing money did not return the same amount, then there would be an opportunity to make arbitrage profits—defined to be either instantaneous profit or sure future profit with zero net investment. In the preceding example, if $(1 + s_1)(1 + f) > (1 + s_2)^2$, meaning that the second method of investment returned more than the first, then an arbitrageur could reverse the first plan (by *borrowing* for 2 years) and then carry out the second plan by investing the money that was borrowed. This arbitrageur would have zero net investment because he or she used only borrowed capital, but after repaying the loan the arbitrageur would have a profit factor of $(1 + s_1)(1 + f) - (1 + s_2)^2 > 0$. This arbitrage scheme could be carried out at any magnitude, and hence, in theory, the arbitrageur could make very large sums of money from no initial capital. We assume that it is not possible to implement this scheme in the market because potential arbitrageurs are always on the lookout for such discrepancies. If a slight discrepancy does arise, they take advantage of it, and this action tends to close the gap in rates. If the inequality were in the other direction, the arbitageur could just reverse the procedure. Thus equality must hold.

The arbitrage argument assumes that there are no transaction costs—either real costs such as brokerage fees or opportunity costs related to the time and effort of finding the discrepancy and arranging for the trades. The argument also assumes that the borrowing and lending rates are identical. If there were transaction costs or unequal rates, there could be a slight "wedge" between the 2-year rates associated with the two alternative strategies. However, in practice the transaction cost associated with a highly liquid security such as a U.S. Treasury is a very small fraction of the security's total cost, especially if large amounts are involved; and borrowing and lending rates are quite close, again if large amounts of capital are involved. So although the arbitrage argument represents an idealization, it is in practice a reasonable approximation.

The comparison principle can be used to argue that the two overall rates must be equal even in the absence of arbitrageurs. If there were a difference in rates, then investors seeking to loan money for 2 years would choose the best alternative—and so would borrowers. Market forces would tend to equalize the rates.

Example 4.4   Suppose that the spot rates for 1 and 2 years are, respectively, $s_1 = 7\%$ and $s_2 = 8\%$. We then find that the forward rate is $f = (1.08)^2/1.07 - 1 = .0901 = 9.01\%$. Hence the 2-year 8% rate can be obtained either as a direct 2-year investment, or by investing for 1 year at 7% followed by a second year at 9.01%.

---

[1] Forward contracts of this type are actually implemented by the use of futures contracts on Treasury securities, as explained in Chapter 10. They are highly liquid, so forwards of this type are obtained easily.

This discussion can be generalized to define other forward rates between different time periods. The rate f used earlier is more completely labeled as $f_{1,2}$ because it is the forward rate between years 1 and 2. In general we use the following:

Forward rate definition *The forward rate between times t_1 and t_2 with $t_1 < t_2$ is denoted by f_{t_1,t_2}. It is the rate of interest charged for borrowing money at time t_1 which is to be repaid (with interest) at time t_2.*

In general, forward rates are expressed on an annualized basis, like other interest rates, unless another basis is explicitly specified.

In the market there could be more than one rate for any particular forward period. For example, the forward rate for borrowing may differ from that for lending. Thus when discussing market rates one must be specific. However, in theoretical discussions the definition of forward rates is based on an underlying set of spot rates (which themselves generally represent idealizations or averages of market conditions). These calculated forward rates are often termed **implied forward rates** to distinguish them from **market forward rates.**

The implied forward rates are found by extending the logic given earlier for assigning the value $f_{1,2}$. If we use 1-year compounding, the basic forward rates are defined between various yearly periods. They are defined to satisfy the following equation (for $i < j$):

$$(1+s_j)^j = (1+s_i)^i(1+f_{i,j})^{j-i}.$$

The left side of this equation is the factor by which money grows if it is directly invested for j years. This amount is determined by the spot rate s_j. The right side of the equation is the factor by which money grows if it is invested first for i years and then in a forward contract (arranged now) between years i and j. The term $(1+f_{i,j})$ is raised to the $(j-i)$th power because the forward rate is expressed in yearly terms.

The extension to other compounding conventions is straightforward. For completeness, the formulas for forward rates (expressed as yearly rates) under various compounding conventions are listed here:

Forward rate formulas *The implied forward rate between times t_1 and $t_2 > t_1$ is the rate of interest between those times that is consistent with a given spot rate curve. Under various compounding conventions the forward rates are specified as follows:*

(a) **Yearly** *For yearly compounding, the forward rates satisfy, for $j > i$,*

$$(1+s_j)^j = (1+s_i)^i(1+f_{i,j})^{j-i}.$$

Hence,

$$f_{i,j} = \left[\frac{(1+s_j)^j}{(1+s_i)^i}\right]^{1/(j-i)} - 1.$$

(b) *m* **periods per year**   *For m period-per-year compounding, the forward rates satisfy, for j > i, expressed in periods,*

$$(1 + s_j/m)^j = (1 + s_i/m)^i (1 + f_{i,j}/m)^{(j-i)}.$$

Hence,

$$f_{i,j} = m \left[\frac{(1 + s_j/m)^j}{(1 + s_i/m)^i} \right]^{1/(j-i)} - m.$$

(c) **Continuous**   *For continuous compounding, the forward rates f_{t_1,t_2} are defined for all t_1 and t_2, with $t_2 > t_1$, and satisfy*

$$e^{s_{t_2} t_2} = e^{s_{t_1} t_1} e^{f_{t_1,t_2}(t_2 - t_1)}.$$

Hence,

$$f_{t_1,t_2} = \frac{s_{t_2} t_2 - s_{t_1} t_1}{t_2 - t_1}.$$

Note again that continuous compounding produces the simplest formula. As a further convention, it is useful to define spot rates, discount factors, and forward rates when one of the time points is zero, representing current time. Hence we define $s_{t_0} = 0$ and correspondingly $d_{t_0} = 1$, where t_0 is the current time. (Alternatively we write $s_0 = 0$ and $d_0 = 1$ when denoting time by period integers.) For forward rates, we write similarly $f_{t_0,t_1} = s_{t_1}$. The forward rates from time zero are the corresponding spot rates.

There are a large number of forward rates associated with a spot rate curve. In fact, if there are n periods, there are n spot rates (excluding s_0); and there are $n(n+1)/2$ forward rates (including the basic spot rates.) However, all these forward rates are derived from the n underlying spot rates.

The forward rates are introduced partly because they represent rates of actual transactions. Forward contracts do in fact serve a very important hedging role, and their use in this manner is discussed further in Chapter 10. They are introduced here, however, mainly because they are important for the full development of the term structure theory. They are used briefly in the next section and then extensively in the section following that.

4.4 TERM STRUCTURE EXPLANATIONS

The yield curve can be observed, at least roughly, by looking at a series of bond quotes in the financial press. The curve is almost never *flat* but, rather, it usually slopes gradually upward as maturity increases. The spot rate curve has similar characteristics. Typically it, too, slopes rapidly upward at short maturities and continues to slope upward, but more gradually as maturities lengthen. It is natural to ask if there is a simple explanation for this typical shape. Why is the curve not just flat at a common interest rate?

There are three standard explanations (or "theories") for the term structure, each of which provides some important insight. We outline them briefly in this section.

Expectations Theory

The first explanation is that spot rates are determined by expectations of what rates will be in the future. To visualize this process, suppose that, as is usually the case, the spot rate curve slopes upward, with rates increasing for longer maturities. The 2-year rate is greater than the 1-year rate. It is argued that this is so because the market (that is, the collective of all people who trade in the interest rate market) believes that the 1-year rate will most likely go up next year. (This belief may, for example, be because most people believe inflation will rise, and thus to maintain the same real rate of interest, the nominal rate must increase.) This majority belief that the interest rate will rise translates into a market *expectation*. An expectation is only an average guess; it is not definite information—for no one knows for sure what will happen next year—but people on average assume, according to this explanation, that the rate will increase.

This argument is made more concrete by expressing the expectations in terms of forward rates. This more precise formulation is the **expectations hypothesis.** To outline this hypothesis, consider the forward rate $f_{1,2}$, which is the implied rate for money loaned for 1 year, a year from now. According to the expectations hypothesis, this forward rate is *exactly* equal to the market expectation of what the 1-year spot rate will be next year. Thus the expectation can be inferred from existing rates.

Earlier we considered a situation where $s_1 = 7\%$ and $s_2 = 8\%$. We found that the implied forward rate was $f_{1,2} = 9.01\%$. According to the unbiased expectations hypothesis, this value of 9.01% is the market's expected value of next year's 1-year spot rate s_1'.

The same argument applies to the other rates as well. As additional spot rates are considered, they define corresponding forward rates for next year. Specifically, s_1, s_2, and s_3 together determine the forward rates $f_{1,2}$ and $f_{1,3}$. The second of these is the forward rate for borrowing money for 2 years, starting next year. This rate is assumed to be equal to the current expectation of what the 2-year spot rate s_2' will be next year. In general, then, the current spot rate curve leads to a set of forward rates $f_{1,2}, f_{1,3}, \ldots, f_{1,n}$, which define the expected spot rate curve $s_1', s_2', \ldots, s_{n-1}'$ for next year. The expectations are inherent in the current spot rate structure.

There are two ways of looking at this construction. One way is that the current spot rate curve implies an expectation about what the spot rate curve will be next year. The other way is to turn this first view around and say that the expectation of next year's curve determines what the current spot rate curve must be. Both views are intertwined; expectations about future rates are part of today's market and influence today's rates.

This theory or hypothesis is a nice explanation of the spot rate curve, even though it has some important weaknesses. The primary weakness is that, according to this explanation, the market expects rates to increase whenever the spot rate curve slopes upward; and this is practically all the time. Thus the expectations cannot be right even on average, since rates do not go up as often as expectations would imply. Nevertheless, the expectations explanation is plausible, although the expectations may themselves be skewed.

The expectations explanation of the term structure can be regarded as being (loosely) based on the comparison principle. To see this, consider again the 2-year situation. An investor can invest either in a 2-year instrument or in a 1-year instrument followed by another 1-year investment. The follow-on investment can also be carried out two ways. It can be arranged currently through a forward contract at rate $f_{1,2}$, or it can simply be "rolled over" by reinvesting the following year at the then prevailing 1-year rate. A wise investor would compare the two alternatives. If the investor expects that next year's 1-year rate will equal the current value of $f_{1,2}$, then he or she will be indifferent between these two alternatives. Indeed, the fact that both are viable implies that they must seem (approximately) equal.

Liquidity Preference

The liquidity preference explanation asserts that investors usually prefer short-term fixed income securities over long-term securities. The simplest justification for this assertion is that investors do not like to tie up capital in long-term securities, since those funds may be needed before the maturity date. Investors prefer their funds to be **liquid** rather than tied up. However, the term *liquidity* is used in a slightly nonstandard way in this argument. There are large active markets for bonds of major corporations and of the Treasury, so it is easy to sell any such bonds one might hold. Short-term and long-term bonds of this type are equally liquid.

Liquidity is used in this explanation of the term structure shape instead to express the fact that most investors prefer short-term bonds to long-term bonds. The reason for this preference is that investors anticipate that they may need to sell their bonds soon, and they recognize that long-term bonds are more sensitive to interest rate changes than are short-term bonds. Hence an investor who may need funds in a year or so will be be reluctant to place these funds in long-term bonds because of the relatively high near-term risk associated with such bonds. To lessen risk, such an investor prefers short-term investments. Hence to induce investors into long-term instruments, better rates must be offered for long bonds. For this reason, according to the theory, the spot rate curve rises.

Market Segmentation

The market segmentation explanation of the term structure argues that the market for fixed-income securities is segmented by maturity dates. This argument assumes that investors have a good idea of the maturity date that they desire, based on their projected need for future funds or their risk preference. The argument concludes that the group of investors competing for long-term bonds is different from the group competing for short-term bonds. Hence there need be no relation between the prices (defined by interest rates) of these two types of instruments; short and long rates can move around rather independently. Taken to an extreme, this viewpoint suggests that all points on the spot rate curve are mutually independent. Each is determined by the forces of supply and demand in its own market.

A moderated version of this explanation is that, although the market is basically segmented, individual investors are willing to shift segments if the rates in an adjacent segment are substantially more attractive than those of the main target segment. Adjacent rates cannot become grossly out of line with each other. Hence the spot rate curve must indeed be a curve rather than a jumble of disjointed numbers, but this curve can bend in various ways, depending on market forces.

Discussion

Certainly each of the foregoing explanations embodies an element of truth. The whole truth is probably some combination of them all.

The expectations theory is the most analytical of the three, in the sense that it offers concrete numerical values for expectations, and hence it can be tested. These tests show that it works reasonably well with a deviation that seems to be explained by liquidity preference. Hence expectations tempered by the risk considerations of liquidity preference seem to offer a good straightforward explanation.

4.5 EXPECTATIONS DYNAMICS

The concept of market expectations introduced in the previous section as an explanation for the shape of the spot rate curve can be developed into a useful tool in its own right. This tool can be used to form a plausible **forecast** of future interest rates.

Spot Rate Forecasts

The basis of this method is to assume that the expectations implied by the current spot rate curve will actually be fulfilled. Under this assumption we can then predict next year's spot rate curve from the current one. This new curve implies yet another set of expectations for the following year. If we assume that these, too, are fulfilled, we can predict ahead once again. Going forward in this way, an entire future of spot rate curves can be predicted. Of course, it is understood that these predicted spot rate curves are based on the assumption that expectations will be fulfilled (and we recognize that this may not happen), but once made, the assumption does provide a logical forecast.

Let us work out some of the details. We begin with the current spot rate curve $s_1, s_2, \ldots, s_n$, and we wish to estimate next year's spot rate curve $s'_1, s'_2, \ldots, s'_{n-1}$. The current forward rate $f_{1,j}$ can be regarded as the expectation of what the interest rate will be next year—measured from next year's current time to a time $j - 1$ years ahead—in other words, $f_{1,j}$ is next year's spot rate s'_{j-1}. Explicitly,[2]

$$s'_{j-1} = f_{1,j} = \left[\frac{(1+s_j)^j}{1+s_1} \right]^{1/(j-1)} - 1 \tag{4.1}$$

----

[2]Recall that this formula for $f_{i,j}$ was given in Section 4.3. It is derived from the relation $(1 + s_j)^j = (1 + f_{1,j})^{j-1}(1 + s_1)$.

for $1 < j \leq n$. This is the basic formula for updating a spot rate curve under the assumption that expectations are fulfilled. Starting with the current curve, we obtain an estimate of next year's curve.

We term this transformation **expectations dynamics,** since it gives an explicit characterization of the dynamics of the spot rate curve based on the expectations assumption. Other assumptions are certainly possible. For instance, we could assume that the spot rate curve will remain unchanged, or that it will shift upward by a fixed amount, and so forth; however, expectations dynamics has a nice logical appeal.

The expectations process can be carried out for another step to obtain the spot rate curve for the third year, and so forth. Note, however, that if the original curve has finite length, each succeeding curve is shorter by one term—and hence the curves eventually become quite short. This problem can be rectified by initially assuming a very long (or infinite) spot rate curve, or by adding a new s_n term each year. This latter approach would require an additional hypothesis.

Example 4.5 (A simple forecast)   Let us take as given the spot rate curve shown in the first row of the table. The second row is then the forecast of next year's spot rate curve under expectations dynamics. This row is found using (4.1).

	s_1	s_2	s_3	s_4	s_5	s_6	s_7
Current	6.00	6.45	6.80	7.10	7.36	7.56	7.77
Forecast	6.90	7.20	7.47	7.70	7.88	8.06	

The first two entries in the second row were computed as follows:

$$f_{1,2} = \frac{(1.0645)^2}{1.06} - 1 = .069$$

$$f_{1,3} = \left[\frac{(1.068)^3}{1.06}\right]^{1/2} - 1 = .072.$$

All future spot rate curves implied by an initial spot rate curve can be displayed by listing all of the forward rates associated with the initial spot rate curve. Such a list is shown in a triangular array:

$$
\begin{array}{cccccc}
f_{0,1} & f_{0,2} & f_{0,3} & \cdots & f_{0,n-2} & f_{0,n-1} & f_{0,n} \\
f_{1,2} & f_{1,3} & f_{1,4} & \cdots & f_{1,n-1} & f_{1,n} \\
f_{2,3} & f_{2,4} & f_{2,5} & \cdots & f_{2,n} \\
\vdots & \vdots \\
f_{n-2,n-1} & f_{n-2,n} \\
f_{n-1,n}.
\end{array}
$$

The first row of the array lists the forward rates from the initial time. These are identical to the spot rates themselves; that is, $s_j = f_{0,j}$ for all j with $0 < j \leq n$.

The next row lists the forward rates from time 1. These will be next year's spot rates according to expectations dynamics. The third row will be the spot rates for the third year, and so forth.

Discount Factors

Another important concept is that of a **discount factor** between two times. The discount factors are, of course, fundamental quantities used in present value calculations.

It is useful to apply a double indexing system to the discount factors paralleling the system used for forward rates. Accordingly, the symbol $d_{j,k}$ denotes the discount factor used to discount cash received at time k back to an equivalent amount of cash at time j. The normal, time zero, discount factors are $d_1 = d_{0,1}, d_2 = d_{0,2}, \ldots, d_n = d_{0,n}$. The discount factors can be expressed in terms of the forward rates as

$$d_{j,k} = \left[\frac{1}{1 + f_{j,k}}\right]^{k-j}.$$

The discount factors are related by a compounding rule: to discount from time k back to time i, one can first discount from time k back to an intermediate time j and then discount from j back to i. In other words, $d_{i,k} = d_{i,j}d_{j,k}$ for $i < j < k$.

 Discount factor relation *The discount factor between periods i and j is defined as*

$$d_{i,j} = \left[\frac{1}{1 + f_{i,j}}\right]^{j-i}.$$

These factors satisfy the compounding rule

$$d_{i,k} = d_{i,j}d_{j,k}$$

for $i < j < k$.

Short Rates

Short rates are the forward rates spanning a single time period. The short rate at time k is accordingly $r_k = f_{k,k+1}$; that is, it is the forward rate from k to $k+1$. The short rates can be considered fundamental just as spot rates, for a complete set of short rates fully specifies a term structure.

The spot rate s_k is found from the short rates from the fact that interest earned from time zero to time k is identical to the interest that would be earned by rolling over an investment each year. Specifically,

$$(1 + s_k)^k = (1 + r_0)(1 + r_1) \cdots (1 + r_{k-1}).$$

The relation generalizes because all forward rates can be found from the short rates in a similar way. Specifically,

$$(1 + f_{i,j})^{j-i} = (1 + r_i)(1 + r_{i+1}) \cdots (1 + r_{j-1}) .$$

Hence the short rates form a convenient basis for generating all other rates.

The short rates are especially appealing in the context of expectations dynamics, because they do not change from year to year, whereas spot rates do. Given the initial short rates $r_0, r_1, r_2, \ldots, r_{n-1}$, next year (under expectations dynamics) the short rates will be $r_1, r_2, \ldots, r_{n-1}$. The short rate for a specific year does not change; however, that year is 1 year closer to the sliding current time. For example, if we are at the beginning of year 2020, the short rate r_4 is the rate for the year beginning January 2024. A year later, in 2021, the new r_3 will be the rate for the year 2024 and this short rate will be identical (under expectations dynamics) to the previous r_4.

An example of a complete set of forward rates, discount factors, and short rates is shown in Table 4.2. Here the rows represent the rates or factors for a given year: the top row of each array contains the initial rates or factors for 7 years forward. The forward rate array is, as discussed, identical to the spot rate array. Hence the basic spot rate curve is defined by the top line of the forward rate array. Everything else is derived from that single row. The discount factors for the current time are those listed in the top row of the discount factor array. These are the values used to find the present values of future cash flows. Note that successive rows of the short rate table are just shifted versions of the rows above. Short rates remain fixed in absolute time.

TABLE 4.2
Forward Rates, Discount Factors, and Short Rates

Forward rates							Short rates						
6.00	6.45	6.80	7.10	7.36	7.56	7.77	6.00	6.90	7.50	8.00	8.40	8.60	9.00
6.90	7.20	7.47	7.70	7.88	8.06		6.90	7.50	8.00	8.40	8.60	9.00	
7.50	7.75	7.97	8.12	8.30			7.50	8.00	8.40	8.60	9.00		
8.00	8.20	8.33	8.50				8.00	8.40	8.60	9.00			
8.40	8.50	8.67					8.40	8.60	9.00				
8.60	8.80						8.60	9.00					
9.00							9.00						

Discount factors						
.943	.883	.821	.760	.701	.646	.592
.935	.870	.806	.743	.684	.628	
.930	.861	.795	.732	.671		
.926	.854	.787	.722			
.923	.849	.779				
.921	.845					
.917						

The original spot rate curve is defined by the top row of the forward rate array. All other terms are derived from this row.

Invariance Theorem

Suppose that you have a sum of money to invest in fixed-income securities, and you will not draw from these funds for n periods (say, n years). You will invest only in Treasury instruments, and there is a current known spot rate curve for these securities. You have a multitude of choices for structuring a portfolio using your available money. You may select some bonds with long maturities, some zero-coupon bonds, and some bonds with short maturities. If you select a mix of these securities, then, as time passes, you will obtain income from coupons and from the redemption of the short maturity bonds. You may also elect to sell some bonds early, before maturity. As income is generated in these ways, you will reinvest this income in other bonds; again you have a multitude of choices. Finally you will cash out everything at time period n. How should you invest in order to obtain the maximum amount of money at the terminal time?

To address this question, you must have a model of how interest rates will change in the intervening years, since future rates will determine the prices for bonds that you sell early and those that you buy when reinvesting income. There are a variety of models you could select (some of which might involve randomness, as discussed in Chapter 14), but a straightforward choice is to assume expectations dynamics—so let us make that assumption. Let us assume that the initial spot rate curve is transformed, after 1 year, to a new curve in accordance with the updating formula presented earlier. This updating is repeated each year. Now, how should you invest?

The answer is revealed by the title of this subsection. It makes absolutely *no* difference how you invest (as long as you remain fully invested). All choices will produce exactly the same result. In particular, investing in a single zero-coupon bond will produce this invariant amount, which is, accordingly, $(1+s_n)^n$ times your original sum of money. This result is spelled out in the following theorem:

Invariance theorem *Suppose that interest rates evolve according to expectations dynamics. Then (assuming a yearly compounding convention) a sum of money invested in the interest rate market for n years will grow by a factor of $(1 + s_n)^n$ independent of the investment and reinvestment strategy (so long as all funds are fully invested).*

> ***Proof:*** The conclusion is easiest to see from the example used earlier. Suppose that $n = 2$. You have two basic choices for investment. You can invest in a 2-year zero-coupon bond, or you can invest in a 1-year bond and then reinvest the proceeds at the end of the year. Under expectations dynamics, the reinvestment rate after 1 year will be equal to the current forward rate $f_{1,2}$. Both of these choices lead to a growth of $(1 + s_2)^2$. Any other investment, such as a 2-year bond that makes a coupon payment after 1 year that must be reinvested, will be a combination of these two basic strategies. It should be clear that a similar argument applies for any n. ∎

The simplest way to internalize this result is to think in terms of the short rates. Every investment earns the relevant short rates over its duration. A 10-year zero-coupon bond earns the 10 short rates that are defined initially. An investment rolled over year by year for 10 years earns the 10 short rates that happen to occur. Under expectations dynamics, the short rates do not change; that is, the rate initially implied for a specified period in the future will be realized when that period arrives. Hence no matter how an initial sum is invested, it will progress step by step through each of the short rates.

This theorem is very helpful in discussing how to structure an actual portfolio. It shows that the motivation for selecting a mixture of bonds must be due to anticipated deviations from expectations dynamics—deviations of the realized short rates from their originally implied values. Expectations dynamics is, therefore, in a sense the *simplest* assumption about the future because it implies invariance of portfolio growth with respect to strategy.

4.6 RUNNING PRESENT VALUE

The present value of a cash flow stream is easily calculated in the term structure framework. One simply multiplies each cash flow by the discount factor associated with the period of the flow and then sums these discounted values; that is, present value is obtained by appropriately discounting all future cash flows.

There is a special, alternative way to arrange the calculations of present value, which is sometimes quite convenient and which has a useful interpretation. This different way is termed **running present value.** It calculates present value in a recursive manner starting with the final cash flow and working backward to the present. This method uses the concepts of expectations dynamics from the previous section, although it is not necessary to assume that interest rates actually follow the expectations dynamics pattern to use the method. Although this method is presented, at this point, as just an alternative to the standard method of calculation, it will be the preferred—indeed standard—method of calculation in later chapters.

To work out the process, suppose $(x_0, x_1, x_2, \ldots, x_n)$ is a cash flow stream. We denote the present value of this stream PV(0), meaning the present value at time zero. Now imagine that k time periods have passed and we are anticipating the remainder of the cash flow stream, which is $(x_k, x_{k+1}, \ldots, x_n)$. We could calculate the present value (as viewed at time k) using the discount factors that would be applicable then. We denote this present value by PV(k). In general, then, we can imagine the present value running along in time—each period's value being the present value of the remaining stream, but calculated using that period's discount factors. These running values are related to each other in a simple way, which is the basis for the method we describe.

The original present value can be expressed explicitly as

$$\text{PV}(0) = x_0 + d_1 x_1 + d_2 x_2 + \cdots + d_n x_n$$

where the d_k's are the discount factors at time zero. This formula can be written in the alternative form

$$\text{PV}(0) = x_0 + d_1[x_1 + (d_2/d_1)x_2 + \cdots + (d_n/d_1)x_n]. \tag{4.2}$$

The values d_k/d_1, $k = 2, 3, \ldots, n$, are the discount factors *1 year from now* under an assumption of expectations dynamics (as shown later). Hence,

$$PV(0) = x_0 + d_1 PV(1).$$

To show how this works in general, for arbitrary time points, we employ the double-indexing system for discount factors introduced in the previous section. The present values at time k is

$$PV(k) = x_k + d_{k,k+1} x_{k+1} + d_{k,k+2} x_{k+2} + \cdots + d_{k,n} x_n.$$

Using the discount compounding formula, it follows that $d_{k,k+j} = d_{k,k+1} d_{k+1,k+j}$. Hence we may write this equation as

$$PV(k) = x_k + d_{k,k+1}(x_{k+1} + d_{k+1,k+2} x_{k+2} + \cdots + d_{k+1,n} x_n).$$

We can therefore write

$$PV(k) = x_k + d_{k,k+1} PV(k + 1).$$

This equation states that the present value at time k is the sum of the current cash flow and a one-period discount of the next present value. Note that $d_{k,k+1} = 1/(1 + f_{k,k+1})$, where $f_{k,k+1}$ is the short rate at time k. Hence in this method discounting always uses short rates to determine the discount factors.

 Present value updating   *The running present values satisfy the recursion*

$$PV(k) = x_k + d_{k,k+1} PV(k + 1)$$

where $d_{k,k+1} = 1/(1 + f_{k,k+1})$ is the discount factor for the short rate at k.

To carry out the computation in a recursive manner, the process is initiated by starting at the *final* time. One first calculates $PV(n)$ as $PV(n) = x_n$ and then $PV(n - 1) = x_{n-1} + d_{n-1,n} PV(n)$, and so forth until $PV(0)$ is found.

You can visualize the process in terms of n people standing strung out, on a time line. You are at the head of the line, at time zero. Each person can observe only the cash flow that occurs at that person's time point. Hence you can observe only the current, time zero, cash flow. How can you compute the present value? Use the running method.

The last person, person n, computes the present value seen then and passes that value to the first person behind. That person, using the short rate at that time, discounts the value announced by person n, then adds the observed cash flow at $n - 1$ and passes this new present value back to person $n - 2$. This process continues, each person discounting according to their short rate, until the running present value is passed to you. Once you hear what the person in front of you announces, you discount it using the initial short rate and add the current cash flow. That is the overall present value.

The running present value $PV(k)$ is, of course, somewhat of a fiction. It will be the actual present value of the remaining stream at time k only if interest rates follow expectations dynamics. Otherwise, entirely different discount rates will apply at that

TABLE 4.3
Example of Running Present Value

	Year k							
	0	**1**	**2**	**3**	**4**	**5**	**6**	**7**
Cash flow	20	25	30	35	40	30	20	10
Discount	.943	.935	.93	.926	.923	.921	.917	
PV(k)	168.95	157.96	142.20	120.64	92.49	56.87	29.17	10.00

The present value is found by starting at the final time and working backward, discounting one period at a time.

time. However, when computing a present value at time zero, that is, when computing PV(0), the running present value method can be used since it is a mathematical identity.

Example 4.6 (Constant running rate) Suppose that the spot rate curve is flat, with $s_k = r$ for all $k = 1, 2, \ldots, n$. Let $(x_0, x_1, x_2, \ldots, x_n)$ be a cash flow stream. In the flat case, all forward rates are also equal to r. (See Exercise 9.) Hence the present value can be calculated as

$$PV(n) = x_n$$

$$PV(k) = x_k + \frac{1}{1+r}PV(k+1).$$

This recursion is run from the terminal time backward to $k = 0$.

Example 4.7 (General running) A sample present value calculation is shown in Table 4.3. The basic cash flow stream is the first row of the table. We assume that the current term structure is that of Table 4.2, and the appropriate one-period discount rates (found in the first column of the discount factor table in Table 4.2) are listed in the second row of Table 4.3.

The present value at any year k is computed by multiplying the discount factor listed under that year times the present value of the next year, and then adding the cash flow for year k. This is done by beginning with the final year and working backward to time zero. Thus we first find PV(7) = 10.00. Then PV(6) = $20 + .917 \times 10.00 = 29.17$, PV(5) = $30 + .921 \times 29.17 = 56.87$, and so forth. The present value of the entire stream is PV(0) = 168.95.

4.7 FLOATING RATE BONDS

A floating rate note or bond has a fixed face value and fixed maturity, but its coupon payments are tied to current (short) rates of interest. Consider, for example, a floating rate bond that makes coupon payments every 6 months. When the bond is issued, the coupon rate for the first 6 months is set equal to the current 6-month interest rate. At the end of 6 months a coupon payment at that rate is paid; specifically, the coupon is the rate times the face value divided by 2 (because of the 6-month schedule). Then, after that payment, the rate is **reset**: the rate for the next 6 months is set equal to the then current 6-month (short) rate. The process continues until maturity.

Clearly, the exact values of future coupon payments are uncertain until 6 months before they are due. It seems, therefore, that it may be difficult to assess the value of such a bond. In fact at the reset times, the value is easy to deduce—it is equal to par. We highlight this important result.

Theorem 4.1 (Floating rate value)   *The value of a floating rate bond is equal to par at any reset point.*

> ***Proof:*** It is simplest to prove this by working backward using a running present value argument. Look first at the last reset point, 6 months before maturity. We know that the final payment, in 6 months, will be the face value plus the 6-month rate of interest on this amount. The present value at the last reset point is obtained by discounting the total final payment at the 6-month rate—leading to the face value—so the present value is par at that point. Now move back another 6 months to the previous reset point. The present value there is found by discounting the sum of the next present value and the next coupon payment, again leading to a value of par. We can continue this argument back to time zero. ∎

4.8 DURATION

The concept of duration presented in Chapter 3, Section 3.5, can be extended to a term structure framework. We recall that duration is a measure of interest rate sensitivity, which in the earlier development was expressed as sensitivity with respect to yield. In the term structure framework, yield is not a fundamental quantity, but a different, yet similar, measure of risk can be constructed.

The alternative is to consider parallel shifts in the spot rate curve. Specifically, given the spot rates $s_1, s_2, \ldots, s_n$ we imagine that these rates all change together by an additive amount λ. Hence the new spot rates are $s_1+\lambda, s_2+\lambda, \ldots, s_n+\lambda$. This is a hypothetical *instantaneous* change, for the new spot rates are for the same periods as before. This parallel shift of the spot rate curve generalizes a change in the yield because if the spot rate curve were flat, all spot rates would be equal to the common value of yield. Figure 4.3 shows the shifted spot rate curve in the case of a continuous spot rate curve.

Given this notion of a potential change in spot rates, we then can measure the sensitivity of price with respect to the change.

Fisher–Weil Duration

The details work out most nicely for the case of continuous compounding, and we shall present that case first. Given a cash flow sequence $(x_{t_0}, x_{t_1}, x_{t_2}, \ldots, x_{t_n})$ and the

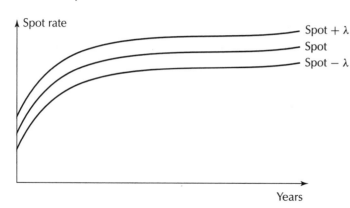

FIGURE 4.3 Shifted spot rate curves. The original spot rate curve is the middle curve. This curve is shifted upward and downward by an amount λ to obtain the other curves. It is possible to immunize a portfolio against such shifts for small values of λ.

spot rate curve s_t, $t_0 \leq t \leq t_n$, the present value is

$$PV = \sum_{i=0}^{n} x_{t_i} e^{-s_{t_i} t_i} .$$

The **Fisher–Weil duration** is then defined as

$$D_{FW} = \frac{1}{PV} \sum_{i=0}^{n} t_i x_{t_i} e^{-s_{t_i} t_i} .$$

Note that this corresponds exactly to the general definition of duration as a present-value-weighted average of the cash flow times. Clearly D_{FW} has the units of time and satisfies $t_0 \leq D \leq t_n$ when all $x_{t_i} \geq 0$.

We now consider the sensitivity of price (present value) to a parallel shift of the yield curve and show that it is determined by the Fisher–Weil duration. For arbitrary λ the price is

$$P(\lambda) = \sum_{i=0}^{n} x_{t_i} e^{-(s_{t_i} + \lambda)t_i} .$$

We then differentiate to find

$$\left. \frac{dP(\lambda)}{d\lambda} \right|_{\lambda=0} = -\sum_{i=0}^{n} t_i x_{t_i} e^{-s_{t_i} t_i}$$

so immediately we find that the **relative price sensitivity** is

$$\frac{1}{P(0)} \frac{dP(0)}{d\lambda} = -D_{FW} .$$

This essentially duplicates the formula that holds for yield sensitivity presented in Chapter 3.

 Fisher–Weil formulas   *Under continuous compounding, the Fisher–Weil duration of a cash flow stream* $(x_{t_0}, x_{t_1}, \ldots, x_{t_n})$ *is*

$$D_{FW} = \frac{1}{PV} \sum_{i=0}^{n} t_i x_{t_i} e^{-s_{t_i} t_i}$$

where PV *denotes the present value of the stream. If all spot rates change to* $s_{t_i} + \lambda$, $i = 0, 1, 2, \ldots, n$, *the corresponding present value function* $P(\lambda)$ *satisfies*

$$\frac{1}{P(0)} \frac{dP(0)}{d\lambda} = -D_{FW}.$$

Discrete-Time Compounding*

Now we work out the details under the convention of compounding m times per year. The spot rate in period k is s_k (expressed as a yearly rate). Again, we have a cash flow stream $(x_0, x_1, x_2, \ldots, x_n)$ (where the indexing is by period). The price is

$$P(\lambda) = \sum_{k=0}^{n} x_k \left(1 + \frac{s_k + \lambda}{m}\right)^{-k}.$$

We then find that

$$\frac{dP(0)}{d\lambda} \equiv \frac{dP(\lambda)}{d\lambda}\bigg|_0 = \sum_{k=1}^{n} -\left(\frac{k}{m}\right) x_k \left(1 + \frac{s_k}{m}\right)^{-(k+1)}.$$

We can relate this to a duration measure by dividing by $-P(0)$. Thus we define

$$D_Q \equiv -\frac{1}{P(0)} \frac{dP(0)}{d\lambda} = \frac{\sum_{k=1}^{n}(k/m)x_k(1 + s_k/m)^{-(k+1)}}{\sum_{i=0}^{n} x_k(1 + s_k/m)^{-k}}. \tag{4.3}$$

We term the quantity D_Q the **quasi-modified duration.** It does have the units of time; however, it is not exactly an average of the cash flow times because $(1 + s_k/m)^{-(k+1)}$ appears in the numerator instead of $(1 + s_k/m)^{-k}$, which is the discount factor. There is an extra factor of $(1 + s_k/m)^{-1}$ in each numerator term. In the earlier case, where s_k was constant for all k, it was possible to pull this extra term outside the summation sign. That led to modified duration. Here such a step is not possible, since the extra factor depends on k, so we call this rather cumbersome expression by an equally cumbersome name—the quasi-modified duration. It does give the relative price sensitivity to a parallel shift in the spot rate curve. An example is given in the next section.

 Quasi-modified duration *Under compounding m times per year, the quasi-modified duration of a cash flow stream* $(x_0, x_1, \ldots, x_n)$ *is*

$$D_Q = \frac{1}{PV} \sum_{k=1}^{n} \left(\frac{k}{m}\right) x_k \left(1 + \frac{s_k}{m}\right)^{-(k+1)}$$

where PV *denotes the present value of the stream. If all spot rates change to* $s_k + \lambda$, $k = 1, 2, \ldots, n$, *the corresponding present value function* $P(\lambda)$ *satisfies*

$$\frac{1}{P(0)} \frac{dP(0)}{d\lambda} = -D_Q.$$

Duration is used extensively by investors and professional bond portfolio managers. It serves as a convenient and accurate proxy for interest rate risk. Frequently an institution specifies a guideline that duration should not exceed a certain level, or sometimes a target duration figure is prescribed.

4.9 IMMUNIZATION

The term structure of interest rates leads directly to a new, more robust method for portfolio immunization. This new method does not depend on selecting bonds with a common yield, as in Chapter 3; indeed, yield does not even enter the calculations. The process is best explained through an example.

Example 4.8 (A million dollar obligation)   Suppose that we have a $1 million obligation payable at the end of 5 years, and we wish to invest enough money today to meet this future obligation. We wish to do this in a way that provides a measure of protection against interest rate risk. To solve this problem, we first determine the current spot rate curve. A hypothetical spot rate curve s_k is shown as the column labeled **spot** in Table 4.4.

We use a yearly compounding convention in this example in order to save space in the table. We decide to invest in two bonds described as follows: B_1 is a 12-year 6% bond with price 65.95 (in decimal form), and B_2 is a 5-year 10% bond with price 101.66. The prices of these bonds are consistent with the spot rates; and the details of the price calculation are given in Table 4.4. The cash flows are multiplied by the discount factors (column d), and the results are listed and summed in columns headed PV_1 and PV_2 for the two bonds.

TABLE 4.4
Worksheet for Immunization Problem

Year	Spot	d	B_1	PV_1	$-PV_1'$	B_2	PV_2	$-PV_2'$
1	7.67	.929	6	5.57	5.18	10	9.29	8.63
2	8.27	.853	6	5.12	9.45	10	8.53	15.76
3	8.81	.776	6	4.66	12.84	10	7.76	21.40
4	9.31	.700	6	4.20	15.38	10	7.00	25.63
5	9.75	.628	6	3.77	17.17	110	69.08	314.73
6	10.16	.560	6	3.36	18.29			
7	10.52	.496	6	2.98	18.87			
8	10.85	.439	6	2.63	18.99			
9	11.15	.386	6	2.32	18.76			
10	11.42	.339	6	2.03	18.26			
11	11.67	.297	6	1.78	17.55			
12	11.89	.260	106	27.53	295.26			
Total				65.95	466.00		101.66	386.15
Duration					7.07			3.80

The present values and durations of two bonds are found as transformations of cash flows.

We decide to immunize against a parallel shift in the spot rate curve. We calculate $dP/d\lambda$, denoted by $-PV'$ in Table 4.4, by multiplying each cash flow by t and by $(1+s_t)^{-(t+1)}$ and then summing these. The quasi-modified duration is then the quotient of these two numbers; that is, it equals $-(1/P)\,dP/d\lambda$. The quasi-modified duration of bond 1 is, accordingly, $466/65.95 = 7.07$.

We also find the present value of the obligation to be \$627,903.01 and the corresponding quasi-modified duration is $5/(1 + s_5) = 4.56$.

To determine the appropriate portfolio we let x_1 and x_2 denote the number of units of bonds 1 and 2, respectively, in the portfolio (assuming, for simplicity, face values of \$100). We then solve the two equations[3]

$$P_1 x_1 + P_2 x_2 = PV$$

$$P_1 D_1 x_1 + P_2 D_2 x_2 = PV \times D$$

where the D's are the quasi-modified durations. This leads to $x_1 = 2{,}208.17$ and $x_2 = 4{,}744.03$. We round the solutions to determine the portfolio. The results are shown in the first column of Table 4.5, where it is clear that, to within rounding error, the present value condition is met.

To check the immunization properties of this portfolio we change the spot rate curve by adding 1% to each of the spot rate numbers in the first column of Table 4.4. Using these new spot rates, we can again calculate all present values. Likewise, we subtract 1% from the spot rates and calculate present values. The results are shown in the final two columns of Table 4.5. These results show that the immunization property does hold: the change in net present value is only a second-order effect.

TABLE 4.5
Immunization Results

	Lambda		
	0	**1%**	**−1%**
Bond 1			
Shares	2,208.00	2,208.00	2,208.00
Price	65.94	51.00	70.84
Value	145,602.14	135,805.94	156,420.00
Bond 2			
Shares	4,744.00	4,744.00	4,744.00
Price	101.65	97.89	105.62
Value	482,248.51	464,392.47	501,042.18
Obligation value	627,903.01	600,063.63	657,306.77
Bonds minus obligation	−\$52.37	\$134.78	\$155.40

The overall portfolio of bonds and obligations is immunized against parallel shifts in the spot rate curve.

---

[3] Alternatively, but equivalently, one could solve the equations $V_1 + V_2 = PV$ and $D_1 V_1 + D_2 V_2 = PV \times D$. Then let $x_1 = V_1/P_1$ and $x_2 = V_2/P_2$.

Of course, the portfolio is immunized only against parallel shifts in the spot rate curve. It is easy to develop other immunization procedures, which protect against other kinds of shifts as well. Such procedures are discussed in the exercises.

4.10 SUMMARY

If observed yield is plotted as a function of time to maturity for a variety of bonds within a fixed risk class, the result is a scatter of points that can be approximated by a curve—the yield curve. This curve typically rises gradually with increasing maturity, reflecting the fact that long maturity bonds typically offer higher yields than short maturity bonds. The shape of the yield curve varies continually, and occasionally it may take on an inverted shaped, where yields decrease as the time to maturity increases.

Fixed-income securities are best understood through the concept of the term structure of interest rates. In this structure there is, at any time, a specified interest rate for every maturity date. This is the rate, expressed on an annual basis, that would apply to a zero-coupon bond of the specified maturity. These underlying interest rates are termed spot rates, and if they are plotted as a function of time to maturity, they determine a spot rate curve, similar in character to the yield curve. However, spot rates are fundamental to the whole interest rate market—unlike yields, which depend on the payout pattern of the particular bonds used to calculate them. Once spot rates are determined, it is straightforward to define discount factors for every time, and the present value of a future cash flow is found by discounting that cash flow by the appropriate discount factor. Likewise, the present value of a cash flow stream is found by summing the present values of the individual flow elements.

A series of forward rates can be inferred from a spot rate curve. The forward rate between future times t_1 and t_2 is the interest rate that would be charged for borrowing money at time t_1 and repaying it at time t_2, but at terms arranged today. These forward rates are important components of term structure theory.

There are three main explanations of the characteristic upward sloping spot rate curve. The first is expectations theory. It asserts that the current implied forward rates for 1 year ahead—that is, the forward rates from year 1 to future dates—are good estimates of next year's spot rates. If these estimates are higher than today's values, the current spot rate curve must slope upward. The second explanation is liquidity preference theory. It asserts that people prefer short-term maturities to long-term maturities because the interest rate risk is lower with short-term maturities. This preference drives up the prices of short-term maturities. The third explanation is the market segmentation theory. According to this theory, there are separate supply and demand forces in every range of maturities, and prices are determined in each range by these forces. Hence the interest rate within any maturity range is more or less independent of that in other ranges. Overall it is believed that the factors in all three of these explanations play a role in the determination of the observed spot rate curve.

Expectations theory forms the basis of the concept of expectations dynamics, which is a particular model of how spot rates might change with time. According to expectations dynamics, next year's spot rates will be equal to the current implied forward rates for 1 year ahead—the rates between year 1 and future years. In other words, the forward rates for 1 year ahead actually will be realized in 1 year. This prediction can be repeated for the next year, and so on. This means that all future spot rates are determined by the set of current forward rates. Expectations dynamics is only a model, and future rates will most likely deviate from the values it delivers; but it provides a logical simple prediction of future rates. As a special case, if the current spot rate curve is flat—say, at 12%—then according to expectations dynamics, the spot rate curve next year will also be flat at 12%. The invariance theorem states that if spot rates evolve according to expectations dynamics, the interest earned on funds committed to the interest rate market for several years is independent of how those funds are invested.

Present value can be calculated by the running method, which starts from the final cash flow and works backward toward the first cash flow. At any stage k of the process, the present value is calculated by discounting the next period's present value using the short rate at time k that is implied by the term structure. This backward moving method of evaluation is fundamental to advanced methods of calculation in various areas of investment science.

Duration can be extended to the term structure framework. The key idea is to consider parallel shifts of the spot rate curve, shifts defined by adding a constant λ to every spot rate. Duration is then defined as $(-1/P)\, dP/d\lambda$ evaluated at $\lambda = 0$. Fisher–Weil duration is based on continuous-time compounding, which leads to a simple formula. In discrete time, the appropriate, somewhat complicated formula is termed quasi-modified duration.

Once duration is defined, it is possible to extend the process of immunization to the term structure framework. A portfolio of assets designed to fund a stream of obligations can be immunized against a parallel shift in the spot rate curve by matching both the present values and the durations of the assets and the obligations.

EXERCISES

1. (One forward rate)   If the spot rates for 1 and 2 years are $s_1 = 6.3\%$ and $s_2 = 6.9\%$, what is the forward rate $f_{1,2}$?

2. (Spot update)   Given the (yearly) spot rate curve $\mathbf{s} = (5.0, 5.3, 5.6, 5.8, 6.0, 6.1)$, find the spot rate curve for next year.

3. (Construction of a zero)   Consider two 5-year bonds: one has a 9% coupon and sells for 101.00; the other has a 7% coupon and sells for 93.20. Find the price of a 5-year zero-coupon bond.

4. (Spot rate project ⊕)   It is November 5 in the year 2011. The bond quotations of Table 4.6 are available. Assume that all bonds make semiannual coupon payments on the 15th of the month. The fractional part of a bond's price is quoted in 1/32nd's. Estimate the (continuous-time) term structure in the form of a 4th-order polynomial,

$$r(t) = a_0 + a_1 t + a_2 t^2 + a_3 t^3 + a_4 t^4$$

TABLE 4.6
Bond Quotes

Coupon	Maturity	Ask price
$6\frac{5}{8}$	Feb-2012	100:0
$9\frac{1}{8}$	Feb-2012	100:22
$7\frac{7}{8}$	Aug-2012	100:24
$8\frac{1}{4}$	Aug-2012	101:1
$8\frac{1}{4}$	Feb-2013	101:7
$8\frac{3}{8}$	Feb-2013	101:12
8	Aug-2013	100:26
$8\frac{3}{4}$	Aug-2013	102:1
$6\frac{7}{8}$	Feb-2014	98:5
$8\frac{7}{8}$	Feb-2014	102:9
$6\frac{7}{8}$	Aug-2014	97:13
$8\frac{5}{8}$	Aug-2014	101:23
$7\frac{3}{4}$	Feb-2015	99:5
$11\frac{1}{4}$	Feb-2015	109:4
$8\frac{1}{2}$	Aug-2015	101:13
$10\frac{1}{2}$	Aug-2015	107:27
$7\frac{7}{8}$	Feb-2016	99:13
$8\frac{7}{8}$	Feb-2016	103:0

where t is time in units of years from today. The discount rate for cash flows at time t is accordingly $d(t) = e^{-r(t)t}$. Recall that accrued interest must be added to the price quoted to get the total price. Estimate the coefficients of the polynomial by minimizing the sum of squared errors between the total price and the price predicted by the estimated term structure curve. Plot the curve and give the five polynomial coefficients.

5. (Instantaneous rates ◇)   Let $s(t)$, $0 \leq t \leq \infty$, denote a spot rate curve; that is, the present value of a dollar to be received at time t is $e^{-s(t)t}$. For $t_1 < t_2$, let $f(t_1, t_2)$ be the forward rate between t_1 and t_2 implied by the given spot rate curve.

   (a) Find an expression for $f(t_1, t_2)$.
   (b) Let $r(t) = \lim_{t_2 \to t} f(t, t_2)$. We can call $r(t)$ the instantaneous interest rate at time t. Show that $r(t) = s(t) + s'(t)t$.
   (c) Suppose an amount x_0 is invested in a bank account at $t = 0$ which pays the instantaneous rate of interest $r(t)$ at all t (compounded). Then the bank balance $x(t)$ will satisfy $dx(t)/dt = r(t)x(t)$. Find an expression for $x(t)$. [*Hint:* Recall in general that $y\,dz + z\,dy = d(yz)$.]

6. (Discount conversion)   At time zero the one-period discount rates $d_{0,1}, d_{1,2}, d_{2,3}, \ldots, d_{5,6}$ are known to be 0.950, 0.940, 0.932, 0.925, 0.919, 0.913. Find the time zero discount factors $d_{0,1}, d_{0,2}, \ldots, d_{0,6}$.

7. (Bond taxes)   An investor is considering the purchase of 10-year U.S. Treasury bonds and plans to hold them to maturity. Federal taxes on coupons must be paid during the year they are received, and tax must also be paid on the capital gain realized at maturity (defined as the difference between face value and original price). Federal bonds are exempt from state taxes. This investor's federal tax bracket rate is $t = 30\%$, as it is for most individuals. There are two bonds that meet the investor's requirements. Bond 1 is a 10-year, 10% bond with a price (in decimal form) of $P_1 = 92.21$. Bond 2 is a 10-year, 7% bond with a price of $P_2 = 75.84$. Based on the price information contained in those two bonds, the investor would like to compute the theoretical price of a hypothetical 10-year zero-coupon bond that had no coupon payments and required tax payment only at maturity equal in amount to 30% of the realized capital gain (the face value minus the original price). This theoretical price should be such that the price of this bond and those of bonds 1 and 2 are mutually consistent on an after-tax basis. Find this theoretical price, and show that it does not depend on the tax rate t. (Assume all cash flows occur at the end of each year.)

8. (Real zeros)   Actual zero-coupon bonds are taxed as if implied coupon payments were made each year (or really every 6 months), so tax payments are made each year, even though no coupon payments are received. The implied coupon rate for a bond with n years to maturity is $(100 - P_0)/n$, where P_0 is the purchase price. If the bond is held to maturity, there is no realized capital gain, since all gains are accounted for in the implied coupon payments. Compute the theoretical price of a real 10-year zero-coupon bond. This price is to be consistent on an after-tax basis with the prices of bonds 1 and 2 of Exercise 7.

9. (Flat forwards)   Show explicitly that if the spot rate curve is flat [with $s(k) = r$ for all k], then all forward rates also equal r.

10. (Orange County blues)   Orange County managed an investment pool into which several municipalities made short-term investments. A total of $7.5 billion was invested in this pool, and this money was used to purchase securities. Using these securities as collateral, the pool borrowed $12.5 billion from Wall Street brokerages, and these funds were used to purchase additional securities. The $20 billion total was invested primarily in long-term fixed-income securities to obtain a higher yield than the short-term alternatives. Furthermore, as interest rates slowly declined, as they did in 1992–1994, an even greater return was obtained. Things fell apart in 1994, when interest rates rose sharply.

   Hypothetically, assume that initially the duration of the invested portfolio was 10 years, the short-term rate was 6%, the average coupon interest on the portfolio was 8.5% of face value, the cost of Wall Street money was 7%, and short-term interest rates were falling at $\frac{1}{2}\%$ per year.

   (a) What was the rate of return that pool investors obtained during this early period? Does it compare favorably with the 6% that these investors would have obtained by investing normally in short-term securities?

   (b) When interest rates had fallen two percentage points and began increasing at 2% per year, what rate of return was obtained by the pool?

11. (Running PV example)   A (yearly) cash flow stream is $\mathbf{x} = (-40, 10, 10, 10, 10, 10, 10)$. The spot rates are those of Exercise 2.

   (a) Find the current discount factors $d_{0,k}$ and use them to determine the (net) present value of the stream.

(b) Find the series of expectations dynamics short-rate discount factors and use the running present value method to evaluate the stream.

12. (Pure duration ◇)   It is sometimes useful to introduce variations of the spot rates that are different from an additive variation. Let $s^0 = (s_1^0, s_2^0, s_3^0, \ldots, s_n^0)$ be an initial spot rate sequence (based on m periods per year). Let $s(\lambda) = (s_1, s_2, \ldots, s_n)$ be spot rates parameterized by λ, where

$$1 + s_k/m = e^{\lambda/m} (1 + s_k^0/m)$$

for $k = 1, 2, \ldots, n$. Suppose a bond price $P(\lambda)$, is determined by these spot rates. Show that

$$-\frac{1}{P}\frac{dP}{d\lambda} = D$$

is a pure duration; that is, find D and describe it in words.

13. (Stream immunization ⊕)   A company faces a stream of obligations over the next 8 years as shown: where the numbers denote thousands of dollars. The spot rate curve is that of

Year	1	2	3	4	5	6	7	8
	500	900	600	500	100	100	100	50

Example 4.8. Find a portfolio, consisting of the two bonds described in that example, that has the same present value as the obligation stream and is immunized against an additive shift in the spot rate curve.

14. (Mortgage division)   Often a mortgage payment stream is divided into a principal payment stream and an interest payment stream, and the two streams are sold separately. We shall examine the component values. Consider a standard mortgage of initial value $M = M(0)$ with equal periodic payments of amount B. If the interest rate used is r per period, then the mortgage principal after the kth payment satisfies

$$M(k) = (1 + r) M(k - 1) - B$$

for $k = 0, 1, \ldots$. This equation has the solution

$$M(k) = (1 + r)^k M - \left[\frac{(1 + r)^k - 1}{r}\right] B.$$

Let us suppose that the mortgage has n periods and B is chosen so that $M(n) = 0$; namely,

$$B = \frac{r(1 + r)^n M}{(1 + r)^n - 1}.$$

The kth payment has an interest component of

$$I(k) = r M(k - 1)$$

and a principal component of

$$P(k) = B - r M(k - 1).$$

(a) Find the present value V (at rate r) of the principal payment stream in terms of B, r, n, M.

(b) Find V in terms of r, n, M only.

(c) What is the present value W of the interest payment stream?

(d) What is the value of V as $n \to \infty$?

(e) Which stream do you think has the larger duration—principal or interest?

15. (Short rate sensitivity)   Gavin Jones sometimes has flashes of brilliance. He asked his instructor if duration would measure the sensitivity of price to a parallel shift in the short rate curve. (That is, $r_k \to r_k + \lambda$.) His instructor smiled and told him to work it out. He was unsuccessful at first because his formulas became very complicated. Finally he discovered a simple solution based on the running present value method. Specifically, letting P_k be the present value as seen at time k and $S_k = \mathrm{d}P_k/\mathrm{d}\lambda|_{\lambda=0}$, the S_k's can be found recursively by an equation of the form $S_{k-1} = -a_k P_k + b_k S_k$, while the P_k's are found by the running method. Find a_k and b_k.

REFERENCES

For general discussions of term structure theory, see [1–3]. Critical analyses of the expectations explanation are contained in [4] and [5]. The liquidity preference explanation is explored in [6]. Immunization in a term structure environment was originated in [7].

1. Fabozzi, F. J., and F. Modigliani (1992), *Capital Markets: Institutions and Instruments*, Prentice Hall, Englewood Cliffs, NJ.

2. Homer, S., and M. Liebowitz (1972), *Inside the Yield Book: New Tools for Bond Market Strategy*, Prentice Hall, Englewood Cliffs, NJ.

3. Van Horne, J. C. (1990), *Financial Market Rates & Flows*, Prentice Hall, Englewood Cliffs, NJ.

4. Russell, S. (July/August 1992), "Understanding the Term Structure of Interest Rates: The Expectations Theory," *Federal Reserve Bank of St. Louis Review*, 36–51.

5. Cox, J., J. Ingersoll, and S. Ross (September 1981), "A Reexamination of Traditional Hypotheses about the Term Structure of Interest Rates," *Journal of Finance*, **36,** 769–99.

6. Fama, E. (1984), "The Information in the Term Structure," *Journal of Financial Economics*, **13,** 509–28.

7. Fisher, L., and R. L. Weil (October 1977), "Coping with the Risk of Market-Rate Fluctuations: Returns to Bondholders from Naive and Optimal Strategies," *Journal of Business*, **44,** 408–431.

5 APPLIED INTEREST RATE ANALYSIS

Ultimately, the practical purpose of investment science is to improve the investment process. This process includes identification, selection, combination, and ongoing management. In the ideal case, these process components are integrated and handled as a craft—a craft rooted in scientific principles and meaningful experience, and executed through a combination of intuition and formal problem-solving procedures. This chapter highlights the formal procedures for structuring investments.

The previous chapters provide the groundwork for the analysis of a surprisingly broad set of investment problems. Indeed, interest rate theory alone provides the basis of the vast majority of actual investment studies. Therefore mastery of the previous chapters is adequate preparation to address a wide assortment of investment situations—and appropriate analyses can be conducted with simple practical tools, such as spreadsheet programs, or more complex tools, such as parallel processor computers. To illustrate the range of problems that can be meaningfully treated by the theory developed in earlier chapters, this chapter considers a few typical problem areas. Our treatment of these subjects is only introductory, for indeed there are textbooks devoted to each of these topics. Nevertheless, the solid grounding of the previous chapters allows us to enter these problems at a relatively high level, and to convey quickly the essence of the subject. We consider capital budgeting, bond portfolio construction, management of dynamic investments, and valuation of firms from accounting data. These subjects all represent important investment issues.

To resolve an investment issue with quantitative methods, the issue must first be formulated as a specific problem. There are usually a number of ways to do this, but frequently the best formulation is a version of **optimization.** It is entirely consistent with general investment objectives to try to devise the "ideal" portfolio, to select the "best" combination of projects, to manage an investment to attain the "most favorable" outcome, or to hedge assets to attain the "least" exposure to risk. All of these are, at least loosely, statements of optimization. Indeed, optimization and investment seem like perfect partners. We begin to explore the possibilities of this happy relationship in this chapter.

5.1 CAPITAL BUDGETING

The capital allocation problem consists of allocating a (usually fixed) budget among a number of investments or projects. We distinguish between **capital budgeting** treated here and **portfolio problems** treated in the next section, although the two are related. Capital budgeting typically refers to allocation among projects or investments for which there are not well-established markets and where the projects are *lumpy* in that they each require discrete lumps of cash (as opposed to securities, where virtually any number of shares can be purchased).

Capital budgeting problems often arise in a firm where several proposed projects compete for funding. The projects may differ considerably in their scale, their cash requirements, and their benefits. The critical point, however, is that even if all proposed projects offer attractive benefits, they cannot all be funded because of a budget limitation. Our earlier study of investment choice, in Chapter 2, focused on situations where the budget was not fixed, and the choice options were mutually exclusive, such as the choice between a red and a green car. In capital budgeting the alternatives may or may not be mutually exclusive, and budget is a definite limitation.

Independent Projects

The simplest, and classic, type of a capital budgeting problem is that of selecting from a list of independent projects. The projects are independent in the sense that it is reasonable to select any combination from the list. It is not a question of selecting between a red and a green car; we can choose both if we have the required budget. Likewise, the value of one project does not depend on another project also being funded. This standard capital budgeting problem is quite easy to formulate.

Suppose that there are m potential projects. Let b_i be the total benefit (usually the net present value) of the ith project, and let c_i denote its initial cost. Finally, let C be the total capital available—the budget. For each $i = 1, 2, \ldots, m$ we introduce the **zero–one variable** x_i, which is zero if the project is rejected and one if it is accepted. The problem is then that of solving

$$\text{maximize} \sum_{i=1}^{m} b_i x_i$$

$$\text{subject to} \sum_{i=1}^{m} c_i x_i \leq C$$

$$x_i = 0 \text{ or } 1 \quad \text{for } i = 1, 2, \ldots, m.$$

This is termed a **zero–one programming problem,** since the variables are zero–one variables. It is a formal representation of the fact that projects can either be selected or not, but for those that are selected, both the benefits and the costs are directly additive.

There is an easy way to obtain an approximate solution to this problem, which is quite accurate in many cases. We shall describe this method under the assumption (which can be weakened) that each project requires an initial outlay of funds (a negative cash flow) that is followed by a stream of benefits (a stream of positive cash flows). We define the **benefit–cost ratio** as the ratio of the present worth of the benefits to the magnitude of the initial cost. We then rank projects in terms of this benefit–cost ratio. Projects with the highest ratios offer the best return per dollar invested—the biggest "bang for the buck"—and hence are excellent candidates for inclusion in the final list of selected projects. Once the projects are ranked this way, they are selected one at a time, by order of the ranking, until no additional project can be included without violating the given budget. This method will produce the best value for the amount spent. However, despite this property, the solution found by this approximate method is not always optimal since it may not use the entire available budget. Better solutions may be found by skipping over some high-cost projects so that other projects, with almost as high a benefit–cost ratio, can be included. To obtain true optimality, the zero–one optimization problem can be solved exactly by readily available software programs. However, the simpler method based on the benefit–cost ratio is helpful in a preliminary study. (Some spreadsheet packages have integer programming routines suitable for modest-sized problems.)

Example 5.1 (A selection problem)   During its annual budget planning meeting, a small computer company has identified several proposals for independent projects that could be initiated in the forthcoming year. These projects include the purchase of equipment, the design of new products, the lease of new facilities, and so forth. The projects all require an initial capital outlay in the coming year. The company management believes that it can make available up to $500,000 for these projects. The financial aspects of the projects are shown in Table 5.1.

For each project the required initial outlay, the present worth of the benefits (the present value of the remainder of the stream after the initial outlay), and the ratio of these two are shown. The projects are already listed in order of decreasing benefit–cost ratio. According to the approximate method the company would select projects 1, 2, 3, 4, and 5 for a total expenditure of $370,000 and a total net

TABLE 5.1
Project Choices

Project	Outlay ($1,000)	Present worth ($1,000)	Benefit–cost ratio
1	100	300	3.00
2	20	50	2.50
3	150	350	2.33
4	50	110	2.20
5	50	100	2.00
6	150	250	1.67
7	150	200	1.33

The outlays are made immediately, and the present worth is the present value of the future benefits. Projects with a high benefit–cost ratio are desirable.

Project	Outlay	Present worth	Net PV	Optimal x-value	Cost	Optimal PV
1	100	300	200	1	100	200
2	20	50	30	0	0	0
3	150	350	200	1	150	200
4	50	110	60	1	50	60
5	50	100	50	1	50	50
6	150	250	100	1	150	100
7	150	200	50	0	0	0
Totals					500	610

FIGURE 5.1 Spreadsheet for project choices. The x-values are listed in one column. These values are multiplied by the corresponding elements of outlay and net present value to obtain the components of cost and optimal present value in the total package of projects. A zero–one program (within the spreadsheet) adjusts these x-values to find the optimal set.

present value of $910,000 - $370,000 = $540,000$. However, this solution is not optimal.

The proper method of solution is to formulate the problem as a zero–one optimization problem. Accordingly, we define the variables x_i, $i = 1, 2, \ldots, 7$, with x_i equal to 1 if it is to be selected and 0 if not. The problem is then

$$\text{maximize } 200x_1 + 30x_2 + 200x_3 + 60x_4 + 50x_5 + 100x_6 + 50x_7$$

$$\text{subject to } 100x_1 + 20x_2 + 150x_3 + 50x_4 + 50x_5 + 150x_6 + 150x_7 \leq 500$$

$$x_i = 0 \text{ or } 1 \quad \text{for each } i.$$

Note that the terms of the objective for maximization are present worth minus outlay—present value.

The problem and its solution are displayed in spreadsheet form in Figure 5.1. It is seen that the solution is to select projects 1, 3, 4, 5, and 6 for a total expenditure of $500,000 and a total net present value of $610,000. The approximate method does not account for the fact that using project 2 precludes the use of the more costly, but more beneficial, project 6. Specifically, by replacing 2 by 6 the full budget can be used and, hence, a greater total benefit achieved.

Interdependent Projects*

Sometimes various projects are interdependent, the feasibility of one being dependent on whether others are undertaken. We formulate a problem of this type by assuming that there are several independent goals, but each goal has more than one possible method of implementation. It is these implementation alternatives that define the projects. This formulation generalizes the problems studied in Chapter 2, where there was only one goal (such as buying a new car) but several ways to achieve that goal. The more general problem can be treated as a zero–one programming problem.

As an example of the formulation using goals and projects, suppose a transportation authority wishes to construct a road between two cities. Corresponding projects might detail whether the road were concrete or asphalt, two lanes or four, and so forth. Another, independent, goal might be the improvement of a bridge.

In general, assume that there are m goals and that associated with the ith goal there are n_i possible projects. Only one project can be selected for any goal. As before, there is a fixed available budget.

We formulate this problem by introducing the zero–one variables x_{ij} for $i = 1, 2, \ldots, m$ and $j = 1, 2, \ldots, n_i$. The variable x_{ij} equals 1 if goal i is chosen and implemented by project j; otherwise it is 0. The problem is then

$$\text{maximize} \ \sum_{i=1}^{m} \sum_{j=1}^{n_i} b_{ij} x_{ij}$$

$$\text{subject to} \ \sum_{i=1}^{m} \sum_{j=1}^{n_i} c_{ij} x_{ij} \leq C$$

$$\sum_{j=1}^{n_i} x_{ij} \leq 1, \quad \text{for } i = 1, 2, \ldots, m$$

$$x_{ij} = 0 \text{ or } 1 \quad \text{for all } i \text{ and } j.$$

The exclusivity of the individual projects is captured by the second set of constraints—one constraint for each objective. This constraint states that the sum of the x_{ij} variables over j (the sum of the variables corresponding to projects associated with objective i) must not exceed 1. Since the variables are all either 0 or 1, this means that at most one x_{ij} variable can be 1 for any i. In other words, at most one project associated with goal i can be chosen.

In general this is a more difficult zero–one programming problem than that for independent projects. This new problem has more constraints, hence it is not easy to obtain a solution by inspection. In particular, the approximate solution based on benefit–cost ratios is not applicable. However, even large-scale problems of this type can be readily solved with modern computers.

Example 5.2 (County transportation choices)   Suppose that the goals and specific projects shown in Table 5.2 are being considered by the County Transportation Authority.

There are three independent goals and a total of 10 projects. Table 5.2 shows the cost and the net present value (after the cost has been deducted) for each of the projects. The total available budget is $5 million. To formulate this problem we introduce a zero–one variable for each project. (However, for simplicity we index these variables consecutively from 1 through 10, rather than using the double indexing procedure of the general formulation presented earlier.) The problem formulation can be expressed as

$$\text{maximize} \ \ 4x_1 + 5x_2 + 3x_3 + 4.3x_4 + x_5 + 1.5x_6 + 2.5x_7 + .3x_8 + x_9 + 2x_{10}$$

$$\text{subject to} \ \ 2x_1 + 3x_2 + 1.5x_3 + 2.2x_4 + .5x_5 + 1.5x_6 + 2.5x_7 + .1x_8 + .6x_9 + x_{10} \leq 5$$

$$x_1 + x_2 + x_3 + x_4 \leq 1$$

$$x_5 + x_6 + x_7 \leq 1$$

$$x_8 + x_9 + x_{10} \leq 1$$

$$x_1, x_2, x_3, x_4, x_5, x_6, x_7, x_8, x_9, x_{10} = 0 \text{ or } 1.$$

TABLE 5.2
Transportation Alternatives

	Cost ($1,000)	NPV ($1,000)
Road between Augen and Burger		
1 Concrete, 2 lanes	2,000	4,000
2 Concrete, 4 lanes	3,000	5,000
3 Asphalt, 2 lanes	1,500	3,000
4 Asphalt, 4 lanes	2,200	4,300
Bridge at Cay Road		
5 Repair existing	500	1,000
6 Add lane	1,500	1,500
7 New structure	2,500	2,500
Traffic Control in Downsberg		
8 Traffic lights	100	300
9 Turn lanes	600	1,000
10 Underpass	1,000	2,000

At most one project can be selected for each major objective.

This problem and its solution are clearly displayed by a spreadsheet, as illustrated in Figure 5.2. The solution is that projects 2, 5, and 10 should be selected, for a cost of $4,500,000 and a total present value of $8,000,000.

This method for treating dependencies among projects can be extended to situations where precedence relations apply (that is, where one project cannot be chosen unless another is also chosen) and to capital budgeting problems with additional

	Project	Cost ($1,000)	NPV ($1,000)	Optimal x-values	Cost	NPV	Goals
1	Concrete, 2 lanes	2,000	4,000	0	0	0	
2	Concrete, 4 lanes	3,000	5,000	1	3,000	5,000	
3	Asphalt, 2 lanes	1,500	3,000	0	0	0	
4	Asphalt, 4 lanes	2,200	4,300	0	0		1
5	Repair existing	500	1,000	1	500	1,000	
6	Add lane	1,500	1,500	0	0	0	
7	New structure	2,500	2,000	0	0	0	1
8	Traffic lights	100	300	0	0	0	
9	Turn lanes	600	1,000	0	0	0	
10	Underpass	1,000	2,000	1	1,000	2,000	1
Totals					4,500	8,000	

FIGURE 5.2 Transportation spreadsheet. The x-values are shown in one column; the corresponding elements of cost and net present value in the next columns. Also, the number of projects included for each goal are shown in the final column. These numbers are constrained to be less than or equal to 1. The optimal x-values are found by a zero–one programming package.

financial constraints. Typically these more general problems merely impose additional constraints among the variables.

Although capital budgeting is a useful concept, its basic formulation is somewhat flawed. The *hard* budget constraint is inconsistent with the underlying assumption that it is possible for the investor (or organization) to borrow unlimited funds at a given interest rate. Indeed, in theory one should carry out *all* projects that have positive net present value. In practice, however, the assumption that an unlimited supply of capital is available at a fixed interest rate does not hold. A bank may impose a limited credit line, or in a large organization investment decisions may be decentralized by passing down budgets to individual organizational units. It is therefore often useful to in fact solve the capital budgeting problem. However, it is usually worth solving the problem for various values of the budget to measure the sensitivity of the benefit to the budget level.

5.2 OPTIMAL PORTFOLIOS

Portfolio optimization is another capital allocation problem, similar to capital budgeting. The term **optimal portfolio** usually refers to the construction of a portfolio of financial securities. However, the term is also used more generally to refer to the construction of any portfolio of financial assets, including a "portfolio" of projects. When the assets are freely traded in a market, certain pricing relations apply that may not apply to more general, nontraded assets. This feature is an important distinction that is highlighted by using the term **portfolio optimization** for problems involving securities.

This section considers only portfolios of fixed-income instruments. As we know, a fixed-income instrument that returns cash at known points in time can be described by listing the stream of promised cash payments (and future cash outflows, if any). Such an instrument can be thought of as corresponding to a list or a vector, with the payments as components, defining an associated cash flow stream. A portfolio is just a combination of such streams, and can be represented as a combination of the individual lists or vectors representing the securities. Spreadsheets offer one convenient way to handle such combinations.

The Cash Matching Problem

A simple optimal portfolio problem is the **cash matching problem.** To describe this problem, suppose that we face a known sequence of future monetary obligations. (If we manage a pension fund, these obligations might represent required annuity payments.) We wish to invest now so that these obligations can be met as they occur; and accordingly, we plan to purchase bonds of various maturities and use the coupon payments and redemption values to meet the obligations. The simplest approach is to design a portfolio that will, without future alteration, provide the necessary cash as required.

To formulate this problem mathematically, we first establish a basic time period length, with cash flows occurring at the end of these periods. For example, we might use 6-month periods. Our obligation is then a stream $\mathbf{y} = (y_1, y_2, \ldots, y_n)$, starting one period from now. (We use boldface letters to denote an entire stream.) Likewise each bond has an associated cash flow stream of receipts, starting one period from now. If there are m bonds, we denote the stream associated with one unit of bond j by $\mathbf{c}_j = (c_{1j}, c_{2j}, \ldots, c_{nj})$. The price of bond j is denoted by p_j. We denote by x_j the amount of bond j to be held in the portfolio. The cash matching problem is to find the x_j's of minimum total cost that guarantee that the obligations can be met. Specifically,

$$\text{minimize} \sum_{j=1}^{m} p_j x_j$$

$$\text{subject to} \sum_{j=1}^{m} c_{ij} x_j \geq y_i \quad \text{for } i = 1, 2, \ldots, n$$

$$x_j \geq 0 \quad \text{for } j = 1, 2, \ldots, m.$$

The objective function to be minimized is the total cost of the portfolio, which is equal to the sum of the prices of the bonds times the amounts purchased. The main set of constraints are the cash matching constraints. For a given i the corresponding constraint states that the total amount of cash generated in period i from all m bonds must be at least equal to the obligation in period i. The final constraint rules out the possibility of selling bonds short.

This problem can be clearly visualized in terms of an array of numbers in a spreadsheet, as in the following example.

Example 5.3 (A 6-year match) We wish to match cash obligations over a 6-year period. We select 10 bonds for this purpose (and for simplicity all accounting is done on a yearly basis). The cash flow structure of each bond is shown in the corresponding column in Table 5.3. Below this column is the bond's current price. For example, the first column represents a 10% bond that matures in 6 years. This bond is selling at 109. The second to last column shows the yearly cash requirements (or obligations) for cash to be generated by the portfolio. We formulate the standard cash matching problem as a linear programming problem and solve for the optimal portfolio. (The solution can be found easily by use of a standard linear programming package such as those available on some spreadsheet programs.) The solution is given in the bottom row of Table 5.3. The actual cash generated by the portfolio is shown in the right-hand column. This column is computed by multiplying each bond column j by its solution value x_j and then summing these results. The minimum total cost of the portfolio is also indicated in the table.

Note that in two of the years extra cash, beyond what is required, is generated. This is because there are high requirements in some years, and so a large number of bonds must be purchased that mature at those dates. However, these bonds generate coupon payments in earlier years and only a portion of these payments is needed to

TABLE 5.3
Cash Matching Example

Yr	|	1	2	3	4	5	6	7	8	9	10	Req'd	Actual
						Bonds							
1		10	7	8	6	7	5	10	8	7	100	100	171.74
2		10	7	8	6	7	5	10	8	107		200	200.00
3		10	7	8	6	7	5	110	108			800	800.00
4		10	7	8	6	7	105					100	119.34
5		10	7	8	106	107						800	800.00
6		110	107	108								1,200	1,200.00
p		109	94.8	99.5	93.1	97.2	92.9	110	104	102	95.2	2,381.14	
x		0	11.2	0	6.81	0	0	0	6.3	0.28	0	Cost	

A spreadsheet layout clearly shows the problem and its solution. In this example, the cash flow streams of 10 different bonds are shown, year by year, as 10 columns in the array. The current price of each bond is listed below the stream, and the amount to be included in a portfolio is listed below the price. Cash flows required to be generated by the portfolio are shown in the penultimate column, and those actually generated are shown in the last column.

meet obligations in those early years. A smoother set of cash requirements would not lead to such surpluses.

There is a fundamental flaw in the cash matching problem as formulated here, as evidenced by the surpluses generated in our example. The surpluses amount to extra cash, which is essentially thrown away since it is not used to meet obligations and is not reinvested. In reality, such surpluses would be immediately reinvested in instruments that were available at that time. Such reinvestment can be accommodated by a slight modification of the problem formulation, but some assumptions about the nature of future investment opportunities must be introduced. The simplest is to assume that extra cash can be carried forward at zero interest; that it can, so to speak, be put under the mattress to be recovered when needed. This flexibility is introduced by adjoining artificial "bonds" having cash flow streams of the form $(0, \ldots, 0, -1, 1, 0, \ldots, 0)$. Such a bond is "purchased" in the year with the -1 (since it absorbs cash) and is "redeemed" the next year. An even better formulation would allow surplus cash to be invested in actual bonds, but to incorporate this feature an assumption about future interest rates (or, equivalently, about future bond prices) must be made. One logical approach is to assume that prices follow expectations dynamics based on the current spot rate curve. Then if r' is the estimate of what the 1-year interest rate will be a year from now, which under expectations dynamics is the current forward rate $f_{1,2}$, a bond of the form $(0, -1, 1 + r', 0, \ldots, 0)$ would be introduced. The addition of such future bonds allows surpluses to be reinvested, and this addition will lead to a different solution than the simple cash matching solution given earlier.

Other modifications to the basic cash matching problem are possible. For example, if the sums involved are not large, then account might be made of the integer nature of the required solution; that is, the x_i variables might be restricted to be integers. Other modifications combine immunization with cash matching.

5.3 DYNAMIC CASH FLOW PROCESSES

To produce excellent results, many investments require deliberate ongoing management. For example, the course of a project within a firm might be guided by a series of operational decisions. Likewise, a portfolio of financial instruments might (and should be) modified systematically over time. The selection of an appropriate sequence of actions that affect an investment's cash flow stream is the problem of dynamic management.

Imagine, for example, that you have purchased an oil well. This is an investment project, and to obtain good results from it, it must be carefully managed. In this case you must decide, each month, whether to pump oil from your well or not. If you do pump oil, you will incur operational costs and receive revenue from the sale of oil, leading to a profit; but you will also reduce the oil reserves. Your current pumping decision clearly influences the future possibilities of production. If you believe that current oil prices are low, you may wisely choose not to pump now, but rather to save the oil for a time of higher prices.

Discussion of this type of problem within the context of deterministic cash flow streams is especially useful—both because it is an important class of problems, and because the method used to solve these problems, **dynamic programming,** is used also in Part 3 of the book. This simpler setting provides a good foundation for that later work.

Representation of Dynamic Choice

A deterministic investment is defined by its cash flow stream, say, $\mathbf{x} = (x_0, x_1, x_2, \ldots, x_n)$, but the magnitudes of the cash flows in this stream often depend on management choices in a complex fashion. In order to solve dynamic management problems, we need a way to represent the possible choices at each period, and the effect that those choices have on future cash flows. In short, we need a **dynamic model.** There are several mathematical structures that can be used to construct such a model, but the simplest is a **graph.** In this structure, the time points at which cash flows occur are represented by points along the horizontal direction, as usual. In the vertical direction above each such time point is laid out a set of **nodes,** which represent the different possible **states** or conditions of the process at that time. Nodes from one time to the next are connected by **branches** or **arcs.** A branch represents a possible path from a node at one time to another node at the next time. Different branches correspond to different management actions, which guide the course of the process. Simple examples of such graphs are that of a **binomial tree** and a **binomial lattice,** illustrated in Figure 5.3(*a*) and (*b*). In such a tree there are exactly two branches leaving each node. The leftmost node corresponds to the situation at the initial time, the next vertical pair of nodes represent the two possibilities at time 1, and so forth. (In the figure only four time points are shown.)

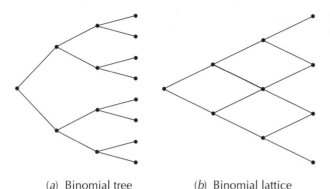

FIGURE 5.3 Graph representations. A tree is a general way to represent dynamic choice.

(a) Binomial tree   (b) Binomial lattice

The best way to describe the meaning of the tree is to walk through an example. Let us again consider the management of the oil well you recently purchased. At any time you can either pump oil or not. A node in the tree represents the condition of the well, defined by the size of its reserves, the state of repair, and so forth. To model your choices as a tree, you should start at the leftmost node of the tree, which represents the initial condition of the well. You have only two choices at that time: pump or don't pump. Assign one of these choices to an upward movement and the other to a downward movement; suppose that pumping corresponds to moving upward and nonpumping corresponds to moving downward. At the next time point your well is at one of the two nodes for that time. Again you make a choice and move either up or down. As you make your decisions, you move through the tree, from left to right, from node to node, along a particular path of branches. The path is uniquely determined by your choices; that is, the condition of the well through time and the magnitude of your overall profit are determined by your choices and represented by this unique path through the tree.

Suppose, specifically, that the well has initial reserves of 10 million barrels of oil. Each year it is possible to pump out 10% of the current reserves, but to do so a crew must be hired and paid. However, if a crew is already on hand, because it was used in the previous year, the hiring expenses are avoided. Therefore, to calculate the profit that can be obtained in any year, it is necessary to know the level of oil reserves and whether a crew is already on hand. Hence we label each node of the tree showing the reserve level and the status of a crew. For example, the label (9, YES) means that the reserves are 9,000,000 barrels and there is a crew on hand. A complete tree for the two periods is shown in Figure 5.3(a).

If crews can be assembled with no hiring cost, it is not necessary to keep track of the crew status. We can therefore drop one component from the node labels and keep only the reserve level. If we do that, some nodes that had distinct labels in the original tree will now have identical labels. In the example illustrated in Figure 5.4, two of the nodes at the final time both have a reserve level of 9 (meaning 9 million barrels). Since the labels are identical, we can combine these nodes into a single node, as shown in Figure 5.4(b). If the tree were extended for additional time periods, this combining effect would happen frequently, and as a

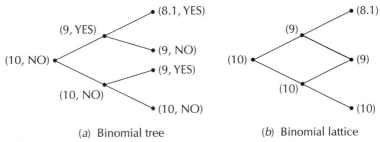

(a) Binomial tree

(b) Binomial lattice

FIGURE 5.4   Trees showing oil well states. Pumping corresponds to an upward movement; no pumping corresponds to a downward movement. The tree in (a) accounts for both the level of reserves and the status of a crew. If only the reserve levels affect the profit, some nodes combine, forming a binomial lattice, as shown in (b).

result the tree could be collapsed to a binomial lattice. A typical binomial lattice is shown in Figure 5.3(b). In such a graph, moving up and then down leads to the same node as moving down and then up. There are fewer nodes in a binomial lattice than in a binomial tree.

In terms of the oil well, if the only relevant factor for determining profit is the reserve level, it is clear that starting at any node, an upward movement in the tree (corresponding to pumping) followed by a downward movement (corresponding to not pumping) is identical in its influence on reserves to a downward movement followed by an upward movement. Both combinations deplete the reserves by the same amount. Hence a binomial lattice can be used to represent the management choices, as in Figure 5.4(b).

We used a binomial tree or a binomial lattice for the oil well example, which is appropriate when there are only two possible choices at each time. If there were three choices, we could form a **trinomial tree** or a **trinomial lattice,** having three branches emanating from each node. Clearly, any finite number of choices can be accommodated. (It is only reasonable to draw small trees on paper, but a computer can handle larger trees quite effectively, up to a point.)

Cash Flows in Graphs

The description of the nodes of a graph as states of a process is only an intermediate step in the representation of a dynamic investment situation. The essential part of the final representation is an assignment of cash flows to the various branches of the graph. These cash flows are used to evaluate management alternatives.

In the first oil well example, where crew hiring costs are not zero, suppose that the cost of hiring a crew is $100,000. (This represents just the initial hiring cost, not the wages paid.) Suppose the profit from oil production is $5.00 per barrel. Finally, suppose that at the beginning of a year the level of reserves in the well is x. Then the net profit for a year of production is $\$5 \times .10 \times x - \$100,000$ if a crew must be hired, and $\$5 \times .10 \times x$ if a crew is already on hand. We can enter these values on the branches of the tree, indicating that much profit is attained if that branch is selected. These values are shown in Figure 5.5 in units of millions of dollars.

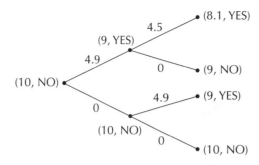

Since only the cash flow values on the branches are important for analysis, it would be possible (conceptually) to bypass the step of describing the nodes as states of the process. However, in practice the node description is important because the cash flow values are determined from these descriptions by an accounting formula. If someone gave us the tree with cash flow values specified on all branches, that would be sufficient; we would not need the node descriptions. In practice, someone must first characterize the nodes, as we did earlier, so that the cash flows can be determined.

In representations of this kind it must also be stated whether the cash flow of a branch occurs at the beginning or at the end of the corresponding time period. In reality, a branch cash flow is often spread out over the entire period, but the model assigns a lump value at one end or the other (or sometimes a part at the beginning and another part at the end). The choice may vary with the situation being represented.

In some cases there is cash flow associated with the termination of the process, whose value varies with the final node achieved. This is a **final reward** or **salvage value.** These values are placed on the graph at the corresponding final nodes. In the oil well example, the final value might be the value for which the well could be sold.

5.4 OPTIMAL MANAGEMENT

Once we have a graph representation of the cash flow process associated with an investment, we can apply the principles of earlier chapters to determine the optimal management plan. Each path through the tree determines a specific cash flow stream; hence it is only necessary to select the path that is best. Usually this is the path that has the largest present value. So one way to solve the problem is to list all the possible streams, corresponding to all the possible paths, compute their respective present values, and select the largest one. We then manage the investment by following the path that corresponds to that maximal present value.

Although this method will work well for small problems, it is plagued by the **curse of dimensionality** for large problems. The number of possible paths in a tree grows exponentially with the number of periods. For example, in an n-period binomial tree the number of nodes is $2^{n+1} - 1$. So if $n = 12$ (say, 1 year of monthly decisions), there are 8,191 possible paths. And if there were 10 possible choices each month, this figure would rise to $10^{13} - 1$, which is beyond the capability of straightforward computation. We can use the computational procedure of **dynamic programming** to search much more efficiently.

Running Dynamic Programming

Dynamic programming solves a problem step by step, starting at the termination time and working back to the beginning. For this reason, dynamic programming is sometimes characterized by the phrase, "it solves the problem backward."

A special version of dynamic programming, based on the running present value method of Section 4.6, is especially convenient for investment problems. We call this method **running dynamic programming.** It is the method that we develop here and that is used throughout the text.

Suppose an investment with a dynamic cash flow is represented by a graph as described earlier. For simplicity, we assume periods are 1 year in length, and we use yearly compounding. A path through the graph generates a cash flow stream $c_0, c_1, \ldots, c_{n-1}$ (with each flow occurring at the beginning of the period), corresponding to the arcs that it passes along, and the path also determines a termination flow V_n at the final node. The present value of this complete stream is

$$\text{PV} = c_0 + \frac{c_1}{1 + s_1} + \frac{c_2}{(1 + s_2)^2} + \cdots + \frac{c_{n-1}}{(1 + s_{n-1})^{n-1}} + \frac{V_n}{(1 + s_n)^n}$$

where the s_k's are the spot rates. A path is defined by a particular series of decisions—one choice at each node. We wish to determine those choices that maximize the resulting present value.

In the running method, we use the one-period discount factors $d_k = 1/(1 + r_k)$, where r_k is the short rate $r_k = f_{k,k+1}$, and we evaluate the present value step by step. In particular, in running dynamic programming we assign to each node a value equal to the best running present value that can be obtained from that node, neglecting all previous cash flows. For the ith node at time k, denoted by (k, i), the best running value is called V_{ki}. We refer to these values as V-values.

The V-values at the final nodes are just the terminal values of the investment process. These values are clearly the present values—as seen at time n—that can be attained neglecting the past. Hence the V-values at the final nodes are already given as part of the problem description.

The dynamic programming procedure next addresses the nodes at time $n - 1$. For any node i at time $n - 1$, we pretend that the underlying investment process has taken us to that node. The decisions for previous nodes have already been made, and the corresponding previous cash flows $c_0, c_1, \ldots, c_{n-2}$ have already occurred. Only one decision remains: we must determine which arc to follow from node $(n - 1, i)$ to some final node at time n. Since we can do nothing about past decisions (in this pretending viewpoint), it is clear that we should select the arc that maximizes the present value as seen at time $n - 1$ (the running present value). Specifically, if we index the arcs by the node number a they reach at time n, we should look at the values $c_{n-1}^a + d_n V_{n,a}$. (Here c_{n-1}^a is the cash flow associated with arc a and $V_{n,a}$ is the V-value at the node

$$V_{n-1,1} = \max_{a=1,2} \left(c_{n-1}^a + d_{n-1} V_{n,a} \right)$$

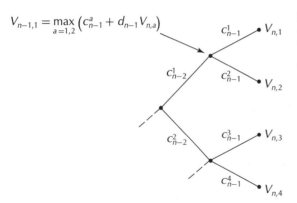

FIGURE 5.6   First recursive step of dynamic programming. Assuming that the first $n-1$ steps of the process have been completed, we evaluate the best that can be done for the last step. For any node at time $n-1$ we find the maximum running present value from that node.

to which arc a leads.) After calculating these sums for every arc a emanating from node $(n-1, i)$, we select the largest of these values and denote that value by $V_{n-1,i}$. This is the best running present value that can be attained from node $(n-1, i)$; and hence it is the correct V-value. This procedure, illustrated in Figure 5.6, is repeated for each of the nodes at time $n-1$.

Next the same procedure is carried out at time $n-2$. We assume that the investment process is at a particular node $(n-2, i)$. Each branch a emanating from that node produces a cash flow and takes the process to a corresponding node a at time $n-1$. If c_{n-2}^a is the cash flow associated with this choice, the total contribution to (running) present value, accounting for the future as well, is $c_{n-2}^a + d_{n-2} V_{n-1,a}$ because the running present value is equal to the current cash flow plus a discounted version of the running present value of the next period. We compute these new values for all possible arcs and select the largest. This maximal value is defined to be $V_{n-2,i}$. This procedure, illustrated in Figure 5.7, is carried out for every node at time $n-2$.

This procedure is continued, working backward until time zero is reached, where there is only one node. The V-value determined there is the optimal present value as seen at time zero, and hence it is the overall best value. The optimal decisions and cash flows can easily be determined as a by-product of the dynamic programming

$$V_{n-2,1} = \max_{a=1,2} \left(c_{n-2}^a + d_{n-2} V_{n-1,a} \right)$$

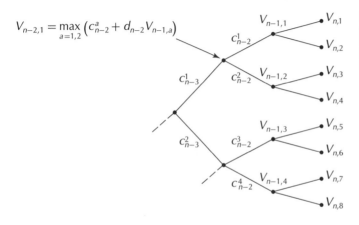

FIGURE 5.7   Second stage of dynamic programming. Assuming that the first $n-2$ stages of the process have been completed, we evaluate the best running present value for the remaining two stages.

procedure, either by recording them at the nodes as the V-values are computed, or by working forward, using the known future V-values.

The running dynamic programming method can be written very succinctly by a recurrence relation. Define c_{ki}^a to be the cash flow generated by moving from node (k, i) to node $(k + 1, a)$. The recursion procedure is

$$V_{ki} = \underset{a}{\text{maximize}} \left(c_{ki}^a + d_k V_{k+1,a} \right) .$$

An example will make all of this clear.

Examples

Example 5.4 (Fishing problem)   Suppose that you own both a lake and a fishing boat as an investment package. You plan to profit by taking fish from the lake. Each season you decide either to fish or not to fish. If you do not fish, the fish population in the lake will flourish, and in fact it will double by the start of the next season. If you do fish, you will extract 70% of the fish that were in the lake at the beginning of the season. The fish that were not caught (and some before they are caught) will reproduce, and the fish population at the beginning of the next season will be the same as at the beginning of the current season. So corresponding to whether you abstain or fish, the fish population will either double or remain the same, and you get either nothing or 70% of the beginning-season fish population. The initial fish population is 10 tons. Your profit is $1 per ton. The interest rate is constant at 25%, which means that the discount factor is .8 each year. Unfortunately you have only three seasons to fish. The management problem is that of determining in which of those seasons you should fish.

The situation can be described by the binomial lattice shown in Figure 5.8. The nodes are marked with the fish population. A lattice, rather than a tree, is appropriate because only the fish population in the lake is relevant at any time. The manner by which that population was achieved has no effect on future cash flows. The value on

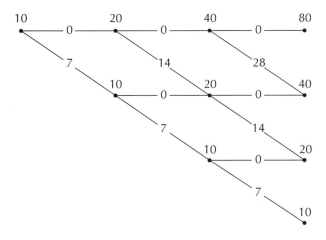

FIGURE 5.8   Fishing problem. The node values are the tonnage of fish in the lake; the branch values are cash flows.

a branch indicates the catch (and hence the cash flow) associated with that branch. Horizontal branches correspond to no fishing and no catch, whereas downward directed branches correspond to fishing.

The problem is solved by working backward. We assign the value of 0 to each of the final nodes, since once we are there we can no longer fish. Then at each of the nodes one step from the end we determine the maximum possible cash flow. (Clearly, we fish in every case.) This determines the cash flow received that season, and we assume that we obtain that cash at the beginning of the season. Hence we do *not* discount the profit. The value obtained is the (running) present value, as viewed from that time. These values are indicated on a copy of the lattice in Figure 5.9.

Next we back up one time period and calculate the maximum present values at that time. For example, for the node just to the right of the initial node, we have

$$V = \max(.8 \times 28, \quad 14 + .8 \times 14).$$

The maximum is attained by the second choice, corresponding to the downward branch, and hence $V = 14 + .8 \times 14 = 25.2$. The discount rate of $1/1.25 = .8$ is applicable at every stage since the spot rate curve is flat. (See Section 4.6.) Finally, a similar calculation is carried out for the initial node. The value there gives the maximum present value. The optimal path is the path determined by the optimal choices we discovered in the procedure. The optimal path for this example is indicated in Figure 5.9 by the heavy line. In words, the solution is not to fish the first season (to let the fish population increase) and then fish the next two seasons (to harvest the population).

The lattice structure can accommodate any finite number of branches emanating from a node. The limit of this kind of construction is a continuous lattice, having a continuum of nodes at any stage and a continuum of possible decisions at any node. For example, in the case of the oil well discussed in the previous section, from a total reserve R you might pump any amount z between, say, 0 and M, leading to a new reserve of

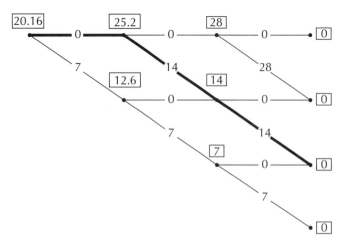

FIGURE 5.9   Calculations for fish problem. The node values are now the optimal running present values, found by working backward from the terminal nodes. The branch values are cash flows.

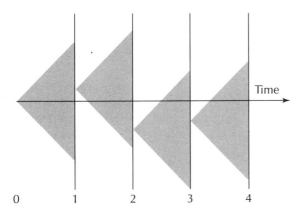

FIGURE 5.10 Continuous lattice. A continuous lattice is a powerful way to represent situations where there is a continuum of possible choices every period.

Time

0   1   2   3   4

$R - z$. Your choice z is continuous, and so is the level of reserves. This type of lattice is illustrated schematically in Figure 5.10. Here each vertical line represents the continuum of nodes possible at a particular time. (At the initial time there is only one node.) The fan emanating from a node represents the fan of possibilities for traveling to a subsequent node. Only one fan is indicated for each time, whereas actually there is such a fan emanating from every point on the vertical line. This dynamic structure works very much like the finite-node case: The process starts at the initial node, and one of the possible choices is selected. This leads to a specific node point on the line for the next time, and the process continues. Optimizing such a process by dynamic programming works in the reverse direction, just like in the finite case, but is made more difficult by the fact that a V-value must be assigned to every point on each node line. Hence V is a function defined on the line. In some cases this function has a simple analytic form, and then the dynamic programming procedure can be carried out explicitly. An illustration of this kind is shown in the next example, which, by the way, is the next in our continuing sequence of gold mine examples.

Example 5.5 (Complexico mine) The Complexico mine is for lease. This mine has been worked heavily and is approaching depletion. It is becoming increasingly difficult to extract rich ore. In fact, if x is the amount of gold remaining in the mine at the beginning of a year, the cost to extract $z < x$ ounces of gold in that year is $\$500z^2/x$. (Note that as x decreases, it becomes more difficult to obtain gold.) It is estimated that the current amount of gold remaining in the mine is $x_0 = 50{,}000$ ounces. The price of gold is $\$400$/oz. We are contemplating the purchase of a 10-year lease of the Complexico mine. The interest rate is 10%. How much is this lease worth?

To solve this problem we must know how to operate the mine optimally over the 10-year period. In particular, we must determine how much gold to mine each year in order to obtain the maximum present value. To find this optimal operating plan, we represent the mine by a continuous lattice, with the nodes at any time representing the amount of gold remaining in the mine at the beginning of that year. We denote this amount by x. This amount determines the optimal value of the remaining lease from that point on.

We index the time points by the number of years since the beginning of the lease. The initial time is 0, the end of the first year is 1, and so forth. The end of the lease is time 10. We also assume, for simplicity, that the cash flow from mining operations is obtained at the *beginning* of the year.

We begin by determining the value of a lease on the mine at time 9, when the remaining deposit is x_9. Only 1 year remains on the lease, so the value is obtained by maximizing the profit for that year. If we extract z_9 ounces, the revenue from the sale of the gold will be gz_9, where g is the price of gold, and the cost of mining will be $500z_9^2/x_9$. Hence the optimal value of the mine at time 9 if x_9 is the remaining deposit level is

$$V_9(x_9) = \max_{z_9} \ (gz_9 - 500z_9^2/x_9).$$

We find the maximum by setting the derivative with respect to z_9 equal to zero. This yields[1]

$$z_9 = gx_9/1,000.$$

We substitute this value in the formula for profit to find

$$V_9(x_9) = \frac{g^2x_9}{1,000} - \frac{500g^2x_9}{1,000 \times 1,000} = \frac{g^2x_9}{2,000}.$$

We write this as $V_9(x_9) = K_9x_9$, where $K_9 = g^2/2,000$ is a constant. Hence the value of the lease is directly proportional to how much gold remains in the mine; the proportionality factor is K_9.

Next we back up and solve for $V_8(x_8)$. In this case we account for the profit generated during the ninth year and also for the value that the lease will have at the end of that year—a value that depends on how much gold we leave in the mine. Hence,

$$V_8(x_8) = \max_{z_8} \left[gz_8 - 500z_8^2/x_8 + d \cdot V_9(x_8 - z_8) \right].$$

Note that we have discounted the value associated with the mine at the next year by a factor d. As in the previous example, the discount rate is constant because the spot rate curve is flat. In this case $d = 1/1.1$.

Using the explicit form for the function V_9, we may write

$$V_8(x_8) = \max_{z_8} \left[gz_8 - 500z_8^2/x_8 + d K_9(x_8 - z_8) \right].$$

We again set the derivative with respect to z_8 equal to zero and obtain

$$z_8 = \frac{(g - d K_9)x_8}{1,000}.$$

This value can be substituted into the expression for V_8 to obtain

$$V_8(x_8) = \left[\frac{(g - d K_9)^2}{2,000} + d K_9 \right] x_8.$$

This is proportional to x_8, and we may write it as $V_8(x_8) = K_8x_8$.

---

[1] We should check that $z_9 \leq x_9$, which does hold with the values we use.

TABLE 5.4
K-Values for
Complexico Mine

Years	K-values
0	213.81
1	211.45
2	208.17
3	203.58
4	197.13
5	187.96
6	174.79
7	155.47
8	126.28
9	80.00

We can continue backward in this way, determining the functions V_7, V_6, ..., V_0. Each of these functions will be of the form $V_j(x_j) = K_j x_j$. It should be clear that the same algebra applies at each step, and hence we have the recursive formula

$$K_j = \frac{(g - dK_{j+1})^2}{2,000} + dK_{j+1}.$$

If we use the specific values $g = 400$ and $d = 1/1.1$, we begin the recursion with $K_9 = g^2/2,000 = 80$. We can then easily solve for all the other values, as shown in Table 5.4, working from the bottom to the top.

It is the last value calculated (that is, K_0) that determines the value of the original lease. That value is determined by finding the value of the lease when there is 50,000 ounces of gold remaining. Hence $V_0(50,000) = 213.82 \times 50,000 = \$10,691,000$.

The optimal plan is determined as a by-product of the dynamic programming procedure. At any time j, the amount of gold to extract is the value z_j found in the optimization problem. Hence $z_9 = gx_9/1,000$ and $z_8 = (g - dK_9)x_8/1,000$. In general, $z_j = (g - dK_{j+1})x_j/1,000$.

Dynamic programming problems using a continuous lattice do not always work out as well as in the preceding example, because it is not always possible to find a simple expression for the V functions. (The specific functional form for the cost in the gold mine example led to the linear form for the V functions.) But dynamic programming is a general problem-solving technique that has many variations and many applications. The general idea is used repeatedly in Parts 3 and 4 of this book.

5.5 THE HARMONY THEOREM*

We know that there is a difference between the present value criterion for selecting investment opportunities and the internal rate of return criterion, and that it is strongly believed by theorists that the present value criterion is the better of the two, provided that account is made for the entire cash flow stream of the investment over all its periods. But if you are asked to consider an investment of a fixed amount of dollars (say, in your friend's new venture), you probably would not evaluate this proposition in terms of present value; you would more likely focus on potential return. In fact, if you do make the investment, you are likely to encourage your friend to maximize the return on your investment, not the present value of the firm. Your friend might insist on maximizing present value. Is there a conflict here?

We will try to shed some light on this important issue by working through a hypothetical situation. Suppose your friend has invented a new gismo for which he holds the patent rights. To profit from this invention, he must raise capital and carry out certain operations. The cost for the operations occurs immediately; the reward occurs at the end of a year. In other words, the cash flow stream has just two elements: a negative amount now and a positive amount at the end of a year.

Your friend recognizes that there are many different ways that he can operate his venture, and these entail different costs and different rewards. Hence there are many possible cash flow streams corresponding to different operating plans. He must select one. The possibilities can be described by points on a graph showing the reward (at the end of a year) versus the current cost of operations, as in Figure 5.11(a). Your friend can select any one of the points.

Suppose also that the 1-year interest rate is $r = 10\%$. The possibility of depositing money in the bank can be represented on the graph as a straight line with slope 1.10: the current deposit is a cost, and the reward is 1.10 times that amount. This slope will be used to evaluate the present value of a cash flow stream.

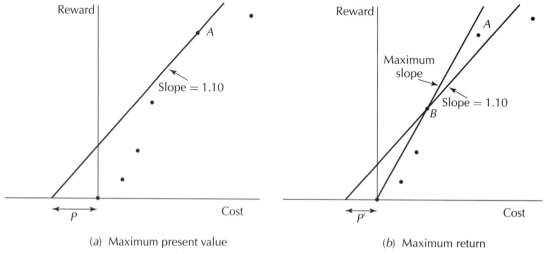

(a) Maximum present value   (b) Maximum return

FIGURE 5.11 Comparison of criteria. (a) Plan A is selected because it has the greatest present value. It is the point corresponding to the highest line of slope, equal to 1.10. (b) Plan B is selected because it is the point on the line from the origin of greatest slope. As the text demonstrates, the analysis in (b) is faulty, and when corrected, the maximum return criterion will correspond to the present value criterion.

If your friend decides to maximize the present value of his venture, he will draw lines with slopes $1 + r = 1.10$ and find the highest one that goes through a possible operating plan. The plan that lies on that line is the optimal one. This optimal line and plan are shown in Figure 5.11(a); point A is the optimal plan. Using a bank, it is possible to move along the line through A. In particular, it is possible to move all the way down to the horizontal axis. At this point, no money will be received next year, but an amount P of net profit is obtained now.

Suppose your friend asks you to invest in his venture, supplying a portion of the operating cost and getting that portion of the reward. You would measure the return on your investment. The operating point that achieves the maximum return is found by swinging a line upward, pivoting around the origin, reaching an operating point of greatest possible slope. The result of this process is shown in Figure 5.11(b). The optimal point according to this criterion is the point B in the figure. The maximum return is the slope of this maximum-slope line. Note that this slope is greater than 110%. So point B achieves a higher rate of return than point A. Its present value, however, is just P', which is less than P. There seems to be a conflict.

Here is how the conflict is resolved. Your friend currently owns the rights to his gismo. He has not yet committed any money for operations; but his present value analysis shows that he could go to the bank, take out a loan sufficient to cover the expenses for plan A, and then, at the end of the year, he could pay back the loan and pocket the profit of $1.10P$ (which is worth P now). He doesn't care about the rate of return, since he is not investing any money; he is just taking out a loan. Alternatively, he could borrow the money from you, but he would not pay you any more than the current interest rate.

But you are not being asked to make a loan; you are being asked to invest in the venture—to have ownership in it. As an extreme case, suppose your friend asks you to buy the whole venture. You will then have the rights to the gismo. He is willing to stay on and operate the venture (if you provide the necessary operating costs), but you will have the power to decide what operating plan to use.

If your friend sells you the venture, he will charge you an amount P because that is what it would be worth to him if he kept ownership. So if you decide to buy the venture, the total expense of an operating plan is now P plus the actual operating cost. If you want to maximize your return, you will maximize reward/(cost + P). You can find this new best operating plan by swinging a line upward, pivoting around the point $-P$, reaching the operating point with the greatest possible slope. That point will be point A, the point that maximized the present value. [Look again at Figure 5.11(a).] Alternatively, once you are the owner, you might consider maximizing the present value. That will lead to point A as well. Therefore if you decide to buy the venture, and you pay the full value P, you will maximize the return on your investment by operating under plan A; and your return will be 110%. (It does not matter if you decide to borrow some of the operating costs instead of funding them yourself; still you will want to operate at A, and your return will still be 110%.)

We summarize the preceding discussion by a general result that we term the *harmony theorem*. It states that there is harmony between the present value criterion and the rate of return criterion when account is made for ownership.

Harmony theorem   *Current owners of a venture should want to operate the venture to maximize the present value of its cash flow stream. Potential new owners, who must pay the full value of their prospective share of the venture, will want the company to operate in the same way, in order to maximize the return on their investment.*

The harmony theorem is justification for operating a venture (such as a company) in the way that maximizes the present value of the cash flow stream it generates. Both current owners and potential investors will agree on this policy.

The presentation in this section considered only deterministic cash flow streams with two flows. The harmony theorem generalizes to multiple periods and to random streams as well—under certain conditions. A multiperiod generalization is discussed in Exercise 10.

5.6 VALUATION OF A FIRM*

The principles of cash flow analysis can be used to evaluate the worth of publicly traded corporations; indeed almost all analytic valuation methods do use some form of cash flow analysis. However, as straightforward as that may sound, the general idea is subject to a variety of interpretations, each leading to a different result. These differences spring from the question of just which cash flows should form the basis of analysis: should they be the dividends that flow to a stockholder, the net earnings to the company, or the flow that could be captured by a single individual or group who owned the company and was free to extract the cash according to the group's own policy? If these various quantities are defined by standard accounting practice, they can lead to significantly different inferred firm values.

Another weakness of this kind of analysis is that it is based on an assumption that future cash flows are known deterministically, which, of course, is usually not the case. Often uncertainty is recognized in an analysis, but treated in a simplistic way (for instance, by increasing the interest rate used for discounting above the risk-free rate). We discuss other, more solidly based approaches to evaluation under uncertainty in later chapters. This section assumes that the cash flows are deterministic.

Dividend Discount Models

The owner of a share of stock in a company can expect to receive periodic dividends. Suppose that it is known that in year k, $k = 1, 2, \ldots$, a dividend of D_k will be received. If the interest rate (or the discount rate) is fixed at r, it is reasonable to assign a value of the firm to the stock holders as the present value of this dividend stream; namely,

$$V_0 = \frac{D_1}{1+r} + \frac{D_2}{(1+r)^2} + \frac{D_3}{(1+r)^3} + \cdots .$$

This formula is straightforward, but it requires that the future dividends be known.

A popular way to specify dividends is to use the **constant-growth dividend model,** where dividends grow at a constant rate g. In particular, given D_1 and the relation $D_{k+1} = (1+g)D_k$, the present value of the stream is

$$V_0 = \frac{D_1}{1+r} + \frac{D_1(1+g)}{(1+r)^2} + \frac{D_1(1+g)^2}{(1+r)^3} + \cdots = D_1 \sum_{k=1}^{\infty} \frac{(1+g)^{k-1}}{(1+r)^k}.$$

This summation is similar to that of an annuity, except that there is the extra growth term in the numerator. The summation will have finite value only if the dividend growth rate is less than the rate used for discounting; that is, if $g < r$. In that case we have the explicit **Gordon formula** (see Exercise 11) for the summation

$$V_0 = \frac{D_1}{r - g}. \tag{5.1}$$

Note that, according to this formula, the value of a firm's stock increases if g increases, if the current dividend D_1 increases, or if the discount rate r decreases. All of these properties are intuitively clear.

If we project D_1 from a current dividend (already paid) of D_0, we can rewrite (5.1) by including the first-year's growth. We highlight this as follows:

Discounted growth formula *Consider a dividend stream that grows at a rate of g per period. Assign $r > g$ as the discount rate per period. Then the present value of the stream, starting one period from the present, with the dividend D_1, is*

$$V_0 = \frac{(1+g)D_0}{r - g} \tag{5.2}$$

where D_0 is the current dividend.

To use the constant-growth dividend model one must estimate the growth rate g and assign an appropriate value to the discount rate r. Estimation of g can be based on the history of the firm's dividends and on future prospects. Frequently a value is assigned to r that is larger than the actual risk-free interest rate to reflect the idea that uncertain cash flows should be discounted more heavily than certain cash flows. (In Chapters 15 and 16, we study better ways to account for uncertainty.)

Example 5.6 (The XX Corporation)   The XX Corporation has just paid a dividend of $1.37M. The company is expected to grow at 10% for the foreseeable future, and hence most analysts project a similar growth in dividends. The discount rate used for this type of company is 15%. What is the value of a share of stock in the XX Corporation?

The total value of all shares is given by (5.2). Hence this value is

$$V_0 = \frac{1.37M \times 1.10}{.15 - .10} = \$30,140,000.$$

Assume that there are 1 million shares outstanding. Each share is worth $30.14 according to this analysis.

Free Cash Flow*

A conceptual difficulty with the dividend discount method is that the dividend rate is set by the board of directors of the firm, and this rate may not be representative of the firm's financial status. A different perspective to valuation is obtained by imagining that you were the sole owner and could take out cash as it is earned. From this perspective the value of the firm might be the discounted value of the net earnings stream.

The net earnings of a firm is defined by accounting practice. In the simplest case it is just revenue minus cost, and then minus taxes; but things are rarely this simple. Account must be made for depreciation of plant and equipment, payment of interest on debt, taxes, and other factors. The final net earnings figure may have little relation to the cash flow that can be extracted from the firm.

Within the limitations of a deterministic approach, the best way to value a firm is to determine the cash flow stream of maximum present value that can be taken out of the company and distributed to the owners. The corresponding cash flow in any year is termed that year's **free cash flow** (FCF). Roughly, free cash flow is the cash generated through operations minus the investments necessary to sustain those operations and their anticipated growth.

It is difficult to obtain an accurate measure of the free cash flow. First, it is necessary to assess the firm's potential for generating cash under various policies. Second, it is necessary to determine the optimal rate of investment—the rate that will generate the cash flow stream of maximum present value. Usually this optimal rate is merely estimated; but since the relation between growth rate and present value is complex, the estimated rate may be far from the true optimum. We shall illustrate the ideal process with a highly idealized example.

Suppose that a company has gross earnings of Y_n in year n and decides to invest a portion u of this amount each year in order to attain earnings growth. The growth rate is determined by the function $g(u)$, which is a property of the firm's characteristics. On a (simplified) accounting basis, depreciation is a fraction α of the current capital account ($\alpha \approx .10$, for example). In this case the capital C_n follows the formula $C_{n+1} = (1 - \alpha)C_n + uY_n$. With these ideas we can set up a general income statement for a firm, as shown in Table 5.5.

Example 5.7 (Optimal growth)   We can go further with the foregoing analysis and calculate Y_n and C_n in explicit form. Since $Y_{n+1} = [1 + g(u)]Y_n$, it is easy to see that $Y_n = [1 + g(u)]^n Y_0$. Likewise, it can be shown that

$$C_n = (1 - \alpha)^n C_0 + uY_0 \left\{ \frac{-(1 - \alpha)^n + [1 + g(u)]^n}{g(u) + \alpha} \right\}.$$

If we ignore the two terms having $(1 - \alpha)^n$ (since they will nearly cancel) we have

$$C_n = \frac{uY_0[1 + g(u)]^n}{g(u) + \alpha}. \tag{5.3}$$

TABLE 5.5
Free Cash Flow

Income statement	
Before-tax cash flow from operations	Y_n
Depreciation	αC_n
Taxable income	$Y_n - \alpha C_n$
Taxes (34%)	$.34(Y_n - \alpha C_n)$
After-tax income	$.66(Y_n - \alpha C_n)$
After-tax cash flow (after-tax income plus depreciation)	$.66(Y_n - \alpha C_n) + \alpha C_n$
Sustaining investment	$u Y_n$
Free cash flow	$.66(Y_n - \alpha C_n) + \alpha C_n - u Y_n$

Depreciation is assumed to be α times the amount in the capital account.

Putting the expressions for Y_n and C_n in the bottom line of Table 5.5, we find the free cash flow at time n to be

$$\text{FCF} = \left[.66 + .34 \frac{\alpha u}{g(u) + \alpha} - u \right] [1 + g(u)]^n Y_0. \tag{5.4}$$

This is a growing geometric series. We can use the Gordon formula to calculate its present value at interest rate r. This gives

$$\text{PV} = \left[.66 + .34 \frac{\alpha u}{g(u) + \alpha} - u \right] \frac{1}{r - g(u)} Y_0. \tag{5.5}$$

It is not easy to see by inspection what value of u would be best. Let us consider another example.

Example 5.8 (XX Corporation) Assume that the XX Corporation has current earnings of $Y_0 = \$10$ million, and the initial capital[2] is $C_0 = \$19.8$ million. The interest rate is $r = 15\%$, the depreciation factor is $\alpha = .10$, and the relation between investment rate and growth rate is $g(u) = .12[1 - e^{5(\alpha - u)}]$. Notice that $g(\alpha) = 0$, reflecting the fact that an investment rate of α times earnings just keeps up with the depreciation of capital.

Using (5.5) we can find the value of the company for various choices of the investment rate u. For example, for $u = 0$, no investment, the company will slowly shrink, and the present value under that policy will be $29 million. If $u = .10$, the company will just maintain its current level, and the present value under that plan will be $39.6 million. Or if $u = .5$, the present value will be $52 million.

It is possible to maximize (5.5) (by trial and error or by a simple optimization routine as is available in some spreadsheet packages). The result is $u = 37.7\%$ and $g(u) = 9.0\%$. The corresponding present value is $58.3 million. This is the company value.

---

[2]This value of C_0 will make the terms that were canceled in deriving (5.3) cancel exactly.

Here is a question to consider carefully. Suppose that during the first year, the firm operates according to this plan, investing 37.7% of its gross earnings in new capital. Suppose also, for simplicity, that no dividends are paid that year. What will be the value of the company after 1 year? Recall that during this year, capital and earnings expand by 9%. Would you guess that the company value will increase by 9% as well? Remember the harmony theorem. Actually, the value will increase by the rate of interest, which is 15%. Investors must receive this rate, and they do. The reason this may seem strange is that we assumed that no dividends were paid. The free cash flow that was generated, but not taken out of the company, is held for the year (itself earning 15%), and this must be added to the present value calculation of future cash flows. If the free cash flow generated in the first year were distributed as dividends, the company value would increase by 9%, but the total return to investors, including the dividend and the value increase, again would be 15%.

Although this example is highly idealized, it indicates the character of a full valuation procedure (under an assumption of certainty). The free cash flow stream must be projected, accounting for future opportunities. Furthermore, this cash flow stream must be optimized by proper selection of a capital investment policy. Because the impact of current investment on future free cash flow is complex, effective optimization requires the use of formal models and formal optimization techniques.

5.7 SUMMARY

Interest rate theory is probably the most widely used financial tool. It is used to determine the value of projects, to allocate money among alternatives, to design complex bond portfolios, to determine how to manage investments effectively, and even to determine the value of a firm.

Interest rate theory is most powerful when it is combined with general problem-solving methods, particularly methods of optimization. With the aid of such methods, interest rate theory provides more than just a static measure of value; it guides us to find the decision or structure with the highest value.

One class of problems that can be approached with this combination is capital budgeting problems. In the classic problem of this class, a fixed budget is to be allocated among a set of independent projects in order to maximize net present value. This problem can be solved approximately by selecting projects with the highest benefit–cost ratio. The problem can be solved exactly by formulating it as a zero–one optimization problem and using an integer programming package. More complex capital budgeting problems having dependencies among projects can be also be solved by the zero–one programming method.

The selection of a bond portfolio to meet certain requirements can be conveniently formulated as an optimization problem—but there are several possible formulations. A particularly simple problem within this class is the cash-matching problem, where a portfolio is constructed to generate a required cash flow in each period. This formulation has the weakness that in some periods extra cash may be generated, beyond that required, and this extra cash is essentially wasted. More complex formulations do not have this weakness.

To produce excellent results, many investments require deliberate ongoing management. The relation between a series of management decisions and the resulting cash flow stream frequently can be modeled as a graph. (Especially useful types of graphs are trees and lattices.) In such a graph the nodes correspond to states of the process, and a branch leading from a node corresponds to a particular choice made from that node. Associated with each branch is a cash flow value.

Optimal dynamic management consists of following the special path of arcs through the graph that produces the greatest present value. This optimal path can be found efficiently by the method of dynamic programming. A particularly useful version of dynamic programming for investment problems uses the running method for evaluation of present value.

Dynamic programming works backward in time. For a problem with n time periods, the running version of the procedure starts by finding the best decision at each of the nodes i at time $n - 1$ and assigns a V-value, denoted by $V_{n-1,i}$, to each such node. This V-value is the optimal present value that could be obtained if the investment process were initiated at that node. To find that value, each possible arc emanating from node i is examined. The sum of the cash flow of the arc and the one-period discounted V-value at the node reached by the arc is evaluated. The V-value of the originating node i is the maximum of those sums. After completing this procedure for all the nodes at $n - 1$, the procedure then steps back to the nodes at time $n - 2$. Optimal V-values are found for each of those nodes by a procedure that exactly parallels that for the nodes at $n - 1$. The procedure continues by working backward through all time periods, and it ends when an optimal V-value is assigned to the initial node at time zero.

When operating a venture it is appropriate to maximize the present value. On the other hand, investors may be most interested in the rate of return. These criteria might seem to be in conflict, but the harmony theorem states that the criteria are equivalent under the assumption that investors pay the full value for their ownership of the venture.

Present value analysis is commonly used to estimate the value of a firm. One such procedure is the dividend discount method, where the value to a stockholder is assumed to be equal to the present value of the stream of future dividend payments. If dividends are assumed to grow at a rate g per year, a simple formula gives the present value of the resulting stream.

The better method of firm evaluation bases the evaluation on free cash flow, which is the amount of cash that can be taken out of the firm while maintaining optimal operations and investment strategies. In idealized form, this method requires that the present value of free cash flow be maximized with respect to all possible management decisions, especially those related to investment that produces earnings growth.

Valuation methods based on present value suffer the defect that future cash flows are treated as if they were known with certainty, when in fact they are usually uncertain. The deterministic theory is therefore not adequate. This defect is widely recognized; and to compensate for it, it is common practice to discount predicted, but uncertain, cash flows at higher interest rates than the risk-free rate. There is some theoretical justification for this, but a completely consistent approach to uncertainty is more subtle. The exciting story of uncertainty in investment begins with the next chapter and continues throughout the remainder of the text.

EXERCISES

1. (Capital budgeting)   A firm is considering funding several proposed projects that have the financial properties shown in Table 5.6. The available budget is $600,000. What set of projects would be recommended by the approximate method based on benefit–cost ratios? What is the optimal set of projects?

TABLE 5.6
Financial Properties of Proposed Projects

Project	Outlay ($1,000)	Present worth ($1,000)
1	100	200
2	300	500
3	200	300
4	150	200
5	150	250

2. (The road ⊕)   Refer to the transportation alternatives problem of Example 5.2. The bridge at Cay Road is actually part of the road between Augen and Burger. Therefore it is not reasonable for the bridge to have fewer lanes than the road itself. This means that if projects 2 or 4 are carried out, either projects 6 or 7 must also be carried out. Formulate a zero–one programming problem that includes this additional requirement. Solve the problem.

3. (Two-period budget ⊕)   A company has identified a number of promising projects, as indicated in Table 5.7. The cash flows for the first 2 years are shown (they are all negative).

TABLE 5.7
A List of Projects

Project	Cash flow 1	2	NPV
1	−90	−58	150
2	−80	−80	200
3	−50	−100	100
4	−20	−64	100
5	−40	−50	120
6	−80	−20	150
7	−80	−100	240

The cash flows in later years are positive, and the net present value of each project is shown. The company managers have decided that they can allocate up to $250,000 in each of the first 2 years to fund these projects. If less than $250,000 is used the first year, the balance can be invested at 10% and used to augment the next year's budget. Which projects should be funded?

4. (Bond matrix ◇)   The cash matching and other problems can be conveniently represented in matrix form. Suppose there are m bonds. We define for each bond j its associated yearly cash flow stream (column) vector $\mathbf{c}_j$, which is n-dimensional. The yearly obligations are likewise represented by the n-dimensional vector $\mathbf{y}$. We can stack the $\mathbf{c}_j$ vectors side by side to form the columns of a bond matrix $\mathbf{C}$. Finally we let $\mathbf{p}$ and $\mathbf{x}$ be m-dimensional column vectors. The cash matching problem can be expressed as

$$\text{minimize} \ \ \mathbf{p}^T\mathbf{x}$$

$$\text{subject to} \ \ \mathbf{Cx} \geq \mathbf{y}$$

$$\mathbf{x} \geq \mathbf{0}.$$

(a) Identify $\mathbf{C, y, p,}$ and $\mathbf{x}$ in Table 5.3.

(b) Show that if all bonds are priced according to a common term structure of interest rates, there is a vector $\mathbf{v}$ satisfying

$$\mathbf{C}^T\mathbf{v} = \mathbf{p}.$$

What are the components of $\mathbf{v}$?

(c) Suppose $\mathbf{b}$ is a vector whose components represent obligations in each period. Show that a portfolio $\mathbf{x}$ meeting these obligations exactly satisfies

$$\mathbf{Cx} = \mathbf{b}.$$

(d) With $\mathbf{x}$ and $\mathbf{v}$ defined as before, show that the price of the portfolio $\mathbf{x}$ is $\mathbf{v}^T\mathbf{b}$. Interpret this result.

5. (Trinomial lattice)   A trinomial lattice is a special case of a trinomial tree. From each node three moves are possible: up, middle, and down. The special feature of the lattice is that certain pairs of moves lead to identical nodes two periods in the future. We can express these equivalences as

$$\begin{aligned} \text{up–down} \ &= \ \text{down–up} \ = \ \text{middle–middle} \\ \text{middle–down} \ &= \ \text{down–middle} \\ \text{middle–up} \ &= \ \text{up–middle.} \end{aligned}$$

Draw a trinomial lattice spanning three periods. How many nodes does it contain? How many nodes are contained in a full trinomial tree of the same number of periods?

6. (A bond project ⊕)   You are the manager of XYZ Pension Fund. On November 5, 2011, XYZ must purchase a portfolio of U.S. Treasury bonds to meet the fund's projected liabilities in the future. The bonds available at that time are those of Exercise 4 in Chapter 4. Short selling is not allowed. Following the procedure of the earlier exercise, a 4th-order polynomial estimate of the term structure is constructed as $r(t) = \alpha_0 + \alpha_1 t + \alpha_2 t^2 + \alpha_3 t^3 + \alpha_4 t^4$. The liabilities of XYZ are as listed in Table 5.8.

TABLE 5.8
Liabilities of XYC Pension Fund

Liabilities	Occur on 15th
Feb 2012	$2,000
Aug 2012	$20,000
Feb 2013	$0
Aug 2013	$25,000
Feb 2014	$1,000
Aug 2014	$0
Feb 2015	$20,000
Aug 2015	$1,000
Feb 2016	$15,000

(a) (Simple cash matching)   Construct a minimum-cost liability-matching portfolio by buying Treasury bonds assuming that excess periodic cash flows may be held only at *zero* interest to meet future liabilities.

(b) (Complex cash matching)   Construct a minimum-cost liability-matching portfolio by buying Treasury bonds assuming that all excess periodic cash flows may be reinvested at the expected interest rates (implied by the current term structure) to meet future liabilities. No borrowing is allowed.

(c) (Duration matching)   Construct a minimum-cost portfolio with present value equal to that of the liability stream. Immunize against a change in the term structure parameters. Do this for five cases. Case 1 is to guard against a change in α_1, case 2 to guard against changes in α_1 and α_2, and so on.

7. (The fishing problem)   Find the solution to the fishing problem of Example 5.4 when the interest rate is 33%. Are the decisions different than when the interest rate is 25%? At what critical value of the discount factor does the solution change?

8. (Complexico mine ⊕)   Consider the Complexico mine and assume a 10% constant interest rate; also assume the price of gold is constant at $400/oz.

(a) Find the value of the mine (not a 10-year lease) if the current deposit is x_0. In particular, how much is the mine worth initially when $x_0 = 50,000$ ounces? [*Hint:* Consider the recursive equation for K_k as $k \to \infty$.]

(b) For the 10-year lease considered in the text, how much gold remains in the mine at the end of the lease; and how much is the mine worth at that time?

(c) If the mine were not leased, but instead operated optimally by an owner, what would the mine be worth after 10 years?

9. (Little Bear Oil)   You have purchased a lease for the Little Bear Oil well. This well has initial reserves of 100 thousand barrels of oil. In any year you have three choices of how to operate the well: (a) you can *not* pump, in which case there is no operating cost and no change in oil reserves; (b) you can pump normally, in which case the operating cost is $50 thousand and you will pump out 20% of what the reserves were at

the beginning of the year; or (c) you can use enhanced pumping using water pressure, in which case the operating cost is $120 thousand and you will pump out 36% of what the reserves were at the beginning of the year. The price of oil is $10 per barrel and the interest rate is 10%. Assume that both your operating costs and the oil revenues come at the beginning of the year (through advance sales). Your lease is for a period of 3 years.

(a) Show how to set up a trinomial lattice to represent the possible states of the oil reserves.
(b) What is the maximum present value of your profits, and what is the corresponding optimal pumping strategy?

10. (Multiperiod harmony theorem ◇) The value of a firm is the maximum present value of its possible cash flow streams. This can be expressed as

$$V_0 = \max \left[x_0 + \frac{x_1}{1 + s_1} + \frac{x_2}{(1 + s_2)^2} + \cdots + \frac{x_n}{(1 + s_n)^n} \right]$$

where the maximization is with respect to all possible streams $x_0, x_1, \ldots, x_n$, and the s_i's are the spot rates. Let x_0^* be the first cash flow in the optimal plan. If the firm chooses an arbitrary plan that results in an initial cash flow of x_0 (distributed to the owners), the value of the firm after 1 year is

$$V_1(x_0) = \max \left\{ x_1 + \frac{x_2}{1 + s_1'} + \frac{x_3}{(1 + s_2')^2} + \cdots + \frac{x_n}{(1 + s_n')^{n-1}} \right\}$$

where now that maximum is with respect to all feasible cash flows that start with x_0 and the s_i''s are the spot rates after 1 year. An investor purchasing the firm at its full fair price has initial cash flow $x_0 - V_0$ and achieves a value of $V_1(x_0)$ after 1 year. Hence the 1-year total return to the investor is

$$R = \frac{V_1(x_0)}{V_0 - x_0}.$$

The investor would urge that x_0 be chosen to maximize R. Call this value $\bar{x}_0$. Assuming that interest rates follow expectation dynamics and that $V_1(\bar{x}_0) > 0$, show that the maximum R is $1 + s_1$ and that this return is achieved by the same x_0^* that determines V_0.

11. (Growing annuity) Show that for $g < r$,

$$\sum_{k=1}^{\infty} \frac{(1 + g)^{k-1}}{(1 + r)^k} = \frac{1}{r - g}.$$

$\left[\textit{Hint: Let } S \textit{ be the value of the sum. Note that } S = 1/(1 + r) + S(1 + g)/(1 + r). \right]$

12. (Two-stage growth) It is common practice in security analysis to modify the basic dividend growth model by allowing more than one stage of growth, with the growth factors being different in the different stages. As an example consider company Z, which currently distributes dividends of $10M annually. The dividends are expected to grow at the rate of 10% for the next 5 years and at a rate of 5% thereafter.

(a) Using a dividend discount approach with an interest rate of 15%, what is the value of the company?
(b) Find a general formula for the value of a company satisfying a two-stage growth model. Assume a growth rate of G for k years, followed by a growth rate of g thereafter, and an initial dividend of D_1.

REFERENCES

Capital budgeting is a classic topic in financial planning. Some good texts are [1–4]; good surveys are [5], [6]. Bond portfolio construction is considered in [6–8] and in other references given for Chapters 3 and 4. Dynamic programming was developed by Bellman (see [9, 10]). The classic reference on stock valuation is [11]. See [12–16] for other presentations. A vivid discussion of how improper analysis techniques led to disastrous overvaluation in the 1980s is in [17].

1. Dean, J. (1951), *Capital Budgeting,* Columbia University Press, New York.
2. Brealey, R., and S. Myers (1984), *Principles of Corporate Finance,* McGraw-Hill, New York.
3. Bierman, H., Jr., and S. Smidt (1984), *The Capital Budgeting Decision*, 6th ed., Macmillan, New York.
4. Martin, J. D., S. H. Cox, Jr., and R. D. MacMinn (1988), *The Theory of Finance, Evidence and Applications*, Dryden Press, Chicago, IL.
5. Schall, L. D., G. L. Sundem, and W. R. Geijsbeek (1978), "Survey and Analysis of Capital Budgeting Methods," *Journal of Finance*, **33**, 281–287.
6. Weingartner, H. M. (1966), "Capital Budgeting of Interrelated Projects: Survey and Synthesis," *Management Science*, **12**, 485–516.
7. Bierwag, G. O., G. G. Kaufman, R. Schweitzer, and A. Toevs (1981), "The Art of Risk Management in Bond Portfolios," *Journal of Portfolio Management*, **7**, 27–36.
8. Fabozzi, F. J., and T. D. Fabozzi (1989), *Bond Markets, Analysis and Strategies,* Prentice Hall, Englewood Cliffs, NJ.
9. Bellman, R. (1957), *Dynamic Programming,* Princeton University Press, Princeton, NJ.
10. Bellman R., and S. Dreyfus (1962), *Applied Dynamic Programming*, Princeton University Press, Princeton, NJ.
11. Graham, B., D. L. Dodd, and S. Cottle (1962), *Security Analysis*, McGraw-Hill, New York.
12. Williams, J. B. (1938), *The Theory of Investment Value,* North-Holland, Amsterdam, The Netherlands.
13. Gordon, M. J. (1959), "Dividends, Earnings, and Stock Prices," *Review of Economics and Statistics*, **41**, 99–195.
14. Molodovsky, N., C. May, and S. Chottiner (1965), "Common Stock Valuation: Principles, Tables and Application," *Financial Analysts Journal*, **21**, 104–123.
15. Foster, G. (1986), *Financial Statement Analysis,* Prentice Hall, Englewood Cliffs, NJ.
16. Black, F. (1980), "The Magic in Earnings: Economic Earnings versus Accounting Earnings," *Financial Analysts Journal*, **36**, 19–24.
17. Klarman, S. A. (1991), *Margin of Safety: Risk-Averse Value Investing Strategies for the Thoughtful Investor,* Harper Business.

PART II

SINGLE-PERIOD RANDOM CASH FLOWS

6 MEAN–VARIANCE PORTFOLIO THEORY

Typically, when making an investment, the initial outlay of capital is known, but the amount to be returned is uncertain. Such situations are studied in this part of the text. In this part, however, we restrict attention to the case of a single investment period: money is invested at the initial time, and payoff is attained at the end of the period.

The assumption that an investment situation comprises a single period is sometimes a good approximation. An investment in a zero-coupon bond that will be held to maturity is an example. Another is an investment in a physical project that will not provide payment until it is completed. However, many common investments, such as publicly traded stocks, are not tied to a single period, since they can be liquidated at will and may return dividends periodically. Nevertheless, such investments are often analyzed on a single period basis as a simplification; but this type of analysis should be regarded only as a prelude to Parts 3 and 4 of the text, which are more comprehensive.

This part of the text treats uncertainty with three different mathematical methods: (1) mean–variance analysis, (2) utility function analysis, and (3) arbitrage (or comparison) analysis. Each of these methods is an important component of investment science.

This first chapter of the second part of the text treats uncertainty by **mean–variance** analysis. This method uses probability theory only slightly, and leads to convenient mathematical expressions and procedures. Mean–variance analysis forms the basis for the important *capital asset pricing model* discussed in Chapter 7.

6.1 ASSET RETURN

An investment instrument that can be bought and sold is frequently called an **asset.** We introduce a fundamental concept concerning such assets.

Suppose that you purchase an asset at time zero, and 1 year later you sell the asset. The **total return** on your investment is defined to be

$$\text{total return} = \frac{\text{amount received}}{\text{amount invested}}.$$

Or if X_0 and X_1 are, respectively, the amounts of money invested and received and R is the total return, then

$$R = \frac{X_1}{X_0}.$$

Often, for simplicity, the term *return* is used for total return.

The **rate of return** is

$$\text{rate of return} = \frac{\text{amount received} - \text{amount invested}}{\text{amount invested}}.$$

Or, again, if X_0 and X_1 are, respectively, the amounts of money invested and received and r is the rate of return, then

$$r = \frac{X_1 - X_0}{X_0}. \tag{6.1}$$

The shorter expression *return* is also frequently used for the rate of return.

We distinguish the two definitions by using upper- or lowercase letters, such as R and r, respectively, for total return and rate of return; and usually the context makes things clear if we use the shorthand phrase *return*.

It is clear that the two notions are related by

$$R = 1 + r$$

and that (6.1) can be rewritten as

$$X_1 = (1 + r)X_0.$$

This shows that a rate of return acts much like an interest rate.

Short Sales

Sometimes it is possible to sell an asset that you do not own through the process of **short selling,** or **shorting,** the asset. To do this, you borrow the asset from someone who owns it (such as a brokerage firm). You then sell the borrowed asset to someone else, receiving an amount X_0. At a later date, you repay your loan by purchasing the asset for, say, X_1 and return the asset to your lender. If the later amount X_1 is lower than the original amount X_0, you will have made a profit of $X_0 - X_1$. Hence short selling is profitable if the asset price declines.

Short selling is considered quite risky—even dangerous—by many investors. The reason is that the potential for loss is unlimited. If the asset value increases, the loss is $X_1 - X_0$; since X_1 can increase arbitrarily, so can the loss. For this reason (and others) short selling is prohibited within certain financial institutions, and it is purposely avoided as a policy by many individuals and institutions. However, it is not universally forbidden, and there is, in fact, a considerable level of short selling of stock market securities.

When short selling a stock, you are essentially duplicating the role of the issuing corporation. You sell the stock to raise immediate capital. If the stock pays dividends during the period that you have borrowed it, you too must pay that same dividend to the person from whom you borrowed the stock.

In practice, the pure process of short selling is supplemented by certain restrictions and safeguards. (For example, you must post a security deposit with the broker from whom you borrowed the asset.) But for theoretical work, we typically assume that the pure shorting of an asset is allowed.

Let us determine the return associated with short selling. We *receive* X_0 initially and *pay* X_1 later, so the outlay is $-X_0$ and the final receipt is $-X_1$, and hence the total return is

$$R = \frac{-X_1}{-X_0} = \frac{X_1}{X_0}.$$

The minus signs cancel out, so we obtain the same expression as that for purchasing the asset. Hence the return value R applies algebraically to both purchases and short sales. We can write this as

$$-X_1 = -X_0 R = -X_0(1 + r)$$

to show that final receipt is related to initial outlay.

Example 6.1 (A short sale)   Suppose I decide to short 100 shares of stock in company CBA. This stock is currently selling for $10 per share. I borrow 100 shares from my broker and sell these in the stock market, receiving $1,000. At the end of 1 year the price of CBA has dropped to $9 per share. I buy back 100 shares for $900 and give these shares to my broker to repay the original loan. Because the stock price fell, this has been a favorable transaction for me. I made a profit of $100.

Someone who purchased the stock at the beginning of the year and sold it at the end would have lost $100. That person would easily compute

$$R = \frac{900}{1,000} = .90$$

or

$$r = \frac{900 - 1,000}{1,000} = -.10.$$

The rate of return is clearly negative as $r = -10\%$. Shorting converts a negative rate of return into a profit because the original investment is also negative. For my shorting activity on CBA my original outlay was $-\$1,000$; hence my profit is $-\$1,000 \times r = \$100$.

It is a bit strange to refer to a rate of return associated with the idealized shorting procedure, since there is no initial commitment of resources. Nevertheless, it is the proper notion. In practice, shorting does require an initial commitment of margin, and the proceeds from the initial sale are held until the short is cleared. This modified procedure will have a different rate of return. (See Exercise 1.) For basic theoretical work, however, we shall often assume that the idealized procedure is available.

Portfolio Return

Suppose now that n different assets are available. We can form a **master asset,** or **portfolio,** of these n assets. Suppose that this is done by apportioning an amount X_0 among the n assets. We then select amounts X_{0i}, $i = 1, 2, \ldots, n$, such that $\sum_{i=1}^{n} X_{0i} = X_0$, where X_{0i} represents the amount invested in the ith asset. If we are allowed to sell an asset short, then some of the X_{0i}'s can be negative; otherwise we restrict the X_{0i}'s to be nonnegative.

The amounts invested can be expressed as fractions of the total investment. Thus we write

$$X_{0i} = w_i X_0, \qquad i = 1, 2, \ldots, n$$

where w_i is the **weight** or fraction of asset i in the portfolio. Clearly,

$$\sum_{i=1}^{n} w_i = 1$$

and some w_i's may be negative if short selling is allowed.

Let R_i denote the total return of asset i. Then the amount of money generated at the end of the period by the ith asset is $R_i X_{0i} = R_i w_i X_0$. The total amount received by this portfolio at the end of the period is therefore $\sum_{i=1}^{n} R_i w_i X_0$. Hence we find that the overall total return of the portfolio is

$$R = \frac{\sum_{i=1}^{n} R_i w_i X_0}{X_0} = \sum_{i=1}^{n} w_i R_i .$$

Equivalently, since $\sum_{i=1}^{n} w_i = 1$, we have

$$r = \sum_{i=1}^{n} w_i r_i .$$

This is a basic result concerning returns, and so we highlight it here:

Portfolio return   *Both the total return and the rate of return of a portfolio of assets are equal to the weighted sum of the corresponding individual asset returns, with the weight of an asset being its relative weight (in purchase cost) in the portfolio; that is,*

$$R = \sum_{i=1}^{n} w_i R_i , \qquad r = \sum_{i=1}^{n} w_i r_i .$$

An example calculation of portfolio weights and the associated expected rate of return of the portfolio are shown in Table 6.1.

TABLE 6.1
Calculation of Portfolio Return

Security	Number of shares	Price	Total cost	Weight in portfolio
Jazz, Inc.	100	$40	$4,000	0.25
Classical, Inc.	400	$20	$8,000	0.50
Rock, Inc.	200	$20	$4,000	0.25
Portfolio total values			$16,000	1.00

Security	Weight in portfolio	Rate of return	Weighted rate
Jazz, Inc.	.25	17%	4.25%
Classical, Inc.	.50	13%	6.50%
Rock, Inc.	.25	23%	5.75%
Portfolio rate of return			16.50%

The weight of a security in a portfolio is its proportion of total cost, as shown in the upper table. These weights then determine the rate of return of the portfolio, as shown in the lower table.

6.2 RANDOM VARIABLES

Frequently the amount of money to be obtained when selling an asset is uncertain at the time of purchase. In that case the return is random and can be described in probabilistic terms. In preparation for the study of random returns, we briefly introduce some concepts of probability. (For more detail on basic probability theory, see Appendix A.)

Suppose x is a random quantity that can take on any one of a finite number of specific values, say, $x_1, x_2, \ldots, x_m$. Assume further that associated with each possible x_i, there is a probability p_i that represents the relative chance of an occurrence of x_i. The p_i's satisfy $\sum_{i=1}^{m} p_i = 1$ and $p_i \geq 0$ for each i. Each p_i can be thought of as the relative frequency with which x_i would occur if an experiment of observing x were repeated infinitely often. The quantity x, characterized in this way before its value is known, is called a **random variable.**

A simple example is that of rolling an ordinary six-sided die, with the number of spots obtained being x. The six possibilities are 1, 2, 3, 4, 5, 6, and each has probability $1/6$.

It is common to display the probabilities associated with a random variable graphically as a density. The possible values of x are indicated on the horizontal axis, and the height of the line at a point represents the probability of that point. Some examples are shown in Figure 6.1. Figure 6.1(*a*) shows the density corresponding to the outcome of a roll of a die, where the six possibilities each have a probability of $1/6$. Figure 6.1(*b*) shows a more general case with several possible outcomes of various probabilities.

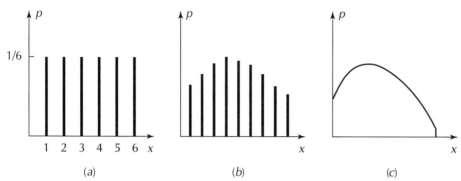

FIGURE 6.1 Probability distributions. Probability distributions are shown for (a) the outcome of a roll of a die, (b) another random variable with a finite number of possible outcomes, and (c) a continuous random variable.

If the outcome variable can take any real value in an interval as, for example, the temperature of a room, a **probability density function** $p(x)$ describes the probability. The probability that the variable's value will lie in any segment of the line is equal to the area of the vertical region bounded by this segment and the density function. An example is shown in Figure 6.1(c).

Expected Value

The **expected value** of a random variable x is just the average value obtained by regarding the probabilities as frequencies. For the case of a finite number of possibilities, it is defined as

$$\mathrm{E}(x) = \sum_{i=1}^{m} x_i \, p_i \, .$$

For convenience $\mathrm{E}(x)$ is often denoted by $\overline{x}$. Also the terms **mean** or **mean value** are often used for the expected value. So we say x has mean $\overline{x}$.

Example 6.2 (A roll of the die)   The expected value of the number of spots on a roll of a die is

$$\tfrac{1}{6}(1 + 2 + 3 + 4 + 5 + 6) = 3.5 \, .$$

Note that the expected value is not necessarily a possible outcome of a roll.

The expected value operation is the main operation used in probability calculations, so it is useful to note its basic properties:

1. Certain value   If y is a known value (not random), then $\mathrm{E}(y) = y$.

   This states that the expected value of a nonrandom quantity is equal to the quantity itself.

2. **Linearity** If y and z are random, then $E(\alpha y + \beta z) = \alpha E(y) + \beta E(z)$ for any real values of α and β.

This states that the expected (or mean) value of the sum of two random variables is the sum of their corresponding means; and the mean value of the multiple of a random variable is the same multiple of the original mean. For example, the expected value for the total number of spots on two dice is $3.5 + 3.5 = 7$.

3. **Nonnegativity** If x is random but never less than zero, then $E(x) \geq 0$.

This is a sign-preserving property.

Variance

The expected value of a random variable provides a useful summary of the probabilistic nature of the variable. However, typically one wants, in addition, to have a measure of the degree of possible deviation from the mean. One such measure is the **variance.**

Given a random variable y with expected value $\bar{y}$, the quantity $y - \bar{y}$ is itself random, but has an expected value of zero. [This is because $E(y - \bar{y}) = E(y) - E(\bar{y}) = \bar{y} - \bar{y} = 0$.] The quantity $(y - \bar{y})^2$ is always nonnegative and is large when y deviates greatly from $\bar{y}$ and small when it is near $\bar{y}$. The expected value of this squared variable $(y - \bar{y})^2$ is a useful measure of how much y tends to vary from its expected value.

In general, for any random variable y the variance of y is defined as

$$\text{var}(y) = E\left[(y - \bar{y})^2\right].$$

In mathematical expressions, variance is represented by the symbol σ^2. Thus we write $\sigma_y^2 = \text{var}(y)$, or if y is understood, we simply write $\sigma^2 = \text{var}(y)$.

We frequently use the square root of the variance, denoted by σ and called the **standard deviation.** It has the same units as the quantity y and is another measure of how much the variable is likely to deviate from its expected value. Thus, formally,

$$\sigma_y = \sqrt{E\left[(y - \bar{y})^2\right]}.$$

There is a simple formula for variance that is useful in computations. We note that

$$\text{var}(x) = E\left[(x - \bar{x})^2\right]$$
$$= E(x^2) - 2E(x)\bar{x} + \bar{x}^2$$
$$= E(x^2) - \bar{x}^2. \tag{6.2}$$

This result is used in the following example.

Example 6.3 (A roll of the die) Let us compute the variance of the random variable y defined as the number of spots obtained by a roll of a die. Recalling that $\bar{y} = 3.5$

we find

$$\sigma^2 = E(y^2) - \bar{y}^2$$
$$= \tfrac{1}{6}[1 + 4 + 9 + 16 + 25 + 36] - (3.5)^2 = 2.92.$$

Hence $\sigma = \sqrt{2.92} = 1.71$.

Several Random Variables

Suppose we are interested in two random variables, such as the outside temperature and the barometric pressure. To describe these random variables we must have probabilities for all possible combinations of the two values. If we denote the variables by x and y, we must consider the possible pairs (x, y). Suppose x can take on the possible values $x_1, x_2, \ldots, x_n$ and y can take on the values $y_1, y_2, \ldots, y_m$. (By assuming limited measurement precision, temperature and pressure can easily be assumed to take on only a finite number of values.) Then we must specify the probabilities p_{ij} for combinations (x_i, y_j) for $i = 1, 2, \ldots, n$ and $j = 1, 2, \ldots, m$. Hence for temperature and barometric pressure we need the probabilities of all possible combinations.

If we are interested in three random variables, such as outside temperature, barometric pressure, and humidity, we would need probabilities over all possible combinations of the three variables. For more variables, things get progressively more complicated.

There is an important special case where the probability description of several variables simplifies. Two random variables x and y are said to be **independent random variables** if the outcome probabilities for one variable do not depend on the outcome of the other. For example, consider the roll of two dice. The probability of an outcome of, say, 4 on the second die is 1/6, no matter what the outcome of the first die. Hence the two random variables corresponding to the spots on the two dice are independent. On the other hand, outside temperature and barometric pressure are not independent, since if pressure is high, temperature is more likely to be high as well.

Covariance

When considering two or more random variables, their mutual dependence can be summarized conveniently by their **covariance.**

Let x_1 and x_2 be two random variables with expected values $\bar{x}_1$ and $\bar{x}_2$. The covariance of these variables is defined to be

$$\text{cov}(x_1, x_2) = E\big[(x_1 - \bar{x}_1)(x_2 - \bar{x}_2)\big].$$

The covariance of two random variables x and y is frequently denoted by σ_{xy}. Hence for random variables x_1 and x_2 we write $\text{cov}(x_1, x_2) = \sigma_{x_1, x_2}$ or, alternatively, $\text{cov}(x_1, x_2) = \sigma_{12}$. Note that, by symmetry, $\sigma_{12} = \sigma_{21}$.

Analogous to (6.2), there is an alternative shorter formula for covariance that is easily derived; namely,

$$\text{cov}(x_1, x_2) = \text{E}(x_1 x_2) - \bar{x}_1 \bar{x}_2. \tag{6.3}$$

This is useful in computations.

If two random variables x_1 and x_2 have the property that $\sigma_{12} = 0$, then they are said to be **uncorrelated.** This is the situation (roughly) where knowledge of the value of one variable gives no information about the other. If two random variables are independent, then they are uncorrelated. If $\sigma_{12} > 0$, the two variables are said to be **positively correlated.** In this case, if one variable is above its mean, the other is likely to be above its mean as well. On the other hand, if $\sigma_{12} < 0$, the two variables are said to be **negatively correlated.**

Figure 6.2 illustrates the concept of correlation by showing collections of random samples of two variables x and y under the conditions (a) positive correlation, (b) negative correlation, and (c) no correlation.

The following result gives an important bound on the covariance.

Covariance bound   *The covariance of two random variables satisfies*

$$|\sigma_{12}| \leq \sigma_1 \sigma_2 .$$

In the preceding inequality, if $\sigma_{12} = \sigma_1 \sigma_2$, the variables are **perfectly correlated.** In this situation, the covariance is as large as possible for the given variances. If one variable were a fixed positive multiple of the other, the two would be perfectly correlated. Conversely, if $\sigma_{12} = -\sigma_1 \sigma_2$, the two variables exhibit **perfect negative correlation.**

Another useful construct is the **correlation coefficient** of two variables, defined as

$$\rho_{12} = \frac{\sigma_{12}}{\sigma_1 \sigma_2} .$$

From the covariance bound above, we see that $|\rho_{12}| \leq 1$.

Note that the variance of a random variable x is the covariance of that variable with itself. Hence we write $\sigma_x^2 = \sigma_{xx}$.

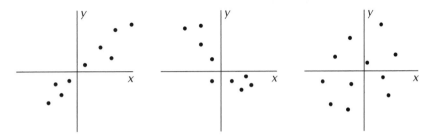

(a) Positively correlated   (b) Negatively correlated   (c) Uncorrelated

FIGURE 6.2   Correlations of data. Samples are drawn of the pair of random variables x and y, and these pairs are plotted on an x–y diagram. A typical pattern of points obtained is shown in the three cases: (a) positive correlation, (b) negative correlation, and (c) no correlation.

Variance of a Sum

When we know the covariance between two random variables, it is possible to compute the variance of the sum of the variables. This is a computation that is used frequently in what follows.

Suppose that x and y are random variables. We have, by linearity, that $E(x+y) = \overline{x} + \overline{y}$. Also by definition,

$$
\begin{aligned}
\text{var}\,(x + y) &= E[(x - \overline{x} + y - \overline{y})^2] \\
&= E[(x - \overline{x})^2] + 2E[(x - \overline{x})(y - \overline{y})] + E[(y - \overline{y})^2] \\
&= \sigma_x^2 + 2\sigma_{xy} + \sigma_y^2.
\end{aligned}
\tag{6.4}
$$

This formula is easy to remember because it looks similar to the standard expression for the square of the sum of two algebraic quantities. We just substitute variance for the square and the covariance for the product.

An important special case is where the two variables are uncorrelated. In that case $\sigma^2 = \sigma_x^2 + \sigma_y^2$.

Example 6.4 (Two rolls of the die)   Suppose that a die is rolled twice and the average of the two numbers of spots is recorded as a quantity z. What are the mean value and the variance of z? We let x and y denote the values obtained on the first and second rolls, respectively. Then $z = \frac{1}{2}(x + y)$. Also x and y are uncorrelated, since the rolls of the die are independent. Therefore $\overline{z} = \frac{1}{2}(\overline{x}+\overline{y}) = 3.5$, and var$(z) = \frac{1}{4}(\sigma_x^2 + \sigma_y^2) = 2.92/2 = 1.46$. Hence $\sigma_z = 1.208$, which is somewhat smaller than the corresponding 1.71 value for a single roll.

6.3 RANDOM RETURNS

When an asset is originally acquired, its rate of return is usually uncertain. Accordingly, we consider the rate of return r to be a random variable. For analytical purposes we shall, in this chapter, summarize the uncertainty of the rate of return by its expected value (or mean) $E(r) \equiv \overline{r}$, by its variance $E[(r - \overline{r}^2)] \equiv \sigma^2$, and by its covariance with other assets of interest. We can best illustrate how rates of return are represented by considering a few examples.

Example 6.5 (Wheel of fortune)   Consider the wheel of fortune shown in Figure 6.3. It is unlike any wheel you are likely to find in an amusement park since its payoffs are quite favorable. If you bet $1 on the wheel, the payoff you receive is that shown in the segment corresponding to the landing spot. The chance of landing on a given segment is proportional to the area of the segment. For this wheel the probability of each segment is 1/6.

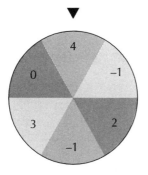

FIGURE 6.3   Wheel of fortune. If you bet $1 on the wheel, you will receive the amount equal to the value shown in the segment under the marker after the wheel is spun.

Let us first compute the mean and the variance of the payoff of the wheel. We denote the payoff of segment i by Q_i. Therefore the expected payoff is

$$\overline{Q} = \sum_i p_i Q_i = \tfrac{1}{6}(4 - 1 + 2 - 1 + 3) = 7/6.$$

The variance can be found from the short formula (6.2) to be

$$\sigma_Q^2 = \mathrm{E}(Q^2) - \overline{Q}^2 = \tfrac{1}{6}(16 + 1 + 4 + 1 + 9) - (7/6)^2 = 3.81\,.$$

The payoff of the wheel is the same as the total return under the assumption of a $1 bet. Therefore $Q = R$ and the rate of return is $r = Q - 1$. From this we find

$$\overline{r} = \mathrm{E}(r) = \overline{Q} - 1 = 1/6$$

$$\sigma_r^2 = \mathrm{E}\left[(r - \overline{r})^2\right] = \mathrm{E}\left\{[Q - 1 - (\overline{Q} - 1)]^2\right\} = \sigma_Q^2 = 3.81\,.$$

Example 6.6 (Rate of return on a stock)   Let us consider a share of stock in a major corporation (such as General Motors, AT&T, or IBM) as an asset. Imagine that we are attempting to describe the rate of return that applies if we were to buy it now and sell it at the end of one year. We ignore transactions costs. As an estimate, we might take $\mathrm{E}(r) = .12$; that is, we estimate that the expected rate of return is 12%. This is a reasonable value for the stock of a major corporation, based on the past performance of stocks in the overall market. Now what about the standard deviation? We recognize that the 12% figure is not likely to be hit exactly, and that there can be significant deviations. In fact it is quite possible that the 1-year rate of return could be -5% in one year and $+25\%$ in the next. A reasonable estimate for the standard deviation is about .15, or 15%. Hence, loosely, we might say that the rate of return is likely to be 12% plus or minus 15%. We discuss the process of estimating expected values and standard deviations for stocks in Chapter 8, but this example gives a rough idea of typical magnitudes.

The probability density for the rate of return of this typical stock is shown in Figure 6.4. It has a mean value of .12, but the return can become arbitrarily large. However, the rate of return can never be less than -1, since that represents complete loss of the original investment.

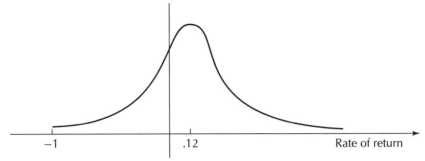

FIGURE 6.4 Probability density of the rate of return of a stock. The mean rate of return may be about 12% and the standard deviation about 15%. The rate of return cannot be less than −1.

Example 6.7 (Betting wheel)   Two kinds of wheels are useful for the study of investment problems. The wheel of fortune of Example 6.5 is one form of wheel. For that type, one bets on (invests in) the wheel as a whole, and the payoff is determined by the landing segment.

The other kind of wheel is a **betting wheel,** an example of which is shown in Figure 6.5. For this kind of wheel one bets on (invests in) the individual segments of the wheel. For example, for the wheel shown, if one invests $1 in the white segment, then $3 will be the payoff if white is the landing segment; otherwise the payoff is zero and the original $1 is lost. One is allowed to bet different amounts on different segments. A roulette wheel is a betting wheel. From a theoretical viewpoint, a betting wheel is interesting because the returns from different segments are correlated.

For the wheel shown, we may bet on: (1) white, (2) black, or (3) gray, with payoffs 3, 2, or 6, respectively. Note that the bet on white has quite favorable odds.

We can work out the expected rates of return for the three possible bets. It is much easier here to work first with total returns and then subtract 1. For example, for white the return is $3 with probability $\frac{1}{2}$ and 0 with probability $\frac{1}{2}$.

The three expected values are:

$$\overline{R}_1 = \tfrac{1}{2}(3) + \tfrac{1}{2}(0) = \tfrac{3}{2}$$

$$\overline{R}_2 = \tfrac{1}{3}(2) + \tfrac{2}{3}(0) = \tfrac{2}{3}$$

$$\overline{R}_3 = \tfrac{1}{6}(6) + \tfrac{5}{6}(0) = 1 \,.$$

Likewise, the three variances are, from (6.2),

$$\sigma_1^2 = \tfrac{1}{2}(3^2) - (\tfrac{3}{2})^2 = 2.25$$

$$\sigma_2^2 = \tfrac{1}{3}(2)^2 - (\tfrac{2}{3})^2 = .889$$

$$\sigma_3^2 = \tfrac{1}{6}6^2 - 1 = 5 \,.$$

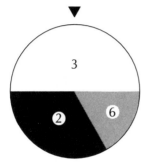

FIGURE 6.5 Betting wheel. It is possible to bet on any segment of the wheel. If that segment is chosen by the spin, the better receives the amount indicated times the bet.

Finally, we can calculate the covariances using (6.3). The expected value of products such as $E(R_1 R_2)$ are all zero, so we easily find

$$\sigma_{12} = -\tfrac{3}{2}(\tfrac{2}{3}) = -1.0$$

$$\sigma_{13} = -\tfrac{3}{2}(1) = -1.5$$

$$\sigma_{23} = -\tfrac{2}{3}(1) = -.67.$$

Mean–Standard Deviation Diagram

The random rates of return of assets can be represented on a two-dimensional diagram, as shown in Figure 6.6. An asset with mean rate of return $\bar{r}$ [or m or $E(r)$] and standard deviation σ is represented as a point in this diagram. The horizontal axis is used for the standard deviation, and the vertical axis is used for the mean. This diagram is called a mean–standard deviation diagram, or simply $\bar{r}$–σ diagram.

In such a diagram the standard deviation, rather than the variance, is used as the horizontal axis. This gives both axes comparable units (such as percent per year). Such diagrams are used frequently in mean–variance investment analysis.

FIGURE 6.6 Mean–standard deviation diagram. Assets are described as points on the diagram.

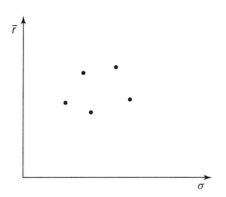

6.4 PORTFOLIO MEAN AND VARIANCE

Now that we have the concepts of expected value (or mean) and variance for returns of individual assets and covariances between pairs of assets, we show how these can be used to determine the corresponding mean and variance of the return of a portfolio.

Mean Return of a Portfolio

Suppose that there are n assets with (random) rates of return $r_1, r_2, \ldots, r_n$. These have expected values $E(r_1) = \bar{r}_1, E(r_2) = \bar{r}_2, \ldots, E(r_n) = \bar{r}_n$.

Suppose that, as in Section 6.1, we form a portfolio of these n assets using the weights w_i, $i = 1, 2, \ldots, n$. The rate of return of the portfolio in terms of the return of the individual returns is

$$r = w_1 r_1 + w_2 r_2 + \cdots + w_n r_n .$$

We may take the expected values of both sides, and using linearity (property 2 of the expected value in Section 6.2), we obtain

$$E(r) = w_1 E(r_1) + w_2 E(r_2) + \cdots + w_n E(r_n) .$$

In other words, the expected rate of return of the portfolio is found by taking the weighted sum of the individual expected rates of return. So, finding the expected return of a portfolio is easy once we have the expected rates of return of the individual assets from which the portfolio is composed.

Variance of Portfolio Return

Now let us determine the variance of the rate of return of the portfolio.

We denote the variance of the return of asset i by σ_i^2, the variance of the return of the portfolio by σ^2, and the covariance of the return of asset i with asset j by σ_{ij}. We perform a straightforward calculation:

$$\sigma^2 = E\left[(r - \bar{r})^2\right]$$

$$= E\left[\left(\sum_{i=1}^{n} w_i r_i - \sum_{i=1}^{n} w_i \bar{r}_i\right)^2\right]$$

$$= E\left[\left(\sum_{i=1}^{n} w_i (r_i - \bar{r}_i)\right)\left(\sum_{j=1}^{n} w_j (r_j - \bar{r}_j)\right)\right]$$

$$= E\left[\sum_{i,j=1}^{n} w_i w_j (r_i - \bar{r}_i)(r_j - \bar{r}_j)\right]$$

$$= \sum_{i,j=1}^{n} w_i w_j \sigma_{ij} .$$

This important result shows how the variance of a portfolio's return can be calculated easily from the covariances of the pairs of asset returns and the asset weights used in the portfolio. (Recall, $\sigma_{ii} = \sigma_i^2$.)

Example 6.8 (Two-asset portfolio)   Suppose that there are two assets with $\bar{r}_1 = .12$, $\bar{r}_2 = .15$, $\sigma_1 = .20$, $\sigma_2 = .18$, and $\sigma_{12} = .01$ (values typical for two stocks). A portfolio is formed with weights $w_1 = .25$ and $w_2 = .75$. We can calculate the mean and the variance of the portfolio. First we have the mean,

$$\bar{r} = .25(.12) + .75(.15) = .1425.$$

Second we calculate the variance,

$$\sigma^2 = (.25)^2(.20)^2 + .25(.75)(.01) + .75(.25)(.01) + (.75)^2(.18)^2 = .024475.$$

Note that the two cross terms are equal (since $w_i w_j = w_j w_i$). Hence,

$$\sigma = .1564.$$

Diversification*

Portfolios with only a few assets may be subject to a high degree of risk, represented by a relatively large variance. As a general rule, the variance of the return of a portfolio can be reduced by including additional assets in the portfolio, a process referred to as **diversification.** This process reflects the maxim, "Don't put all your eggs in one basket."

The effects of diversification can be quantified by using the formulas for combining variances. Suppose as an example that there are many assets, all of which are mutually uncorrelated. That is, the return of each asset is uncorrelated with that of any other asset in the group. Suppose also that the rate of return of each of these assets has mean m and variance σ^2. Now suppose that a portfolio is constructed by taking equal portions of n of these assets; that is, $w_i = 1/n$ for each i. The overall rate of return of this portfolio is

$$r = \frac{1}{n} \sum_{i=1}^{n} r_i.$$

The mean value of this is $\bar{r} = m$, which is independent of n. The corresponding variance is

$$\mathrm{var}(r) = \frac{1}{n^2} \sum_{i=1}^{n} \sigma^2 = \frac{\sigma^2}{n}$$

where we have used the fact that the individual returns are uncorrelated. The variance decreases rapidly as n increases, as shown in Figure 6.7(a). This chart shows the variance as a function of n, the number of assets (when $\sigma^2 = 1$). Note that considerable improvement is obtained by including about six uncorrelated assets.

The situation is somewhat different if the returns of the available assets are correlated. As a simple example suppose again that each asset has a rate of return with mean

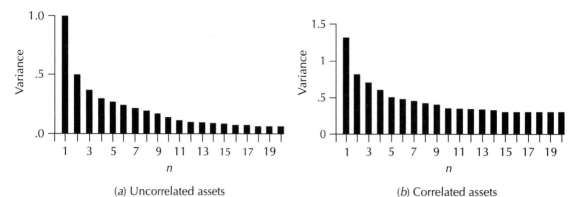

(a) Uncorrelated assets   (b) Correlated assets

FIGURE 6.7   Effects of diversification. If assets are uncorrelated, the variance of a portfolio can be made very small. If assets are positively correlated, there is likely to be a lower limit to the variance that can be achieved.

m and variance σ^2, but now each return pair has a covariance of $\text{cov}(r_i, r_j) = .3\sigma^2$ for $i \neq j$. Again we form a portfolio by taking equal portions of n of these assets. In this case,

$$\text{var}(r) = \text{E}\left[\sum_{i=1}^{n} \frac{1}{n}(r_i - \bar{r})\right]^2$$

$$= \frac{1}{n^2}\text{E}\left\{\left[\sum_{i=1}^{n}(r_i - \bar{r})\right]\left[\sum_{j=i}^{n}(r_j - \bar{r})\right]\right\}$$

$$= \frac{1}{n^2}\sum_{i,j}\sigma_{ij} = \frac{1}{n^2}\left\{\sum_{i=j}\sigma_{ij} + \sum_{i\neq j}\sigma_{ij}\right\}$$

$$= \frac{1}{n^2}\left\{n\sigma^2 + .3(n^2 - n)\sigma^2\right\}$$

$$= \frac{\sigma^2}{n} + .3\sigma^2\left(1 - \frac{1}{n}\right)$$

$$= \frac{.7\sigma^2}{n} + .3\sigma^2$$

This result is shown in Figure 6.7(b) (where again $\sigma^2 = 1$). In this case it is impossible to reduce the variance below $.3\sigma^2$, no matter how large n is made.

This analysis of diversification is somewhat crude, for we have assumed that all expected rates of return are equal. In general, diversification may reduce the overall expected return while reducing the variance. Most people do not want to sacrifice much expected return for a small decrease in variance, so blind diversification, without an understanding of its influence on both the mean and the variance of return, is not necessarily desirable. This is the motivation behind the general mean–variance approach developed by Markowitz. It makes the trade-offs between mean and variance explicit.

Nevertheless, there is an important lesson to be learned from this simple analysis. Namely, if returns are uncorrelated, it is possible through diversification to reduce portfolio variance essentially to zero by taking n large. Conversely, if returns are positively correlated, it is more difficult to reduce variance, and there may be a lower limit to what can be achieved.

Diagram of a Portfolio

Suppose that two assets are represented on a mean–standard deviation diagram. These two assets can be combined, according to some weights, to form a portfolio—a new asset. The mean value and the standard deviation of the rate of return of this new asset can be calculated from the mean, variances, and covariances of the returns of the original assets. However, since covariances are not shown on the diagram, the exact location of the point representing the new asset cannot be determined from the location on the diagram of the original two assets. There are many possibilities, depending on the covariance of these asset returns.

We analyze the possibilities as follows. We begin with two assets as indicated in Figure 6.8. We then define a whole family of portfolios by introducing the variable α, which defines weights as $w_1 = 1-\alpha$ and $w_2 = \alpha$. Thus as α varies from 0 to 1, the portfolio goes from one that contains only asset 1 to one that contains a mixture of assets 1 and 2, and then to one that contains only asset 2. Values of α outside the range $0 \leq \alpha \leq 1$ make one or the other of the weights negative, corresponding to short selling.

As α varies, the new portfolios trace out a curve that includes assets 1 and 2. This curve will look something like the curved shape shown in Figure 6.8, but its exact shape depends on σ_{12}. The solid portion of the curve corresponds to positive combinations of the two assets; the dashed portion corresponds to the shorting of one of them (the one at the opposite end of the solid curve). It can be shown in fact that the solid portion of the curve must lie within the shaded region shown in the figure; that is, it must lie within a triangular region defined by the vertices 1, 2, and a point A on the

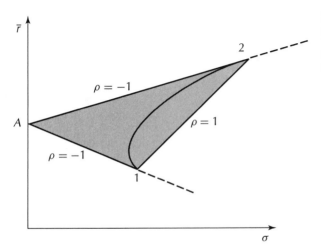

FIGURE 6.8 Combinations of two assets. When two assets are combined in various combinations, the resulting portfolios sweep out a curve between the points representing the original assets. This curve must lie in the shaded triangular region shown.

vertical axis. We state this property formally, but it is not essential that you absorb the details at first reading. It is only necessary to understand the general shape of the curve.

 Portfolio diagram lemma   *The curve in an $\bar{r}$–σ diagram defined by nonnegative mixtures of two assets 1 and 2 lies within the triangular region defined by the two original assets and the point on the vertical axis of height $A = (\bar{r}_1\sigma_2 + \bar{r}_2\sigma_1)/(\sigma_1 + \sigma_2)$.*

Proof: The rate of return of the portfolio defined by α is $r(\alpha) = (1-\alpha)r_1 + \alpha r_2$. The mean value of this return is

$$\bar{r}(\alpha) = (1 - \alpha)\bar{r}_1 + \alpha\bar{r}_2 .$$

This says that the mean value is between the original means, in direct proportion to the proportions of the assets. In a 50–50 mix, for example, the new mean will be midway between the original means.

Let us compute the standard deviation of the portfolio. We have, from the general formula of the previous section,

$$\sigma(\alpha) = \sqrt{(1 - \alpha)^2\sigma_1^2 + 2\alpha(1 - \alpha)\sigma_{12} + \alpha^2\sigma_2^2}.$$

Using the definition of the correlation coefficient $\rho = \sigma_{12}/(\sigma_1\sigma_2)$, this equation can be written

$$\sigma(\alpha) = \sqrt{(1 - \alpha)^2\sigma_1^2 + 2\rho\alpha(1 - \alpha)\sigma_1\sigma_2 + \alpha^2\sigma_2^2}.$$

This is quite a messy expression. However, we can determine its bounds. We know that ρ can range over $-1 \le \rho \le 1$. Using $\rho = 1$ we find the upper bound

$$\sigma(\alpha)^* = \sqrt{(1 - \alpha)^2\sigma_1^2 + 2\alpha(1 - \alpha)\sigma_1\sigma_2 + \alpha^2\sigma_2^2}$$

$$= \sqrt{[(1 - \alpha)\sigma_1 + \alpha\sigma_2]^2}$$

$$= (1 - \alpha)\sigma_1 + \alpha\sigma_2 .$$

Using $\rho = -1$ we likewise obtain the lower bound

$$\sigma(\alpha)_* = \sqrt{(1 - \alpha)^2\sigma_1^2 - 2\alpha(1 - \alpha)\sigma_1\sigma_2 + \alpha^2\sigma_2^2}$$

$$= \sqrt{[(1 - \alpha)\sigma_1 - \alpha\sigma_2]^2}$$

$$= |(1 - \alpha)\sigma_1 - \alpha\sigma_2| .$$

Notice that the upper bound expression is linear in α, just like the expression for the mean. If we use these two linear expressions, we deduce that both the mean and the standard deviation move proportionally to α between their values at $\alpha = 0$ and $\alpha = 1$, provided that $\rho = 1$. This implies that as α varies from 0 to 1, the portfolio point will trace out a straight line between the two points. This is the direct line between 1 and 2 indicated in the figure.

The lower bound expression is nearly linear as well, except for the absolute-value sign. When α is small, the term inside the absolute-value sign is positive, so we can replace that term by $(1 - \alpha)\sigma_1 - \alpha\sigma_2$. This remains positive until $\alpha = \sigma_1/(\sigma_1 + \sigma_2)$. After that it reverses sign, and so the absolute value becomes $\alpha\sigma_2 - (1 - \alpha)\sigma_1$. The reversal occurs at the point A given by the expression in the proposition statement. The two linear expressions, together with the linear expression for the mean, imply that the lower bound traces out the kinked line shown in Figure 6.8. We conclude that the curve traced out by the portfolio points must lie within the shaded region; and for an intermediate value of ρ, it looks like the curve shown. ∎

6.5 THE FEASIBLE SET

Suppose now that there are n basic assets. We can plot them as points on the mean–standard deviation diagram. Next imagine forming portfolios from these n assets, using every possible weighting scheme. Hence there are portfolios consisting of each of the n assets alone, combinations of two assets, combinations of three, and so forth, all the way to arbitrary combinations of all n. These portfolios are made by letting the weighting coefficients w_i range over all possible combinations such that $\sum_{i=1}^{n} w_i = 1$.

The set of points that correspond to portfolios is called the **feasible set** or **feasible region.** The feasible set satisfies two important properties.

1. If there are at least three assets (not perfectly correlated and with different means), the feasible set will be a solid two-dimensional region.

Figure 6.9 shows why the region will be solid. There are three basic assets: 1, 2, and 3. We know that any two assets define a (curved) line between them as combination portfolios are formed. The three lines between the possible three pairs are shown in Figure 6.9. Now if a combination of, say, assets 2 and 3 is formed to produce asset 4, this can be combined with 1 to form a line connecting 1 and 4. As 4 is moved between 2 and 3, the line between 1 and 4 traces out a solid region.

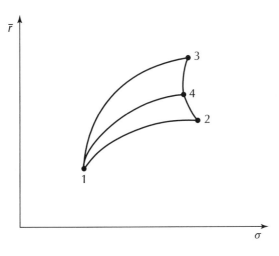

FIGURE 6.9   Three points form a region. Combinations of assets 2 and 3 sweep out a curve between them. Combination of one of these assets, such as 4, together with asset 1 sweeps out another curve. The family of all these curves forms a solid region.

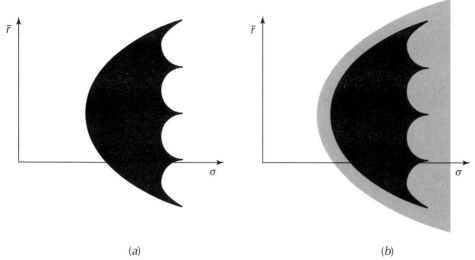

(a) (b)

FIGURE 6.10   Feasible region. The feasible region is the set of all points representing portfolios made from n original assets. Two such regions can be defined: (a) no shorting and (b) shorting allowed.

2. The feasible region is convex to the left.

This means that given any two points in the region, the straight line connecting them does not cross the left boundary of the feasible set. This follows from the fact that all portfolios (with positive weights) made from two assets lie on or to the left of the line connecting them. A typical feasible region is shown in Figure 6.10(a).

There are two natural, but alternative, definitions of the feasible region, corresponding to whether short selling of assets is allowed or not allowed. The two general conclusions about the shape of the region hold in either case. However, in general the feasible region defined with short selling allowed will contain the region defined without short selling, as shown in Figure 6.10(b). (In general, the leftmost edges of these two regions may partially coincide—unlike the case shown in Figure 6.10.)

The Minimum-Variance Set and the Efficient Frontier

The left boundary of a feasible set is called the **minimum-variance set,** since for any value of the mean rate of return, the feasible point with the smallest variance (or standard deviation) is the corresponding left boundary point. The minimum-variance set has a characteristic **bullet** shape, as shown in Figure 6.11(a). There is a special point on this set having minimum variance. It is termed the **minimum-variance point** (MVP).

Suppose that an investor's choice of portfolio is restricted to the feasible points on a given horizontal line in the $\bar{r}$–σ plane. All portfolios on this line have the same mean rate of return, but different standard deviations (or variances). Most investors will prefer the portfolio corresponding to the leftmost point on the line; that is, the point with the smallest standard deviation for the given mean. An investor who agrees

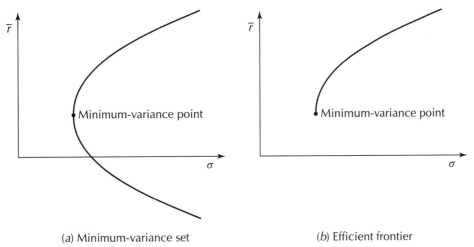

(a) Minimum-variance set   (b) Efficient frontier

FIGURE 6.11   **Special sets.** The minimum-variance set has a characteristic bullet shape. The minimum-variance point is the point with lowest possible variance. The efficient frontier is the upper portion of the minimum-variance set.

with this viewpoint is said to be **risk averse,** since he or she seeks to minimize risk (as measured by standard deviation). An investor who would select a point other than the one of minimum standard deviation is said to be **risk preferring.** We direct our analysis to risk-averse investors who, accordingly, prefer to minimize the standard deviation. Such investors are interested in points on the minimum-variance set.

We can turn the argument around 90 degrees and consider portfolios corresponding to the various points on a vertical line; that is, the portfolios with a fixed standard deviation and various mean values. Most investors will prefer the highest point on such a line. In other words, they would select the portfolio of the largest mean for a given level of standard deviation. This property of investors is termed **nonsatiation,** which reflects the idea that, everything else being equal, investors always want more money; hence they want the highest possible expected return for a given standard deviation.

These arguments imply that only the upper part of the minimum-variance set will be of interest to investors who are risk averse and satisfy nonsatiation. This upper portion of the minimum-variance set is termed the **efficient frontier** of the feasible region. It is illustrated in Figure 6.11(b). These are the efficient portfolios, in the sense that they provide the best mean–variance combinations for most investors. We can therefore limit our investigation to this frontier. The next section explains how to calculate points on this frontier.

6.6 THE MARKOWITZ MODEL

We are now in a position to formulate a mathematical problem that leads to minimum-variance portfolios. Again assume that there are n assets. The mean (or expected) rates of return are $\bar{r}_1, \bar{r}_2, \ldots, \bar{r}_n$ and the covariances are σ_{ij}, for $i, j = 1, 2, \ldots, n$. A portfolio is defined by a set of n weights w_i, $i = 1, 2, \ldots, n$, that sum to 1. (We allow negative weights, corresponding to short selling.) To find a minimum-variance portfolio, we fix the mean value at some arbitrary value $\bar{r}$. Then we find the feasible portfolio of minimum variance that has this mean. Hence we formulate the problem

$$\text{minimize} \quad \tfrac{1}{2} \sum_{i,j=1}^{n} w_i w_j \sigma_{ij}$$

$$\text{subject to} \quad \sum_{i=1}^{n} w_i \bar{r}_i = \bar{r}$$

$$\sum_{i=1}^{n} w_i = 1 .$$

The factor of $\tfrac{1}{2}$ in front of the variance is for convenience only. It makes the final form of the equations neater.

The Markowitz problem provides the foundation for single-period investment theory. The problem explicitly addresses the trade-off between expected rate of return and variance of the rate of return in a portfolio. Once the Markowitz problem is formulated, it can be solved numerically to obtain a specific numerical solution. It is also useful to solve the problem analytically because some strong additional conclusions are obtained from the analytic solution. However, as we move to the next chapter, the Markowitz problem is used mainly when a risk-free asset as well as risky assets are available. The existence of a risk-free asset greatly simplifies the nature of the feasible set and also simplifies the analytic solution.

Solution of the Markowitz Problem*

We can find the conditions for a solution to this problem using **Lagrange multipliers** λ and μ. We form[1] the **Lagrangian**

$$L = \tfrac{1}{2} \sum_{i,j=1}^{n} w_i w_j \sigma_{ij} - \lambda \left(\sum_{i=1}^{n} w_i \bar{r}_i - \bar{r} \right) - \mu \left(\sum_{i=1}^{n} w_i - 1 \right).$$

We then differentiate the Lagrangian with respect to each variable w_i and set this derivative to zero.

The differentiation may be a bit difficult if this type of structure is unfamiliar to you. Therefore we shall do it for the two-variable case, after which it will be easy to generalize to n variables. For two variables,

$$L = \tfrac{1}{2} \left(w_1^2 \sigma_1^2 + w_1 w_2 \sigma_{12} + w_2 w_1 \sigma_{21} + w_2^2 \sigma_2^2 \right)$$
$$- \lambda(\bar{r}_1 w_1 + \bar{r}_2 w_2 - \bar{r}) - \mu(w_1 + w_2 - 1) .$$

---

[1]In general, the Lagrangian is formed by first converting each constraint to one with a zero right-hand side. Then each left-hand side is multiplied by its Lagrange multiplier and subtracted from the objective function. In our problem, λ and μ are the multipliers for the first and second constraints, respectively. (See Appendix B.)

Hence,

$$\frac{\partial L}{\partial w_1} = \tfrac{1}{2}\left(2\sigma_1^2 w_1 + \sigma_{12}w_2 + \sigma_{21}w_2\right) - \lambda\bar{r}_1 - \mu$$

$$\frac{\partial L}{\partial w_2} = \tfrac{1}{2}\left(\sigma_{12}w_1 + \sigma_{21}w_1 + 2\sigma_2^2 w_2\right) - \lambda\bar{r}_2 - \mu.$$

Using the fact that $\sigma_{12} = \sigma_{21}$ and setting these derivatives to zero, we obtain

$$\sigma_1^2 w_1 + \sigma_{12}w_2 - \lambda\bar{r}_1 - \mu = 0$$

$$\sigma_{21}w_1 + \sigma_2^2 w_2 - \lambda\bar{r}_2 - \mu = 0.$$

This gives us two equations. In addition, there are the two equations of the constraints, so we have a total of four equations. These can be solved[2] for the four unknowns w_1, w_2, λ, and μ.

The general form for n variables now can be written by obvious generalization. We state the conditions here:

Equations for efficient set   *The n portfolio weights w_i for $i = 1, 2, \ldots, n$ and the two Lagrange multipliers λ and μ for an efficient portfolio (with short selling allowed) having mean rate of return $\bar{r}$ satisfy*

$$\sum_{j=1}^{n} \sigma_{ij}w_j - \lambda\bar{r}_i - \mu = 0 \quad \text{for } i = 1, 2, \ldots, n \tag{6.5a}$$

$$\sum_{i=1}^{n} w_i\bar{r}_i = \bar{r} \tag{6.5b}$$

$$\sum_{i=1}^{n} w_i = 1. \tag{6.5c}$$

We have n equations in (6.5a), plus the two equations of the constraints (6.5b) and (6.5c), for a total of $n + 2$ equations. Correspondingly, there are $n + 2$ unknowns: the w_i's, λ, and μ. The solution to these equations will produce the weights for an efficient portfolio with mean $\bar{r}$. Notice that all $n + 2$ equations are linear, so they can be solved with linear algebra methods.

Example 6.9 (Three uncorrelated assets)   Suppose there are three uncorrelated assets. Each has variance 1, and the mean values are 1, 2, and 3, respectively. There is

---

[2]The case of two assets is actually degenerate because the two unknowns w_1 and w_2 are uniquely determined by the two constraints. The degeneracy (usually) disappears when there are three or more assets. Nevertheless, the equations obtained for the two-asset case foreshadow the pattern of the corresponding equations for n assets.

a bit of simplicity and symmetry in this situation, which makes it relatively easy to find an explicit solution.

We have $\sigma_1^2 = \sigma_2^2 = \sigma_3^2 = 1$ and $\sigma_{12} = \sigma_{23} = \sigma_{13} = 0$. Thus (6.5a–c) become

$$w_1 - \lambda - \mu = 0$$
$$w_2 - 2\lambda - \mu = 0$$
$$w_3 - 3\lambda - \mu = 0$$
$$w_1 + 2w_2 + 3w_3 = \bar{r}$$
$$w_1 + w_2 + w_3 = 1 .$$

The top three equations can be solved for w_1, w_2, and w_3 and substituted into the bottom two equations. This leads to

$$14\lambda + 6\mu = \bar{r}$$
$$6\lambda + 3\mu = 1 .$$

These two equations can be solved to yield $\lambda = (\bar{r}/2) - 1$ and $\mu = 2\frac{1}{3} - \bar{r}$. Then

$$w_1 = \tfrac{4}{3} - (\bar{r}/2)$$
$$w_2 = \tfrac{1}{3}$$
$$w_3 = (\bar{r}/2) - \tfrac{2}{3} .$$

The standard deviation at the solution is $\sqrt{w_1^2 + w_2^2 + w_3^2}$, which by direct substitution gives

$$\sigma = \sqrt{\frac{7}{3} - 2\bar{r} + \frac{\bar{r}^2}{2}}. \tag{6.6}$$

The minimum-variance point is, by symmetry, at $\bar{r} = 2$, with $\sigma = \sqrt{3}/3 = .58$. The feasible region is the region bounded by the bullet-shaped curve shown in Figure 6.12.

The foregoing analysis assumes that shorting of assets is allowed. If shorting is not allowed, the feasible set will be smaller, as discussed in the next subsection.

Nonnegativity Constraints*

In the preceding derivation, the signs of the w_i variables were not restricted, which meant that short selling was allowed. We can prohibit short selling by restricting

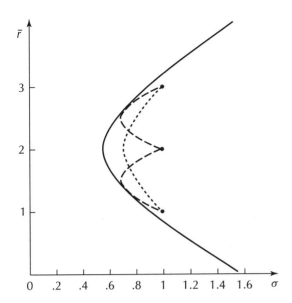

FIGURE 6.12 Three-asset example. The feasible region with shorting contains the feasible region without shorting. The outside curve is the minimum-variance set with shorting allowed. The short curved lines are portfolios made up of two of the assets at a time.

each w_i to be nonnegative. This leads to the following alternative statement of the Markowitz problem:

$$\text{minimize} \quad \tfrac{1}{2} \sum_{i,j=1}^{n} \sigma_{ij} w_i w_j \tag{6.7a}$$

$$\text{subject to} \quad \sum_{i=1}^{n} \bar{r}_i w_i = \bar{r} \tag{6.7b}$$

$$\sum_{i=1}^{n} w_i = 1 \tag{6.7c}$$

$$w_i \geq 0 \quad \text{for } i = 1, 2, \ldots, n. \tag{6.7d}$$

This problem cannot be reduced to the solution of a set of linear equations. It is termed a **quadratic program,** since the objective is quadratic and the constraints are linear equalities and inequalities. Special computer programs are available for solving such problems, but small to moderate-sized problems of this type can be solved readily with spreadsheet programs. In the financial industry there are a multitude of special-purpose programs designed to solve this problem for hundreds or even thousands of assets.

A significant difference between the two formulations is that when short selling is allowed, most, if not all, of the optimal w_i's have nonzero values (either positive or negative), so essentially all assets are used. By contrast, when short selling is not allowed, typically many weights are equal to zero.

Example 6.10 (The three uncorrelated assets) Consider again the assets of Example 6.9, but with shorting not allowed. Efficient points must solve problem (6.7a) with the parameters of the earlier example. In this case the problem cannot be reduced to a system of equations, but by considering combinations of pairs of assets, the efficient frontier can be found. The general solution is as follows:

$1 \leq \bar{r} \leq \frac{4}{3}$	$\frac{4}{3} \leq \bar{r} \leq \frac{8}{3}$	$\frac{8}{3} \leq \bar{r} \leq 3$
$w_1 = 2 - \bar{r}$	$\frac{4}{3} - \dfrac{\bar{r}}{2}$	0
$w_2 = \bar{r} - 1$	$\frac{1}{3}$	$3 - \bar{r}$
$w_3 = 0$	$\dfrac{\bar{r}}{2} - \frac{2}{3}$	$\bar{r} - 2$
$\sigma = \sqrt{2\bar{r}^2 - 6\bar{r} + 5}$	$\sqrt{\dfrac{2}{3} - 2\bar{r}_1 + \dfrac{\bar{r}^2}{2}}$	$\sqrt{2\bar{r}^2 - 10\bar{r} + 13}$.

6.7 THE TWO-FUND THEOREM*

The minimum-variance set has an important property that greatly simplifies its computation. Recall that points in this set satisfy the system of $n + 2$ linear equations [Eqs. (6.5a–c)], which is repeated here:

$$\sum_{j=1}^{n} \sigma_{ij} w_j - \lambda \bar{r}_i - \mu = 0 \quad \text{for } i = 1, 2, \ldots, n \tag{6.8a}$$

$$\sum_{i=1}^{n} w_i \bar{r}_i = \bar{r} \tag{6.8b}$$

$$\sum_{i=1}^{n} w_i = 1. \tag{6.8c}$$

Suppose that there are two known solutions, $\mathbf{w}^1 = (w_1^1, w_2^1, \ldots, w_n^1)$, λ^1, μ^1 and $\mathbf{w}^2 = (w_1^2, w_2^2, \ldots, w_n^2)$, λ^2, μ^2, with expected rates of return $\bar{r}^1$ and $\bar{r}^2$, respectively. Let us form a combination by multiplying the first by α and the second by $(1 - \alpha)$. By direct substitution, we see that the result is also a solution to the $n + 2$ equations, corresponding to the expected value $\alpha \bar{r}^1 + (1 - \alpha)\bar{r}^2$. To check this in detail, notice that $\alpha \mathbf{w}^1 + (1 - \alpha)\mathbf{w}^2$ is a legitimate portfolio with weights that sum to 1; hence (6.8c) is satisfied. Next notice that the expected return is in fact $\alpha \bar{r}_1 + (1 - \alpha)\bar{r}_2$; hence (6.8b) is satisfied for that value. Finally, notice that since both solutions make the left side of (6.8a) equal to zero, their combination does also; hence (6.8a) is satisfied. This implies that the combination portfolio $\alpha \mathbf{w}^1 + (1 - \alpha)\mathbf{w}^2$ is also a solution; that is, it also represents a point in the minimum-variance set. This simple result is usually quite surprising to most people on their first exposure to the subject, but it highlights an important property of the minimum-variance set.

To use this result, suppose $\mathbf{w}^1$ and $\mathbf{w}^2$ are two different portfolios in the minimum-variance set. Then as α varies over $-\infty < \alpha < \infty$, the portfolios defined by $\alpha\mathbf{w}^1 + (1 - \alpha)\mathbf{w}^2$ sweep out the entire minimum-variance set. We can, of course, select the two original solutions to be efficient (that is, on the upper portion of the minimum-variance set), and these will generate all other efficient points (as well as all other points in the minimum-variance set). This result is often stated in a form that has operational significance for investors:

The two-fund theorem   *Two efficient funds (portfolios) can be established so that any efficient portfolio can be duplicated, in terms of mean and variance, as a combination of these two. In other words, all investors seeking efficient portfolios need only invest in combinations of these two funds.*

This result has dramatic implications. According to the two-fund theorem, two **mutual funds**[3] could provide a complete investment service for everyone. There would be no need for anyone to purchase individual stocks separately; they could just purchase shares in the mutual funds. This conclusion, however, is based on the assumption that everyone cares only about mean and variance; that everyone has the same assessment of the means, variances, and covariances; and that a single-period framework is appropriate. All of these assumptions are quite tenuous. Nevertheless, if you are an investor without the time or inclination to make careful assessments, you might choose to find two funds managed by people whose assessments you trust, and invest in those two funds.

The two-fund theorem also has implications for computation. In order to solve (6.5a–c) for all values of $\bar{r}$ it is only necessary to find two solutions and then form combinations of those two. A particularly simple way to specify two solutions is to specify values of λ and μ. Convenient choices are (a) $\lambda = 0$, $\mu = 1$ and (b) $\lambda = 1$, $\mu = 0$. In either of these solutions the constraint $\sum_{i=1}^{n} w_i = 1$ may be violated, but this can be remedied later by normalizing all w_i's by a common scale factor. The solution obtained by choice (a) ignores the constraint on the expected mean rate of return; hence this is the minimum-variance point. The overall procedure is illustrated in the following example.

Example 6.11 (A securities portfolio)   The information concerning the 1-year co-variances and mean values of the rates of return on five securities is shown in the top part of Table 6.2. The mean values are expressed on a percentage basis, whereas the covariances are expressed in units of (percent)^2/100. For example, the first security has an expected rate of return of 15.1% = .151 and a variance of return of .023, which translates into a standard deviation of $\sqrt{.023} = .152 = 15.2\%$ per year.

---

[3] A mutual fund is an investment company that accepts investment capital from individuals and reinvests that capital in a diversity of individual stocks. Each individual is entitled to his or her proportionate share of the fund's portfolio value, less certain operating fees and commissions.

TABLE 6.2
A Securities Portfolio

Security	Covariance V					$\bar{r}$
1	2.30	.93	.62	.74	−.23	15.1
2	.93	1.40	.22	.56	.26	12.5
3	.62	.22	1.80	.78	.27	14.7
4	.74	.56	.78	3.40	−.56	9.02
5	−.23	.26	−.27	−.56	2.60	17.68

	$\mathbf{v}^1$	$\mathbf{v}^2$	$\mathbf{w}^1$	$\mathbf{w}^2$
	.141	3.652	.088	.158
	.401	3.583	.251	.155
	.452	7.248	.282	.314
	.166	.874	.104	.038
	.440	7.706	.275	.334
Mean			14.413	15.202
Variance			.625	.659
Std. dev.			.791	.812

The covariances and mean rates of return are shown for five securities. The portfolio $\mathbf{w}^1$ is the minimum-variance point, and $\mathbf{w}^2$ is another efficient portfolio made from these five securities.

We shall find two funds in the minimum-variance set. First we set $\lambda = 0$ and $\mu = 1$ in (6.5). We thus solve the system of equations

$$\sum_{j=1}^{5} \sigma_{ij} v_j^1 = 1$$

for the vector $\mathbf{v}^1 = (v_1^1, v_2^1, \ldots, v_5^1)$. This solution can be found using a spreadsheet package that solves linear equations. The coefficients of the equation are those of the covariance matrix, and the right-hand sides are all 1's. The resulting v_j^2's are listed in the first column of the bottom part of Table 6.2 as components of the vector $\mathbf{v}^1$.

Next we normalize the v_i^1's so that they sum to 1, obtaining w_i^1's as

$$w_i^1 = \frac{v_i^1}{\sum_{j=1}^{n} v_j^1}.$$

The vector $\mathbf{w}^1 = (w_1^1, w_2^1, \ldots, w_5^1)$ defines the minimum-variance point.
Second we set $\mu = 0$ and $\lambda = 1$. We thus solve the system of equations

$$\sum_{j=1}^{5} \sigma_{ij} v_j^2 = \bar{r}_i, \qquad i = 1, 2, \ldots, 5$$

for a solution $\mathbf{v}^2 = (v_1^2, v_2^2, \ldots, v_5^2)$. Again we normalize the resulting vector $\mathbf{v}^2$ so its components sum to 1, to obtain $\mathbf{w}^2$. The vectors $\mathbf{v}^1$, $\mathbf{v}^2$, $\mathbf{w}^1$, $\mathbf{w}^2$ are shown in the bottom part of Table 6.2. Also shown are the means, variances, and standard deviations corresponding to the portfolios defined by $\mathbf{w}^1$ and $\mathbf{w}^2$. All efficient portfolios are combinations of these two.

6.8 INCLUSION OF A RISK-FREE ASSET

In the previous few sections we have implicitly assumed that the n assets available are all risky; that is, they each have $\sigma > 0$. A **risk-free asset** has a return that is deterministic (that is, known with certainty) and therefore has $\sigma = 0$. In other words, a risk-free asset is a pure interest-bearing instrument; its inclusion in a portfolio corresponds to lending or borrowing cash at the risk-free rate. Lending (such as the purchase of a bond) corresponds to the risk-free asset having a positive weight, whereas borrowing corresponds to its having a negative weight.

The inclusion of a risk-free asset in the list of possible assets is necessary to obtain realism. Investors invariably have the opportunity to borrow or lend. Fortunately, as we shall see shortly, inclusion of a risk-free asset introduces a mathematical degeneracy that greatly simplifies the shape of the efficient frontier.

To explain the degeneracy condition, suppose that there is a risk-free asset with a (deterministic) rate of return r_f. Consider any other risky asset with rate of return r, having mean $\bar{r}$ and variance σ^2. Note that the covariance of these two returns must be zero. This is because the covariance is defined to be $\mathrm{E}\big[(r - \bar{r})(r_f - r_f)\big] = 0$.

Now suppose that these two assets are combined to form a portfolio using a weight of α for the risk-free asset and $1 - \alpha$ for the risky asset, with $\alpha \leq 1$. The mean rate of return of this portfolio will be $\alpha r_f + (1 - \alpha)\bar{r}$. The standard deviation of the return will be $\sqrt{(1 - \alpha)^2 \sigma^2} = (1 - \alpha)\sigma$. This is because the risk-free asset has no variance and no covariance with the risky asset. The only term left in the formula is that due to the risky asset.

If we define, just for the moment, $\sigma_f = 0$, we see that the portfolio rate of return has

$$\text{mean} = \alpha r_f + (1 - \alpha)\bar{r}$$

$$\text{standard deviation} = \alpha \sigma_f + (1 - \alpha)\sigma.$$

These equations show that both the mean and the standard deviation of the portfolio vary linearly with α. This means that as α varies, the point representing the portfolio traces out a straight line in the $\bar{r}$–σ plane.

Suppose now that there are n risky assets with known mean rates of return $\bar{r}_i$ and known covariances σ_{ij}. In addition, there is a risk-free asset with rate of return r_f. The inclusion of the risk-free asset in the list of available assets has a profound effect on the shape of the feasible region. The reason for this is shown in Figure 6.13(a). First we construct the ordinary feasible region, defined by the n risky assets. (This region may be either the one constructed with shorting allowed or the one constructed without shorting.) This region is shown as the darkly shaded region in the figure. Next,

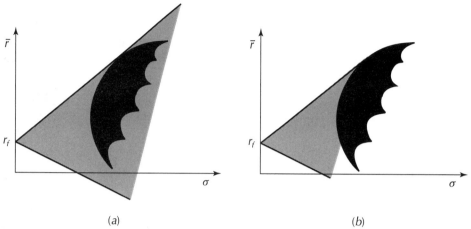

FIGURE 6.13   Effect of a risk-free asset. Inclusion of a risk-free asset adds lines to the feasible region. (*a*) If both borrowing and lending are allowed, a complete infinite triangular region is obtained. (*b*) If only lending is allowed, the region will have a triangular front end, but will curve for larger σ.

for each asset (or portfolio) in this region we form combinations with the risk-free asset. In forming these combinations we allow borrowing or lending of the risk-free asset, but only purchase of the risky asset. These new combinations trace out the infinite straight line originating at the risk-free point, passing through the risky asset, and continuing indefinitely. There is a line of this type for every asset in the original feasible set. The totality of these lines forms a triangularly shaped feasible region, indicated by the light shading in the figure.

This is a beautiful result. The feasible region is an infinite triangle whenever a risk-free asset is included in the universe of available assets.

If borrowing of the risk-free asset is not allowed (no shorting of this asset), we can adjoin only the finite line segments between the risk-free asset and points in the original feasible region. We cannot extend these lines further, since this would entail borrowing of the risk-free asset. The inclusion of these finite line segments leads to a new feasible region with a straight-line front edge but a rounded top, as shown in Figure 6.13(*b*).

6.9 THE ONE-FUND THEOREM

When risk-free borrowing and lending are available, the efficient set consists of a single straight line, which is the top of the triangular feasible region. This line is tangent to the original feasible set of risky assets. (See Figure 6.14.) There will be a point *F* in the original feasible set that is on the line segment defining the overall efficient set. It is clear that *any* efficient point (any point on the line) can be expressed as a combination of this asset and the risk-free asset. We obtain different efficient points by changing the weighting between these two (including negative weights of the risk-free asset to borrow money in order to leverage the buying of the risky asset). The portfolio

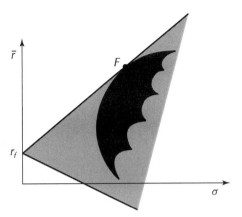

FIGURE 6.14 One-fund theorem. When both borrowing and lending at the risk-free rate are allowed, there is a unique fund F of risky assets that is efficient. All points on the efficient frontier are combinations of F and the risk-free asset.

represented by the tangent point can be thought of as a fund made up of assets and sold as a unit. The role of this fund is summarized by the following statement:

The one-fund theorem   *There is a single fund F of risky assets such that any efficient portfolio can be constructed as a combination of the fund F and the risk-free asset.*

This is a final conclusion of mean–variance portfolio theory, and this conclusion is the launch point for the next chapter. It is fine to stop reading here, and (after doing some exercises) to go on to the next chapter. But if you want to see how to calculate the special efficient point F, read the specialized subsection that follows.

Solution Method*

How can we find the tangent point that represents the efficient fund? We just characterize that point in terms of an optimization problem. Given a point in the feasible region, we draw a line between the risk-free asset and that point. We denote the angle between that line and the horizontal axis by θ. For any feasible (risky) portfolio p, we have

$$\tan \theta = \frac{\bar{r}_p - r_f}{\sigma_p}.$$

The tangent portfolio is the feasible point that maximizes θ or, equivalently, maximizes $\tan \theta$. It turns out that this problem can be reduced to the solution of a system of linear equations.

To develop the solution, suppose, as usual, that there are n risky assets. We assign weights $w_1, w_2, \ldots, w_n$ to the risky assets such that $\sum_{i=1}^{n} w_i = 1$. There is zero weight on the risk-free asset in the tangent fund. (Note that we are allowing short selling among the risky assets.) For $r_p = \sum_{i=1}^{n} w_i r_i$, we have $\bar{r}_p = \sum_{i=1}^{n} w_i \bar{r}_i$ and $r_f = \sum_{i=1}^{n} w_i r_f$. Thus,

$$\tan \theta = \frac{\sum_{i=1}^{n} w_i (\bar{r}_i - r_f)}{\left(\sum_{i,j=1}^{n} \sigma_{ij} w_i w_j \right)^{1/2}}.$$

It should be clear that multiplication of all w_i's by a constant will not change the expression, since the constant will cancel. Hence it is not necessary to impose the constraint $\sum_{i=1}^{n} w_i = 1$ here.

We then set the derivative of $\tan\theta$ with respect to each w_k equal to zero. This leads (see Exercise 10) to the following equations:

$$\sum_{i=1}^{n} \sigma_{ki} \lambda w_i = \bar{r}_k - r_f, \qquad k = 1, 2, \ldots, n \qquad (6.9)$$

where λ is an (unknown) constant. Making the substitution $v_i = \lambda w_i$ for each i, (6.9) becomes

$$\sum_{i=1}^{n} \sigma_{ki} v_i = \bar{r}_k - r_f, \qquad k = 1, 2, \ldots, n. \qquad (6.10)$$

We solve these linear equations for the v_i's and then normalize to determine the w_i's; that is,

$$w_i = \frac{v_i}{\sum_{k=1}^{n} v_k}.$$

Example 6.12 (Three uncorrelated assets)   We consider again Example 6.9, where the three risky assets were uncorrelated and each had variance equal to 1. The three mean rates of return were $\bar{r}_1 = 1$, $\bar{r}_2 = 2$, and $\bar{r}_3 = 3$. We assume in addition that there is a risk-free asset with rate $r_f = .5$.

We apply (6.9), which is very simple in this case because the covariances are all zero, to find

$$v_1 = 1 - .5 = .5$$
$$v_2 = 2 - .5 = 1.5$$
$$v_3 = 3 - .5 = 2.5.$$

We then normalize these values by dividing by their sum, 4.5, and find

$$w_1 = \tfrac{1}{9}, \qquad w_2 = \tfrac{1}{3}, \qquad w_3 = \tfrac{5}{9}.$$

Example 6.13 (A larger portfolio)   Consider the five risky assets of Example 6.11. Assume also that there is a risk-free asset with $r_f = 10\%$. We can easily find the special fund F.

We note that the system of equations (6.10) is identical to those used to find $\mathbf{v}^1$ and $\mathbf{v}^2$ in Example 6.11, but with a different right-hand side. Actually the right-hand side is a linear combination of those used for $\mathbf{v}^1$ and $\mathbf{v}^2$; namely, $\bar{r}_k - r_f = 1 \times \bar{r}_k - r_f \times 1$. Therefore the solution to (6.10) is $\mathbf{v} = \mathbf{v}^2 - r_f \mathbf{v}^1$. Thus (using $r_f = 10$ to be consistent with the units used in the earlier example), $\mathbf{v} = (2.242, -.427, 2.728, -.786, 3.306)$. We normalize this to obtain the final result $\mathbf{w} = (.317, -.060, .386, -.111, .468)$.

Basically, we have used the fact that portfolio F is a combination of two known efficient points.

6.10 SUMMARY

The study of one-period investment situations is based on asset and portfolio returns. Both total returns and rates of return are used. The return of an asset may be uncertain, in which case it is useful to consider it formally as a random variable. The probabilistic properties of such random returns can be summarized by their expected values, their variances, and their covariances with each other.

A portfolio is defined by allocating fractions of initial wealth to individual assets. The fractions (or weights) must sum to 1; but some of these weights may be negative if short selling is allowed. The return of a portfolio is the weighted sum of the returns of its individual assets, with the weights being those that define the portfolio. The expected return of the portfolio is, likewise, equal to the weighted average of the expected returns of the individual assets. The variance of the portfolio is determined by a more complicated formula: $\sigma^2 = \sum_{i,j=1}^{n} w_i w_j \sigma_{ij}$, where the w_i's are the weights and the σ_{ij}'s are the covariances.

From a given collection of n risky assets, there results a set of possible portfolios made from all possible weights of the n individual assets. If the mean and the standard deviation of these portfolios are plotted on a diagram with vertical axis $\bar{r}$ (the mean) and horizontal axis σ (the standard deviation), the region so obtained is called the feasible region. Two alternative feasible regions are defined: one allowing shorting of assets and one not allowing shorting.

It can be argued that investors who measure the value of a portfolio in terms of its mean and its standard deviation, who are risk averse, and who have the nonsatiation property will select portfolios on the upper left-hand portion of the feasible region—the efficient frontier.

Points on the efficient frontier can be characterized by an optimization problem originally formulated by Markowitz. This problem seeks the portfolio weights that minimize variance for a given value of mean return. Mathematically, this is a problem with a quadratic objective and two linear constraints. If shorting is allowed (so that the weights may be negative as well as positive), the optimal weights can be found by solving a system of $n+2$ linear equations and $n+2$ unknowns. Otherwise if shorting is not allowed, the Markowitz problem can be solved by special quadratic programming packages.

An important property of the Markowitz problem, when shorting is allowed, is that if two solutions are known, then any weighted combination of these two solutions is also a solution. This leads to the fundamental two-fund theorem: investors seeking efficient portfolios need only invest in two master efficient funds.

Usually it is appropriate to assume that, in addition to n risky assets, there is available a risk-free asset with fixed rate of return r_f. The inclusion of such an asset greatly simplifies the shape of the feasible region, transforming the upper boundary into a straight line. This line is the efficient frontier. The straight-line frontier touches the original feasible region (the region defined by the risky assets only) at a single point F. This leads to the important one-fund theorem: investors seeking efficient portfolios need only invest in one master fund of risky assets and in the risk-free asset. Different investors may prefer different combinations of these two.

The single efficient fund of risky assets F can be found by solving a system of n linear equations and n unknowns. When the solution to this system is normalized so that its components sum to 1, the resulting components are the weights of the risky assets in the master fund.

EXERCISES

1. (Shorting with margin) Suppose that to short a stock you are required to deposit an amount equal to the initial price X_0 of the stock. At the end of 1 year the stock price is X_1 and you liquidate your position. You receive your profit from shorting equal to $X_0 - X_1$ and you recover your original deposit. If R is the total return of the stock, what is the total return on your short?

2. (Dice product) Two dice are rolled and the two resulting values are multiplied together to form the quantity z. What are the expected value and the variance of the random variable z? [*Hint:* Use the independence of the two separate dice.]

3. (Two correlated assets) The correlation ρ between assets A and B is .1, and other data are given in Table 6.3. [*Note:* $\rho = \sigma_{AB}/(\sigma_A\sigma_B)$.]

TABLE 6.3
Two Correlated Cases

Asset	$\bar{r}$	σ
A	10.0%	15%
B	18.0%	30%

(*a*) Find the proportions α of A and $(1-\alpha)$ of B that define a portfolio of A and B having minimum standard deviation.
(*b*) What is the value of this minimum standard deviation?
(*c*) What is the expected return of this portfolio?

4. (Two stocks) Two stocks are available. The corresponding expected rates of return are $\bar{r}_1$ and $\bar{r}_2$; the corresponding variances and covariances are σ_1^2, σ_2^2, and σ_{12}. What percentages of total investment should be invested in each of the two stocks to minimize the total variance of the rate of return of the resulting portfolio? What is the mean rate of return of this portfolio?

5. (Rain insurance) Gavin Jones's friend is planning to invest $1 million in a rock concert to be held 1 year from now. The friend figures that he will obtain $3 million revenue from his $1 million investment—unless, my goodness, it rains. If it rains, he will lose his entire investment. There is a 50% chance that it will rain the day of the concert. Gavin suggests that he buy rain insurance. He can buy one unit of insurance for $.50, and this unit pays $1 if it rains and nothing if it does not. He may purchase as many units as he wishes, up to $3 million.

(a) What is the expected rate of return on his investment if he buys u units of insurance? (The cost of insurance is in addition to his $1 million investment.)

(b) What number of units will minimize the variance of his return? What is this minimum value? And what is the corresponding expected rate of return? [*Hint:* Before calculating a general expression for variance, think about a simple answer.]

6. (Wild cats)   Suppose there are n assets which are uncorrelated. (They might be n different "wild cat" oil well prospects.) You may invest in any one, or in any combination of them. The mean rate of return $\bar{r}$ is the same for each asset, but the variances are different. The return on asset i has a variance of σ_i^2 for $i = 1, 2, \ldots, n$.

(a) Show the situation on an $\bar{r}$–σ diagram. Describe the efficient set.

(b) Find the minimum-variance point. Express your result in terms of

$$\bar{\sigma}^2 = \left(\sum_{i=1}^{n} \frac{1}{\sigma_i^2} \right)^{-1}.$$

7. (Markowitz fun)   There are just three assets with rates of return r_1, r_2, and r_3, respectively. The covariance matrix and the expected rates of return are

$$\mathbf{V} = \begin{bmatrix} 2 & 1 & 0 \\ 1 & 2 & 1 \\ 0 & 1 & 2 \end{bmatrix}, \qquad \bar{\mathbf{r}} = \begin{bmatrix} .4 \\ .8 \\ .8 \end{bmatrix}.$$

(a) Find the minimum-variance portfolio. [*Hint:* By symmetry $w_1 = w_3$.]

(b) Find another efficient portfolio by setting $\lambda = 1$, $\mu = 0$.

(c) If the risk-free rate is $r_f = .2$, find the efficient portfolio of risky assets.

8. (Tracking)   Suppose that it is impractical to use all the assets that are incorporated into a specified portfolio (such as a given efficient portfolio). One alternative is to find the portfolio, made up of a given set of n stocks, that tracks the specified portfolio most closely—in the sense of minimizing the variance of the difference in returns.

Specifically, suppose that the target portfolio has (random) rate of return r_M. Suppose that there are n assets with (random) rates of return $r_1, r_2, \ldots, r_n$. We wish to find the portfolio rate of return

$$r = \alpha_1 r_1 + \alpha_2 r_2 + \cdots + \alpha_n r_n$$

(with $\sum_{i=1}^{n} \alpha_i = 1$) minimizing $\operatorname{var}(r - r_M)$.

(a) Find a set of equations for the α_i's.

(b) Although this portfolio tracks the desired portfolio most closely in terms of variance, it may sacrifice the mean. Hence a logical approach is to minimize the variance of the tracking error subject to achieving a given mean return. As the mean is varied, this results in a family of portfolios that are efficient in a new sense—say, tracking efficient. Find the equation for the α_i's that are tracking efficient.

9. (Betting wheel)   Consider a general betting wheel with n segments. The payoff for a $1 bet on a segment i is A_i. Suppose you bet an amount $B_i = 1/A_i$ on segment i for each i. Show that the amount you win is independent of the outcome of the wheel. What is the risk-free rate of return for the wheel? Apply this to the wheel in Example 6.7.

10. (Efficient portfolio $\diamond$) Derive (6.9). [*Hint:* Note that

$$\frac{\partial}{\partial w_i} \left(\sum_{ij}^{n} \sigma_{ij} w_i w_j \right)^{1/2} = \left(\sum_{ij}^{n} \sigma_{ij} w_i w_j \right)^{-1/2} \sum_{j=1}^{n} \sigma_{ij} w_j. \Bigg]$$

REFERENCES

Mean–variance portfolio theory was initially devised by Markowitz [1–4]. Other important developments were presented in [5–8]. The one-fund argument is due to Tobin [9]. For comprehensive textbook presentations, see [10–11] and the other general investment textbooks listed as references for Chapter 2.

1. Markowitz, H. M. (1952), "Portfolio Selection," *Journal of Finance*, **7**, no. 1, 77–91.
2. Markowitz, H. M. (1956), "The Optimization of a Quadratic Function Subject to Linear Constraints," *Naval Research Logistics Quarterly*, **3**, nos. 1–2, 111–133.
3. Markowitz, H. M. (1987), *Portfolio Selection*, Wiley, New York.
4. Markowitz, H. M. (1987), *Mean-Variance Analysis in Portfolio Choice and Capital Markets*, Basil Blackwell, New York.
5. Hester, D. D., and J. Tobin (1967), *Risk Aversion and Portfolio Choice*, Wiley, New York.
6. Fama, E. F. (1976), *Foundations of Finance*, Basic Books, New York.
7. Sharpe, W. F. (1967), "Portfolio Analysis," *Journal of Financial and Quantitative Analysis*, **2**, 76–84.
8. Levy, H. (1979), "Does Diversification Always Pay?" *TIMS Studies in Management Science*.
9. Tobin, J. (1958), "Liquidity Preference as Behavior Toward Risk," *Review of Economic Studies*, **26**, February, 65–86.
10. Francis, J. C., and G. Alexander (1986), *Portfolio Analysis*, 3rd ed., Prentice Hall, Englewood Cliffs, NJ.
11. Elton, E. J., and M. J. Gruber (1991), *Portfolio Theory and Investment Analysis*, 4th ed., Wiley, New York.

7 THE CAPITAL ASSET PRICING MODEL

Two main problem types dominate the discipline of investment science. The first is to determine the best course of action in an investment situation. Problems of this type include how to devise the best portfolio, how to devise the optimal strategy for managing an investment, how to select from a group of potential investment projects, and so forth. Several examples of such problems were treated in Part 1 of this book. The second type of problem is to determine the correct, arbitrage-free, fair, or equilibrium price of an asset. We saw examples of this in Part 1 as well, such as the formula for the correct price of a bond in terms of the term structure of interest rates, and the formula for the appropriate value of a firm.

This chapter concentrates mainly on the pricing issue. It deduces the correct price of a risky asset within the framework of the mean–variance setting. The result is the **capital asset pricing model** (CAPM) developed primarily by Sharpe, Lintner, and Mossin, which follows logically from the Markowitz mean–variance portfolio theory described in the previous chapter. Later in this chapter we discuss how this result can be applied to investment decision problems.

7.1 MARKET EQUILIBRIUM

Suppose that everyone is a mean–variance optimizer as described in the previous chapter. Suppose further that everyone agrees on the probabilistic structure of assets; that is, everyone assigns to the returns of assets the same mean values, the same variances, and the same covariances. Furthermore, assume that there is a unique risk-free rate of borrowing and lending that is available to all, and that there are no transactions costs. With these assumptions what will happen?

From the one-fund theorem we know that everyone will purchase a single fund of risky assets, and they may, in addition, borrow or lend at the risk-free rate. Furthermore, since everyone uses the same means, variances, and covariances, everyone will use the same risky fund. The mix of these two assets, the risky fund and the risk-free asset, will likely vary across individuals according to their individual tastes for risk. Some will seek to avoid risk and will, accordingly, have a high percentage of the risk-free asset in their portfolios; others, who are more aggressive, will have a high percentage of the risky fund. However, every individual will form a portfolio that is a mix of the risk-free asset and the single, risky *one fund*. Hence the *one fund* in the theorem is really the *only fund* that is used.

If everyone purchases the same fund of risky assets, what must that fund be? The answer to this question is the key insight underlying the CAPM. A bit of reflection reveals that the answer is that this fund must equal the **market portfolio.** The market portfolio is the summation of all assets. In the world of equity securities, it is the totality of shares of IBM, GM, DIS, and so forth. If everyone buys just one fund, and their purchases add up to the market, then that one fund must be the market as well; that is, it must contain shares of every stock in proportion to that stock's representation in the entire market.

An asset's weight in a portfolio is defined as the proportion of portfolio capital that is allocated to that asset. Hence the weight of an asset in the market portfolio is equal to the proportion of that asset's total capital value to the total market capital value. These weights are termed **capitalization weights.** It is these weights that we usually denote by w_i. In other words, the w_i's of the market portfolio are the capitalization weights of the assets.

The exact definition of the market portfolio is illustrated as follows. Suppose there are only three stocks in the market: Jazz, Inc., Classical, Inc., and Rock, Inc. Their outstanding shares and prices are shown in Table 7.1. The market weights are proportional to the total market capitalization, not to the number of shares.

In the situation where everyone follows the mean–variance methodology with the same estimates of parameters, we know that the efficient fund of risky assets will be the market portfolio. Hence under these assumptions there is no need for us to formulate the mean–variance problem, to estimate the underlying parameters, or to solve the system of equations that define the optimal portfolio. We know that the optimal portfolio will turn out to be the market portfolio.

TABLE 7.1
Market Capitalization Weights

Security	Shares outstanding	Relative shares in market	Price	Capitalization	Weight in market
Jazz, Inc.	10,000	1/8	$6.00	$60,000	3/20
Classical, Inc.	30,000	3/8	$4.00	$120,000	3/10
Rock, Inc.	40,000	1/2	$5.50	$220,000	11/20
Total	80,000	1		$400,000	1

The percentage of shares of a stock in the market portfolio is a share-weighted proportion of total shares. These percentages are not *the market portfolio weights. The market portfolio weight of a stock is proportional to capitalization. If the price of an asset changes, the share proportions do not change, but the capitalization weights do change.*

How does this happen? How can it be that we solve the problem even without knowing the required data? The answer is based on an **equilibrium** argument. If everyone else (or at least a large number of people) solves the problem, we do not need to. It works like this: The return on an asset depends on both its initial price and its final price. The other investors solve the mean–variance portfolio problem using their common estimates, and they place orders in the market to acquire their portfolios. If the orders placed do not match what is available, the prices must change. The prices of assets under heavy demand will increase; the prices of assets under light demand will decrease. These price changes affect the estimates of asset returns directly, and hence investors will recalculate their optimal portfolios. This process continues until demand exactly matches supply; that is, it continues until there is equilibrium.

In the idealized world, where every investor is a mean–variance investor and all have the same estimates, everyone buys the same portfolio, and that must be equal to the market portfolio. In other words, prices adjust to drive the market to efficiency. Then after other people have made the adjustments, we can be sure that the efficient portfolio is the market portfolio, so we need not make any calculations.

This theory of equilibrium is usually applied to assets that are traded repeatedly over time, such as the stock market. In this case it is argued that individuals adjust their return estimates slowly, and only make a series of minor adjustments to their calculations rather than solving the entire portfolio optimization problem at one time.

Finally, in such equilibrium models it is argued that the appropriate equilibrium need be calculated by only a few devoted (and energetic) individuals. They move prices around to the proper value, and other investors follow their lead by purchasing the market portfolio.

These arguments about the equilibrium process all have a degree of plausibility, and all have weaknesses. Deeper analysis can be carried out, but for our purposes we will merely consider that equilibrium occurs. Hence the ultimate conclusion of the mean–variance approach is that the *one fund* must be the market portfolio.

7.2 THE CAPITAL MARKET LINE

Given the preceding conclusion that the single efficient fund of risky assets is the market portfolio, we can label this fund on the $\bar{r}$–σ diagram with an M for *market*. The efficient set therefore consists of a single straight line, emanating from the risk-free point and passing through the market portfolio. This line, shown in Figure 7.1, is called the **capital market line.**

This line shows the relation between the expected rate of return and the risk of return (as measured by the standard deviation) for efficient assets or portfolios of assets. It is also referred to as a pricing line, since prices should adjust so that efficient assets fall on this line.

The line has great intuitive appeal. It states that as risk increases, the corresponding expected rate of return must also increase. Furthermore, this relationship can be

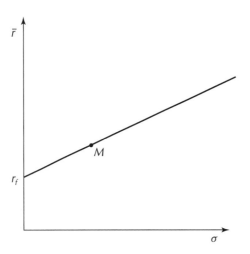

FIGURE 7.1   Capital market line. Efficient assets must all lie on the line determined by the risk-free rate and the market portfolio.

described by a straight line if risk is measured by standard deviation. In mathematical terms the capital market line states that

$$\bar{r} = r_f + \frac{\bar{r}_M - r_f}{\sigma_M}\sigma \tag{7.1}$$

where $\bar{r}_M$ and σ_M are the expected value and the standard deviation of the market rate of return and $\bar{r}$ and σ are the expected value and the standard deviation of the rate of return of an arbitrary efficient asset.

The slope of the capital market line is $K = (\bar{r}_M - r_f)/\sigma_M$, and this value is frequently called the **price of risk.** It tells by how much the expected rate of return of a portfolio must increase if the standard deviation of that rate increases by one unit.

Example 7.1 (The impatient investor)   Mr. Smith is young and impatient. He notes that the risk-free rate is only 6% and the market portfolio of risky assets has an expected return of 12% and a standard deviation of 15%. He figures that it would take about 60 years for his $1,000.00 nest egg to increase to $1 million if it earned the market rate of return. He can't wait that long. He wants that $1 million in 10 years.

Mr. Smith easily determines that he must attain an average rate of return of about 100% per year to achieve his goal (since $1,000 \times 2^{10} = \$1,048,000$). Correspondingly, his yearly standard deviation according to the capital market line would be the value of σ satisfying

$$1.0 = .06 + \frac{.12 - .06}{.15}\sigma$$

or $\sigma = 10$. This corresponds to $\sigma = 1,000\%$. So this young man is certainly not guaranteed success (even if he could borrow the amount required to move far beyond the market on the capital market line).

Example 7.2 (An oil venture)   Consider an oil drilling venture. The price of a share of this venture is \$875. It is expected to yield the equivalent of \$1,000 after 1 year, but due to high uncertainty about how much oil is at the drilling site, the standard deviation of the return is $\sigma = 40\%$. Currently the risk-free rate is 10%. The expected rate of return on the market portfolio is 17%, and the standard deviation of this rate is 12%.

Let us see how this venture compares with assets on the capital market line. Given the level of σ, the expected rate of return predicted by the capital market line is

$$\bar{r} = .10 + \frac{.17 - .10}{.12}.40 = 33\%.$$

However, the actual expected rate of return is only $\bar{r} = 1,000/875 - 1 = 14\%$. Therefore the point representing the oil venture lies well below the capital market line. (This does *not* mean that the venture is necessarily a poor one, as we shall see later, but it certainly does not, by itself, constitute an efficient portfolio.)

7.3 THE PRICING MODEL

The capital market line relates the expected rate of return of an efficient portfolio to its standard deviation, but it does not show how the expected rate of return of an individual asset relates to its individual risk. This relation is expressed by the capital asset pricing model.

We state this major result as a theorem. The reader may wish merely to glance over the proof at first reading since it is a bit involved. We shall discuss the implications of the result following the proof.

 The capital asset pricing model (CAPM)   *If the market portfolio M is efficient, the expected return $\bar{r}_i$ of any asset i satisfies*

$$\bar{r}_i - r_f = \beta_i(\bar{r}_M - r_f) \tag{7.2}$$

where

$$\beta_i = \frac{\sigma_{iM}}{\sigma_M^2}. \tag{7.3}$$

Proof: For any α consider the portfolio consisting of a portion α invested in asset i and a portion $1 - \alpha$ invested in the market portfolio M. (We allow $\alpha < 0$, which corresponds to borrowing at the risk-free rate.) The expected rate of return of this portfolio is

$$\bar{r}_\alpha = \alpha\bar{r}_i + (1 - \alpha)\bar{r}_M$$

and the standard deviation of the rate of return is

$$\sigma_\alpha = [\alpha^2\sigma_i^2 + 2\alpha(1 - \alpha)\sigma_{iM} + (1 - \alpha)^2\sigma_M^2]^{1/2}.$$

As α varies, these values trace out a curve in the $\bar{r}$–σ diagram, as shown in Figure 7.2. In particular, $\alpha = 0$ corresponds to the market portfolio M. This

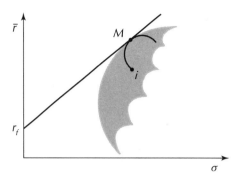

FIGURE 7.2 Portfolio curve. The family of portfolios traces out a curve on the diagram. This curve cannot cross the capital market line, and hence must be tangent to that line.

curve cannot cross the capital market line. If it did, the portfolio corresponding to a point above the capital market line would violate the very definition of the capital market line as being the efficient boundary of the feasible set. Hence as α passes through zero, the curve must be tangent to the capital market line at M. This tangency is the condition that we exploit to derive the formula.

The tangency condition can be translated into the condition that the slope of the curve is equal to the slope of the capital market line at the point M. To set up this condition we need to calculate a few derivatives.

First we have

$$\frac{d\bar{r}_\alpha}{d\alpha} = \bar{r}_i - \bar{r}_M$$

$$\frac{d\sigma_\alpha}{d\alpha} = \frac{\alpha\sigma_i^2 + (1 - 2\alpha)\sigma_{iM} + (\alpha - 1)\sigma_M^2}{\sigma_\alpha}.$$

Thus,

$$\left.\frac{d\sigma_\alpha}{d\alpha}\right|_{\alpha=0} = \frac{\sigma_{iM} - \sigma_M^2}{\sigma_M}.$$

We then use the relation

$$\frac{d\bar{r}_\alpha}{d\sigma_\alpha} = \frac{d\bar{r}_\alpha/d\alpha}{d\sigma_\alpha/d\alpha}$$

to obtain

$$\left.\frac{d\bar{r}_\alpha}{d\sigma_\alpha}\right|_{\alpha=0} = \frac{(\bar{r}_i - \bar{r}_M)\sigma_M}{\sigma_{iM} - \sigma_M^2}.$$

This slope must equal the slope of the capital market line. Hence,

$$\frac{(\bar{r}_i - \bar{r}_M)\sigma_M}{\sigma_{iM} - \sigma_M^2} = \frac{\bar{r}_M - r_f}{\sigma_M}.$$

We now just solve for $\bar{r}_i$, obtaining the final result

$$\bar{r}_i = r_f + \left(\frac{\bar{r}_M - r_f}{\sigma_M^2}\right)\sigma_{iM} = r_f + \beta_i(\bar{r}_M - r_f).$$

This is clearly equivalent to the stated formula. ∎

The value β_i is referred to as the **beta** of an asset. When the asset is fixed in a discussion, we often just write beta without a subscript—β. An asset's beta is all that need be known about the asset's risk characteristics to use the CAPM formula.

The value $\bar{r}_i - r_f$ is termed the **expected excess rate of return** of asset i; it is the amount by which the rate of return is expected to exceed the risk-free rate. Likewise, $\bar{r}_M - r_f$ is the expected excess rate of return of the market portfolio. In terms of these expected excess rates of return, the CAPM says that the expected excess rate of return of an asset is proportional to the expected excess rate of return of the market portfolio, and the proportionality factor is β. So with r_f taken as a base point, the expected returns of a particular asset and of the market above that base are proportional.

An alternative interpretation of the CAPM formula is based on the fact that β is a normalized version of the covariance of the asset with the market portfolio. Hence the CAPM formula states that the expected excess rate of return of an asset is directly proportional to its covariance with the market. It is this covariance that determines the expected excess rate of return.

To gain insight into this result, let us consider some extreme cases. Suppose, first, that the asset is completely *uncorrelated* with the market; that is, $\beta = 0$. Then, according to the CAPM, we have $\bar{r} = r_f$. This is perhaps at first sight a surprising result. It states that even if the asset is very risky (with large σ), the expected rate of return will be that of the risk-free asset—there is no premium for risk. The reason for this is that the risk associated with an asset that is uncorrelated with the market can be diversified away. If we had many such assets, each uncorrelated with the others and with the market, we could purchase small amounts of each of them, and the resulting total variance would be small. Since the final composite return would have small variance, the corresponding expected rate of return should be close to r_f.

Even more extreme is an asset with a negative value of β. In that case $\bar{r} < r_f$; that is, even though the asset may have very high risk (as measured by its σ), its expected rate of return should be even less than the risk-free rate. The reason is that such an asset reduces the overall portfolio risk when it is combined with the market. Investors are therefore willing to accept the lower expected value for this risk-reducing potential. Such assets provide a form of insurance. They do well when everything else does poorly.

The CAPM changes our concept of the risk of an asset from that of σ to that of β. It is still true that, overall, we measure the risk of a portfolio in terms of σ, but this does not translate into a concern for the σ's of individual assets. For those, the proper measure is their β's.

Example 7.3 (A simple calculation)   We illustrate how simple it is to use the CAPM formula to calculate an expected rate of return. Let the risk-free rate be $r_f = 8\%$. Suppose the rate of return of the market has an expected value of 12% and a standard deviation of 15%.

Now consider an asset that has covariance of .045 with the market. Then we find $\beta = .045/(.15)^2 = 2.0$. The expected return of the asset is $\bar{r} = .08 + 2 \times (.12 - .08) = .16 = 16\%$.

Betas of Common Stocks

The concept of beta is well established in the financial community, and it is referred to frequently in technical discussions about particular stocks. Beta values are estimated by various financial service organizations. Typically, these estimates are formed by using a record of past stock values (usually about 6 or 18 months of weekly values) and computing, from the data, average values of returns, products of returns, and squares of returns in order to approximate expected returns, covariances, and variances. The beta values so obtained drift around somewhat over time, but unless there are drastic changes in a company's situation, its beta tends to be relatively stable.

Table 7.2 lists some well-known U.S. companies and their corresponding beta (β) and volatility (σ) values as estimated at a particular date. Try scanning the list and see if the values given support your intuitive impression of the company's market

TABLE 7.2
Some U.S. Companies: Their Betas and Sigmas

Ticker sym	Company name	Beta	Volatility
KO	Coca-Cola Co	1.19	18%
DIS	Disney Productions	2.23	22%
EK	Eastman Kodak	1.43	34%
XON	Exxon Corp	.67	18%
GE	General Electric CO	1.26	15%
GM	General Motors Corp	.81	19%
GS	Gillette Co	1.09	21%
HWP	Hewlett-Packard Co	1.65	21%
HIA	Holiday Inns Inc	2.56	39%
KM	K-Mart Corp	.82	20%
LK	Lockheed Corp	3.02	43%
MCD	McDonalds Corp	1.56	21%
MRK	Merck & Co	.94	20%
MMM	Minnesota Mining & Mfg	1.00	17%
JCP	Penny J C Inc	1.22	20%
MO	Phillip Morris Inc.	.87	21%
PG	Procter & Gamble	.70	14%
SA	Safeway Stores Inc	.72	14%
S	Sears Roebuck & Co	1.04	19%
SD	Standard Oil of Calif	.85	24%
SYN	Syntex Corp	1.18	31%
TXN	Texas Instruments	1.46	23%
X	US Steel Corp	1.03	26%
UNP	Union Pacific Corp	.65	18%
ZE	Zenith Radio Corp	2.01	32%

Source: *Dailygraph Stock Option Guide*, William O'Neil & Co, Inc., Los Angeles, December 7, 1979. Reprinted with permission of Daily Graphs, P.O. Box 66919, Los Angeles, CA 90066.

properties. Generally speaking, we expect aggressive companies or highly leveraged companies to have high betas, whereas conservative companies whose performance is unrelated to the general market behavior are expected to have low betas. Also, we expect that companies in the same business will have similar, but not identical, beta values. Compare, for instance, JC Penny with Sears Roebuck, or Exxon with Standard Oil of California.

Beta of a Portfolio

It is easy to calculate the overall beta of a portfolio in terms of the betas of the individual assets in the portfolio. Suppose, for example, that a portfolio contains n assets with the weights $w_1, w_2, \ldots, w_n$. The rate of return of the portfolio is $r = \sum_{i=1}^{n} w_i r_i$. Hence $\text{cov}(r, r_M) = \sum_{i=1}^{n} w_i \, \text{cov}(r_i, r_M)$. It follows immediately that

$$\beta_p = \sum_{i=1}^{n} w_i \beta_i . \tag{7.4}$$

In other words, the portfolio beta is just the weighted average of the betas of the individual assets in the portfolio, with the weights being identical to those that define the portfolio.

7.4 THE SECURITY MARKET LINE

The CAPM formula can be expressed in graphical form by regarding the formula as a linear relationship. This relationship is termed the **security market line.** Two versions are shown in Figure 7.3.

Both graphs show the linear variation of $\bar{r}$. The first expresses it in covariance form, with $\text{cov}(r, r_M)$ being the horizontal axis. The market portfolio corresponds to the point σ_M^2 on this axis. The second graph shows the relation in beta form, with beta being the horizontal axis. In this case the market corresponds to the point $\beta = 1$.

Both of these lines highlight the essence of the CAPM formula. Under the equilibrium conditions assumed by the CAPM, any asset should fall on the security market line.

The security market line expresses the risk–reward structure of assets according to the CAPM, and emphasizes that the risk of an asset is a function of its covariance with the market or, equivalently, a function of its beta.

Systematic Risk

The CAPM implies a special structural property for the return of an asset, and this property provides further insight as to why beta is the most important measure of risk. To develop this result we write the (random) rate of return of asset i as

$$r_i = r_f + \beta_i (r_M - r_f) + \varepsilon_i . \tag{7.5}$$

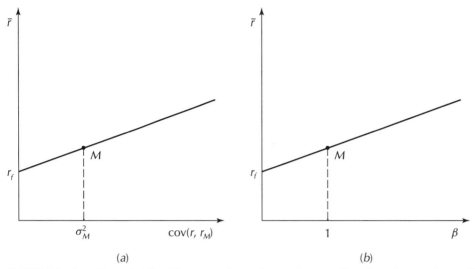

FIGURE 7.3   Security market line. The expected rate of return increases linearly as the covariance with the market increases or, equivalently, as β increases.

This is just an arbitrary equation at this point. The random variable ε_i is chosen to make it true. However, the CAPM formula tells us several things about ε_i.

First, taking the expected value of (7.5), the CAPM says that $E(\varepsilon_i) = 0$. Second, taking the correlation of (7.5) with r_M (and using the definition of β_i), we find $\text{cov}(\varepsilon_i, \sigma_M) = 0$. We can therefore write

$$\sigma_i^2 = \beta_i^2 \sigma_M^2 + \text{var}(\varepsilon_i)$$

and we see that σ_i^2 is the sum of two parts. The first part, $\beta_i^2 \sigma_M^2$, is termed the **systematic risk.** This is the risk associated with the market as a whole. This risk cannot be reduced by diversification because every asset with nonzero beta contains this risk. The second part, $\text{var}(\varepsilon_i)$, is termed the **nonsystematic, idiosyncratic,** or **specific risk.** This risk is uncorrelated with the market and can be reduced by diversification. It is the systematic (or nondiversifiable) risk, measured by beta, that is most important, since it directly combines with the systematic risk of other assets.

Consider an asset on the capital market line[1] with a value of β. The standard deviation of this asset is $\beta\sigma_M$. It has only systematic risk; there is no nonsystematic risk. This asset has an expected rate of return equal to $\bar{r} = r_f + \beta(\bar{r}_M - r_f)$. Now consider a whole group of other assets, all with the same value of β. According to CAPM, these all have the same expected rate of return, equal to $\bar{r}$. However, if these assets carry nonsystematic risk, they will not fall on the capital market line. Indeed, as the nonsystematic risk increases, the points on the $\bar{r}$–σ plane representing these assets drift to the right, as shown in Figure 7.4. The horizontal distance of a point from the capital market line is therefore a measure of the nonsystematic risk.

---

[1] Of course, to be exactly on the line, the asset must be equivalent to a combination of the market portfolio and the risk-free asset.

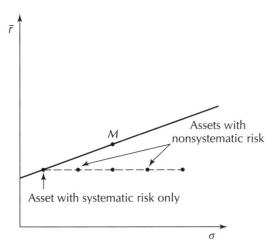

FIGURE 7.4 Systematic and nonsystematic risk. An asset on the capital market line has only systematic risk. Assets with nonsystematic risk fall to the right of the capital market line.

7.5 INVESTMENT IMPLICATIONS

The question of interest for the investor is: Can the CAPM help with investment decisions? There is not a simple answer to this question.

The CAPM states (or assumes), based on an equilibrium argument, that the solution to the Markowitz problem is that the market portfolio is the *one fund* (and *only fund*) of risky assets that anyone need hold. This fund is supplemented only by the risk-free asset. The investment recommendation that follows this argument is that an investor should simply purchase the market portfolio. That is, ideally, an investor should purchase a little bit of every asset that is available, with the proportions determined by the relative amounts that are issued in the market as a whole. If the world of equity securities is taken as the set of available assets, then each person should purchase some shares in every available stock, in proportion to the stocks' monetary share of the total of all stocks outstanding. It is not necessary to go to the trouble of analyzing individual issues and computing a Markowitz solution. Just buy the market portfolio.

Since it would be rather cumbersome for an individual to assemble the market portfolio, mutual funds have been designed to match the market portfolio closely. These funds are termed **index funds,** since they usually attempt to duplicate the portfolio of a major stock market index, such as the *Standard & Poor's 500* (S&P 500), an average of 500 stocks that as a group is thought to be representative of the market as a whole. Other indices use even larger numbers of stocks. A CAPM purist (that is, one who fully accepts the CAPM theory as applied to publicly traded securities) could just purchase one of these index funds (to serve as the *one fund*) as well as some risk-free securities such as U.S. Treasury bills.

Some people believe that they can do better than blindly purchasing the market portfolio. The CAPM, after all, assumes that everyone has identical information about the (uncertain) returns of all assets. Clearly, this is not the case. If someone believes that he or she possesses superior information, then presumably that person could form a portfolio that would outperform the market. We return to this issue in the next chapter, where questions concerning data and information are explicitly addressed. It is shown there that it is not at all easy to obtain accurate data for use in a Markowitz model, and hence the solution computed from such a model is likely to be somewhat nonsensical. For now we just state that the best designs seem to be those formulated as deviations or extensions of the basic CAPM idea, rather than as bold new beginnings. In other words, in constructing a portfolio, one probably should begin with the market portfolio and alter it systematically, rather than attempting to solve the full Markowitz problem from scratch.

One area where the CAPM approach has direct application is in the analysis of assets that do not have well-established market prices. In this case the CAPM can be used to find a *reasonable* price. An important class of problems of this type are the project evaluation problems (variations of capital budgeting problems) that arise in firms. This application is considered explicitly in Section 7.8.

7.6 PERFORMANCE EVALUATION

The CAPM theory can be used to evaluate the performance of an investment portfolio, and indeed it is now common practice to evaluate many institutional portfolios (such as pension funds and mutual funds) using the CAPM framework. We shall present the main ideas by going through a simple hypothetical example. The primary purpose of this section, however, is to use these performance measure ideas to illustrate the CAPM.

Example 7.4 (ABC fund analysis)   The ABC mutual fund has the 10-year record of rates of return shown in the column labeled ABC in Table 7.3. We would like to evaluate this fund's performance in terms of mean–variance portfolio theory and the CAPM. Is it a good fund that we could recommend? Can it serve as the *one fund* for a prudent mean–variance investor?

Step 1. We begin our analysis by computing the three quantities shown in Table 7.3 below the given return data: the average rate of return, the standard deviation of the rate as implied by the 10 samples, and the geometric mean rate of return. These quantities are estimates based on the available data.

In general, given $r_i, i = 1, 2, \ldots, n$, the average rate of return is

$$\hat{\bar{r}} = \frac{1}{n} \sum_{i=1}^{n} r_i$$

and this serves as an estimate of the true expected return $\bar{r}$. The average variance is[2]

$$s^2 = \frac{1}{n-1} \sum_{i=1}^{n} (r_i - \hat{\bar{r}})^2$$

---

[2]The reason that $n - 1$ is used in the denominator instead of n is discussed in the next chapter.

TABLE 7.3
ABC Fund Performance

| | Rate of return percentages | | |
Year	ABC	S&P	T-bills
1	14	12	7
2	10	7	7.5
3	19	20	7.7
4	−8	−2	7.5
5	23	12	8.5
6	28	23	8
7	20	17	7.3
8	14	20	7
9	−9	−5	7.5
10	19	16	8
Average	13	12	7.6
Standard deviation	12.4	9.4	.5
Geometric mean	12.3	11.6	7.6
Cov(ABC, S&P)	.0107		
Beta	1.20375	1	
Jensen	0.00104	0.00000	
Sharpe	0.43577	0.46669	

The top part of the table shows the rate of return achieved by ABC, S&P 500, and T-bills over a 10-year period. The lower portion shows the Jensen and Sharpe indices.

and the estimate s of the standard deviation is the square root of that. It is also useful to calculate the geometric mean rate of return, which is

$$\mu = \left[(1 + r_1)(1 + r_2) \cdots (1 + r_n)\right]^{1/n} - 1.$$

This measures the actual rate of return over the n years, accounting for compounding. This value will generally be somewhat lower than the average rate of return.

Step 2. Next we obtain data on both the market portfolio and the risk-free rate of return over the 10-year period. We use the *Standard & Poor's 500* stock average and the 1-year Treasury bill rate, respectively. These are shown in Table 7.3. We calculate average rates of return and standard deviations of these by the same method as for ABC. We also calculate an estimate of the covariance of the ABC fund with the S&P 500 by using the estimate

$$\text{cov}(r, r_M) = \frac{1}{n-1} \sum_{i=1}^{n} (r_i - \hat{\bar{r}})(r_{Mi} - \hat{\bar{r}}_M).$$

We then calculate beta from the standard formula,

$$\beta = \frac{\text{cov}(r, r_M)}{\text{var}(r_M)}.$$

This gives us enough information to carry out an interesting analysis.

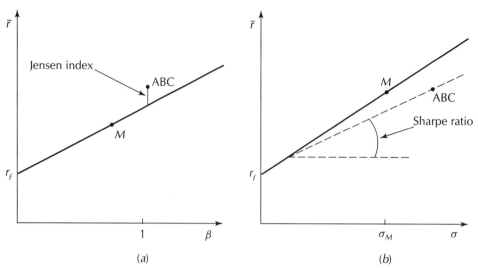

FIGURE 7.5   Performance indices for ABC. The Jensen index measures the height above the security market line; the Sharpe ratio measures the angle in the $\bar{r}$–σ plane.

Step 3. (The Jensen index)   We write the formula

$$\hat{\bar{r}} - r_f = J + \beta(\hat{\bar{r}}_M - r_f).$$

This looks like the CAPM pricing formula (7.2), except that we have replaced expected rates of return by measured average returns (for that is the best that can be done in this situation), and we have added an error term J. The J here stands for **Jensen's index.**

According to the CAPM, the value of J should be zero when true expected returns are used. Hence J measures, approximately, how much the performance of ABC has deviated from the theoretical value of zero. A positive value of J presumably implies that the fund did better than the CAPM prediction (but of course we recognize that approximations are introduced by the use of a finite amount of data to estimate the important quantities).

The Jensen index can be indicated on the security market line, as shown in Figure 7.5(a). For ABC, we find that indeed $J > 0$, and hence we might conclude that ABC is an excellent fund. But is this really a correct inference?

Aside from the difficulties inherent in using short histories of data this way, the inference that ABC is a good mutual fund is not entirely warranted. It is *not* clear that it can serve as the one fund of risky assets in an efficient portfolio. The fact that $J > 0$ is nice, and may tell us that ABC is a good *asset,* but it does not say that the ABC fund is, by itself, efficient.[3]

---

[3]It can be argued that the Jensen index tells us nothing about the fund, but instead is a measure of the validity of the CAPM. If the CAPM is valid, then every security (or fund) must satisfy the CAPM formula exactly, since the formula is an identity if the market portfolio is efficient. If we find a security with a nonzero Jensen index, then that is a sign that the market is not efficient. The CAPM formula is often applied to (new) financial instruments or projects that are not traded and hence not part of the market portfolio. In this case, the Jensen index can be a useful measure.

Step 4. (The Sharpe index)   In order to measure the efficiency of ABC we must see where it falls relative to the capital market line. Only portfolios on that line are efficient. We do this by writing the formula

$$\hat{\bar{r}} - r_f = S\sigma.$$

The value of S is the slope of the line drawn between the risk-free point and the ABC point on the $\bar{r}$–σ diagram. The S stands for **Sharpe index.** For ABC we find $S = .43577$. This must be compared with the corresponding value for the market—represented by the S&P 500. We find the value for the S&P 500 is $S = .46669$. The situation is shown in Figure 7.5(b). Clearly ABC is not efficient, at least as revealed by the available data.

We conclude that ABC may be worth holding in a portfolio. By itself it is not quite efficient, so it would be necessary to supplement this fund with other assets or funds to achieve efficiency. Or, to attain efficiency, an investor could simply invest in a broad-based fund instead of the ABC fund.

7.7 CAPM AS A PRICING FORMULA

The CAPM is a **pricing model.** However, the standard CAPM formula does not contain prices explicitly—only expected rates of return. To see why the CAPM is called a pricing model we must go back to the definition of return.

Suppose that an asset is purchased at price P and later sold at price Q. The rate of return is then $r = (Q - P)/P$. Here P is known and Q is random. Putting this in the CAPM formula, we have

$$\frac{\overline{Q} - P}{P} = r_f + \beta(\bar{r}_M - r_f).$$

Solving for P we obtain

$$P = \frac{\overline{Q}}{1 + r_f + \beta(\bar{r}_M - r_f)}.$$

This gives the price of the asset according to the CAPM. We highlight this important result:

Pricing form of the CAPM   *The price P of an asset with payoff Q is*

$$P = \frac{\overline{Q}}{1 + r_f + \beta(\bar{r}_M - r_f)} \tag{7.6}$$

where β is the beta of the asset.

This pricing formula has a form that very nicely generalizes the familiar discounting formula for deterministic situations. In the deterministic case, it is appropriate to discount the future payment at the interest rate r_f, using a factor of $1/(1 + r_f)$. In the random case the appropriate interest rate is $r_f + \beta(\bar{r}_M - r_f)$, which can be regarded as a risk-adjusted interest rate.

Example 7.5 (The price is right)   Gavin Jones is good at math, but his friends tell him that he doesn't always see the *big picture*. Right now, Gavin is thinking about investing in a mutual fund. This fund invests 10% of its funds at the risk-free rate of 7% and the remaining 90% in a widely diversified portfolio that closely approximates the market portfolio, which has an expected rate of return equal to 15%. One share of the mutual fund represents $100 of assets in the fund. Having just studied the CAPM, Gavin wants to know how much such a share should cost.

   Gavin figures out that the beta of the fund must be .90. The value of a share after 1 year is expected to be $10 \times 1.07 + 90 \times 1.15 = 114.20$. Hence, according to (7.6),

$$P = \frac{114.20}{1.07 + .90 \times .08} = \$100.$$

Yes, the price of a share will be equal to the value of the funds it represents. Gavin is reassured (but suspects he could have figured that out more simply).

Example 7.6 (The oil venture)   Consider again, as in Example 7.2, the possibility of investing in a share of a certain oil well that will produce a payoff that is random because of the uncertainty associated with whether or not there is oil at that site and because of the uncertainty in future oil prices. The expected payoff is $1,000 and the standard deviation of return is a relatively high 40%. The beta of the asset is $\beta = .6$, which is relatively low because, although the uncertainty in return due to oil prices is correlated with the market portfolio, the uncertainty associated with exploration is not. The risk-free rate is $r_f = 10\%$, and the expected return on the market portfolio is .17. What is the value of this share of the oil venture, based on CAPM? (Recall that earlier it was stated that the offered price was $875.) We have immediately

$$P = \frac{\$1,000}{1.10 + .6(.17 - .10)} = \$876$$

and σ does not enter the calculation.

   The venture may be quite risky in the traditional sense of having a high standard deviation associated with its return. But, nevertheless, it is fairly priced because of the relatively low beta.

Linearity of Pricing and the Certainty Equivalent Form

We now discuss a very important property of the pricing formula—namely, that it is **linear.** This means that the price of the sum of two assets is the sum of their prices, and the price of a multiple of an asset is the same multiple of the price. This is really quite startling because the formula does not *look* linear at all (at least for sums). For example, if

$$P_1 = \frac{\overline{Q}_1}{1 + r_f + \beta_1(\overline{r}_M - r_f)}, \qquad P_2 = \frac{\overline{Q}_2}{1 + r_f + \beta_2(\overline{r}_M - r_f)}$$

it does not seem obvious that

$$P_1 + P_2 = \frac{\overline{Q}_1 + \overline{Q}_2}{1 + r_f + \beta_{1+2}(\overline{r}_M - r_f)}$$

where β_{1+2} is the beta of a new asset, which is the sum of assets 1 and 2. Furthermore, based on our recognition that the covariance between assets is important in assessing how to use them in a portfolio, it may seem *unreasonable* that the pricing formula should be linear. We can easily take care of the first doubt by converting the formula into another form, which appears linear; then we will discuss the intuition behind the result.

The form of the CAPM pricing formula that clearly displays linearity is called the **certainty equivalent form.** Suppose that we have an asset with price P and final value Q. Here again P is known and Q is uncertain. Using the fact that $r = Q/P - 1$, the value of beta is

$$\beta = \frac{\text{cov}[(Q/P - 1), r_M]}{\sigma_M^2}.$$

This becomes

$$\beta = \frac{\text{cov}(Q, r_M)}{P\sigma_M^2}.$$

Substituting this into the pricing formula (7.6) and dividing by P yields

$$1 = \frac{\overline{Q}}{P(1 + r_f) + \text{cov}(Q, r_M)(\overline{r}_M - r_f)/\sigma_M^2}.$$

Finally, solving for P we obtain the following formula:

Certainty equivalent pricing formula   *The price P of an asset with payoff Q is*

$$P = \frac{1}{1 + r_f}\left[\overline{Q} - \frac{\text{cov}(Q, r_M)(\overline{r}_M - r_f)}{\sigma_M^2}\right]. \qquad (7.7)$$

The term in brackets is called the **certainty equivalent** of Q. This value is treated as a certain amount, and then the normal discount factor $1/(1 + r_f)$ is applied to obtain P. The certainty equivalent form shows clearly that the pricing formula is linear because both terms in the brackets depend linearly on Q.

The reason for linearity can be traced back to the principle of no arbitrage: if the price of the sum of two assets were not equal to the sum of the individual prices, it would be possible to make arbitrage profits. For example, if the combination asset were priced lower than the sum of the individual prices, we could buy the combination (at the low price) and sell the individual pieces (at the higher price), thereby making a profit. By doing this in large quantities, we could make arbitrarily large profits. If the reverse situation held—if the combination asset were priced higher than the sum of the two assets—we would buy the assets individually and sell the combination, again making arbitrage profits. Such arbitrage opportunities are ruled out if and only if the pricing of assets is linear. This linearity of pricing is therefore a fundamental tenet of financial theory (in the context of perfect markets), and we shall return to it frequently throughout the text.

Example 7.7 (Gavin tries again)   Gavin Jones decides to use the certainty equivalent form of the pricing equation to calculate the share price of the mutual fund considered in Example 7.5. In this case he notes that $\text{cov}(Q, r_M) = 90\sigma_M^2$, where Q is the value of the fund after 1 year. Hence,

$$P = \frac{114.20 - 90 \times .08}{1.07} = \$100.$$

All is well again, according to his math.

7.8 PROJECT CHOICE*

A firm can use the CAPM as a basis for deciding which projects it should carry out. Suppose, for example, that a potential project requires an initial outlay of P and will generate a net amount Q after 1 year. As usual, P is known and Q is random, with expected value $\overline{Q}$. It is natural to define the net present value (NPV) of this project by the formula

$$\text{NPV} = -P + \frac{1}{1 + r_f}\left[\overline{Q} - \frac{\text{cov}(Q, r_M)(\overline{r}_M - r_f)}{\sigma_M^2}\right]. \qquad (7.8)$$

This formula is based on the certainty equivalent form of the CAPM: the first (negative) term is the initial outlay and the second term is the certainty equivalent of the final payoff.

The firm may have many different projects from which it will select a few. What criterion should the firm employ in making its selection? Extending our knowledge of the deterministic case, it seems appropriate for the firm to select the group of projects that maximize NPV. Indeed this is the advice that is normally given to firms.

How would potential investors view the situation? For them a particular firm is only one of a whole group of firms in which they may choose to invest. Investors are concerned with the overall performance of their portfolios, and only incidentally with the internal decisions of a particular firm. If investors base their investment decisions on a mean–variance criterion, they want an individual firm to operate so as to push the efficient frontier, of the entire universe of assets, as far upward and leftward as possible. This would improve the efficient frontier and hence the performance of a mean–variance efficient portfolio. Therefore potential investors will urge the management teams of firms to select projects that will shift the efficient frontier outward as far as possible, then they will invest in the efficient portfolio. For firms to do this, they must account for the selections made by all other firms, for it is the combined effect, accounting for interactions, that determines the efficient frontier.

The two criteria—net present value and maximum expansion of the efficient frontier—may, it seems, be in conflict. The NPV criterion focuses on the firm itself; the efficient frontier criterion focuses on the joint effect of all firms. But really, there is no conflict. The two criteria are essentially equivalent, as stated by the following version of the harmony theorem:

Harmony theorem   *If a firm does not maximize* NPV, *then the efficient frontier can be expanded.*

Proof: Suppose firm i is planning to operate in a manner that leads to a net present value of Δ which does not maximize the net present value available. The initial cost of the project is P_i^0. Investors pay $P_i = P_i^0 + \Delta$ and plan to receive the reward Q_i, obtaining a rate of return $r_i = (Q_i - P_i)/P_i$. We assume that firm i has a very small weight in the market portfolio of risky assets and that projects have positive initial cost.

The current rate of return r_i satisfies the CAPM relation

$$\bar{r}_i - r_f = \beta_i(\bar{r}_M - r_f)$$

which as shown earlier is equivalent to

$$0 = -P_i + \frac{\overline{Q} - \mathrm{cov}(Q, r_M)(\bar{r}_M - r_f)/\sigma_M^2}{1 + r_f}.$$

Hence from the viewpoint of investors, the current net present value is zero.

Suppose now that the firm could operate to increase the present value by using a project with cost $P_i^{0\prime}$ and reward Q_i'. Investors pay Δ to buy the company and pay the operating cost $P_i^{0\prime}$. The total $P_i' = P_i^{0\prime} + \Delta$ satisfies

$$-P_i' + \frac{\overline{Q}_i' - \mathrm{cov}(Q_i', r_M)(\bar{r}_M - r_f)/\sigma_M^2}{1 + r_f} > 0$$

which, since $P_i' > 0$, implies that

$$r_i' - r_f - \mathrm{cov}(r_i', r_M)(\bar{r}_M - r_f)/\sigma_M^2 > 0.$$

Now consider the portfolio with return $r_\alpha = r_M + \alpha r_i' - \alpha r_i$ where α is the original weight of the firm i in the market portfolio. This portfolio corresponds to dropping the old firm project and replacing it by the same weight of the new.

We want to show that this portfolio lies above the old efficient frontier. To show this we evaluate

$$\tan \theta_\alpha = \frac{\bar{r}_\alpha - r_f}{\sigma_\alpha}$$

for small $\alpha > 0$. Differentiation gives

$$\frac{d \tan \theta_\alpha}{d\alpha} = \frac{1}{\sigma_\alpha}\frac{d\bar{r}_\alpha}{d\alpha} - \frac{\bar{r}_\alpha - r_f}{\sigma_\alpha^2}\frac{d\sigma_\alpha}{d\alpha}.$$

Using

$$\left.\frac{d\bar{r}_\alpha}{d\alpha}\right|_{\alpha=0} = \bar{r}'_i - \bar{r}_i$$

$$\left.\frac{d\sigma_\alpha}{d\alpha}\right|_{\alpha=0} = \frac{\sigma_{Mi'} - \sigma_{Mi}}{\sigma_M}$$

we find

$$\left.\frac{d\tan\theta_\alpha}{d\alpha}\right|_{\alpha=0} = \frac{\bar{r}'_i - \bar{r}_i}{\sigma_M} - \frac{\bar{r}_M - r_f}{\sigma_M^2}\frac{\sigma_{Mi'} - \sigma_{Mi}}{\sigma_M}$$

$$= \frac{1}{\sigma_M}[\bar{r}'_i - \beta'_i(\bar{r}_M - r_f)] - \frac{1}{\sigma_M}[\bar{r}_i - \beta_i(\bar{r}_M - r_f)] > 0.$$

The final inequality follows because the first bracketed term is positive and the second is zero. Since α is small this means that $\tan\theta_\alpha > \tan\theta_0$. Hence the efficient frontier is larger than it was originally. ∎

7.9 SUMMARY

If everybody uses the mean–variance approach to investing, and if everybody has the same estimates of the asset's expected returns, variances, and covariances, then everybody must invest in the same fund F of risky assets and in the risk-free asset. Because F is the same for everybody, it follows that, in equilibrium, F must correspond to the market portfolio M—the portfolio in which each asset is weighted by its proportion of total market capitalization. This observation is the basis for the capital asset pricing model (CAPM).

If the market portfolio M is the efficient portfolio of risky assets, it follows that the efficient frontier in the $\bar{r}$–σ diagram is a straight line that emanates from the risk-free point and passes through the point representing M. This line is the capital market line. Its slope is called the market price of risk. Any efficient portfolio must lie on this line.

The CAPM is derived directly from the condition that the market portfolio is a point on the edge of the feasible region that is tangent to the capital market line; in other words, the CAPM expresses the tangency conditions in mathematical form. The CAPM result states that the expected rate of return of any asset i satisfies

$$\bar{r}_i - r_f = \beta_i(\bar{r}_M - r_f)$$

where $\beta_i = \text{cov}(r_i, r_M)/\sigma_M^2$ is the beta of the asset.

The CAPM can be represented graphically as a security market line: the expected rate of return of an asset is a straight-line function of its beta (or, alternatively, of its covariance with the market); greater beta implies greater expected return. Indeed, from the CAPM view it follows that the risk of an asset is fully characterized by its beta. It follows, for example, that an asset that is uncorrelated with the market ($\beta = 0$) will have an expected rate of return equal to the risk-free rate.

The beta of the market portfolio is by definition equal to 1. The betas of other stocks take other values, but the betas of most U.S. stocks range between .5 and 2.5.

The beta of a portfolio of stocks is equal to the weighted average of the betas of the individual assets that make up the portfolio.

One application of CAPM is to the evaluation of mutual fund performance. The Jensen index measures the historical deviation of a fund from the security market line. (This measure has dubious value for funds of publicly traded stocks, however.) The Sharpe index measures the slope of the line joining the fund and the risk-free asset on the $\bar{r}$–σ diagram, so that this slope can be compared with the market price of risk.

The CAPM can be converted to an explicit formula for the price of an asset. In the simplest version, this formula states that price is obtained by discounting the expected payoff, but the interest rate used for discounting must be $r_f + \beta(\bar{r}_M - r_f)$, where β is the beta of the asset. An alternative form expresses the price as a discounting of the certainty equivalent of the payoff, and in this formula the discounting is based on the risk-free rate r_f.

It is important to recognize that the pricing formula of CAPM is linear, meaning that the price of a sum of assets is the sum of their prices, and the price of a multiple of an asset is that same multiple of the basic price. The certainty equivalent formulation of the CAPM clearly exhibits this linear property.

The CAPM can be used to evaluate single-period projects within firms. Managers of firms should maximize the net present value of the firm, as calculated using the pricing form of the CAPM formula. This policy will generate the greatest wealth for existing owners and provide the maximum expansion of the efficient frontier for all mean–variance investors.

EXERCISES

1. **(Capital market line)**   Assume that the expected rate of return on the market portfolio is 23% and the rate of return on T-bills (the risk-free rate) is 7%. The standard deviation of the market is 32%. Assume that the market portfolio is efficient.

   (a) What is the equation of the capital market line?

   (b) (i) If an expected return of 39% is desired, what is the standard deviation of this position? (ii) If you have $1,000 to invest, how should you allocate it to achieve the above position?

   (c) If you invest $300 in the risk-free asset and $700 in the market portfolio, how much money should you expect to have at the end of the year?

2. **(A small world)**   Consider a world in which there are only two risky assets, A and B, and a risk-free asset F. The two risky assets are in equal supply in the market; that is, $M = \frac{1}{2}(A + B)$. The following information is known: $r_F = .10$, $\sigma_A^2 = .04$, $\sigma_{AB} = .01$, $\sigma_B^2 = .02$, and $\bar{r}_M = .18$.

   (a) Find a general expression (without substituting values) for σ_M^2, β_A, and β_B.

   (b) According to the CAPM, what are the numerical values of $\bar{r}_A$ and $\bar{r}_B$?

3. **(Bounds on returns)**   Consider a universe of just three securities. They have expected rates of return of 10%, 20%, and 10%, respectively. Two portfolios are known to lie on

the minimum-variance set. They are defined by the portfolio weights

$$\mathbf{w} = \begin{bmatrix} .60 \\ .20 \\ .20 \end{bmatrix}, \qquad \mathbf{v} = \begin{bmatrix} .80 \\ -.20 \\ .40 \end{bmatrix}.$$

It is also known that the market portfolio is efficient.

(a) Given this information, what are the minimum and maximum possible values for the expected rate of return on the market portfolio?

(b) Now suppose you are told that $\mathbf{w}$ represents the minimum-variance portfolio. Does this change your answers to part (a)?

4. (Quick CAPM derivation)   Derive the CAPM formula for $\bar{r}_k - r_f$ by using Equation (6.9) in Chapter 6. [*Hint:* Note that

$$\sum_{i=1}^{n} \sigma_{ik} w_i = \text{cov}(r_k, r_M).]$$

Apply (6.9) both to asset k and to the market itself.

5. (Uncorrelated assets)   Suppose there are n mutually uncorrelated assets. The return on asset i has variance σ_i^2. The expected rates of return are unspecified at this point. The total amount of asset i in the market is X_i. We let $T = \sum_{i=1}^{n} X_i$ and then set $x_i = X_i/T$, for $i = 1, 2, \ldots, n$. Hence the market portfolio in normalized form is $\mathbf{x} = (x_1, x_2, \ldots, x_n)$. Assume there is a risk-free asset with rate of return r_f. Find an expression for β_j in terms of the x_i's and σ_i's.

6. (Simpleland)   In Simpleland there are only two risky stocks, A and B, whose details are listed in Table 7.4.

TABLE 7.4
Details of Stocks A and B

	Number of shares outstanding	Price per share	Expected rate of return	Standard deviation of return
Stock A	100	$1.50	15%	15%
Stock B	150	$2.00	12%	9%

Furthermore, the correlation coefficient between the returns of stocks A and B is $\rho_{AB} = \frac{1}{3}$. There is also a risk-free asset, and Simpleland satisfies the CAPM exactly.

(a) What is the expected rate of return of the market portfolio?

(b) What is the standard deviation of the market portfolio?

(c) What is the beta of stock A?

(d) What is the risk-free rate in Simpleland?

7. (Zero-beta assets)   Let $\mathbf{w}_0$ be the portfolio (weights) of risky assets corresponding the minimum-variance point in the feasible region. Let $\mathbf{w}_1$ be any other portfolio on the efficient frontier. Define r_0 and r_1 to be the corresponding returns.

(a) There is a formula of the form $\sigma_{01} = A\,\sigma_0^2$. Find A. [*Hint:* Consider the portfolios $(1-\alpha)\mathbf{w}_0 + \alpha\mathbf{w}_1$, and consider small variations of the variance of such portfolios near $\alpha = 0$.]

(b) Corresponding to the portfolio $\mathbf{w}_1$ there is a portfolio $\mathbf{w}_z$ on the minimum-variance set that has zero beta with respect to $\mathbf{w}_1$; that is, $\sigma_{1,z} = 0$. This portfolio can be expressed as $\mathbf{w}_z = (1-\alpha)\mathbf{w}_0 + \alpha\mathbf{w}_1$. Find the proper value of α.

(c) Show the relation of the three portfolios on a diagram that includes the feasible region.

(d) If there is no risk-free asset, it can be shown that other assets can be priced according to the formula

$$\bar{r}_i - \bar{r}_z = \beta_{iM}\left(\bar{r}_M - \bar{r}_z\right)$$

where the subscript M denotes the market portfolio and $\bar{r}_z$ is the expected rate of return on the portfolio that has zero beta with the market portfolio. Suppose that the expected returns on the market and the zero-beta portfolio are 15% and 9%, respectively. Suppose that a stock i has a correlation coefficient with the market of .5. Assume also that the standard deviation of the returns of the market and stock i are 15% and 5%, respectively. Find the expected return of stock i.

8. (Wizards $\diamond$)   Electron Wizards, Inc. (EWI) has a new idea for producing TV sets, and it is planning to enter the development stage. Once the product is developed (which will be at the end of 1 year), the company expects to sell its new process for a price p, with expected value $\bar{p} = \$24M$. However, this sale price will depend on the market for TV sets at the time. By examining the stock histories of various TV companies, it is determined that the final sales price p is correlated with the market return as $E[(p-\bar{p})(r_M - \bar{r}_M)] = \$20M\sigma_M^2$.

To develop the process, EWI must invest in a research and development project. The cost c of this project will be known shortly after the project is begun (when a technical uncertainty will be resolved). The current estimate is that the cost will be either $c = \$20M$ or $c = \$16M$, and each of these is equally likely. (This uncertainty is uncorrelated with the final price and is also uncorrelated with the market.) Assume that the risk-free rate is $r_f = 9\%$ and the expected return on the market is $\bar{r}_M = 33\%$.

(a) What is the expected rate of return of this project?

(b) What is the beta of this project? [*Hint:* In this case, note that

$$E\left[\left(\frac{p-\bar{p}}{c}\right)(r_M - \bar{r}_M)\right] = E\left(\frac{1}{c}\right)E[(p-\bar{p})(r_M - \bar{r}_M)].]$$

(c) Is this an acceptable project based on a CAPM criterion? In particular, what is the excess rate of return (+ or −) above the return predicted by the CAPM?

9. (Gavin's problem)   Prove to Gavin Jones that the results he obtained in Examples 7.5 and 7.7 were not accidents. Specifically, for a fund with return $\alpha r_f + (1-\alpha)r_M$, show that both CAPM pricing formulas give the price of $100 worth of fund assets as $100.

REFERENCES

The CAPM theory was developed independently in references [1–4]. There are now numerous extensions and textbook accounts of that theory. Consult any of the basic finance textbooks listed as references for Chapter 2. The application of this theory to mutual fund performance evaluation was presented in [5, 6]. An alternative measure, not discussed in this chapter, is due to Treynor [7]. For summaries of the application of CAPM to corporate analysis, see [8, 9]. The idea of using a zero-beta asset, as in Exercise 7, is due to Black [10].

1. Sharpe, W. F. (1964), "Capital Asset Prices: A Theory of Market Equilibrium under Conditions of Risk," *Journal of Finance*, **19**, 425–442.
2. Lintner, J. (1965), "The Valuation of Risk Assets and the Selection of Risky Investment in Stock Portfolios and Capital Budgets," *Review of Economics and Statistics*, **47**, 13–37.
3. Mossin, J. (1966), "Equilibrium in a Capital Asset Market," *Econometrica*, **34**, no. 4, 768–783.
4. Treynor, J. L. (1961), "Towards a Theory of Market Value of Risky Assets," unpublished manuscript.
5. Sharpe, W. F. (1966), "Mutual Fund Performance." *Journal of Business*, **39**, January, 119–138.
6. Jensen, M. C. (1969), "Risk, the Pricing of Capital Assets, and the Evaluation of Investment Portfolios," *Journal of Business*, **42**, April, 167–247.
7. Treynor, J. L. (1965), "How to Rate Management Investment Funds," *Harvard Business Review*, **43**, January–February, 63–75.
8. Rubinstein, M. E. (1973), "A Mean–Variance Synthesis of Corporate Financial Theory," *Journal of Finance*, **28**, 167–182.
9. Fama, E. F. (1977), "Risk-Adjusted Discount Rates and Capital Budgeting under Uncertainty," *Journal of Financial Economics*, **5**, 3–24.
10. Black, F. (1972), "Capital Market Equilibrium with Restricted Borrowing," *Journal of Business*, **45**, 445–454.

8 MODELS AND DATA

8.1 INTRODUCTION

The theory of the previous two chapters is quite general, for it can be applied to bets on a wheel of fortune, to analysis of an oil wild cat venture, to construction of a portfolio of stocks, and to many other single-period investment problems. However, the primary application of mean–variance theory is to stocks, and this chapter focuses primarily on those special securities, although much of the material is applicable to other assets as well.

A major obstacle in the application of mean–variance theory to stocks is the determination of the parameter values that the theory requires: the mean values of each of the assets and the covariances among them. These parameter values are not readily available for stocks and other financial securities; nor can they be surmised by logical deduction as they can be for a wheel of fortune, which has clear payoffs and associated probabilities. For stocks and other financial securities, we must use indirect and subtle methods to obtain the information required for a mean–variance formulation.

This chapter examines how models of stock returns, suitable for mean–variance analysis, can be specified. It shows how to build a **factor model** of the return process to simplify the structure and reduce the number of required parameters. Along the way a new theory of asset pricing, termed **arbitrage pricing theory** (APT), is obtained. Later we turn directly to the issue of determining parameter values. We consider the possibility of using historical data to determine parameter values, but we discover that this approach is of limited value.

It should become clear that the application of mean–variance theory and the CAPM to the design of a portfolio of stocks is not straightforward, but is fraught with many practical and conceptual difficulties. Understanding these difficulties and developing strategies for alleviating them is an essential element of investment science.

8.2 FACTOR MODELS

The information required by the mean–variance approach grows substantially as the number n of assets increases. There are n mean values, n variances, and $n(n-1)/2$ covariances—a total of $2n + n(n-1)/2$ parameters. When n is large, this is a very large set of required values. For example, if we consider a universe of 1,000 stocks, 501,500 values are required to fully specify a mean–variance model. Clearly it is a formidable task to obtain this information directly. We need a simplified approach.

Fortunately the randomness displayed by the returns of n assets often can be traced back to a smaller number of underlying basic sources of randomness (termed factors) that influence the individual returns. A factor model that represents this connection between factors and individual returns leads to a simplified structure for the covariance matrix, and provides important insight into the relationships among assets.

The factors used to explain randomness must be chosen carefully—and the proper choice depends on the universe of assets being considered. For real estate parcels within a city, the underlying factors might be population, employment rate, and school budgets. For common stocks listed on an exchange, the factors might be the stock market average, gross national product, employment rate, and so forth. Selection of factors is somewhat of an art, or a trial-and-error process, although formal analysis methods can also be helpful. (See Exercise 3.)

This section introduces the factor model concept and shows how it simplifies the covariance structure.

Single-Factor Model

Single-factor models are the simplest of the factor models, but they illustrate the concept quite well. Suppose that there are n assets, indexed by i, with rates of return $r_i, i = 1, 2, \ldots, n$. There is a single factor f which is a random quantity (such as the stock market average rate of return for the period). We assume that the rates of return and the factor are related by the following equation:

$$r_i = a_i + b_i f + e_i \tag{8.1}$$

for $i = 1, 2, \ldots, n$. In this equation, the a_i's and the b_i's are fixed constants. The e_i's are random quantities which represent **errors.** Without loss of generality, it can be assumed that the errors each have zero mean, that is, $\mathrm{E}(e_i) = 0$, since any nonzero mean could be transferred to a_i. In addition, however, it is usually assumed that the errors are uncorrelated with f and with each other; that is, $\mathrm{E}[(f - \overline{f})e_i] = 0$ for each i and $\mathrm{E}(e_i e_j) = 0$ for $i \neq j$. These are idealizing assumptions which may not actually be true, but are usually assumed to be true for purposes of analysis. It is also assumed that variances of the e_i's are known, and they are denoted by $\sigma_{e_i}^2$.

An individual factor model equation can be viewed graphically as defining a linear fit to (potential) data, as shown in Figure 8.1. Imagine that several independent observations are made of both the rate of return r_i and the factor f. These points are plotted on the graph. Since both are random quantities, the points are likely to be

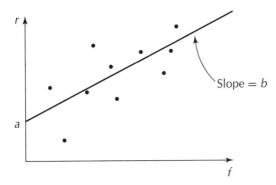

FIGURE 8.1 Single-factor model. Returns are related linearly to the factor f, except that random errors are added to the return.

scattered. A straight line is fitted through these points in such a way that the average value of the error, as measured by the vertical distance from a point to the line, is zero.

It is helpful to view Figure 8.1 in two ways. First, given the model (8.1), we can draw the line on the diagram before obtaining data points. Then if we believe the model, we believe that the data points will fall in the kind of pattern shown in the diagram. In the second view, we imagine that we first obtain the data points, then we construct the line that fits the data. When we draw the line, however, we are implying that additional data are likely to support it in the sense of falling in the same pattern.

When applied to a group of assets, the fitting process is carried out for each asset separately. As a result, we obtain for each asset i an a_i and b_i. The a_i's are termed **intercepts** because a_i is the intercept of the line for asset i with the vertical axis. The b_i's are termed **factor loadings** because they measure the sensitivity of the return to the factor.

If an historical record of asset returns and the factor values are available, the parameters of a single-factor model can be estimated by actually fitting straight lines, as suggested before. Note, however, that different values of the a_i's and b_i's are likely to be obtained for different sets of data. For example, if we use monthly data on returns and the factor f for one year to obtain values of the a_i's and b_i's, and then we do it again the next year, we are likely to get different values. In what follows, we assume that the model is given, and that it represents our understanding of how the returns are related to the factor f. We ignore the question of where this model comes from—at least for now.

If we agree to use a single-factor model, then the standard parameters for mean–variance analysis can be determined directly from that model. We calculate

$$\bar{r}_i = a_i + b_i \bar{f} \tag{8.2a}$$

$$\sigma_i^2 = b_i^2 \sigma_f^2 + \sigma_{e_i}^2 \tag{8.2b}$$

$$\sigma_{ij} = b_i b_j \sigma_f^2, \qquad i \neq j \tag{8.2c}$$

$$b_i = \text{cov}(r_i, f)/\sigma_f^2. \tag{8.2d}$$

These equations reveal the primary advantage of a factor model. In the usual representation of asset returns, a total of $2n + n(n - 1)/2$ parameters are required to specify means, variances, and covariances. In a single-factor model, only the a_i's, b_i's, $\sigma_{e_i}^2$'s, and $\overline{f}$ and σ_f^2 are required—a total of just $3n + 2$ parameters.

Portfolio Parameters

When asset returns are described by a single-factor model, the return of any portfolio of these assets is described by a corresponding factor model equation of its own. To verify this important property, suppose that there are n assets with rates of return governed by the factor model

$$r_i = a_i + b_i f + e_i, \qquad i = 1, 2, \ldots, n.$$

Suppose that a portfolio is constructed with weights w_i, with $\sum_{i=1}^{n} w_i = 1$. Then the rate of return r of the portfolio is just the corresponding combination of individual rates of return; namely,

$$r = \sum_{i=1}^{n} w_i a_i + \sum_{i=1}^{n} w_i b_i f + \sum_{i=1}^{n} w_i e_i.$$

We can write this as

$$r = a + bf + e$$

where

$$a = \sum_{i=1}^{n} w_i a_i$$

$$b = \sum_{i=1}^{n} w_i b_i$$

$$e = \sum_{i=1}^{n} w_i e_i.$$

Both a and b are constants, which are weighted averages of the individual a_i's and b_i's. The error term e is random, but it, too, is an average. Under the assumptions that $E(e_i) = 0$, $E[(f - \overline{f})e_i] = 0$, and $E(e_i e_j) = 0$ for all $i \neq j$, it is clear that $E(e) = 0$ and $E[(f - \overline{f})e] = 0$; that is, e and f are uncorrelated. The variance of e is

$$\sigma_e^2 = E(e^2) = E\left[\left(\sum_{i=1}^{n} w_i e_i\right)\left(\sum_{j=1}^{n} w_j e_j\right)\right] = E\left(\sum_{i=1}^{n} w_i^2 e_i^2\right) = \sum_{i=1}^{n} w_i^2 \sigma_{e_i}^2$$

where we have used the fact that the e_i's are uncorrelated with each other. Thus we have a simple and full description of the portfolio return as a factor equation.

A factor model is a good model to use to explore the effects of diversification, showing how risk can be reduced but not entirely eliminated. For simplicity, let us assume that in the one-factor model $\sigma_{e_i}^2$ is the same for all i; say, $\sigma_{e_i}^2 = s^2$. Suppose that a portfolio is formed by taking equal fractions of each asset; that is, we put $w_i = 1/n$ for each i. In that case, from before, we find

$$\sigma_e^2 = \frac{1}{n}s^2.$$

Hence as $n \to \infty$ we see that $\sigma_e^2 \to 0$. So in a well-diversified portfolio the error term in the factor equation is small.

The overall variance of the portfolio is

$$\sigma^2 = b^2\sigma_f^2 + \sigma_e^2.$$

The σ_e^2 term goes to zero, but since b is an average of the b_i's, the $b^2\sigma_f^2$ term remains more or less constant. Hence the variance of the portfolio tends to decrease as n increases because σ_e^2 goes to zero, but the portfolio variance does not go to zero.

This observation leads to a general conclusion. For any one asset with a rate of return described by a factor model

$$r_i = a_i + b_i f + e_i$$

there are two sources of risk: that due to the $b_i f$ term and that due to e_i. The risk due to e_i is said to be **diversifiable** because this term's contribution to overall risk is essentially zero in a well-diversified portfolio. On the other hand, the $b_i f$ term is said to be a **systematic** or **nondiversifiable risk,** since it is present even in a diversified portfolio. The systematic risk is due to the factor that influences every asset, so diversification cannot eliminate it. The risks due to the e_i's are independent and, hence, each can be reduced by diversification.

Example 8.1 (Four stocks and one index)   The upper portion of Table 8.1 shows the historical rates of return (in percent) for four stocks over a period of 10 years. Also shown is a record of an industrial price index over this same period. We shall build a single-index model for each of the stocks using this index as the factor. As a first step, we calculate the historical averages of the returns and the index. We denote the averages by $\hat{\bar{r}}_i$ and $\hat{\bar{f}}$ to distinguish these values from the true (but unknown) values $\bar{r}_i$ and $\bar{f}$.

Let r_i^k, for $k = 1, 2, \ldots, 10$, denote the 10 samples of the rate of return r_i. Then the estimate of $\bar{r}_i$ is

$$\hat{\bar{r}}_i = \frac{1}{10}\sum_{k=1}^{10} r_i^k.$$

We estimate the variances with the formula

$$\text{var}(r_i) = \frac{1}{9}\sum_{k=1}^{10}\left(r_i^k - \hat{\bar{r}}_i\right)^2$$

which is the standard way to estimate variance.[1] Analogous formulas are used to calculate estimates of the mean and the variance of the index.

---

[1] See Section 8.6 for details on this estimation formula.

TABLE 8.1
Factor Model

Year	Stock 1	Stock 2	Stock 3	Stock 4	Index
1	11.91	29.59	23.27	27.24	12.30
2	18.37	15.25	19.47	17.05	5.50
3	3.64	3.53	−6.58	10.20	4.30
4	24.37	17.67	15.08	20.26	6.70
5	30.42	12.74	16.24	19.84	9.70
6	−1.45	−2.56	−15.05	1.51	8.30
7	20.11	25.46	17.80	12.24	5.60
8	9.28	6.92	18.82	16.12	5.70
9	17.63	9.73	3.05	22.93	5.70
10	15.71	25.09	16.94	3.49	3.60
aver	15.00	14.34	10.90	15.09	6.74
var	90.28	107.24	162.19	68.27	6.99
cov	2.34	4.99	5.45	11.13	6.99
b	0.33	0.71	0.78	1.59	1.00
a	12.74	9.53	5.65	4.36	0.00
e-var	89.49	103.68	157.95	50.55	

The record of the rates of return for four stocks and an index of industrial prices are shown. The averages and variances are all computed, as well as the covariance of each with the index. From these quantities, the b_i's and the a_i's are calculated. Finally, the computed error variances are also shown. The index does not explain the stock price variations very well.

Next the covariances of the returns with the index are estimated. The formula used for this purpose is

$$\operatorname{cov}(r_i, f) = \frac{1}{9} \sum_{k=1}^{10} \left(r_i^k - \hat{\bar{r}}_i \right) \left(f^k - \hat{\bar{f}} \right). \tag{8.3}$$

Once the covariances are estimated, we find the values of b_i and a_i from the formulas

$$b_i = \frac{\operatorname{cov}(r_i, f)}{\operatorname{var}(f)}$$

$$a_i = \hat{\bar{r}}_i - b_i \hat{\bar{f}}.$$

(The first of these is obtained by forming the covariance with respect to f of both sides of the factor equation.)

After the model is constructed, we estimate the variance of the error under the assumption that the errors are uncorrelated with each other and with the index. Hence using (8.2b) we write

$$\operatorname{var}(e_i) = \operatorname{var}(r_i) - b_i^2 \operatorname{var}(f).$$

These values are shown in the last row of Table 8.1. Notice that these error variances are almost as large as the variances of the stock returns themselves, and hence the factor does not explain much of the variation in returns. In other words, there is high nonsystematic risk. Furthermore, by applying a version of (8.3) to estimate $\text{cov}(e_i, e_j)$, it turns out that the errors are highly correlated. For example, the estimation formula gives $\text{cov}(e_1, e_2) = 44$ and $\text{cov}(e_2, e_3) = 91$, whereas the factor model was constructed under the assumption that these error covariances are zero. Hence this single-index model is not a very accurate representation of the stock returns. (A better model for these data is given in the next section.)

Multifactor Models

The preceding development can be extended to include more than one factor. For example, if there are two factors f_1 and f_2, with perhaps the first factor being a broad index of the market return and the second an index of the change since the previous period of consumer spending, the model for the rate of return of asset i would have the form

$$r_i = a_i + b_{1i} f_1 + b_{2i} f_2 + e_i.$$

Again the constant a_i is called the intercept, and b_{1i} and b_{2i} are the factor loadings. The factors f_1 and f_2 and the error e_i are random variables. It is assumed that the expected value of the error is zero, and that the error is uncorrelated with the two factors and with the errors of other assets. However, it is not assumed that the two factors are uncorrelated with each other. These factors are presumably observable variables, and their statistical properties can be studied independently of the asset returns.

In the case of the two-factor model we easily derive the following values for the expected rates of return and the covariances:

$$\overline{r}_i = a_i + b_{1i}\overline{f}_1 + b_{2i}\overline{f}_2$$

$$\text{cov}(r_i, r_j) = \begin{cases} b_{1i}b_{1j}\sigma_{f_1}^2 + (b_{1i}b_{2j} + b_{2i}b_{1j})\text{cov}(f_1, f_2) + b_{2i}b_{2j}\sigma_{f_2}^2, & i \neq j \\ b_{1i}^2\sigma_{f_1}^2 + 2b_{1i}b_{2i}\text{cov}(f_1, f_2) + b_{2i}^2\sigma_{f_2}^2 + \sigma_{e_i}^2, & i = j. \end{cases}$$

The b_{1i}'s and b_{2i}'s can be obtained by forming the covariance of r_i with f_1 and f_2, leading to

$$\text{cov}(r_i, f_1) = b_{1i}\sigma_{f_1}^2 + b_{2i}\sigma_{f_1, f_2}$$

$$\text{cov}(r_i, f_2) = b_{1i}\sigma_{f_1, f_2} + b_{21}\sigma_{f_2}^2.$$

These give two equations that can be solved for the two unknowns b_{1i} and b_{2i}.

A two-factor model is often an improvement of a single-factor model. For example, suppose a single-factor model were proposed and the a_i's and b_i's determined by fitting data. It might be found that the resulting error terms are large and that they exhibit correlation with the factor and with each other. In this case the single-factor model is not a good representation of the actual returns structure. A two-factor model may lead to smaller error terms, and these terms may exhibit the assumed correlation properties. The two-factor model will still be much simpler than a full unstructured covariance matrix.

It should be clear how to extend the model to include a greater number of factors. Quite comprehensive models of this type have been constructed. It is generally agreed that for models of U.S. stocks, it is appropriate to use between 3 and 15 factors.

Selection of Factors

The selection of appropriate factors for a factor model is part science and part art (like most practical analyses). It is helpful, however, to place factors in three categories. Once these categories are recognized, you will no doubt be able to dream up additional useful factors. Here are the categories:

1. External factors Very commonly, factors are chosen to be variables that are external to the securities being explicitly considered in the model. Examples are gross national product (GNP), consumer price index (CPI), unemployment rate, or a new construction index. The U.S. Government publishes numerous such statistics. It is possible to use other external variables as well, such as the number of traffic accidents in a month or sun spot activity.

2. Extracted factors It is possible to extract factors from the known information about security returns. For example, the factor used most frequently is the rate of return on the market portfolio. This factor is constructed directly from the returns of the individual securities. As another example, the rate of return of one security can be used as a factor for others. More commonly, an average of the returns of the securities in an industry is used as a factor; for example, there might be an industrial factor, a utilities factor, and a transportation factor. Factors can also be extracted by the method of principal components. (See Exercise 3.) This method uses the covariance matrix of the returns to find combinations of securities that have large variances. Indeed, extracted factors are usually linear combinations of the returns of individual securities (as in the preceding examples). Factors can be extracted in more complex ways. For example, a factor might be defined as the ratio of the returns of two stocks, the number of days since the last market peak, or a moving average of the market return.

3. Firm characteristics Firms are characterized financially by a number of firm-specific values, such as the price–earnings ratio, the dividend-payout ratio, an earnings forecast, and many other variables. About 50 such variables for each major security are available from various data services. These characteristics can be used in a factor model. The characteristics do not serve as factors in the usual sense, but they play a similar role. As an example, suppose that we decide to use a single factor f (of the normal kind) and a single firm characteristic g (such as last quarter's price–earnings ratio). We then represent the rate of return on security i as

$$r_i = a_i + b_i f + c g_i + e_i. \tag{8.4}$$

In this model, the constant c is the same for each security, but g_i (the value of the characteristic) varies. The characteristic term does not contribute to systematic (or nondiversifiable) risk, but rather it may reduce the variance of the error term e_i. In other words, the term cg_i can be regarded as an estimate of the error term that would appear in the standard single-factor model. Firm characteristics are effective additions to factor models.

8.3 THE CAPM AS A FACTOR MODEL

The CAPM can be derived as a special case of a single-factor model. This view adds considerable insight to the CAPM development.

The Characteristic Line

Let us hypothesize a single-factor model for stock returns, with the factor being the market rate of return r_M. For convenience we can subtract the constant r_f from this factor and also from the rate of return r_i, thereby expressing the model in terms of the excess returns $r_i - r_f$ and $r_M - r_f$. The factor model then becomes

$$r_i - r_f = \alpha_i + \beta_i(r_M - r_f) + e_i. \tag{8.5}$$

It is conventional to use the notation α_i and β_i for the coefficients of this special model, rather than the a_i's and b_i's that are being used more generally. Again it is assumed that $E(e_i) = 0$ and that e_i is uncorrelated with the market return (the factor) and with other e_j's.

The **characteristic equation** or **characteristic line** corresponding to (8.5) is the line formed by putting $e_i = 0$; that is, it is the line $r_i - r_f = \alpha_i + \beta_i(r_M - r_f)$ drawn on a diagram of r_i versus r_M. Such a line is shown in Figure 8.2. A single typical point is indicated on the line. If measurements of $r_i - r_f$ and $r_M - r_f$ were taken and plotted on this diagram, they would fall at various places, but the characteristic line would presumably define a good fit through the scatter of points.

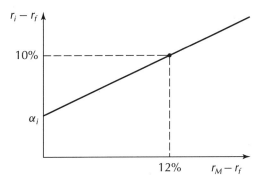

FIGURE 8.2   Characteristic line. This line represents a single-factor model that has $r_M - r_f$ as the factor for the variable $r_i - r_f$.

The expected value of this equation is

$$\overline{r}_i - r_f = \alpha_i + \beta_i(\overline{r}_M - r_f)$$

which is identical to the CAPM except for the presence of α_i. The CAPM predicts that $\alpha_i = 0$.

The value of β_i in this model can be calculated directly. We take the covariance of both sides of (8.5) with r_M. This produces

$$\sigma_{iM} = \beta_i \sigma_M^2$$

and hence

$$\beta_i = \frac{\sigma_{iM}}{\sigma_M^2}.$$

This is exactly the same expression that holds for the β_i used in the CAPM (and that is why we use the same notation).

The characteristic line is in a sense more general than the CAPM because it allows α_i to be nonzero. From the CAPM viewpoint, α_i can be regarded as a measure of the amount that asset i is mispriced. A stock with a positive α_i is, according to this view, performing better than it should, and a stock with a negative α_i is performing worse than it should. Some financial services organizations (and some highly technical investors) estimate α as well as β for a large assortment of stocks. Note, however, that the single-factor model that leads to the CAPM formula is not equivalent to the general model underlying the CAPM, since the general model is based on an arbitrary covariance matrix, but assumes that the market is efficient. The single-factor model has a very simple covariance structure, but makes no assumption about efficiency.

Example 8.2 (Four stocks and the market)   Let us rework Example 8.1 by using the excess market return as a factor. We assume that the market consists of just the four stocks, with equal weights. Therefore the market return in any year is just the average of the returns of the four stocks. These are shown in the upper portion of Table 8.2. We also adjoin the historical value of the risk-free rate of return for each of the 10 years. The relevant statistical quantities are computed by the same estimating formulas as in the earlier example, except that the factor is taken to be the excess return on the market, which will change the formula for a_i to α_i. As seen from the table, a large portion of the variability of the stock returns is explained by the factor. In other words, there is relatively low nonsystematic risk. Furthermore, a side calculation shows that the errors are close to being uncorrelated with each other and with the market return. For example, the data provide the estimates $\text{cov}(e_1, e_2) = -14$ and $\text{cov}(e_2, e_3) = 2$, which are much smaller than for the earlier model. We conclude that this single-factor model is an excellent representation of the stock returns of the four stocks. In other words, for this example, the market return serves as a much better factor than the industrial index factor used earlier. However, this may not be true for other examples.

TABLE 8.2
Factor Model with Market

Year	Stock 1	Stock 2	Stock 3	Stock 4	Market	Riskless
1	11.91	29.59	23.27	27.24	23.00	6.20
2	18.37	15.25	19.47	17.05	17.54	6.70
3	3.64	3.53	−6.58	10.20	2.70	6.40
4	24.37	17.67	15.08	20.26	19.34	5.70
5	30.42	12.74	16.24	19.84	19.81	5.90
6	−1.45	−2.56	−15.05	1.51	−4.39	5.20
7	20.11	25.46	17.80	12.24	18.90	4.90
8	9.28	6.92	18.82	16.12	12.78	5.50
9	17.63	9.73	3.05	22.93	13.34	6.10
10	15.71	25.09	16.94	3.49	15.31	5.80
aver	15.00	14.34	10.90	15.09	13.83	5.84
var	90.28	107.24	162.19	68.27	72.12	
cov	65.08	73.62	100.78	48.99	72.12	
β	.90	1.02	1.40	.68	1.00	
α	1.95	.34	−6.11	3.82	0.00	
e-var	31.54	32.09	21.37	34.99		

Now the factor is taken to be the excess return on the market portfolio. The variation in stock returns is largely explained by this return, and the errors are uncorrelated with each other and with the market. This model provides an excellent fit to the data.

8.4 ARBITRAGE PRICING THEORY*

The factor model framework leads to an alternative theory of asset pricing, termed **arbitrage pricing theory** (APT). This theory does not require the assumption that investors evaluate portfolios on the basis of means and variances; only that, when returns are certain, investors prefer greater return to lesser return. In this sense the theory is much more satisfying than the CAPM theory, which relies on both the mean–variance framework and a strong version of equilibrium, which assumes that everyone uses the mean–variance framework.

The APT does, however, require a special assumption of its own. This is the assumption that the universe of assets being considered is large. For the theory to work exactly, we must, in fact, assume that there are an infinite number of securities, and that these securities differ from each other in nontrivial ways. This assumption is generally felt to be satisfied well enough by, say, the universe of all publicly traded U.S. stocks.

Simple Version of APT

To explain the concept underlying the APT, we first consider an idealized special case. Assume that all asset rates of return satisfy the following one-factor model:

$$r_i = a_i + b_i f.$$

Different assets will have different a_i's and b_i's. This factor model is special because there is no error term. The uncertainty associated with a return is due only to the uncertainty in the factor f. The point of APT is that the values of a_i and b_i must be related if arbitrage opportunities are to be excluded. To work out the relationship between a_i and b_i we write the model for two assets i (as before) and j, which is

$$r_j = a_j + b_j f.$$

The only requirement in the selection of these two securities is that $b_i \neq b_j$. Now form a portfolio with weights $w_i = w$ and $w_j = 1 - w$. We know that the rate of return of this portfolio is

$$r = wa_i + (1 - w)a_j + [wb_i + (1 - w)b_j]f.$$

We shall select w so that the coefficient of f in this equation is zero. Specifically, we select $w = b_j/(b_j - b_i)$. This yields a rate of return of

$$r = wa_i + (1 - w)a_j = \frac{a_i b_j}{b_j - b_i} + \frac{a_j b_i}{b_i - b_j}. \tag{8.6}$$

This special portfolio is risk free because the equation for r contains no random element. If there is a separate risk-free asset with rate of return r_f, it is clear that the portfolio constructed in (8.6) must have this same rate—otherwise there would be an arbitrage opportunity. Even if there is no explicit risk-free asset, all portfolios constructed this way, with no dependence on f, must have the same rate of return. We denote this rate by λ_0, recognizing that $\lambda_0 = r_f$ if there is an explicit risk-free asset.

Setting the right-hand side of (8.6) equal to λ_0, we find

$$\lambda_0(b_j - b_i) = a_i b_j - a_j b_i$$

which can be rearranged to

$$\frac{a_j - \lambda_0}{b_j} = \frac{a_i - \lambda_0}{b_i}.$$

This is a general relation that must hold for all i and j. Therefore,

$$\frac{a_i - \lambda_0}{b_i} = c$$

holds for all i for some constant c. This shows explicitly that the values of a_i and b_i are not independent. Indeed, $a_i = \lambda_0 + b_i c$.

To see that such a relation is reasonable, suppose we take f to be the rate of return on the S&P 500 average. If a_i and b_i were arbitrary, we might specify a stock i with $a_i = .50$ and $b_i = 1.0$, which would give i a rate of return of 50% plus the S&P 500 rate. Clearly this is unreasonably high. No stock does this well. More realistically, if we have $a_i = .50$, then b_i will be negative so that, overall, r_i makes sense. As another case, if a_i is the risk-free rate, then b_i should be zero. The relation $a_i = \lambda_0 + b_i c$ keeps things in proper alignment.

We can use this information to write a simple formula for the expected rate of return of asset i. We have

$$\bar{r}_i = a_i + b_i \bar{f} = \lambda_0 + b_i c + b_i \bar{f}$$

or, alternatively,

$$\bar{r}_i = \lambda_0 + b_i \lambda_1 \tag{8.7}$$

for the constant $\lambda_1 = c + \bar{f}$. We see that once the constants λ_0 and λ_1 are known, the expected return of an asset is determined entirely by the factor loading b_i (since a_i must follow b_i).

Notice that the pricing formula (8.7) looks similar to the CAPM. If the factor f is chosen to be the rate of return on the market r_M, then we can set $\lambda_0 = r_f$ and $\lambda_1 = \bar{r}_M - r_f$, and the APT is identical to the CAPM with $b_i = \beta_i$.

For additional factors the result is similar. We now give a more general statement and proof:

Simple APT *Suppose that there are n assets whose rates of return are governed by $m < n$ factors according to the equation*

$$r_i = a_i + \sum_{j=1}^{m} b_{ij} f_j$$

for $i = 1, 2, \ldots, n$. Then there are constants $\lambda_0, \lambda_1, \ldots, \lambda_m$ such that

$$\bar{r}_i = \lambda_0 + \sum_{j=1}^{m} b_{ij} \lambda_j$$

for $i = 1, 2, \ldots, n$.

> *Proof:* We prove the statement for the case of two factors. Suppose we invest a dollar amount x_i in asset i, $i = 1, 2, \ldots, n$, in order to satisfy $\sum_{i=1}^{n} x_i = 0$, $\sum_{i=1}^{n} x_i b_{i1} = 0$, and $\sum_{i=1}^{n} x_i b_{i2} = 0$. This portfolio requires zero net investment and has zero risk. Therefore its expected payoff must be zero. Hence $\sum_{i=1}^{n} x_i \bar{r}_i = 0$. Defining the vectors $\mathbf{x} = (x_1, x_2, \ldots, x_n)$, $\mathbf{b}_1 = (b_{11}, b_{21}, \ldots, b_{n1})$, $\mathbf{b}_2 = (b_{12}, b_{22}, b_{32}, \ldots, b_{n2})$, $\mathbf{1} = (1, 1, \ldots, 1)$, and $\bar{\mathbf{r}} = (\bar{r}_1, \bar{r}_2, \ldots, \bar{r}_n)$, we can restate the foregoing as follows: For any $\mathbf{x}$ satisfying $\mathbf{x}^T \mathbf{1} = 0$, $\mathbf{x}^T \mathbf{b}_1 = 0$, and $\mathbf{x}^T \mathbf{b}_2 = 0$ it follows that $\mathbf{x}^T \bar{\mathbf{r}} = 0$; that is, any $\mathbf{x}$ orthogonal to $\mathbf{1}$, $\mathbf{b}_1$, and $\mathbf{b}_2$ is also orthogonal to $\bar{\mathbf{r}}$. It follows from a standard result in linear algebra[2] that $\bar{\mathbf{r}}$ must be a linear combination of the vectors $\mathbf{1}$, $\mathbf{b}_1$, and $\mathbf{b}_2$. Thus there are constants $\lambda_0, \lambda_1, \lambda_2$ such that $\bar{\mathbf{r}} = \lambda_0 \mathbf{1} + \mathbf{b}_1 \lambda_1 + \mathbf{b}_2 \lambda_2$. This is identical to the given statement. ∎

To understand this result, let us look at some special cases. If all the b_{ij}'s are zero, then there is no risk and we have $a_i = \lambda_0$, which is appropriate. If a b_{ij} is nonzero, then $\bar{r}_i$ increases in proportion to b_{ij}; the value λ_j is the **price of risk** associated with the factor f_i, often called the **factor price**. As one accepts greater amounts of f_i, one obtains greater expected return.

---

[2] You can visualize this in the three dimensions of a room. Fix a vector $\mathbf{b}$, say, running along the floor and perpendicular to a wall. Suppose that for *all* $\mathbf{x}$ with $\mathbf{x}^T \mathbf{b} = 0$, there also holds $\mathbf{x}^T \bar{\mathbf{r}} = 0$. The set of $\mathbf{x}$'s are those on the wall. Then you should see that $\bar{\mathbf{r}} = \lambda \mathbf{b}$ for some λ.

Well-Diversified Portfolios

We now consider more realistic factor models, which have error terms as well as factor terms. Suppose there are a total of n assets and the rate of return on asset i satisfies

$$r_i = a_i + \sum_{j=1}^{m} b_{ij} f_j + e_i$$

where $E(e_i) = 0$ and $E[e_i]^2 = \sigma_{e_i}^2$. Also assume that e_i is uncorrelated with the factors and with the error terms of other assets. Let us form a portfolio using the weights $w_1, w_2, \ldots, w_n$ with $\sum_{i=1}^{n} w_i = 1$. The rate of return of the portfolio is

$$r = a + \sum_{j=1}^{m} b_j f_j + e$$

where

$$a = \sum_{i=1}^{n} w_i a_i$$

$$b_j = \sum_{i=1}^{n} w_i b_{ij}$$

$$\sigma_e^2 = \sum_{i=1}^{n} w_i^2 \sigma_{e_i}^2 .$$

Suppose that for each i there holds $\sigma_{e_i}^2 \leq S^2$ for some constant S. Suppose also that the portfolio is **well diversified** in the sense that for each i there holds $w_i \leq W/n$ for some constant $W \approx 1$. This assures that no one asset is heavily weighted in the portfolio. We then find that

$$\sigma_e^2 \leq \frac{1}{n^2} \sum_{i=1}^{n} W^2 S^2 \leq \frac{1}{n} W^2 S^2 .$$

We now let $n \to \infty$. While doing this we assume that the bound $\sigma_{e_i}^2 \leq S^2$ remains valid for all i. Also for each n, we select a portfolio that is well diversified. As $n \to \infty$, we see that $\sigma_e^2 \to 0$. In other words, the error term associated with a well-diversified portfolio of an infinite number of assets has a variance of zero. For a finite, but large, number of assets the error term has approximately zero variance.

General APT

We now combine the ideas of the preceding two subsections. We imagine forming thousands of different well-diversified portfolios, each being (essentially) error free. These portfolios form a collection of assets, the return on each satisfying a factor model without error. We therefore can apply the simple APT to conclude that there are constants $\lambda_0, \lambda_1, \ldots, \lambda_m$ such that for any well-diversified portfolio having a rate of return

$$r = a + \sum_{j=1}^{m} b_j f_j$$

the expected rate of return is

$$\bar{r} = \lambda_0 + \sum_{j=1}^{m} b_j \lambda_j .$$

Since various well-diversified portfolios can be formed with weights that differ on only a small number of basic assets, it follows that these individual assets must also satisfy

$$\bar{r}_i = \lambda_0 + \sum_{j=1}^{m} b_{ij} \lambda_j .$$

(This argument is not completely rigorous; but a more rigorous argument is quite complex.)

This is again basically a relation that says that a_i is not independent of the b_{ij}'s. The risk-free term must be related to the factor loadings. This is true even when there are error terms, provided there is a large number of assets so that error terms can be effectively diversified away.

APT and CAPM

The factor model underlying APT can be applied to the CAPM framework to derive a relation between the two theories.

Using a two-factor model we have

$$r_i = a_i + b_{i1} f_1 + b_{i2} f_2 + e_i.$$

We find the covariance of this asset with the market portfolio to be

$$\text{cov}(r_M, r_i) = b_{i1}\text{cov}(r_M, f_1) + b_{i2}\text{cov}(r_M, f_2) + \text{cov}(r_M, e_i).$$

If the market represents a well-diversified portfolio, it will contain essentially no error term, and hence it is reasonable to ignore the term $\text{cov}(r_M, e_i)$ in the foregoing expression. We can then write the beta of the asset as

$$\beta_i = b_{i1}\beta_{f_1} + b_{i2}\beta_{f_2}$$

where

$$\beta_{f_1} = \sigma_{M, f_1}/\sigma_M^2$$

$$\beta_{f_2} = \sigma_{M, f_2}/\sigma_M^2 .$$

Hence the overall beta of the asset can be considered to be made up from underlying factor betas that do not depend on the particular asset. The weight of these factor betas in the overall asset beta is equal to the factor loadings. Hence in this framework, the reason that different assets have different betas is that they have different loadings.

8.5 DATA AND STATISTICS

Mean–variance portfolio theory and the related models of the CAPM and APT are frequently applied to equity securities (that is, to publicly traded stocks). Typically, when using mean–variance theory to construct a portfolio, a nominal investment period, or planning horizon, is chosen—say, 1 year or 1 month—and the portfolio is optimized with respect to the mean and the variance for this period. However, to carry out this procedure, it is necessary to assign specific numerical values to the parameters of the model: the expected returns, the variances of those returns, and the covariances between the returns of different securities. Where do we obtain these parameter values?

One obvious source is historical data of security returns. For example, to obtain the expected monthly rate of return of a particular stock, we might average the monthly rates of return of that stock over a long period of time, say, 3 years. This average over the past should, hopefully, give a reasonable estimate of the true expected value of the rate of return over the next month. Likewise, we might estimate the variance of the stock by averaging the square of the month's deviations from the expected value. The covariances could be estimated in a similar manner.

This method of extracting the basic parameters from historical returns data is commonly used to structure mean–variance models. It is a convenient method since suitable sources of data are readily available. Some financial service organizations either supply the data or provide the parameter estimates based on the data. The method is also reasonably reliable for certain of the parameters such as the variances and covariances; but it is decidedly *unreliable* for other parameters, such as the expected returns. The lack of reliability is not due to faulty data or difficult computation, it is due to a fundamental limitation of the process of extracting estimates from data. It is a statistical limitation, which we loosely term the **blur of history.** It is important to understand the basic statistics of data processing and this fundamental limitation.

Period-Length Effects

Suppose that the yearly return of a stock is $1+r_y$. This yearly return can be considered to be the result of 12 monthly returns and thus can be written as

$$1 + r_y = (1 + r_1)(1 + r_2) \cdots (1 + r_{12}).$$

In this equation the monthly returns are *not* measured in yearly terms; they are the actual returns for the month. For small values of the r_i's we can expand the product and keep only the first-order terms, as

$$1 + r_y \approx 1 + r_1 + r_2 + \cdots + r_{12}. \tag{8.8}$$

In other words, $r_y \approx \sum_{i=1}^{n} r_i$, which means that the yearly rate of return is approximately equal to the sum of the 12 individual monthly returns. This approximation ignores the compounding effect, but it is good enough for our present purpose, which is to estimate the rough magnitudes of the parameters.

Assume that the monthly returns of a given stock all have the same statistical properties and are mutually uncorrelated; that is, each monthly r_i has the same expected value $\bar{r}$ and the same variance σ^2. Using the approximation (8.8) we find that

$$\bar{r}_y = 12\bar{r}.$$

Likewise, we find

$$\sigma_y^2 = \mathrm{E}\left[\sum_{i=1}^{12}(r_i - \bar{r})\right]^2 = \mathrm{E}\left[\sum_{i=1}^{12}(r_i - \bar{r})^2\right] = 12\sigma^2$$

where in the second step we used the fact that the returns are uncorrelated. Turning these equations around and taking the square root of the variance, we obtain an expression for the monthly values in terms of the yearly values,

$$\bar{r} = \frac{1}{12}\bar{r}_y$$

$$\bar{\sigma} = \frac{1}{\sqrt{12}}\sigma_y.$$

This analysis can be generalized to any length of period, such as a week or a day. If we assume that the returns in different (identical length) periods have identical statistical properties and are uncorrelated, we obtain a similar result. Specifically, if the period is p part of a year (expressed as a fraction of a year), then the expected return and the standard deviation of the 1-period rate of return can be found by generalizing from monthly periods where $p = 1/12$. We have for general p

$$\bar{r}_p = p\bar{r}_y \qquad (8.9a)$$

$$\sigma_p = \sqrt{p}\sigma_y. \qquad (8.9b)$$

It is the square-root term that causes the difficulty in estimation problems, as we shall see.

The effect of the period length on the expected rate of return and the standard deviation of the period returns is shown in Figure 8.3. The values for a 1-year period are normalized to unity for both the expected rate of return and the standard deviation. As the period is reduced, both the expected rate of return and the standard deviation of

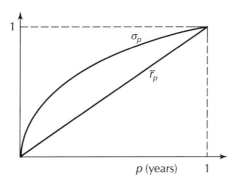

FIGURE 8.3 Period effects. The expected rate of return over a period increases approximately linearly with the length of the period. The standard deviation increases as the square root of the length of the period.

the period returns decrease. The expected rate of return is directly proportional to the length of the period. However, the standard deviation is proportional to the square root of the length of the period. This means that the ratio of the two—the ratio of standard deviation to expected rate of return—*increases* dramatically as the period length is reduced. In fact, this ratio goes to infinity as the period length goes to zero. Therefore the rates of return for small periods have very high standard deviations compared to their expected values.

Let us apply this analysis to a typical stock. The mean yearly rate of return for stocks ranges from around 6% to 30%, with a typical value being about 12%. These mean values change with time, so any particular value is meaningful only for about 2 or 3 years. The standard deviation of yearly stock returns ranges from around 10% to 60%, with 15% being somewhat typical.

Now let us translate the values of mean and variance into corresponding monthly values. Accordingly, we set $p = 1/12$ in the formulas (8.9a) and (8.9b). Let us use the nominal values of $\bar{r}_y = 12\%$ for the yearly expected rate of return, and $\sigma_y = 15\%$ for the yearly standard deviation. This leads to $\bar{r}_{1/12} = 1\%$ and $\sigma_{1/12} = 4.33\%$ for the corresponding monthly values. Hence the standard deviation of the monthly return is 4.3 times the expected rate of return, whereas for the yearly figures the ratio is 1.25. The relative error is amplified as the period is shortened. Let us go a bit further and assume that returns are generated through independent *daily* returns. Assuming 250 trading days per year, we set $p = 1/250$. Then $\bar{r}_{1/250} = .048\%$ and $\sigma_{1/250} = .95\%$ are the corresponding daily values. The ratio of the two is now $.95/.048 = 19.8$. This result is confirmed by ordinary experience with the stock market. On any given day a stock value may easily move 3 to 5%, whereas the expected change is only about .05%. The daily mean is low compared to the daily variance.

Mean Blur

We now show how this amplification effect makes the estimation of expected (or mean) rates nearly impossible.

Let us select a basic period length p (such as $p = 1/12$ for a monthly period). We shall try to estimate the mean rate of return for this period. That is, we assume that the statistical properties of the returns in each of the periods are identical, with mean value $\bar{r}$ and standard deviation σ. We also assume that the individual returns are mutually uncorrelated. We wish to estimate the common mean value by using historical data.

Suppose that we have n samples of these period returns. The best estimate of the mean rate of return is obtained by averaging the samples. Hence,

$$\hat{\bar{r}} = \frac{1}{n} \sum_{i=1}^{n} r_i . \tag{8.10}$$

The value of $\hat{\bar{r}}$ that we obtain this way is itself random. If we were to use a different set of n data points, we would obtain a different value of $\hat{\bar{r}}$, even if the probabilistic character of the stock did not change (that is, if the true mean remained constant).

However, the expected value of the estimate (8.10) is the true value $\bar{r}$ since

$$E(\hat{\bar{r}}) = E\left(\frac{1}{n}\sum_{i=1}^{n} r_i\right) = \bar{r}.$$

We want to calculate the standard deviation of the estimate $\hat{\bar{r}}$, for it shows how accurate the estimate is likely to be. We have immediately

$$\sigma_{\hat{\bar{r}}}^2 = E[(\hat{\bar{r}} - \bar{r})^2] = E\left[\frac{1}{n}\sum_{i=1}^{n}(r_i - \bar{r})\right]^2 = \frac{1}{n}\sigma^2.$$

Hence,

$$\sigma_{\hat{\bar{r}}} = \frac{\sigma}{\sqrt{n}}. \tag{8.11}$$

This is the basic formula for the error in the estimate of the mean value.

Let us put a few numbers into the formula. We take the period length to be 1 month. For the numbers used earlier, the monthly values are $\bar{r} = 1\%$ and $\sigma = 4.33\%$. If we use 12 months of data, we obtain $\sigma_{\hat{\bar{r}}} = 4.33\%/\sqrt{12} = 1.25\%$. Hence the standard deviation of the estimated mean is larger than the mean itself. If, using 1 year of data, we find $\hat{\bar{r}} = 1\%$, we are only able to say, roughly, "the mean is 1% plus or minus 1.25%." This is not a good estimate. If we use 4 years of data, we cut this standard deviation down by a factor of only 2—which is still poor. In order to get a good estimate, we need a standard deviation of about one-tenth of the mean value itself. This would require $n = (43.3)^2 = 1,875$, or about 156 years of data. However, the mean values are not likely to be constant over that length of time, and hence the estimation procedure is not really improved by much.

This is the historical blur problem for the measurement of $\bar{r}$. It is basically *impossible* to measure $\bar{r}$ to within workable accuracy using historical data. Furthermore, the problem cannot be improved much by changing the period length. If longer periods are used, each sample is more reliable, but fewer independent samples are obtained in any year. Conversely, if smaller periods are used, more samples are available, but each is worse in terms of the ratio of standard deviation to mean value. (See Exercise 5.) The problem of mean blur is a fundamental difficulty.

Example 8.3 (A statistical try)   We simulated 8 years of monthly rates of return of a stock that had a monthly mean of 1% and a monthly standard deviation of 4.33%, corresponding approximately to yearly values of 12% and 15%, respectively. Random monthly returns were generated using a normal distribution with these parameters, and these returns are shown in the upper portion of Table 8.3. The sample means were calculated each year for the entire 8-year period. The sample means for each year are indicated below the monthly returns for that year. The sample standard deviation is also indicated. (Note that the sample standard deviations are also estimates—the accuracy of these is discussed in the following subsection.) Note how the individual yearly estimates of the mean, as determined by the sample averages, jump around

TABLE 8.3
Monthly Rates of Return and Estimation of Mean (Expressed as Percent)

| | \multicolumn{8}{c}{Year of return} | | | | | | | | Overall |
	1	2	3	4	5	6	7	8	
Jan	−8.65	2.61	6.39	−4.52	1.28	4.49	−1.44	3.30	
Feb	8.61	−2.38	−1.22	2.30	.14	7.58	−4.34	3.75	
Mar	5.50	−3.28	1.12	−3.96	−2.63	5.02	1.24	3.95	
Apr	2.04	7.45	3.69	−.84	3.15	−.51	8.92	−3.13	
May	7.51	7.96	.28	.35	−.47	−.19	−.46	−.31	
Jun	−2.50	−9.37	3.61	6.96	7.04	1.18	8.28	−.89	
Jul	2.28	−7.27	−1.45	4.23	3.68	1.61	−5.33	−6.39	
Aug	1.85	−5.30	6.83	.21	2.74	2.62	−1.01	−.60	
Sep	5.86	5.69	2.32	.14	−2.08	−2.32	3.77	−.76	
Oct	1.37	5.24	−3.79	−6.48	1.73	−3.08	4.18	1.92	
Nov	3.17	2.94	−.52	−1.11	6.18	5.42	−2.27	−3.97	
Dec	9.23	1.94	2.77	2.86	.38	2.93	4.91	5.18	
Mean	3.02	.52	1.67	.01	1.76	2.06	1.37	.17	1.32
σ	5.01	5.88	3.21	3.81	2.98	3.24	4.66	3.55	4.12

Each column represents a year of randomly generated returns. The true mean values are all 1%, but the estimates deviate significantly from this value.

quite a bit from year to year. From this analysis we expect these estimates to have a standard deviation of 1.25%, and the results appear to be consistent with that. Even the 8-year estimate is quite far from the true value. We certainly should hesitate to use these estimates in a mean–variance optimization problem.

A histogram of the individual monthly returns is shown in Figure 8.4. Note that the standard deviation of the samples is large compared to the mean. One can see, visually, that it is impossible to determine an accurate estimate of the true mean from these samples. The mean value is too close to zero compared to the breadth of the distribution; hence one cannot pin down the estimate to within a small fraction of its actual value.

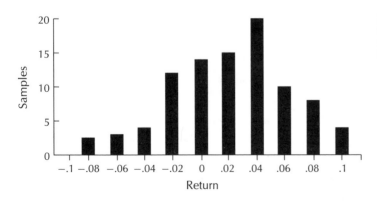

FIGURE 8.4 Histogram of monthly returns. The distribution is too broad to pin down the true mean of .01 to within a small fraction of its value.

8.6 ESTIMATION OF OTHER PARAMETERS

Estimates of other parameters from historical data are also subject to error. In some cases the error level is tolerable and in others it is not. In any event it is important to recognize the presence of errors and to determine their rough magnitudes—otherwise one might propose elaborate but fundamentally flawed procedures for portfolio construction.

Estimation of σ

The blurring effect is not nearly as strong for the estimation of variances and covariances as it is for the mean. Suppose again that we have n samples of period rates of return $r_1, r_2, \ldots, r_n$. We calculate the sample mean

$$\hat{\bar{r}} = \frac{1}{n} \sum_{i=1}^{n} r_i$$

and the sample variance

$$s^2 = \frac{1}{n-1} \sum_{i=1}^{n} (r_i - \hat{\bar{r}})^2 .$$

The use of $n-1$ in the denominator instead of n compensates for the fact that $\hat{\bar{r}}$ is used instead of the true (but unknown) $\bar{r}$. It then follows that $E(s^2) = \sigma^2$. (See Exercise 4.) Hence s^2 provides an unbiased estimate of the variance.

The accuracy of the estimate s^2 is given by its variance (or its standard deviation). It can be shown that if the original samples are normally distributed, the variance of s^2 is

$$\mathrm{var}(s^2) = \frac{2\sigma^4}{n-1}$$

or, equivalently,

$$\mathrm{stdev}(s^2) = \frac{\sqrt{2}\sigma^2}{\sqrt{n-1}} .$$

This shows that the standard deviation of the variance is the fraction $\sqrt{2/(n-1)}$ times the true variance, and hence the relative error in the estimate of σ^2 is not too extreme if n is reasonably large.

Example 8.4 (One year of data) Suppose we again use a period length of 1 month. Using 12 months of data, we obtain $\mathrm{stdev}(s^2) = \sigma^2/2.35$, which is already less than half of the value of σ^2 itself. Hence the variance can be estimated with reasonable accuracy with about 1 year of historical data.

This conclusion is validated by the experiment shown in Table 8.3. The yearly estimates of σ shown in the bottom row are all reasonably close to the true value of 4.33% (certainly they are much better than the estimates of $\bar{r}$), and the full 8-year estimate is really quite good.

a Blur

The blur phenomenon applies to the parameters of a factor model, but mainly to the determination of *a*. In fact the presence of *a* blur can be deduced from the mean-blur phenomenon, but we omit the (somewhat complicated) details.

The inherently poor accuracy of α estimates is reflected in a so-called *Beta Book*, published by Merrill Lynch, a page of which is shown in Table 8.4. Note that the reported standard deviation for α is typically larger than the value of α itself. The relative error in estimating β is somewhat better.

8.7 TILTING AWAY FROM EQUILIBRIUM*

One way to use mean–variance theory is to rely on the insight of the CAPM that if everyone followed the mean–variance approach and everyone agreed on the parameters, then *the* efficient fund of risky assets would be the market portfolio. Using this idea, you need not compute anything; just purchase a mixture of the market portfolio and the risk-free asset.

Many investors are not completely satisfied with this solution and believe that a superior solution can be computed by solving the Markowitz mean–variance portfolio problem directly, using appropriate parameters. We have seen, however, that it is fundamentally impossible to obtain accurate estimates of expected returns of common stocks using historical data. The standard deviation (or volatility) is just too great. Furthermore, the solution of the Markowitz mean–variance portfolio problem tends to be fairly sensitive to these values. This, unfortunately, makes it essentially meaningless to compute the solution to the Markowitz problem using historical data alone. The Markowitz approach to portfolio construction can be salvaged only if better estimates of the mean values are obtained.

Better estimates can only be obtained if there is information regarding the future prospects of the stock available that supplements the information contained in the historical record. Such information can be obtained in a variety of ways, including: (1) from detailed fundamental analyses of the firm, including an analysis of its future projects, its management, its financial condition, its competition, and the projected market for its products or services, (2) as a composite of other analysts' conclusions, or (3) from intuition and hunches based on news reports and personal experience. Such information can be systematically combined with the estimates derived from historical data to develop superior estimates.

However, the solution to the Markowitz problem will still be sensitive to the estimates used, and it is therefore likely that the solution obtained using the new estimates will differ substantially from the market portfolio. An investor might feel uncomfortable departing so significantly from the CAPM's recommendation to select the market portfolio. A compromise uses both the CAPM view and additional information. This is the idea presented in this section.

TABLE 8.4
A Page from a Beta Book

TICKER SYMBOL	SECURITY NAME		93/12 CLOSE PRICE	BETA	ALPHA	R-SQR	RESID STD DEV-N	STD. ERR. OF BETA	STD. ERR. OF ALPHA	ADJUSTED BETA	NUMBER OF OBSERV
COH	COHU INC		19.125	0.99	1.67	0.09	10.87	0.38	1.45	0.99	60
CLN	COLEMAN INC NEW		28.000	0.62	0.34	0.01	5.72	0.65	1.28	0.75	22
CM	COLES MYER LTD	SPNSRD ADR NEW	30.000	0.61	0.19	0.09	6.88	0.24	0.92	0.74	60
COFD	COLLECTIVE BANCORP INC		21.750	1.49	2.32	0.19	10.90	0.38	1.45	1.32	60
CL	COLGATE PALMOLIVE CO		62.375	1.01	0.88	0.36	4.96	0.17	0.66	1.01	60
CL P	COLGATE PALMOLIVE CO	PFD $4.25	74.000	0.08	0.38	0.01	3.04	0.11	0.41	0.39	60
CRIC	COLLABORATIVE RESH INC		3.750	0.47	3.10	0.01	25.08	0.88	3.34	0.65	60
CGEN	COLLAGEN CORP		27.750	1.30	0.94	0.11	12.86	0.45	1.71	1.20	60
COLL	COLLINS INDS INC		2.500	0.57	0.88	0.00	15.51	0.54	2.07	0.71	60
CLBGA	COLONIAL BANCGROUP INC	CLASS A	18.750	0.67	0.55	0.09	7.27	0.25	0.97	0.78	60
CCOM	COLONIAL COML CORP		0.313	0.01	0.27	0.02	19.06	0.67	2.54	0.35	60
CDT	COLONIAL DATA TECH CORP EC		4.313	0.01	3.63	0.02	28.01	1.09	3.98	0.34	51
CGES	COLONIAL GAS CO		22.500	0.19	0.85	0.01	4.65	0.16	0.62	0.46	60
COGRA	COLONIAL GROUP INC	CLASS A	28.000	1.07	0.76	0.21	7.46	0.26	0.99	1.05	60
CLOR -	COLOR Q INC		0.430	0.32	-3.16	0.02	14.03	0.74	2.44	0.55	38
CMED	COLORADO MEDTECH INC		1.125	-0.66	3.76	0.01	35.63	1.25	4.75	-0.10	60
COT	COLTEC INDS INC		18.750	2.45	-1.45	0.31	6.39	0.77	1.50	1.96	21
COLB	COLUMBIA BKG SYS INC		10.500	0.07	1.37	0.06	10.82	1.42	2.77	0.39	18
CLBF -	COLUMBIA FINL CORP		31.000	-0.02	0.40	0.03	5.50	0.22	0.90	0.32	40
CG	COLUMBIA GAS SYSTEM		22.375	0.18	-0.17	0.01	11.04	0.39	1.47	0.46	60
COL	COLUMBIA HEALTHCARE CORP		33.125	0.94	2.21	0.06	10.96	0.49	1.70	0.96	43
COB	COLUMBIA LABS INC		6.000	1.76	2.07	0.05	24.31	0.85	3.24	1.50	60
CFFS	COLUMBIA 1ST BK FSB WASH D C		33.000	1.57	1.02	0.11	15.61	0.55	2.08	1.37	60
CIV	COLUMBIA REAL ESTATE INVTS I		8.125	0.05	0.42	0.02	4.98	0.17	0.66	0.37	60
EGY	COLUMBIA ENERGY CORP		9.500	-0.20	1.22	0.01	8.04	0.28	1.07	0.21	60
COMR	COMAIR HOLDINGS INC		22.875	1.32	2.57	0.13	12.15	0.43	1.62	1.22	60
CMRO	COMARCO INC		4.875	1.29	0.18	0.11	12.65	0.44	1.69	1.19	60
CCPI	COMCAST CABLEVISION PHILA IN		103.000	0.21	1.75	0.00	7.25	0.25	0.97	0.48	60
CMCSA	COMCAST CORP CL A	CLASS A	36.375	1.69	1.03	0.29	9.72	0.34	1.29	1.46	60
CMCSK	COMCAST CORP CL A	CL A SPL	36.000	1.67	1.02	0.30	9.18	0.32	1.22	1.44	60

BASED ON S & P 500 INDEX   USING STRAIGHT REGRESSION   PAGE   53

Note that the standard deviations of the errors in the estimates of α are in many cases larger than the estimate itself.

Source: Security Risk Evaluation, Merrill Lynch, Pierce, Fenner & Smith, Inc., January 1994. Reprinted with permission.

Equilibrium Means

The first part of the approach uses the CAPM in a reverse fashion. It determines the expected rates of return that would be required to produce the market portfolio. That is, a set of expected rates of return is found, which, when used as the rates in the mean–variance problem, will lead to the market portfolio as the solution. Let us see how that works.

The required CAPM rates are given by the CAPM formula; namely,

$$\bar{r}_i^e = r_f + \beta_i(\bar{r}_M - r_f).$$

We have added the superscript e to emphasize that this is the value of $\bar{r}_i$ obtained through the equilibrium argument. Note that this value of $\bar{r}_i^e$ is fairly easy to obtain. It is only necessary to estimate β_i (which can be estimated quite reliably) and $\bar{r}_M$ (which is more difficult, but often a consensus view can be used). No equations need be solved.

Information

The true expected rates of return are random variables that we cannot know with certainty. The equilibrium values computed before give us some information about these values, but these too are only estimates. We expect that these estimates each have some variance and they are correlated with each other. We therefore write the equation

$$\bar{r}_i = \bar{r}_i^e + \varepsilon_i$$

for each stock i to express the fact that the true value of $\bar{r}_i$ is equal to the values obtained by the equilibrium argument plus some error. The error ε_i has zero mean. For convenience, often all the error variances are set to some small value τ, and the error covariances are assumed to be zero.

Other information about expected rates of return can be expressed in a similar way. For example, to incorporate historical data on asset i, we might write an equation of the form $\bar{r}_i = \bar{r}_i^h + e_i$, where $\bar{r}_i^h$ is the value of $\bar{r}_i$ obtained from historical data and e_i has variance equal to that implied by the length of the historical record.

Likewise, we might include subjective information about the expected return, or information based on a careful analysis of the firm. In each case we also assign a variance to the estimate.

We can imagine building up the estimate in steps. We can start with the estimate based on the equilibrium expected returns. This will lead to the market portfolio as the solution to the Markowitz problem. As additional information is added, the solution will **tilt** away from that initial solution. The degree of departure, or tilt, will depend on the nature of the adjoined equations and the degree of confidence we have in them, as expressed by the variances and covariances of the error terms.

Example 8.5 (A double use of data)   Refer to Example 8.2 and the data of Table 8.2. Most of the summary part of this table is repeated here in Table 8.5. The first row of the table gives the 10-year average returns. It is easy to calculate the corresponding CAPM

TABLE 8.5
Data for Tilting

	Stock 1	Stock 2	Stock 3	Stock 4	Market	Riskless
aver	15.00	14.34	10.90	15.09	13.83	5.84
var	90.28	107.24	162.19	68.27	72.12	
cov	65.08	73.62	100.78	48.99	72.12	
β	.90	1.02	1.40	.68	1.00	
CAPM	13.05	14.00	17.01	11.27		
tilt	13.82	14.14	14.17	12.52		

The historical average returns are not equal to the average returns predicted by CAPM. Both estimates have errors, but they can be combined to form new estimates, called tilt.

estimates. For example, for stock 1 we have $\bar{r}_1^e = 5.84 + .90(13.83 - 5.84) = 13.05$. These estimates are clearly not equal to the historical averages.

To form new, combined, estimates, we assign a variance to each estimate. Since there are 10 years of data, it is appropriate to use (8.11) to write $\sigma_i^h = \sigma_i/\sqrt{10}$ for the standard deviation of the error in the historical estimate of $\bar{r}_i$. For stock 1, this is $\sigma_1^h = \sqrt{90.28/10} = 3.00$.

To assign error magnitudes to the CAPM estimates, we notice that these estimates are based on our estimates of r_f, β_i, and $\bar{r}_M$. Let us ignore all errors except that contained $\bar{r}_M$. The standard deviation of the error in $\bar{r}_1^e$ is thus $\beta_1 \times \sigma_M/\sqrt{10} = .90\sqrt{72.12/10} = 2.42$.

For stock 1, if we treat these two estimates of $\bar{r}_1$, the historical and the CAPM (equilibrium) estimates, as independent, then they are best combined by[3]

$$\bar{r}_1 = \left[\frac{\bar{r}_1^h}{(3.00)^2} + \frac{\bar{r}_1^e}{(2.42)^2} \right] \left[\frac{1}{(3.00)^2} + \frac{1}{(2.42)^2} \right]^{-1} = 13.82.$$

(See Exercise 8.) The new estimates for the other stocks are found in a similar fashion.

8.8   A MULTIPERIOD FALLACY

The CAPM theory is a beautiful and simple theory that follows very logically from the single-period mean–variance theory of Markowitz. In practice, however, both mean–variance theory and the derived CAPM are applied to situations that are inherently multiperiod, such as the construction of portfolios of common stocks that can be traded at any time.

The simplest way to apply mean–variance theory to the multiperiod case is that implied by the statistical procedures used to estimate parameters. Specifically, a basic

---

[3]These two estimates are not really independent since the historical market return is based in part on the historical return of stock 1. Furthermore, the CAPM errors of different stocks are highly correlated since they all depend on the market. We ignore these correlations for the sake of simplicity.

period length—say, 1 month—is selected. The Markowitz problem is formulated for this period. If this problem is solved, it should, according to the CAPM assumption, prescribe that the optimal portfolio weighting vector **w** is equal to the market portfolio. This idea can then be carried forward another period. If it is assumed that the statistical properties of the returns for the next period are identical to those of the previous period and the new returns are uncorrelated with those of the previous period, the new weighting vector **w** will be equal to that of the previous period. However, in the meantime the prices will have changed relative to each other; and hence the vector **w** will no longer correspond to the market portfolio since the market weights are capitalization weights, and a price variation changes the capitalization. This is a basic fallacy, or contradiction, since the Markowitz model keeps giving the same weights, but the market portfolio weights change every period.

Let us consider a simple example. Suppose that there are only two stocks, each having the same initial price of, say, $1, the same mean and variance of return, and zero correlation with each other. Both stocks are in equal supply in the market—say, 1,000 shares of each. Suppose that we have an amount X_0 to invest. By symmetry, the mean–variance solution will be $\mathbf{w} = (\frac{1}{2}, \frac{1}{2})$; hence we should purchase equal amounts of both assets (equal dollar amounts, which is equivalent to equal numbers of shares since the prices of the two stocks are equal). This solution corresponds to the market portfolio.

Suppose that during the first period the first stock doubles in value and the second does not change. Hence now $p_1 = \$2$ and $p_2 = \$1$, and our total wealth has increased to $1.5X_0$. Since the statistical properties remain unchanged, the optimal mean–variance solution will still have $\mathbf{w} = (\frac{1}{2}, \frac{1}{2})$. This implies that we should again divide our money evenly between the two stocks. But if we do that we will purchase $\frac{1}{4}1.5X_0$ shares of stock 1 and $\frac{1}{2}1.5X_0$ shares of stock 2. This does *not* correspond to the market portfolio, which still has equal numbers of shares of the two stocks. In general, as prices change relative to each other, the dollar proportions represented in the market also change; but a repeating mean–variance model dictates that the dollar proportions of an optimal portfolio should remain fixed, which is a contradiction.

The fallacy can be repaired by assuming that the expected returns change each period in a way that keeps the market portfolio optimal; but this destroys the elegance of the model. It is more satisfying to develop a full multiperiod approach (as in Part 4 of this text). The multiperiod approach reverses some conclusions of the single-period theory. For example, the multiperiod theory suggests that price volatility is actually desirable, rather than undesirable. Nevertheless, the single-period framework of Markowitz and the CAPM are beautiful theories that ushered in an era of quantitative analysis and have provided an elegant foundation to support further work.

8.9 SUMMARY

Special analytical procedures and modeling techniques can make mean–variance portfolio theory more practical than it would be if the theory were used in its barest form. The procedures and techniques discussed in this chapter include: (1) factor models to reduce the number of parameters required to specify a mean–variance structure, (2) use of APT to add factors to the CAPM and also to avoid the equilibrium assumption that underlies the CAPM, (3) recognition of the errors inherent in computing parameter estimates from historical records of returns, and (4) blending of different types of parameter estimates to obtain informed and reasonable numerical results.

A factor model expresses the rate of return of each asset as a linear combination of certain specified (random) factor variables. The same factors are used for each asset, but the coefficients of the linear combination of these factors are different for different assets. In addition to the factor terms, there are a constant term a_i and an error term e_i. The coefficients of the factors are called factor loadings. In making calculations with the model, it is usually assumed that the error terms are uncorrelated with each other and with the factors.

A great advantage of a factor model is that it has far fewer parameters than a standard mean–variance representation. In practice, between three and fifteen factors can provide a good representation of the covariance properties of the returns of thousands of U.S. stocks.

There are several choices for factors. The most common choice is the return on the market portfolio. A factor model using this single factor is closely related to the CAPM. Other choices include various economic indicators published by the U.S. Government or factors extracted as combinations of certain asset returns. It is also helpful to supplement a factor model by including combinations of company-specific financial characteristics.

When the excess market return is used as the single factor, the resulting factor model can be interpreted as defining a straight line on a graph with $r_M - r_f$ being the horizontal axis and $r - r_f$ the vertical axis. This line is called the characteristic line of the asset. Its vertical intercept is called alpha, and its slope is the beta of the CAPM. The CAPM predicts that alpha is zero (but in practice it may be nonzero).

Arbitrage pricing theory (APT) is built directly on a factor model. For the theory to be useful, it is important that the underlying factor model be a good representation in the sense that the error terms are uncorrelated with each other and with the factors. In that case, the error terms can be diversified away by forming combinations of a large number of assets.

The result of APT is that the coefficients of the underlying factor model must satisfy a linear relation. In the special case where the underlying factor model has the single factor equal to the excess return on the market portfolio, the CAPM theory states that $\alpha = 0$. This is a special case of APT, which states that the constant a in the expression for the return of an asset is a linear combination of the factor loadings of that asset. Again, the difficult part of applying APT is the determination of appropriate factors.

It is tempting to assume that the parameter values necessary to implement mean–variance theory—the expected returns, variances, and covariances for a Markowitz formulation, or the a_i's and b_{ij}'s for a factor model representation—can be estimated from historical returns data. Although some parameter values can be estimated this way, others cannot. In particular, for stocks the variances and covariances can be estimated to within reasonable accuracy by using about 1 year of weekly or daily returns data. However, the expected rates of return (the means) are subject to a blurring phenomenon and therefore cannot be estimated to within workable accuracy, even if a record of 10 years of returns is employed. This blurring phenomenon applies to the estimation of the a coefficients in factor models as well.

The statistical analysis of estimates based on historical data tells us that we must supplement such estimates of expected returns with estimates obtained by other methods. This conclusion is not altogether surprising. It asserts that active portfolio management (as opposed to a passive strategy of investing only in the market portfolio and the risk-free asset) cannot be relegated to a pure computer analysis of historical data. Some additional intelligence is required. If this intelligence can be cast into the form of estimates, with associated variances, these estimates can be logically combined with the estimates based on historical data to produce refined estimates with smaller errors. An additional estimate of this type is provided by the CAPM formula itself.

The Markowitz mean–variance formulation of portfolio theory and the subsequent theories of CAPM, factor models, and APT provide an elegant foundation for single-period investment analysis. These developments have elaborated the benefits of diversification and deepened our understanding of risk in a market environment. These theories have also provided approaches that can be implemented. Indeed, this whole area has had a profound influence on the practice of portfolio management: index funds now abound, betas are computed and widely discussed in the financial community, large quadratic programming programs have been written to solve the Markowitz problem, numerous factor models have been constructed and tested, and trillions of dollars have been managed with at least some guidance from these ideas and methods.

But mean–variance theory is not a universal investment panacea. The assumption that all investors focus exclusively on mean and variance is questionable, it is hard to estimate the required parameter values, it seems unlikely (as required of the equilibrium argument) that everyone has the same estimates of the parameter values, and the approach must be modified in a multiperiod framework. Each of these difficulties can be overcome to some extent by extending the model, living with approximations, or looking deeper into the properties of the assets under consideration. A great deal of innovative effort has been so devoted. But ultimately, to make significant progress, we must expand the fundamental tools of analysis beyond mean–variance. We must formulate a theory that, built on the insights of the mean–variance approach, treats uncertainty more explicitly and is directed at multiperiod situations.

EXERCISES

1. (A simple portfolio)   Someone who believes that the collection of all stocks satisfies a single-factor model with the market portfolio serving as the factor gives you information on three stocks which make up a portfolio. (See Table 8.6.) In addition, you know that the market portfolio has an expected rate of return of 12% and a standard deviation of 18%. The risk-free rate is 5%.

   (a) What is the portfolio's expected rate of return?
   (b) Assuming the factor model is accurate, what is the standard deviation of this rate of return?

TABLE 8.6
Simple Portfolio

Stock	Beta	Standard deviation of random error term	Weight in portfolio
A	1.10	7.0%	20%
B	0.80	2.3%	50%
C	1.00	1.0%	30%

2. **(APT factors)** Two stocks are believed to satisfy the two-factor model

$$r_1 = a_1 + 2f_1 + f_2$$
$$r_2 = a_2 + 3f_1 + 4f_2.$$

In addition, there is a risk-free asset with a rate of return of 10%. It is known that $\bar{r}_1 = 15\%$ and $\bar{r}_2 = 20\%$. What are the values of λ_0, λ_1, and λ_2 for this model?

3. **(Principal components ⊕)** Suppose there are n random variables $x_1, x_2, \ldots, x_n$ and let $\mathbf{V}$ be the corresponding covariance matrix. An **eigenvector** of $\mathbf{V}$ is a vector $\mathbf{v} = (v_1, v_2, \cdots, v_n)$ such that $\mathbf{V}\mathbf{v} = \lambda\mathbf{v}$ for some λ (called an eigenvalue of $\mathbf{V}$). The random variable $v_1x_1 + v_2x_2 + \cdots + v_nx_n$ is a **principal component**. The first principal component is the one corresponding to the largest eigenvalue of $\mathbf{V}$, the second to the second largest, and so forth.

  A good candidate for the factor in a one-factor model of n asset returns is the first principal component extracted from the n returns themselves; that is, by using the principal eigenvector of the covariance matrix of the returns. Find the first principal component for the data of Example 8.2. Does this factor (when normalized) resemble the return on the market portfolio? [*Note:* For this part, you need an eigenvector calculator as available in most matrix operations packages.]

4. **(Variance estimate)** Let r_i, for $i = 1, 2, \ldots, n$, be independent samples of a return r of mean $\bar{r}$ and variance σ^2. Define the estimates

$$\hat{\bar{r}} = \frac{1}{n}\sum_{i=1}^{n} r_i$$

$$s^2 = \frac{1}{n-1}\sum_{i=1}^{n}(r_i - \hat{\bar{r}})^2.$$

Show that $E(s^2) = \sigma^2$.

5. **(Are more data helpful? ◇)** Suppose a stock's rate of return has annual mean and variance of $\bar{r}$ and σ^2. To estimate these quantities, we divide 1 year into n equal periods and record the return for each period. Let $\bar{r}_n$ and σ_n^2 be the mean and the variance for the rate of return for each period. Specifically, assume that $\bar{r}_n = \bar{r}/n$ and $\sigma_n^2 = \sigma^2/n$. If $\hat{\bar{r}}_n$ and $\hat{\sigma}_n^2$ are the estimates of these, then $\hat{\bar{r}} = n\hat{\bar{r}}_n$ and $\hat{\sigma}^2 = n\hat{\sigma}_n^2$. Let $\sigma(\hat{\bar{r}})$ and $\sigma(\hat{\sigma}^2)$ be the standard deviations of these estimates.

  (*a*) Show that $\sigma(\hat{\bar{r}})$ is independent of n.
  (*b*) Show how $\sigma(\hat{\sigma}^2)$ depends on n. (Assume the returns are normal random variables.) Answer the question posed as the title to this exercise.

TABLE 8.7
Record of Rates of Return

Month	Percent rate of return	Month	Percent rate of return
1	1.0	13	4.2
2	.5	14	4.5
3	4.2	15	−2.5
4	−2.7	16	2.1
5	−2.0	17	−1.7
6	3.5	18	3.7
7	−3.1	19	3.2
8	4.1	20	−2.4
9	1.7	21	2.7
10	.1	22	2.9
11	−2.4	23	−1.9
12	3.2	24	1.1

6. (A record) A record of annual percentage rates of return of the stock S is shown in Table 8.7.

(a) Estimate the arithmetic mean rate of return, expressed in percent per year.
(b) Estimate the arithmetic standard deviation of these returns, again as percent per year.
(c) Estimate the accuracy of the estimates found in parts (a) and (b).
(d) How do you think the answers to (c) would change if you had 2 years of weekly data instead of monthly data? (See Exercise 5.)

7. (Clever, but no cigar ◇) Gavin Jones figured out a clever way to get 24 samples of monthly returns in just over one year instead of only 12 samples; he takes overlapping samples; that is, the first sample covers Jan. 1 to Feb. 1, and the second sample covers Jan. 15 to Feb. 15, and so forth. He figures that the error in his estimate of $\bar{r}$, the mean monthly return, will be reduced by this method. Analyze Gavin's idea. How does the variance of his estimate compare with that of the usual method of using 12 nonoverlapping monthly returns?

8. (General tilting ◇) A general model for information about expected returns can be expressed in vector–matrix form as

$$\mathbf{p} = \mathbf{P}\bar{\mathbf{r}} + \mathbf{e}.$$

In the model $\mathbf{P}$ is an $m \times n$ matrix, $\bar{\mathbf{r}}$ is an n-dimensional vector, and $\mathbf{p}$ and $\mathbf{e}$ are m-dimensional vectors. The vector $\mathbf{p}$ is a set of observation values and $\mathbf{e}$ is a vector of errors having zero mean. The error vector has a covariance matrix $\mathbf{Q}$. The best (minimum-variance) estimate of $\bar{\mathbf{r}}$ is

$$\hat{\bar{\mathbf{r}}} = (\mathbf{P}^T\mathbf{Q}^{-1}\mathbf{P})^{-1}\mathbf{P}^T\mathbf{Q}^{-1}\mathbf{p}. \tag{8.12}$$

(a) Suppose there is a single asset and just one measurement of the form $p = \bar{r} + e$. Show that according to (8.12), we have $\hat{\bar{r}} = p$.
(b) Suppose there are two uncorrelated measurements with values p_1 and p_2, having variances σ_1^2 and σ_2^2. Show that

$$\hat{\bar{r}} = \left(\frac{p_1}{\sigma_1^2} + \frac{p_2}{\sigma_2^2}\right)\left(\frac{1}{\sigma_1^2} + \frac{1}{\sigma_2^2}\right)^{-1}.$$

(c) Consider Example 8.5. There are measurements of the form

$$\bar{r}_1 = p_1 + e_1$$

$$\bar{r}_2 = p_2 + e_2$$

$$\bar{r}_3 = p_3 + e_3$$

$$\bar{r}_4 = p_4 + e_4$$

$$\bar{r}_1 = r_f + \beta_1 f_M$$

$$\bar{r}_2 = r_f + \beta_2 f_M$$

$$\bar{r}_3 = r_f + \beta_3 f_M$$

$$\bar{r}_4 = r_f + \beta_4 f_M$$

where the e_i's are uncorrelated, but where $\text{cov}(e_i, f_M) = .25\sigma_i^2$. Using the data of the example, and assuming the β_i's are known exactly, find the best estimates of the $\bar{r}_i$'s. [*Note:* You should only need to invert 2×2 matrices.]

REFERENCES

The factor analysis approach to structuring a family of returns is quite well developed. A good survey is contained in [1]. Also see [2]. The APT was devised by Ross [3]. For a practical application see [4]. For introductory presentations of factor models and the APT consult the finance textbooks listed as references for Chapter 2. The analysis of errors in the estimation of return parameters from historical data has long been available, but is not widely employed. See [5] for a good treatment. A detailed example of tilting applied to global asset management is contained in [6].

1. Sharpe, W. F. (1982), "Factors in New York Stock Exchange Security Returns 1931–1979," *Journal of Portfolio Management*, **8,** Summer, 5–19.
2. King, B. F. (1966), "Market and Industry Factors in Stock Price Behavior," *Journal of Business*, **39**, January, 137–170.
3. Ross, S. A. (1976), "The Arbitrage Theory of Capital Asset Pricing," *Journal of Economic Theory*, **13,** 341–360.
4. Chen, N. F., R. Roll, and S. A. Ross (1986), "Economic Forces and the Stock Market," *Journal of Business*, **59,** 383–403.
5. Ingersoll, J. E. (1987), *Theory of Financial Decision Making*, Rowman and Littlefield, Savage, MD.
6. Black, F., and R. Litterman (1992), "Global Portfolio Optimization," *Financial Analysts Journal*, September/October, 28–43.

9 GENERAL PRINCIPLES

9.1 INTRODUCTION

Fundamentally, there are two ways to evaluate a random cash flow: (1) directly, using measures such as expected value and variance; and (2) indirectly, by reducing the flow to a combination of other flows which already have been evaluated. This chapter focuses on these two approaches, showing how they apply to single-period investment problems—and showing how they work together to produce strong and useful pricing relationships.

This chapter is more abstract than the previous chapters and serves primarily as preparation for the study of general multiperiod problems in Parts 3 and 4. The reader may wish to skip ahead to Chapter 10 (or even Chapter 11) since most of the material in Part 3 can be understood without studying this chapter. One strategy is to study the first part of this chapter—the first five sections, which cover expected utility theory. Then later, when approaching Part 4, the reader can come back to the second part of this chapter to study general pricing theory. Other readers may wish to study this chapter in sequence, for it is a logical culmination of the single-period framework.

9.2 UTILITY FUNCTIONS

Suppose that, sitting here today, you have a number of different investment opportunities that could influence your wealth at the end of the year. Once you decide how to allocate your money among the alternatives, your future wealth is governed by corresponding random variables. If the outcomes from all alternatives were certain, it would be easy to rank the choices—you would select the one that produced the greatest wealth. In the general random case, however, the choice is not so obvious. You need a procedure for ranking random wealth levels. A utility function provides such a procedure.

Formally, a utility function is a function U defined on the real numbers (representing possible wealth levels) and giving a real value. Once a utility function is defined, all alternative random wealth levels are ranked by evaluating their expected utility values. Specifically, you compare two outcome random wealth variables x and y by comparing the corresponding values $E[U(x)]$ and $E[U(y)]$; the larger value is preferred.

The specific utility function used varies among individuals, depending on their individual risk tolerance and their individual financial environment. The simplest utility function is the linear one $U(x) = x$. An individual using this utility function ranks random wealth levels by their expected values. This utility function (and an individual who employs it) is said to be **risk neutral** since, as will become clear later, no account for risk is made. Other utility functions do account for risk.

The one general restriction that is placed on the form of the utility function is that it is an *increasing* continuous function. That is, if x and y are (nonrandom) real values with $x > y$, then $U(x) > U(y)$. Other than this restriction, the utility function can, at least in theory, take any form. In practice, however, certain standard types are popular. Here are some of the most commonly used utility functions (see Figure 9.1):

1. Exponential

$$U(x) = -e^{-ax}$$

for some parameter $a > 0$. Note that this utility has negative values. This negativity does not matter, since only the *relative* values are important. The function is increasing toward zero.

2. Logarithmic

$$U(x) = \ln(x).$$

Note that this function is defined only for $x > 0$. It has a severe penalty for $x \approx 0$. In fact, if there is any positive probability of obtaining an outcome of 0, the expected utility will be $-\infty$.

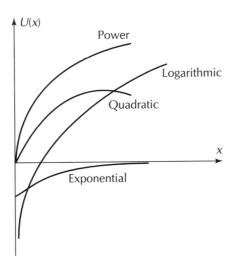

FIGURE 9.1 **Some popular utility functions.** Utility functions should increase with wealth, since greater wealth is preferred to less wealth. Functions with simple analytic forms are convenient for representation and analysis.

3. Power

$$U(x) = bx^b$$

for some parameter $b \leq 1$, $b \neq 0$. This family includes (for $b = 1$) the risk-neutral utility.

4. Quadratic

$$U(x) = x - bx^2$$

for some parameter $b > 0$. Note that this function is increasing only for $x < 1/(2b)$.

We shall discuss how an investor might select an appropriate utility function after we examine a few more properties of utility functions and study some examples of their use.

Example 9.1 (The venture capitalist)   Sybil, a venture capitalist, is considering two possible investment alternatives for the coming year. Her first alternative is to buy Treasury bills, which will give her a wealth of $6M for sure. The second alternative has three possible outcomes. They will produce wealth levels $10M, $5M, and $1M with corresponding probabilities of .2, .4, and .4. She decides to use the power utility $U(x) = x^{1/2}$ to evaluate these alternatives (where x is in millions of dollars).

The first alternative has an expected utility of $\sqrt{6} = 2.45$. The second has an expected utility of $.2 \times \sqrt{10} + .4 \times \sqrt{5} + .4 \times \sqrt{1} = .2 \times 3.16 + .4 \times 2.24 + .4 = 1.93$. Hence the first alternative is preferred to the second.

There is good justification for using the expected value of a utility function as a basis for decision making. Indeed, the approach can be derived from a set of reasonable axioms that describe rational behavior.[1] Overall, this method has the merit of simplicity, good flexibility due to the possibility of selecting a variety of utility functions, and strong theoretical justification.

Equivalent Utility Functions

Since a utility function is used to provide a ranking among alternatives, its actual numerical value (its cardinal value) has no real meaning. All that matters is how it ranks alternatives when an expected utility is computed. It seems clear that a utility function can be modified in certain elementary ways without changing the rankings that it provides. We investigate this property here.

First, it is clear that the addition of a constant to a utility function does not affect its rankings. That is, if we use a utility function $U(x)$ and then define the alternative

---

[1] There are several axiomatic frameworks that lead to the conclusion that rational investors use utility functions. The earliest set is the von Neumann–Morgenstern axioms. Another important set is the Savage axioms. (See the references at the end of the chapter.)

function $V(x) = U(x) + b$, this new function provides exactly the same rankings as the original. This follows from the linearity of the expected value operation. Specifically, $E[V(x)] = E[U(x) + b] = E[U(x)] + b$. Hence the new expected utility values are equal to the old values plus the constant b. This addition does not change the rankings of various alternatives.

In a similar fashion it can be seen that the use of the function $V(x) = aU(x)$ for a constant $a > 0$ does not change the ranking because $E[V(x)] = E[aU(x)] = aE[U(x)]$.

In general, given a utility function $U(x)$, any function of the form

$$V(x) = aU(x) + b \qquad (9.1)$$

with $a > 0$ is a utility function **equivalent** to $U(x)$. Equivalent utility functions give identical rankings. [It can be shown that the transformation (9.1) is the only transformation that leaves the rankings of all random outcomes the same.] As an example, the utility function $V(x) = \ln(cx^a)$ with $a > 0$ is equivalent to the logarithmic utility function $U(x) = \ln x$ because $\ln(cx^a) = a \ln x + \ln c$.

In practice, we recognize that a utility function can be changed to an equivalent one, and we may use this fact to scale a utility function conveniently.

9.3 RISK AVERSION

The main purpose of a utility function is to provide a systematic way to rank alternatives that captures the principle of risk aversion. This is accomplished whenever the utility function is concave. We spell out this definition formally:

Concave utility and risk aversion *A function U defined on an interval [a, b] of real numbers is said to be **concave** if for any α with $0 \le \alpha \le 1$ and any x and y in [a, b] there holds*

$$U[\alpha x + (1 - \alpha)y] \ge \alpha U(x) + (1 - \alpha)U(y). \qquad (9.2)$$

*A utility function U is said to be **risk averse on** [a, b] if it is concave on [a, b]. If U is concave everywhere, it is said to be **risk averse**.*

This definition is illustrated in Figure 9.2. The figure shows a utility function that is concave. To check the concavity we take two arbitrary points x and y as shown, and any α, $0 \le \alpha \le 1$. The point $x^* = \alpha x + (1 - \alpha)y$ is a weighted average of x and y, and hence x^* is between x and y. The value of the function at this point is greater than the value at x^* of the straight line connecting the function values at $U(x)$ and $U(y)$. In general, the condition for concavity is that the straight line drawn between two points on the function must lie below (or on) the function itself. In simple terms, an increasing concave function has a slope that flattens for increasing values.

The same figure can be used to show how concavity of the utility function is related to risk aversion. Suppose that we have two alternatives for future wealth. The first is that we obtain either x or y, each with a probability of $\frac{1}{2}$. The second is that we obtain $\frac{1}{2}x + \frac{1}{2}y$ with certainty. Suppose our utility function is the one shown in

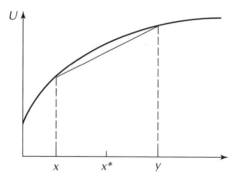

FIGURE 9.2   Concavity and risk aversion. The straight line connecting x and y lies below the function at any intermediate point. As a special case, a sure value of $x^* = \frac{1}{2}x + \frac{1}{2}y$ is preferred to a 50–50 chance of x or y.

Figure 9.2. The expected utility of the first alternative (the 50–50 chance) is equal to the value of the straight line at the point $x^* = \frac{1}{2}x + \frac{1}{2}y$, because this is the weighting of the two utility values. The expected utility of the second option (the riskless one) is equal to the value of the function at the point $x^* = \frac{1}{2}x + \frac{1}{2}y$. This value is greater than that of the first alternative when the utility function is concave. Hence the sure wealth of $\frac{1}{2}x + \frac{1}{2}y$ is preferred to a 50–50 chance of x or y. Both alternatives have the same expected value, but the one without risk is preferred.

A special case is the risk-neutral utility function $U(x) = x$ [and its equivalent forms $V(x) = ax + b$ with $a > 0$]. This function is concave according to the preceding definition, but it is a limiting case. Strictly speaking, this function represents risk aversion of zero. Frequently we reserve the phrase *risk averse* for the case where U is *strictly concave,* which means that there is strict inequality in (9.2) whenever $x \neq y$.

Example 9.2 (A coin toss)   As a specific example suppose that you face two options. The first is based on a toss of a coin—heads, you win $10; tails, you win nothing. The second option is that you can have an amount M for certain. Your utility function for money is $x - .04x^2$. Let us evaluate these two alternatives. The first has expected utility $E[U(x)] = \frac{1}{2}(10 - .04 \times 10^2) + \frac{1}{2}0 = 3$. The second alternative has expected utility $M - .04M^2$. If $M = 5$, for example, then this value is 4, which is greater than the value of the first alternative. This means that you would favor the second alternative; that is, you would prefer to have $5 for sure rather than a 50–50 chance of getting $10 or nothing.

We can go a step further and determine what value of M would give the same utility as the first option. We solve $M - .04M^2 = 3$. This gives $M = \$3.49$. Hence you would be indifferent between getting $3.49 for sure and having a 50–50 chance of getting $10 or 0.

Derivatives

We can relate important properties of a utility function to its derivatives. First, $U(x)$ is increasing with respect to x if $U'(x) > 0$. Second, $U(x)$ is strictly concave with respect to x if $U''(x) < 0$. For example, consider the exponential utility function

$U(x) = -e^{-ax}$. We find $U'(x) = ae^{-ax} > 0$, so U is increasing. Also, $U''(x) = -a^2 e^{-ax} < 0$, so U is concave.

Risk Aversion Coefficients

The degree of risk aversion exhibited by a utility function is related to the magnitude of the bend in the function—the stronger the bend, the greater the risk aversion. This notion can be quantified in terms of the second derivative of the utility function.

The degree of risk aversion is formally defined by the **Arrow–Pratt absolute risk aversion coefficient,** which is

$$a(x) = -\frac{U''(x)}{U'(x)}.$$

The term $U'(x)$ appears in the denominator to normalize the coefficient. With this normalization $a(x)$ is the same for all equivalent utility functions. Basically, the coefficient function $a(x)$ shows how risk aversion changes with the wealth level. For many individuals, risk aversion decreases as their wealth increases, reflecting the fact that they are willing to take more risk when they are financially secure.

As a specific example consider again the exponential utility function $U(x) = -e^{-ax}$. We have $U'(x) = ae^{-ax}$ and $U''(x) = -a^2 e^{-ax}$. Therefore $a(x) = a$. In this case the risk aversion coefficient is constant for all x. If we make the same calculation for the equivalent utility function $U(x) = 1 - be^{-ax}$, we find that $U'(x) = bae^{-ax}$ and $U''(x) = -ba^2 e^{-ax}$. So again $a(x) = a$.

As another example, consider the logarithmic utility function $U(x) = \ln x$. Here $U'(x) = 1/x$ and $U''(x) = -1/x^2$. Therefore $a(x) = 1/x$; and in this case, risk aversion decreases as wealth increases.

Certainty Equivalent

Although the actual value of the expected utility of a random wealth variable is meaningless except in comparison with that of another alternative, there is a derived measure with units that do have intuitive meaning. This measure is the **certainty equivalent.**[2]

The certainty equivalent of a random wealth variable x is defined to be the amount of a certain (that is, risk-free) wealth that has a utility level equal to the expected utility of x. In other words, the certainty equivalent C of a random wealth variable x is that value C satisfying

$$U(C) = \mathrm{E}[U(x)].$$

The certainty equivalent of a random variable is the same for all equivalent utility functions and is measured in units of wealth.

---

[2] This general concept of certainty equivalent is indirectly related to the concept with the same name used in Section 7.7.

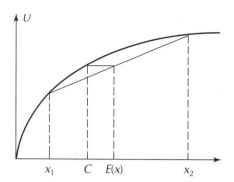

FIGURE 9.3   Certainty equivalent. The certainty equivalent is always less than the expected value for a risk-averse investor. Reprinted with permission of Fidelity Investments.

As an example, consider the coin toss example discussed earlier. Our computation at the end of the example found that the certainty equivalent of the 50–50 chance of winning $10 or $0 is $3.49 because that is the value that, if obtained with certainty, would have the same utility as the reward based on the outcome of the coin toss.

For a concave utility function it is always true that the certainty equivalent of a random outcome x is less than or equal to the expected value; that is, $C \leq E(x)$. Indeed, this inequality is another (equivalent) way to define risk aversion.

The certainty equivalent is illustrated in Figure 9.3 for the case of two outcomes x_1 and x_2. The certainty equivalent is found by moving horizontally leftward from the point where the line between $U(x_1)$ and $U(x_2)$ intersects the vertical line drawn at $E(x)$.

9.4 SPECIFICATION OF UTILITY FUNCTIONS*

There are systematic procedures for assigning an appropriate utility function to an investor, some of which are quite elaborate. We outline a few general approaches in simple form.

Direct Measurement of Utility

One way to measure an individual's utility function is to ask the individual to assign certainty equivalents to various risky alternatives. One particularly elegant way to organize this process is to select two fixed wealth values A and B as reference points. A lottery is then proposed that has outcome A with probability p and outcome B with probability $1 - p$. For various values of p the investor is asked how much certain wealth C he or she would accept in place of the lottery. C will vary as p changes. Note that the values A, B, and C are values for total wealth, not just increments based on a bet. A lottery with probability p has an expected value of $e = pA + (1 - p)B$. However, a risk-averse investor would accept less than this amount to avoid the risk of the lottery. Hence $C < e$.

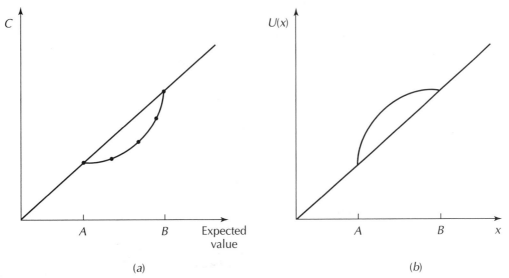

FIGURE 9.4 Experimental determination of utility function. (a) For lotteries that pay either A or B and have expected value e, a person is asked to state the certainty equivalent C. (b) Inverting this relation gives the utility function.

The values of C reported by the investor for various p's are plotted in Figure 9.4(a). The value of C is placed above the corresponding e. A curve is drawn through these points, giving a function $C(e)$. To define a utility function from this diagram, we normalize by setting $U(A) = A$ and $U(B) = B$ (which is legitimate because a utility function has two degrees of scaling freedom). With this normalization, the expected utility of the lottery is $pU(A) + (1 - p)U(B) = pA + (1 - p)B$, which is exactly the same as the expected value e. Therefore since C is defined so that $U(C)$ is the expected utility of the lottery, we have the relation $U(C) = e$. Hence $C = U^{-1}(e)$, and thus the curve defined by $C(e)$ is the inverse of the utility function. The utility function is obtained by flipping the axes to obtain the inverse function, as shown in Figure 9.4(b).[3]

Example 9.3 (The venture capitalist) Sybil, a moderately successful venture capitalist, is anxious to make her utility function explicit. A consultant asks her to consider lotteries with outcomes of either $1M or $9M. She is asked to follow the direct procedure as the probability p of receiving $1M varies. For a 50–50 chance of the two outcomes, the expected value is $5M, but she assigns a certainty equivalent of $4M. Other values she assigns are shown in Table 9.1.

The utility function is also shown in Table 9.1, since $U(C) = e$. (We just read from the bottom row up to the next row to evaluate U.) For example, $U(4) = 5$. However, the values of C in the table are not all whole numbers, so the table is not in the form that one would most desire. A new table of utility values could be constructed

---

[3] If different values of A and B are used, a new utility function is obtained, which is equivalent to the original one; that is, it is just a linear transformation of the original one. (See Exercise 5.)

TABLE 9.1
Expected Utility Values and Certainty Equivalents

p	0	.1	.2	.3	.4	.5	.6	.7	.8	.9	1
e	9	8.2	7.4	6.6	5.8	5	4.2	3.4	2.6	1.8	1
C	9	7.84	6.76	5.76	4.84	4	3.24	2.56	1.96	1.44	1

by interpolating in Table 9.1. For example (although perhaps not obviously),

$$U(2) = \frac{3.4(2.00 - 1.96) + 2.6(2.56 - 2.00)}{2.56 - 1.96} = 2.65.$$

Parameter Families

Another simple method of assigning a utility function is to select a parameterized family of functions and then determine a suitable set of parameter values.

This technique is often carried out by assuming that the utility function is of the exponential form $U(x) = -e^{-ax}$. It is then only necessary to determine the parameter a, which is the risk aversion coefficient for this utility function. This parameter can be determined by evaluating a single lottery in certainty equivalent terms. For example, we might ask an investor how much he or she would accept in place of a lottery that offers a 50–50 chance of winning $1 million or $100,000. Suppose the investor felt that this was equivalent to a certain wealth of $400,000. We then set

$$-e^{-400,000a} = -.5e^{-1,000,000a} - .5e^{-100,000a}.$$

We can solve this (by an iterative procedure) to obtain $a = 1/\$623,426$.

Many people prefer to use a logarithmic or power utility function, since these functions have the property that risk aversion decreases with wealth. Indeed, for the logarithmic utility, the risk aversion coefficient is $a(x) = 1/x$, and for the power utility function $U(x) = \gamma x^\gamma$ the coefficient is $a(x) = (1 - \gamma)/x$. There are also good arguments based on the theory of Chapter 15, which suggest that these are appropriate utility functions for investors concerned with long-term growth of their wealth.

A compromise, or composite, approach that is commonly used is to recognize that while utility is a function of total wealth, most investment decisions involve relatively small increments to that wealth. Hence if x_0 is the initial wealth and w is the increment, the proper function is $U(x_0 + w)$. This is approximated by evaluating increments directly with an exponential utility function $-e^{-aw}$. However, if we assume that the true utility function is $\ln x$, then we use $a = 1/x_0$ in the exponential approximation.

Example 9.4 (Curve fitting)   The tabular results of Example 9.3 (for the venture capitalist Sybil) can be expressed compactly by fitting a curve to the results. If we assume a power utility function, it will have the form $U(x) = ax^\gamma + c$. Our normalization requires

$$a + c = 1$$

$$a9^\gamma + c = 9.$$

Thus $a = 8/(9^\gamma - 1)$ and $c = (9^\gamma - 9)/(9^\gamma - 1)$. Therefore it only remains to determine γ. We can find the best value to fit the values matching $U(C)$ to e in Table 9.1. We find (using a spreadsheet optimizer) that, in fact, $\gamma = \frac{1}{2}$ provides an excellent fit. Hence we set $U(x) = 4\sqrt{x} - 3$; or as an equivalent form, $V(x) = \sqrt{x}$.

Questionnaire Method

The risk aversion characteristics of an individual depend on the individual's feelings about risk, his or her current financial situation (such as net worth), the prospects for financial gains or requirements (such as college expenses), and the individual's age. One way, therefore, to attempt to deduce the appropriate risk factor and utility function for wealth increments is to administer a questionnaire such as the one shown in Figure 9.5, prepared by Fidelity Investments, Inc. This gives a good qualitative evaluation, and the results can be used to assign a specific function if desired.

In the questionnaire, note that five items (numbers 1, 6, 7, 8, 9) concern the investor's situation, five others (numbers 2, 4, 5, 11, 12) concern the investor's investment approach (mainly characterizing the level of comfort for risk), one item characterizes the market, and one item asks about the value of a managed fund. This questionnaire therefore reflects the notion that risk tolerance is determined both by internal feelings toward risk and by an investor's financial environment.

9.5 UTILITY FUNCTIONS AND THE MEAN–VARIANCE CRITERION*

The mean–variance criterion used in the Markowitz portfolio problem can be reconciled with the expected utility approach in either of two ways: (1) using a quadratic utility function, or (2) making the assumption that the random variables that characterize returns are normal (Gaussian) random variables. These two special cases are examined here.

Quadratic Utility

The quadratic utility function can be defined as $U(x) = ax - \frac{1}{2}bx^2$, where $a > 0$ and $b \geq 0$. This function is shown in Figure 9.6.

This utility function is really meaningful only in the range $x \leq a/b$, for it is in this range that the function is increasing. Note also that for $b > 0$ the function is strictly concave everywhere and thus exhibits risk aversion.

We assume that all random variables of interest lie in the feasible range $x \leq a/b$; that is, within the meaningful range of the quadratic utility function.

WHAT'S YOUR INVESTMENT "RQ"—RISK QUOTIENT?

This "Risk Quiz" is intended as a starting point at sessions between a client and a financial planner to help evaluate your tolerance for risk. It shouldn't be used to make specific investment decisions. Even if you haven't experienced a specific situation addressed here, answer based on what you think your decision would be if you faced the issue today.

1. My salary and overall earnings from my job are likely to grow significantly in the coming years.
a) Disagree strongly
b) Disagree
c) Neither agree nor disagree
d) Agree
e) Agree strongly

2. If I were deciding how to invest contributions in my retirement plan, I would choose investments that offered fixed yields and stability.
a) Agree strongly
b) Agree
c) Neither agree nor disagree
d) Disagree
e) Disagree strongly

3. I believe investing in today's volatile stock market is like spinning a roulette wheel in Las Vegas—the odds are against you.
a) Agree strongly
b) Agree
c) Neither agree nor disagree
d) Disagree
e) Disagree strongly

4. If I were picking a stock to invest in, I would look for companies that are involved in developing the hot products of the future, such as the next penicillin.
a) Disagree strongly
b) Disagree
c) Neither agree nor disagree
d) Agree
e) Agree strongly

5. If I were selecting an investment for my child's college education fund, I would choose:
a) Certificate of deposit
b) Government-backed mortgage securities or municipal bonds
c) Corporate bonds
d) Stocks equity mutual funds
e) Commodities futures contracts

6. The following number of dependents rely on me for their financial welfare.
a) Four or more
b) Three
c) Two
d) One
e) Only myself

7. The number of years remaining until I expect to retire is approximately:
a) Currently retired
b) Less than 5 years
c) 5–14 years
d) 15–24 years
e) 25 or more

8. My total net worth (the value of my assets less my debts) is:
a) Under $15,000
b) $15,001–$50,000
c) $50,001–$150,000
d) $150,001–$350,000
e) Over $350,000

9. The amount I have saved to handle emergencies, such as a job loss or unexpected medical expenses, equates to:
a) One month's salary or less
b) Two to six months' salary
c) Seven months' to one year's salary
d) One to two years' salary
e) More than two years' salary

10. I would rather invest in a stock mutual fund than buy individual stocks because a mutual fund provides professional management and diversification.
a) Agree strongly
b) Agree
c) Neither agree nor disagree
d) Disagree
e) Disagree strongly

11. I want and need to reduce the overall level of debt in my personal finances.
a) Agree strongly
b) Agree
c) Neither agree nor disagree
d) Disagree
e) Disagree strongly

12. When making investments, I am willing to settle for a lower yield if it is guaranteed, as opposed to higher yields that are less certain.
a) Strongly agree
b) Agree
c) Neither agree nor disagree
d) Disagree
e) Strongly disagree

Scoring System

SCORING: Give yourself one point for every "a" answer, two points for every "b," three points for every "c," four points for every "d" and five points for every "e."

46 AND HIGHER: You probably have the money and the inclination to take risks. High-risk investments include growth stocks, start-up companies, commodities, junk bonds and limited partnerships, as well as stock options and investment real estate. But be sure to diversify at least some of your portfolio into safer investments. Even you could lose everything and regret your high-risk tolerance.

41–45: You have an above-average tolerance for risk and probably enough time and income to cover your losses. Investors in this category are wise to mix high-risk and low-risk options.

36–40: You have an average tolerance for risk, but don't like to gamble. Consider a mix of long-term investments that have a history of strong and steady performance. Blue chip stocks, high-grade corporate bonds, mutual funds and real estate are all possible options.

31–35: You have below-average tolerance for risk, either because of your age or your income and family circumstances. Comfortable investments for you would probably include your home, high-quality bonds, government-backed securities and federally insured savings accounts.

30 and below: You have virtually no tolerance for risk. Look for investments that have government backing, such as bank and thrift certificates of deposit, Treasury bills, bonds and notes.

FIGURE 9.5   Risk quiz. An investor's attitude toward risk and toward type of investment might be inferred from responses to a questionnaire such as this one. Source: *Fidelity Investments,* 1991. Developed in association with Andrew Comrey, Ph.D., Professor of Psychology, University of California at Los Angeles.

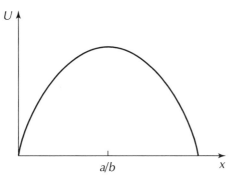

FIGURE 9.6   Quadratic utility function. This function is meaningful as a utility function only for $x < a/b$.

Suppose that a portfolio has a random wealth value of y. Using the expected utility criterion we evaluate the portfolio using the value

$$E[U(y)] = E(ay - \tfrac{1}{2}by^2)$$

$$= a\,E(y) - \tfrac{1}{2}bE(y^2)$$

$$= a\,E(y) - \tfrac{1}{2}b\left[E(y)\right]^2 - \tfrac{1}{2}b\,\mathrm{var}(y)\,.$$

The optimal portfolio is the one that maximizes this value with respect to all feasible choices of the random wealth variable y.

This can be seen to be equivalent to a mean–variance approach. First, for convenience, suppose that the initial wealth is 1. Then y corresponds exactly to the return R. Suppose also that the solution has an expected value $E(y) = M$. Then clearly, y must have minimum variance with respect to all feasible y's with $E(y) = M = 1 + m$ (where m is the mean rate of return). Since $y = R$, it follows that the solution must correspond to a mean–variance efficient point.

Different mean–variance efficient points are obtained by selecting different values for the parameters a and b. Likewise, if the initial wealth is not 1, a different factor is introduced. (See Exercise 5.)

Normal Returns

When all returns are normal random variables, the mean–variance criterion is also equivalent to the expected utility approach for any risk-averse utility function. To deduce this, select a utility function U. Consider a random wealth variable y that is a normal random variable with mean value M and standard deviation σ. Since the probability distribution is completely defined by M and σ, it follows that the expected utility is a function of M and σ; that is,

$$E[U(y)] = f(M, \sigma).$$

(It may be impossible to determine the function f in closed form, but that does not matter.) If U is risk averse, then $f(M, \sigma)$ will be increasing with respect to M and decreasing with respect to σ. Now suppose that the returns of all assets are normal random variables. Then (and this is the key property) any linear combination of these assets is a normal random variable, with some mean and standard deviation. (See Appendix A.) Hence any portfolio of these assets will have a return that is a normal random variable. The portfolio problem is therefore equivalent to the selection of that combination of assets that maximizes the function $f(M, \sigma)$ with respect to all feasible combinations. For a risk-averse utility this again implies that the variance should be minimized for any given value of the mean. In other words, the solution must be mean–variance efficient. Therefore the mean–variance criterion is appropriate when all returns are normal random variables.

9.6 LINEAR PRICING

We now turn attention to a fundamental property of security pricing—namely, that of linearity. We shall find that this property has profound implications and by itself explains much of the theory developed in previous chapters. (The remaining sections of the chapter might be best read after completing Part 3.)

We formalize the definition of a **security** as a random payoff variable, say, d. The payoff is revealed and obtained at the end of the period. (The payoff can be thought of as a dividend, which justifies the use of the letter d.) Associated with a security is a price P. As an example, we can imagine a security that pays $d = \$10$ if it rains tomorrow or $d = -\$10$ if it is sunny, with zero initial price. (This would correspond to a $10 bet that it will rain.) Or we could consider a share of IBM stock whose value at the end of a year is unknown. The payoff d is that random value. The price is the current price of a share of IBM.

Type A Arbitrage

Linear pricing of securities follows from an assumption that the most basic form of arbitrage is not possible. We define this basic form of arbitrage as follows. If an investment produces an immediate positive reward with no future payoff (either positive or negative), that investment is said to be a **type A arbitrage.**

In other words, if you invest in a type A arbitrage, you obtain money immediately and never have to pay anything. You invest in a security that pays zero with certainty but has a negative price. It seems quite reasonable to assume that such things do not exist.

To see that linear pricing follows from the assumption that there is no possibility of type A arbitrage, suppose that d is a security with price P. Consider the security $2d$ that always pays exactly twice what d pays. Suppose that its price were $P' < 2P$. Then we could buy this double security at the reduced price, and then break it apart and sell the two halves at price P for each half. We would obtain a net profit of $2P - P'$ and then have no further obligation, since we sold what we bought. We have an immediate profit, and hence have found a type A arbitrage. This argument can be reversed to show that the price of the double security cannot be greater than $2P$. The argument also can be extended to show that for any real number α the price of αd must be αP.

Likewise, if d_1 and d_2 are securities with prices P_1 and P_2, the price of the security $d_1 + d_2$ must be $P_1 + P_2$. For if the price of $d_1 + d_2$ were $P' < P_1 + P_2$, we could purchase the combined security for P', then break it into d_1 and d_2 and sell these for P_1 and P_2, respectively. As a result we would obtain a profit of $P_1 + P_2 - P' > 0$. As before, this argument can be reversed if $P' > P_1 + P_2$. Hence the price of $d_1 + d_2$ must be $P_1 + P_2$. In general, therefore, the price of $\alpha d_1 + \beta d_2$ must be equal to $\alpha P_1 + \beta P_2$. This is **linear pricing.**[4]

In addition to the absence of type A arbitrage, the preceding argument assumes an ideal functioning of the market: it assumes that securities can be arbitrarily divided into two pieces, and it assumes that there are no transactions costs. In practice these requirements are not met perfectly, but when dealing with large numbers of shares of traded securities in highly liquid markets, they are closely met.

Portfolios

Suppose now that there are n securities $d_1, d_2, \ldots, d_n$. A **portfolio** of these securities is represented by an n–dimensional vector $\theta = (\theta_1, \theta_2, \ldots, \theta_n)$. The ith component θ_i represents the amount of security i in the portfolio. The payoff of the portfolio is the random variable

$$d = \sum_{i=1}^{n} \theta_i d_i.$$

Under the assumption of no type A arbitrage, the price of the portfolio θ is found by linearity. Thus the total price is

$$P = \sum_{i=1}^{n} \theta_i P_i$$

which is a more general expression of linear pricing.

Recall that the CAPM formula in pricing form is linear.

Type B Arbitrage

Another form of arbitrage can be identified. If an investment has nonpositive cost but has a positive probability of yielding a positive payoff and no probability of yielding a negative payoff, that investment is said to be a **type B arbitrage.**

In other words, a type B arbitrage is a situation where an individual pays nothing (or a negative amount) and has a chance of getting something. An example would be a free lottery ticket—you pay nothing for the ticket, but have a chance of winning a prize. Clearly, such tickets are rare in securities markets.

The two types of arbitrage are distinguished only for clarity of the concepts involved. In further developments we shall usually assume that neither type A nor

---

[4]Linear pricing also follows from the **law of one price:** if $d_1 = d_2$ then $P_1 = P_2$.

type B is possible, and we shall just say that there is **no arbitrage possibility.** However, we have shown that ruling out type A is all that is needed to establish linear pricing. Ruling out type B as well allows us to develop stronger relations, as shown in the next section.

9.7 PORTFOLIO CHOICE

We are now prepared to put many of the earlier sections of this chapter together and consider the portfolio problem of an investor who uses an expected utility criterion to rank alternatives.

If x is a random variable, we write $x \geq 0$ to indicate that the variable is never less than zero. We write $x > 0$ to indicate that the variable is never less than zero and it is strictly positive with some positive probability.

Suppose that an investor has a strictly increasing utility function U and an initial wealth W. There are n securities $d_1, d_2, \ldots, d_n$. The investor wishes to form a portfolio to maximize the expected utility of final wealth, say, x. We let the portfolio be defined by $\theta = (\theta_1, \theta_2, \ldots, \theta_n)$, which gives the amounts of the various securities. The investor's problem is

$$\text{maximize} \quad E[U(x)] \tag{9.3a}$$

$$\text{subject to} \quad \sum_{i=1}^{n} \theta_i d_i = x \tag{9.3b}$$

$$x \geq 0 \tag{9.3c}$$

$$\sum_{i=1}^{n} \theta_i P_i \leq W. \tag{9.3d}$$

This problem states that the investor must select a portfolio with total cost no greater than the initial wealth W (the last constraint), that the final wealth x is defined by the portfolio choice (the first constraint), that this final wealth must be nonnegative in every possible outcome (the second constraint), and that the investor wishes to maximize the expected utility of this final wealth.

We now show how this problem is connected to the arbitrage concepts.

 Portfolio choice theorem   *Suppose that $U(x)$ is continuous and increases toward infinity as $x \to \infty$. Suppose also that there is a portfolio θ^0 such that $\sum_{i=1}^{n} \theta_i^0 d_i > 0$. Then the optimal portfolio problem (9.3a) has a solution if and only if there is no arbitrage possibility.*

> **Proof:**   We shall only prove the *only if* portion of the theorem. Suppose that there is a type A arbitrage produced by a portfolio $\theta = (\theta_1, \theta_2, \ldots, \theta_n)$. Using this portfolio, it is possible to obtain additional initial wealth without affecting the final payoff. Hence arbitrary amounts of the portfolio θ^0 can be purchased. This implies that $E[U(x)]$ does not have a maximum, because given a feasible portfolio, that portfolio can be supplemented by arbitrary amounts of θ^0 to

increase $E[U(x)]$. If there is a type B arbitrage, it is possible to obtain (at zero or negative cost) an asset that has payoff $\overline{x} > 0$ (with nonzero probability of being positive). We can acquire arbitrarily large amounts of this asset to increase $E[U(x)]$ arbitrarily. Hence if there is a solution, there can be no type A or type B arbitrage. ∎

We can go further than the preceding result on the existence of a solution and actually characterize the solution. We assume that there are no arbitrage opportunities and hence there is an optimal portfolio, which we denote by θ^*. We also assume that the corresponding payoff $x^* = \sum_{i=1}^{n} \theta_i^* d_i$ satisfies $x^* > 0$. We can immediately deduce that the inequality $\sum_{i=1}^{n} \theta_i P_i \leq W$ will be met with equality at the solution; otherwise some positive fraction of the portfolio θ^0 (or θ^*) could be added to improve the result.

To derive the equations satisfied by the solution, we substitute $x = \sum_{i=1}^{n} \theta_i d_i$ in the objective and ignore the constraint $x \geq 0$ since we have assumed that it is satisfied by strict inequality. The problem therefore becomes

$$\text{maximize} \quad E\left[U\left(\sum_{i=1}^{n} \theta_i d_i\right)\right]$$

$$\text{subject to} \quad \sum_{i=1}^{n} \theta_i P_i = W.$$

By introducing a Lagrange multiplier λ for the constraint, and using $x^* = \sum_{i=1}^{n} \theta_i^* d_i$ for the payoff of the optimal portfolio, the necessary conditions are found by differentiating the Lagrangian (see Appendix B)

$$L = E\left[U\left(\sum_{i=1}^{n} \theta_i d_i\right)\right] - \lambda\left(\sum_{i=1}^{n} \theta_i P_i - W\right)$$

with respect to each θ_i. This gives

$$E[U'(x^*)d_i] = \lambda P_i \tag{9.4}$$

for $i = 1, 2, \ldots, n$. This represents n equations. The original budget constraint $\sum_{i=1}^{n} \theta_i P_i = W$ is one more equation. Altogether, therefore, there are $n + 1$ equations for the $n + 1$ unknowns $\theta_1, \theta_2, \ldots, \theta_n$ and λ. It can be shown that $\lambda > 0$.

These equations are *very* important because they serve two roles. First, and most obviously, they give enough equations to actually solve the optimal portfolio problem. An example of such a solution is given soon in Example 9.5. Second, since these equations are valid if there are no arbitrage opportunities, they provide a valuable characterization of prices under the assumption of no arbitrage. This use of the equations is explained in the next section.

If there is a risk-free asset with total return R, then (9.4) must apply when $d_i = R$ and $P_i = 1$. Thus,

$$\lambda = E[U'(x^*)]R.$$

Substituting this value of λ in (9.4) yields

$$\frac{E[U'(x^*)d_i]}{R\,E[U'(x^*)]} = P_i.$$

Because of the importance of these equations, we now highlight them:

 Portfolio pricing equation   *If $x^* = \sum_{i=1}^{n} \theta_i^* d_i$ is a solution to the optimal portfolio problem (9.3a), then*

$$E[U'(x^*)d_i] = \lambda P_i \qquad (9.5)$$

for $i = 1, 2, \ldots, n$, where $\lambda > 0$. If there is a risk-free asset with return R, then

$$\frac{E[U'(x^*)d_i]}{R\,E[U'(x^*)]} = P_i \qquad (9.6)$$

for $i = 1, 2, \ldots, n$.

Example 9.5 (A film venture)   An investor is considering the possibility of investing in a venture to produce an entertainment film. He has learned that such ventures are quite risky. In this particular case he has learned that there are essentially three possible outcomes, as shown in Table 9.2: (1) with probability .3 his investment will be multiplied by a factor of 3, (2) with probability .4 the factor will be 1, and (3) with probability .3 he will lose the entire investment. One of these outcomes will occur in 2 years. He also has the opportunity to earn 20% risk free over this period. He wants to know whether he should invest money in the film venture; and if so, how much?

This is a simplification of a fairly realistic situation. The expected return is $.3 \times 3 + .4 \times 1 + .3 \times 0 = 1.3$, which is somewhat better than what can be obtained risk free. How much would *you* invest in such a venture? Think about it for a moment.

The investor decides to use $U(x) = \ln x$ as a utility function. This is an excellent general choice (as will be explained in Chapter 15). His problem is to select amounts θ_1 and θ_2 of the two available securities, the film venture and the risk-free opportunity,

TABLE 9.2
The Film Venture

	Return	Probability
High success	3.0	0.3
Moderate success	1.0	0.4
Failure	0.0	0.3
Risk free	1.2	1.0

There are three possible outcomes with associated total returns and probabilities shown. There is also a risk-free opportunity with total return 1.2.

each of which has a unit price of 1. Hence his problem is to select (θ_1, θ_2) to solve

$$\text{maximize } [.3 \ln(3\theta_1 + 1.2\theta_2) + .4 \ln(\theta_1 + 1.2\theta_2) + .3 \ln(1.2\theta_2)]$$

$$\text{subject to } \theta_1 + \theta_2 = W.$$

The necessary conditions from (9.5), or by direct calculation, are

$$\frac{.9}{3\theta_1 + 1.2\theta_2} + \frac{.4}{\theta_1 + 1.2\theta_2} = \lambda$$

$$\frac{.36}{3\theta_1 + 1.2\theta_2} + \frac{.48}{\theta_1 + 1.2\theta_2} + \frac{.36}{1.2\theta_2} = \lambda.$$

These two equations, together with the constraint $\theta_1 + \theta_2 = W$, can be solved for the unknowns θ_1, θ_2, and λ. (A quadratic equation must be solved.) The result is $\theta_1 = .089W$, $\theta_2 = .911W$, and $\lambda = 1/W$. In other words, the investor should commit 8.9% of his wealth to this venture; the rest should be placed in the risk-free security.

Example 9.6 (Residual rights) While pondering the possibility of investing in the film venture of the previous example, an investor discovers that it is also possible to invest in film residuals, which have a large payoff if the film is highly successful. Each dollar invested in residual rights produces \$6 if the venture has high success and zero in the other two cases. Now what should the investor do?

He must solve the portfolio optimization problem again with this new information. There are now three securities: the original film venture, the risk-free alternative, and residual rights. He will purchase these in amounts θ_1, θ_2, and θ_3, respectively. The necessary equations are

$$\frac{.9}{3\theta_1 + 1.2\theta_2 + 6\theta_3} + \frac{.4}{\theta_1 + 1.2\theta_2} = \lambda$$

$$\frac{.36}{3\theta_1 + 1.2\theta_2 + 6\theta_3} + \frac{.48}{\theta_1 + 1.2\theta_2} + \frac{.36}{1.2\theta_2} = \lambda$$

$$\frac{1.8}{3\theta_1 + 1.2\theta_2 + 6\theta_3} = \lambda.$$

In addition there is the wealth constraint $\theta_1 + \theta_2 + \theta_3 = W$. These equations have solution $\theta_1 = -1.0W, \theta_2 = 1.5W, \theta_3 = .5W$, and $\lambda = 1/W$. In other words, the investor should short the ordinary film venture by an amount equal to his total wealth in order to invest in the other two alternatives.

9.8 LOG-OPTIMAL PRICING*

The portfolio pricing formula

$$\text{E}[U'(x^*)d_i] = \lambda P_i, \qquad i = 1, 2, \ldots, n \tag{9.7}$$

of the previous section is a general result with many important ramifications. It can be transformed to produce a variety of convenient special pricing formulas. This section presents one especially elegant version.

The main idea of these pricing relations is to turn the equation around to give an expression for the prices P_i. Remember that the prices were already known, and we used them to find the optimal x^*. Now we are going to use the optimal x^* to recover the prices. That is all there is to it.

We shall choose $U(x) = \ln x$ and $W = 1$ as a special case to investigate. The final wealth variable x^* is then the one that is associated with the portfolio that maximizes the expected logarithm of final wealth. In this special case we denote this x^* by R^*, since R^* is the return that is optimal for the logarithmic utility. We refer to R^* as the **log-optimal return.**

Since $d \ln x / dx = 1/x$, the pricing equation (9.7) becomes

$$E\left(\frac{d_i}{R^*}\right) = \lambda P_i \tag{9.8}$$

for all i. Since this is valid for every security i, it is, by linearity, valid for the log-optimal portfolio itself. This portfolio has price 1, and therefore we find that

$$1 = E\left(\frac{R^*}{R^*}\right) = \lambda.$$

Thus we have found the value of λ for this case.

If there is a risk-free asset, the portfolio pricing equation (9.7) is valid for it as well. The risk-free asset has a payoff identically equal to 1 and price $1/R$, where R is the total risk-free return. Hence we find

$$E(1/R^*) = 1/R.$$

Therefore we know that the expected value of $1/R^*$ is equal to $1/R$.

Using the value of $\lambda = 1$, the pricing equation (9.8) becomes

$$P_i = E\left(\frac{d_i}{R^*}\right).$$

Since this is true for any security i, it is, by linearity, also true for any portfolio. Hence we have the following general pricing result:

Log-optimal pricing   *The price P of any security (or portfolio) with dividend d is*

$$P = E\left(\frac{d}{R^*}\right) \tag{9.9}$$

where R^* is the return on the log-optimal portfolio.

Isn't this a simple and easily remembered result? The formula looks very similar to the expression $P = d/R$ that would hold in the case where d is deterministic. In the random case we just substitute R^* for R and put an expected value in front. If d happens to be deterministic, this more general result reduces to the simple one because $E(1/R^*) = 1/R$.

Example 9.7 (Film variations)   Suppose that a new security is proposed with payoffs that depend only on the possible outcomes of the film venture. For example, one might propose an investment that paid back something even if the venture was a failure. A general security of this type will have payoffs d^1, d^2, and d^3, corresponding to high success, moderate success, and failure, respectively. We can find the appropriate price of such a security by using the log-optimal portfolio that we calculated in Example 9.6.

Note that we cannot use the simple log-optimal portfolio of the first film venture example, because that example only considered the film venture and the risk-free security. If a new security were a combination of those two, then we could use the simple log-optimal portfolio for pricing. But if the new security is a general one, we must use the log-optimal portfolio of the second example, since it includes a complete set of three securities for the three possibilities. Any new security will be a combination of these three.

The log-optimal portfolio has the following return:

	High Success	Moderate Success	Failure
R^*	1.8	.8	1.8

These returns are calculated from the θ_i's found in the residual rights example. For example, under high success $R^* = -1.0 \times 3 + 1.5 \times 1.2 + .5 \times 6 = 1.8$.

The value of a security with payoffs d^1, d^2, d^3 is $\mathrm{E}(d/R^*)$, which is

$$P = .3\frac{d^1}{1.8} + .4\frac{d^2}{.8} + .3\frac{d^3}{1.8}.$$

You can try this on the three securities we have used before; their prices should all turn out to be 1. For example, for the original venture, $P = .3\frac{3}{1.8} + .4\frac{1}{.8} = \frac{1}{2} + \frac{1}{2} = 1$.

We shall return to this log-optimal pricing equation in Chapter 15. For the moment we may regard it simply as a special version of the general pricing equation—the version obtained by using $\ln x$ as the utility function.

Remember what is happening here. The prices of the original securities were used to find x^*. Now we use x^* to find those prices again. However, since pricing is linear, we can find the price of any security that is a linear combination of the original ones by the same formula.

What about a new security d that is not a linear combination of the original ones? We could enter it into the pricing equation as well, but the price obtained this way may not be correct. The formula is valid only for the securities used to derive it, or for a linear combination of those original securities.

9.9 FINITE STATE MODELS

Suppose that there are a finite number of possible **states** that describe the possible outcomes of a specific investment situation (see Figure 9.7). At the initial time it is known only that one of these states will occur. At the end of the period, one specific state will be revealed. Sometimes states describe certain physical phenomena. For example, we might define two weather states for tomorrow: sunny and rainy. We do not know today which of these will occur, but tomorrow this uncertainty will be

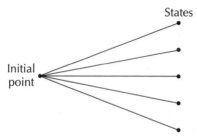

States   **FIGURE 9.7   States.** States represent uncertainty in a simple but effective manner.

Initial point

resolved. Or, as another example, the states may correspond to economic events, as in the film venture example, which has the three possible states of high success, moderate success, and failure. Normally we index the possible states by numbers $\{1, 2, \ldots, S\}$.

States define uncertainty in a very basic manner. It is not even necessary to introduce probabilities of the states, although this will be done later. Indeed, one of the main points of this section is that a great deal can be said without reference to probabilities. In an important sense, probabilities are irrelevant for pricing relations.

A **security** is defined within the context of states as a set of payoffs—one payoff for each possible state (again without reference to probabilities). Hence a security is represented by a vector of the form $d = \langle d^1, d^2, \ldots, d^S \rangle$. We use the notation $\langle \ \rangle$ to denote vectors whose components are state payoffs. In this case, the component $d^s, s = 1, 2, \ldots, S$, represents the payoff that is obtained if state s occurs. As before, associated with a security is a price P. Our earlier example, at the beginning of Section 9.6, of a security that pays \$10 if it rains tomorrow and $-\$10$ if it is sunny (with zero price), works here as well; and it is not necessary to specify probabilities. This security is represented as $\langle 10, -10 \rangle$.

State Prices

A special form of security is one that has a payoff in only one state. Indeed, we can define the S **elementary state securities** $e_s = \langle 0, 0, \ldots, 0, 1, 0, \ldots, 0 \rangle$, where the 1 is the component s for $s = 1, 2, \ldots, S$. If such a security exists, we denote its price by ψ_s.

When a complete set of state securities exists (one for each state), it is easy to determine the price of any other security. The security $d = \langle d^1, d^2, \ldots, d^S \rangle$ can be expressed as a combination of the elementary state securities as $d = \sum_{s=1}^{S} d^s e_s$, and hence by the linearity of pricing, the price of d must be

$$P = \sum_{s=1}^{S} d^s \psi_s. \tag{9.10}$$

If the elementary state securities do not exist, it may be possible to construct them artificially by combining securities that do exist. For example, in a two-state world, if $\langle 1, 1 \rangle$ and $\langle 1, -1 \rangle$ exist, then one-half the sum of these two securities is equivalent to the first elementary state security $\langle 1, 0 \rangle$.

Positive State Prices

If a complete set of elementary securities exists or can be constructed as a combination of existing securities, it is important that their prices be positive. Otherwise there would be an arbitrage opportunity. To see this, suppose an elementary state security e_s had a zero or negative price. That security would then present the possibility of obtaining something (a payoff of 1 if the state s occurs) for nonpositive cost. This is type B arbitrage. So if elementary state securities actually exist or can be constructed as combinations of other securities, their prices must be positive to avoid arbitrage.

Actually, the condition of no arbitrage possibility is equivalent to the existence of positive state prices as established by the following theorem:

Positive state prices theorem *A set of positive state prices exists if and only if there are no arbitrage opportunities.*

Proof: Suppose first that there are positive state prices. Then it is clear that no arbitrage is possible. To see this, suppose a security d can be constructed with $d \geq 0$. We have $d = (d^1, d^2, \ldots, d^S)$ with $d^s \geq 0$ for each $s = 1, 2, \ldots, S$. The price of d is $P = \sum_{s=1}^{S} \psi_s d^s$, which since $\psi_s > 0$ for all s, gives $P \geq 0$. Indeed $P > 0$ if $d \neq 0$ and $P = 0$ if $d = 0$. Hence there is no arbitrage possibility.

To prove the converse, we assume that there are no arbitrage opportunities, and we make use of the result on the portfolio choice problem of Section 9.7. This proof requires some additional assumptions. (A more general proof is outlined in Exercise 12.) We assume there is a portfolio θ^0 such that $\sum_{i=1}^{n} \theta_i^0 d_i > 0$. We assign positive probabilities $p_s, s = 1, 2, \ldots, S$, to the states arbitrarily, with $\sum_{s=1}^{S} p_s = 1$, and we select a strictly increasing utility function U. Since there is no arbitrage, there is, by the portfolio choice theorem of Section 9.8, a solution to the optimal portfolio choice problem. We assume that the optimal payoff has $x^* > 0$. The necessary conditions (9.5) show that for any security d with price P,

$$E[U'(x^*)d] = \lambda P \qquad (9.11)$$

where x^* is the (random) payoff of the optimal portfolio and $\lambda > 0$ is the Lagrange multiplier.

If we expand this equation to show the details of the expected value operation, we find

$$P = \frac{1}{\lambda} \sum_{s=1}^{S} p_s U'(x^*)^s d^s$$

where $U'(x^*)^s$ is the value of $U'(x^*)$ in state s.

Now we define

$$\psi_s = \frac{p_s U'(x^*)^s}{\lambda}. \qquad (9.12)$$

We see that $\psi_s > 0$ because $p_s > 0$, $U'(x^*)^s > 0$, and $\lambda > 0$. We also have

$$P = \sum_{s=1}^{S} \psi_s d^s$$

showing that the ψ_s's are state prices. They are all positive. ∎

Note that the theorem says that such positive prices exist—it does not say that they are unique. If there are more states than securities, there may be many different ways to assign state prices that are consistent with the prices of the existing securities. The theorem only says that for one of these ways the state prices are positive.

Example 9.8 (The plain film venture) Consider again the original film venture. There are three states, but only two securities: the venture itself and the riskless security. Hence state prices are not unique.

We can find a set of positive state prices by using (9.12) and the values of the θ_i's and $\lambda = 1$ found in Example 9.5 (with $W = 1$). We have

$$\psi_1 = \frac{.3}{3\theta_1 + 1.2\theta_2} = .221$$

$$\psi_2 = \frac{.4}{\theta_1 + 1.2\theta_2} = .338$$

$$\psi_3 = \frac{.3}{1.2\theta_2} = .274.$$

These state prices can be used only to price combinations of the original two securities. They could not be applied, for example, to the purchase of residual rights. To check the price of the original venture we have $P = 3 \times .221 + .338 = 1$, as it should be.

Example 9.9 (Expanded film venture) Now consider the film venture with three available securities, as discussed in Example 9.6, which introduces residual rights. Since there are three states and three securities, the state prices are unique. Indeed we may find the state prices by setting the price of the three securities to 1, obtaining

$$
\begin{aligned}
3\psi_1 + \psi_2 &= 1 \\
1.2\psi_1 + 1.2\psi_2 + 1.2\psi_3 &= 1 \\
6\psi_1 &= 1.
\end{aligned}
$$

This system has the solution

$$\psi_1 = \tfrac{1}{6}, \qquad \psi_2 = \tfrac{1}{2}, \qquad \psi_3 = \tfrac{1}{6}.$$

Therefore the price of a security with payoff $\langle d^1, d^2, d^3 \rangle$ is

$$P = \tfrac{1}{6}d^1 + \tfrac{1}{2}d^2 + \tfrac{1}{6}d^3.$$

You can compare this with the formula for P given at the end of Example 9.7. It is exactly the same.

Note also that these state prices, although different from those of the preceding example, give the same values for prices of securities that are combinations of just the two in the original film venture. For example, the price of the basic venture itself is $P = \frac{3}{6} + \frac{1}{2} = 1$.

9.10 RISK-NEUTRAL PRICING

Suppose there are positive state prices $\psi_s, s = 1, 2, \ldots, S$. Then the price of any security $d = \langle d^1, d^2, \ldots, d^S \rangle$ can be found from

$$P = \sum_{s=1}^{S} d^s \psi_s.$$

We now normalize these state prices so that they sum to 1. Hence we let $\psi_0 = \sum_{s=1}^{S} \psi_s$, and let $q_s = \psi_s / \psi_0$. We can then write the pricing formula as

$$P = \psi_0 \sum_{s=1}^{S} q_s d^s. \tag{9.13}$$

The quantities $q_s, s = 1, 2, \ldots, S$, can be thought of as (artificial) probabilities, since they are positive and sum to 1. Using these as probabilities, we can write the pricing formula as

$$P = \psi_0 \hat{E}(d) \tag{9.14}$$

where $\hat{E}$ denotes expectation with respect to the artificial probabilities q_s.

The value ψ_0 has a useful interpretation. Since $\psi_0 = \sum_{s=1}^{S} \psi_s$, we see that ψ_0 is the price of the security $\langle 1, 1, \ldots, 1 \rangle$ that pays 1 in every state—a risk-free bond. By definition, its price is $1/R$, where R is the risk-free return. Thus we can write the pricing formula as

$$P = \frac{1}{R}\hat{E}(d). \tag{9.15}$$

This equation states that the price of a security is equal to the discounted expected value of its payoff, under the artificial probabilities. We term this **risk-neutral pricing** since it is exactly the formula that we would use if the q_s's were real probabilities and we used a risk-neutral utility function (that is, the linear utility function). We also refer to the q_s's as **risk-neutral probabilities.**

This artifice is deceptive in its simplicity; we shall find in the coming chapters that it has profound consequences. In fact a major portion of Part 3 is elaboration of this simple idea. Here are three ways to find the risk-neutral probabilities q_s:

(a) The risk-neutral probabilities can be found from positive state prices by multiplying those prices by the risk-free rate. This is how we defined the risk-neutral probabilities at the beginning of this section.

(b) If the positive state prices were found from a portfolio problem and there is a risk-free asset, we can use (9.6) to define

$$q_s = \frac{p_s U'(x^*)^s}{\sum_{t=1}^{S} p_t U'(x^*)^t} \, . \tag{9.16}$$

This formula will be useful in our later work.

(c) If there are n states and at least n independent securities with known prices, and no arbitrage possibility, then the risk-neutral probabilities can be found directly by solving the system of equations

$$P_i = \frac{1}{R} \sum_{s=1}^{S} q_s d_i^s, \qquad i = 1, 2, \dots, n$$

for the n unknown q_s's.

Example 9.10 (The film venture)   We found the state prices of the full film venture (with three securities) to be

$$\psi_1 = \tfrac{1}{6}, \qquad \psi_2 = \tfrac{1}{2}, \qquad \psi_3 = \tfrac{1}{6}.$$

Multiplying these by the risk-free rate 1.2, we obtain the risk-neutral probabilities

$$q_1 = .2, \qquad q_2 = .6, \qquad q_3 = .2.$$

Hence the price of a security with payoff $\langle d^1, d^2, d^3 \rangle$ is

$$P = \frac{.2d^1 + .6d_2 + .2d_3}{1.2}.$$

Here again, this pricing formula is valid only for the original securities or linear combinations of those securities. The risk-neutral probabilities were derived explicitly to price the original securities.

The risk-neutral pricing result can be extended to the general situation that does not assume that there are a finite number of states. (See Exercise 15.)

9.11 PRICING ALTERNATIVES*

Let us review some alternative pricing methods. Suppose that there is an environment of n securities for which prices are known, and then a new security is introduced, defined by the (random) cash flow d to be obtained at the end of the period. What is the correct price of that new security? Listed here are five alternative ways we might assign it a price. In each case R is the one-period risk-free return.

1. *Discounted expected value:*

$$P = \frac{E(d)}{R}.$$

2. *CAPM pricing:*

$$P = \frac{E(d)}{R + \beta(\overline{R}_M - R)}$$

where β is the beta of the asset with respect to the market, and R_M is the return on the market portfolio. We assume that the market portfolio is equal to the Markowitz fund of risky assets.

3. *Certainty equivalent form of CAPM:*

$$P = \frac{E(d) - \text{cov}(R_M, d)(\overline{R}_M - R)/\sigma_M^2}{R}.$$

4. *Log-optimal pricing:*

$$P = E\left(\frac{d}{R^*}\right)$$

where R^* is the return on the log-optimal portfolio.

5. *Risk-neutral pricing:*

$$P = \frac{\hat{E}(d)}{R}$$

where the expectation $\hat{E}$ is taken with respect to the risk-neutral probabilities.

Method 1 is the simplest extension of what is true for the deterministic case. In general, however, the price determined this way is too large (at least for assets that are positively correlated with all others). The price usually must be reduced. Method 2 reduces the answer obtained in 1 by increasing the denominator. This method essentially increases the discount rate. Method 3 reduces the answer obtained in 1 by decreasing the numerator, replacing it with a certainty equivalent. Method 4 reduces the answer obtained in 1 by putting the return R^* inside the expectation. Although $E(1/R^*) = 1/R$, the resulting price usually will be smaller than that of method 1. Method 5 reduces the answer obtained in 1 by changing the probabilities used to calculate the expected value.

Methods 2–5 represent four different ways to modify method 1 to get a more appropriate result. What are the differences between these four modified methods? That is, how will the prices obtained by the different formulas differ? Think about it for a moment. The answer, of course, is that if the new security is a linear combination of the original n securities, all four of the modified methods give *identical* prices. Each method is a way of expressing linear pricing.

If d is not a linear combination of these n securities, the prices assigned by the different formulas may differ, for these formulas are then being applied outside the domain for which they were derived. Methods 2 and 3 will always yield identical values. Methods 3 and 4 will yield identical values if the log-optimal formula is used to calculate the risk-neutral probabilities. Otherwise they will differ as well.

If the cash flow d is completely independent of the n original securities, then *all five* methods, including the first, will produce the identical price. (Check it!)

We can obtain additional methods by specifying other utility functions in the optimal portfolio problem. For the n original securities, the price so obtained is independent of the utility function employed. However, the methods presented here seem to be the most useful.

9.12 SUMMARY

This chapter is devoted to general theory, and hence it is somewhat more abstract than other chapters, but the tools presented are quite powerful. The chapter should be reviewed after reading Part 3 and again after reading Part 4.

The first part of the chapter presents the basics of expected utility theory. Utility functions account for risk aversion in financial decision making, and provide a more general and more useful approach than does the mean–variance framework. In this new approach, an uncertain final wealth level is evaluated by computing the expected value of the utility of the wealth. One random wealth level is preferred to another if the expected utility of the first is greater than that of the second. Often the utility function is expressed in analytic form. Commonly used functions are: exponential, logarithmic, power, and quadratic. A utility function $U(x)$ can be transformed to $V(x) = aU(x)+b$ with $a > 0$, and the new function V is equivalent to U for decision-making purposes.

It is generally assumed that a utility function is increasing, since more wealth is preferred to less. A utility function exhibits risk aversion if it is concave. If the utility function has derivatives and is both increasing and concave, then $U'(x) > 0$ and $U''(x) < 0$.

Corresponding to a random wealth level, there is a number C, called the certainty equivalent of that random wealth. The certainty equivalent is the minimum (nonrandom) amount that an investor with utility function U would accept in place of the random wealth under consideration. The value C is defined such that $U(C)$ is equal to the expected utility due to the random wealth level.

In order to use the utility function approach, an appropriate utility function must be selected. One way to make this selection is to assess the certain equivalents of various lotteries, and then work backward to find the underlying utility function that would assign those certain equivalent values.

Frequently the utility function is assumed to be either the exponential form $-e^{-ax}$ with a approximately equal to the reciprocal of total wealth, the logarithmic form $\ln x$, or a power form γx^γ with $\gamma < 1$ but close to 0. The parameters of the function are either fit to lottery responses or deduced from the answers to a series of questions about an investor's financial situation and attitudes toward risk.

The second part of the chapter presents the outline of a general theory of linear pricing. In perfect markets (without transactions costs and with the possibility of buying or selling any amount of each security), security prices must be linear—meaning that the price of a bundle of securities must equal the sum of the prices of the component securities in the bundle—otherwise there is an arbitrage opportunity.

Two types of arbitrage are distinguished in the chapter: type A, which rules out the possibility of obtaining something for nothing—right now; and type B, which rules out the possibility of obtaining a chance for something later—at no cost now.

Ruling out type A arbitrage leads to linear pricing. Ruling out both types A an B implies that the problem of finding the portfolio that maximizes the expected utility has a well-defined solution.

The optimal portfolio problem can be used to solve realistic investment problems (such as the film venture problem). Furthermore, the necessary conditions of this general problem can be used in a backward fashion to express a security price as an expected value. Different choices of utility functions lead to different pricing formulas, but all of them are equivalent when applied to securities that are linear combinations of those considered in the original optimal portfolio problem. Utility functions that lead to especially convenient pricing equations include quadratic functions (which lead to the CAPM formula) and the logarithmic utility function.

Insight and practical advantage can be derived from the use of finite state models. In these models it is useful to introduce the concept of state prices. A set of positive state prices consistent with the securities under consideration exists if and only if there are no arbitrage opportunities. One way to find a set of positive state prices is to solve the optimal portfolio problem. The state prices are determined directly by the resulting optimal portfolio.

A concept of major significance is that of risk-neutral pricing. By introducing artificial probabilities, the pricing formula can be written as $P = \hat{E}(d)/R$, where R, is the return of the riskless asset and $\hat{E}$ denotes expectation with respect to the artificial (risk-neutral) probabilities. A set of risk-neutral probabilities can be found by multiplying the state prices by the total return R of the risk-free asset.

The pricing process can be visualized in a special space. Starting with a set of n securities defined by their (random) outcomes d_i, define the space S of all linear combinations of these securities. A major consequence of the no-arbitrage condition is that there exists another random variable v, not necessarily in S, such that the price of any security d in the space S is $E(vd)$. In particular, for each i, we have $P_i = E(vd_i)$. Since v is not required to be in S, there are many choices for it. One choice is embodied in the CAPM; and in this case v is in the space S. Another choice is $v = 1/R^*$, where R^* is the return on the log-optimal portfolio, and in this case v is often not in S. The optimal portfolio problem can be solved using other utility functions to find other v's. If the formula $P = E(vd)$ is applied to a security d outside of S, the result will generally be different for different choices of v.

If the securities are defined by a finite state model and if there are as many (independent) securities as states, then the market is said to be complete. In this case the space S contains all possible random vectors (in this model), and hence v must be in S as well. Indeed, v is unique. It may be found by solving an optimal portfolio problem; all utility functions will produce the same v.

EXERCISES

1. (Certainty equivalent) An investor has utility function $U(x) = x^{1/4}$ for salary. He has a new job offer which pays $80,000 with a bonus. The bonus will be $0, $10,000, $20,000, $30,000, $40,000, $50,000, or $60,000, each with equal probability. What is the certainty equivalent of this job offer?

2. (Wealth independence) Suppose an investor has exponential utility function $U(x) = -e^{-ax}$ and an initial wealth level of W. The investor is faced with an opportunity to invest an amount $w \leq W$ and obtain a random payoff x. Show that his evaluation of this incremental investment is independent of W.

3. (Risk aversion invariance)   Suppose $U(x)$ is a utility function with Arrow–Pratt risk aversion coefficient $a(x)$. Let $V(x) = c + bU(x)$. What is the risk aversion coefficient of V?

4. (Relative risk aversion)   The Arrow–Pratt relative risk aversion coefficient is

$$\mu(x) = \frac{xU''(x)}{U'(x)}.$$

Show that the utility functions $U(x) = \ln x$ and $U(x) = \gamma x^{\gamma}$ have constant relative risk aversion coefficients.

5. (Equivalency)   A young woman uses the first procedure described in Section 9.4 to deduce her utility function $U(x)$ over the range $A \leq x \leq B$. She uses the normalization $U(A) = A$, $U(B) = B$. To check her result, she repeats the whole procedure over the range $A' \leq x \leq B'$, where $A < A' < B' < B$. The result is a utility function $V(x)$, with $V(A') = A'$, $V(B') = B'$. If the results are consistent, U and V should be equivalent; that is, $V(x) = aU(x) + b$ for some $a > 0$ and b. Find a and b.

6. (HARA ◇)   The HARA (for hyperbolic absolute risk aversion) class of utility functions is defined by

$$U(x) = \frac{1-\gamma}{\gamma}\left(\frac{ax}{1-\gamma} + b\right)^{\gamma}, \qquad b > 0.$$

The functions are defined for those values of x where the term in parentheses is nonnegative. Show how the parameters γ, a, and b can be chosen to obtain the following special cases (or an equivalent form).

(a) Linear or risk neutral: $U(x) = x$
(b) Quadratic: $U(x) = x - \frac{1}{2}cx^2$
(c) Exponential: $U(x) = -e^{-ax}$ $\left[\text{Try } \gamma = -\infty.\right]$
(d) Power: $U(x) = cx^{\gamma}$
(e) Logarithmic: $U(x) = \ln x$ $\left[\text{Try } U(x) = (1-\gamma)^{1-\gamma}((x^{\gamma} - 1)/\gamma).\right]$

Show that the Arrow–Pratt risk aversion coefficient is of the form $1/(cx + d)$.

7. (The venture capitalist)   A venture capitalist with a utility function $U(x) = \sqrt{x}$ carried out the procedure of Example 9.3. Find an analytical expression for C as a function of e, and for e as a function of C. Do the values in Table 9.1 of the example agree with these expressions?

8. (Certainty approximation ◇)   There is a useful approximation to the certainty equivalent that is easy to derive. A second-order expansion near $\overline{x} = E(x)$ gives

$$U(x) \approx U(\overline{x}) + U'(\overline{x})(x - \overline{x}) + \tfrac{1}{2}U''(\overline{x})(x - \overline{x})^2.$$

Hence,

$$E[U(x)] \approx U(\overline{x}) + \tfrac{1}{2}U''(\overline{x})\mathrm{var}(x).$$

On the other hand, if we let c denote the certainty equivalent and assume it is close to $\overline{x}$, we can use the first-order expansion

$$U(c) \approx U(\overline{x}) + U'(\overline{x})(c - \overline{x}).$$

Using these approximations, show that

$$c \approx \overline{x} + \frac{U''(\overline{x})}{U'(\overline{x})} \operatorname{var}(x).$$

9. (Quadratic mean–variance)   An investor with unit wealth maximizes the expected value of the utility function $U(x) = ax - bx^2/2$ and obtains a mean–variance efficient portfolio. A friend of his with wealth W and the same utility function does the same calculation, but gets a different portfolio return. However, changing b to b' does yield the same result. What is the value of b'?

10. (Portfolio optimization)   Suppose an investor has utility function U. There are n risky assets with rates of return r_i, $i = 1, 2, \ldots, n$, and one risk-free asset with rate of return r_f. The investor has initial wealth W_0. Suppose that the optimal portfolio for this investor has (random) payoff x^*. Show that

$$\mathrm{E}\big[U'(x^*)(r_i - r_f)\big] = 0$$

for $i = 1, 2, \ldots, n$.

11. (Money-back guarantee)   The promoter of the film venture offers a new investment designed to attract reluctant investors. One unit of this new investment has a payoff of \$3,000 if the venture is highly successful, and it refunds the original investment otherwise. Assuming that the other three investment alternatives described in Example 9.6 are also available, what is the price of this money-back guaranteed investment?

12. (General positive state prices result ◇)   The following is a general result from matrix theory: Let $\mathbf{A}$ be an $m \times n$ matrix. Suppose that the equation $\mathbf{A}\mathbf{x} = \mathbf{p}$ can achieve no $\mathbf{p} \geq \mathbf{0}$ except $\mathbf{p} = \mathbf{0}$. Then there is a vector $\mathbf{y} > \mathbf{0}$ with $\mathbf{A}^T\mathbf{y} = \mathbf{0}$. Use this result to show that if there is no arbitrage, there are positive state prices; that is, prove the positive state price theorem in Section 9.9. [*Hint:* If there are S states and N securities, let $\mathbf{A}$ be an appropriate $(S+1) \times N$ matrix.]

13. (Quadratic pricing ◇)   Suppose an investor uses the quadratic utility function $U(x) = x - \frac{1}{2}cx^2$. Suppose there are n risky assets and one risk-free asset with total return R. Let R_M be the total return on the optimal portfolio of risky assets. Show that the expected return of any asset i is given by the formula

$$\overline{R}_i - R = \beta_i(\overline{R}_M - R)$$

where $\beta_i = \operatorname{cov}(R_M, R_i)/\sigma_M^2$. [*Hint:* Use Exercise 10. Apply the result to R_M itself.]

14. (At the track)   At the horse races one Saturday afternoon Gavin Jones studies the racing form and concludes that the horse No Arbitrage has a 25% chance to win and is posted at 4 to 1 odds. (For every dollar Gavin bets, he receives \$5 if the horse wins and nothing if it loses.) He can either bet on this horse or keep his money in his pocket. Gavin decides that he has a square-root utility for money.

(a) What fraction of his money should Gavin bet on No Arbitrage?

(b) What is the implied winning payoff of a \$1 bet against No Arbitrage?

15. (General risk-neutral pricing)   We can transform the log-optimal pricing formula into a risk-neutral pricing equation. From the log-optimal pricing equation we have

$$P = \mathrm{E}\left(\frac{d}{R^*}\right)$$

where R^* is the return on the log-optimal portfolio. We can then define a new expectation operation $\hat{\mathrm{E}}$ by

$$\hat{\mathrm{E}}(x) = \mathrm{E}\left(\frac{Rx}{R^*}\right).$$

This can be regarded as the expectation of an artificial probability. Note that the usual rules of expectation hold. Namely:

(a) If x is certain, then $\hat{\mathrm{E}}(x) = x$. This is because $\mathrm{E}(1/R^*) = 1/R$.

(b) For any random variables x and y, there holds $\hat{\mathrm{E}}(ax + by) = a\,\hat{\mathrm{E}}(x) + b\,\hat{\mathrm{E}}(y)$.

(c) For any nonnegative random variable x, there holds $\hat{\mathrm{E}}(x) \geq 0$.

Using this new expectation operation, with the implied artificial probabilities, show that the price of any security d is

$$P = \frac{\hat{\mathrm{E}}(d)}{R}.$$

This is risk neutral pricing.

REFERENCES

The systematic use of expected utility as a basis for financial decision making was originated by von Neumann and Morgenstern in [1]. Another set of axioms is due to Savage [2]. The practical application of the theory was elaborated in [3]. For a comprehensive treatment explicitly aimed at finance problems, see [4]. The presentation of the second half of this chapter, related to linear pricing, draws heavily on the first chapter of [5]. The idea of linear pricing was developed in [6]. The use of the log-optimal portfolio to determine prices is explained in [7]. The idea of risk-neutral evaluation emerged from the pioneering approach to options by Black and Scholes in [8] and was formalized explicitly in [9]. The concept was generalized in [10] and now is a fundamental part of modern investment science.

1. von Neumann, J., and O. Morgenstern (1944), *Theory of Games and Economic Behavior,* Princeton University Press, Princeton, NJ.

2. Savage, L. J. (1954, 1972), *Foundations of Statistics,* Wiley, New York, 1954; 2nd ed., Dover, New York, 1972.

3. Luce, R. D., and H. Raiffa (1957), *Games and Decisions,* Wiley, New York.

4. Ingersoll, J. E., Jr. (1987), *Theory of Financial Decision Making,* Rowman and Littlefield, Savage, MD.

5. Duffie, D. (1996), *Dynamic Asset Pricing,* 2nd ed., Princeton University Press, Princeton, NJ.

6. Cox, J., S. Ross, and M. Rubinstein (1979), "Option Pricing: A Simplified Approach," *Journal of Financial Economics*, **7**, 229–263.

7. Long, J. B., Jr. (1990), "The Numeraire Portfolio," *Journal of Financial Economics,* **26,** 29–69.

8. Black, F., and M. Scholes (1973), "The Pricing of Options and Corporate Liabilities," *Journal of Political Economy,* **81,** 637–654.

9. Ross, S. (1961), "A Simple Approach to the Valuation of Risky Streams," *Journal of Business*, **34,** 411–433.

10. Harrison, J. M., and D. Kreps (1979), "Martingales and Arbitrage in Multiperiod Securities Markets," *Journal of Economic Theory,* **20,** 381–408.

PART III

DERIVATIVE SECURITIES

10 FORWARDS, FUTURES, AND SWAPS

10.1 INTRODUCTION

A derivative security is a security whose payoff is explicitly tied to the value of some other variable. In practice, however, this broad definition is often restricted to securities whose payoffs are explicitly tied to the price of some other financial security. A hypothetical example of such a derivative security is a certificate that can be redeemed in 6 months for an amount equal to the price, then, of a share of IBM stock. The certificate is a derivative security since its payoff depends on the future price of IBM. Most real derivatives are fashioned to have important risk control features, and the payoff relation is more subtle than that of the hypothetical certificate example. A more realistic example is a **forward contract** to purchase 2,000 pounds of sugar at 12 cents per pound in 6 weeks. There is no reference to a payoff—the contract just guarantees the purchase of sugar—but in fact a payoff is implied. The payoff is determined by the price of sugar in 6 weeks. If the price of sugar then were, say, 13 cents per pound, the contract would have a value of 1 cent per pound, or $20, since the owner of the contract could buy sugar at 12 cents according to the contract and then turn around and sell that sugar in the sugar market at 13 cents. The contract is a derivative security because its value is derived from the price of sugar. Another realistic example is a contract that gives one the right, but not the obligation, to purchase 100 shares of GM stock for $60 per share in exactly 3 months. This is an **option** to buy GM. The payoff of this option will be determined in 3 months by the price of GM stock at that time. If GM is selling then for $70, the option will be worth $1,000 because the owner of the option could at that time purchase 100 shares of GM for $60 per share according to the option contract, and immediately sell those shares for $70 each. As a final example of a derivative security, suppose you take out a mortgage whose interest rate is adjusted periodically according to a weighted average of the rates on new mortgages offered by major banks. Your mortgage is a derivative security since its value at later times is determined by other financial prices, namely, prevailing interest rates.

As mentioned earlier, the payoff of a derivative security is usually based on the price of some other financial security. In the foregoing examples these were the price of IBM shares, the price of sugar, the price of GM shares, and the prevailing interest rates. The security that determines the value of a derivative security is called the **underlying security.** However, according to the broad definition, derivatives may have payoffs that are functions of nonfinancial variables, such as the weather or the outcome of an election. The main point is that the payments derived from a derivative security are deterministic functions of some other variable whose value will be revealed before or at the time of the payoff.

The main types of derivative securities are forward contracts, futures contracts, options, options on futures, and swaps.[1] Such securities play an important role in everyday commerce, since they provide effective tools for hedging risks involving the underlying variables. For example, a business that deals with a lot of sugar—perhaps a sugar producer, a processor, a marketeer, or a commercial user—typically faces substantial risks associated with possible sugar price fluctuations. Such users can control that risk through the use of derivative securities (in this case mainly through the use of sugar futures contracts). Indeed, the primary function of derivative securities in a portfolio—for businesses, institutions, or individuals—is to control risk.

This third part of the text addresses several aspects of derivative securities. First, these chapters explain what these different types of securities are; that is, how forwards, futures, swaps, and options are structured. Second, these chapters show, through theory and example, how derivative securities are used to control risk; that is, how derivatives can enhance the overall structure of a portfolio that contains risky components. Third, these chapters present the special pricing theory that applies to derivative securities. This is the aspect that receives the most attention in the text. Finally, an important technical subject presented in this part of the text is concerned with how to model security price fluctuations. This is the primary topic of the next chapter. This current chapter is devoted to forward and futures contracts, which are among the simplest and most useful derivative securities.

Before starting this topic, we offer a small warning and a suggestion. This chapter is not difficult page by page, but it contains many new concepts. You may find that your progress through the chapter is slower than in other chapters. Since the next three chapters do not depend on this one, one reading strategy is to scan the chapter briefly and then skip to Chapter 11, returning to this one later. However, the study of forwards, futures, and swaps is both practical and fascinating, so this chapter should be studied in depth at some point.

10.2 FORWARD CONTRACTS

Forward and futures contracts are closely related structures, but forward contracts are the simpler of the two. A **forward contract** on a commodity is a contract to purchase or

---

[1]In addition to the primary types listed here, there are *many* other derivative securities, such as variable-rate preferred stock, variable-rate mortgages, prime-rate loans, and LIBOR-based notes. New derivative securities are created and marketed every year by financial institutions. Fortunately most of these various financial products can be analyzed by using just a few common principles.

sell a specific amount of the commodity at a specific price and at a specific time in the future. For example, a typical forward contract might be to purchase 100,000 pounds of sugar at 12 cents per pound on the 15th of March next year. The contract is between two parties, the buyer and the seller. The buyer is said to be **long** 100,000 pounds of sugar, and the seller is said to be **short.** Being long or short a given amount is the **position** of the party. Forward contracts for commodities have existed for thousands of years, for they are indeed a natural adjunct to commerce. Both suppliers and consumers of large quantities of a commodity frequently find it advantageous to lock in the price associated with a future commodity delivery.

A forward contract is specified by a legal document, the terms of which bind the two parties involved to a specific transaction in the future. However, a forward contract on a priced asset, such as sugar, is also a financial instrument, since it has an intrinsic value determined by the market for the underlying asset. Forward contracts have been extended in modern times to include underlying assets other than physical commodities. For example, many corporations use forward contracts on foreign currency or on interest rate instruments.

Most forward contracts specify that all claims are settled at the defined future date (or dates); both parties must carry out their side of the agreement at that time. Almost always, the initial payment associated with a forward contract is zero. Neither party pays any money to obtain the contract (although a security deposit is sometimes required of both parties). The **forward price** is the price that applies at delivery. This price is negotiated so that the initial payment is zero; that is, the *value* of the contract is zero when it is initiated.

The open market for immediate delivery of the underlying asset is called the **spot market.** This is distinguished from the **forward market,** which trades contracts for future delivery. During the course of a forward contract, the spot market price may fluctuate. Hence, although the initial value of a forward contract is zero, its later values will vary as a function of the spot price of the underlying asset (or assets). Later we shall explore the relation between the current value and the forward price.

Forward Interest Rates

We discussed a rather advanced form of forward contract in Chapter 4 when studying the term structure of interest rates. The forward rate was defined as the rate of interest associated with an agreement to loan money over a specified interval of time in the future. It may not be apparent how to arrange for such a loan using standard financial securities; but actually it is quite simple, as the following example illustrates.

Example 10.1 (A T-bill forward) Suppose that you wish to arrange to loan money for 6 months beginning 3 months from now. Suppose that the forward rate for that period is 10%. A suitable contract that implements this loan would be an agreement for a bank to deliver to you, 3 months from now, a 6-month Treasury bill (that is, a T-bill with 6 months to run from the delivery date). The price would be agreed upon today for this delivery, and the Treasury bill would pay its face value of, say,

$1,000 at maturity. The correct price for a Treasury bill of face value $1,000 would be determined by the forward rate, which is 10% in annual terms, or 5% for 6 months. Hence the value of the T-bill would be $1,000/1.05 = $952.38, so this is the price that today you would agree to pay in 3 months when the T-bill is delivered to you. Six months later you receive the $1,000 face value. Hence, overall, you have loaned $952.38 for 6 months, with repayment of $1,000. This agreement exactly parallels that of other forward contracts, the special feature being that the underlying asset to be delivered is a T-bill. The price associated with this contract directly reflects the forward interest rate.

The forward rates can be determined from the term structure of interest rates, which in turn can be determined from current bond prices. These forward rates are basic to the pricing of forward contracts on *all* commodities and assets because they provide a point of comparison. The payoff associated with a given forward contract on, say, sugar can be compared with one associated with pure lending and borrowing. Consistency (or lack of arbitrage opportunities) dictates the (theoretical) forward price, as we show next.

10.3 FORWARD PRICES

As discussed earlier, there are two prices or values associated with a forward contract. The first is the **forward price** F. This is the delivery price of a unit of the underlying asset to be delivered at a specific future date. It is the delivery price that would be specified in a forward contract written today. The second price or value of a forward contract is its current value, which is denoted by f. The forward price F is determined such that $f = 0$ initially, so that no money need be exchanged when completing the contract agreement. After the initial time, the value f may vary, depending on variations of the spot price of the underlying asset, the prevailing interest rates, and other factors. Likewise the forward price F of new contracts with delivery terms identical to that of the original contract will also vary.

In this section we determine the theoretical forward price F associated with a forward contract written at time $t = 0$ to deliver an asset at time T. Our analysis depends on the standard assumptions that there are no transactions costs, and that assets can be divided arbitrarily. Also we assume initially that it is possible to store the underlying asset without cost and that it is possible to sell the asset short. Later we will allow for storage costs, but still require that it be possible to store the underlying asset for the duration of the contract. This is a good assumption for many assets, such as gold or sugar or T-bills, but perhaps not good for perishable commodities such as oranges.

Suppose that at time $t = 0$ the underlying asset has spot price S and a forward contract is being designed today for delivery at time T. How can we determine the value of the forward contract? The key is to recognize that a forward contract on a commodity can be used in conjunction with the spot market for that commodity to borrow or lend money indirectly. The interest rate implied by this operation must be equal to the normal interest rate; otherwise arbitrage can be set up between the direct and indirect methods of lending.

Specifically, suppose we buy one unit of the commodity at price S on the spot market and simultaneously enter a forward contract to deliver at time T one unit at price F (that is, we short one unit). We store the commodity until T and then deliver it to meet our obligation and obtain F. The cash flow sequence associated with these two market operations is $(-S, F)$, which is fully determined at $t = 0$. This must be consistent with the interest rate between $t = 0$ and $t = T$. Hence,

$$S = d(0, T)F$$

where $d(0, T)$ is the discount factor between 0 and T. In other words, because storage is costless, buying the commodity at price S is exactly the same as lending an amount S of cash for which we will receive an amount F at time T.

We can assert the relation $S = d(0, T)F$ using elementary present value analysis: the present value of the stream $(-S, F)$ must be zero. However, this type of present value analysis is based on an assumption of perfect markets, no transactions costs, and the absence of arbitrage possibilities. Next we formalize the arbitrage argument, not because it is really necessary here, but to set the stage for later situations where the present value formula breaks down because of a market imperfection.

Forward price formula *Suppose an asset can be stored at zero cost and also sold short. Suppose the current spot price (at $t = 0$) of the asset is S. The theoretical forward price F (for delivery at $t = T$) is*

$$F = S/d(0, T) \tag{10.1}$$

where $d(0, T)$ is the discount factor between 0 and T.

Proof: First suppose to the contrary that $F > S/d(0, T)$. Then we construct a portfolio as follows: At the present time borrow S amount of cash, buy one unit of the underlying asset on the spot market at price S, and take a one-unit short position in the forward market. The total cost of this portfolio is zero. At time T we deliver the asset (which we have stored), receiving a cash amount F, and we repay our loan in the amount $S/d(0, T)$. As a result we obtain a positive profit of $F - S/d(0, T)$ for zero net investment. This is an arbitrage, which we assume is impossible. The details of these transactions are shown in Table 10.1.

TABLE 10.1

At $t = 0$	Initial cost	Final receipt
Borrow $\$S$	$-S$	$-S/d(0, T)$
Buy 1 unit and store	S	0
Short 1 forward	0	F
Total	0	$F - S/d(0, T)$

TABLE 10.2

At $t = 0$	Initial cost	Final receipt
Lend $\$S$	S	$S/d(0, T)$
Short 1 unit	$-S$	0
Go long 1 forward	0	$-F$
Total	0	$S/d(0, T) - F$

If $F < S/d(0, T)$, we can construct the reverse portfolio. However, this requires that we short one unit of the asset. The shorting is executed by borrowing the asset from someone who plans to store it during this period, then selling the borrowed asset at the spot price, and replacing the borrowed asset at time T. The arbitrage portfolio is constructed by shorting one unit, lending the proceeds S from time 0 to T, and taking a one-unit long position in the forward market. The net cash flow at time zero of this portfolio is zero. At time T we receive $S/d(0, T)$ from our loan, pay F to obtain one unit of the asset, and we return this unit to the lender who made the short possible. The details are shown in Table 10.2.

Our profit is $S/d(0, T) - F$ (which we might share with the asset lender for making the short possible).

Since either inequality leads to an arbitrage opportunity, equality must hold. ∎

The relationship between the spot price S and the forward price F is illustrated in Figure 10.1. The spot price starts at $S(0)$ and varies randomly, arriving at $S(T)$. However, the forward price at time zero is based on extrapolating the current spot price forward at the prevailing rate of interest.

Example 10.2 (Copper forward) A manufacturer of heavy electrical equipment wishes to take the long side of a forward contract for delivery of copper in 9 months. The current price of copper is 84.85 cents per pound, and 9-month T-bills are selling at 970.87. What is the appropriate forward price of the copper contract?

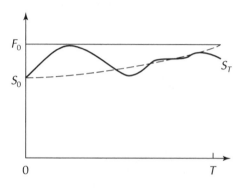

FIGURE 10.1 Forward price. The forward price at time zero is equal to the projected future value of cash of amount $S(0)$.

If we ignore storage costs and use the T-bill rate, the appropriate price is $84.85/.97087 = 87.40$ cents per pound.

Example 10.3 (Continuous-time compounding) If there is a constant interest rate r compounded continuously, the forward rate formula becomes

$$F = Se^{rT}.$$

The discount rate $d(0, T)$ used in the forward price formula should be the one consistent with one's access to the interest rate market. Professional traders of forwards and futures commonly use the **repo rate** associated with repurchase agreements. (These are agreements to sell a security and repurchase it a short time later for a slightly higher price.) This repo rate is only slightly higher than the Treasury bill rate.

Costs of Carry

The preceding analysis assumed that there are no storage costs associated with holding the underlying asset. This is not always the case. Holding a physical asset such as gold entails storage costs, such as vault rental and insurance fees. Holding a security may, alternatively, entail negative costs, representing dividend or coupon payments. These costs (or incomes) affect the theoretical forward price.

We shall use a discrete-time (multiperiod) model to describe this situation. The delivery date T is M periods (say, months) in the future. We assume that storage is paid periodically, and we measure time according to these periods. The carrying cost is $c(k)$ per unit for holding the asset in the period from k to $k + 1$ (payable at the beginning of the period). The forward price of the asset is then determined by the structure of the forward interest rates applied to the holding costs and the asset itself.

Forward price formula with carrying costs *Suppose an asset has a holding cost of* $c(k)$ *per unit in period k, and the asset can be sold short. Suppose the initial spot price is S. Then the theoretical forward price is*

$$F = \frac{S}{d(0, M)} + \sum_{k=0}^{M-1} \frac{c(k)}{d(k, M)} \qquad (10.2)$$

where $d(k, M)$ *is the discount factor from k to M. Equivalently,*

$$S = -\sum_{k=0}^{M-1} d(0, k)c(k) + d(0, M)F. \qquad (10.3)$$

Proof: The simple version of the proof is this: Buy one unit of the commodity on the spot market and enter a forward contract to deliver one unit at time T. The cash flow stream associated with this is $(-S-c(0), -c(1), -c(2), \ldots,$

$-c(M-1)$, F). The present value of this stream must be zero, and this gives the stated formula for F. We shall also give a detailed proof based on the no-arbitrage condition.

Suppose that F is greater than that given by (10.2). We can set up an arbitrage as follows. At the initial time, short one unit of a forward contract with forward price F and buy one unit of the asset for price S. Simultaneously, borrow an amount of cash S and arrange to borrow amounts $c(k)$ each time $k = 0, 1, \dots, M-1$. All of these loans are to be repaid at the final time M, so each is governed by the corresponding forward interest rate between k and M. The initial cash flow associated with this plan is zero, since we immediately borrow enough to pay for the asset. Furthermore, the cash flow during each period is also zero, because we borrow enough to cover the carrying charge. Hence there is no net cash flow until the final period.

At the final period we deliver the asset as required, receive F, and repay all loans, which now total $S/d(0, M) + \sum_{k=0}^{M-1} c(k)/d(k, M)$. Under our inequality assumption this will represent an arbitrage profit, so our original assumption of inequality must be false. The details are shown in Table 10.3. Assuming short selling is possible, we may reverse this argument to prove that the opposite inequality is likewise not possible. (See Exercise 5.) ∎

The alternative formula (10.3) is obtained from (10.2) by multiplying through by $d(0, M)$ and using the fact that $d(0, M) = d(0, k)d(k, M)$ for any k. This alternative formula is probably the simplest to understand, since it is a standard present value equation. We recognize that we can buy the commodity at price S and deliver it according to a forward contract at time M in a completely deterministic fashion. The cash flow incurred while holding the commodity will be the carrying charges and the delivery price. The present value of this stream must equal the price S.

TABLE 10.3
Details of Arbitrage

Time 0 action	Time 0 cost	Time k cost	Receipt at time M
Short 1 forward	0	0	F
Borrow $\$S$	$-S$	0	$\dfrac{-S(0, M)}{d(0, M)}$
Buy 1 unit spot	S	0	0
Borrow $c(k)$'s forward	$-c(0)$	$-c(k)$	$-\displaystyle\sum_{k=0}^{M-1} \dfrac{c(k)}{d(k, M)}$
Pay storage	$c(0)$	$c(k)$	0
Total	0	0	$F - \dfrac{S}{d(0, M)} - \displaystyle\sum_{k=0}^{M-1} \dfrac{c(k)}{d(k, M)}$

Example 10.4 (Sugar with storage cost) The current price of sugar is 12 cents per pound. We wish to find the forward price of sugar to be delivered in 5 months. The carrying cost of sugar is .1 cent per pound per month, to be paid at the beginning of the month, and the interest rate is constant at 9% per annum.

The interest rate is $.09/12 = .0075$ per month. The reciprocal of the 1-month discount rate (for any month) is 1.0075. Therefore we find

$$F = (1.0075)^5(.12) + [(1.0075)^5 + (1.0075)^4 + (1.0075)^3$$
$$+ (1.0075)^2 + 1.0075](.001)$$
$$= .1295 = 12.95 \text{ cents}.$$

Example 10.5 (A bond forward) Consider a Treasury bond with a face value of $10,000, a coupon of 8%, and several years to maturity. Currently this bond is selling for $9,260, and the previous coupon has just been paid. What is the forward price for delivery of this bond in 1 year? Assume that interest rates for 1 year out are flat at 9%.

We recognize that there will be two coupons before delivery: one in 6 months and one just prior to delivery. Hence using the present value form (10.3) and a 6-month compounding convention, we have immediately

$$\$9,260 = \frac{F + \$400}{(1.045)^2} + \frac{\$400}{1.045}.$$

This can be solved [or turned around to the form (10.2)] to give

$$F = \$9,260(1.045)^2 - \$400 - \$400(1.045) = \$9,294.15$$

(in decimal form, not 32nd's).

Tight Markets

At any one time it is possible to define several different forward contracts on a given commodity, each contract having a different delivery date. If the commodity is a physical commodity such as soybean meal, the preceding theory implies that the forward prices of these various contracts will increase smoothly as the delivery date is increased because the value of F in (10.2) increases with M. In fact, however, this is frequently *not* the case.

Consider, for example, the prices for soybean contracts shown in Table 10.4. This table[2] shows that the prices actually decrease with time over a certain range. How do we explain this? Certainly the holding cost for soybean meal is not negative. In fact, holders of soybean meal are giving up an opportunity to make arbitrage profit.

To verify this opportunity, note that someone, say, a farmer with soybean meal could sell it now (in December) at $188.20 and arrange now to buy it back in March

---

[2]These are actually futures market prices, but they can be assumed to be forward prices.

TABLE 10.4
Soybean Meal Forward Prices

Dec	188.20	Aug	185.50
Jan	185.60	Sept	186.20
Mar	184.00	Oct	188.00
May	183.70	Dec	189.00
July	184.80		

The delivery prices do not increase
continuously as the delivery date is
increased.

at \$184.00, thereby making a sure profit and avoiding any holding costs that would otherwise be incurred. Why does the farmer not do this? The reason is that soybean meal is frequently in short supply; those that hold it do so because they need it to supply other contracts or for their own use. It is true that they could make a small profit by selling their holdings and purchasing a forward contract, but this small potential profit is less than the costs incurred by not having soybean meal on hand.

Likewise, arbitrageurs are unable to short a forward contract because no one will lend them soybean meal. Hence the theoretical price relationship that assumes that shorting is possible does not apply.

The theoretical relation does hold in one direction as long as storage is possible. This is the case for most assets (including soybean meal). When storage is possible, the first direction of the proofs of (10.1) and (10.2) applies. In other words,

$$F \leq \frac{S}{d(0, M)} + \sum_{k=0}^{M-1} \frac{c(k)}{d(k, M)} \tag{10.4}$$

must hold if there are no arbitrage opportunities.

Shorting, on the other hand, relies on there being a positive amount of storage available for borrowing over the period from 0 to T. Someone, or some group, must plan on having excess stocks over this entire period, no matter how the market changes. If stocks are low, or potentially low, short selling at the spot price is essentially infeasible. That means that the second direction of the proofs of (10.1) and (10.2) does not apply. Hence only the inequality (10.4) can be inferred. As shown by the example of soybean meal, this is, in fact, a fairly common situation.

The inequality can be converted to an equality by the artifice of defining a **convenience yield,** which measures the benefit of holding the commodity. In the case of soybean meal, for example, the convenience yield may represent the value of having meal on hand to keep a farm operating. The convenience yield can be thought of as a negative holding cost, so if incorporated into (10.4), it reduces the right-hand side to the point of equality. One way to incorporate it is to modify (10.4) as

$$F = \frac{S}{d(0, M)} + \sum_{k=0}^{M-1} \frac{c(k)}{d(k, M)} - \sum_{k=0}^{M-1} \frac{y}{d(k, M)}$$

where y is the convenience yield per period.

10.4 THE VALUE OF A FORWARD CONTRACT

Suppose a forward contract was written in the past with a delivery price of F_0. At the present time t the forward price for the same delivery date is F_t. We would like to determine the current value f_t of the initial contract. This value is given by the following statement.

The value of a forward *Suppose a forward contract for delivery at time T in the future has a delivery price F_0 and a current forward price F_t. The value of the contract is*

$$f_t = (F_t - F_0)d(t, T)$$

where $d(t, T)$ is the risk-free discount factor over the period from t to T.

Proof: Consider forming the following portfolio at time t: one unit long of a forward contract with delivery price F_t maturing at time T, and one unit short of the contract with delivery price F_0. The initial cash flow of this portfolio is f_t. The final cash flow at time T is $F_0 - F_t$. This is a completely deterministic stream, because the short and long delivery requirements cancel. The present value of this portfolio is $f_t + (F_0 - F_t)d(t, T)$, and this must be zero. The stated result follows immediately. ∎

10.5 SWAPS*

Motivating most investment problems is a desire to transform one cash flow stream into another by appropriate market or technological activity. A **swap** accomplishes this directly—for a swap is an agreement to exchange one cash flow stream for another. The attraction of this direct approach is evidenced by the fact that the swap market amounts to hundreds of billions of dollars. Swaps are often tailored for a specific situation, but the most common is the **plain vanilla swap,** in which one party swaps a series of fixed-level payments for a series of variable-level payments. It is this form that we consider in this section. As we shall see, such swaps can be regarded as a series of forward contracts, and hence they can be priced using the concepts of forwards.

As an example, consider a plain vanilla interest rate swap. Party A agrees to make a series of semiannual payments to party B equal to a fixed rate of interest on a notional principal. (The term **notional principal** is used because there is no loan. This principal simply sets the level of the payments.) In return, party B makes a series of semiannual payments to party A based on a floating rate of interest (such as the current 6-month LIBOR rate) and the same notional principal. Usually, swaps are **netted** in the sense that only the difference of required payments is made by the party that owes the difference.

This swap might be motivated by the fact that party B has loaned money to a third party C under floating rate terms; but party B would rather have fixed payments. The swap with party A effectively transforms the floating rate stream to one with fixed payments.

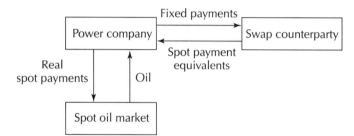

FIGURE 10.2 Commodity swap. The power company buys oil on the spot market every month. The company arranges a swap with a counterparty (or a swap dealer) to exchange fixed payments for spot price payments. The net effect is that the power company has eliminated the variability of its payments.

As an example of a commodity swap, consider an electric power company that must purchase oil every month for its power generation facility. If it purchases oil on the spot market, the company will experience randomly fluctuating cash flows caused by fluctuating spot prices. The company may wish to swap this payment stream for one that is constant. It can do this if it can find a counterparty willing to swap. This is shown in Figure 10.2. The swap counterparty agrees to pay the power company the spot price of oil times a fixed number of barrels, and in return the power company pays a fixed price per barrel for the same number of barrels over the life of the swap. The variable cash flow stream is thereby transformed to a fixed stream.

Value of a Commodity Swap

Consider an agreement where party A receives spot price for N units of a commodity each period while paying a fixed amount X per unit for N units. If the agreement is made for M periods, the net cash flow stream received by A is $(S_1 - X, S_2 - X, S_3 - X, \ldots, S_M - X)$ multiplied by the number of units N, where S_i denotes the spot price of the commodity at time i.

We can value this stream using the concepts of forward markets. At time zero the forward price of one unit of the commodity to be received at time i is F_i. This means that we are indifferent between receiving S_i (which is currently uncertain) at i and receiving F_i at i. By discounting back to time zero we conclude that the current value of receiving S_i at time i is $d(0, i)F_i$, where $d(0, i)$ is the discount factor at time zero for cash received at i.

If we apply this argument each period, we find that the total value of the stream is

$$V = \sum_{i=1}^{M} d(0, i)(F_i - X)N. \tag{10.5}$$

Hence the value of the swap can be determined from the series of forward prices. Usually X is chosen to make the value zero, so that the swap represents an equal exchange.

Example 10.6 (A gold swap)   Consider an agreement by an electronics firm to receive spot value for gold in return for fixed payments. We assume that gold is in ample supply and can be stored without cost—which implies that the swap formula takes an almost trivial form. In that case we know that the forward price is $F_i = S_0/d(0, i)$. Therefore (10.5) becomes

$$V = \left[M S_0 - \sum_{i=1}^{M} d(0, i) X \right] N.$$

The summation is identical to the value of the coupon payment stream of a bond. Using this fact, it is easy to convert the value formula to

$$V = \left\{ M S_0 - \frac{X}{C} [B(M, C) + 100 d(0, M)] \right\} N \qquad (10.6)$$

where $B(M, C)$ denotes the price (relative to 100) of a bond of maturity M and coupon C per period. Any value of C can be used. (See Exercise 8.)

Value of an Interest Rate Swap

Consider a plain vanilla interest rate swap in which party A agrees to make payments of a fixed rate r of interest on a notional principal N while receiving floating rate payments on the same notional principal for M periods. The cash flow stream received by A is $(c_0 - r, c_1 - r, c_2 - r, \ldots, c_M - r)$ times the principal N. The c_i's are the floating rates.

We can value the floating portion of this swap with a special trick derived from our knowledge of floating rate bonds. (For a direct proof using forward pricing concepts, see Exercise 10.) The floating rate cash flow stream is exactly the same as that generated by a floating rate bond of principal N and maturity M, except that no final principal payment is made. We know that the initial value of a floating rate bond (including the final principal payment) is par; hence the value of the floating rate portion of the swap is par minus the present value of the principal received at M. In other words, the value of the floating rate portion of the swap stream is $N - d(0, M)N$.

The value of the fixed rate portion of the stream is the sum of the discounted fixed payments, discounted according to the current term structure discount rates. Hence overall, the value of the swap is[3]

$$V = \left[1 - d(0, M) - r \sum_{i=1}^{M} d(0, i) \right] N.$$

The summation can be reduced using the method in the gold swap example.

10.6 BASICS OF FUTURES CONTRACTS

Because forward trading is so useful, it became desirable long ago to standardize the contracts and trade them on an organized exchange. An exchange helps define universal

---

[3]Typically, account must be made for other details. For example, interest rates for fixed payments are usually quoted on the basis of 365 days per year, whereas for floating rates they are quoted on the basis of 360 days per year.

prices and provides convenience and security because individuals do not themselves need to find an appropriate counterparty and need not face the risk of counterparty default. Individual contracts are made with the exchange, the exchange itself being the counterparty for both long and short traders. But standardization presents an interesting challenge. Consider the likely mechanics of forward contract trading on an exchange. It is a relatively simple matter to standardize a set of delivery dates, quantities to be delivered, quality of delivered goods, and delivery locations (although there are some subtleties even in these items). But standardization of forward prices is impossible. To appreciate the issue, suppose that contracts were issued today at a delivery price of F_0. The exchange would keep track of all such contracts. Then tomorrow the forward price might change and contracts initiated that day would have a different delivery price F_1. In fact, the appropriate delivery price might change continuously throughout the day. The thousands of outstanding forward contracts could each have a different delivery price, even though all other terms were identical. This would be a bookkeeping nightmare.

The way that this has been solved is through the brilliant invention of a **futures market** as an alternative to a forward market. Multiple delivery prices are eliminated by revising contracts as the price environment changes. Consider again the situation where contracts are initially written at F_0 and then the next day the price for new contracts is F_1. At the second day, the clearinghouse associated with the exchange revises all the earlier contracts to the new delivery price F_1. To do this, the contract holders either pay or receive the difference in the two prices, depending on whether the change in price reflects a loss or a gain. Specifically, suppose $F_1 > F_0$ and I hold a one-unit long position with price F_0. My contract price is then changed to F_1 and I receive $F_1 - F_0$ from the clearinghouse because I will later have to pay F_1 rather than F_0 when I receive delivery of the commodity.

The process of adjusting the contract is called **marking to market.** In more detail it works like this: An individual is required to open a **margin account** with a broker. This account must contain a specified amount of cash for each futures contract (usually on the order of 5–10% of the value of the contract). All contract holders, whether short or long, must have such an account. These accounts are marked to market at the end of each trading day. If the price of the futures contract (the price determined on the exchange) increased that day, then the long parties receive a profit equal to the price change times the contract quantity. This profit is deposited in their margin accounts. The short parties lose the same amount, and this amount is deducted from their margin accounts. Hence each margin account value fluctuates from day to day according to the change in the futures price. With this procedure, every long futures contract holder has the same contract, as does every short contract holder. At the delivery date, delivery is made at the futures contract price at that time, which may be quite different from the futures price at the time the contract was first purchased.

Actually, delivery of commodities under the terms of a futures contract is quite rare; over 90% of all parties close out their positions before the delivery date. Even commercial organizations that need the commodity for production frequently close out their long positions and purchase the commodity from their conventional suppliers on the spot market.

GRAINS AND OILSEEDS

FIGURE 10.3   Corn futures quotations. Contracts for various delivery dates are shown. Source: *The Wall Street Journal,* November 10, 1995.

	Open	High	Low	Settle	Change	Lifetime High	Lifetime Low	Open Interest
CORN (CBT) 5,000 bu.; cents per bu.								
Dec	336	337	326½	327¼	− 3¾	339	235½	162,928
Mr96	344	344	333½	334½	− 3¼	344¼	249½	215,702
May	344½	345	333½	334	− 4½	345	259½	36,974
July	342	342	331	331¾	− 4¼	342	254	47,422
Sept	299	299	294½	295	− 1¼	300	260	8,173
Dec	284	284½	280½	281	− ¾	284½	239	23,244
Mr97	289½	289¾	286½	286¾	− 1¼	289¾	279¼	796
Jly	292	293¼	290	290	− 1¾	293¼	284	176
Dec	272	273	271	271½	−	273	249¾	325

Est vol 100,000; vol Wd 85,650; open int 495,740, + 145.

Futures prices are listed in financial newspapers such as *The Wall Street Journal.* An example listing for corn futures is shown in Figure 10.3. The heading explains that a standard contract for corn is for 5,000 bushels, and that prices are quoted in cents per bushel. The first column of the table lists the delivery dates for the various contracts, with the earliest date being first. The next columns indicate various prices for the previous trading day: Open, High, Low, Settle, and Change, followed by Lifetime High and Low. The last column is Open Interest, which is the total number of contracts outstanding. (Both the long and short positions are counted, so open interest really reflects twice the number of contracts committed.) Delivery of the commodity may be made anytime within the specified month.

Margin accounts not only serve as accounts to collect or pay out daily profits, they also guarantee that contract holders will not default on their obligations. Margin accounts usually do not pay interest, so the cash in these accounts is, in effect, losing money. However, many brokers allow Treasury bills or other securities, as well as cash, to serve as margin, so interest can be earned indirectly. If the value of a margin account should drop below a defined maintenance margin level (usually about 75% of the initial margin requirement), a **margin call** is issued to the contract holder, demanding additional margin. Otherwise the futures position will be closed out by taking an equal and opposite position.

Example 10.7 (Margin)   Suppose that Mr. Smith takes a long position of one contract in corn (5,000 bushels) for March delivery at a price of $2.10 (per bushel). And suppose the broker requires margin of $800 with a maintenance margin of $600.

The next day the price of this contract drops to $2.07. This represents a loss of $.03 \times 5,000 = \$150$. The broker will take this amount from the margin account, leaving a balance of $650. The following day the price drops again to $2.05. This represents an additional loss of $100, which is again deducted from the margin account. At this point the margin account is $550, which is below the maintenance level. The broker calls Mr. Smith and tells him that he must deposit at least $50 in his margin account, or his position will be closed out, meaning that Mr. Smith will be forced to give up his contract, leaving him with $550 in his account.

10.7 FUTURES PRICES

There is, at any one time, only one price associated with a futures contract—the delivery price. The value of existing contracts is always zero because they are marked to market. The delivery price will in general be different from the spot price of the underlying asset, but the two must bear some relation to each other. In fact, as the maturity date approaches, the futures price and the spot price must approach each other, actually converging to the same value. This effect, termed **convergence,** is illustrated in Figure 10.4.

As a general rule we expect that the (theoretical) futures price should have a close relation to the forward price, the delivery price at which forward contracts would be written. Both are prices for future delivery. However, even if we idealize the mechanics of forward and futures trading by assuming no transactions costs and by assuming that no margin is required (or that margin earns competitive interest), there remains a fundamental difference between the cash flow processes associated with forwards and futures. With forwards, there is no cash flow until the final period, where either delivery is made or the contract is settled in cash according to the difference between the spot price and the previously established delivery price. With futures, there is cash flow every period after the first, the cash flow being derived from the most recent change in futures price. It seems likely that this difference in cash flow pattern will cause forward and futures prices to differ. In fact, however, under the assumption that interest rates are deterministic and follow expectations dynamics, as described in Chapter 4, the forward and futures prices must be identical if arbitrage opportunities are precluded. This important result is established here:

 Futures–forward equivalence   *Suppose that interest rates are known to follow expectations dynamics. Then the theoretical futures and forward prices of corresponding contracts are identical.*

> *Proof:*   Let F_0 be the initial futures price (but remember that no payment is made initially). Let G_0 be the corresponding forward price (to be paid at

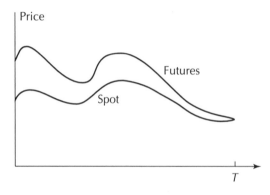

FIGURE 10.4   Convergence of spot and futures prices. The futures price converges to the spot price as time approaches the delivery date.

delivery time). Assume that there are $T + 1$ time points and corresponding futures prices, as indicated:

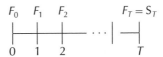

Let $d(j, k)$ denote the discount rate at time j for a bond of unit face value maturing at time k (with $j < k$).

We now consider two strategies for participation in the futures and forward markets, respectively.

Strategy A

- At time 0:   Go long $d(1, T)$ futures.
- At time 1:   Increase position to $d(2, T)$

$$\vdots$$

- At time k: Increase position to $d(k + 1, T)$
- At time $T - 1$:   Increase position to 1.

The profit at time $k + 1$ from the previous period is

$$\left(F_{k+1} - F_k\right)d(k + 1, T).$$

As part of strategy A we invest this profit at time $k + 1$ in the interest rate market until time T. It is thereby transformed to the final amount

$$\frac{d(k + 1, T)}{d(k + 1, T)}\left(F_{k+1} - F_k\right) = F_{k+1} - F_k.$$

The total profit from strategy A is therefore

$$\text{profit}_A = \sum_{k=0}^{T-1} F_{k+1} - F_k = F_T - F_0 = S_T - F_0.$$

Note that at each step before the end, there is zero net cash flow because all profits (or losses) are absorbed in the interest rate market. Hence a zero investment produces profit$_A$.

Strategy B   Take a long position in one forward contract. This requires no initial investment and produces a profit of

$$\text{profit}_B = S_T - G_0.$$

We can now form a new strategy, which is A $-$ B. This combined strategy also requires no cash flow until the final period, at which point it produces profit of $G_0 - F_0$. This is a deterministic amount, and hence must be zero if there is no opportunity for arbitrage. Hence $G_0 = F_0$. ∎

When interest rates are not deterministic, the equivalence may not hold, but the equivalence is considered quite accurate for purposes of routine analysis. The result is important because it at least partially justifies simplifying an analysis of futures hedging by considering the corresponding hedge with forward contracts, where the cash flow occurs only at the delivery or settlement date.

Example 10.8 (Wheat contracts)   In January a large producer of commercial flour and bread wishes to lock in the price for a large order of wheat. The producer would like to buy 500,000 bushels of wheat forward for May delivery. Although this producer could probably arrange a special forward contract, he decides instead to use the futures market, since it is organized and more convenient. The producer recognizes (and verifies) that the futures price is equal to the forward price he could negotiate.

The current futures (or forward) price for May delivery is $3.30 per bushel. The size of a standard wheat futures contract is 5,000 bushels. Hence the producer decides that he needs 100 contracts.

Details of the futures market transaction are shown in Table 10.5. For simplicity this table shows accounting on a monthly basis, rather than on a daily basis.

The left part of the table shows the dates and the corresponding hypothetical prices (in cents) for a futures contract for May delivery. The next section, headed "Forward," shows the result of entering a forward contract for the delivery of 500,000 bushels of wheat in May, followed by the subsequent closing out of that contract so that delivery is not actually taken. There is no cash flow associated with this contract until May. Then there is the profit in May of 22 cents per bushel, or a total of $110,000.

The next section of the table, headed "Futures contracts 1," shows the accounting details of entering a 100 contract long futures position in January and closing out this position in May. It is assumed that an account is established to hold all profits and losses. It is also assumed that the prevailing interest rate is 12%, or 1% per month, and that there are no margin requirements. Note that no money is required when the

TABLE 10.5
Futures and Forward Transactions

		Forward	Futures contracts 1				Futures contracts 2			
Date	Price	Profit	Pos.	Profit	Interest	Balance	Pos.	Profit	Interest	Balance
Jan 1	330	$0	100	$0	$0	$0	97	$0	$0	$0
Feb 1	340	0	100	50,000	0	50,000	98	48,500	0	48,500
Mar 1	355	0	100	75,000	500	125,500	99	73,500	485	122,485
Apr 1	345	0	100	−50,000	1,255	76,755	100	−49,500	1,225	74,210
May 1	352	110,000	0	35,000	768	112,523	0	35,000	742	109,952
Total		$110,000		$110,000				$107,500		

The details of a forward contract, a fixed futures contract, and a futures contract strategy designed to mimic a forward are shown.

order is placed. A profit of $50,000 is obtained in the second month because the futures price increased by 10 cents. This profit enters the account. The next month's balance reflects the additional profit and interest of the account. The total cash flow is $110,000, exactly as in the case of the forward contract. However, because the cash flow occurs at various times, the actual final balance is $112,523. (The result is more favorable in this case because prices rose early, but that is not the point.)

The third section of the table, headed "Futures contracts 2," shows how futures can be used to duplicate a forward contract more precisely, by using the construction in the proof of the futures–forward equivalence result. Since interest is 1% a month, the discount rate increases by about 1% per month as well. Hence in this approach the producer initially goes long 97 contracts and increases this by 1 contract per month, finally reaching 100 contracts. Exactly the same accounting system is used as in the previous method. In this case the resulting final balance is $109,952, which is very close to the $110,000 figure obtained by a pure forward contract—the slight difference being due to rounding of the discount rate to even percentages so that integral numbers of contracts could be used.

This example illustrates that there is indeed a slight difference between forward and futures contract implementation if a constant contract level is used. In practice, however, the difference between using forward and futures contracts is small over short intervals of time, such as a few months. Furthermore, if interest rates are deterministic and follow expectations dynamics, then the difference between using futures and using forwards can be reduced to zero within rounding errors caused by the restriction to integral numbers of contracts.

10.8 RELATION TO EXPECTED SPOT PRICE*

At time zero it is logical to form an opinion, or expectation, about the spot price of a commodity at time T. Is the current futures price for delivery at time T a good estimate of the future spot price; that is, is $F = E(S_T)$?

If there were inequality, say, $F < E(S_T)$, a speculator might take a long position in futures and then at time T purchase the commodity at F according to the contract and sell the commodity at S_T for an expected profit of $E(S_T) - F$. If the inequality were in the other direction, the investor could carry out the reverse plan by taking a short position in futures. Hence speculators are likely to respond to any inequality.

Hedgers, on the other hand, participate in futures mainly to reduce the risks of commercial operations, not to speculate on commodity prices. Hence hedgers are unlikely to be influenced by small discrepancies between futures prices and expected spot prices.

Now suppose that there happen to be many more hedgers that are short in futures than those that are long. For the market to balance, speculators must enter the market and take long positions. They will do so only if they believe $F < E(S_T)$. Conversely, if there are more hedgers that are long in futures than those that are short, speculators will take the corresponding short position only if they believe $F > E(S_T)$.

The two situations have been given special names. If the futures price is below the expected future spot price, that is **normal backwardation.** If the futures price is above the expected future spot price, that is **contango.**

10.9 THE PERFECT HEDGE

The primary use of futures contracts is to hedge against risk. Hedging strategies can be simple or complex; we shall illustrate some of the main approaches to their design in the remainder of this chapter.

The simplest hedging strategy is the **perfect hedge,** where the risk associated with a future commitment to deliver or receive an asset is completely eliminated by taking an **equal and opposite** position in the futures market. Equivalently, the hedge is constructed to effectively make anticipated future market purchases or sales immediately. This locks in the price of the futures transaction; there is absolutely no price risk. Such a strategy is possible only if there is a futures contract that exactly matches, with respect to the nature of the asset and the terms of delivery, the obligation that is being hedged.

Example 10.9 (A wheat hedge)   Consider again the producer of flour and bread of Example 10.8. The producer has received a large order for delivery on May 20 at a specified price. To satisfy this order, the producer will purchase 500,000 bushels of wheat on the spot market shortly before the order is due. The producer has calculated its profit on the basis of current prices for wheat, but if the wheat price should measurably increase, the order may become unprofitable. The producer can hedge by taking an equal and opposite position in wheat futures. (That is, the producer is obligated to supply processed wheat, so it goes opposite the obligation and purchases wheat. Alternatively, the producer may think of it as *purchasing early* wheat that it must ultimately purchase.)

If we ignore the slight discrepancy between futures and forwards due to differences in cash flow timing, we can treat the futures contract just like a forward. The producer will close out the position in the futures market and then purchase wheat in the spot market. Since the price in the spot market will be the same as the closing futures price, the net effect is that the producer pays the original price of $3.30 per bushel.

Example 10.10 (A foreign currency hedge)   A U.S. electronics firm has received an order to sell equipment to a German customer in 90 days. The price of the order is specified as 500,000 Deutsche mark, which will be paid upon delivery. The U.S. firm faces risk associated with the exchange rate between Deutsche mark and U.S. dollars.

The firm can hedge this foreign exchange risk with four Deutsche mark contracts (125,000 DM per contract) with a 90-day maturity date. Since the firm will be receiving Deutsche mark in 90 days, it hedges by taking an equal and opposite position now— that is, it goes *short* four contracts. (Viewed alternatively, after receiving Deutsche mark the firm will want to sell them, so it sells them early by going short.)

10.10 THE MINIMUM-VARIANCE HEDGE

It is not always possible to form a perfect hedge with futures contracts. There may be no contract involving the exact asset whose value must be hedged, the delivery dates of the available contracts may not match the asset obligation date, the amount of the asset obligated may not be an integral multiple of the contract size, there may be a lack of liquidity in the futures market, or the delivery terms may not coincide with the those of the obligation. In these situations, the original risk cannot be eliminated completely with a futures contract, but usually the risk can be reduced.

One measure of the lack of hedging perfection is the **basis,** defined as the mismatch between the spot and futures prices. Specifically,

basis = spot price of asset to be hedged − futures price of contract used.

If the asset to be hedged is identical to that of the futures contract, then the basis will be zero at the delivery date. However, in general, for the reasons mentioned, the final basis may not be zero as anticipated. Usually the final basis is a random quantity, and this precludes the possibility of a perfect hedge. The basis risk calls for alternative hedging techniques.

One common method of hedging in the presence of basis risk is the minimum-variance hedge. The general formula for this hedge can be deduced quite readily. Suppose that at time zero the situation to be hedged is described by a cash flow x to occur at time T. For example, if the obligation is to purchase W units of an asset at time T, we have $x = WS$, where S is the spot price of the asset at T. Let F denote the futures price of the contract that is used as a hedge, and let h denote the futures position taken. We neglect interest payments on margin accounts by assuming that all profits (or losses) in the futures account are settled at T. The cash flow at time T is therefore equal to the original obligation plus the profit in the futures account. Hence,

$$\text{cash flow} = y = x + (F_T - F_0)h.$$

We find the variance of the cash flow as

$$\text{var}(y) = \text{E}[x - \overline{x} + (F_T - \overline{F}_T)h]^2 = \text{var}(x) + 2\,\text{cov}(x, F_T)h + \text{var}(F_T)h^2.$$

This is minimized by setting the derivative with respect to h equal to zero. This leads to the following result:

Minimum-variance hedging formula   *The minimum-variance hedge and the resulting variance are*

$$h = -\frac{\text{cov}(x, F_T)}{\text{var}(F_T)} \tag{10.7}$$

$$\text{var}(y) = \text{var}(x) - \frac{\text{cov}(x, F_T)^2}{\text{var}(F_T)}. \tag{10.8}$$

When the obligation has the form of a fixed amount W of an asset whose spot price is S_T, (10.7) becomes

$$h = -\beta W \tag{10.9}$$

where

$$\beta = \frac{\text{cov}(S_T, F_T)}{\text{var}(F_T)}.$$

This, of course, reminds us of the general mean–variance formulas of Chapter 7; and indeed it is closely related to them.

Example 10.11 (The perfect hedge)   As a special case, suppose that the futures commodity is identical to the spot commodity being hedged. In that case $F_T = S_T$. Suppose that the obligation is W units of the commodity, so that $x = WS_T$. In that case $\text{cov}(x, F_T) = \text{cov}(S_T, F_T)W = \text{var}(F_T)W$. Therefore, according to (10.7) we have $h = -W$, and according to (10.8) we find $\text{var}(y) = 0$. In other words, the minimum-variance hedge reduces to the perfect hedge when the futures price is perfectly correlated with the spot price of the commodity being hedged.

Example 10.12 (Hedging foreign currency with alternative futures)   The BIG H Corporation (a U.S. corporation) has obtained a large order from a Danish firm. Payment will be in 60 days in the amount of 1 million Danish kroner. BIG H would like to hedge the exchange risk, but there is no futures contract for Danish kroner. The vice president for finance of BIG H decides that the company can hedge with German marks, although DM and kroner do not follow each other exactly.

He notes that the current exchange rates are $K = .164$ dollar/kroner and $M = .625$ dollar/DM. Hence the exchange rate between marks and kroner is $K/M = .164/.625 = .262$ DM/kroner. Therefore receipt of 1 million Danish kroner is equivalent to the receipt of 262,000 DM at the current exchange rate. He deduces that an equal and opposite hedge would be to short 262,000 DM.

An intern working at BIG H suggests that a minimum-variance hedge be considered as an alternative. The intern is given a few days to work out the details. He does some quick historical studies and estimates that the monthly fluctuations in the U.S. exchange rates K and M are correlated with a correlation coefficient of about .8. The standard deviation of these fluctuations is found to be about 3% of its value per month for marks and slightly less, 2.5%, for kroner. In this problem the x of (10.7) denotes the dollar value of 1 million Danish kroner in 60 days, and F_T is the dollar value of a German mark at that time. We may put $x = K \times 1$ million. The intern therefore estimates beta as

$$\beta = \frac{\text{cov}(K, M)}{\text{var}(M)} = \frac{\sigma_{KM}}{\sigma_K \sigma_M} \times \frac{\sigma_K}{\sigma_M} = \rho \frac{\sigma_K}{\sigma_M} = .8 \times \frac{.025K}{.03M}.$$

Hence the minimum-variance hedge is

$$h = -\frac{\text{cov}(x, F)}{\text{var}(F)} = -\frac{\text{cov}(k, M) \times 1,000,000}{\text{var}(M)}$$

$$= \left[-.8 \times \frac{2.5}{3.0} \times .262 \times 1,000,000 \right] = -175,000 \, \text{DM} \, .$$

The minimum-variance hedge is smaller than that implied by a full hedge based on the exchange ratios; it is reduced by the correlation coefficient and by the ratio of standard deviations.

We can go a bit further and find out how effective this hedge really is, compared to doing nothing. We have $x = K \times 1$ million. Hence $\text{cov}(x, M) = 1$ million $\times \sigma_{KM}$ and $\sigma_x = 1$ million $\times \sigma_K$. Combining these two, we have $\text{cov}(x, M) = \sigma_{KM} \sigma_x / \sigma_K$. Using the minimum-variance hedging formula, we find

$$\text{var}(y) = \text{var}(x) - \frac{\text{cov}(x, M)^2}{\sigma_M^2} = \left[1 - \left(\frac{\sigma_{MK}}{\sigma_K \sigma_M} \right)^2 \right] \text{var}(x) \, .$$

Hence,

$$\text{stdev}(y) = \left(\sqrt{1 - .8^2} \right) \text{stdev}(x) = .6 \times \text{stdev}(x).$$

Hence the minimum-variance hedge reduces risk by a factor of .6. A hedge with lower risk would be obtained if a hedging instrument could be found that was more highly correlated with Danish kroner.

Example 10.13 (Changing portfolio beta with stock index futures) Mrs. Smith owns a large portfolio that is heavily weighted toward high technology stocks. She believes that these securities will perform exceedingly well compared to the market as a whole over the next several months. However, Mrs. Smith realizes that her portfolio, which has a beta (with respect to the market) of 1.4, is exposed to a significant degree of market risk. If the general market declines, her portfolio will also decline, even if her securities do achieve significant excess return above that predicted by, say, CAPM, as she believes they will.

Mrs. Smith decides to hedge against this market risk. She can change the beta of her portfolio by selling some stock index futures. She might decide to construct a minimum-variance hedge of her $2 million portfolio by shorting $2 million $\times 1.4 =$ $2.8 million of S&P 500 stock index futures with maturity in 120 days. Since the normal beta of her portfolio is based on the S&P 500, this beta is the same beta as that in the general equation, (10.9). The overall new beta of her hedged portfolio, after taking the short position in the stock index futures, is zero.

10.11 OPTIMAL HEDGING*

Although the minimum-variance hedge is useful and fairly simple, it can be improved by viewing the hedging problem from a portfolio perspective. Suppose again that there is an existing cash flow commitment x at time T. And suppose that this will be hedged by futures contracts in the amount h, leading to a final cash flow of $x - h(F_T - F_0)$. If a utility function is assigned, it is appropriate to solve the problem[4]

$$\underset{h}{\text{maximize}} \, \text{E}\{U[x + h(F_T - F_0)]\}. \tag{10.10}$$

This approach fully accounts for the basis risk and is perfectly tailored to the risk aversion characteristics of the person or institution facing the risk.

Example 10.14 (Mean–variance hedging)   One obvious choice for the utility function is the quadratic function

$$U(x) = x - \frac{b}{2}x^2$$

with $b > 0$. Then (10.10) leads to a maximization problem involving the means, variances, and covariances of the variables. Smoother derivations and neater formulas are obtained, however, by recognizing that this is essentially equivalent to maximizing the expression

$$V(x) = \text{E}(x) - r \, \text{var}(x)$$

for some positive constant r. The function V can be thought of as an altered mean–variance utility.

For meaningful results, the magnitude of r must be determined by the problem itself. One reasonable choice is $r = 1/(2\hat{x})$, where $\hat{x}$ is a rough estimate of the final value of $\text{E}(x)$. This then weights variance and one-half of $[\text{E}(x)]^2$ about equally.

Using $V(x)$ as the objective, the optimal hedging problem becomes

$$\text{maximize} \, \{\text{E}[x + h(F_T - F_0)] - r \, \text{var}(x + hF_T)\}. \tag{10.11}$$

This leads directly, after some algebra, to the solution

$$h = \frac{\overline{F}_T - F_0}{2r \, \text{var}(F_T)} - \frac{\text{cov}(x, F_T)}{\text{var}(F_T)}. \tag{10.12}$$

Note that the second term is exactly the minimum-variance solution. The first term augments this by accounting for the expected gain due to futures participation. In other words, the second term is a pure hedging term, whereas the first term accounts for the fact that hedging is a form of investment, and the expected return of that investment should be incorporated into the portfolio.

This simple formula illustrates, however, the practical difficulty associated with optimal hedging. It is quite difficult to obtain meaningful estimates of $\overline{F}_T - F_0$. In fact, in many cases a reasonable estimate is that this difference is zero, so it is understandable why many hedgers prefer to use only the minimum-variance portion of the solution.

---

[4] Ideally, we should express utility in terms of total wealth; but we may assume here that the additional wealth simply changes the definition of U.

Example 10.15 (The wheat hedge) Consider the producer of flour and bread of Example 10.8. It is likely that this producer, being a large player in the market, has a good knowledge of wheat market conditions. Suppose that this producer expects the price of wheat to increase by 5% in 3 months. However, the producer recognizes that the wheat market has approximately 30% volatility (per year), so the producer assigns a 15% variation to the 3-month forecast ($15\% = 30\%/\sqrt{4}$).

Using $x = 500,000 F_T$ and applying (10.12), we find

$$h = -500,000 + \frac{1}{2r \operatorname{var}(F_T)}(\overline{F}_T - F_0)$$

$$= -500,000 + \frac{1}{2r F_0 \operatorname{var}(F_T/F_0)}\left(\frac{\overline{F}_T}{F_0} - 1\right)$$

$$= -500,000 + \frac{1}{6.60(.15)^2 r} \times .05$$

$$= -500,000 + \frac{.336}{r}.$$

Note that the term $-500,000$ represents the equal and opposite position of perfect hedging. This is augmented by a speculative term, determined by the estimate of return on the futures price, and by the value of r.

Using the method of selecting r suggested earlier, we have $r = 1/1,000,000$. Hence the final hedge is $h = -500,000 + 336,000 = -164,000$.

10.12 HEDGING NONLINEAR RISK⋆

In our examples so far the risk being hedged was linear, in the sense that final wealth x was a linear function of an underlying market variable, such as a commodity price. The general theory of hedging does not depend on this assumption, and indeed nonlinear risks frequently occur. For example, immunization of a bond portfolio with T-bills (see Exercise 15) is a nonlinear hedging problem—because the change in the value of a bond portfolio is a nonlinear function of the future T-bill price.

Nonlinear risk can arise in complex contracts. For example, suppose a U.S. firm is negotiating to sell a commodity to a Japanese company at a future date for a price specified in Japanese yen. Both parties recognize that the U.S. firm would face exchange rate risk. Hence an agreement might be made where the U.S. firm absorbs adverse rate changes up to 10%, while beyond that the two companies share the impact equally.

Nonlinear risks also arise when the price of a good is influenced by the quantity being bought or sold. This situation occurs in farming when the magnitudes of all farmers' crops are mutually correlated, and hence any particular farmer finds that his harvest size is correlated to the market price. We give a detailed example of this type.

Example 10.16 (A corn farmer) A certain commodity, which we call corn, is grown by many farmers, but the amount of corn harvested by every farmer depends on the

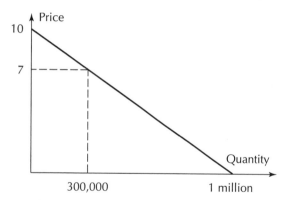

FIGURE 10.5   Demand for corn. The price of corn varies from \$10 to \$0 per bushel, depending on the total quantity produced.

weather: sunny weather yields more corn than cloudy weather during the growing season. All corn is harvested simultaneously, and the price per bushel is determined by a market demand function, which is shown in Figure 10.5. This demand function is

$$P = 10 - D/100{,}000$$

where D is the demand (which is also equal, through supply and demand equality, to the total crop size). Each farmer's crop will produce an amount of corn C which is random. We assume that the amount of corn grown on each farm can vary between 0 and 6,000 bushels, with expected value $\overline{C} = 3{,}000$. The amounts produced on different farms are all perfectly correlated. There are a total of 100 farms, and thus $\overline{D} = 300{,}000$. The revenue to a farmer will be

$$R = PC = \left(10 - \frac{D}{100{,}000}\right) C = 10\,C - \frac{C^2}{1{,}000}. \tag{10.13}$$

This shows that the revenue is a nonlinear function of the underlying uncertain variable C. Since C is random, each farmer faces nonlinear risk.

Can a farmer hedge this risk in advance by participating in the futures market for corn? Try to think this through before we present the analysis. Since the farmer is ultimately going to sell his corn harvest at the (risky) spot price, it might be prudent to sell some corn now at a known price in the futures market. Indeed, if the farmer knew exactly how much corn he would produce, and only the price were uncertain, he could implement an equal and opposite policy by shorting this amount in the corn futures market. Perhaps in this actual situation where both amount and price are uncertain, he should short some lesser amount. What do you think?

The way to find the best hedge is to work out the relationships between revenue, production, and the futures position. We assume for simplicity that interest rates are zero. If each farm produces the expected value of $\overline{C} = 3{,}000$, then $D = 300{,}000$ and we find $P = \$7$ per bushel. Hence \$7 represents a nominal anticipated price. Let us assume that \$7 is also the current futures price P_0. We want to determine the best futures participation.

Let h be the futures market position. With this position the farmer's revenue will be

$$R = PC + h(P - P_0).$$

Substituting for P in terms of C, we find

$$R = 10C - \frac{C^2}{1,000} + \frac{\overline{C} - C}{1,000}h.$$

This is the equation that the farmer should consider. One simple way to study this equation is to display it in a spreadsheet array, as shown in Table 10.6. This table has the farm's production of corn across the columns, and the futures position (in hundreds of bushels) running along the rows. The entries are the corresponding revenues. For example, note that if the final production is 3,000 bushels (the expected value), then the revenue is $21,000, independent of the futures position. This is because the final price will be $7, which is equal to the current futures price; hence the futures contract makes no profit or loss.

TABLE 10.6
Revenue from Production and Hedging

Futures position	Corn production (in 100's of bushels)								
	10	15	20	25	30	35	40	45	50
50	19000	20250	21000	21250	21000	20250	19000	17250	15000
45	18000	19500	20500	21000	21000	20500	19500	18000	16000
40	17000	18750	20000	20750	21000	20750	20000	18750	17000
35	16000	18000	19500	20500	21000	21000	20500	19500	18000
30	15000	17250	19000	20250	21000	21250	21000	20250	19000
25	14000	16500	18500	20000	21000	21500	21500	21000	20000
20	13000	15750	18000	19750	21000	21750	22000	21750	21000
15	12000	15000	17500	19500	21000	22000	22500	22500	22000
10	11000	14250	17000	19250	21000	22250	23000	23250	23000
5	10000	13500	16500	19000	21000	22500	23500	24000	24000
0	9000	12750	16000	18750	21000	22750	24000	24750	25000
−5	8000	12000	15500	18500	21000	23000	24500	25500	26000
−10	7000	11250	15000	18250	21000	23250	25000	26250	27000
−15	6000	10500	14500	18000	21000	23500	25500	27000	28000
−20	5000	9750	14000	17750	21000	23750	26000	27750	29000
−25	4000	9000	13500	17500	21000	24000	26500	28500	30000
−30	3000	8250	13000	17250	21000	24250	27000	29250	31000
−35	2000	7500	12500	17000	21000	24500	27500	30000	32000
−40	1000	6750	12000	16750	21000	24750	28000	30750	33000
−45	0	6000	11500	16500	21000	25000	28500	31500	34000
−50	−1000	5250	11000	16250	21000	25250	29000	32250	35000

Revenue can be calculated for various futures positions and production outcomes using a spreadsheet.

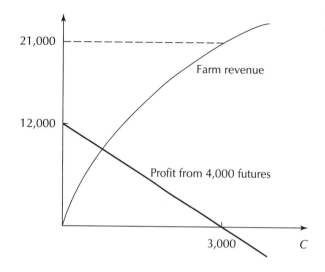

FIGURE 10.6   Farm revenue and hedging. The best futures position is obtained when the slope of its payoff is equal to and opposite the slope of the revenue.

The equal and opposite hedge would correspond to a futures position of $-3,000$ (or -30 in the table). Note that this is actually a very risky position—much more so than the zero position—for the revenue varies widely from \$3,000 to \$31,000. What is the least risky position? We find that position by scanning the rows, looking for the row with the least variation. It is the row marked 40, corresponding to a position of $+4,000$. Wow! The optimal position has a sign opposite to that which we might have expected, and a magnitude much greater than the expected value of the crop.[5]

How can we understand the nature of this solution? The original revenue function (10.13), is shown in Figure 10.6. Also shown in the figure is the profit from a $+4,000$ futures position as a function of the amount of corn grown. Note that the profit from the futures contract *decreases* as more corn is grown. This is because as more corn is grown, the final spot price of corn decreases. The revenue increases as more corn is produced (although eventually the revenue curve bends downward). At the nominal value of $C = 3,000$, the slopes of the two functions are exactly opposite—the slope of the revenue curve is 4 and the slope of the futures profit line is -4. The two slopes cancel, meaning that the net revenue curve is flat at the nominal point. This is the best linear approximation to the nonlinear hedging problem.

Here is one way to think about the situation, to resolve the apparent conundrum. The farmer has a natural hedge against price movements. If the price of corn should go down, the farmer's revenue from corn will go *up* because of his increased harvest, instead of down as it would if the harvest were unaffected. This natural hedge is, in fact, of greater magnitude than an equal and opposite hedge, which would keep net revenue constant. Hence the farmer must counteract the natural hedge by taking a positive position in the futures market.

---

[5]It can be shown that this position is indeed optimal for any concave increasing utility function if the probabilities of different-size harvests are symmetric. (See Exercise 16.)

10.13 SUMMARY

A forward contract is a contract to buy or sell an asset at a fixed date in the future. The intrinsic value of a forward contract may vary from day to day, but there are no cash flows until the delivery date. A futures contract is similar, except that it is marked to market daily, with profits or losses flowing to a margin account so that the contract continues to have zero value. The price of a forward contract, in the absence of carrying costs and assuming that the commodity can be shorted, is just $F = S/d$, where S is the current value of the asset and d is the discount rate that applies for the interval of time until delivery. In other words, F is the future value of the current spot price S. If there are carrying costs, F is the future value of these costs plus the future value of S. If shorting is not possible, as is frequently the case, the forward price is restricted only to be less than S/d.

If interest rates follow expectation dynamics, the prices of a forward contract and a corresponding futures contract are identical, even though their cash flow patterns are slightly different. For analysis purposes, a futures contract can therefore be approximated by the corresponding forward contract.

Forwards and futures are used to hedge risk in commercial transactions. The simplest type of hedge is the perfect, or equal and opposite, hedge, where an obligation to buy or sell a commodity in a future spot market is essentially executed early at a known price by entering a futures contract for the same quantity. If there is no hedging instrument available that matches the commodity of the obligation exactly, a minimum-variance hedge can be constructed using instruments that are correlated with the obligation. A relatively high correlation is required, however, to produce a significant hedging effect.

More sophisticated hedging is obtained by taking an optimal portfolio viewpoint, maximizing expected utility subject to the constraints implied by obligations and market conditions. This approach has the advantage that it can handle essentially any situation, even those where the decisions affect portfolio value nonlinearly, but it has the disadvantage that detailed information is required. In any case, futures market participation is an important aspect of many hedging operations.

EXERCISES

1. (Gold futures)   The current price of gold is $412 per ounce. The storage cost is $2 per ounce per year, payable quarterly in advance. Assuming a constant interest rate of 9% compounded quarterly, what is the theoretical forward price of gold for delivery in 9 months?

2. (Proportional carrying charges ◊)   Suppose that a forward contract on an asset is written at time zero and there are M periods until delivery. Suppose that the carrying charge in period k is $qS(k)$, where $S(k)$ is the spot price of the asset in period k. Show that the forward price is

$$F = \frac{(1-q)^M S}{d(0, M)}.$$

[*Hint:* Consider a portfolio that pays all carrying costs by selling a fraction of the asset as required. Let the number of units of the asset held at time k be $x(k)$ and find $x(M)$ in terms of $x(0)$.]

3. **(Silver contract)**   At the beginning of April one year, the silver forward prices (in cents per troy ounce) were as follows:

Apr	406.50
July	416.64
Sept	423.48
Dec	433.84

(Assume that contracts settle at the end of the given month.) The carrying cost of silver is about 20 cents per ounce per year, paid at the beginning of each month. Estimate the interest rate at that time.

4. **(Continuous-time carrying charges)**   Suppose that a continuous-time compounding framework is used with a fixed interest rate r. Suppose that the carrying charge per unit of time is proportional to the spot price; that is, the charge is $qS(t)$. Show that the theoretical forward price of a contract with delivery date T is

$$F = S e^{(r-q)T}.$$

[*Hint:* Use Exercise 2.]

5. **(Carrying cost proof)**   Complete the second half of the proof of the "forward price formula with carrying cost" in Section 10.3. To construct the arbitrage, go long one unit of a forward and short one unit spot. To execute the short, it is necessary to borrow the asset from someone, say, Mr. X. As part of our arrangement with Mr. X we ask that he give us the carrying costs as they would normally occur, since he would have to pay them if we did not borrow the asset. We then invest these cash flows. At the final time we buy one unit as obligated by our forward and repay Mr. X. Show the details of this argument.

6. **(Foreign currency alternative)**   Consider the situation of Example 10.10. Rather than shorting a futures contract, the U.S. firm could borrow $500/(1 + r_G)$ Deutsche mark (where r_G is the 90-day interest rate in Germany), sell these marks into dollars, invest the dollars in T-bills, and then later repay the Deutsche mark loan with the payment received for the German order. Discuss how this procedure is related to the original one.

7. **(A bond forward)**   A certain 10-year bond is currently selling for $920. A friend of yours owns a forward contract on this bond that has a delivery date in 1 year and a delivery price of $940. The bond pays coupons of $80 every 6 months, with one due 6 months from now and another just before maturity of the forward. The current interest rates for 6 months and 1 year (compounded semiannually) are 7% and 8%, respectively (annual rates compounded every 6 months). What is the current value of the forward contract?

8. **(Simple formula)**   Derive the formula (10.6) by converting a cash flow of a bond to that of the fixed portion of the swap.

9. (Equity swap ◇) Mr. A. Gaylord manages a pension fund and believes that his stock selection ability is excellent. However, he is worried because the market could go down. He considers entering an equity swap where each quarter i, up to quarter M, he pays counterparty B the previous quarter's total rate of return r_i on the S&P 500 index times some notional principal and receives payments at a fixed rate r on the same principal. The total rate of return includes dividends. Specifically, $1 + r_i = (S_i + d_i)/S_{i-1}$, where S_i and d_i are the values of the index at i and the dividends received from $i - 1$ to i, respectively. Derive the value of such a swap by the following steps:

(a) Let $V_{i-1}(S_i + d_i)$ denote the value at time $i - 1$ of receiving $S_i + d_i$ at time i. Argue that $V_{i-1}(S_i + d_i) = S_{i-1}$ and find $V_{i-1}(r_i)$.
(b) Find $V_0(r_i)$.
(c) Find $\sum_{i=1}^{M} V_0(r_i)$.
(d) Find the value of the swap.

10. (Forward vanilla) The floating rate portion of a plain vanilla interest rate swap with yearly payments and a notional principal of one unit has cash flows at the end of each year defining a stream starting at time 1 of $(c_0, c_1, c_2, \ldots, c_{M-1})$, where c_i is the actual short rate at the beginning of year i. Using the concepts of forwards, argue that the value at time zero of c_i to be received at time $i + 1$ is $d(0, i + 1)r_i$, where r_i is the short rate for time i implied by the current (time zero) term structure and $d(0, i + 1)$ is the implied discount factor to time $i + 1$. The value of the stream is therefore $\sum_{i=0}^{M-1} d(0, i + 1)r_i$. Show that this reduces to the formula for V at the end of Section 10.5.

11. (Specific vanilla) Suppose the current term structure of interest rates is (.070, .073, .077, .081, .084, .088). A plain vanilla interest rate swap will make payments at the end of each year equal to the floating short rate that was posted at the beginning of that year. A 6-year swap having a notional principal of $10 million is being configured.

(a) What is the value of the floating rate portion of the swap?
(b) What rate of interest for the fixed portion of the swap would make the two sides of the swap equal?

12. (Derivation) Derive the mean–variance hedge formula given by (10.12).

13. (Grapefruit hedge) Farmer D. Jones has a crop of grapefruit that will be ready for harvest and sale as 150,000 pounds of grapefruit juice in 3 months. Jones is worried about possible price changes, so he is considering hedging. There is no futures contract for grapefruit juice, but there is a futures contract for orange juice. His son, Gavin, recently studied minimum-variance hedging and suggests it as a possible approach. Currently the spot prices are $1.20 per pound for orange juice and $1.50 per pound for grapefruit juice. The standard deviation of the prices of orange juice and grapefruit juice is about 20% per year, and the correlation coefficient between them is about .7. What is the minimum-variance hedge for farmer Jones, and how effective is this hedge as compared to no hedge?

14. (Opposite hedge variance) Assume that cash flow is given by $y = S_T W + (F_T - F_0)h$. Let $\sigma_S^2 = \text{var}(S_T)$, $\sigma_F^2 = \text{var}(F_T)$, and $\sigma_{ST} = \text{cov}(S_T, F_T)$.

(a) In an equal and opposite hedge, h is taken to be an opposite equivalent dollar value of the hedging instrument. Therefore $h = -kW$, where k is the price ratio between the asset and the hedging instrument. Express the standard deviation of y with the equal and opposite hedge in the form

$$\sigma_y = W \sigma_S \times B.$$

(That is, find B.)

(b) Apply this to Example 10.12 and compare with the minimum-variance hedge.

15. (Immunization as hedging ◇)   A pension fund has just paid some of its liabilities, and as a result of this transaction the fund is no longer fully immunized. The fund manager decides that instead of changing the portfolio, the firm should hedge its position using a futures contract on a Treasury bond. The fund manager wants to hedge against parallel changes to the spot rate curve. Use the following set of information to determine the numerical values of the hedging position:

- Yearly spot rate sequence: .05, .053, .056, .058, .06, .061.
- Liabilities: $1 million in 1 year, $2 million in 2 years, and $1 million in 3 years.
- Current bond portfolio: $4.253 million in par value of zero-coupon bonds maturing in 2 years. (Use the continuous-time formulas for discounting: e^{-rt}.)
- The hedge is to be constructed using futures contracts on zero-coupon bonds maturing in 6 years, with a contract delivery date in 1 year.

16. (Symmetric probability ◇)   Suppose the wealth that is to be received at a time T in the future has the form

$$W = a + hx + cx^2$$

where a is a constant and x is a random variable. The value of the variable h can be selected by the investor. Suppose that the investor has a utility function that is increasing and strictly concave. Suppose also that the probability distribution of x is symmetric; that is, x and $-x$ have the same distribution. It follows that $E(x) = 0$ and that the investor cannot influence the expected value of wealth.

(a) Show that the optimal choice is $h = 0$.

(b) Apply this result to the corn farm problem to show that the optimal futures position is $+4,000$.

17. (Double symmetric probability ◇)   Suppose that revenue has the form

$$R = Axy + Bx - hy$$

where h can be chosen and x and y are random variables. The distribution of x and y is symmetric about $(0, 0)$; that is, $-x, -y$ has the same distribution as x, y. Show that the choice of h that minimizes the variance of R is

$$h = B\sigma_{xy}/\sigma_y^2.$$

18. (A general farm problem ◇)   Suppose that, as in the corn farm example, the farm has random production and the final spot price is governed by the same demand function. However, the crop of the farm is not perfectly correlated to total demand, but σ_{CD} and σ_D^2 are known. The current futures price is also equal to the expected final spot price. Show that the minimum-variance hedging position is

$$h = 100,000 \left(\frac{-3}{100} + \frac{7\sigma_{CD}}{\sigma_D^2} \right).$$

Check the solution for the special cases (a) $D = 100C$ and (b) $\sigma_{CD} = 0$. [*Hint:* Use Exercise 17.]

REFERENCES

There are several books devoted to futures markets; for example, [1–3]. An excellent book, similar in level to this textbook, is [4]. The futures–forward equivalence result was proved in [5] for the case of a constant interest rate. See [6] for a discussion of hedging techniques, and [7] for the use of interest rate futures similar to that of Exercise 15.

1. Duffie, D. (1989), *Futures Markets*, Prentice Hall, Englewood Cliffs, NJ.
2. Teweles, R. J., and F. J. Jones (1987), *The Futures Game.* McGraw-Hill, New York.
3. Stoll, H. R., and R. E. Whaley (1993), *Futures and Options*, South-West Publishing, Cincinnati, OH.
4. Hull, J. C. (1993), *Options, Futures, and Other Derivative Securities*, 2nd ed., Prentice Hall, Englewood Cliffs, NJ.
5. Cox, J. C., J. E. Ingersoll, and S. A. Ross (1981), "The Relation between Forward Prices and Futures Prices," *Journal of Financial Economics*, **9,** 321–346.
6. Figlewski, S. (1986), *Hedging with Financial Futures for Institutional Investors*, Ballenger Publishing, Cambridge, MA.
7. Kolb, R. W., and G. D. Gay (1982), "Immunizing Bond Portfolios with Interest Rate Futures," *Financial Management*, **11,** 81–89.

11 MODELS OF ASSET DYNAMICS

Tue multiperiod investments fluctuate in value, distribute random dividends, exist in an environment of variable interest rates, and are subject to a continuing variety of other uncertainties. This chapter initiates the study of such investments by showing how to model asset price fluctuations conveniently and realistically. This chapter therefore contains no investment principles as such. Rather it introduces the mathematical models that form the foundation for the analyses developed in later chapters.

Two primary model types are used to represent asset dynamics: binomial lattices and Ito processes. Binomial lattices are analytically simpler than Ito processes, and they provide an excellent basis for computational work associated with investment problems. For these reasons it is best to study binomial lattice models first. The important investment concepts can all be expressed in terms of these models, and many real investment problems can be formulated and solved using the binomial lattice framework. Indeed, roughly 80% of the material in later chapters is presented in terms of binomial lattice models.

Ito processes are more realistic than binomial lattice models in the sense that they have a continuum of possible stock prices at each period, not just two. Ito process models also allow some problems to be solved analytically, as well as computationally. They also provide the foundation for constructing binomial lattice models in a clear and consistent manner. For these reasons Ito process models are fundamental to dynamic problems. For a complete understanding of investment principles, it is important to understand these models.

The organization of this chapter is based on the preceding viewpoint concerning the roles of different models. The first section presents the binomial lattice model directly. With this background most of the material in later chapters can be studied. Therefore you may wish to read only this first section and then skip to the next chapter.

The remaining sections consider models that have a continuum of price values. These models are developed progressively from discrete-time models to continuous-time models based on Ito processes.

11.1 BINOMIAL LATTICE MODEL

To define a binomial lattice model, a basic period length is established (such as 1 week). According to the model, if the price is known at the beginning of a period, the price at the beginning of the next period is one of only two possible values. Usually these two possibilities are defined to be multiples of the price at the previous period—a multiple u (for up) and a multiple d (for down). Both u and d are positive, with $u > 1$ and (usually) $d < 1$. Hence if the price at the beginning of a period is S, it will be either uS or dS at the next period. The probabilities of these possibilities are p and $1 - p$, respectively, for some given probability p, $0 < p < 1$. That is, if the current price is S, there is a probability p that the new price will be uS and a probability $1 - p$ that it will be dS. This model continues on for several periods.

The general form of such a lattice is shown in Figure 11.1. The stock price can be visualized as moving from node to node in a rightward direction. The probability of an upward movement from any node is p and the probability of a downward movement is $1 - p$. A lattice is the appropriate structure in this case, rather than a tree, because an up movement followed by a down is identical to a down followed by an up. Both produce ud times the price.

The model may at first seem too simple because it permits only two possible values at the next period. But if the period length is small, many values are possible after several short steps.

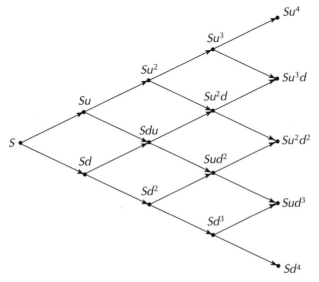

FIGURE 11.1 Binomial lattice stock model. At each step the stock price S either increases to uS or decreases to dS.

To specify the model completely, we must select values for u and d and the probability p. These should be chosen in such a way that the true stochastic nature of the stock is captured as faithfully as possible, as will be discussed.

Because the model is multiplicative in nature (the new value being uS or dS, with $u > 0$, $d > 0$), the price will never become negative. It is therefore possible to consider the logarithm of price as a fundamental variable. For reasons discussed in later sections, use of the logarithm is in fact very helpful and leads to simple formulas for selecting the parameters.

Accordingly, we define v as the expected yearly growth rate.[1] Specifically,

$$v = E[\ln(S_T/S_0)]$$

where S_0 is the initial stock price and S_T is the price at the end of 1 year.

Likewise, we define σ as the yearly standard deviation. Specifically,

$$\sigma^2 = \text{var}[\ln(S_T/S_0)].$$

If a period length of Δt is chosen, which is small compared to 1, the parameters of the binomial lattice can be selected as

$$p = \frac{1}{2} + \frac{1}{2}\left(\frac{v}{\sigma}\right)\sqrt{\Delta t}$$

$$u = e^{\sigma\sqrt{\Delta t}} \tag{11.1}$$

$$d = e^{-\sigma\sqrt{\Delta t}}.$$

With this choice, the binomial model will closely match the values of v and σ (as shown later); that is, the expected growth rate of $\ln S$ in the binomial model will be nearly v, and the variance of that rate will be nearly σ^2. The closeness of the match improves if Δt is made smaller, becoming exact as Δt goes to zero.

Example 11.1 (A volatile stock)   Consider a stock with the parameters $v = 15\%$ and $\sigma = 30\%$. We wish to make a binomial model based on weekly periods. According to (11.1), we set

$$u = e^{.30/\sqrt{52}} = 1.04248, \qquad d = 1/u = .95925$$

and

$$p = \frac{1}{2}\left(1 + \frac{.15}{.30}\sqrt{\frac{1}{52}}\right) = .534669.$$

The lattice for this example is shown in Figure 11.2, assuming $S(0) = 100$.

We shall return to the binomial lattice later in this chapter after studying models that allow a continuum of prices. The binomial model will be found to be a natural approximation to these models.

---

[1] If the process were deterministic, then $v = \ln(S_T/S_0)$ implies $S_T = S_0 e^{vT}$, which shows that v is the exponential growth rate.

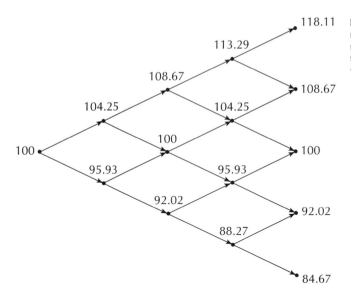

FIGURE 11.2   Lattice for Example 11.1. The parameters are chosen so that the expected growth rate of the logarithm of price and the variance of that growth rate match the known corresponding values for the asset.

11.2 THE ADDITIVE MODEL

We now study models with the property that price can range over a continuum. First we shall consider discrete-time models, beginning with the additive model of this section, and then later we shall consider continuous-time models defined by Ito processes.

Let us focus on $N + 1$ time points, indexed by k, $k = 0, 1, 2, \ldots, N$. We also focus on a particular asset that is characterized by a price at each time. The price at time k is denoted by $S(k)$. Our model will recognize that the price in any one time is dependent to some extent on previous prices.

The simplest model is the **additive model,**

$$S(k + 1) = aS(k) + u(k) \tag{11.2}$$

for $k = 0, 1, 2, \ldots, N$. In this equation a is a constant (usually $a > 1$) and the quantities $u(k)$, $k = 0, 1, \ldots, N - 1$, are random variables. The $u(k)$'s can be thought of as "shocks" or "disturbances" that cause the price to fluctuate. To operate or run this model, an initial price $S(0)$ is specified; then once the random variable $u(0)$ is given, $S(1)$ can be determined. The process then repeats progressively in a stepwise fashion, determining $S(2), S(3), \ldots, S(N)$.

The key ingredient of this model is the sequence of random variables $u(k)$, $k = 1, 2, \ldots, N$. We assume that these are mutually statistically independent.

Note that the price at any time depends only on the price at the most recent previous time and the random disturbance. It does not explicitly depend on other previous prices.

Normal Price Distribution

It is instructive to solve explicitly for a few of the prices from (11.2). By direct substitution we have

$$S(1) = aS(0) + u(0)$$

$$S(2) = aS(1) + u(1)$$

$$= a^2 S(0) + au(0) + u(1).$$

By simple induction it can be seen that for general k,

$$S(k) = a^k S(0) + a^{k-1} u(0) + a^{k-2} u(1) + \cdots + u(k-1). \tag{11.3}$$

Hence $S(k)$ is $a^k S(0)$ plus the sum of k random variables.

Frequently we assume that the random variables $u(k)$, $k = 0, 1, 2, \ldots, N - 1$, are independent normal random variables with a common variance σ^2. Then, since a linear combination of normal random variables is also normal (see Appendix A), it follows from (11.3) that $S(k)$ is itself a normal random variable.

If the expected values of all the $u(k)$'s are zero, then the expected value of $S(k)$ is

$$E[S(k)] = a^k S(0).$$

When $a > 1$, this model has the property that the expected value of the price increases geometrically (that is, according to a^k). Indeed, the constant a is the growth rate factor of the model.

The additive model is structurally simple and easy to work with. The expected value of price grows geometrically, and all prices are normal random variables. However, the model is seriously flawed because it lacks realism. Normal random variables can take on negative values, which means that the prices in this model might be negative as well; but real stock prices are never negative. Furthermore, if a stock were to begin at a price of, say, $1 with a σ of, say, $.50 and then drift upward to a price of $100, it seems very unlikely that the σ would remain at $.50. It is more likely that the standard deviation would be proportional to the price. For these reasons the additive model is not a good general model of asset dynamics. The model is useful for localized analyses, over short periods of time (perhaps up to a few months for common stocks), and it is a useful building block for other models, but it cannot be used alone as an ongoing model representing long- or intermediate-term fluctuations. For this reason we must consider a better alternative, which is the multiplicative model. (However, our understanding of the additive model will be important for that more advanced model.)

11.3 THE MULTIPLICATIVE MODEL

The **multiplicative model** has the form

$$S(k + 1) = u(k)S(k) \tag{11.4}$$

for $k = 0, 1, \ldots, N - 1$. Here again the quantities $u(k)$, $k = 0, 1, 2, \ldots, N - 1$, are mutually independent random variables. The variable $u(k)$ defines the *relative* change in price between times k and $k + 1$. This relative change is $S(k + 1)/S(k)$, which is independent of the overall magnitude of $S(k)$. It is also independent of the units of price. For example, if we change units from U.S. dollars to German marks, the relative price change is still $u(k)$.

The multiplicative model takes a familiar form if we take the natural logarithm of both sides of the equation. This yields

$$\ln S(k + 1) = \ln S(k) + \ln u(k) \tag{11.5}$$

for $k = 0, 1, 2, \ldots, N - 1$. Hence in this form the model is of the additive type with respect to the logarithm of the price, rather than the price itself. Therefore we can use our knowledge of the additive model to analyze the multiplicative model.

It is now natural to specify the random disturbances directly in terms of the $\ln u(k)$'s. In particular we let

$$w(k) = \ln u(k)$$

for $k = 0, 1, 2, \ldots, N - 1$, and we specify that these $w(k)$'s be normal random variables. We assume that they are mutually independent and that each has expected value $\overline{w}(k) = v$ and variance σ^2.

We can express the original multiplicative disturbances as

$$u(k) = e^{w(k)} \tag{11.6}$$

for $k = 0, 1, 2, \ldots, N - 1$. Each of the variables $u(k)$ is said to be a **lognormal** random variable since its logarithm is in fact a normal random variable.

Notice that now there is no problem with negative values. Although the normal variable $w(k)$ may be negative, the corresponding $u(k)$ given by (11.6) is always positive. Since the random factor by which a price is multiplied is $u(k)$, it follows that prices remain positive in this model.

Lognormal Prices

The successive prices of the multiplicative model can be easily found to be

$$S(k) = u(k - 1)u(k - 2) \cdots u(0)S(0).$$

Taking the natural logarithm of this equation we find

$$\ln S(k) = \ln S(0) + \sum_{i=0}^{k-1} \ln u(i) = \ln S(0) + \sum_{i=0}^{k-1} w(i).$$

The term $\ln S(0)$ is a constant, and the $w(i)$'s are each normal random variables. Since the sum of normal random variables is itself a normal random variable (see Appendix A), it follows that $\ln S(k)$ is normal. In other words, all prices are lognormal under the multiplicative model.

If each $w(i)$ has expected value $\overline{w}(i) = v$ and variance σ^2, and all are mutually independent, then we find

$$E[\ln S(k)] = \ln S(0) + vk \tag{11.7a}$$

$$\text{var}[\ln S(k)] = k\sigma^2. \tag{11.7b}$$

Hence both the expected value and the variance increase linearly with k.

Real Stock Distributions

At this point it is natural to ask how well this theoretical model fits actual stock price behavior. Are real stock prices lognormal?

The answer is that, based on an analysis of past stock price records, the price distributions of most stocks are actually quite close to lognormal. To verify this, we select a nominal period length of, say, 1 week and record the differences $\ln S(k+1) - \ln S(k)$ for many values of k; that is, we record the weekly changes in the logarithm of the prices for many weeks. We then construct a histogram of these values and compare it with that of a normal distribution of the same variance. Typically, the measured distribution is quite close to being normal, except that the observed distribution often is slightly smaller near the mean and larger at extremely large values (either positive or negative large values). This slight change in shape is picturesquely termed **fat tails.** (See Figure 11.3.[2]) The observed distribution is larger in the tails than a normal

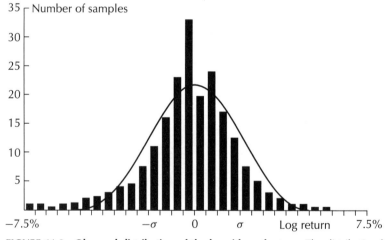

FIGURE 11.3   Observed distribution of the logarithm of return. The distribution has "fatter tails" than a normal distribution of the same variance.

---

[2]The figure shows a histogram of American Airlines weekly log stock returns for the 10-year period of 1982–1992. Shown superimposed is the normal distribution with the same (sample) mean and standard deviation. Along with fat tails there is invariably a "skinny middle."

distribution. This implies that large price changes tend to occur somewhat more frequently than would be predicted by a normal distribution of the same variance. For most applications (but not all) this slight discrepancy is not important.

11.4 TYPICAL PARAMETER VALUES*

The return of a stock over the period between k and $k+1$ is $S(k+1)/S(k)$, which under the multiplicative model is equal to $u(k)$. The value of $w(k) = \ln u(k)$ is therefore the logarithm of the return. The mean value of $w(k)$ is denoted by v and the variance of $w(k)$ by σ^2. Typical values of these parameters for assets such as common stocks can be inferred from our knowledge of corresponding values for returns. Thus for stocks, typical values of $v = E[w(k)]$ and $\sigma = \text{stdev}[w(k)]$ might be

$$v = 12\%, \qquad \sigma = 15\%$$

when the length of a period is 1 year. If the period length is less than a year, these values scale downward;[3] that is, if the period length is p part of a year, then

$$v_p = pv, \qquad \sigma_p = \sqrt{p}\sigma.$$

The values can be estimated from historical records in the standard fashion (but with caution as to the validity of these estimates, as raised in Chapter 8). If we have $N + 1$ time points of data, spanning N periods, the estimate of the single-period v is

$$\hat{v} = \frac{1}{N} \sum_{k=0}^{N-1} \ln \left[\frac{S(k+1)}{S(k)} \right] = \frac{1}{N} \sum_{k=0}^{N-1} [\ln S(k+1) - \ln S(k)]$$

$$= \frac{1}{N} \ln \left[\frac{S(N)}{S(0)} \right].$$

Hence all that matters is the ratio of the last to the first price.

The standard estimate of σ^2 is

$$\hat{\sigma}^2 = \frac{1}{N-1} \sum_{k=0}^{N-1} \left\{ \ln \left[\frac{S(k+1)}{S(k)} \right] - \hat{v} \right\}^2.$$

As with the estimation of return parameters, the error in these estimates can be characterized by their variances. For v this variance is

$$\text{var}(\hat{v}) = \sigma^2/N$$

and for σ^2 it is [assuming $w(k)$ is normal]

$$\text{var}(\hat{\sigma}^2) = 2\sigma^4/(N - 1).$$

---

[3] Using log returns, the scaling is *exactly* proportional. There is no error due to compounding as with returns (without the log). (See Exercise 2.)

Hence for the values assumed earlier, namely, $\nu = .12$ and $\sigma = .15$, we find that 10 years of data is required to reduce the standard deviation of the estimate[4] of ν to .05 (which is still a sizable fraction of the true value). On the other hand, with only 1 year of weekly data we can obtain a fairly good estimate[5] of σ^2.

11.5 LOGNORMAL RANDOM VARIABLES

If u is a lognormal random variable, then the variable $w = \ln u$ is normal. In this case we found that the prices in the multiplicative model are all lognormal random variables. It is therefore useful to study a few important properties of such random variables.

The general shape of the probability distribution of a lognormal random variable is shown in Figure 11.4. Note that the variable is always nonnegative and the distribution is somewhat skewed.

Suppose that w is normal and has expected value $\overline{w}$ and variance σ^2. What is the expected value of $u = e^w$? A quick guess might be $\overline{u} = e^{\overline{w}}$, but this is wrong. Actually $\overline{u}$ is greater than this by the factor $e^{\frac{1}{2}\sigma^2}$; that is,

$$\overline{u} = e^{\overline{w}+\frac{1}{2}\sigma^2}. \tag{11.8}$$

This result can be intuitively understood by noting that as σ is increased, the lognormal distribution will spread out. It cannot spread downward below zero, but it can spread upward unboundedly. Hence the mean value increases as σ increases.

The extra term $\frac{1}{2}\sigma^2$ is actually fairly small for low-volatility stocks. For example, consider a stock with a yearly $\overline{w} = .12$ and a yearly σ of .15. The correction term is

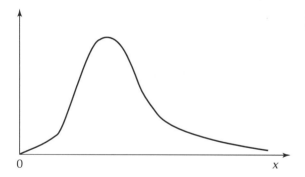

FIGURE 11.4   Lognormal distribution. The lognormal distribution is nonzero only for $x > 0$.

[4] $\sigma(\hat{\nu}) = \dfrac{\sigma}{\sqrt{N}} = \dfrac{\sigma}{\sqrt{10}} = \dfrac{.15}{3.16} = .05.$

[5] $\text{var}(\hat{\sigma}^2) = (52)^2 \, \text{var}(\hat{\sigma}_w^2) = \dfrac{(52)^2 \times 2\sigma_w^4}{N-1} = \dfrac{(52)^2 \times 2\sigma^4}{(52)^2 \times 51} = \dfrac{2\sigma^4}{51}.$ Hence $\sigma(\hat{\sigma}^2) = \dfrac{\sqrt{2}\sigma^2}{\sqrt{51}} \approx \dfrac{\sigma^2}{5}.$

$\frac{1}{2}\sigma^2 = .0225$, which is small compared to $\overline{w}$. For stocks with high volatility, however, the correction can be significant.

11.6 RANDOM WALKS AND WIENER PROCESSES

In Section 11.7 we will shorten the period length in a multiplicative model and take the limit as this length goes to zero. This will produce a model in continuous time. In preparation for that step, we introduce special random functions of time, called random walks and Wiener processes.

Suppose that we have N periods of length Δt. We define the additive process z by

$$z(t_{k+1}) = z(t_k) + \epsilon(t_k)\sqrt{\Delta t} \tag{11.9}$$

$$t_{k+1} = t_k + \Delta t \tag{11.10}$$

for $k = 0, 1, 2, \ldots, N$. This process is termed a **random walk.** In these equations $\epsilon(t_k)$ is a normal random variable with mean 0 and variance 1—a **standardized normal random variable.** These random variables are mutually uncorrelated; that is, $E[\epsilon(t_j)\epsilon(t_k)] = 0$ for $j \neq k$. The process is started by setting $z(t_0) = 0$. Thereafter a particular realized path wanders around according to the happenstance of the random variables $\epsilon(t_k)$. [The reason for using $\sqrt{\Delta t}$ in (11.9) will become clear shortly.] A particular path of a random walk is shown in Figure 11.5.

Of special interest are the difference random variables $z(t_k) - z(t_j)$ for $j < k$. We can write such a difference as

$$z(t_k) - z(t_j) = \sum_{i=j}^{k-1} \epsilon(t_i)\sqrt{\Delta t}\,.$$

This is a normal random variable because it is the sum of normal random variables. We find immediately that

$$E[z(t_k) - z(t_j)] = 0.$$

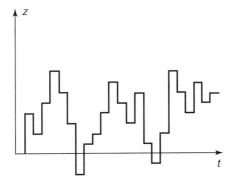

FIGURE 11.5   Possible random walk. The movements are determined by normal random variables.

Also, using the independence of the $\epsilon(t_k)$'s, we find

$$\text{var}[z(t_k) - z(t_j)] = \text{E}\left[\sum_{i=j}^{k-1} \epsilon(t_i)\sqrt{\Delta t}\right]^2$$

$$= \text{E}\left[\sum_{i=j}^{k-1} \epsilon(t_i)^2 \Delta t\right]$$

$$= (k-j)\Delta t \ = \ t_k - t_j.$$

Hence the variance of $z(t_k) - z(t_j)$ is exactly equal to the time difference $t_k - t_j$ between the points. This calculation also shows why $\sqrt{\Delta t}$ was used in the definition of the random walk so that Δt would appear in the variance.

It should be clear that the difference variables associated with two different time intervals are uncorrelated if the two intervals are nonoverlapping. That is, if $t_{k_1} < t_{k_2} \leq t_{k_3} < t_{k_4}$, then $z(t_{k_2}) - z(t_{k_1})$ is uncorrelated with $z(t_{k_4}) - z(t_{k_3})$ because each of these differences is made up of different ϵ's, which are themselves uncorrelated.

A Wiener process is obtained by taking the limit of the random walk process (11.9) as $\Delta t \to 0$. In symbolic form we write the equations governing a Wiener process as

$$dz = \epsilon(t)\sqrt{dt} \tag{11.11}$$

where each $\epsilon(t)$ is a standardized normal random variable. The random variables $\epsilon(t')$ and $\epsilon(t'')$ are uncorrelated whenever $t' \neq t''$.

This description of a Wiener process is not rigorous because we have no assurance that the limiting operations are defined; but it provides a good intuitive description. An alternative definition of a Wiener process can be made by simply listing the required properties. In this approach we say a process $z(t)$ is a **Wiener process** (or, alternatively, **Brownian motion**) if it satisfies the following:

1. For any $s < t$ the quantity $z(t) - z(s)$ is a normal random variable with mean zero and variance $t - s$.

2. For any $0 \leq t_1 < t_2 \leq t_3 < t_4$, the random variables $z(t_2) - z(t_1)$ and $z(t_4) - z(t_3)$ are uncorrelated.

3. $z(t_0) = 0$ with probability 1.

These properties parallel the properties of the random walk process given earlier.

It is fun to try to visualize the outcome of a Wiener process. A sketch of a possible path is shown in Figure 11.6. Remember that given $z(t)$ at time t, the value of $z(s)$ at time $s > t$ is, on average, the same as $z(t)$ but will vary from that according to a standard deviation equal to $\sqrt{s - t}$.

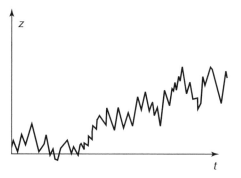

FIGURE 11.6 Path of a Wiener process. A Wiener process moves continuously but is not differentiable.

A Wiener process is not differentiable with respect to time. We can roughly verify this by noting that for $t < s$,

$$\mathrm{E}\left[\frac{z(s) - z(t)}{s - t}\right]^2 = \frac{s - t}{(s - t)^2} = \frac{1}{s - t} \to \infty$$

as $s \to t$.

It is, however, useful to have a word for the term $\mathrm{d}z/\mathrm{d}t$ since this expression appears in many stochastic equations. A common word used, arising from the systems engineering field (the field that motivated Wiener's work), is **white noise.** It is really fun to try to visualize white noise. One depiction is presented in Figure 11.7.

Generalized Wiener Processes and Ito Processes

The Wiener process (or Brownian motion) is the fundamental building block for a whole collection of more general processes. These generalizations are obtained by inserting white noise in an ordinary differential equation.

The simplest extension of this kind is the **generalized Wiener process,** which is of the form

$$\mathrm{d}x(t) = a\,\mathrm{d}t + b\,\mathrm{d}z \tag{11.12}$$

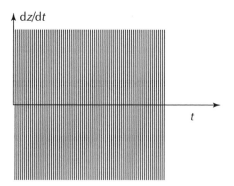

FIGURE 11.7 Fantasizing white noise. White noise is the derivative of a Wiener process, but that derivative does not exist in the normal sense.

where $x(t)$ is a random variable for each t, z is a Wiener process, and a and b are constants.

A generalized Wiener process is especially important because it has an analytic solution (which can be found by integrating both sides). Specifically,

$$x(t) = x(0) + at + bz(t). \tag{11.13}$$

An **Ito process** is somewhat more general still. Such a process is described by an equation of the form

$$dx(t) = a(x, t)\,dt + b(x, t)\,dz. \tag{11.14}$$

As before, z denotes a Wiener process. Now, however, the coefficients $a(x, t)$ and $b(x, t)$ may depend on x and t, and a general solution cannot be written in an analytic form. A special form of Ito process is used frequently to describe the behavior of financial assets, as discussed in the next section.

11.7 A STOCK PRICE PROCESS

We now have the tools necessary to extend the multiplicative model of stock prices to a continuous-time model. Recall that the multiplicative model is

$$\ln S(k + 1) - \ln S(k) = w(k)$$

where the $w(k)$'s are uncorrelated normal random variables. The continuous-time version of this equation is

$$d\ln S(t) = v\,dt + \sigma\,dz \tag{11.15}$$

where v and $\sigma \geq 0$ are constants and z is a standard Wiener process. The whole right-hand side of the equation can be regarded as playing the role of the random variable $w(k)$ in the discrete-time model. This side can be thought of as a constant plus a normal random variable with zero mean, and hence, overall it is a normal random variable. (Although all terms in the equation are differentials or multiples of differentials and thus do not themselves have magnitude in the usual sense, it is helpful to think of dt and dz as being "small" like Δt and Δz.) The term $v\,dt$ is, accordingly, the mean value of the right-hand side. This mean value is proportional to dt, consistent with the fact that in the logarithm version of the multiplicative model the mean value of the change in $\ln S$ is proportional to the length of one period. The standard deviation of the right-hand side is σ times the standard deviation of dz. Hence it is of order of magnitude $\sigma\sqrt{dt}$, which is consistent with the fact that in the logarithm version of the multiplicative model the standard deviation of the change in $\ln S$ is proportional to the square root of the length of one period, as reflected by (11.7a) and (11.7b).

Since equation (11.15) is expressed in terms of $\ln S(t)$, it is actually a generalized Wiener process. Hence we can solve it explicitly using (11.13) as

$$\ln S(t) = \ln S(0) + vt + \sigma z(t). \tag{11.16}$$

This shows that $E[\ln S(t)] = E[\ln S(0)] + vt$, and hence $E[\ln S(t)]$ grows linearly with t. Because the expected logarithm of this process increases linearly with t, just as a continuously compounded bank account, this process is termed **geometric Brownian motion.**

Lognormal Prices

Like the discrete-time multiplicative model, the geometric Brownian motion process described by (11.15) is a lognormal process. This can be seen easily from the solution (11.16). The right-hand side of that equation is a normal random variable with expected value $\ln S(0) + vt$ and standard deviation $\sigma\sqrt{t}$.

We conclude that the price $S(t)$ itself has a lognormal distribution. We can express this formally by $\ln S(t) \sim N(\ln S(0) + vt, \sigma^2 t)$, where $N(m, \sigma^2)$ denotes the normal distribution with mean m and variance σ^2.

Although we can write $S(t) = \exp[\ln S(t)] = S(0)\exp[vt + \sigma z(t)]$, it does *not* follow that the expected value of $S(t)$ is $S(0)e^{vt}$. The mean value must instead be determined by equation (11.8), the general formula that applies to lognormal variables. Hence,

$$E[S(t)] = S(0)e^{(v + \frac{1}{2}\sigma^2)t}.$$

If we define $\mu = v + \frac{1}{2}\sigma^2$, we have

$$E[S(t)] = S(0)e^{\mu t}.$$

The standard deviation of $S(t)$ is also given by a general relation for lognormal variables. In the case of the standard deviation, the required calculation is a bit more complex. The formula is (see Exercise 5)

$$\text{stdev}[S(t)] = S(0)e^{vt + \frac{1}{2}\sigma^2 t}\left(e^{\sigma^2 t} - 1\right)^{1/2}.$$

Standard Ito Form

We have defined the random process for $S(t)$ in terms of $\ln S(t)$ rather than directly in terms of $S(t)$. The use of $\ln S(t)$ facilitated the development, and it highlights the fact that the process is a straightforward generalization of the multiplicative model that leads to lognormal distributions. It is, however, useful to express the process in terms of $S(t)$ itself.

In ordinary calculus we know that

$$d\ln[S(t)] = \frac{dS(t)}{S(t)}.$$

Hence we might be tempted to substitute $dS(t)/S(t)$ for $d\ln S(t)$ in the basic equation [Eq. (11.15)], obtaining $dS(t)/S(t) = v\, dt + \sigma\, dz$. This would be almost correct, but there is a correction term that must be applied when changing variables in Ito processes (because Wiener processes are not ordinary functions and do not follow the rules of ordinary calculus). The appropriate Ito process in terms of $S(t)$ is

$$\frac{dS(t)}{S(t)} = \left(v + \frac{1}{2}\sigma^2\right)dt + \sigma\, dz. \qquad (11.17)$$

Note that the correction term $\frac{1}{2}\sigma^2$ is exactly the same as needed in the expression for the expected value of a lognormal random variable. Putting $\mu = v + \frac{1}{2}\sigma^2$, we may write the equation in the standard Ito form for price dynamics,

$$\frac{dS(t)}{S(t)} = \mu \, dt + \sigma \, dz. \tag{11.18}$$

The term $dS(t)/S(t)$ can be thought of as the differential return of the stock; hence in this form the differential return has a simple form.

The correction term required when transforming the equation from $\ln S(t)$ to $S(t)$ is a special instance of a general transformation equation defined by **Ito's lemma,** which applies to variables defined by Ito processes. Ito's lemma is discussed in the next section.

Note that if the equation in standard form is written with S in the denominator, as in (11.17), it is an equation for dS/S. This term can be interpreted as the instantaneous rate of return on the stock. Hence the standard form is often referred to as an equation for the instantaneous return.

Example 11.2 (Bond price dynamics)   Let $P(t)$ denote the price of a bond that pays \$1 at time $t = T$, with no other payments. Assume that interest rates are constant at r. The price of this bond satisfies

$$\frac{dP(t)}{P(t)} = r \, dt$$

which is a deterministic Ito equation, paralleling the equation for stock prices. The solution to this equation is $P(t) = P(0)e^{rt}$. Using $P(T) = 1$, we find that $P(t) = e^{r(t-T)}$.

We now summarize the relations between $S(t)$ and $\ln S(t)$:

Relations for geometric Brownian motion   *Suppose the geometric Brownian motion process $S(t)$ is governed by*

$$dS(t) = \mu S(t) \, dt + \sigma S(t) \, dz$$

where z is a standard Wiener process. Define $v = \mu - \frac{1}{2}\sigma^2$. Then $S(t)$ is lognormal and

$$E\{\ln[S(t)/S(0)]\} = vt$$

$$\text{stdev}\{\ln[S(t)/S(0)]\} = \sigma\sqrt{t}$$

$$E\{S(t)/S(0)\} = e^{\mu t}$$

$$\text{stdev}\{S(t)/S(0)\} = e^{\mu t}\left(e^{\sigma^2 t} - 1\right)^{1/2}.$$

Simulation

A continuous-time price process can be simulated by taking a series of small time periods and then stepping the process forward period by period. There are two natural ways to do this, and they are *not* exactly equivalent.

First, consider the process in standard form defined by (11.18). We take a basic period length Δt and set $S(t_0) = S_0$, a given initial price at $t = t_0$. The corresponding simulation equation is

$$S(t_{k+1}) - S(t_k) = \mu S(t_k)\Delta t + \sigma S(t_k)\epsilon(t_k)\sqrt{\Delta t}$$

where the $\epsilon(t_k)$'s are uncorrelated normal random variables of mean 0 and standard deviation 1. This leads to

$$S(t_{k+1}) = \left[1 + \mu\,\Delta t + \sigma\epsilon(t_k)\sqrt{\Delta t}\right]S(t_k) \qquad (11.19)$$

which is a multiplicative model, but the random coefficient is normal rather than log-normal, so this simulation method does not produce the lognormal price distributions that are characteristic of the underlying Ito process (in either of its forms).

A second approach is to use the log (or multiplicative) form (11.15). In discrete form this is

$$\ln S(t_{k+1}) - \ln S(t_k) = \nu\,\Delta t + \sigma\epsilon(t_k)\sqrt{\Delta t}.$$

This leads to

$$S(t_{k+1}) = e^{\nu\Delta t + \sigma\epsilon(t_k)\sqrt{\Delta t}}S(t_k) \qquad (11.20)$$

which is also a multiplicative model, but now the random coefficient *is* lognormal.

The two methods are different, but it can be shown that their differences tend to cancel in the long run. Hence in practice, either method is about as good as the other.

Example 11.3 (Simulation by two methods)   Consider a stock with an initial price of $10 and having $\nu = 15\%$ and $\sigma = 40\%$. We take the basic time interval to be 1 week ($\Delta t = 1/52$), and we simulate the stock behavior for 1 year. Both methods described in this subsection were applied using the same random ϵ's, which were generated from a normal distribution of mean 0 and standard deviation 1. Table 11.1 gives the results. The first column shows the random variables $dz = \epsilon\sqrt{\Delta t}$ for that week. The second column lists the corresponding multiplicative factors. The value P_1 is the simulated price using the standard method as represented by (11.19). The fourth column shows the appropriate exponential factors for the second method, (11.20). The value P_2 is the simulated price using that method. Note that even at the first step the results are not identical. However, overall the results are fairly close.

TABLE 11.1
Simulation of Price Dynamics

Week	dz	$\mu + \sigma\,dz$	P_1	$\nu + \sigma\,dz$	P_2
0			10.0000		10.0000
1	.06476	.00802	10.0802	.00648	10.0650
2	−.19945	−.00664	10.0132	−.00818	9.9830
3	−.83883	−.04211	9.5916	−.04365	9.5567
4	.49609	.03194	9.8980	.03040	9.8517
5	−.33892	−.01438	9.7557	−.01592	9.6961
6	1.39485	.08180	10.5536	.08026	10.5064
7	.61869	.03874	10.9625	.03720	10.9046
8	.40201	.02672	11.2554	.02518	11.1827
9	−.71118	−.03503	10.8612	−.03656	10.7812
10	.16937	.01382	11.0113	.01228	10.9144
11	1.19678	.07081	11.7910	.06927	11.6973
12	−.14408	−.00357	11.7489	−.00511	11.6377
13	.80590	.04913	12.3261	.04759	12.2049
26	−1.23335	−.06399	13.1428	−.06553	12.9157
39	.68140	.04222	17.6850	.04068	17.3668
52	.69955	.04323	15.1230	.04169	14.7564

The price process is simulated by two methods. Although they differ step by step, the overall results are similar.

11.8 ITO'S LEMMA*

We saw that the two Ito equations—for $S(t)$ and for $\ln S(t)$—are different, and that the difference is not exactly what would be expected from the application of ordinary calculus to the transformation of variables from $S(t)$ to $\ln S(t)$; an additional term $\frac{1}{2}\sigma^2$ is required. This extra term arises because the random variables have order $\sqrt{dt}$, and hence their squares produce first-order, rather than second-order, effects. There is a systematic method for making such transformations in general, and this is encapsulated in Ito's lemma:

Ito's lemma *Suppose that the random process x is defined by the Ito process*

$$dx(t) = a(x, t)\,dt + b(x, t)\,dz \tag{11.21}$$

where z is a standard Wiener process. Suppose also that the process y(t) is defined by $y(t) = F(x, t)$. *Then y(t) satisfies the Ito equation*

$$dy(t) = \left(\frac{\partial F}{\partial x}a + \frac{\partial F}{\partial t} + \frac{1}{2}\frac{\partial^2 F}{\partial x^2}b^2\right)dt + \frac{\partial F}{\partial x}b\,dz \tag{11.22}$$

where z is the same Wiener process as in Eq. (11.21).

Proof: Ordinary calculus would give a formula similar to (11.22), but without the term with $\frac{1}{2}$.

We shall sketch a rough proof of the full formula. We expand y with respect to a change Δy. In the expansion we keep terms up to first order in Δt, but since Δx is of order $\sqrt{\Delta t}$, this means that we must expand to second order in Δx. We find

$$y + \Delta y = F(x, t) + \frac{\partial F}{\partial x}\Delta x + \frac{\partial F}{\partial t}\Delta t + \frac{1}{2}\frac{\partial^2 F}{\partial x^2}(\Delta x)^2$$

$$= F(x, t) + \frac{\partial F}{\partial x}(a\,\Delta t + b\,\Delta z) + \frac{\partial F}{\partial t}\Delta t + \frac{1}{2}\frac{\partial^2 F}{\partial x^2}(a\,\Delta t + b\,\Delta z)^2.$$

The quadratic expression in the last term must be treated in a special way. When expanded, it becomes $a^2(\Delta t)^2 + 2ab\,\Delta t\,\Delta z + b^2(\Delta z)^2$. The first two terms of this expression are of order higher than 1 in Δt, so they can be dropped. The term $b^2(\Delta z)^2$ is all that remains. However, Δz has expected value zero and variance Δt, and hence this last term is of order Δt and cannot be dropped. Indeed, it can be shown that, in the limit as Δt goes to zero, the term $(\Delta z)^2$ is nonstochastic and is equal to Δt. Substitution of this into the previous expansion leads to

$$y + \Delta y = F(x, t) + \left(\frac{\partial F}{\partial x}a + \frac{\partial F}{\partial t} + \frac{1}{2}\frac{\partial^2 F}{\partial x^2}b^2\right)\Delta t + \frac{\partial F}{\partial x}b\,\Delta z.$$

Taking the limit and using $y = F(x, t)$ yields Ito's equation, (11.22). ∎

Example 11.4 (Stock dynamics)   Suppose that $S(t)$ is governed by the geometric Brownian motion

$$dS = \mu S\,dt + \sigma S\,dz.$$

Let us use Ito's lemma to find the equation governing the process $F(S(t)) = \ln S(t)$.

We have the identifications $a = \mu S$ and $b = \sigma S$. We also have $\partial F/\partial S = 1/S$ and $\partial^2 F/\partial S^2 = -1/S^2$. Therefore according to (11.22),

$$d\ln S = \left(\frac{a}{S} - \frac{1}{2}\frac{b^2}{S^2}\right)dt + \frac{b}{S}\,dz$$

$$= \left(\mu - \frac{1}{2}\sigma^2\right)dt + \sigma\,dz$$

which agrees with our earlier result.

11.9 BINOMIAL LATTICE REVISITED

Let us consider again the binomial lattice model shown in Figure 11.8 (which is identical to Figure 11.1). The model is analogous to the multiplicative model discussed earlier in this chapter, since at each step the price is multiplied by a random variable.

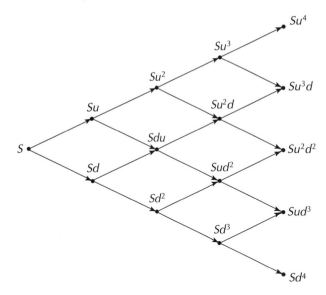

Su^4

FIGURE 11.8   Binomial lattice stock model. At each step the stock price S either increases to uS or decreases to dS.

In this case, the random variable takes only the two possible values u and d. We can find suitable values for u, d, and p by matching the multiplicative model as closely as possible. This is done by matching both the expected value of the logarithm of a price change and the variance of the logarithm of the price change.[6]

To carry out the matching, it is only necessary to ensure that the random variable S_1, which is the price after the first step, has the correct properties since the process is identical thereafter. Taking $S(0) = 1$, we find by direct calculation that

$$E(\ln S_1) = p \ln u + (1 - p) \ln d$$

$$\text{var}(\ln S_1) = p(\ln u)^2 + (1 - p)(\ln d)^2 - [p \ln u + (1 - p) \ln d]^2$$

$$= p(1 - p)(\ln u - \ln d)^2.$$

Therefore the appropriate parameter matching equations are

$$pU + (1 - p)D = v\,\Delta t \tag{11.23}$$

$$p(1 - p)(U - D)^2 = \sigma^2 \Delta t \tag{11.24}$$

where $U = \ln u$ and $D = \ln d$.

Notice that three parameters are to be chosen: U, D, and p; but there are only two requirements. Therefore there is one degree of freedom. One way to use this freedom is to set $D = -U$ (which is equivalent to setting $d = 1/u$). In this case the

---

[6]For the lattice, the probability of attaining the various end nodes of the lattice is given by the binomial distribution. Specifically, the probability of reaching the value $Su^k d^{n-k}$ is $\binom{n}{k} p^k (1 - p)^{n-k}$, where $\binom{n}{k} = \dfrac{n!}{(n-k)!k!}$ is the binomial coefficient. This distribution approaches (in a certain sense) a normal distribution for large n. The logarithm of the final prices is of the form $k \ln u + (n-k) \ln d$, which is linear in k. Hence the distribution of the end point prices can be considered to be nearly lognormal.

equations (11.23) and (11.24) reduce to

$$(2p - 1)U = v\,\Delta t$$

$$4p(1 - p)U^2 = \sigma^2 \Delta t\,.$$

If we square the first equation and add it to the second, we obtain

$$U^2 = \sigma^2\,\Delta t + (v\,\Delta t)^2\,.$$

Substituting this in the first equation, we may solve for p directly, and then $U = \ln u$ can be determined. The resulting solutions to the parameter matching equations are

$$p = \frac{1}{2} + \frac{\frac{1}{2}}{\sqrt{\sigma^2/(v^2\Delta t) + 1}}$$

$$\ln u = \sqrt{\sigma^2\Delta t + (v\,\Delta t)^2} \qquad (11.25)$$

$$\ln d = -\sqrt{\sigma^2\Delta t + (v\,\Delta t)^2}\,.$$

For small Δt (11.25) can be approximated as

$$p = \tfrac{1}{2} + \tfrac{1}{2}\left(\frac{v}{\sigma}\right)\sqrt{\Delta t}$$

$$u = e^{\sigma\sqrt{\Delta t}} \qquad (11.26)$$

$$d = e^{-\sigma\sqrt{\Delta t}}\,.$$

These are the values presented in Section 11.1.

11.10 SUMMARY

A simple and versatile model of asset dynamics is the binomial lattice. In this model an asset's price is assumed to be multiplied either by the factor u or by the factor d, the choice being made each period according to probabilities p and $1-p$, respectively. This model is used extensively in theoretical developments and as a basis for computing solutions to investment problems.

Another broad class of models are those where the asset price may take on values from a continuum of possibilities. The simplest model of this type is the additive model. If the random inputs of this model are normal random variables, the asset prices are also normal random variables. This model has the disadvantage, however, that prices may be negative.

A better model is the multiplicative model of the form $S(k+1) = u(k)S(k)$. If the multiplicative inputs $u(k)$ are lognormal, then the future prices $S(k)$ are also lognormal. The model can be expressed in the alternative form as $\ln S(k+1) - \ln S(k) = \ln u(k)$.

By letting the period length tend to zero, the multiplicative model becomes the Ito process $d \ln S(t) = v\,dt + \sigma^2 dz(t)$, where z is a normalized Wiener process. This special form of an Ito process is called geometric Brownian motion. This model can be expressed in the alternative (but equivalent) form $dS(t) = \mu S(t)dt + \sigma^2 S(t)dz(t)$, where $\mu = v + \tfrac{1}{2}\sigma^2$.

Ito processes are useful representations of asset dynamics. An important tool for transforming such processes is Ito's lemma: If $x(t)$ satisfies an Ito process, and $y(t)$ is defined by $y(t) = F(x, t)$, Ito's lemma specifies the process satisfied by $y(t)$.

A binomial lattice model can be considered to be an approximation to an Ito process. The parameters of the lattice can be chosen so that the mean and standard deviation of the logarithm of the return agree in the two models.

EXERCISES

1. **(Stock lattice)** A stock with current value $S(0) = 100$ has an expected growth rate of its logarithm of $v = 12\%$ and a volatility of that growth rate of $\sigma = 20\%$. Find suitable parameters of a binomial lattice representing this stock with a basic elementary period of 3 months. Draw the lattice and enter the node values for 1 year. What are the probabilities of attaining the various final nodes?

2. **(Time scaling)** A stock price S is governed by the model

$$\ln S(k + 1) = \ln S(k) + w(k)$$

where the period length is 1 month. Let $v = E[w(k)]$ and $\sigma^2 = \text{var}[w(k)]$ for all k. Now suppose the basic period length is changed to 1 year. Then the model is

$$\ln S(K + 1) = \ln S(K) + W(K)$$

where each movement in K corresponds to 1 year. What is the natural definition of $W(K)$? Show that $E[W(K)] = 12v$ and $\text{var}[W(K)] = 12\sigma^2$. Hence parameters scale in proportion to time.

3. **(Arithmetic and geometric means)** Suppose that $v_1, v_2, \ldots, v_n$ are positive numbers. The *arithmetic mean* and the *geometric mean* of these numbers are, respectively,

$$v_A = \frac{1}{n} \sum_{i=1}^{n} v_i \quad \text{and} \quad v_G = \left(\prod_{i=1}^{n} v_i \right)^{1/n}.$$

(a) It is always true that $v_A \geq v_G$. Prove this inequality for $n = 2$.

(b) If $r_1, r_2, \ldots, r_n$ are rates of return of a stock in each of n periods, the arithmetic and geometric mean rates of return are likewise

$$r_A = \frac{1}{n} \sum_{i=1}^{n} r_i \quad \text{and} \quad r_G = \left(\prod_{i=1}^{n} (1 + r_i) \right)^{1/n} - 1.$$

Suppose $40 is invested. During the first year it increases to $60 and during the second year it decreases to $48. What are the arithmetic and geometric mean rates of return over the 2 years?

(c) When is it appropriate to use these means to describe investment performance?

4. **(Complete the square ◇)** Suppose that $u = e^w$, where w is normal with expected value $\overline{w}$ and variance σ^2. Then

$$\overline{u} = \frac{1}{\sqrt{2\pi\sigma^2}} \int_{-\infty}^{\infty} e^w e^{-(w-\overline{w})^2/2\sigma^2} \, dw \, .$$

Show that

$$w - \frac{(w - \overline{w})^2}{2\sigma^2} = -\frac{1}{2\sigma^2}\left[w - (\overline{w} + \sigma^2)\right]^2 + \overline{w} + \frac{\sigma^2}{2}.$$

Use the fact that

$$\frac{1}{\sqrt{2\pi\sigma^2}} \int_{-\infty}^{\infty} e^{-(x-\bar{x}^2)/2\sigma^2}\, dx = 1$$

to evaluate $\overline{u}$.

5. (Log variance ◊)   Use the method of Exercise 4 to find the variance of a lognormal variable in terms of the parameters of the underlying normal variable.

6. (Expectations)   A stock price is governed by geometric Brownian motion with $\mu = .20$ and $\sigma = .40$. The initial price is $S(0) = 1$. Evaluate the four quantities

$$E[\ln S(1)], \qquad \text{stdev}[\ln S(1)]$$

$$E[S(1)], \qquad \text{stdev}[S(1)].$$

7. (Application of Ito's lemma)   A stock price S is governed by

$$dS = aS\, dt + bS\, dz$$

where z is a standardized Wiener process. Find the process that governs

$$G(t) = S^{1/2}(t).$$

8. (Reverse check)   Gavin Jones was mystified by Ito's lemma when he first studied it, so he tested it. He started with S governed by

$$dS = \mu S\, dt + \sigma S\, dz$$

and found that $Q = \ln S$ satisfies

$$dQ = (\mu - \tfrac{1}{2}\sigma^2)\, dt + \sigma\, dz.$$

He then applied Ito's lemma to this last equation using the change of variable $S = e^Q$. Duplicate his calculations. What did he get?

9. (Two simulations ◊)   A useful expansion is

$$e^x = 1 + x + \tfrac{1}{2}x^2 + \cdots.$$

Use this to express the exponential in equation (11.20) in linear terms of powers of Δt up to first order. Note that this differs from the expression in (11.19), so conclude that the standard form and the multiplicative (or lognormal) form of simulation are different even to first order. Show, however, that the expected values of the two expressions *are* identical to first order, and hence, over the long run the two methods should produce similar results.

10. (A simulation experiment ⊕)   Consider a stock price S governed by the geometric Brownian motion process

$$\frac{dS}{S(t)} = .10\, dt + .30\, dz.$$

(a) Using $\Delta t = 1/12$ and $S(0) = 1$, simulate several (i.e., *many*) years of this process using either method, and evaluate

$$\frac{1}{t} \ln[S(t)]$$

as a function of t. Note that it tends to a limit p. What is the theoretical value of this limit?

(b) About how large must t be to obtain two-place accuracy?

(c) Evaluate

$$\frac{1}{t} \Big[\ln S(t) - pt \Big]^2$$

as a function of t. Does this tend to a limit? If so, what is its theoretical value?

REFERENCES

For a good overview of stock models similar to this chapter, see [1]. For greater detail on stochastic processes see [2], and for general information of how stock prices actually behave, see [3].

There are numerous textbooks on probability theory that discuss the normal distribution and the lognormal distribution. A classic is [4]. The book by Wiener [5] was responsible for inspiring a great deal of serious theoretical and practical work on issues involving Wiener processes. Ito's lemma was first published in [6] and later in [7].

1. Hull, J. C. (1993), *Options, Futures, and Other Derivative Securities*, 2nd ed., Prentice Hall, Englewood Cliffs, NJ.
2. Malliaris, A. G., and W. A. Brock (1982), *Stochastic methods in Economics and Finance*, North-Holland, Amsterdam, The Netherlands.
3. Cootner, P. H., Ed. (1964), *The Random Character of Stock Market Prices*, M.I.T. Press, Cambridge, MA.
4. Feller, W. (1950), *Probability Theory and Its Applications*, vols 1 and 2, Wiley, New York.
5. Wiener, N. (1950), *Extrapolation, Interpolation, and Smoothing of Stationary Time Series*, Technology Press, M.I.T., Cambridge, MA, and Wiley, New York.
6. Ito, K. (1951), "On a Formula Concerning Stochastic Differentials," *Nagoya Mathematics Journal*, **3**, 55–65.
7. Ito, K. (1961), *Lectures on Stochastic Processes,* Tata Institute of Fundamental Research, India.

12 BASIC OPTIONS THEORY

An **option** is the right, but not the obligation, to buy (or sell) an asset under specified terms. Usually there are a specified price and a specified period of time over which the option is valid. An example is the option to purchase, for a price of $200,000, a certain house, say, the one you are now renting, anytime within the next year. An option that gives the right to purchase something is called a **call** option, whereas an option that gives the right to sell something is called a **put.** Usually an option itself has a price; frequently we refer to this price as the option **premium,** to distinguish it from the purchase or selling price specified in the terms of the option. The premium may be a small fraction of the price of the optioned asset. For example, you might pay $15,000 for the option to purchase the house at $200,000. If the option holder actually does buy or sell the asset according to the terms of the option, the option holder is said to **exercise** the option. The original premium is not recovered in any case.

An option is a derivative security whose underlying asset is the asset that can be bought or sold, such as the house in our example. The ultimate financial value of an option depends on the price of the underlying asset at the time of possible exercise. For example, if the house is worth $300,000 at the end of the year, the $200,000 option is then worth $100,000, because you could buy the house for $200,000 and immediately sell it for $300,000 for a profit of $100,000.

Options have a long history in commerce, since they provide excellent mechanisms for controlling risk, or for locking up resources at a minimal fee. The following story, quoted from Aristotle,[1] is a favorite of professors who write about investments.

> There is an anecdote of Thales the Milesian and his financial device, which involves
> a principle of universal application, but is attributed to him on account of his reputation
> for wisdom. He was reproached for his poverty, which was supposed to show that
> philosophy was of no use. According to the story, he knew by his skill in the stars

---

[1] Aristotle, *Politics*, Book 1, Chapter 11, Jowett translation. Quoted in Gastineau (1975).

while it was yet winter that there would be a great harvest of olives in the coming year; so, having a little money, he gave deposits for the use of all the olive presses in Chios and Miletus, which he hired at a low price because no one bid against him. When the harvest time came, and many wanted them all at once and of a sudden, he let them out at any rate which he pleased, and made a quantity of money. Thus he showed the world that philosophers can easily be rich if they like ...

Another classic example is associated with the Dutch *tulip mania* in about 1600. Tulips were prized for their beauty, and this led to vigorous speculation and escalation of prices. Put options were used by growers to guarantee a price for their bulbs, and call options were used by dealers to assure future prices. The market was not regulated in any way and finally crashed in 1636, leaving options with a bad reputation.

Options are now available on a wide assortment of financial instruments (such as stocks and bonds) through regulated exchanges. However, options on physical assets are still very important. In addition, there are many implied or hidden options in other financial situations. An example is the option to extract oil from an oil well or leave it in the ground until a better time, or the option to accept a mortgage guarantee or renegotiate. These situations can be fruitfully analyzed using the theory of options explained in this chapter.

12.1 OPTION CONCEPTS

The specifications of an option include, first, a clear description of what can be bought (for a call) or sold (for a put). For options on stock, each option is usually for 100 shares of a specified stock. Thus a call option on IBM is the option to buy 100 shares of IBM. Second, the exercise price, or **strike price,** must be specified. This is the price at which the asset can be purchased upon exercise of the option. For IBM stock the exercise price might be $70, which means that each share can be bought at $70. Third, the period of time for which the option is valid must be specified—defined by the expiration date. Hence an option may be valid for a day, a week, or several months. There are two primary conventions regarding acceptable exercise dates before expiration. An **American option** allows exercise at any time before and including the expiration date. A **European option** allows exercise only on the expiration date. The terms *American* and *European* refer to the different ways most stock options are structured in America and in Europe, but the words have become standard for the two different types of structures, no matter where they are issued. There are some European-style options in America. For example, if the option to buy a house in one year states that the sale must be made in exactly one year and not sooner, the house option can be referred to as a European option.

These four features—the description of the asset, whether a call or a put, the exercise price, and the expiration date (including whether American or European in style)—specify the details of an option. A final, but somewhat separate, feature is the price of the option itself—the premium. If an option is individually tailored, this premium price is established as part of the original negotiation and is part of the contract. If the option is traded on an exchange, the premium is established by the

Option/strike	Exp.	Call Vol.	Call Last	Put Vol.	Put Last
GM	35	Dec	529	$2\frac{7}{8}$	...	...
$37\frac{7}{8}$	35	Jan	93	$3\frac{5}{8}$	90	$\frac{1}{2}$
$37\frac{7}{8}$	35	Mar	36	$4\frac{1}{4}$	49	1
$37\frac{7}{8}$	35	Jun	31	$5\frac{1}{2}$	...	...
$37\frac{7}{8}$	40	Dec	24	$\frac{1}{16}$	549	$2\frac{1}{16}$
$37\frac{7}{8}$	40	Jan	407	$\frac{11}{16}$	284	$2\frac{5}{8}$
$37\frac{7}{8}$	40	Mar	746	$1\frac{5}{8}$	40	3
$37\frac{7}{8}$	40	Jun	91	$2\frac{11}{16}$	135	$3\frac{7}{8}$
$37\frac{7}{8}$	45	Jan	104	$\frac{1}{8}$	49	7
$37\frac{7}{8}$	45	Mar	50	$\frac{1}{2}$	...	...
$37\frac{7}{8}$	45	Jun	110	$1\frac{1}{4}$	15	$7\frac{5}{8}$
$37\frac{7}{8}$	50	Jun	94	$\frac{1}{2}$	...	...

FIGURE 12.1 Options quotations on General Motors stock (December 15, 1995). The first column shows the closing price of the stock. The other columns give information about available options. Source: *The Wall Street Journal,* December 15, 1994.

market through supply and demand, and this premium will vary according to trading activity.

There are two sides to any option: the party that grants the option is said to **write** an option, whereas the party that obtains the option is said to purchase it. The party purchasing an option faces no risk of loss other than the original purchase premium. However, the party that writes the option may face a large loss, since this party must buy or sell this asset at the specified terms if the option is exercised. In the case of an exercised call option, if the writer does not already own the asset, he must purchase it in order to deliver it at the specified strike price, which may be much higher than the current market price. Likewise, in the case of an exercised put option, the writer must accept the asset for the strike price, which could be much lower than the current market price.

Options on many stocks are traded on an exchange. In this case individual option trades are made through a broker who trades on the exchange. The exchange clearinghouse guarantees the performance of all parties. Because of the risk associated with options, an option writer is required to post **margin** (a security deposit) guaranteeing performance.[2]

Exchange-traded options are listed in the financial press. A listing of GM (General Motors) options is shown in Figure 12.1. There are several different options available for GM stock. Some are calls and some are puts, and they have a variety of strike prices and expiration dates. In the figure, the first column shows the symbol for the underlying stock and the closing price of the stock itself. The second column shows the exercise (or strike) price of the option. The third column shows the month in

---

[2]The initial margin level is often 50% of the stock value of the option, with a maintenance level of 25%.

which the option expires. The exact expiration date during that month is the Saturday following the third Friday. The fourth and fifth columns give data on a call, showing the volume traded on the day reported and the last reported price for that option. The final two columns give the analogous information for the put. All prices are quoted on a per-share basis, although a single option contract is for 100 shares.

As with futures contracts, options on financial securities are rarely exercised, with the underlying security being bought or sold. Instead, if the price of the security moves in a favorable direction, the option price (the premium) will increase accordingly, and most option holders will elect to sell their options before maturity.

There are many details with regard to options trading, governing special situations such as stock splits, dividends, position limits, and specific margin requirements. These must be checked before engaging in serious trading of options. However, the present overview is sufficient for understanding the basic mechanics of options.

12.2 THE NATURE OF OPTION VALUES

A primary objective of this chapter is to show how to determine the value of an option on a financial security. Such a determination is a fascinating and creative application of the fundamental principles that we have studied so far. Hence options theory is important *partly* because options themselves are important financial instruments, but also partly because options theory shows how the fundamental principles of investment science can be taken to a new level—a level where dynamic structure is fundamental. In this section we examine in a qualitative manner the nature of option prices. This will prepare us for the deeper analysis that follows in subsequent sections.

Suppose that you own a call option on a stock with a strike price of K. Suppose that on the expiration date the price of the underlying stock is S. What is the value of the option at that time? It is easy to see that if $S < K$, then the option value is zero. This is because under the terms of the option, you could exercise the option and purchase the stock for K, but by not exercising the option you could buy the stock on the open market for the lower price of S. Hence you would not exercise the option. The option is worthless. On the other hand, if $S > K$, then the option does have value. By exercising the option you could buy the stock at a price K and then sell that stock on the market for the larger price S. Your profit would be $S - K$, which is therefore the value of the option. We handle both cases together by writing the value of the call at expiration as

$$C = \max(0, S - K) \tag{12.1}$$

which means that C is equal to the maximum of the values 0 or $S - K$. We therefore have an explicit formula for the value of a call option at expiration as a function of the price of the underlying security S. This function is shown in Figure 12.2(a). The figure shows that for $S < K$, the value is zero, but for $S > K$, the value of the option increases linearly with the price, on a one–for–one basis.

The result is reversed for a put option. A put option gives one the right, but not the obligation, to sell an asset at a given strike price. Suppose you own a put

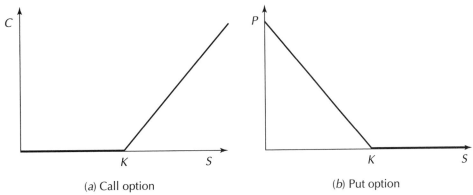

(a) Call option   (b) Put option

FIGURE 12.2   **Value of option at expiration.** A call has value if $S > K$. A put has value if $S < K$.

option on a stock with a strike price of K. In this case if the price S of the stock at expiration satisfies $S > K$, then this option is worthless. By exercising the option you could sell the stock for a price K, whereas in the open market you could sell the stock for the greater price S. Hence you would not exercise the option. On the other hand, if the price of the stock is less than the strike price, the put option does have value. You could buy the stock on the market for a price S and then exercise the option to sell that same stock for a greater price K. Your profit would be $K - S$, which is therefore the value of the option. The general formula for the value of a put at expiration is

$$P = \max (0, \ K - S) . \tag{12.2}$$

This function is illustrated in Figure 12.2(*b*). Note that the value of a put is bounded, whereas the payoff of a call is unbounded. Conversely, when writing a call, the potential for *loss* is unbounded.

We say that a call option is **in the money, at the money,** or **out of the money,** depending on whether $S > K$, $S = K$, or $S < K$, respectively. The terminology applies at any time; but at expiration the terms describe the nature of the option value. Puts have the reverse terminology, since the payoffs at exercise are positive if $S < K$.

Time Value of Options

The preceding analysis focused on the value of an option at expiration. This value is derived from the basic structure of an option. However, even European options (which cannot be exercised except at expiration) have value at earlier times, since they provide the potential for future exercise. Consider, for example, an option on GM stock with a strike price of $40 and 3 months to expiration. Suppose the current price of GM stock is $37.88. (This situation is approximately that of Figure 12.1 represented by the March 40 call.) It is clear that there is a chance that the price of GM stock might increase to over $40 within 3 months. It would then be possible to exercise the option and obtain a profit. Hence this option has value even though it is currently

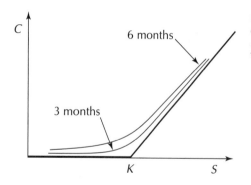

FIGURE 12.3 Option price curve with various times to expiration. At a given stock price S, the value of a call option increases as the time to expiration increases.

out of the money. (In the example represented by the figure, the 40 call is selling for $1.63.)

When there is a positive time to expiration, the value of a call option as a function of the stock price is a smooth curve rather than the decidedly kinked curve that applies at expiration. This smooth curve can be determined by estimation, using data of actual option prices. Such estimation shows that the option price curve for any given expiration period looks something like the curves shown in Figure 12.3. In this figure the heavy kinked line represents the value of a call at expiration. The higher curves correspond to different times to expiration. The first curve is for a call with 3 months to expiration, whereas the next higher one is for 6 months. The curves get higher with increasing length to expiration, since additional time provides a greater chance for the stock to rise in value, increasing the final payoff. However, the effect of additional time is diminished when the stock price is either much smaller or much greater than the strike price K. When the stock price S is much lower than K, there is little chance that S will rise above K, so the option value remains close to zero. When S is much greater than K, there is little advantage in owning the option over owning the stock itself.

A major objective of this chapter is to determine a theory for option prices. This theory will imply a specific set of curves, such as the ones shown in Figure 12.3.

Other Factors Affecting the Value of Options

The volatility of the underlying stock is another factor that influences the value of an option significantly. To see this, imagine that you own similar options on two different stocks. Suppose the prices of the two stocks are both $90, the options have strike prices of $100, and there are 3 months to expiration. Suppose, however, that one of these stocks is very volatile and the other is quite placid. Which option has more value? It is clear that the stock with the high volatility has the greatest chance of rising above $90 in the short period remaining to expiration, and hence its option is the more valuable of the two. We expect therefore that the value of a call option increases with volatility, and we shall verify this in our theoretical development.

What other factors might influence the value of an option? One is the prevailing interest rate (or term structure pattern). Purchasing a call option is in some way a method of purchasing the stock at a reduced price. Hence one saves interest expense. We expect therefore that option prices depend on interest rates.

Another factor that would seem to be important is the growth rate of the stock. It seems plausible that higher values of growth would imply larger values for the option. However, perhaps surprisingly, the growth rate does *not* influence the theoretical value of an option. The reason for this will become clear when the theoretical formula is developed.

12.3 OPTION COMBINATIONS AND PUT–CALL PARITY

It is common to invest in combinations of options in order to implement special hedging or speculative strategies. The payoff curve of such a combination may have any number of connected straight-line segments. This overall payoff curve is formed by combining the payoff functions defined by calls, puts, and the underlying stock itself. The process is best illustrated by an example and a corresponding graph.

Example 12.1 (A butterfly spread) One of the most interesting combinations of options is the butterfly spread. It is illustrated in Figure 12.4. The spread is constructed by buying two calls, one with strike price K_1 and another with strike price K_3, and by selling two units of a call with strike price K_2, where $K_1 < K_2 < K_3$. Usually K_2 is chosen to be near the current stock price. The figure shows with dashed lines the *profit* (including the payoff and original cost) associated with each of the components. The overall profit function of the combination is the sum of the individual component functions. This particular combination yields a positive profit if the stock price at expiration is close to K_2; otherwise the loss is quite small. The payoff of this spread is obtained by lifting the curve up so that the horizontal portions touch the axis, the displacement distance corresponding to the net cost of the options.

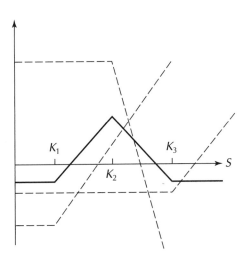

FIGURE 12.4 Profit of butterfly spread. This spread is formed by buying calls with strike prices K_1 and K_3 and writing two units of a call at K_2. This combination is useful if one believes that the underlying stock price will stay in a region near K_2.

The main point here is that by forming combinations of options and stock it is possible to approximate virtually any payoff function by a sequence of straight-line segments. The cost of such a payoff is then just the sum of the costs of the individual components.

Put–Call Parity

For European options there is a simple theoretical relationship between the prices of corresponding puts and calls. The relationship is found by noting that a combination of a put, a call, and a risk-free loan has a payoff identical to that of the underlying stock.

The combination can be easily imagined: buy one call, sell one put, and lend an amount dK. The combination of the first two has a payoff that is a straight line at $45°$, passing through K on the horizontal axis. By lending dK, we obtain an additional payoff of K, which lifts the payoff line up so that it is now a $45°$ line originating at the origin. This final payoff is exactly that of the stock itself, so it must have the value S of the stock. In other words,

$$C - P + dK = S.$$

(See Exercise 3 for more detail.)

Put–call parity   *Let C and P be the prices of a European call and a European put, both with a strike price of K and both defined on the same stock with price S. Put–call parity states that*

$$C - P + dK = S$$

where d is the discount factor to the expiration date.

Example 12.2 (Parity almost)   Consider the GM options of Figure 12.1, and focus on the two 35 March options (with 3 months to expiration). These have $C = 4.25$ and $P = 1.00$, respectively. The interest rate for this period is about 5.5%, so over 3 months we have $d = 1/(1 + .055/4) = .986$. Thus,

$$C - P + dK = 4.25 - 1.0 + .986 \times 35.00 = 37.78 .$$

This is a close, but not exact, match with the actual stock price of $37.88. There are several possible explanations for the mismatch. One of the most important is that the stock quotes and option quotes do not come from the same sources. The stock price is the closing price on the stock exchange, whereas the option prices are from the last traded options on the options exchanges; the last trades can occur at different times. Dividends also can influence the parity relation, as discussed in Exercise 2.

12.4 EARLY EXERCISE

An American option offers the possibility of early exercise, that is, exercise before the expiration date of the option. We prove in this section that for call options on a stock that pays no dividends prior to expiration, early exercise is never optimal, provided that prices are such that no arbitrage is possible.

The result can be seen intuitively as follows. Suppose that we are holding a call option at time t and expiration is at time $T > t$. If the current stock price $S(t)$ is less than the strike price K, we would not exercise the option, since we would lose money. If, on the other hand, the stock price is greater than K, we might be tempted to exercise. However, if we do so we will have to pay K now to obtain the stock. If we hold the option a little longer and then exercise, we will still obtain the stock for a price of K, but we will have earned additional interest on the exercise money K—in fact, if the stock declines below K in this waiting period, we will not exercise and be happy that we did not do so earlier.

12.5 SINGLE-PERIOD BINOMIAL OPTIONS THEORY

We now turn to the issue of calculating the theoretical value of an option—an area of work that is called **options pricing theory.** There are several approaches to this problem, based on different assumptions about the market, about the dynamics of stock price behavior, and about individual preferences. The most important theories are based on the no arbitrage principle, which can be applied when the dynamics of the underlying stock take certain forms. The simplest of these theories is based on the binomial model of stock price fluctuations discussed in Chapter 11. This theory is widely used in practice because of its simplicity and ease of calculation. It is a beautiful culmination of the principles discussed in previous chapters.

The basic theory of binomial options pricing has been hinted at in our earlier discussions. We shall develop it here in a self-contained manner, but the reader should notice the connections to earlier sections.

We shall first develop the theory for the single-period case. A single step of a binomial process is all that is used. Accordingly, we suppose that the initial price of a stock is S. At the end of the period the price will either be uS with probability p or dS with probability $1 - p$. We assume $u > d > 0$. Also at every period it is possible to borrow or lend at a common risk-free interest rate r. We let $R = 1 + r$. To avoid arbitrage opportunities, we must have

$$u > R > d.$$

To see this, suppose $R \geq u > d$ and $0 < p < 1$. Then the stock performs worse than the risk-free asset, even in the "up" branch of the lattice. Hence one could short $1.00 of the stock and loan the proceeds, thereby obtaining a profit of either $R - u$ or $R - d$, depending on the outcome state. The initial cost is zero, but in either case the profit is positive, which is not possible if there are no arbitrage opportunities. A similar argument rules out $u > d \geq R$.

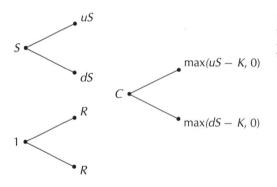

FIGURE 12.5 Three related lattices. The stock price, the value of a risk-free loan, and the value of a call option all move together on a common lattice, represented here as three separate lattices.

Now suppose also that there is a call option on this stock with exercise price K and expiration at the end of the period. To find the value of the call option, we use a no-arbitrage argument by referring to Figure 12.5. This figure shows the binomial lattices for the stock price, the value of a risk-free asset, and the value of the option. All three of these lattices have common arcs, in the sense that all move together along the same arcs. If the stock price moves along the upward arc, then the risk-free asset and the call option both move along their upward arcs as well. The risk-free value is deterministic, but this is treated as if it were a (degenerate) derivative of the stock by just making the value at the end of each arc the same.

Assuming that we know the stock price S, then all values of these one-step lattices are known except the value of the call C. This value will be determined from the other values.

The insight that we use is to note that each of the lattices on the left has only two possible outcomes. By combining various proportions of these two lattices, we can construct any other pattern of outcomes. In particular, we can construct the pattern corresponding to the outcomes of the option.

Let us denote

$$C_u = \max(uS - K, 0) \tag{12.3}$$

$$C_d = \max(dS - K, 0). \tag{12.4}$$

To duplicate these two outcomes, let us purchase x dollars worth of stock and b dollars worth of the risk-free asset. At the next time period, this portfolio will be worth either $ux + Rb$ or $dx + Rb$, depending on which path is taken. To match the option outcomes we therefore require

$$ux + Rb = C_u \tag{12.5a}$$

$$dx + Rb = C_d. \tag{12.5b}$$

To solve these equations we subtract the second from the first, obtaining

$$x = \frac{C_u - C_d}{u - d}.$$

From this we easily find

$$b = \frac{C_u - ux}{R} = \frac{uC_d - dC_u}{R(u - d)}.$$

Combining these we find that the value of the portfolio is

$$x + b = \frac{C_u - C_d}{u - d} + \frac{uC_d - dC_u}{R(u - d)}$$

$$= \frac{1}{R}\left(\frac{R - d}{u - d}C_u + \frac{u - R}{u - d}C_d\right).$$

We now use the comparison principle (or, equivalently, the no-arbitrage principle) to assert that the value $x + b$ must be the value of the call option C. The reason is that the portfolio we constructed produces exactly the same outcomes as the call option. If the cost of this portfolio were less than the price of the call, we would never purchase the call. Indeed, we could make arbitrage profits by buying this portfolio and selling the call for an immediate gain and no future consequence. If the prices were unequal in the reverse direction, we could just reverse the argument. We conclude therefore that the price of the call is

$$C = \frac{1}{R}\left(\frac{R - d}{u - d}C_u + \frac{u - R}{u - d}C_d\right). \tag{12.6}$$

The portfolio made up of the stock and the risk-free asset that duplicates the outcome of the option is often referred to an a **replicating portfolio.** It replicates the option. This replicating idea can be used to find the value of any security defined on the same lattice; that is, any security that is a derivative of the stock.

There is a simplified way to view equation (12.6). We define the quantity

$$q = \frac{R - d}{u - d}. \tag{12.7}$$

From the relation $u > R > d$ assumed earlier, it follows that $0 < q < 1$. Hence q can be considered to be a probability. Also (12.6) can be written as follows:

Option pricing formula   *The value of a one-period call option on a stock governed by a binomial lattice is*

$$C = \frac{1}{R}[qC_u + (1 - q)C_d]. \tag{12.8}$$

Note that (12.8) can be interpreted as stating that C is found by taking the expected value of the option using the probability q, and then discounting this value according to the risk-free rate. The probability q is therefore a **risk-neutral probability.** This procedure of valuation works for all securities. In fact q can be calculated by making sure that the risk-neutral formula holds for the underlying stock itself; that is, we want

$$S = \frac{1}{R}[quS + (1 - q)dS].$$

Solving this equation gives (12.7).

As a suggestive notation, we write (12.8) as

$$C(T - 1) = \frac{1}{R}\hat{E}[C(T)].$$

Here $C(T)$ and $C(T-1)$ are the call values at T and $T-1$, respectively, and $\hat{E}$ denotes expectation with respect to the risk-neutral probabilities q and $1-q$.

An important, and perhaps initially surprising, feature of the pricing formula (12.6) is that it is *independent* of the probability p of an upward move in the lattice. This is because no trade-off among probabilistic events is made. The value is found by perfectly matching the outcomes of the option with a combination of stock and the risk-free asset. Probability never enters this matching calculation.

This derivation of the option pricing formula is really a special case of the risk-neutral pricing concept discussed in Chapter 9. At this point it would be useful for the reader to review that earlier section.

12.6 MULTIPERIOD OPTIONS

We now extend the solution method to multiperiod options by working backward one step at a time.

A two-stage lattice representing a two-period call option is shown in Figure 12.6. It is assumed as before that the initial price of the stock is S, and this price is modified by the up and down factors u and d while moving through the lattice. The values shown in the lattice are those of the corresponding call option with strike price K and expiration time corresponding to the final point in the lattice. The value of the option is known at the final nodes of the lattice. In particular,

$$C_{uu} = \max\left(u^2 S - K, 0\right) \tag{12.9a}$$

$$C_{ud} = \max\left(udS - K, 0\right) \tag{12.9b}$$

$$C_{dd} = \max\left(d^2 S - K, 0\right). \tag{12.9c}$$

We again define the risk-neutral probability as

$$q = \frac{R - d}{u - d}$$

where R is the one-period return on the risk-free asset. Then, assuming that we do not exercise the option early (which we already know is optimal, but will demonstrate

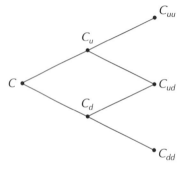

FIGURE 12.6   **Two-period option.** The value is found by working backward a step at a time.

again shortly), we can find the values of C_u and C_d from the single-period calculation given earlier. Specifically,

$$C_u = \frac{1}{R}[qC_{uu} + (1-q)C_{ud}] \tag{12.10}$$

$$C_d = \frac{1}{R}[qC_{ud} + (1-q)C_{dd}]. \tag{12.11}$$

Then we find C by another application of the same risk-neutral discounting formula. Hence,

$$C = \frac{1}{R}[qC_u + (1-q)C_d].$$

For a lattice with more periods, a similar procedure is used. The single-period, risk-free discounting is just repeated at every node of the lattice, starting from the final period and working backward toward the initial time.

Example 12.3 (A 5-month call)   Consider a stock with a volatility of its logarithm of $\sigma = .20$. The current price of the stock is 62. The stock pays no dividends. A certain call option on this stock has an expiration date 5 months from now and a strike price of 60. The current rate of interest is 10%, compounded monthly. We wish to determine the theoretical price of this call using the binomial option approach.

First we must determine the parameters for the binomial model of the stock price fluctuations. We shall take the period length to be 1 month, which means $\Delta t = 1/12$. The parameters are found from Eqs. (11.1) to be

$$
\begin{aligned}
u &= e^{\sigma\sqrt{\Delta t}} &&= 1.05943 \\
d &= e^{-\sigma\sqrt{\Delta t}} &&= .94390 \\
R &= 1 + .1/12 &&= 1.00833.
\end{aligned}
$$

Then the risk-neutral probability is

$$q = (R-d)/(u-d) = .55770.$$

We now form the binomial lattice corresponding to the stock price at the beginning of each of six successive months (including the current month). This lattice is shown in Figure 12.7, with the number above a node being the stock price at that node. Note that an up followed by a down always yields a net multiple of 1.

Next we calculate the call option price. We start at the final time and enter the expiration values of the call below the final nodes. This is the maximum of 0 and $S - K$. For example, the entry for the top node is $82.75 - 60 = 22.75$.

The values for the previous time are found by the single-step pricing relation. The value of any node at this time is the discounted expected value of two successive values at the next time. The expected value is calculated using the risk-neutral

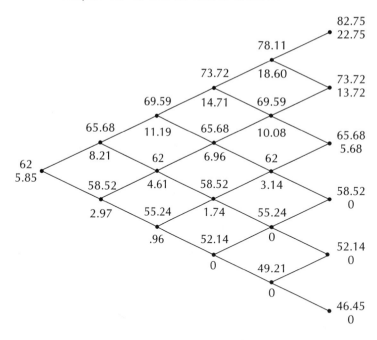

FIGURE 12.7   5-month call using a binomial lattice. The upper numbers are the stock prices, the lower numbers the option values. The option values are found by working backward through the lattice.

probabilities q and $1 - q$. For example, the value at the top node is $[.5577 \times 22.75 + (1 - .5577) \times 13.72]/1.00833 = 18.60$.

We work toward the left, one period at a time, until finally the initial value is reached. In this case we conclude that the price of the option computed this way is $5.85.

Note that the entire process is independent of the expected growth rate of the stock. This value only enters the binomial model of the stock through the probability p; but this probability is not used in the option calculation. Instead it is the risk-neutral probability q that is used. Note, however, that this independence results from using the small Δt approximation for parameter matching. And indeed, in practice this approximation is almost invariably used (even for Δt equal to 1 year). If the more general matching formula were used, the growth rate would (slightly) influence the result.

No Early Exercise*

In the preceding example we assumed (rightly) that the option would never be exercised early. We can prove this directly from the binomial equations. From the basic payoff structure we see that

$$C_{uu} \geq u^2 S - K$$
$$C_{ud} \geq udS - K$$
$$C_{dd} \geq d^2 S - K.$$

Hence,

$$
\begin{aligned}
C_u &\geq [u^2 q S + ud(1-q)S - K]/R \\
&= u\big[qu + (1-q)d\big]S/R - K/R \\
&> uS - K .
\end{aligned}
$$

Likewise,

$$
C_d > dS - K .
$$

If the option were exercised at the end of the first period of the two-period lattice shown in Figure 12.6, we would obtain $uS - K$ or $dS - K$, depending on which node was active at the time. These inequalities show that the value of the option at the end of one period is greater than the amount that would be obtained by exercise at that period. Hence we should not exercise the option.

If the lattice had more periods, these inequalities would extend to the next forward period as well. Hence, in general, by an inductive process it can be shown that it is never optimal to exercise the option.

The argument against early exercise does not hold for all options; in some cases an additional operation must be incorporated in the recursive process of value calculation. This is explained in the next section.

12.7 MORE GENERAL BINOMIAL PROBLEMS

The binomial lattice method for calculating the value of an option is extremely simple and highly versatile. For this reason it has become a common tool in the investment and financial community. The method is simplest when applied to a call option on a non-dividend-paying stock, as illustrated in the previous section. This section shows how the basic method can be extended to more complex situations.

Put Options

The method for calculating the values of European put options is analogous to that for call options. The main difference is that the terminal values for the option are different. But once these are specified, the recursive procedure works in a similar way.

For an American put, early exercise may be optimal. This is easily accounted for in the recursive process as follows: At each node, first calculate the value of the put using the discounted risk-neutral formula; then calculate the value that would be obtained by immediate exercise of the put; finally, select the larger of these two values as the value of the put at that node.

Example 12.4 (A 5-month put)   We consider the same stock that was used to evaluate the 5-month call option of Example 12.3, but now we evaluate a 5-month American

62.00	65.68	69.59	73.72	78.11	82.75
	58.52	62.00	65.68	69.59	73.72
		55.24	58.52	62.00	65.68
	Stock price		52.14	55.24	58.52
				49.21	52.14
					46.45

1.56	0.61	0.12	0.00	0.00	0.00
	2.79	1.23	0.28	0.00	0.00
		4.80	2.45	0.65	0.00
	Put option		**7.86**	**4.76**	**1.48**
			10.79	**7.86**
				13.55

FIGURE 12.8 Calculation of a 5-month put option price. The put values in the lower portion of the figure are found by working backward. Boldface entries indicate points where it is optimal to exercise the option.

put option with a strike price of $K = \$60$. Recall that the critical parameters were $R = 1.008333$, $q = .55770$, $u = 1.05943$, and $d = .94390$. Binomial lattice calculations can be very conveniently carried out with a spreadsheet program. Hence we often show lattices in spreadsheet form rather than as graphical diagrams. This allows us to show larger lattices in a restricted space, and it also indicates more directly how calculations are organized.

The binomial lattice for the stock price is shown in the top portion of Figure 12.8. In this figure an up move is made by moving directly to the right, and a down move is made by moving to the right and down one step.

To calculate the value of the put option, we again work backward, constructing a new lattice below the stock price lattice. The final values (those of the last column) are, in this case, the maximum of 0 and $K - S$. We then work toward the left, one column at a time. To find the value of an element we first calculate the discounted expected value as before, using the risk-neutral probabilities. Now, however, we must also check whether this value would be exceeded by $K - S$, which is what could be obtained by exercising the option at the current point. We assign the larger of the two values to this current node. For example, consider the fourth entry in the second to last column. The discounted expected value there is $[.5577 \times 1.48 + (1 - .5577) \times 7.86]/1.00833 = 4.266$. The exercise value is $60 - 55.24 = 4.76$. The larger of these is 4.76, and that is what is entered in the value lattice. If the larger value is obtained by exercising, we may also wish to indicate this on the lattice, which in our figure is done by using boldface for the entries corresponding to exercise points. (Alternatively, a separate lattice consisting of 0's and 1's can be constructed to indicate the exercise points.) In our example we see that there are several points at which exercise is optimal. The value of the put is the first entry of the lattice, namely, $1.56.

Intuitively, early exercise of a put may be optimal because the upside profit is bounded. Clearly, for example, if the stock price falls to zero, one should exercise there, since no greater profit can be achieved. A continuity argument can be used to infer that it is optimal to exercise if the stock price gets close to zero.

Dividend and Term Structure Problems*

Many other problems can be treated with the binomial lattice model by allowing the parameters of the model to vary from node to node. This does not change the basic structure of the computational method. It merely means that the risk-neutral probabilities and the discount factor may differ from period to period.

One example is the evaluation of a call option on a stock that pays a dividend. If the dividend is proportional to the value of the stock—say, the dividend is δS and is paid at time k—then in the stock price lattice we just change the factors u and d for the period ending at k to $u(1 - \delta)$ and $d(1 - \delta)$. If the dividend is known in advance to be a fixed amount D, then this technique will not work directly, but the lattice approach can still be used. (See Exercise 5.)

The parameters also vary when the interest rate is not constant. In this case the appropriate single-period rate for a given period (the implied short rate) should be used. This will change the value of R and hence also the value of q.

Futures Options*

Are we ready to consider a futures option—that is, an option on a futures contract? This may at first sound complicated; but we shall find that futures options are quite simple to analyze, and study of the analysis should help develop a fuller understanding of the risk-neutral pricing process. The best way to study the analysis is to consider an example.

Example 12.5 (A futures contract) Suppose that a certain commodity (which can be stored without cost and is in ample supply) has a current price of $100, and the price process is described by a monthly binomial lattice with parameters $u = 1.02$, $d = .99$, and $R = 1.01$. The actual probabilities are not important for our analysis. This lattice, for 6 months into the future, is shown in the upper left-hand corner of Figure 12.9. We can immediately calculate the risk-neutral probabilities to be $q = (R-d)/(u-d) = \frac{2}{3}$ and $1 - q = \frac{1}{3}$.

Let us compute the lattice of the corresponding futures prices for a futures contract that expires in the sixth month. This lattice is shown in the lower left-hand side of Figure 12.9. One way to compute this lattice is to use the result of Chapter 10 that the futures price is equal to the current commodity price amplified by interest rate growth over the remaining period of the contract. Hence the futures price at time zero is $100(1.01)^6 = 106.15, as shown in the lattice. The futures price for any node in the lattice can be found by the same technique: just multiply the corresponding commodity price by the factor of interest rate growth for the remaining time.

The futures price can also be found recursively by using the risk-neutral probabilities. We know that the final futures price, at month 6, must be identical to the price of the commodity itself at that time, so we can fill in the last column of the array with those values. Let us denote the futures price at the top of the previous column,

0	1	2	3	4	5	6	0	1	2	3	4	5	6
100.00	102.00	104.04	106.12	108.24	110.41	112.62	4.16	5.05	6.04	7.12	8.25	9.42	10.62
	99.00	100.98	103.00	105.06	107.16	109.30		2.50	3.21	4.07	5.07	6.17	7.30
		98.01	99.97	101.97	104.01	106.09			1.14	1.59	2.20	3.02	4.09
Commodity price			97.03	98.97	100.95	102.97	Commodity option			0.28	0.42	0.64	0.97
				96.06	97.98	99.94					0.00	0.00	0.00
					95.10	97.00						0.00	0.00
						94.15							0.00

0	1	2	3	4	5	6	0	1	2	3	4	5	6
106.15	107.20	108.26	109.34	110.42	111.51	112.62	4.28	5.21	**6.26**	**7.34**	**8.42**	**9.51**	10.62
	104.05	105.08	106.12	107.17	108.23	109.30		2.54	3.27	4.15	**5.17**	**6.23**	7.30
		101.99	103.00	104.02	105.05	106.09			1.15	1.61	2.22	**3.05**	4.09
Futures price			99.97	100.96	101.96	102.97	Futures option			0.28	0.42	0.64	0.97
				97.99	98.96	99.94					0.00	0.00	0.00
					96.05	97.00						0.00	0.00
						94.15							0.00

FIGURE 12.9   Lattices associated with a commodity. The upper left lattice is the price lattice of a commodity. All other lattices are computed from it by backward risk-neutral evaluation.

at time 5, by F. If one took the long side of a one-period contract with this assigned price, the payoff in the next period would be either $112.62 - F$ or $109.30 - F$, depending on which of the two nodes was attained. These two values should be multiplied by q and $1 - q$, respectively, and the sum discounted one period to find the initial value, at time 5, of such a contract. But since futures contracts are arranged so that the initial value is zero, it follows that $q(112.62 - F) + (1 - q)(109.30 - F) = 0$, which gives $F = q112.62 + (1 - q)109.30$. In other words, F is the weighted average of the next period's prices; the weighting coefficients are the risk-neutral probabilities. We do *not* discount the average.

This process is continued backward a column at a time, computing the weighted average (or expected value) using the risk-neutral probabilities. The final result is again 106.15.

Notice that the original commodity price lattice also can be reconstructed backward by using risk-neutral pricing. Given the final prices, we compute the expected values using the risk-neutral probabilities, but now we *do* discount to find the value at the previous node. Working backward we fill in the entire lattice, duplicating the original figures in the upper left-hand corner.

The backward process for calculating the futures prices and the backward process for computing the commodity prices are identical, except that no discounting is applied in the calculation of futures prices. Hence futures prices will be the same as the commodity prices, but inflated by interest rate growth.

Example 12.6 (Some options)   Now let us consider some options related to the commodity in Example 12.5. First let us consider a call option on the commodity itself, with a strike price of $102 and expiration in month 6. This is now easy for us to calculate using binomial lattice methodology, as shown in the upper right-hand part of Figure 12.9. We just fill in the final column and then work backward with the risk-neutral discounting process. The fair price of the option is $4.16.

Next let us consider a call option on a futures contract with a strike price of $102. If this option is exercised, the call writer must deliver a futures contract with a futures price of $102, but marked to market. Suppose the actual futures price at the time of exercise is $110.42. Then the writer can purchase the futures contract (at zero cost) with the futures price $110.42 and deliver this contract together with the difference of $110.42 − $102.00 = $8.42 to the option holder. This payment compensates for the fact that the writer is delivering a contract at $110.42, instead of at $102.00 as promised. In other words, if the option is exercised, the call holder obtains a current futures contract and cash equal to the difference between the current futures price and the option strike price.

We can compute the value of such a call in the same manner as other calls, as shown in the lattice in the lower right-hand portion of Figure 12.9. At each node we must check whether or not it is desirable to exercise the option. This is done by seeing whether the corresponding futures price minus the strike price is greater than the risk-neutral value that would be obtained by holding the option. If it is optimal to exercise the option, we record the option value in boldface. The option price is found to be $4.28. Notice that even though the final payoff values are identical for the two options. The futures option has a higher value because the higher intermediate futures prices lead to the possibility of early exercise.

12.8 EVALUATING REAL INVESTMENT OPPORTUNITIES

Options theory can be used to evaluate investment opportunities that are not pure financial instruments. We shall illustrate this by again considering our gold mine lease problems. Now, however, the price of gold is assumed to fluctuate randomly, and this fluctuation must be accounted for in our evaluation of the lease prospect.

Example 12.7 (Simplico gold mine)   Recall the Simplico gold mine from Chapter 2. Gold can be extracted from this mine at a rate of up to 10,000 ounces per year at a cost of $200 per ounce. Currently the market price of gold is $400 per ounce, but we recognize that the price of gold fluctuates randomly. The term structure of interest rates is assumed to be flat at 10%. As a convention, we assume that the price obtained for gold mined in a given year is the price that held at the beginning of the year; but all cash flows occur at the end of the year. We wish to determine the value of a 10-year lease of this mine.

We represent future gold prices by a binomial lattice. Each year the price either increases by a factor of 1.2 (with probability .75) or decreases by a factor of .9 (with probability .25). The resulting lattice is shown in Figure 12.10.

How do we solve the problem of finding the lease value by the methods developed for options pricing? The trick is to notice that the gold mine lease can be regarded as a financial instrument. It has a value that fluctuates in time as the price of gold fluctuates. Indeed, the value of the mine lease at any given time can only be

0	1	2	3	4	5	6	7	8	9	10
400.0	480.0	576.0	691.2	829.4	995.3	1194.4	1433.3	1719.9	2063.9	2476.7
	360.0	432.0	518.4	622.1	746.5	895.8	1075.0	1289.9	1547.9	1857.5
		324.0	388.8	466.6	559.9	671.8	806.2	967.5	1161.0	1393.1
			291.6	349.9	419.9	503.9	604.7	725.6	870.7	1044.9
				262.4	314.9	377.9	453.5	544.2	653.0	783.6
Gold price (dollars)					236.2	283.4	340.1	408.1	489.8	587.7
						212.6	255.1	306.1	367.3	440.8
							191.3	229.6	275.5	330.6
								172.2	206.6	247.9
									155.0	186.0
										139.5

FIGURE 12.10   Gold price lattice. Each year the price either increases by a factor of 1.2 or decreases by a factor of .9. The resulting possible values each year are shown in spreadsheet form.

a function of the price of gold and the interest rate (which we assume is fixed). In other words, the lease on the gold mine is a derivative instrument whose underlying security is gold. Therefore the value of the lease can be entered node by node on the gold price lattice.

The lease values on the lattice are determined easily for the final nodes, at the end of the 10 years: the values are zero there because we must return the mine to the owners. At a node representing 1 year to go, the value of the lease is equal to the profit that can be made from the mine that year, discounted back to the beginning of the year. For example, the value at the top node for year 9 is $10,000(2,063.9 - 200)/1.1 = 16.94$ million. For an earlier node, the value of the lease is the sum of the profit that can be made that year and the risk-neutral expected value of the lease in the next period, both discounted back one period. The risk-neutral probabilities are $q = (1.1 - .9)/(1.2 - .9) = \frac{2}{3}$, and $1 - q = \frac{1}{3}$. The lease values can therefore be calculated by backward recursion using these values. (At nodes where the price of gold is less than $200, we do not mine.) The resulting values are indicated in Figure 12.11. We conclude that the value of the lease is $24,074,548 (showing all the digits).

0	1	2	3	4	5	6	7	8	9	10
24.1	27.8	31.2	34.2	36.5	37.7	37.1	34.1	27.8	16.9	0.0
	17.9	20.7	23.3	25.2	26.4	26.2	24.3	20.0	12.3	0.0
		12.9	15.0	16.7	17.9	18.1	17.0	14.1	8.7	0.0
			8.8	10.4	11.5	12.0	11.5	9.7	6.1	0.0
				5.6	6.7	7.4	7.4	6.4	4.1	0.0
Lease value (millions)					3.2	4.0	4.3	3.9	2.6	0.0
						1.4	2.0	2.1	1.5	0.0
							0.4	0.7	0.7	0.0
								0.0	0.1	0.0
									0.0	0.0
										0.0

FIGURE 12.11   Simplico gold mine. The value of the lease is found by working backward. If the price of gold is greater than $200 per ounce, it is profitable to mine; otherwise no mining is undertaken.

Many readers will be able to see from this example that they have a deeper understanding of investment than they did when they began to study this book. Earlier, in Chapter 2, we discussed the Simplico gold mine under the assumption that the price of gold would remain constant at $400 over the course of the lease. We also assumed a constant 10% interest rate. These assumptions, which are fairly commonly employed in problems of this type, were probably not regarded as being seriously incongruous by most readers. Now, however, we see that they are not just a simplification, but an actual inconsistency. If the price of gold were known to be constant, gold would act as a risk-free asset with zero rate of return. This is incompatible with the assumption that the risk-free rate is 10%. Indeed, in our lattice of gold prices we must select u, d, and R such that $u > R > d$.

Now that we have "mastered" the Simplico gold mine, it is time to move on to even greater challenges. (If you think you have really mastered the Simplico mine, try Exercise 8.)

Example 12.8 (Complexico gold mine★) [3]   The Complexico gold mine was discussed in Chapter 5. In this mine the cost of extraction depends on the amount of gold remaining. Hence if you lease this mine, you must decide how much to mine each period, taking into account that mining in one period affects future mining costs. We also assume now that the price of gold fluctuates according to the binomial lattice of the previous example.

The cost of extraction in any year is $500z^2/x$, where x is the amount of gold remaining at the beginning of the year and z is the amount of gold extracted in ounces. Initially there are $x_0 = 50,000$ ounces of gold in the mine. We again assume that the term structure of interest rates is flat at 10%. Also, the profit from mining is determined on the basis of the price of gold at the beginning of the period, and in this example all cash flows occur at the beginning of the period.

To solve this problem we must do some preliminary analysis. At the final time the value of the lease is clearly zero. If we are at a node representing the end of year 9, we must determine the optimal amount of gold to mine during the tenth year. Accordingly, we must compute the profit

$$V_9(x_9) = \max_{z_9}(gz_9 - 500z_9^2/x_9)$$

where g is the price of gold at that particular node. From the calculations of Example 5.5 we know that the maximization gives

$$V_9(x_9) = \frac{g^2 x_9}{2,000}.$$

This shows that the value of the lease is proportional to x_9, the amount of gold remaining. We therefore write $V_9(x_9) = K_9 x_9$, where

$$K_9 = \frac{g^2}{2,000}.$$

---

[3]This is a more difficult example, which should be studied only after you are fairly comfortable with the material of this chapter.

0	1	2	3	4	5	6	7	8	9	10
324.4	393.8	478.1	580.8	706.6	862.3	1058.7	1313.4	1656.1	2129.9	0.0
	272.5	329.9	398.6	480.7	578.4	694.4	831.7	995.0	1198.0	0.0
		225.8	272.2	327.0	390.7	463.4	542.9	621.9	673.9	0.0
			182.8	218.9	260.0	305.2	351.1	387.3	379.1	0.0
				143.6	169.5	197.0	222.5	237.3	213.2	0.0
K-value					108.1	124.4	138.1	142.8	119.9	0.0
						76.9	84.1	84.6	67.5	0.0
							50.3	49.5	37.9	0.0
								28.7	21.3	0.0
									12.0	0.0
										0.0

FIGURE 12.12   Complexico gold mine solution. The value of the mine is proportional to the amount of gold remaining in the mine. The proportionality factor K is found by backward recursion.

We set up a lattice of K values with nodes corresponding to various gold prices. We put $K_{10} = 0$ for all elements in the last column and put the values of K_9 in the ninth column. In a similar way, following the analysis of the earlier example, we find that for a node at time 8,

$$V_8(x_8) = \max_{z_8}[gz_8 - 500z_8^2/x_8 + d\hat{K}_9 \times (x_8 - z_8)]$$

where

$$\hat{K}_9 = qK_9 + (1 - q)K_9'$$

and where K_9 is the value on the node directly to the right, and K_9' is the value on the node just below that. This leads to

$$z_8 = \frac{(g - d\hat{K}_9)x_8}{1,000}$$

and $V_8(x_8) = K_8 x_8$, where

$$K_8 = \frac{(g - \hat{K}_9/R)^2}{2,000} + \hat{K}_9/R \ .$$

Again, there will be a different value of K_8 for each node at period 8. We work backward with this same formula to complete the lattice shown in Figure 12.12, obtaining $K_0 = 324.4$. The value of the lease is then found as $V_0 = 50,000 \times K_0 = \$16,220,000$.

Real Options

Sometimes options are associated with investment opportunities that are not financial instruments. For example, when operating a factory, a manager may have the option of hiring additional employees or buying new equipment. As another example, if one acquires a piece of land, one has the option to drill for oil, and then later the option of extracting oil if oil is found. In fact, it is possible to view almost any process that allows control as a process with a series of operational options. These operational options are often termed **real options** to emphasize that they involve *real* activities or *real* commodities, as opposed to purely financial commodities, as in the case, for instance, of stock options. The term *real option* when applied to a general investment problem is also used to imply that options theory can (and should) be used to analyze the problem.

Example 12.9 (A plant manager's problem)   Some manufacturing plants can be described by a **fixed cost** per month (for equipment, management, and rent) and a **variable cost** (for material, labor, and utilities) that is proportional to the level of production. The total cost is therefore $T = F + Vx$, where F is the fixed cost, V is the rate of variable cost, and x is the amount of product produced. The profit of the plant in a month in which it operates at level x is $\pi = px - F - Vx$, where p is the market price of its product. Clearly, if $p > V$, the firm will operate at x equal to the maximum capacity of the plant; if $p < V$, it will not operate. Hence the firm has a continuing option to operate, with a strike price equal to the rate of variable cost. (The Simplico gold mine in Example 12.7 is of this type.)

Real options usually can be analyzed by the same methods used to analyze financial options. Specifically, one sets up an appropriate representation of uncertainty, usually with a binomial lattice, and works backward to find the value. This solution process is really more fundamental than its particular application to options, so it seems unnecessary and sometimes artificial to force all opportunities for control into options—real or otherwise. Instead, the seasoned analyst takes problems as they come and attacks them directly.

The Simplico mine can be used to illustrate a complex real option associated with the timing of an investment.

Example 12.10 (Enhancement of the Simplico mine★)   Recall that the Simplico mine is capable of producing 10,000 ounces of gold per year at a cost of $200 per ounce. This mine already consists of a whole series of real options—namely, the yearly options to carry out mining operations. In fact, the value of the lease can be expressed as a sum of the values of these individual options (although this viewpoint is not particularly helpful). In this example we wish to consider another option, which is truly in the spirit of a real option.

Suppose that there is a possibility of enhancing the production rate of the Simplico mine by purchasing a new mining machine and making some structural changes in the mine. This enhancement would cost $4 million but would raise the mine capability by 25% to 12,500 ounces per year, at a total operating cost of $240 per ounce.

This enhancement alternative is an option, since it need not be carried out. Furthermore, it is an option that is available throughout the term of the lease. The enhancement can be undertaken (that is, exercised) at the beginning of any year, and once in place it applies to all future years. We assume, however, that at the termination of the lease, the enhancement becomes the property of the original mine owner.

Figure 12.13 shows how to calculate the value of the lease when the enhancement option is available. We first calculate the value of the lease assuming that the enhancement is already in place. This calculation is made by constructing the upper lattice of the figure, using exactly the same technique used for the Simplico mine of Example 12.7, but with the new capacity and operating cost figures. The value of the mine under these conditions is $27.0 million. This figure does not include the cost of the enhancement, so if we were to enhance the mine at time zero, the net value of the lease would be $23.0 million, which is somewhat less than the value of $24.1 found earlier without the enhancement. Hence it is not useful to carry out the enhancement immediately.

To find the value of the enhancement option, we construct another lattice, as shown in the lower part of the figure. Here we use the original parameters for production capability and operating cost: 100,000 ounces per year and $200 per ounce. However, at each node, in addition to the usual calculation of value, we see if it would be useful to jump up to the upper lattice by paying $4 million. Specifically, we first calculate the value at a node in the lower lattice in the normal way using risk-neutral probabilities. Then we compare this value with the value at the corresponding node in the upper lattice minus $4 million. We then put the larger of these two values at the node in the lower lattice.

0	1	2	3	4	5	6	7	8	9	10
27.0	31.8	36.4	40.4	43.5	45.2	44.8	41.4	33.9	20.7	0.0
	19.5	23.3	26.6	29.3	31.0	31.2	29.2	24.1	14.9	0.0
		13.5	16.3	18.7	20.4	21.0	20.0	16.8	10.5	0.0
			8.6	10.8	12.5	13.4	13.2	11.3	7.2	0.0
				4.9	6.5	7.7	8.0	7.2	4.7	0.0
Lease value					2.3	3.4	4.1	4.1	2.8	0.0
assuming enhancement						0.8	1.3	1.8	1.4	0.0
in place							0.1	0.2	0.4	0.0
								0.0	0.0	0.0
									0.0	0.0
										0.0

24.6	28.6	32.6	**36.4**	**39.5**	**41.2**	**40.8**	**37.4**	**29.9**	16.9	0
	18.0	20.9	23.5	25.6	**27.0**	**27.2**	**25.2**	**20.1**	12.3	0
		12.9	15.0	16.7	17.9	18.1	17.0	14.1	8.7	0
			8.8	10.4	11.5	12.0	11.5	9.7	6.1	0
				5.6	6.7	7.4	7.4	6.4	4.1	0
Lease with option					3.1	4.0	4.3	3.9	2.6	0
for enhancement						1.3	2.0	2.1	1.5	0
							0.0	0.7	0.7	0
								0.0	0.1	0
									0.0	0
										0

FIGURE 12.13 Option to enhance mine operation. The top array is computed just as for the Simplico mine, but with parameters of enhancement. The lower array refers to the top one to determine when to carry out the enhancement.

The figures in boldface type show nodes where it is advantageous to jump to the upper lattice by carrying out the enhancement. Note that these values are exactly $4 million less than their upper counterparts.

The overall value of the lease with the option is given by the value at the first node, and the $4 million is already taken out. Hence the value of the lease with the enhancement option is $24.6 million—a slight improvement over the original value of $24.1 million.

Linear Pricing

Although we generally use risk-neutral pricing to evaluate derivative securities, it is important to recognize that this evaluation is based on linear pricing; that is, we match a particular derivative to securities we know and then add up the values. The following example highlights the basic simplicity of the method.

Example 12.11 (Gavin explains)   Mr. D. Jones was curious about quantitative work on Wall Street. He brought it up with his son Gavin.

"What are they calculating with all those fancy computers?"

Gavin said that it was all based on linear pricing. "They break a security into its separate pieces, price each piece, and then add them up."

"Are you kidding me? I don't see why you need a supercomputer to do that."

"It gets complicated quickly." Gavin remembered something he had worked out when studying options theory. "I'll show you an example," he said, as he fished in his pocket for a twenty-five cent piece.

Holding the coin up, Gavin began, "Consider this proposition: You pay $1. I flip this coin. If it is heads, you get $3; if it is tails, you get nothing. You can participate at any level you wish, and the payoff scales accordingly."

Mr. Jones nodded. Gavin continued. "The coin flip is like a stock. It has a price, and its outcome is uncertain; but it has a positive expected value—otherwise nobody would invest in it."

"That's simple enough."

"Alternatively, as a second proposition, you can just keep your dollar in your pocket. This is equivalent to paying $1. I flip the coin. If it is heads, you get $1; if it is tails you get $1. Clear?"

"Sure."

"Those are the basic ones. Now here is a new proposition to evaluate: I flip the coin twice. If at least one of the flips is a head, you get $9; otherwise you get nothing. How much is this proposition worth?"

Mr. Jones scratched his head, and after a few seconds said, "I could work out the probabilities."

"It has nothing to do with actual probabilities. This proposition can be expressed as combinations of the other two. We just add up the pieces."

"Okay, show me."

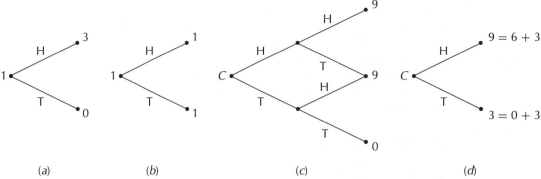

FIGURE 12.14   A proposition and its parts. Tree (a) is a basic risky proposition; tree (b) is a risk-free opportunity; and tree (c) represents a new, more complex proposition. The value C can be found by breaking it into its parts. The final piece is shown in (d).

Gavin drew four trees on the edge of a newspaper, as shown in Figure 12.14. He explained that tree (a) is the original proposition; (b) is keeping money in your pocket, and (c) is the new proposition, with an unknown price C.

If the first flip is heads, the tree from that point has payoff of $9 in each direction, which looks like nine times the payoff of the pocket alternative. It is worth $9 to be there. If the first flip is tails, the tree from that point looks like three times the original proposition, so it is worth $3 to be there. Hence the whole thing is equivalent to tree (d) having payoffs of $9 and $3. "Clear?"

"Very."

Gavin showed that the payoff of 9 and 3 could be broken into 6 and 0 plus 3 and 3. The first of these is twice the original proposition. The second is three times the pocket alternative. Hence $C = 2 + 3 = \$5$. "Okay?"

"Well, I'll be."

Gavin concluded. "That is what those computers are doing. Derivative securities are evaluated by using hundreds of coin flips to represent the daily movements of a stock. The computers work through the big tree just like we did in this example."

[As an exercise, it is useful to determine the risk-neutral probabilities for this example and work through the risk-neutral valuation.]

12.9 GENERAL RISK-NEUTRAL PRICING*

A general principle of risk-neutral pricing can be inferred from the analysis and methods of the previous few sections. This principle provides a compact formula for the price of a derivative security under the binomial lattice formulation.

Suppose that the price S of an asset is described by a binomial lattice, and suppose that f is a security whose cash flow at any time k is a function only of the node at time k. Then the arbitrage-free price of the asset is

$$f_{\text{val}} = \hat{\text{E}}\left(\sum_{k=0}^{N} d_k f_k\right).$$ (12.12)

In this equation the summation represents the discounted cash flow, with the d_k's being the risk-free discount factors as seen at time 0. The f_k's are the period cash flows, which depend on the particular node at k that occurs. Hence the f_k's are random. The expectation $\hat{\text{E}}$ is taken with respect to the risk-neutral probabilities associated with the lattice of the underlying asset.

Consider a European call option with strike price K. The pricing formula, Eq. (12.12), becomes

$$C = \frac{1}{R_T}\hat{\text{E}}[\max(S_T - K, 0)]$$ (12.13)

where R_T is the risk-free return for the whole time to expiration. In this case there is only a single cash flow, $\max(S_T - K, 0)$, occurring at the final time. We take the risk-neutral expected value of this and discount it to the present. Note that actual calculation using this formula is best done by working backward from the end. We use the running present value method to back the formula up one stage at a time.

In many situations the cash flow stream can be influenced by our actions as well as by chance. For instance, we may have the opportunity to exercise an option before expiration, decide how much gold to mine, or add enhancements. In such cases the general pricing formula becomes

$$f_{\text{val}} = \max\left[\hat{\text{E}}\left(\sum_{k=0}^{N} d_k f_k\right)\right]$$

where the maximization is taken with respect to the available actions. We have seen in the examples of this chapter how this maximization can in many cases be carried out as part of the backward recursion process, although the size of the lattice sometimes must be increased. This general formula has great power, for it provides a way to formulate and solve many interesting and important investment problems.

12.10 SUMMARY

An option is the right, but not the obligation, to buy (or sell) an asset under specified terms. Options have had a checkered past, but for the past two decades they have played an important role in finance. Used wisely, they can control risk and enhance the performance of a portfolio. Used carelessly, options can greatly increase risk and lead to substantial losses.

Options terminology includes: call, put, exercise, strike price, expiration, writing a call, premium, in the money, out of the money, American option, and European option.

A major topic of options theory is the determination of the correct price (or premium) of an option. This price depends on the price of the underlying asset, the strike price, the time to expiration, the volatility of the underlying asset, the cash flow generated by the asset (such as dividend payments), and the prevailing interest rate. Although determination of an appropriate option price can be difficult, certain relations can be derived from simple no-arbitrage arguments. For example, for European-style options there is parity between a put and a call with the same strike price. Likewise, the value of a combination of options (such as in a butterfly spread) must be the same combination of the prices of the component options.

One important result is that it is never optimal to exercise, before expiration, an American call option on a stock that does not pay a dividend before expiration.

A general way to find the price of an option is to use the binomial lattice methodology. The random process of the underlying asset is modeled as a binomial lattice. The value of the option at expiration is entered on the final nodes of a corresponding option lattice. The other nodes in the option lattice are computed one at a time by working backward through the periods. For a European-style option (without the possibility of early exercise) the value at any node in the option lattice is found by computing the expected value of the value next period using risk-neutral probabilities. This expected value is then discounted by the effect of one period's interest rate. If the option is an American-style option, the value computed as before must be compared with the value that could be obtained by exercise at that time, and the greater of the two compared values is taken to be the final value for that node.

The risk-neutral probabilities are easy to calculate. The risk-neutral probability for an up move is $q = (R - d)/(u - d)$. The easiest way to derive this formula is to find the q that makes the price of the underlying security equal to the discounted expected value of its next period value.

The binomial lattice methodology can be used to find the value of other investments besides options. Indeed, it can be used to evaluate any project whose cash flow stream is determined by an underlying traded asset. Examples include futures on options, gold mine leases, oil wells, and tree farms. With ingenuity, even complex real options can be evaluated by constructing two or more interrelated binomial lattices.

EXERCISES

1. (Bull spread)   An investor who is bullish about a stock (believing that it will rise) may wish to construct a *bull spread* for that stock. One way to construct such a spread is to buy a call with strike price K_1 and sell a call with the same expiration date but with a strike price of $K_2 > K_1$. Draw the payoff curve for such a spread. Is the initial cost of the spread positive or negative?

2. (Put–call parity)   Suppose over the period $[0, T]$ a certain stock pays a dividend whose present value at interest rate r is D. Show that the put–call parity relation for European options at $t = 0$, expiring at T, is

$$C + D + Kd = P + S$$

where d is the discount factor from 0 to T.

3. (Parity formula)   To derive the put–call parity formula, the payoff associated with buying one call option, selling one put option, and lending dK is $Q = \max(0, S - K) - \max(0, K - S) + K$. Show that $Q = S$, and hence derive the put–call parity formula.

4. (Call strikes $\diamond$)   Consider a family of call options on a non-dividend-paying stock, each option being identical except for its strike price. The value of the call with strike price K is denoted by $C(K)$. Prove the following three general relations using arbitrage arguments:

(a) $K_2 > K_1$ implies $C(K_1) \geq C(K_2)$.
(b) $K_2 > K_1$ implies $K_2 - K_1 \geq C(K_1) - C(K_2)$.
(c) $K_3 > K_2 > K_1$ implies

$$C(K_2) \leq \left(\frac{K_3 - K_2}{K_3 - K_1}\right) C(K_1) + \left(\frac{K_2 - K_1}{K_3 - K_1}\right) C(K_3).$$

5. (Fixed dividend $\oplus$)   Suppose that a stock will pay a dividend of amount D at time τ. We wish to determine the price of a European call option on this stock using the lattice method. Accordingly, the time interval $[0, T]$ covering the life of the option is divided into N intervals, and hence $N + 1$ time periods are assigned. Assume that the dividend date τ occurs somewhere between periods k and $k + 1$. One approach to the problem would be to establish a lattice of stock prices in the usual way, but subtract D from the nodes at period k. This produces a tree with nodes that do not recombine, as shown in Figure 12.15.

The problem can be solved this way, but there is another representation that does recombine. Since the dividend amount is known, we regard it as a nonrandom component of the stock price. At any time before the dividend we regard the price as having two components: a random component S^* and a deterministic component equal to the present value of the future dividend. The random component S^* is described by a lattice with initial value $S(0) - De^{-r\tau}$ and with u and d determined by the volatility σ of the stock. The option is evaluated on this lattice. The only modification that must be made in the computation is that when valuing the option at a node, the stock price used in the valuation formula is not just S^* at that node, but rather $S = S^* + De^{-r(\tau-t)}$ for $t < \tau$. Use this technique to find the value of a 6-month call option with $S(0) = 50$, $K = 50$, $\sigma = 20\%$, $R = 10\%$, and $D = \$3$ to be paid in $3\frac{1}{2}$ months.

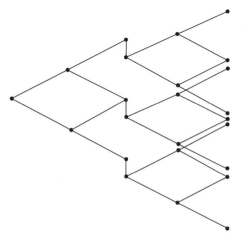

FIGURE 12.15 Nonrecombining dividend tree.

6. (Call inequality)   Consider a European call option on a non-dividend-paying stock. The strike price is K, the time to expiration is T, and the price of one unit of a zero-coupon bond maturing at T is $B(T)$. Denote the price of the call by $C(S, T)$. Show that

$$C(S, T) \geq \max [0, S - K B(T)].$$

[*Hint:* Consider two portfolios: (*a*) purchase one call, (*b*) purchase one share of stock and sell K bonds.]

7. (Perpetual call)   A perpetual option is one that never expires. (Such an option must be of American style.) Use Exercise 6 to show that the value of a perpetual call on a non-dividend-paying stock is $C = S$.

8. (A surprise ⊕)   Consider a deterministic cash flow stream $(x_0, x_1, x_2, \ldots, x_n)$ with all positive flows. Let $\mathrm{PV}(r)$ denote the present value of this stream at an interest rate r.

(*a*) If r decreases, does $\mathrm{PV}(r)$ increase or decrease?
(*b*) Solve the Simplico gold mine problem with $r = 4\%$ and find that the value of the lease is $22.1 million. Can you explain why the value decreased relative to its value with $r = 10\%$?

9. (My coin)   There are two propositions: (*a*) I flip a coin. If it is heads, you are paid $3; if it is tails, you are paid $0. It costs you $1 to participate in this proposition. You may do so at any level, or repeatedly, and the payoffs scale accordingly. (*b*) You may keep your money in your pocket (earning no interest). Here is a third proposition: (*c*) I flip the coin three times. If at least two of the flips are heads, you are paid $27; otherwise zero. How much is this proposition worth?

10. (The happy call)   A New York firm is offering a new financial instrument called a "happy call." It has a payoff function at time T equal to $\max(.5S, S - K)$, where S is the price of a stock and K is a fixed strike price. You always get something with a happy call. Let P be the price of the stock at time $t = 0$ and let C_1 and C_2 be the prices of ordinary calls with strike prices K and $2K$, respectively. The fair price of the happy call is of the form

$$C_H = \alpha P + \beta C_1 + \gamma C_2.$$

Find the constants α, β, and γ.

11. (You are a president)   It is August 6. You are the president of a small electronics company. The company has some cash reserves that will not be needed for about 3 months, but interest rates are very low. Your chief financial officer (CFO) tells you that a progressive securities firm has an investment that guarantees no losses and allows participation in upward movements of the stock market. In fact, the total rate of return until the third week of November is to be determined by the formula $\max(0, .25r)$, where r is the rate of return on the S&P 100 stock index during the 3-month period (ignoring dividends). The CFO suggests that this conservative investment might be an ideal alternative to participation in the interest rate market and asks for your opinion. You pick up *The Wall Street Journal* and make a few simple calculations to check whether it is, in fact, a good deal. Show these calculations and the conclusion. Use the data in Table 12.1. (Note that 410c denotes a call with strike price 410.)

TABLE 12.1
Data for the President

S&P 100 index	Options		S&P index = 414.74
Nov	410c	13	Treasury bills
Nov	410p	$8\frac{1}{4}$	Nov 12: yield = 3.11
Nov	420c	$7\frac{1}{2}$	
Nov	420p	$11\frac{1}{4}$	

Source: Standard & Poor's, a division of the McGraw-Hill Companies. Reprinted with permission.

12. (Simplico invariance)   If the Simplico mine is solved with all parameters remaining the same except that $u = 1.2$ is changed to $u = 1.3$, the value of the lease remains unchanged to within three decimal places. Indeed, quite wide variations in u and d have almost no influence on the lease price. Give an intuitive explanation for this.

13. (Change of period length ⊕)   A stock has volatility $\sigma = .30$ and a current value of $36. A put option on this stock has a strike price of $40 and expiration is in 5 months. The interest rate is 8%. Find the value of this put using a binomial lattice with 1-month intervals. Repeat using a lattice with half-month intervals.

14. (Average value Complexico ⊕)   Suppose that the price received for gold extracted from time k to $k+1$ is the average of the price of gold at these two times; that is, $(g_k + g_{k+1})/2$. However, costs are incurred at the beginning of the period whereas revenues are received at the end of the period. Find the value of the Complexico mine in this case.

15. ("As you like it" option)   Consider the stock of Examples 12.3 and 12.4, which has $\sigma = .20$ and an initial price of $62. The interest rate is 10%, compounded monthly. Consider a 5-month option with a strike price of $60. This option can be declared, after exactly 3 months, by the purchaser to be either a European call or a European put. Find the value of this "as you like it" option.

16. (Tree harvesting ⊕)   You are considering an investment in a tree farm. Trees grow each year by the following factors:

Year	1	2	3	4	5	6	7	8	9	10
Growth	1.6	1.5	1.4	1.3	1.2	1.15	1.1	1.05	1.02	1.01

The price of lumber follows a binomial lattice with $u = 1.20$ and $d = .9$. The interest rate is constant at 10%. It costs $2 million each year, payable at the beginning of the year, to lease the forest land. The initial value of the trees is $5 million (assuming they were harvested immediately). You can cut the trees at the end of any year and then not pay rent after that. (For those readers who care, we assume that cut lumber can be stored at no cost.)

(a) Argue that if the rent were zero, you would never cut the trees as long as they were growing.

(b) With rent of $2 million per year, find the best cutting policy and the value of the investment opportunity.

REFERENCES

For general background material on options, see [1–3]. The pricing of options was originally addressed mathematically by Bachelier [4] using a statistical approach. The analysis of put–call parity and various price inequalities that hold independently of the underlying stock process was systematically developed in [5]. The rational option price based on the no-arbitrage principle was first discovered by Black and Scholes [6] when the price of the underlying asset was governed by geometric Brownian motion. The simplified approach using a binomial lattice was first presented in [7] and later developed in [8, 9]. The risk-neutral formulation of option evaluation was generalized to other derivatives in [10]. Exercise 4 is adopted from [2].

1. Gastineau, G. L. (1975), *The Stock Options Manual*, McGraw-Hill, New York.
2. Cox, J. C., and M. Rubinstein (1985), *Options Markets*, Prentice Hall, Englewood Cliffs, NJ.
3. Hull, J. C. (1993), *Options, Futures, and Other Derivative Securities*, 2nd ed., Prentice Hall, Englewood Cliffs, NJ.
4. Bachelier, L. (1900), "Théorie de la Spéculation," *Annals de l'Ecole Normale Superieure,* **17,** 21–86. English translation by A. J. Boness (1967) in *The Random Character of Stock Market Prices*, P. H. Cootner, Ed., M.I.T. Press, Cambridge, MA, 17–78.
5. Merton, R. C. (1973), "Theory of Rational Option Pricing," *Bell Journal of Economics and Management Science,* **4,** 141–183.
6. Black, F., and M. Scholes (1973), "The Pricing of Options and Corporate Liabilities," *Journal of Political Economy,* **81,** 637–654.
7. Sharpe, W. F. (1978), *Investments,* Prentice Hall, Englewood Cliffs, NJ.
8. Cox, J. C., S. A. Ross, and M. Rubinstein (1979), "Option Pricing: A Simplified Approach," *Journal of Financial Economics,* **7,** 229–263.
9. Rendleman, R. J., Jr., and B. J. Bartter (1979), "Two-State Option Pricing," *Journal of Finance,* **34,** 1093–1110.
10. Harrison, J. M., and D. M. Kreps (1979), "Martingales and Arbitrage in Multiperiod Securities Markets," *Journal of Economic Theory,* **20,** 381–408.

13 ADDITIONAL OPTIONS TOPICS

13.1 INTRODUCTION

Options theory plays a major role in the modern theory of finance because it so clearly highlights the power of the comparison principle, based on the assumption that there are no arbitrage opportunities. The previous chapter presented the theory in a simple and practical form, using the binomial lattice framework. That material is by itself sufficient to solve most options problems. There is, however, a continuous-time version of the theory and extensions of the lattice theory, which lead to new financial insights, allow consideration of more complex derivative securities, provide alternative computational methods, and prepare the way for the more complete theory of investment presented in the following chapters.

13.2 THE BLACK–SCHOLES EQUATION

The famous Black–Scholes option pricing equation initiated the modern theory of finance based on the no-arbitrage principle. Its development triggered an enormous amount of research and revolutionized the practice of finance. The equation was developed under the assumption that the price fluctuations of the underlying security can be described by an Ito process, as presented in Chapter 11. The logic behind the equation is, however, conceptually identical to that used for the binomial lattice: at each moment two available securities are combined to construct a portfolio that reproduces the local behavior of the derivative security. Historically, the Black–Scholes theory of options predated the binomial lattice theory by several years, the lattice theory being a result of simplification.

To begin the presentation of the Black–Scholes equation, let the price S of an underlying security (which we shall refer to as a stock) be governed by a geometric

Brownian motion process over a time interval $[0, T]$ described by

$$dS = \mu S \, dt + \sigma S \, dz \tag{13.1}$$

where z is standard Brownian motion (or a Wiener process). Suppose also that there is a risk-free asset (a bond) carrying an interest rate of r over $[0, T]$. The value B of this bond satisfies

$$dB = rB \, dt \,. \tag{13.2}$$

Finally consider a security that is derivative to S, which means that its price is a function of S and t. Let $f(S, t)$ denote the price of this security at time t when the stock price is S. We want a (nonrandom) equation for the function $f(S, t)$, which will give the price of the derivative explicitly. This function can be found by solving the Black–Scholes equation as stated:

Black–Scholes equation   *Suppose that the price of a security is governed by (13.1) and the interest rate is r. A derivative of this security has a price $f(S, t)$, which satisfies the partial differential equation*

$$\frac{\partial f}{\partial t} + \frac{\partial f}{\partial S} rS + \frac{1}{2} \frac{\partial^2 f}{\partial S^2} \sigma^2 S^2 = rf \,. \tag{13.3}$$

We present a proof of this result later in this section, but first let us look at its significance.

As a simple example, consider the stock itself. It is (in a trivial way) a derivative of S, so $f(S, t) = S$ should satisfy the Black–Scholes equation. In fact, with this choice of f we have $\partial f/\partial t = 0$, $\partial f/\partial S = 1$, $\partial^2 f/\partial S^2 = 0$. Hence (13.3) becomes $rS = rS$, which shows that $f(S, t) = S$ is a solution.

As another simple example, consider the bond. It also is (in a trivial way) a derivative of S, so $f(S, t) = e^{rt}$ should satisfy the Black–Scholes equation. In fact, with this choice of f we have $\partial f/\partial t = re^{rt}$, $\partial f/\partial S = 0$, $\partial^2 f/\partial S^2 = 0$. Hence (13.3) becomes $re^{rt} = re^{rt}$, which shows that, indeed, $f(S, t) = e^{rt}$ is a solution. There are uncountably more solutions.

In general, the Black–Scholes equation can be thought of in two ways. First, suppose that we arbitrarily specify a function $f(S, t)$ and announce that this is the price of a new security. Since we specify the function, we can arrange for it *not* to satisfy the Black–Scholes equation. What is wrong? If $f(S, t)$ does not satisfy the Black–Scholes equation, then there is an arbitrage opportunity lying somewhere among S, B, and f. By a proper combination of these (and the combination may change with time) it will be possible to extract money, risk free. Hence the first way to look at the Black–Scholes equation is that it establishes a property that must hold for a derivative security's price function.

The second way to view the equation is that it can be used to actually find the price function corresponding to various derivative securities. This is done by specifying appropriate boundary conditions that are used in conjunction with the Black–Scholes partial differential equation to solve for the price function. For example, specifying $f(S, T) = S(T)$ leads to $f(S, t) = S(t)$; specifying $f(S, T) = e^{rT}$ leads to $f(S, t) = e^{rt}$. As a nontrivial example, the price $C(S, t)$ of a European call option on a stock that pays no dividends must satisfy the Black–Scholes equation (with C

playing the role of f) and it must satisfy the boundary conditions

$$C(0, t) = 0 \tag{13.4}$$

$$C(S, T) = \max(S - K, 0). \tag{13.5}$$

Likewise, for a European put with price $P(S, t)$ the boundary conditions are

$$P(\infty, t) = 0 \tag{13.6}$$

$$P(S, T) = \max(K - S, 0). \tag{13.7}$$

Other derivative securities may have different forms of boundary conditions, which are sufficient to determine the entire function $f(S, T)$. For example, the boundary conditions for an American call option and an American put on a non-dividend-paying stock require, in addition to the conditions mentioned, a condition concerning the possibility of early exercise. These are

$$C(S, t) \geq \max(0, S - K) \tag{13.8}$$

$$P(S, t) \geq \max(0, K - S). \tag{13.9}$$

Of course, the additional boundary condition for calls is unnecessary, since an American call on a non-dividend-paying stock is never exercised early.

Example 13.1 (A perpetual call)   Consider a perpetual call option with strike price K. There is no terminal boundary condition since $T = \infty$. However, the early exercise condition $f(S, t) \geq \max(0, S - K)$ for all t must be satisfied by the solution f. In addition, we must have $f(S, t) \leq S$ for all t since the call must cost less than the security itself. As an (informed) guess we might try the simple solution $f = S$. Indeed, we know that this satisfies the Black–Scholes equation. The two boundary conditions are also satisfied.

The solution $f(S) = S$ for the value of a perpetual call does make intuitive sense. If the call is held for a long time, the stock value will almost certainly increase to a very large value, so that the exercise price K is insignificant in comparison. Hence if we owned the call we could obtain the stock later for essentially nothing, duplicating the position we would have if we initially bought the stock.

Proof of the Black–Scholes Equation*

How can we derive the Black–Scholes equation? The key idea is the same idea used in Chapter 12 to derive the binomial lattice pricing method. At any time we form a portfolio with portions of the stock and the bond so that this portfolio exactly matches the (instantaneous) return characteristics of the derivative security. The value of this portfolio must equal the value of the derivative security. In a binomial lattice framework the matching is done period by period, relating the value at one time point to those at the next. In the continuous-time framework, the matching is done at each instant, relating the value at one time to the rates of change at that time. Replication is used in both cases. Here is the proof.

Proof: By Ito's lemma [Eq. (11.22)] we have

$$df = \left(\frac{\partial f}{\partial t} + \frac{\partial f}{\partial S}\mu S + \frac{1}{2}\frac{\partial^2 f}{\partial S^2}\sigma^2 S^2 \right) dt + \frac{\partial f}{\partial S}\sigma S \, dz \qquad (13.10)$$

which is an Ito process for the price of the derivative security. This price fluctuates randomly along with the stock price S and the Brownian motion z.

We form a portfolio of S and B that replicates the behavior of the derivative security. In particular, at each time t we select an amount x_t of the stock and an amount y_t of the bond, giving a total portfolio value of $G(t) = x_t S(t) + y_t B(t)$. We wish to select x_t and y_t so that $G(t)$ replicates the derivative security value $f(S, t)$. The instantaneous gain in value of this portfolio due to changes in security prices (the investment gain) is

$$dG = x_t \, dS + y_t \, dB. \qquad (13.11)$$

Expanding, we write

$$
\begin{aligned}
dG &= x_t \, dS + y_t \, dB \\
&= x_t\{\mu S \, dt + \sigma S \, dz\} + y_t r B \, dt \\
&= (x_t \mu S + y_t r B)dt + x_t \sigma S \, dz .
\end{aligned}
\qquad (13.12)
$$

Since we want the portfolio gain of $G(t)$ to behave just like the gain of f, we match the coefficients of dt and dz in 13.12 to those of (13.10). To do this we first match the dz coefficient by setting

$$x_t = \frac{\partial f}{\partial S}. \qquad (13.13)$$

Requiring $G = x_t S + y_t B$ and $G = f$, gives

$$y_t = \frac{1}{B}\left[f(S, t) - S\frac{\partial f}{\partial S} \right].$$

Substituting these expressions in (13.12) and matching the coefficient of dt in (13.10), we obtain

$$\frac{\partial f}{\partial S}\mu S + \frac{1}{B}\left[f(S, t) - S\frac{\partial f}{\partial S} \right]rB = \frac{\partial f}{\partial t} + \frac{\partial f}{\partial S}\mu S + \frac{1}{2}\frac{\partial^2 f}{\partial S^2}\sigma^2 S^2.$$

Or, finally,[1]

$$\frac{\partial f}{\partial t} + \frac{\partial f}{\partial S}rS + \frac{1}{2}\frac{\partial^2 f}{\partial S^2}\sigma^2 S^2 = rf . \qquad (13.14)$$

This is the Black–Scholes equation. (For an alternate proof based on the bi-

---

[1]This is actually a simplified proof. Equation (13.11) should include $x_t' S + y_t' B$, but it can be shown that this sum is zero.

nomial pricing framework, see the Appendix of this chapter. In that proof the case where cash flow rates occur at intermediate times is included.) ∎

13.3 CALL OPTION FORMULA

Although it is usually impossible to find an analytic solution to the Black–Scholes equation, it *is* possible to find such a solution for a European call option. This analytic solution is of great practical and theoretical use.

The formula uses the function $N(x)$, the standard **cumulative normal probability distribution.** This is the cumulative distribution of a normal random variable having mean 0 and variance 1. It can be expressed as

$$N(x) = \frac{1}{\sqrt{2\pi}} \int_{-\infty}^{x} e^{-y^2/2} \, dy. \qquad (13.15)$$

The function $N(x)$ is illustrated in Figure 13.1. The value $N(x)$ is the area under the familiar bell-shaped curve from $-\infty$ to x. Particular values are $N(-\infty) = 0$, $N(0) = \frac{1}{2}$, and $N(\infty) = 1$.

The function $N(x)$ cannot be expressed in closed form, but there are tables for its values, and there are accurate approximation formulas. (See Exercise 1.)

 Black–Scholes call option formula   *Consider a European call option with strike price K and expiration time T. If the underlying stock pays no dividends during the time $[0, T]$ and if interest is constant and continuously compounded at a rate r, the Black–Scholes solution is $f(S, t) = C(S, t)$, defined by*

$$C(S, t) = SN(d_1) - Ke^{-r(T-t)}N(d_2) \qquad (13.16)$$

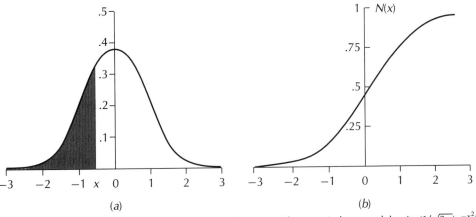

(a)   (b)

FIGURE 13.1   Normal density and cumulative distribution. (a) The curve is the normal density $(1/\sqrt{2\pi})e^{-x^2/2}$. The area under the curve up to the point x gives the value of the cumulative distribution $N(x)$. (b) The cumulative distribution itself rises smoothly from 0 to 1, but it does not have a closed-form representation.

where

$$d_1 = \frac{\ln(S/K) + (r + \sigma^2/2)(T - t)}{\sigma\sqrt{T - t}}$$

$$d_2 = \frac{\ln(S/K) + (r - \sigma^2/2)(T - t)}{\sigma\sqrt{T - t}} = d_1 - \sigma\sqrt{T - t}$$

and where $N(x)$ denotes the standard cumulative normal probability distribution.

Let us examine some special cases. First suppose $t = T$ (meaning the option is at expiration). Then

$$d_1 = d_2 = \begin{cases} +\infty & \text{if } S > K \\ -\infty & \text{if } S < K \end{cases}$$

because the d's depend only on the sign of $\ln(S/K)$. Therefore, since $N(\infty) = 1$ and $N(-\infty) = 0$, we find

$$C(S, T) = \begin{cases} S - K & \text{if } S > K \\ 0 & \text{if } S < K \end{cases}$$

which agrees with the known value at T.

Next let us consider $T = \infty$. Then $d_1 = \infty$ and $e^{-r(T-t)} = 0$. Thus $C(S, \infty) = S$, which agrees with the result derived earlier for a perpetual call.

Example 13.2 (A 5-month option) Let us calculate the value of the same option considered in Chapter 12, Example 12.3. That was a 5-month call option on a stock with a current price of $62 and volatility of 20% per year. The strike price is $60 and the interest rate is 10%. Using $S = 62$, $K = 60$, $\sigma = .20$, and $r = .10$, we find

$$d_1 = \frac{\ln(62/60) + .12 \times 5/12}{.20\sqrt{5/12}} = .641287$$

$$d_2 = d_1 - .2\sqrt{5/12} = .512188.$$

The corresponding values for the cumulative normal distribution are found by the approximation in Exercise 1 to be

$$N(d_1) = .739332, \qquad N(d_2) = .695740.$$

Hence the value for the call option is

$$C = 62 \times .739332 - 60 \times .95918 \times .695740 = \$5.798.$$

This is close to the value of $5.85 found by the binomial lattice method.

Although a formula exists for a call option on a non-dividend-paying stock, analogous formulas do not generally exist for other options, including an American put option. The Black–Scholes equation, incorporating the corresponding boundary conditions, cannot be solved in analytic form.

13.4 RISK-NEUTRAL VALUATION*

In the binomial lattice framework, pricing of options and other derivatives was expressed concisely as discounted risk-neutral valuation. This concept works in the Ito process framework as well.

For the geometric Brownian motion stock price process

$$dS(t) = \mu S \, dt + \sigma S \, dz \tag{13.17}$$

we know from Section 11.7 that

$$E[S(t)] = S(0)e^{\mu t} . \tag{13.18}$$

In a risk-neutral setting, the price of the stock at time zero is found from its price at time t by discounting the risk-neutral expected value at the risk-free rate. This means that there should hold

$$S(0) = e^{-rt}\hat{E}[S(t)] .$$

It is clear that this formula would hold if $\hat{E}[S(t)] = S(0)e^{rt}$. From (13.17) and (13.18) this will be the case if we define the process

$$dS = rS \, dt + \sigma S \, d\hat{z} \tag{13.19}$$

where $\hat{z}$ is a standardized Wiener process, and we define $\hat{E}$ as expectation with respect to the $\hat{z}$ process. In other words, starting with a lognormal Ito process with rate μ, we obtain the equivalent risk-neutral process by constructing a similar process but having rate r.

This change of equation is analogous to having two binomial lattices for a stock process: a lattice for the real process and a lattice for the risk-neutral process. In the first lattice the probabilities of moving up or down are p and $1 - p$, respectively. The risk-neutral lattice has the same values as the stock prices on the nodes, but the probabilities of up and down are changed to q and $1 - q$. For the Ito process we have two processes—like two lattices. Because the probability structures are different, we use z and $\hat{z}$ to distinguish them.

Once the risk-neutral probability structure is defined, we can use risk-neutral valuation to value any security that is a derivative of S. In particular, for a call option the pricing formula is

$$C = e^{-rT}\hat{E}\{\max[S(T) - K, 0]\} . \tag{13.20}$$

This is analogous to (12.13) in Chapter 12.

We know that the risk-neutral distribution of $S(T)$ satisfying (13.19) is lognormal with $E\{\ln[S(T)/S(0)]\} = rT - \frac{1}{2}\sigma^2 T$ and $\text{var}\{\ln[S(T)/S(0)]\} = \sigma^2 T$. We can use this distribution to find the indicated expected value in analytic form. The result will be identical to the value given by the Black–Scholes equation for a call option price. Specifically, writing out the details of the lognormal distribution, we have

$$C = \frac{e^{-rT}}{\sqrt{2\pi\sigma^2 T}} \int_{\ln K}^{\infty} (e^x - K)e^{-[x - \ln S(0) - rT + \sigma^2 T/2]^2/(2\sigma^2 T)} \, dx . \tag{13.21}$$

This is the Black–Scholes formula in integral form.

13.5 DELTA

At any fixed time the value of a derivative security is a function of the underlying asset's price. The sensitivity of this function to changes in the price of the underlying asset is described by the quantity **delta** (Δ). If the derivative security's value is $f(S, t)$, then formally delta is

$$\Delta = \frac{\partial f(S, t)}{\partial S}.$$

Delta is frequently expressed in approximation form as

$$\Delta = \frac{\Delta f}{\Delta S}.$$

The delta of a call option is illustrated in Figure 13.2. It is the slope of the curve that relates the option price to the stock price.

Delta can be used to construct portfolios that hedge against risk. As an example, suppose that an option trader believes that a certain call option is overpriced. The trader would like to write (that is, sell) the option, taking a very large (negative) position in the call option. However, doing so would expose the trader to a great deal of price risk. If the underlying stock price should increase, the trader will lose money on the option even if his assessment of the option value relative to its current price is well founded. The trader may not wish to speculate on the stock itself, but only to profit from his belief that the option is overpriced. The trader can neutralize the effect of stock price fluctuations by offsetting the sale of options with a simultaneous purchase of the stock itself. The appropriate amount of stock to purchase is delta times the value of the options sold. Then if the stock price should rise by $1, the profit on the trader's holding of stock will offset the loss on the options.

The delta of a call option can be calculated from the Black–Scholes formula (13.3) to be

$$\Delta = N(d_1). \tag{13.22}$$

This explicit formula can be used to implement delta hedging strategies that employ call options.

In general, given a portfolio of securities, all components of which are derivative to a common underlying asset, we can calculate the **portfolio delta** as the sum of the

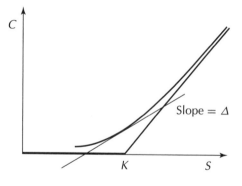

FIGURE 13.2   **Delta of a call option.** Delta measures the sensitivity of the option value to small changes in the price of the underlying security.

deltas of each component of the portfolio. Traders who do not wish to speculate on the underlying asset prices will form a portfolio that is **delta neutral,** which means that the overall delta is zero. In the case of the previous trader, the value of the portfolio was $-C + \Delta \times S$. Since the delta of S is 1, the overall delta of this hedged portfolio is $-\Delta + \Delta = 0$.

Delta itself varies both with S and with t. Hence a portfolio that is delta neutral initially will not remain so. It is necessary, therefore, to **rebalance** the portfolio by changing the proportions of its securities in order to maintain neutrality. This process constitutes a **dynamic hedging strategy.** In theory, rebalancing should occur continuously, although in practice it is undertaken only periodically or when delta has materially changed from zero.

The amount of rebalancing required is related to another constant termed **gamma** (Γ). Gamma is defined as

$$\Gamma = \frac{\partial^2 f(S, t)}{\partial S^2}.$$

Gamma defines the curvature of the derivative price curve. In Figure 13.2 gamma is the second derivative of the option price curve at the point under consideration.

Another useful number is **theta** (Θ). Theta is defined as

$$\Theta = \frac{\partial f(S, t)}{\partial t}.$$

Theta measures the time change in the value of a derivative security. Referring again to Figure 13.2, if time is increased, the option curve will shift to the right. Theta measures the magnitude of this shift.

These parameters are sufficient to estimate the change in value of a derivative security over small time periods, and hence they can be used to define appropriate hedging strategies. In particular, using δf, δS, and δt to represent small changes in f, S, and t, we have

$$\delta f \approx \Delta \cdot \delta S + \tfrac{1}{2}\Gamma \times (\delta S)^2 + \Theta \times \delta t$$

as a first-order approximation to δf.[2]

Example 13.3 (Call price estimation)   Consider a call option with $S = 43$, $K = 40$, $\sigma = .20$, $r = 10$, and a time to expiration of $T - t = 6$ months $= .5$. The Black–Scholes formula yields $C = \$5.56$. We can also calculate that $\Delta = .825$, $\Gamma = .143$, and $\Theta = -6.127$. (See Exercise 7.)

Now suppose that in two weeks the stock price increases to \$44. We have $\delta S = 1$ and $\delta t = 1/26$; therefore the price of the call at that time is approximately

$$C \approx 5.56 + \Delta \times 1 + \tfrac{1}{2}\Gamma \times (1)^2 + \Theta \times (1/26) = \$6.22.$$

The actual value of the call at the later date according to the Black–Scholes formula is $C = \$6.23$.

---

[2] Recall that δS is proportional to $\sqrt{\delta t}$, so we must include the $(\delta S)^2$ term.

13.6 REPLICATION, SYNTHETIC OPTIONS, AND PORTFOLIO INSURANCE*

The derivation of the Black–Scholes equation shows that a derivative security can be duplicated by constructing a portfolio consisting of an appropriate combination of the underlying security and the risk-free asset. We say that this portfolio **replicates** the derivative security. The proportions of stock and the risk-free asset in the portfolio must be adjusted continuously with time, but no additional money need be added or taken away; the portfolio is **self-financing.** This replication can be carried out in practice in order to construct a **synthetic** derivative security using the underlying and the risk-free assets. Of course, the required construction is dynamic, since the particular combination must change every period (or continuously in the context of the Black–Scholes framework).

The process for a call option is this: At the initial time, calculate the theoretical price C. Devote an amount C to the replicating portfolio. This portfolio should have ΔS invested in the stock and the remainder invested in the risk-free asset (although this will usually require *borrowing,* not lending). Then both the delta and the value of the portfolio will match those of the option. Indeed, the short-term behavior of the two will match.

A short time later, delta will be different, and the portfolio must be rebalanced. However, the value of the portfolio will be approximately equal to the corresponding new value of the option, so it will be possible to continue to hold the equivalent of one option. This rebalancing is repeated frequently. As the expiration date of the (synthetic) option approaches, the portfolio will consist mainly of stock if the price of the stock is above K; otherwise the portfolio's value will tend to zero.

Example 13.4 (A replication experiment)   Let us construct, experimentally, a synthetic call option on Exxon stock with a strike price of $35 and a life of 20 weeks. We will replicate this option by buying Exxon stock and selling (that is, borrowing) the risk-free asset. In order to use real data in this experiment, we select the 20-week period from May 11 to September 21, 1983. The actual weekly closing prices of Exxon (with stock symbol XON) are shown in the second column of Table 13.1. The measured sigma corresponding to this period is $\sigma = 18\%$ on an annual basis, so we shall use that value to calculate the theoretical values of call prices and delta. We assume an interest rate of 10%.

Let us walk across the first row of the table. There are 20 weeks remaining in the life of the option. The initial stock price is $35.50. The third column shows that the initial value of the call (as calculated by the Black–Scholes formula) is $2.62. Likewise the initial value of delta is .701. To construct the replicating portfolio we devote a value of $2.62 to it, matching the initial value of the call. This is shown in the column marked "Portfolio value." However, this portfolio consists of two parts, indicated in the next two columns. The amount devoted to Exxon stock is $24.89, which is delta times the current stock value. The remainder $2.62 − $24.89 = −$22.27 is devoted to the risk-free asset. In other words we borrow $22.27, add $2.62, and use the total of $24.89 to buy Exxon stock.

TABLE 13.1
An Experiment in Option Replication

Weeks remaining	XON price	Call price	Delta	Portfolio value	Stock portfolio	Bond portfolio
20	35.50	2.62	.701	2.62	24.89	−22.27
19	34.63	1.96	.615	1.96	21.28	−19.32
18	33.75	1.40	.515	1.39	17.37	−15.98
17	34.75	1.89	.618	1.87	21.47	−19.59
16	33.75	1.25	.498	1.22	16.79	−15.58
15	33.00	0.85	.397	.81	13.09	−12.28
14	33.88	1.17	.494	1.14	16.74	−15.60
13	34.50	1.42	.565	1.41	19.48	−18.07
12	33.75	0.96	.456	.96	15.39	−14.43
11	34.75	1.40	.583	1.38	20.27	−18.89
10	34.38	1.10	.522	1.13	17.94	−16.81
9	35.13	1.44	.624	1.49	21.92	−20.43
8	36.00	1.94	.743	2.00	26.74	−24.75
7	37.00	2.65	.860	2.69	31.80	−29.11
6	36.88	2.44	.858	2.53	31.65	−29.12
5	38.75	4.10	.979	4.08	37.92	−33.84
4	37.88	3.17	.961	3.16	36.39	−33.23
3	38.00	3.21	.980	3.22	37.25	−34.03
2	38.63	3.76	.998	3.76	38.56	−34.79
1	38.50	3.57	1.000	3.57	38.50	−34.93
0	37.50	2.50		2.50		

A call on XON with strike price 35 and 20 weeks to expiration is replicated by buying XON stock and selling the risk-free asset at 10%. The portfolio is adjusted each week according to the value of delta at that time. When the volatility is set at 18% (the actual value during that period), the portfolio value closely matches the Black–Scholes value of the call.

Now walk across the second row, which is calculated in a slightly different way. The first four entries show that there are 19 weeks remaining, the new stock price is $34.63, the corresponding Black–Scholes option price is $1.96, and delta is now .615. The next entry, "Portfolio value," is obtained by updating from the row above it. The earlier stock purchase of $24.89 is now worth $(34.63/35.50) \times \$24.89 = \$24.28$. The debt of $22.27 is now a debt of $(1 + 0.10/52)\$22.27 = \$22.31$. The new value of the portfolio we constructed last week is therefore now $24.28 − $22.31 = $1.96 (adjusting for the round-off error in the table). This new value does not exactly agree with the current call value (although in this case it happens to agree within the two decimal places shown). We do not add or subtract from the value. However, we now rebalance the portfolio by allocating to the stock $21.28 (which is delta times the stock price) and borrowing $19.32 so that the net portfolio value remains at $1.96.

Succeeding rows are calculated in the same fashion. At each step, the updated portfolio value may not exactly match the current value of the call, but it tends to be very close, as is seen by scanning down the table and comparing the call and portfolio values. The maximum difference is 11 cents. At the end of the 20 weeks it happens in this case that the portfolio value is exactly equal (to within a fraction of a cent) to the value of the call.

The results depend on the assumed value of volatility. The choice of $\sigma = 18\%$ represents the actual volatility over the 20-week period, and this choice leads to good results. Study of a longer period of Exxon stock data before the date of this option indicates that volatility is more typically 20%. If this value were used to construct Table 13.1, the resulting final portfolio value would be $2.66 rather than $2.50. If $\sigma = 15\%$ were used, the final portfolio value would be $2.27.

The degree of match would also be affected by transactions costs. The experiment with an Exxon call assumed that transactions costs were zero and that stock could be purchased in any fractional amount. In practice these assumptions are not satisfied exactly. But for large volumes, as might be typical of institutional dealings, the departure from these assumptions is small enough so that replication is in fact practical.

Example 13.5 (Portfolio insurance)   Many institutions with large portfolios of equities (stocks) are interested in insuring against the risk of a major market downturn. They could protect the value of their portfolio if they could buy a put, giving them the right to sell their portfolio at a specified exercise price K.

Puts are available for the major indices, such as the S&P 500, and hence one way to obtain protection is to buy index puts. However, a particular portfolio may not match an index closely, and hence the protection would be imperfect.

Another approach is to construct a synthetic put using the actual stocks in the portfolio and the risk-free asset. Since puts have negative deltas, construction of a put requires a short position in stock and a long position in the risk-free asset. Hence some of the portfolio would be sold and later bought back if the market moves upward. This strategy has the disadvantage of disrupting the portfolio and incurring trading costs.

A third approach is to construct a synthetic put using futures on the stocks held in the portfolio instead of using the stocks themselves. To implement this strategy, one would calculate the total value of the puts required and go long delta times this amount of futures. (Since $\Delta < 0$, we would actually short futures.) The difference between the value of stock shorted and the value of a put is placed in the risk-free asset. The positions must be adjusted periodically as delta changes, just as in the previous example. This method, termed **portfolio insurance,** was quite popular with investment institutions (such as pension funds) for a short time until the U.S. stock market fell substantially in October 1987, and it was not possible to sell futures in the quantities called for by the hedging rule, resulting in loss of protection and actual losses in portfolio value.

13.7 COMPUTATIONAL METHODS

The theory presented in this chapter can be transformed into computational methods in several ways. Some of these methods are briefly outlined in this section.

Monte Carlo Simulation

Monte Carlo simulation is one of the most powerful and most easily implemented methods for the calculation of option values. However, the procedure is essentially only useful for European-style options, where no decisions are made until expiration. Suppose that there is a derivative security that has payoff at the terminal time T of $f(S(T))$ and suppose the stock price $S(t)$ is governed by geometric Brownian motion according to

$$dS = \mu S \, dt + \sigma S \, dz$$

where z is a standardized Wiener process. The basis for the Monte Carlo method is the risk-neutral pricing formula, which states that the initial price of the derivative security should be

$$P = e^{-rT} \hat{E}[f(S(T))].$$

To evaluate the right-hand side by Monte Carlo simulation, the stochastic stock dynamic equation in a risk-free world

$$dS = rS \, dt + \sigma S \, d\hat{z}$$

is simulated over the time interval $[0, T]$ by dividing the entire time period into several periods of length Δt. The simulation equation is

$$S(t_k + \Delta t) = S(t_k) + rS(t_k) \, \Delta t + \sigma S(t_k) \epsilon(t_k)$$

where $\epsilon(t_k)$ is chosen by a random number generator that produces numbers according to a normal distribution having zero mean and variance Δt. (Or the multiplicative version of Section 11.7 can be used.) After each simulation, the value $f(S(T))$ is calculated. An estimate $\hat{P}$ of the true theoretical price of the derivative security is found from the formula

$$\hat{P} = e^{-rT} \text{average}[f(S(T))]$$

where the average is taken over all simulation trials.

A disadvantage of this method is that suitable accuracy may require a very large number of simulation trials. In general, the expected error decreases with the number of trials n by the factor $1/\sqrt{n}$; so one more digit of accuracy requires 100 times as many trials. Often tens of thousands of trials are required to obtain two-place accuracy.

Example 13.6 (The 5-month call)   Simulation is unnecessary for a call option since better methods are available, but this example, which was solved earlier in Example 13.2, provides a simple illustration of the method. For this call $S(0) = \$62$, $K = \$60$, $\sigma = 20\%$, and $r = 12\%$. The time to maturity is 5 months.

To carry out the simulation the 5-month period was divided into 80 equal small time intervals. The stock dynamics were modeled as

$$S(t + \Delta t) = S(t) + rS(t)\Delta t + \sigma S(t)\epsilon(t)\sqrt{\Delta t}$$

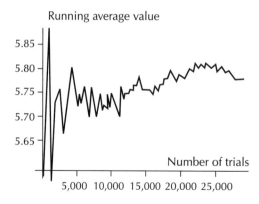

Running average value

FIGURE 13.3 Monte Carlo evaluation of a call. The value of a call is estimated as the discounted average of final payoff when simulations are governed by the risk-neutral process. The method is easy to implement but requires a large number of trials for reasonable accuracy.

where $\epsilon(t)$ is chosen randomly from a normal distribution with mean zero and unit variance.

After each simulation trial, the terminal value of the call, $\max(S - K, 0)$, was determined based on the final stock price, and this value was discounted back to the initial time. A running average of these discounted values was recorded as successive runs were made. Figure 13.3 shows a graph of the discounted average value obtained as a function of the total number of trials. A reasonably accurate and stable result requires about 25,000 simulation trials. From the figure we can conclude that the price of the call is in the neighborhood of $5.80 plus or minus around 10 cents. The Black–Scholes value is in fact $5.80.

The simulation can be improved by various **variance reduction** procedures, the two most common of these being the **control variate method** and the **antithetic variable method.** (See Exercise 9.)

Although it is costly in terms of computer time to use the Monte Carlo method, the method is in fact often used in practice to evaluate European-style derivatives that do not have analytic solutions. The method has the advantages of flexibility and ease of programming, and it is reasonably foolproof.

Finite-Difference Methods

Numerical solution of the Black–Scholes partial differential equation is a second approach to the calculation of option prices. In this method a large rectangular grid is established, a small version of which is shown in Figure 13.4. In this grid the horizontal axis represents time t and the vertical axis represents S. The time difference between horizontally adjacent points is Δt, and the price difference between vertically adjacent points is ΔS. The function $f(S, t)$ is defined at all the corresponding grid points. If the S values on the grid are indexed by i and the t values are indexed by j, then the function at the grid point (i, j) is denoted by $f_{i,j}$.

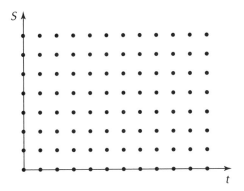

FIGURE 13.4 Grid for finite-difference method. The finite-difference method approximates the Black–Scholes equation by algebraic relations among values at grid points. The method can handle American as well as European options.

The method is implemented by using the finite-difference approximations to partial derivatives as follows:

$$\frac{\partial f}{\partial S} \approx \frac{f_{i+1,j} - f_{i,j}}{\Delta S}$$

$$\frac{\partial^2 f}{\partial S^2} \approx \frac{f_{i+1,j} - f_{i,j} - f_{i,j} + f_{i-1,j}}{(\Delta S)^2} = \frac{f_{i+1,j} - 2f_{i,j} + f_{i-1,j}}{(\Delta S)^2}$$

$$\frac{\partial f}{\partial t} \approx \frac{f_{i,j+1} - f_{i,j}}{\Delta t}.$$

The terminal conditions imply that $f_{i,j}$ is known at the right boundary of the grid. Additional boundary conditions may be specified, depending on the particular derivative security. In the case of a put option, for example, it is known that the value of the put is at least equal to $K - S$ everywhere, and since the value of the put approaches zero as $S \to \infty$, we may specify that the value is zero along the top edge of the grid.

When these approximations are used in the Black–Scholes equation, the result is a large set of algebraic equations and inequalities. These can be solved systematically by working backward from the right edge of the grid toward the left. In fact, the equations are closely related to the equations of backward solution in a lattice.

The finite-difference method has the advantage that it can handle derivative securities such as American puts that impose boundary conditions other than terminal-time conditions. An inherent disadvantage, however, is that the equations are only approximations to the actual partial differential equation, and therefore, aside from the obvious approximation error, their solutions are subject to instabilities and inconsistencies, which are not characteristic of the partial differential equation itself (usually resulting from implied probabilities becoming negative). As a general rule of numerical problem solving, if a problem is to be solved with a finite-step approximation, it is usually better to reformulate the problem itself in finite-step form and then solve that problem directly, rather than to formulate the problem in continuous time and then approximate the solution by a finite-step method. In the case of derivative securities this means that rather than approximating the Black–Scholes equation, it is probably better to use a discrete formulation, such as the discrete-time risk-neutral pricing formula or the binomial lattice formulation. These discrete formulations will introduce approximation error, but will not instill numerical instabilities. Despite these caveats, finite-difference methods, when carefully designed, do have a useful role in the numerical evaluation of derivative securities.

Binomial and Trinomial Lattices

A popular method for finding the value of a derivative security is the binomial lattice method of Section 12.6. The method is straightforward and leads to reasonably accurate results, even if the time divisions are crude (say, 10 or so time periods over the remaining time interval). However, it is also possible to use other tree and lattice structures. For example, a good choice is to use a trinomial lattice, as shown in Figure 13.5. For a given number of time periods, the trinomial lattice has more nodes than a binomial lattice and hence can produce a better approximation to the continuous solution.

At first it might seem that a trinomial lattice cannot replace a binomial lattice because it is impossible to replicate three possible outcomes using only two securities: the stock and the risk-free asset. This is correct; replication is not possible. Hence the trinomial lattice cannot be used as a basis for options theory. However, once the theory is deduced by other methods (such as the Black–Scholes method), we can seek alternative ways to implement it. A trinomial lattice is a convenient structure for implementing the risk-neutral pricing formula.

To set up a suitable trinomial lattice refer to Figure 13.6, which shows one piece of the lattice. There are three paths leaving a node, with probabilities p_1, p_2, and p_3. The three resulting nodes represent multiplication of the stock value by u, 1, and d, respectively, where we set $d = 1/u$, so that an up followed by a down is equal to 1.

To assign the parameters of the trinomial lattice we can arbitrarily select a value for u. Then if the mean value for one step is to be $1 + \mu \, \Delta t$ and the variance is to be

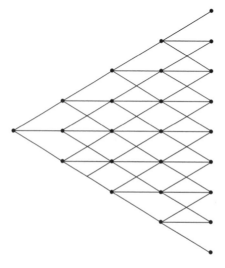

FIGURE 13.5   Trinomial lattice. A trinomial lattice can give a more accurate representation than a binomial lattice for the same number of steps.

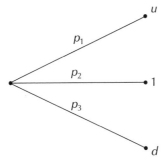

FIGURE 13.6 **One piece of a trinomial lattice.** In this lattice we must have $d = 1/u$ so that the nodes recombine after two steps.

$\sigma^2 \, \Delta t$, we select the probabilities to satisfy

$$
\begin{aligned}
p_1 + p_2 + \quad p_3 &= 1 \\
u p_1 + p_2 + \quad d p_3 &= 1 + \mu \, \Delta t \\
u^2 p_1 + p_2 + d^2 p_3 &= \sigma^2 \, \Delta t + (1 + \mu \, \Delta t)^2.
\end{aligned}
\tag{13.23}
$$

(The last line represents $\mathrm{E}(x^2) = \mathrm{var}(x) + \mathrm{E}(x)^2$, where x is the random factor by which the stock price is multiplied in one period.) This is just a system of three linear equations to be solved for the three probabilities. Once these probabilities are found, we have a good approximation to the underlying stock dynamics. (Note that we are implicitly using the dynamics of (11.19).)

To use this lattice for pricing, we must instead use the risk-neutral probabilities q_1, q_2, and q_3. These are found by solving the same set of equations (13.23), but with the mean value changed from $\mu \, \Delta t$ to $r \, \Delta t$. Once the risk-neutral probabilities are found, the lattice can be solved backward, just as in the binomial procedure.

Example 13.7 (The 5-month call)   Let us find the price of the 5-month call option of Example 12.3 using a trinomial lattice, just to compare the results. We have $S(0) = \$62$, $K = \$60$, $r = 10\%$, and $\sigma = 20\%$. The time to expiration is 5 months $= .416667$. To set up the lattice we must select a value of u and solve the equations (13.23) for the probabilities (when μ is set to r) in the equations. The choice of u requires a bit of experimentation, since for some values the resulting risk-neutral probabilities may not be positive. For example, using $u = 1.06$ leads to $q_1 = .57$, $q_2 = -.03$, and $q_3 = .46$. Instead we use $u = 1.1031277$ and $q_1 = .20947$, $q_2 = .64896$, and $q_3 = .14156$. This leads to the lattice shown in Figure 13.7. Note that the value of the option obtained is $\$5.83$, which is slightly closer to the Black–Scholes result of $\$5.80$ than is the price of $\$5.85$ determined by a binomial lattice.[3]

The lattice of Figure 13.7 has the stock value listed above each node and the option value listed below each node. The final option values are just $\max(0, \, S - K)$. The option values at other nodes are found by discounted risk-neutral pricing. For

---

[3] In this example we assumed monthly compounding, while the Black–Scholes formula implicitly assumes continuous compounding. We can also use the equivalent continuous compounding rate in the example, and the result differs by only one-tenth of a cent from $\$5.83$.

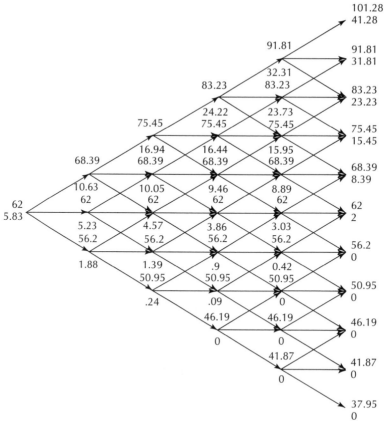

FIGURE 13.7   5-month call using a trinomial lattice. Stock prices are listed above nodes; and option prices are listed below. The discounted risk-neutral valuation is easily generalized to the trinomial lattice.

example, the value at the top node after 4 months is $(1 + .10/12)^{-1}(q_1 \times 41.28 + q_2 \times 31.81 + q_3 \times 23.23) = 32.31$. If in this calculation the stock values 101.28, 91.81, and 83.23 were used instead of the option values, the result would be the stock value of 91.81, but of course it is not necessary to use this backward procedure for the stock prices.

13.8 EXOTIC OPTIONS

Numerous variations on the basic design of options have been proposed. Each variation offers effective control of the risk perceived by a certain group of investors or eases execution and bookkeeping. We list a few of these variations here:

1. **Bermudan option**   In this option, the allowable exercise dates are restricted, in some case to specific dates and in other cases to specific periods within the lifetime of the option. Warrants on stock often have this characteristic.

2. **Forward start options**   These are options that are paid for at one date, but do not begin until a later date.

3. **Compound options**   A compound option is an option on an option.

4. **"As you like it" or "chooser" options**   The holder of an "as you like it" option can, after a specified time, declare the option to be either a put or a call.

5. **CAPs**   These options restrict the amount of profit that can be made by the option holder by automatically exercising once the profit reaches a specified level. A $20 CAP on a call option, means that once the stock price rises to $20 over the strike price, the option is exercised.

6. **LEAPS**   This term stands for "Long-term Equity AnticiPation Securities." They are long-term, exchange-traded options with exercise dates as far as 3 years into the future.

7. **Digital options**   In a digital option the payoff is $1 if the option is in the money and zero otherwise. A European digital call option, for example, has payoff 1 if $S(T) > K$, and 0 if $S(T) < K$, where K is the strike price.

8. **Exchange options**   Such an option gives one the right to exchange one specified security for another.

9. **Yield-based options**   A yield-based option on a bond defines the exercise value in terms of yield rather than price. Hence the holder of a yield-based call option benefits if bond prices **decrease** since yields move in the opposite direction to prices.

10. **Cross-ratio options**   These are foreign-currency options denominated in another foreign currency; for example, a call on German marks with an exercise price in Japanese yen.

11. **Knockout options**   These options terminate (with zero value) once the price of the underlying asset reaches a specified point. For calls these are "down and out" options, which terminate once the price of the underlying asset falls below a specified level. For puts the analogous option is a "up and out" option.

12. **Discontinuous options**   These options have payoffs that are discontinuous functions of the price of the underlying asset. For example, a call option may pay either zero or $20, depending on whether the final price of the underlying asset is below or above a specified strike price.

13. **Lookback options**   In a lookback option the effective strike price is not specified, but is determined by the minimum (in the case of a call) or maximum (in the case of a put) of the price of the underlying asset during the period of the option. For example, a European-style lookback call option has a payoff equal to $\max(S_T - S_{\min}, 0) = S_T - S_{\min}$, where $S_{\min}$ is the minimum value of the price S over the period from initiation to the termination time T. Such options are very attractive to investors, since in fact they always have positive value (unless $S_T = S_{\min}$). Of course their prices reflect the apparent attractiveness.

14. **Asian options**   The payoff of Asian options depends on the average price S_{avg} of the underlying asset during the period of the option. There are basically two ways

that the average can be used. In one, S_{avg} serves as the strike price, so that the payoff of a corresponding call, for example, is max $(S_T - S_{avg}, 0)$. In the second type, S_{avg} is substituted for the final price. Thus the payoff of the corresponding call is max $(S_{avg} - K, 0)$, where K is a specified strike price.

Pricing*

Prices of some of these variations can be worked out computationally by using the theory and methods presented in this chapter. In other cases, formulas analogous to the Black–Scholes formula have been derived. There are cases, however, that present a serious technical challenge to the investment analysis community.

Example 13.8 (A down and outer)   Consider a down and out call option on a non-dividend-paying stock. This option has a strike price of K and a "knockout" price of $N < K$. If the stock price S falls below N, the option is terminated with zero value. A closed-form expression for the original value of such an option can be found using the Black–Scholes framework; however, the details are not neat. We shall consider a simplified case, where the option is perpetual (that is, $T = \infty$) but still has the down and out provision.

Since there is no explicit time dependence in the price of a perpetual option, the Black–Scholes equation reduces to

$$\tfrac{1}{2}\sigma^2 S^2 C''(S) + rSC'(S) - rC(S) = 0. \tag{13.24}$$

The boundary condition is

$$C(N) = 0.$$

We also know that $C(S) \approx S$ as $S \to \infty$.

To solve (13.24) let us try a solution of the form $C(S) = S^\alpha$. This gives the algebraic equation

$$\tfrac{1}{2}\sigma^2\alpha(\alpha - 1) + r\alpha - r = 0$$

which has solutions $\alpha = 1$ and $\alpha = -\gamma$, where $\gamma = 2r/\sigma^2$. We may write the general solution of (13.24) as a linear combination of these two; that is,

$$C(S) = a_1 S + a_2 S^{-\gamma}.$$

Using the boundary condition we find $a_2 = -a_1 N^{\gamma+1}$. Hence $C(S) = a_1[S - N(S/N)^{-\gamma}]$. Using the asymptotic property, we have $a_1 = 1$. Therefore the final result is

$$C(S) = S - N(S/N)^{-\gamma}.$$

Since the value of a perpetual call is S, the second term in this expression can be regarded as a discount for the down and out feature.

The lookback and Asian options are particularly interesting because their payoffs are **path dependent;** that is, their payoffs do not merely depend on the final value of the price of the underlying asset, but also on the way that that price was reached. So the conventional binomial lattice method of evaluation is not applicable. However, there are ways to modify the lattice approach to handle such cases; but as one might expect, the amount of computation required tends to be substantially greater than for a conventional option.

For European-style options that are path dependent, the Monte Carlo method offers a simple and effective procedure. The principle of risk-neutral pricing still applies, so it is only necessary to simulate the process repeatedly, using the risk-neutral probabilities for the underlying asset price fluctuations, and to average the payoffs obtained during the simulations. The control variate method for reducing the number of required simulations is especially useful for these options, and a corresponding non-path-dependent option, for which a solution is readily found, can be used as the control variate. (See Exercise 9.)

13.9 STORAGE COSTS AND DIVIDENDS★

Commodity storage costs and security dividends can complicate an evaluation procedure, but there is an important special case, of proportional costs or dividends, that can be handled easily. This case is useful in applications, and the study of the technique involved should further enhance your understanding of risk-neutral pricing.

Binomial Form

Suppose the commodity price S is governed by a binomial process having an up factor u and a down factor d. There is a storage cost of cS per period, payable at the end of each period. The total risk-free return per period is R.

If you invest in the commodity at the beginning of a period, you must pay the current price S. At the end of the period, you receive the new commodity minus the storage cost; hence you receive either $(u - c)S$ or $(d - c)S$. The new factors $u - c$ and $d - c$ are the legitimate factors that define the result of holding the commodity, and therefore these are the factors that can be used in a replication argument. It follows that the risk-neutral probabilities for up and down are

$$q = \frac{R - d + c}{u - d}, \qquad 1 - q = \frac{u - c - R}{u - d}$$

respectively. (To avoid arbitrage we must have $u - c > R > d - c$.) These risk-neutral probabilities should be used to evaluate securities or ventures that are derivative to the commodity.

Example 13.9 (A foreign currency put)   Mr. Smith, a successful but cautious U.S. businessman, has sold a product to a German firm, and he will receive payment of 1 million German marks in 6 months. Currently the exchange rate M is $.625 per DM. To protect the value of this anticipated payment, Mr. Smith is considering the purchase of a 6-month put of DM 1 million at a strike price of $.60 per DM. Mr. Smith wants to compute the fair value of such a put to see whether the market price is reasonable.

To make the calculation, Mr. Smith notes that the U.S. dollar interest rate is 5% while the German mark interest rate is 8%. The interest on marks acts like a proportional dividend or, equivalently, a negative holding cost. The volatility of the exchange rate is 3% per month.

To find the value of the put, Mr. Smith sets up a binomial lattice with six monthly periods, with $u = e^{.03} = 1.03045$ and $d = 1/u = .97045$. The risk-neutral probability for an up move is

$$q = \frac{(1 + .05/12) - d - .08/12}{u - d} = .387 \, .$$

Mr. Smith then evaluates the put with the usual backward process. Specifically, he sets up a lattice of DM prices using the u and d factors defined by the volatility. He then sets up a corresponding lattice for put prices. The terminal values are found easily, and other values are found by discounted risk-neutral valuation using the risk-neutral probabilities.

Brownian Motion Form*

Suppose a commodity—let's take copper—has a price governed by geometric Brownian motion as

$$dS = \mu S \, dt + \sigma S \, dz \tag{13.25}$$

where z is a standard Wiener process. If an investor buys copper and holds it, there is a proportional storage cost that is paid at the rate of cS per unit time. If at any moment t the investor holds copper with total value $W(t)$, the holding cost can be paid at the rate of $cW(t)dt$ by selling copper at this rate. The process for the value of copper holdings is therefore

$$dW = \mu W \, dt + \sigma W \, dz - cW \, dt$$
$$= (\mu - c)W \, dt + \sigma W \, dz \tag{13.26}$$

where $W(0) = S(0)$. Equation (13.26) can now be regarded as that governing the value of a security with the holding costs accounted for. We might term W the value of *net copper*, since it is the net value after holding costs.

If we consider an investment opportunity that involves copper, such as an option on copper futures or a real option on a project that involves copper as a commodity (such as a copper mining operation or an electrical equipment project), we can value this opportunity by risk-neutral techniques. We change the process for net copper to risk-neutral form since it is net copper that can be used in constructing a replication of other securities. Specifically, in a risk-neutral setting with interest rate r, net copper is governed by

$$dW = rW \, dt + \sigma W \, d\hat{z} \tag{13.27}$$

where $\hat{z}$ is a standard Wiener process.

The appropriate transformation embodied in the foregoing is that from (13.26) to (13.27), which boils down to the change $\mu - c \to r$. This is equivalent to $\mu \to r + c$. Hence the original copper price in a risk-neutral world satisfies

$$dS = (r + c)S \, dt + \sigma S \, d\hat{z} \, . \tag{13.28}$$

This is the equation that should be used for risk-neutral valuation of copper-related investments.

13.10 MARTINGALE PRICING★

Consider any security with a continuous-time price process $S(t)$. Suppose that the interest rate is r and the security makes no payments for $0 \le t \le T$. The theory of risk-neutral pricing states that there is a risk-neutral version of the process on $[0, T]$ such that

$$S(0) = e^{-rt}\hat{E}[S(t)] \tag{13.29}$$

where $\hat{E}$ denotes expectation in the risk-neutral world. We can translate this expression to time t_1 to write

$$S(t_1) = e^{-r(t_2 - t_1)}\hat{E}_{t_1}[S(t_2)]$$

for any $t_2 > t_1$, where $\hat{E}_{t_1}$ denotes risk-neutral expectation as seen[4] at time t_1. We can then rearrange this expression to

$$e^{-rt_1}S(t_1) = e^{-rt_2}\hat{E}_{t_1}[S(t_2)] \, .$$

Equivalently, if for all t we define

$$\overline{S}(t) = e^{-rt}S(t)$$

we have the especially simple expression

$$\overline{S}(t_1) = \hat{E}_{t_1}[\overline{S}(t_2)] \tag{13.30}$$

for all $t_2 > t_1$.

In general, a process $x(t)$ that satisfies $x(t_1) = E_{t_1}[x(t_2)]$ for all $t_2 > t_1$ is called a **martingale** (after the mathematician who first studied these processes). The expected future value of a martingale is equal to the current value of the process—there is no systematic drift.

Equation (13.30) states that the security price $S(t)$ deflated by the discount factor from 0 to t is a martingale under the risk-neutral probability structure.

Furthermore, our results on risk-neutral evaluation imply, in the same way, that the price process P of any security which is derivative to S (and which does not

---

[4]In (13.29) we could write $\hat{E}_0$, but the time reference is understood.

generate intermediate cash flows) must also be a martingale under the same probability structure; that is,

$$\overline{P}(t_1) = \hat{E}[\overline{P}(t_2)].$$ (13.31)

This is just a restatement of the risk-neutral pricing formula because we can unscramble (13.31) to produce

$$P(t_1) = e^{-r(t_2-t_1)}\hat{E}[P(t_2)].$$ (13.32)

Example 13.10 (Forward value)   Consider a forward contract on a security with price process S. The contract is written at $t = 0$ with forward price F_0 for delivery at time T. The initial value of this contract is $f_0 = 0$. At time $t > 0$, new contracts have forward price F_t. What is the value f_t of the original forward contract at t?

The function f_t is a derivative of the security S; hence its deflated price must be a martingale in the risk-neutral world. Hence,

$$\overline{f}_t = \hat{E}_t(f_T).$$

Equivalently,

$$e^{-rt} f_t = e^{-rT}\hat{E}_t(f_T) = e^{-rT}\hat{E}_t(S_T - F_0).$$ (13.33)

The same argument applied to a contract written at t with forward price F_t (and value zero) gives

$$0 = e^{-rT}\hat{E}_t(S_T - F_t)$$

or, equivalently, $\hat{E}(S_T) = F_t$. Using this in (13.33), we find the desired result

$$f_t = e^{-r(T-t)}(F_t - F_0)$$

which agrees with the formula derived in Section 10.4 by more elementary (but less general) arguments.

The martingale formulation can be used in the binomial lattice framework as well. The analog of (13.31) is

$$\overline{P}_k = \hat{E}_k(\overline{P}_j)$$ (13.34)

for $j > k$, where

$$\overline{P}_k = \frac{P_k}{(1+r)^k}$$

and $\hat{E}_k$ denotes expectation at k with respect to the risk-neutral probabilities. Again $\overline{P}$ is P deflated by the discount factor. In the binomial framework (13.34) is usually applied a single step at a time, in which case it is identical, once the interest rate terms are made explicit, to the familiar backward discounted risk-neutral recursive evaluation process.

Because of this association with martingales, the risk-neutral probabilities are often termed **martingale probabilities.** However, in this text we generally prefer risk-neutral terminology to martingale terminology.

13.11 SUMMARY

The Black–Scholes equation is a partial differential equation that must be satisfied by any function $f(S, t)$ that is derivative to the underlying security with price process

$$dS = \mu S\, dt + \sigma S\, dz$$

where z is a standardized Wiener process. In particular, the functions S and e^{rt} both satisfy the Black–Scholes equation. The price functions of other derivative securities, such as options, satisfy the same equation, but with different boundary conditions.

It is usually difficult or impossible to solve the Black–Scholes equation explicitly for a given set of boundary conditions. It can be solved for the special case of a call option on a stock that does not pay dividends during the life of the option. The resulting solution formula $C(S, t)$ is called the Black–Scholes formula for the price of a call option. This formula is expressed in terms of the function N, the cumulative distribution of a standard normal random variable. The function N cannot be evaluated in closed form, but accurate approximations are available.

The Black–Scholes equation can be regarded as an instance of risk-neutral pricing. Indeed, the value of a derivative security with payoff $V(T)$ at T and no other payments can be written as $V = e^{-rT}\hat{E}[V(T)]$, where $\hat{E}$ denotes expectation with respect to the risk-neutral process $dS = rS\, dt + \sigma S\, d\hat{z}$.

Delta is defined as $\Delta = \partial f/\partial S$. Delta therefore measures the sensitivity of a derivative asset to the changes in the underlying stock price S. A portfolio can be hedged by constructing it so that its net delta is zero. Delta can also be used to construct a derivative security synthetically, by replication. To do this, one constructs a special portfolio containing the underlying security in sufficient amount so that its value is equal to the value of delta times the price of the underlying security. The portfolio also contains the risk-free asset (either short or long) in an amount to make the entire portfolio have value equal to the theoretical value of the derivative. The portfolio is rebalanced periodically so that the value continues to track the theoretical value of the derivative closely. Portfolio insurance is an extension of this idea, but it constructs the replicating portfolio with futures contracts on the underlying security rather than with the underlying security itself.

There are several ways to compute the value of options or other derivative securities numerically. Monte Carlo simulation is a simple method that is well suited to European-style options, even those that are path dependent in the sense that the final payoff depends on the particular price path of the underlying security as well as the final price itself (as, for example, a call with strike price equal to the average price of the underlying security during the life of the option). A disadvantage of Monte Carlo is that it may require a very large number of simulation runs.

Finite-difference methods approximate the Black–Scholes equation by a set of algebraic equations, which can be solved numerically. The method can treat American-as well as European-style options, but it cannot treat path-dependent options, except in special cases.

Lattice and tree methods are very popular. A disadvantage is that the size of the lattice or tree often becomes very great. Path-dependent options require trees rather than lattices, and hence the number of nodes can become truly enormous.

Many variations of the option concept exist. Formulas for the theoretical prices of some of these exotic options have been devised, but in most cases the prices must be found numerically.

If storage costs are incurred or dividends are received while holding an asset, those will influence the value of securities derivative to that asset. If the storage costs or dividends are proportional to the asset price, the value of a derivative security can be found by properly adjusting the risk-neutral probabilities or, in the continuous-time case, by adjusting the growth coefficient in the risk-neutral process governing the asset.

If intermediate payments are made or costs incurred while holding a derivative security itself, those additional cash flows can, within the binomial lattice framework, be accounted for at each node during the discounted risk-neutral valuation process, as illustrated in Chapter 12. In the continuous-time framework, additional cash flow rates can be entered as an additional term in the Black–Scholes equation, as shown in the Appendix to this chapter.

The risk-neutral valuation equation can be transformed (easily) to martingale form: the price of a derivative deflated by the discount factor defines a martingale process under the risk-neutral probability structure.

APPENDIX: ALTERNATIVE BLACK–SCHOLES DERIVATION*

Here we derive the Black–Scholes equation using the discrete-time risk-neutral pricing formula and taking the limit as $\Delta t \to 0$. In addition, we shall account for intermediate cash flows.

The price of the underlying security is governed by

$$dS = \mu S\,dt + \sigma S\,dz$$

where z is a standard Wiener process. The derivative security pays cash flow at a rate $h(S, t)$ at time t and has a final cash flow of $g(S, T)$.

To determine the price of the derivative security, we set up a binomial lattice approximating the price process of S. Following the usual procedure (see Chapter 11), we select Δt and put

$$u = e^{\sigma\sqrt{\Delta t}}$$
$$d = e^{-\sigma\sqrt{\Delta t}}$$
$$R = e^{r\Delta t}.$$

The risk-neutral probabilities for up and down moves are

$$q = \frac{R - d}{u - d}, \qquad 1 - q = \frac{u - R}{u - d}.$$

We use the first-order approximations

$$e^{\sigma\sqrt{\Delta t}} = 1 + \sigma\sqrt{\Delta t} + \tfrac{1}{2}\sigma^2\Delta t$$

$$e^{-\sigma\sqrt{\Delta t}} = 1 - \sigma\sqrt{\Delta t} + \tfrac{1}{2}\sigma^2\Delta t$$

$$e^{r\Delta t} = 1 + r\Delta t$$

$$e^{-r\Delta t} = 1 - r\Delta t .$$

Substituting these into the expressions for q and $1 - q$ and keeping terms only up to first order gives

$$q = \frac{1}{2} + \frac{1}{2\sigma}\left(r - \frac{1}{2}\sigma^2\right)\sqrt{\Delta t}$$

$$1 - q = \frac{1}{2} - \frac{1}{2\sigma}\left(r - \frac{1}{2}\sigma^2\right)\sqrt{\Delta t} .$$

Let $f(S, t)$ be the value of the derivative security at S and t. According to the recursive pricing formula we have

$$f(S, t) = h(S, t)\Delta t + (1 - r\Delta t)\left[qf(uS, t + \Delta t) + (1 - q)f(dS, t + \Delta t)\right]. \quad (13.35)$$

However, to first order,

$$f(uS, t + \Delta t) = f(S, t) + \frac{\partial f}{\partial S}\left(\sigma\sqrt{\Delta t} + \frac{\sigma^2}{2}\Delta t\right)S$$

$$+ \frac{1}{2}\frac{\partial^2 f}{\partial S^2}(\sigma^2\Delta t)S^2 + \frac{\partial f}{\partial t}\Delta t$$

$$f(dS, t + \Delta t) = f(S, t) + \frac{\partial f}{\partial S}\left(-\sigma\sqrt{\Delta t} + \frac{\sigma^2}{2}\Delta t\right)S$$

$$+ \frac{1}{2}\frac{\partial^2 f}{\partial S^2}(\sigma^2\Delta t)S^2 + \frac{\partial f}{\partial t}\Delta t .$$

Using these in (13.35), keeping terms up to order Δt, and combining similar terms (requiring a bit of algebra), we obtain

$$f(S, t) = h(S, t)\Delta t + f(S, t) - rf(S, t)\Delta t + \frac{\partial f}{\partial S}rS\Delta t + \frac{1}{2}\frac{\partial^2 f}{\partial S^2}\sigma^2 S^2\Delta t + \frac{\partial f}{\partial t}\Delta t .$$

Canceling $f(S, t)$ and Δt we have

$$h + \frac{\partial f}{\partial t} + \frac{\partial f}{\partial S}rS + \frac{1}{2}\frac{\partial^2 f}{\partial S^2}\sigma^2 S^2 = rf . \quad (13.36)$$

The boundary condition is $f(S, T) = g(S, T)$. This is the Black–Scholes equation when there is cash flow.

EXERCISES

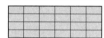

1. (Numerical evaluation of normal distribution ⊕)   The cumulative normal distribution can be approximated (to within about six decimal places) by the modified polynomial relation

$$N(x) = \begin{cases} 1 - N'(x)(a_1 k + a_2 k^2 + a_3 k^3 + a_4 k^4 + a_5 k^5) & \text{for } x \geq 0 \\ 1 - N(-x) & \text{for } x < 0 \end{cases}$$

where

$$N'(x) = \frac{1}{\sqrt{2\pi}} e^{-x^2/2}$$

$$k = \frac{1}{1 + \gamma x}$$

$$\gamma = .2316419$$

$$a_1 = .319381530$$

$$a_2 = -.35653782$$

$$a_3 = 1.781477937$$

$$a_4 = -1.821255978$$

$$a_5 = 1.330274429.$$

Use this formula to find the value of a call option with parameters $T = .5$, $\sigma = .25$, $r = .08$, $K = 35$, and $S_0 = \$34$.

2. (Perpetual put ◇)   Consider a perpetual American put option (with $T = \infty$). For small stock prices it will be advantageous to exercise the put. Let G be the largest such stock price. The time-independent Black–Scholes equation becomes

$$\tfrac{1}{2}\sigma^2 S^2 P''(S) + r S P'(S) - r P(S) = 0$$

for $G \leq S \leq \infty$. The appropriate boundary conditions are $P(\infty) = 0$ and $P(G) = K - G$. G should be chosen to maximize the value of the option.

(a) Show that $P(S)$ has the form

$$P(S) = a_1 S + a_2 S^{-\gamma}$$

where $\gamma = 2r/\sigma^2$.

(b) Use the two boundary conditions to show that

$$P(S) = (K - G)(S/G)^{-\gamma}.$$

(c) Finally, choose G to maximize $P(S)$ to conclude that

$$P(S) = \frac{K}{1+\gamma} \left[\frac{(1+\gamma)S}{\gamma K} \right]^{-\gamma}.$$

3. (Sigma estimation ⊕)   Traders in major financial institutions use the Black–Scholes formula in a backward fashion to infer other traders' estimates of σ from option prices. In fact, traders frequently quote sigmas to each other, rather than prices, to arrange trades. Suppose a call option on a stock that pays no dividend for 6 months has a strike price of $35, a premium of $2.15, and time to maturity of 7 weeks. The current short-term T-bill rate is

7%, and the price of the underlying stock is $36.12. What is the implied volatility of the underlying security?

4. (Black–Scholes approximation ⋄)   Note that to first order $N(d) = \frac{1}{2} + d/\sqrt{2\pi}$. Use this to derive the value of a call option when the stock price is at the present value of the strike price; that is, $S = Ke^{-rT}$. Specifically, show that $C \simeq .4S\sigma\sqrt{T}$. Also show that $\Delta \simeq \frac{1}{2} + .2\sigma\sqrt{T}$. Use these approximations to estimate the value of the call option of Example 13.2.

5. (Delta)   Using the same parameters as in Example 13.2, find the value of the 5-month call if the initial value of the stock is $63. Hence estimate the quantity $\Delta = \Delta C/\Delta S$. Estimate $\Theta = \Delta C/\Delta t$.

6. (A special identity)   Gavin Jones believes that for a derivative security with price $P(S)$, the values of Δ, Γ, and Θ are related. Show that in fact

$$\Theta + rS\Delta + \tfrac{1}{2}\sigma^2 S^2 \Gamma = rP .$$

7. (Gamma and theta ⋄)   Show that for a European call or put on a non-dividend-paying stock

$$\Gamma = \frac{N'(d_1)}{S\sigma\sqrt{T}}.$$

$$\Theta = -\frac{SN'(d_1)\sigma}{2\sqrt{T}} - rKe^{-rT}N(d_2).$$

[*Hint:* Use Exercise 6.]

8. (Great Western CD ⊕)   Great Western Bank has offered a special certificate of deposit (CD) tied to the S&P 500. Funds are deposited into the account at the beginning of a month and are held in the account for 3 years. Interest is credited to the account at the end of each year, and the amount of interest paid is based on the performance of the S&P 500 index during the previous 12 months. Specifically,[5] at the end of the first year, if the value of the index at the end of k months is S_k, $k = 0, 1, 2, \ldots, 12$, the average of the 12-month index values is defined as $A = \frac{1}{12}\sum_{k=1}^{12} S_k$ and the interest paid is

$$I = \max[0, (A - S_0)/S_0]$$

times the initial account balance. Interest in the following years is computed in the same fashion, with new values of account balance and index values. Assuming that monthly changes in the S&P 500 index can be modeled as geometric Brownian motion with $\sigma = .20$, what risk-free rate is equivalent to this CD? [*Hint:* Try a tree. Use 2-month intervals.]

9. (The control variate method)   Suppose that it is desired to estimate the expected value of a random variable x. (This random variable might be the discounted terminal value of a call option on a stock that is following a risk-neutral random process; then the expected value is the value of the option.) One way to do the estimation is to generate numerous samples of x, according to its probability distribution, and then take the average of the results. A difficulty with this method is that it may take a very large number of samples to obtain satisfactory results. The process can be speeded up somewhat by the use of an additional random variable y called a **control variate**. The control variate must be correlated with x,

_____
[5]There were some minor changes in the actual formula.

and its expected value must be known. For example, if x is the terminal value of a call with a down and out feature, we might choose y to be the terminal value of a similar call without the down and out feature. We can determine the value of $E(y) = \bar{y}$ by direct methods such as the Black–Scholes formula or a binomial lattice. But we do expect that if the stock should happen to end high on a particular simulation trial, the value of both x and y will be relatively high as well. Hence the two variables are correlated.

The estimate $\hat{x}$ of $E(x)$ is made with the formula

$$\hat{x} = x_{avg} + a(y_{avg} - \bar{y}).$$

Sometimes a small value of a is selected arbitrarily. However, an optimal value of a can be estimated as well. Find the value of a that minimizes the variance of $\hat{x}$. (The result will depend on certain variances and covariances.)

10. (Control variate application ⊕)   Use the control variate method of Exercise 9 to determine the value of a 5-month Asian call option on a stock with $S_0 = \$62$, $\sigma = 20\%$, and $r = 10\%$ and a strike price of $\$60$.

   (a) As a control variate use the 5-month standard call option treated in Example 12.3.
   (b) Use S_{avg} as a control variate and compare with part (a).

11. (Pay-later options)   Pay-later options are options for which the buyer is not required to pay the premium up front (i.e., at the time that the contract is entered into). At expiration, the holder of a pay-later option *must* exercise the option if it is in the money, in which case he pays the premium at that time. Otherwise the option is left unexercised and no premium is paid.

   The stock of the CCC Corporation is currently valued at $\$12$ and is assumed to possess all the properties of geometric Brownian motion. It has an expected annual return of 15%, an annual volatility of 20%, and the annual risk-free rate is 10%.

   (a) Using a binomial lattice, determine the price of a call option on CCC stock maturing in 10 months' time with a strike price of $\$14$. (Let the distance between nodes on your tree be 1 month in length.)
   (b) Using a similar methodology, determine the premium for a pay-later call with all the same parameters as the call in part (a).
   (c) Compare your answers to parts (a) and (b). Do the answers differ; if so why, if not why not? Under what conditions would you prefer to hold which option?

12. (California housing put ⊕)   Suppose you buy a new home and finance 90% of the price with a mortgage from a bank. Suppose that a few years later the value of your home falls below your mortgage balance and you decide to default on your loan. California has antideficiency judgment legislation that states that the bank can only recover the value of the house itself, not the entire mortgage balance.[6] (Of course, real estate values in California always increase, so this is never an issue!)

   Suppose you take out a 15-year mortgage for 90% of the home price, and suppose that the risk-free rate is constant at 10%. Assume also that the house has a net value to you (perhaps in saved rent) of 5% of its market value each year. Housing prices have a volatility of 18% per year. What is the value of this put option for a loan of $\$90$? What is the fair value for the interest rate on your mortgage? (Use the small Δt approximation.)

---

[6]This is, of course, a simplification of the law.

13. (Forest value)   Solve Exercise 16 in Chapter 12 assuming that the annual storage cost of cut lumber is 5% of its value.

14. (Mr. Smith's put)   Find the value of the put for Mr. Smith described in Example 13.9.

REFERENCES

The classic paper of Black and Scholes [1] initiated the modern approach to options valuation. Another early significant contributor was Merton, many of whose papers are collected in [2]. Merton examined many important special cases, such as perpetual options. Details of options trading are given in [3]. Portfolio insurance is discussed in [4, 5]. The Monte Carlo technique is a classic method for evaluating expected value. Its application to options valuation is treated in [6, 7]. A textbook treatment of general finite-difference methods is [8]. Application to options valuation is discussed in [9, 10]. For a discussion of exotic options see [11, 12]. The idea of Exercise 4 is in [13].

1. Black, F., and M. Scholes (1973), "The Pricing of Options and Corporate Liabilities," *Journal of Political Economy*, **81**, 637–654.
2. Merton, R. C. (1990), *Continuous-Time Finance*, Blackwell, Cambridge, MA.
3. *Characteristics and Risk of Standardized Options*, American Stock Exchange, New York; Chicago Board Options Exchange, Chicago; New York Stock Exchange, New York; Pacific Stock Exchange, San Francisco; Philadelphia Stock Exchange, Philadelphia, February 1994.
4. Leland, H. E. (1980), "Who Should Buy Portfolio Insurance," *Journal of Finance*, **35**, 581–594.
5. Rubinstein, M., and H. E. Leland (1981), "Replicating Options with Positions in Stock and Cash," *Financial Analysts Journal*, **37**, July/August, 63–72.
6. Boyle, P. P. (1977), "Options: A Monte Carlo Approach," *Journal of Financial Economics*, **4**, 323–338.
7. Hull, J. C., and A. White (1988), "The Use of the Control Variate Technique in Option Pricing," *Journal of Financial and Quantitative Analysis*, **23**, 237–251.
8. Mitchell, A., and D. Griffiths (1980), *The Finite Difference Method in Partial Differential Equations*, Wiley, New York.
9. Brennan, M., and E. S. Schwartz (1977), "The Valuation of American Put Options," *Journal of Finance*, **32**, 449–462.
10. Courtadon, G. (1982), "A More Accurate Finite Difference Approximation for the Valuation of Options," *Journal of Financial and Quantitative Analysis*, **17**, 697–705.
11. Rubinstein, M. (1991), "Pay Now, Choose Later," *Risk* (February). (Also see similar articles on other exotic options by the same author in subsequent issues of *Risk*.)
12. Hull, J. C. (1993), *Options, Futures, and Other Derivative Securities*, 2nd ed., Prentice Hall, Englewood Cliffs, NJ.
13. Brenner, M., and M. G. Subrahmanyam (1994), "A Simple Approach to Option Valuation and Hedging in the Black–Scholes Mode," *Financial Analysts Journal*, March/April, 25–28.

INTEREST RATE DERIVATIVES

S ecurities with payoffs that depend on interest rates are called **interest rate derivatives.** Such securities are extremely important because almost every financial transaction entails exposure to interest rate risk—and interest rate derivatives provide the means for controlling that risk. In addition, as with other derivative securities, interest rate derivatives may also be used creatively to enhance the performance of investment portfolios.

Some examples of interest rate derivatives are listed in the next section. These examples illustrate the complexity of the interest rate environment and the range of financial instruments designed to harness that complexity.

The complexity of the interest rate market is reflected in the theoretical structure used for its analysis. Even in the deterministic case, we found that it is necessary to define an entire term structure of interest rates in order to explain bond prices. When uncertainty is introduced, it is necessary to define a randomly changing term structure. We will find, however, that the concepts and methods that we have developed in the past few chapters—namely, risk-neutral pricing, binomial lattices, and Ito processes—can be combined with the ideas of term structure very nicely to develop a coherent approach to the pricing of interest rate derivative securities. The reader should therefore find this chapter quite interesting, both because the topic is itself extremely important in the investment world, and because it brings together much of the previous material and expands it.

14.1 EXAMPLES OF INTEREST RATE DERIVATIVES

Interest rate derivative securities are relevant to many forms of investment. Here are some examples.

1. **Bonds** Bonds themselves can be regarded as being derivative to interest rates, although the dependency is quite direct. In particular, the price of a risk-free zero-coupon bond with maturity in N years is a direct measure of the N-year interest rate. Coupon-bearing bonds can be regarded, as always, as combinations of zero-coupon bonds.

2. **Bond futures** Futures on Treasury bonds, Treasury notes, and other interest rate instruments are traded on exchanges. These were discussed in Chapter 10.

3. **Bond options** An option can be granted on a bond. An American call option on a 10-year Treasury bond would grant the right to purchase the bond at a fixed (strike) price within a fixed period of time.

4. **Bond futures options** More common than actual bond options are options on bond futures. Such options are traded on an exchange that deals with futures on Treasury notes and other interest rate futures contracts. Such options specify delivery of the underlying futures contract.

5. **Embedded bond options** Many bonds are **callable,** which means that the issuer of the bond has the right to repurchase the bond according to certain terms. (Usually a bond is callable only after a specified number of years.) A call provision can be regarded as an option granted to the issuer, the option being embedded within the bond itself. The issuer of such a bond will find it advantageous to exercise the call option if interest rates fall below those of the original issue. Some bonds are **putable,** which means that the owner of the bond can require that the issuer redeem the bond under certain conditions. Such bonds grant an embedded put option to the bond holder.

6. **Mortgages** Typically, a home mortgage carries with it certain prepayment privileges, allowing the mortgagee to repay the loan anytime. (Often there is a repayment penalty for, perhaps, the first 2 years.) The repayment privilege is analogous to a call provision in a bond, with the homeowner taking the role of the issuer. Some mortgages have special features such as rates that adjust with prevailing interest rates.

7. **Mortgage-backed securities** Mortgages are usually packaged together in mortgage pools. A mortgage-backed security is an ownership share of the income generated by such a pool or an obligation secured by such a pool. The individual mortgages in a pool are typically serviced by banks, which receive the monthly mortgage payments and send them to the mortgage owner. For this reason these securities are also termed **pass throughs.** The overall market for mortgage-backed securities is enormous, surpassing that of the corporate bond market.

8. **Interest rate caps and floors** It is quite common for a financial institution to offer loans to businesses in which the outstanding balance is charged an interest rate that is pegged to a standard, such as the prime rate or the LIBOR[1] rate. However, the institution may offer to *cap* the interest rate over a certain time

---

[1] The London Interbank Offered Rate (LIBOR) is the rate used for U.S. dollar borrowing through London intermediaries. There are LIBOR rates for various maturities, such as 1 month, 3 months, 6 months, and so on.

period. For example, it may offer to charge each day, over the next 6 months, the LIBOR rate plus 1%, but the charge will never exceed 10% (annual rate). Similarly a *floor* might be established, where the interest rate will never fall below the floor level. Adjustable-rate mortgages often have cap and floor features. The interest rate is updated periodically according to an interest rate index, but the charge cannot exceed a certain specified amount each period and may be limited over the life of the mortgage by an overall cap.

9. **Swaps**   A swap is an agreement between two parties to exchange the cash flows of two interest rate instruments. For example, party A may swap its fixed-income stream with party B's adjustable-rate stream.

10. **Swaptions**   The term is short for *swap option*. A swaption is an option on an interest rate swap. Such options are quite popular among corporations wishing to hedge interest rate risk. (See Exercise 10.) For the student, they represent an excellent example of how the interest rate market is becoming ever more sophisticated.

14.2 THE NEED FOR A THEORY

Wise investors take interest rate movements into account as a form of risk. To analyze this risk systematically, it is best to develop a model of interest rate fluctuations. Development of a model may seem difficult because the interest rate environment is characterized at any one time, not by a single interest rate, but by an entire term structure, composed of a series of spot rates, or a spot rate curve. This entire curve varies its shape with time.

A simplistic approach to modeling the fluctuations is to assume that the individual spot rates move independently of one another in a completely random fashion. This is perhaps acceptable abstractly, but it is not in accord with the observation that rates for adjacent maturities tend to move together. A realistic theory would account for this observation and build additional structure into the model of allowable fluctuations. However, as soon as a specific model is proposed, a new issue arises—that of potential arbitrage.

To see how this issue arises, let us hypothesize, as a simple model restricting the fluctuations, that the term structure is always flat, but that it moves randomly up and down—all rates moving together by the same amount. This simple model was in fact used in the immunization analysis of Chapter 3. To complete the model we could decide on a probabilistic structure for the up and down movements, assuming either a discrete set of possible jumps or a continuous distribution of movements. For the present argument, however, we do not need to be that specific. No matter how the probabilities are assigned, this simple model of term structure variations implies that arbitrage opportunities exist. The simplest proof of this is to look again at Chapter 3, Example 3.10, which treats the immunization problem of the X Corporation. According to that example, if interest rates are flat at 9%, one can form a portfolio by buying $292,788 worth of bond 1 and $121,854 worth of bond 2 while shorting $414,642 worth of a zero-coupon bond that matures in 10 years. The total cost of this portfolio is zero. However, if the term structure moves either up or down, the net value of the portfolio will increase. Hence there is a chance that a positive profit can be made from the portfolio and no chance of a loss—a classic type B arbitrage situation. (This is a general result for the flat term structure assumption, as shown in Chapter 3, Exercise 16.) This example shows that one cannot arbitrarily select a framework for term structure fluctuation if arbitrage opportunities are to be avoided. How can we find a realistic framework that is arbitrage free?

14.3 THE BINOMIAL APPROACH

Our familiar tool—the binomial lattice—provides a suitable framework for constructing interest rate models. We set up a lattice with a basic time span between successive nodes equal to the period we wish to use for representing the term structure—perhaps a week, a month, a quarter, or a year. We then assign a **short rate** (that is, a one-period rate) to each node of the lattice. The interpretation of this lattice is that if the process reaches a specific node, then the one-period rate, for the next period, is the rate specified at that node. To complete the model we may assign probabilities to the various node transitions so that we have a full probabilistic process for the short rate. However, *real* probabilities for node transitions are not relevant for the pricing theory that follows. Instead we will also *assign* a set of risk-neutral node transition probabilities. The assignment of the short rate values and the corresponding risk-neutral probabilities completely defines an interest rate structure for all maturities, as will be demonstrated shortly. It is important to understand that the risk-neutral probabilities are assigned in this case rather than derived from a replication argument.

Since the risk-neutral probabilities are assigned, rather than computed, it is convenient to set them all equal to one-half. We follow this convention in this section. It is convenient as well to establish an indexing convention for the nodes of the lattice. For this purpose, it is easiest to draw the lattice in the right-triangle form shown in Figure 14.1. Note that at time t there are a total of $t + 1$ nodes, indexed by i from 0

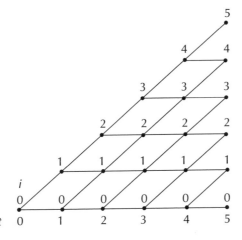

FIGURE 14.1 Indexing system for short rate lattice. Nodes are double indexed in the form (t, i). The t refers to time as shown at the bottom of the lattice, and i refers to the height above the lowest part of the lattice.

to t. A convenient way to visualize this notation is to imagine that the two branches leading from any node are considered to be "up" and "flat." The index i at time t denotes how many ups it has taken to reach the node. A specific node in the lattice is indexed by the pair (t, i), with t being time and i being the node index at that time. At a node (t, i) there is specified a short rate $r_{ti} \geq 0$, which is the one-period rate at that point.

This lattice forms the basis for pricing interest rate securities by using risk-neutral pricing. When the process is at any node, the value of any interest rate security depends only on that node; and we assume that all node values are related by the risk-neutral pricing formula. For example, consider a given node (t, i) somewhere in the middle of the lattice, and any interest rate security. Suppose the value of this security at node (t, i) is V_{ti}. Then according to the rules of the lattice, this value is related to the value of the security at the next two possible successor nodes according to the risk-neutral pricing formula

$$V_{ti} = \frac{1}{1 + r_{ti}} \left(\tfrac{1}{2} V_{t+1,i+1} + \tfrac{1}{2} V_{t+1,i} \right) + D_{ti} \tag{14.1}$$

where D_{ti} is the dividend payment[2] at node (t, i).

Implied Term Structure

It may seem that we are a long way from having specified an entire term structure model, since all we have are short rates—but actually the whole structure is already there. We just have to extract it. The extraction is accomplished in the same way that a spot rate curve is extracted from a series of one-period forward rates in the deterministic case. For the binomial lattice, the extraction is based on risk-neutral pricing. To see how this works, suppose that we are at the initial time, at node $(0, 0)$. The one-period spot rate is simply r_{00}, as defined at that node. To find the two-period spot rate, we consider a bond that pays \$1 at time 2. We find its value in two steps, working backward using the risk-neutral pricing formula. In detail, suppose for simplicity the period length is a full year. Denote the price at node (t, i) of the bond that matures at year 2 by $P_{ti}(2)$. Then,

$$P_{10}(2) = \frac{1}{1 + r_{10}} \left(\tfrac{1}{2} \times 1 + \tfrac{1}{2} \times 1 \right) = \frac{1}{1 + r_{10}}$$

$$P_{11}(2) = \frac{1}{1 + r_{11}} \left(\tfrac{1}{2} \times 1 + \tfrac{1}{2} \times 1 \right) = \frac{1}{1 + r_{11}}$$

and next

$$P_{00}(2) = \frac{1}{1 + r_{00}} \left[\tfrac{1}{2} P_{10}(2) + \tfrac{1}{2} P_{11}(2) \right] .$$

---

[2] This formula assumes that D_{ti} depends only on t and i. For some complex securities, this does not hold and the valuation process is then path dependent. Such cases are illustrated in later sections.

This process can be applied to evaluate the price $P_{00}(k)$ for any k. The corresponding spot rate for period k is then the rate s_k that satisfies

$$\frac{1}{(1 + s_k)^k} = P_{00}(k).$$

Example 14.1 (A simple short rate lattice)   Figure 14.2 shows a short rate lattice giving the rates for 6 years. (The period length is 1 year.) The figure was constructed by using an up factor of $u = 1.3$ and a flat (or down) factor of $d = .9$. Risk-neutral probabilities for the lattice were assigned as $q = .5$ for up and $1 - q = .5$ for flat.

   The entire term structure of interest rates can be determined from this lattice by computing the prices of the zero-coupon bonds of various maturities. An example of such a calculation is shown in the lower part of the figure for a bond maturing at time 4. The value is computed by moving backward through the lattice in the familiar way, at each period weighting the next period's values by the risk-neutral probabilities and discounting by the one-period rate. For example, the top entry in the third column is $P_{22}(4) = \frac{1}{2}(.8667 + .9038)/1.1183 = .7916$. The value of the bond at time zero is found to be .7334 times its face value. This corresponds to a spot rate from time zero to time 4 of $s_4 = (1/.7334)^{.25} - 1 = .0806$. The other spot rates can be calculated in a similar way by constructing a lattice of the corresponding length with 1's in the final column. If this is done, the resulting term structure is found to be (.0700, .0734, .0769, .0806, .0844, .0882). Note how the term structure rises smoothly in a manner that is fairly characteristic of actual term structures.

   A short rate binomial lattice gives birth to a whole family of spot rate curves, depicting the way the term structure varies randomly with time. To see this, imagine the process initially at the node $(0, 0)$. The corresponding term structure (spot rate curve) can be determined by the calculations illustrated in the foregoing example. After one period the process moves to one of the two successor nodes. This successor node is then considered to be the new initial node of a (smaller) short rate lattice that

Short rate						.2599
				.1999	.1799	
			.1538	.1384	.1246	
		.1183	.1065	.0958	.0862	
	.0910	.0819	.0737	.0663	.0597	
.0700	.0630	.0567	.0510	.0459	.0413	

Bond value				1.0000
			.8667	1.0000
		.7916	.9038	1.0000
	.7515	.8481	.9314	1.0000
.7334	.8180	.8909	.9514	1.0000

FIGURE 14.2   Simple short rate lattice and valuation of a 4-year bond. The bond is valued by working backward in the lower lattice, starting from the terminal value of 1.0 and discounting with the short rate values in the upper lattice.

is a sublattice of the original one. A corresponding spot rate curve can be computed exactly as before, but it will have somewhat different values, representing the one-period change. If the process had moved to the other possible node, the corresponding spot rate curve would be somewhat different still. We can therefore visualize a spot rate curve associated with every node in the lattice. As the underlying process moves from node to node, the entire spot rate curve changes.

No Arbitrage Opportunities

Is the term structure determined from the short rate binomial lattice free from arbitrage possibilities? Yes! This important fact follows from the risk-neutral pricing formula. To prove it, first consider the possibility of arbitrage over a single period, starting at node (t, i). Any security at that node is defined by its values $V_{t+1,i}$ and $V_{t+1,i+1}$ at period $t + 1$ and its price P_{ti} at (t, i). These are related by

$$P_{ti} = \frac{1}{2} \frac{V_{t+1,i} + V_{t+1,i+1}}{1 + r_{ti}}.$$

If this security represents an arbitrage, then we must have $P_{ti} \leq 0$ and $V_{t+1,i} \geq 0$, $V_{t+1,i+1} \geq 0$ with one of these inequalities being strict. This is clearly impossible since all coefficients in the equation linking these values are positive. Hence no arbitrage is possible over one period.

The argument for two periods is similar. A security will have price P_{ti} at time t, payouts $D_{t+1,i}$, $D_{t+1,i+1}$ at time $t + 1$, and values $V_{t+2,i}$, $V_{t+2,i+1}$, $V_{t+2,i+2}$ at time $t + 2$. It should be clear (see Figure 14.3) that these values are related by

$$P_{ti} = \frac{1}{2} \frac{D_{t+1,i} + D_{t+1,i+1}}{1 + r_{ti}} + \frac{1}{4} \frac{V_{t+2,i} + V_{t+2,i+1}}{(1 + r_{t+1,i})(1 + r_{ti})} + \frac{1}{4} \frac{V_{t+2,i+1} + V_{t+2,i+2}}{(1 + r_{t+1,i+1})(1 + r_{ti})}.$$

Again for an arbitrage, all variables on the right must be greater than or equal to zero, and P_{ti} must be less than or equal to zero, with at least one strict inequality. Clearly this is not possible. Hence no two-period arbitrage exists. The argument can be extended to an arbitrary number of periods. Therefore the short rate lattice approach to modeling interest rates is arbitrage free, and hence specification of a short rate lattice provides a workable model of interest rate variations.

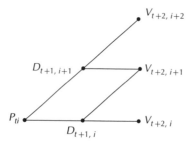

FIGURE 14.3   No arbitrage is possible. The initial price P_{ti} is determined by discounted risk-neutral valuation. If all payoffs are nonnegative, then the initial price must also be nonnegative.

14.4 PRICING APPLICATIONS

Many interesting securities can be priced with the short rate lattice. Sometimes the short rate lattice together with the promised payout pattern on the nodes of the lattice is all that is needed to set up a backward calculation to determine value. Other times somewhat more subtle techniques must be used. But a wide assortment of problems are amenable to fairly quick calculation using the binomial lattice framework. This section discusses and illustrates a representative group of important and interesting applications of this type.

Bond Derivatives

The previous section showed how to calculate the value of zero-coupon bonds using the binomial lattice methodology. It is a straightforward extension to calculate the value of other bonds. To calculate the value of a derivative of a bond, we proceed in two steps: first we calculate the price lattice of the bond itself, then we calculate the value of the derivative. We illustrate the procedure for an option on a bond.

Example 14.2 (A bond option) Consider a zero-coupon bond that has 4 years remaining to maturity and is selling at a current price of 73.34. Suppose that we are granted a European option to purchase this bond in 2 years at a strike price of 84.00. What is the value of this option?

We assume that the term structure is governed by the short rate lattice of Example 14.1. The value of the zero-coupon bond at any node is indicated in the bond price lattice shown in the bottom portion of Figure 14.2. To evaluate the option we only need the first three periods of this lattice. The value at expiration of the option is $\max(0, P - K)$, where P is the price of the bond at expiration and K is the strike price. We can then construct a small lattice to determine the option value, as shown in Figure 14.4. The last column shows the value of the option at expiration. The earlier columns show the value obtained by working backward (as usual), using the risk-neutral probabilities of .5 and discounting according to the corresponding values in the short rate lattice. We conclude that the value of the option is 1.4703.

Forwards and Futures*

Forward and futures contracts on interest rate securities, such as bonds, are easily treated by the binomial lattice method. This method provides additional insight into the

		0
	.3712	.81
1.4703	2.7752	5.09

FIGURE 14.4 Bond option calculation. The standard backward method is applied.

results of Chapter 10 and generalizes those results in important ways, since it is not necessary to assume that interest rates are deterministic. Actually, the results for forward contracts are not influenced much by the introduction of uncertainty, but the results for futures are. This means, in particular, that the futures–forwards equivalence result no longer applies. However, the calculations required for interest rate futures are simple.

Example 14.3 (A bond forward)   Consider a forward contract to purchase a 2-year, 10% Treasury bond 4 years from now. Assume that the interest rate process follows the lattice of the previous examples, as shown in Figure 14.2; and assume that coupons are paid yearly and that the contract specifies that delivery will be made just after the coupon payment at the beginning of year 4.

The first step of the calculation is to find the value of the Treasury bond at the beginning of the fourth year. This is done in the usual way by backward calculation, as shown on the right side of Figure 14.5. In the calculation the coupon payments for years 5 and 6 are included. For example, the top entry in year 5 is $\frac{1}{1.26}(.5 \times 110 + .5 \times 110) + 10 = 97.31$. The column for year 4 is computed in a similar way, but without the coupon. The figures in the column for year 4 are the prices that the bond would sell for that year.

The left part of the lattice continues the backward calculation, but does not include any coupon payments. The resulting value at the initial node is the value of the 2-year bond delivered at year 4, but paid for at year zero. This is 72.90.

With the forward contract there is no initial payment; the payment is at year 4. This delay of payment has time value, which is determined by the value of a 4-year zero-coupon bond. The value of such a zero-coupon bond was calculated in Example 14.1 to be 73.34. We can find the correct forward price of the bond by comparing it with the forward price of $100 cash that is to be delivered in 4 years; this forward price is of course just $100. Hence the correct price of the forward is

$$
\begin{aligned}
F_0 &= \text{forward price of bond} \\
&= \text{forward price of \$100} \times \frac{\text{current value of bond}}{\text{current value of \$100}} \\
&= 100 \times \frac{72.90}{73.34} = 99.40.
\end{aligned}
$$

Year						
0	1	2	3	4	5	6
				Bond		110
					97.31	110
Forward period				83.56	103.23	110
			76.38	92.69	107.82	110
		73.07	87.06	99.96	111.27	110
	72.2	84.46	95.69	105.5	113.80	110
72.9	83.81	93.72	102.4	109.7	115.63	110

FIGURE 14.5 Lattice for bond forward. The value of the bond is calculated backward from year 6 to year 4. The forward price is then computed backward using the year 4 bond values as final values.

		Year		
0	**1**	**2**	**3**	**4**
Futures period				83.56
			88.13	92.69
		92.23	96.33	99.96
	95.88	99.54	102.75	105.53
99.12	102.36	105.18	107.61	109.68

FIGURE 14.6 Lattice for bond future. Futures prices are computed by averaging in backward steps without discounting.

Futures*

The pricing of futures contracts is also easy using a binomial lattice. The method is best described by a continuation of Example 14.3.

Example 14.4 (A bond future)   Consider a futures contract on the 2-year, 10% bond to be purchased in 4 years. As before, we need to know the value of the bond at each node for year 4, when the futures contract is due. This calculation was carried out in the previous example, and we simply enter the values in a new lattice at year 4, as shown in Figure 14.6. Now suppose that you are at the top node of year 3, and that the price of the futures contract is F at that point. You pay nothing then, but next period you would obtain a profit of either $83.56 - F$ or $92.69 - F$. The price you should pay at year 3 is therefore $.5(83.56 - F) + .5(92.69 - F)$, discounted by the short rate at that point. But this price is zero, since you pay nothing for the contract. Hence $F = .5(83.56 + 92.69) = 88.13$. In other words, the futures price is the average of the two next prices (using the risk-neutral probabilities). This argument can be applied to every previous node. So we just work backward, computing averages *without* discounting. The value at the initial node is the price of the futures contract; namely, 99.12. Note that indeed this value is slightly different than the corresponding forward price of 99.40, thus demonstrating that futures–forward equivalence does not hold when interest rates are random (although the discrepancy is likely to be small).

14.5 LEVELING AND ADJUSTABLE-RATE LOANS*

Luckily we have been able to solve most pricing problems in this book using binomial lattices, rather than more complex tree structures. Lattices are very desirable since the number of nodes in a lattice grows only in proportion to n, the number of periods, whereas for more general trees the number of nodes may grow geometrically (such as 2^n for a binomial tree). Hence if a lattice can be used, representation will be relatively easy and computational effort will be relatively small; whereas everything is more difficult if a full tree is required. Not surprisingly, we are willing to work hard to convert tree structures into lattice structures when that is possible. This section describes a method for doing just that, and then applies the method to the evaluation of adjustable-rate loans.

When using a lattice, nodes are typically defined by the value of some underlying variable that uniquely determines the cash flow at that node. For example, for standard options, the stock price serves that function, whereas for a bond the short rate is used. If the cash flows associated with a node depend on the path used to arrive at the node, then the cash flow process is said to be **path dependent** and the lattice is not an appropriate structure. A tree structure, on the other hand, does not have this shortcoming because each node in a tree is reached by a unique path. Hence one way to solve path-dependent problems is to separate all the combined nodes in a lattice, thereby producing a tree that represents the same problem.

Usually, what is going on in a path-dependent case is that more than one variable is needed to describe the cash flow at a node. Sometimes we can collapse these variables into one and salvage the lattice.

We term the technique that we use **leveling** for a reason that will become clear. It applies to situations where cash flow is defined by two variables, say, j and x. The first of these is a discrete variable that by itself would define a lattice. The second variable is a continuous variable that is also needed to define cash flow. As an example, consider the Complexico gold mine with random gold prices (which was treated in Chapter 12, Example 12.8). The gold price can be modeled as a binomial lattice, so this price serves as the lattice variable j. However, after arriving at a lattice node, the cash flow there depends also on the amount of gold remaining in the mine, and hence this amount serves as the x variable. The mine value is path dependent because the amount x at any gold price node depends on the path that led to that node. Problems of this type look discouraging because we fear that we might need a lot more nodes to account for the x dependence.

The path-independent dilemma can be circumvented if the price at a node can be proved to be proportional to the variable x. If this is the case, we can decide on a fixed level x_0 of x and use this one level at all nodes, then later scale the results appropriately. Specifically, when working backward, at any node j we value the security price V at node j using the underlying variable values j and x_0. The resulting value is V_j. The step-by-step backward computation is simple because we can easily keep track of the changes in x for a single step. For example, suppose we are at node j and we need the price at node $j+1$, which is one step ahead, but we need the price at $j+1$ when $x \neq x_0$. By linearity this price is $(x/x_0)V_{j+1}$, where V_{j+1} is the price at $j+1$ when $x = x_0$. Things are especially simple if we choose $x_0 = 1$. Then the price at any node j and level x is of the form $V_j(x) = K_j x$. We just need to keep track of the K_j's; then multiply by the appropriate x.

The method is called leveling because the x variable is kept at a constant level. The Complexico gold mine problem was solved this way, after it was found that the lease value was linear in the gold reserve amount x. The method seems to be especially valuable in interest rate derivative problems. We shall use it to treat adjustable-rate loans in the next subsection. That example should clarify the method.

Adjustable-Rate Loans

Adjustable-rate loans are very common and very important. A typical adjustable-rate loan charges an interest rate in any period that is tied to a standard index, such as the 3-month T-bill rate. For example, the rate charged might be the T-bill rate plus 2 percentage points. However, if the loan is to be amortized over a fixed number of periods (that is, it is to be paid off essentially uniformly), a change in interest rate implies a change in the level of the required payment. The payment in any period is calculated so that the loan will be retired at the maturity date, under the assumption that the interest rate will remain constant until then.

Suppose you were to try to evaluate such a loan. You could take the perspective of the bank that makes the loan, and see how much the bank would pay for the (random) income stream represented by the loan repayment schedule. You would start with a binomial lattice model of the T-bill rate. Then you would be inclined to enter the payments due at any node in the lattice and evaluate this payment structure by backward calculation in the standard way. However, in thinking about this, you would soon discover that the payments could not be entered on the lattice in a unique way because the payment due at any node depends not only on that node, but also on the path taken to get to that node. For example, if a path of high interest rates were taken, the loan balance might be larger than if a path of low interest rates were taken. The loan balance at a node therefore depends on the particular history of interest rates. Your thought at this point would most likely be "Oh, no; it looks like I might have to use a binomial tree, with its thousands of nodes, instead of a lattice. But wait; maybe I can use leveling."

Example 14.5 (The auto buyer's dilemma)   Denise just graduated from college and has agreed to purchase a new automobile. She is now faced with the decision of how to finance the $10,000 balance she owes after her down payment. She has decided on a 5-year loan, but is given two choices: (A) a fixed-rate loan at 10% interest or (B) an adjustable-rate loan with interest that at any year is 2 points above the 1-year T-bill rate at the beginning of that year. Currently the T-bill rate is 7%. She wants to know which is the better deal.

Denise is pretty adept with spreadsheet programs, so she does a little homework that night. First she decides that the T-bill rate can be modeled by the lattice that we used earlier in Example 14.1. She decides to take the viewpoint of the bank and see what the two loans are worth to it. She makes the assumption that all payments are made annually, starting at the end of the first year.

The fixed-rate loan is easy. The payments are found by using the annuity formula in Chapter 3. Namely,

$$A = \frac{r(1+r)^n P}{(1+r)^n - 1}.$$

For $P = \$10,000$, $r = 10\%$, and $n = 5$ this yields $A = \$2,638$, which is the annual payment. The cash flow at each node is shown on the lattice on the left side of Figure 14.7. The lattice on the right side of the figure shows the corresponding value of this cash flow computed using the interest rates of Example 14.1.[3] Denise concludes that the fixed-rate loan is worth $561.10 to the bank.

---

[3] The loan value can equivalently be calculated as $-\$10,000 + \sum_{k=1}^{5}\left[\$2{,}638/(1+s_k)^k\right]$, where the s_k's are the spot rates implied by the short rate lattice.

	Year						Year					
	0	1	2	3	4	5	0	1	2	3	4	5
						2,638						2,638
Payment received					2,638	2,638	Loan value				4,836.5	2,638
				2,638	2,638	2,638				6,881.3	4,955.3	2,638
			2,638	2,638	2,638	2,638			8,914.7	7,157.1	5,045.3	2,638
		2,638	2,638	2,638	2,638	2,638		11,009.0	9,350.8	7,368.0	5,111.9	2,638
	−10,000	2,638	2,638	2,638	2,638	2,638	561.1	11,591.7	9,684.8	7,524.7	5,160.2	2,638

FIGURE 14.7 **Value of fixed-rate loan.** The lattice on the right is found by standard discounted risk-neutral evaluation using the payments shown in the left lattice.

For the adjustable-rate loan, Denise quickly recognizes that the cash flows are not unique at a node, but depend on the particular path by which the node was reached. She could proceed by constructing a tree and recording at each node both the short rate and the loan balance. Cash flow at the node would be uniquely determined by these two values. Instead, she preserves the lattice structure by using the leveling technique, working with loans of the same balance at every node. She uses a balance value of $100. At each node she calculates the required annual payment to amortize a loan of value $100 starting at that time and ending at year 5. These values are shown in the lattice on the left side of Figure 14.8. For example, the top element of year 4 shows $122, which is the amount that must be paid at the end of 1 year to clear a loan of $100 made at an interest rate of 19.99% + 2%. Similarly, the initial node shows $25.71, which is the amount that would have to be paid at the end of each year to amortize a loan of $100 over the entire 5-year period at a fixed interest rate of 7% + 2%. This table is constructed by using the amortization formula. It could be used on an ongoing basis to find the actual payments of the adjustable-rate loan. Denise would simply find the balance of the loan at the node (which depends on the path to the node) and then apply the amount in the lattice as a payment per $100 of balance. This payment would be made at the end of the then current year.

The lattice on the right side of Figure 14.8 contains at each node the value to the bank of initiating an adjustable-rate loan for $100 at that node. But the length of the

	Year						Year					
	0	1	2	3	4	5	0	1	2	3	4	5
						100						0
Payment rate					122	100	Value per 100				1.667	0
				63.38	115.8	100				2.535	1.757	0
			42.95	59.67	111.6	100			3.436	2.665	1.825	0
		32.3	40.35	57.13	108.6	100		4.3744	3.601	2.763	1.876	0
	25.71	30.39	38.57	55.39	106.6	100	5.349	4.56512	3.723	2.835	1.912	0

FIGURE 14.8 **Value of adjustable-rate loan.** The lattice on the right is found using the leveling technique, keeping the loan balance fixed at $100. The payments shown in the left lattice are those associated with a balance of $100.

loan is such that it terminates at the end of the original 5-year period. The lattice has the final values of 0 since loans initiated there would be paid back immediately and no interest payments would be received. At the top node of year 4 the bank could loan $100 at a rate of 22%. This would give it a payment of $122 next year. This payment has a present value of $122/1.20 = $101.67. Subtracting the $100 loan outlay gives a net present value profit of $1.67. The earlier nodes are a bit more complicated. The top node of year 3 is calculated by noting that a new loan of $100 will generate a cash flow of $63.38 next year. Part of this payment is interest payment and part reduces the principal. The remaining principal will be $100 − $63.38 + ($15.38 + $2.00) = $54.00. This principal is received by the bank and then loaned again to Denise during the next period at rates determined then. (In effect, Denise will pay the bank $63.38 + $54, and the bank will then issue her a new loan for $54.) The value of this next loan is either $1.67 per $100 or $1.76 per $100, each with (risk-neutral) probability of one-half. This amount together with the first payment can be discounted back one period and the $100 subtracted to obtain the overall net present value of $2.535. Specifically,

$$\frac{54\left[1 + \frac{1}{2}(1.67 + 1.76)/100\right] + 63.38}{1.1538} - 100 = 2.535\,.$$

Working back through the lattice, Denise finds that a $100 loan made at year zero is worth $5.349. Hence the $10,000 loan is worth $534.90, which is only slightly lower than the $561.10 value found for the fixed rate. Hence she concludes that the adjustable-rate loan is somewhat better than the fixed-rate loan in terms of price (although she may wish to carry out a different analysis to see which is best for her utility function, since she is probably unwilling to engage in active T-bill trading to fully hedge the uncertainty).

14.6 THE FORWARD EQUATION

Backward evaluation through a tree or lattice is a powerful method for evaluating financial instruments. There are times when a dual method—a forward recursion—is even better. This forward method is particularly useful for determining the term structure based on a short rate lattice.

In Section 14.4 we saw that a short rate lattice completely determines the term structure. This term structure can be computed by finding the prices of zero-coupon bonds for each maturity using the backward evaluation method. However, separate recursions and separate price lattices are required for each of these maturities. Hence if there are n periods, n separate recursions must be made in order to compute the entire term structure. For large values of n the number of single-node evaluations is approximately $n^3/6$, as compared to $n^2/2$ for one pass through the entire tree.[4] The forward process described next requires only a single recursion.

---

[4] A recursion at period $j - 1$ requires j single evaluations. Hence to evaluate a bond of maturity k requires $1 + 2 + \cdots + k = (k + 1)k/2$ separate evaluations. Since this must be done for all n maturities, the total is $\sum_{k=1}^{n}(k + 1)k/2 = [n(n + 1)^2/6][1 + 1/(n + 1)]$. For one pass through the entire tree the number of evaluations is $n(n + 1)/2$.

The forward recursion is based on calculating **elementary prices.** The elementary price $P_0(k, s)$ is the price at time zero of a security that pays one unit at time k and state s, and pays nothing at any other time or state. The prices $P_0(k, s)$ are termed elementary prices because they are the prices of elementary securities that have payoff at only one node. We could find $P_0(k, s)$ for any fixed k and s by assigning a 1 at the node (k, s) in the lattice and then working backward to time zero. Alternatively, we can work forward.

Suppose that elementary prices have been found for all nodes in the lattice for times from 0 through k. Consider a node of the form $(k+1, s)$, where $s \neq 0$, $s \neq k+1$; that is, s is not the bottom or the top node of the lattice at time $k + 1$. This situation is illustrated in Figure 14.9. Such a node has two predecessor nodes (nodes leading to it), namely, $(k, s - 1)$ and (k, s). Suppose that a security pays one unit at node $(k + 1, s)$ and nothing elsewhere. If we were to work backward in the lattice, this security would have values $.5d_{k,s-1}$ and $.5d_{k,s}$ at the respective predecessor nodes, where $d_{k,s-1}$ and $d_{k,s}$ are the one-period discount factors (determined from the short rates at those nodes).

At time zero the values at these two predecessor nodes are worth, by definition of the elementary prices, $.5d_{k,s-1}P_0(k, s-1)$ and $.5d_{k,s}P_0(k, s)$, respectively. The total value at time zero is the sum of these two, and this is the elementary price at $(k+1, s)$. Thus $P_0(k + 1, s) = .5d_{k,s-1}P_0(k, s - 1) + .5d_{k,s}P_0(k, s)$. This is a forward recursion because the value at time $k + 1$ is expressed in terms of values at time k. If $s = 0$ or $k + 1$, there is only one predecessor node, and the result is modified accordingly. Overall we obtain the three forms of the forward equation, depending on whether the node is in the middle, at the bottom, or at the top of the lattice,

$$P_0(k + 1, s) = \tfrac{1}{2}[d_{k,s-1}P_0(k, s - 1) + d_{k,s}P_0(k, s)], \qquad 0 < s < k + 1 \quad (14.2a)$$

$$P_0(k + 1, 0) = \tfrac{1}{2}d_{k,0}P_0(k, 0), \qquad\qquad\qquad\qquad s = 0 \qquad (14.2b)$$

$$P_0(k + 1, k + 1) = \tfrac{1}{2}d_{k,k}P_0(k, k), \qquad\qquad\qquad\qquad s = k + 1 .$$

Although we derived this equation through intuitive reasoning, it is possible to derive it algebraically from the backward equation. This forward equation is just a different way of organizing the fundamental risk-neutral pricing equations.

The price of any interest rate security can be found easily once the elementary prices are known. We simply multiply the payoff at any node (k, s) by the price $P_0(k, s)$ and sum the results over all nodes that have payoffs. For example, the price at time zero of a zero-coupon bond with value 1 that matures at time n is

$$P_0 = \sum_{s=0}^{n} P_0(n, s) .$$

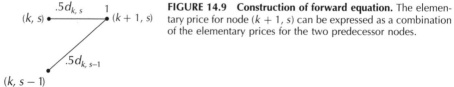

FIGURE 14.9   Construction of forward equation. The elementary price for node $(k + 1, s)$ can be expressed as a combination of the elementary prices for the two predecessor nodes.

Short rate						
						.2599
					.1999	.1799
				.1538	.1384	.1246
			.1183	.1065	.0958	.0862
		.0910	.0819	.0737	.0663	.0597
	.0700	.0630	.0567	.0510	.0459	.0413

Elementary prices							
							.0069
						.0173	.0468
					.0415	.0943	.1302
				.0958	.1754	.2028	.1894
			.2142	.2963	.2757	.2155	.1527
		.4673	.4340	.3046	.1913	.1134	.0648
	1.0000	.4673	.2198	.1040	.0495	.0237	.0114

Bond prices	.9346	.8679	.8006	.7334	.6670	.6021
Spot rates	.0700	.0734	.0769	.0806	.0844	.0882

FIGURE 14.10 Use of elementary prices to find term structure. The elementary prices are determined by a single forward sweep through the lattice. The sum of any column then gives the price of a zero-coupon bond of that maturity. Note that a short rate applies over the coming year while a spot rate applies to the previous years. Hence the initial short rate and the initial spot rate, although equal, are one column apart.

The forward equation can be used to find the entire term structure corresponding to a short rate tree by a single forward recursion—because all zero-coupon bond prices can be determined.

Example 14.6 (The simple lattice) Let us apply the forward equation to Example 14.1. The elementary price lattice can be calculated directly from the short rate lattice. It is shown in Figure 14.10 together with the resulting zero-coupon bond prices and the derived term structure.

As an example of the calculation, both terms in the second column are derived from the single predecessor node; and these terms are equal to one-half times the discount rate at the first period times the elementary price at 0, which is 1. Hence these values are $.5/1.07 = .4673$. The figures directly below the lattice are the sums of the elements above them. These values correspond to prices of zero-coupon bonds. The final figures below the lattice make up the term structure, expressed as spot rates computed directly from the bond prices above. The values agree with those computed in Example 14.1 by the more laborious process.

14.7 MATCHING THE TERM STRUCTURE

Happily we now have an excellent start on a workable methodology for pricing interest rate derivatives, based on the construction of a short rate binomial lattice. From that lattice we can compute the term structure and evaluate interest rate derivatives using the risk-neutral pricing formula and backward recursion. One vital part of this methodology, which we have not yet fully addressed, is how to construct the original short rate lattice so that it is representative of actual interest rate dynamics. This is the subject of this section.

Interest rate fluctuations are similar in character to the fluctuations of stock prices. Therefore a short rate lattice should reflect those basic properties. However, we also know that once a short rate lattice is specified, it implies a certain term structure. It seems appropriate therefore to construct the lattice so that its initial term structure matches the current observed term structure. This is easily accomplished using the concepts and tools developed in the previous sections.

The Ho–Lee Model

Let us index the nodes of a short rate lattice according to our standard format as (k, s), where k is the time, $k = 0, 1, \ldots, n$, and s is the state, with $s = 0, 1, \ldots, k$ at time k. We must make the assignments r_{ks} of short rates at each node.

One simple method of assignment is to set

$$r_{ks} = a_k + b_k s . \tag{14.3}$$

This is the Ho–Lee form. It only remains to select the parameters a_k and b_k for $k = 0, 1, \ldots, n$. The variation among nodes at a given time is completely determined by the parameter b_k. In fact, from any node $(k - 1, s)$ at time $k - 1$, the next rate is either $a_k + b_k s$ or $a_k + b_k(s + 1)$. The difference between the two is b_k. Indeed, it can be shown easily (see Exercise 6) that the (risk-neutral) standard deviation of the one-period rate is exactly $b_k/2$. Hence we refer to b_k as a **volatility parameter.** The parameter a_k is a measure of the **aggregate drift** from period 0 to k. If we remain in state 0, the short rate increases to a_k.

In the standard Ho–Lee model, the volatility parameters are all set equal to a constant b, which is characteristic of the observed volatility of interest rates (accounting for the factor of one-half). It therefore remains only to select the a_k's; and these can be selected to match the observed term structure at time zero.

If the times are $0, 1, \ldots, n$, there are $n + 1$ values of a_k to be chosen and $n + 1$ spot rates to be matched. Hence we have equal numbers of variables and requirements. The only difficulty is that the relation between the a_k's and the spot rates is somewhat indirect; but the matching can be carried out numerically.

Example 14.7 (A 14-year match)   Consider the 14-year term structure used in Chapter 4. We will assume that this is the observed spot rate curve. To match it to a full Ho–Lee model, we must make some assumption concerning volatility. Suppose that we have measured the volatility to be .01 per year, which means that the short rate is likely to fluctuate about 1 percentage point during a year.

We can carry out the match using a spreadsheet package that includes an equation-solving routine. The details are shown in Figure 14.11. The first two lines of the figure show the given spot rates over the 14-year period. The next row shows the parameters a_k that are used in the Ho–Lee model. These parameters are considered variable by the program. Based on these parameters a short rate lattice is constructed, as shown next in Figure 14.11. From this the forward equations are constructed as another lattice, based on the short rate lattice. The sum of the elements in any column gives

Year	0	1	2	3	4	5	6	7	8	9	10	11	12	13	14
Spot	7.67	8.27	8.81	9.31	9.75	10.16	10.52	10.85	11.15	11.42	11.67	11.89	12.09	12.27	
a	7.67	8.863	9.878	10.79	11.49	12.18	12.64	13.12	13.5	13.79	14.1	14.23	14.4	14.51	

Short rates

State	0	1	2	3	4	5	6	7	8	9	10	11	12	13	14
13														14.77	
12														14.75	
11													14.64	14.73	
10												14.45	14.62	14.71	
9											14.30	14.43	14.60	14.69	
8										13.97	14.28	14.41	14.58	14.67	
7									13.66	13.95	14.26	14.39	14.56	14.65	
6								13.26	13.64	13.93	14.24	14.37	14.54	14.63	
5							12.76	13.24	13.62	13.91	14.22	14.35	14.52	14.61	
4						12.28	12.74	13.22	13.60	13.89	14.20	14.33	14.50	14.59	
3					11.57	12.26	12.72	13.20	13.58	13.87	14.18	14.31	14.48	14.57	
2				10.85	11.55	12.24	12.70	13.18	13.56	13.85	14.16	14.29	14.46	14.55	
1			9.92	10.83	11.53	12.22	12.68	13.16	13.54	13.83	14.14	14.27	14.44	14.53	
0	7.67	8.86	9.88	10.79	11.49	12.18	12.64	13.12	13.50	13.79	14.10	14.23	14.40	14.51	

(year 1 also: state 1 = 8.88; year 2 also: state 1 = 9.90, state 0 = 9.88; etc. — upper‑state value is the higher rate)

Elementary prices

State	0	1	2	3	4	5	6	7	8	9	10	11	12	13	14
14															1E-05
13														3E-05	2E-04
12													6E-05	4E-04	.001
11												1E-04	8E-04	.002	.004
10											3E-04	.002	.004	.008	.012
9										8E-04	.003	.008	.014	.02	.024
8									.002	.007	.015	.024	.031	.036	.036
7								.004	.014	.027	.04	.048	.05	.047	.041
6							.009	.027	.048	.063	.069	.067	.059	.048	.036
5						.02	.052	.081	.096	.095	.083	.067	.05	.036	.024
4					.044	.098	.131	.136	.12	.095	.07	.048	.031	.02	.012
3				.097	.175	.196	.175	.136	.096	.063	.04	.024	.014	.008	.004
2			.213	.291	.263	.196	.131	.082	.048	.027	.015	.008	.004	.002	.001
1		.464	.427	.291	.175	.098	.053	.027	.014	.007	.003	.002	8E-04	4E-04	2E-04
0		.464	.213	.097	.044	.02	.009	.004	.002	8E-04	3E-04	1E-04	6E-05	3E-05	1E-05

	0	1	2	3	4	5	6	7	8	9	10	11	12	13	14
P_0	1	.929	.853	.776	.7	.628	.56	.496	.439	.386	.339	.297	.26	.227	.198
Forward rate	7.67	8.27	8.81	9.31	9.75	10.16	10.52	10.85	11.15	11.42	11.67	11.89	12.09	12.27	

FIGURE 14.11 Match of term structure. The observed spot rate curve is given at the top of the figure. Below that are listed some assumed values for the a_k's. Using these a_k's, the short rate lattice is constructed and the elementary prices are computed by the forward equations. The elementary prices are summed column by column to obtain the zero-coupon bond prices, and these are converted to the forward rates shown in the bottom row. An equation-solving routine is run which adjusts the assumed a_k's until the bottom row agrees with the spot rates shown at the top.

the price of a zero-coupon bond with maturity at that date. From these prices, the spot rates can be directly computed. The equation-solving routine is run, adjusting the a_k's until the bottom row matches the assumed spot rate values given in the second row.

The spreadsheet method takes advantage of the forward equation and is an appropriate method when the number of periods is not large. When the number of periods is really large, it is better to take advantage of the fact that the spot rate s_1 depends only on a_0, s_2 depends only on a_0, a_1, and so forth. The a_i's can therefore be found sequentially by a very rapid process.

The Black–Derman–Toy Model

An alternative to the model given by (14.3) is to assume that the values in the short rate lattice are of the form

$$r_{ks} = a_k e^{b_k s}. \tag{14.4}$$

This can be viewed as a Ho–Lee model applied to $\ln r_{ks}$. In this case b_k represents the volatility of the logarithm of the short rate from time $k - 1$ to k.

In the simplest version of the Black–Derman–Toy model, the values of b_k are all equal to a value b. The a_k's are then assigned so that the implied term structure matches the observed forward rates. The computational method is very similar to that for the Ho–Lee model.

Matching Volatilities

The procedure of this section can be extended to match volatilities[5] of the spot rates as well as the spot rates themselves. To carry out this extended match, both the a_k's and the b_k's are varied. The volatilities of the spot rates are first observed by recording a history of each of the spot rates. For example, a history of the rates for 2-year zero-coupon bonds will provide an estimate of both the 2-year spot rate and the volatility of that rate. It is likely that the volatilities associated with different maturities will differ. In fact, it is common to define a term structure volatility curve as well as a term structure rate curve.

14.8 IMMUNIZATION

Our new understanding of interest rate fluctuations and their impact on the term structure provides the basis for a new, more sophisticated approach to bond portfolio

---

[5]The probabilities used are risk-neutral probabilities, so strictly speaking, the b_k's determine risk-neutral volatilities. However, for small time periods the real probabilities are close to one-half, so real and risk-neutral volatilities are approximately equal.

immunization, as discussed in Chapters 3, 4, and 5. In those earlier chapters uncertainty was not treated explicitly; instead, a portfolio was immunized against parallel shifts in the spot rate curve. However, we saw in Section 14.2 that the parallel shift assumption is not only simplistic, but in fact inconsistent with a theory that precludes arbitrage. The new approach does not have that weakness.

The new approach is based on the binomial lattice framework. Suppose that we have a series of cash obligations to be paid at specific times in the future, say, up to year n. Suppose also that we have decided on a specific binomial lattice representation of the short rate. Then we can compute the initial value of the obligation stream using this lattice. One way to compute this value is to first find the term structure at time zero (using the forward equations) and then compute the present value of the obligation stream, just as we learned to do in Chapter 4. Alternatively, but equivalently, we can compute the initial value of the obligation stream by applying the risk-neutral discounting backward process to the obligation stream. The value at the initial node will be the initial (present) value of the stream. To honor the obligation stream, we must have a bond portfolio with this same present value.

After the first period, the value of the obligation stream can take on either of two possible values, corresponding to the values at the two successor nodes. For simplicity assume that no payments must be made at this time. The value at a particular node would correspond to the present value that would be obtained using the new term structure at that node. Likewise, our bond portfolio will have new values at the two successor nodes. Our portfolio is immunized if its value at each of the two successor nodes exactly matches the present value of the obligation at those nodes. In other words, to immunize for one period, we must match the present values at *three* places—the initial node and the two successor nodes.

The matching might seem complex, but because of the no-arbitrage property of the interest rate structure, things fall into place very nicely. To see how this works, imagine two different bonds that are valued at $1 at time zero. One of these bonds is the single-period, risk-free bond that pays $1 + r_{00}$ at each of the two successor nodes. The other is $1 worth of a zero-coupon bond that matures at year n. This second bond will have a relatively low value next period if the spot rate increases, but it will have a relatively large value if the spot rate decreases. The two bonds provide two independent outcomes for the next period, and therefore they can be used in combination to replicate the one-period performance of any other interest rate instrument. In particular, they can be combined to replicate the behavior of the obligation.

The solution to the immunization problem is now clear. Using any two dissimilar bonds, we construct a portfolio having the same values at both of the next two states. By the no-arbitrage property, the initial value of this portfolio will be equal to the initial value of the obligation stream that it replicates. Furthermore, the total portfolio consisting of these bonds and the obligation stream is immunized in the sense that its net value is exactly zero initially and at the next period, no matter which state occurs. After one period, the portfolio can be rebalanced to obtain immunization for the next period as well. By continuing to rebalance each period (with the result dependent on the state that occurs), complete immunization over all periods is possible.

Bond 1		70.96636
	65.95147	71.05353
Bond 2		109.4342
	101.6677	109.497
Obligation		67.59499
	62.80256	67.64404

FIGURE 14.12   Initial branching of values. The initial and next-period values of the two bonds and an obligation are shown. A combination of the bonds will replicate the obligation for one period.

Example 14.8 (Our earlier problem)   We consider again the immunization problem of Example 4.8 in Chapter 4. In this problem we have a $1 million obligation at the end of 5 years. We wish to immunize this obligation with two bonds. Bond 1 is a 12-year 6% bond with a price of $65.95. Bond 2 is a 5-year 10% bond with a price of $101.65. The spot rate curve is known and is equal to that of the Ho–Lee matching problem solved in the last section.

To carry out the immunization we use the short rate lattice found in Example 14.7, since this matches the term structure given in the earlier example. Using this lattice we solve backward for the prices of each of the two bonds and of the obligation. We need to know the results only for the first two periods, which are shown in Figure 14.12. (The initial prices differ slightly from the prices computed earlier due to rounding errors in the lattice.) In each case, the values shown are percentages of the face value.

To construct the immunization, we let x_1 and x_2 be the number of units of bond 1 and bond 2, respectively, in the portfolio. We then solve the equations

$$65.95147x_1 + 101.6677x_2 = 628,025.6 \tag{14.5}$$

$$70.96636x_1 + 109.4342x_2 = 675,949.9 \tag{14.6}$$

(It is not necessary to replicate explicitly state 0 in period 1. This will occur automatically; otherwise there would be an arbitrage opportunity—which is impossible.) The result is that

$$x_1 = 2,165.66 \tag{14.7}$$

$$x_2 = 4,772.38. \tag{14.8}$$

This solution is quite *insensitive* to the volatility assumed when constructing the short rate lattice. Note that the solution is very close to the values of 2,208.17 and 4,744.03 obtained using the standard duration matching method presented in Chapter 4. This seems to be generally true, and hence despite the deeper elegance of the lattice theory, the conventional method of duration matching is frequently used in practice with good results.

14.9 COLLATERALIZED MORTGAGE OBLIGATIONS*

Collateralized mortgage obligations (CMOs) are securities constructed from mortgage pools. The cash flow derived from a pool is sliced up in various ways, and the individual slices define the payout of a particular CMO. The slicing process can be quite intricate, for rather than merely apportioning the principal or the interest payment stream, CMOs are made up of slices that vary the fraction of interest and principal over time. There are numerous variations of the general theme, and new designs are introduced frequently.

The motivating force behind the introduction of CMOs is the prepayment option inherent in real estate mortgages. Homeowners can pay the balance of their mortgage at any time (with some restrictions) and therefore terminate the mortgage. This pre-payment feature means that the payment stream of a mortgage is not fixed in advance because the principal might be paid early. This timing uncertainty is somewhat alle-viated by the averaging effect derived from a pool, but it is not entirely eliminated because the prepayment pattern cannot be fully predicted. CMOs were devised in order to reduce the variability of the of cash flow due to prepayments.

CMOs were first issued by the Federal Home Loan Mortgage Corporation (called Freddie Mac), which buys individual mortgages and forms pools. CMOs issued by Freddie Mac are federally insured against default. Other agencies and corporations now offer CMOs, but those originated by Freddie Mac make up the majority of the market.

The first CMOs were **sequential** CMOs, and they are still very common. In this structure the principal payments are assigned in sequence to different **classes,** or **tranches,** of CMO bonds. Typically there are four to twelve different classes. The total principal of the pool is first divided among the classes. In the early years, mortgage payments received by the pool are used to pay interest to all classes in proportion to their existing unpaid principal balances, unless they are defined to be Z bonds, in which case owed interest is not paid but instead is accrued and added to the principal balance of that class. The remaining portion of the received mortgage payments is paid to the first class to reduce its principal balance. This continues until the first class is fully retired. After that, the principal of the second class is reduced until it is retired, and so on. Once all previous classes are retired, a Z class bond receives income to reduce its (now greater) principal and to pay interest on that principal.

For example, suppose there are three classes A, B, and Z. Then, as the first mortgage payments are received, interest is paid to classes A and B, and the remaining income is distributed to the A class to reduce its principal. The interest that is due to class Z is paid as principal to class A, thereby speeding the retirement of that class. This foregone interest also augments the principal owed to the Z class. When class A is retired, the principal payments pass to class B, and then finally to class Z. The principal balance patterns are illustrated in Figure 14.13 for a 20-year mortgage pool.

The valuation of CMOs depends very much on the assumed prepayment pattern. A simple approach is to assume a fixed pattern over time. There is in fact a benchmark pattern adopted by the Public Securities Association (PSA). This pattern assumes a prepayment rate of .2% (on an annual basis) the first month, .4% the second month, .6% the third month, and so forth until month 30. After that, the prepayment rate is assumed to be fixed at 6% annually = .5% monthly. For this pattern, or those similar to it, it is easy to project the cash flow pattern for any of the CMO classes. The corresponding value of the CMO class can then be obtained by straightforward discounting using the current spot rate curve. No lattice or tree calculations are required.

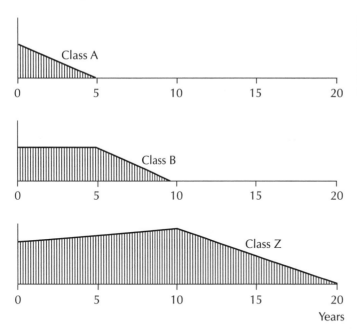

FIGURE 14.13 Principal balance patterns of a three-class sequential CMO. Class A is paid principal before the other classes. When class A is retired, then class B is paid. Class Z does not receive interest until all previous classes are retired. Instead its interest is accrued, augmenting the principal balance.

In actuality, prepayments depend on prevailing interest rates. Homeowners are more likely to refinance their loans (which entails prepayment of the existing loan) when interest rates are relatively low. Using such a model, a CMO class can be valued using the lattice and tree techniques that we have studied.

Example 14.9 (Quick, buy this CMO)   Mr. Johnathan Quick, the city treasurer of White Falls, is young, well educated, and wants to modernize the financial affairs of the city. A major New York bank has urged him to purchase, for White Falls' account, a portion of class A of a CMO originated by Freddie Mac. This CMO has four classes A, B, C, and Z, each entitled to one-fourth of the principal of a pool of 30-year mortgages carrying an interest rate of 12%. He has been told that these mortgages are guaranteed by the federal government. The current short rate is 10% and the price that he is quoted for the class A bonds is 105.00.

Mr. Quick decides to carry out a simple prototype valuation of this CMO. To do this he first makes a few simple calculations. The yearly payment on a 30-year 12% mortgage is found (see Chapter 3) to be 12.41 per hundred. The interest that will be paid to each of the classes B and C while A is not yet retired is $25 \times 12\% = 3$.

He then constructs a short rate lattice covering 4 years, as shown at the top of Figure 14.14. (The lattice starts at the top left node. The successor nodes are the two nodes in the next row.) This lattice has risk-neutral probabilities of .5. Next he assigns estimated prepayment rates. He assigns a 5% annual rate whenever the short rate goes down, and a 2% rate when the short rate goes up. He then puts the remaining pool size fraction on the short rate lattice (shown as a separate array in Figure 14.14).

```
.100                Short rate lattice            1.000           Pool size lattice
.095      .115                                    .950      .980
.090      .110      .130                          .903      .931      .960
.085      .105      .125      .145                .857      .884      .912      .941
```

```
25.000              Principal tree
├─────────────────────────────────────┐
16.436                               19.526
├─────────────────┐                  ├─────────────────┐
7.969           10.756             10.759           13.725
├────────┐      ├────────┐         ├────────┐      ├────────┐
0.000    2.041  2.026    4.704     2.029    4.707  4.703    7.551
```

```
25.758              Value tree
├─────────────────────────────────────┐
28.627                               28.041
├─────────────────┐                  ├─────────────────┐
18.860          18.508             21.969           21.665
├────────┐      ├────────┐         ├────────┐      ├────────┐
9.405    8.953  12.074   12.026    12.078   12.029 15.351   15.207
```

FIGURE 14.14 Quick's CMO valuation. The top of the figure shows the short rate lattice. Next to that is the lattice showing the corresponding pool size fraction. These lattices start at the top and move downward. A down move is a move directly downward, and an up move is a move downward to the right. Below these is the tree of principal due class A, and finally the corresponding tree of values for class A.

Quick must keep track of the principal owed to class A. Unfortunately, this principal is path dependent in the original lattice. So he decides that he must use a binomial tree rather than a lattice. He establishes the initial principal to be 25, since class A is entitled to 25% of the total. He arranges his tree in the downward flowing manner, as shown in Figure 14.14. As an example calculation, the final value in the tree is

$$13.725 \times 1.12 - 12.41 \times .960 + 2 \times 3.00$$
$$-(.960 - .941)[13.725 + 50 + 25(1.12)^3] = 7.551.$$

In words, the new principal is the old principal times 1 plus the interest rate on the loan (12%), minus the total payment made by the remaining pool, plus the interest payments that must go to classes B and C (but not Z), minus the new prepayment amounts (which is the change in pool size times the total remaining principal). The tree is terminated after 3 years. Mr. Quick assumes that the remaining small amounts of principal will be paid to class A the following year.

To find the value of the class A bond, he uses a tree to carry out backward risk-neutral valuation. A year 3 node value is equal to the year 3 cash flow plus a discounted version of next year's principal and interest. The value at an earlier node is equal to the cash flow at that node plus the discounted expected value of the successor node values. For example, the final node value is

$$7.551 \times 1.12/1.145 + 12.41 \times .960 - 2 \times 3.00$$
$$+(.960 - .941)[13.725 + 50 + 25(1.12)^3] = 15.207.$$

The final node in the previous row is

$$12.41 \times .980 - 2 \times 3.00 + (.980 - .960)[19.526 + 50 + 25(1.12)^2]$$
$$+.5(15.351 + 15.207)/1.130 = 21.665.$$

The overall value is 25.758, which when normalized to a base of 100 is $4 \times 25.758 = 103.032$. Mr. Quick concludes that the offered price of 105.00 may be a bit high.

He then runs his spreadsheet program again after adding 1 percentage point to each of the short rates and finds the value of 101.112 and therefore concludes that an effective modified duration is $D_M = 100(103.032 - 101.112)/103.032 = 1.863$ years. This is in accord with the observation that the class A bond is retired very quickly.

Mr. Quick decides to investigate other classes, which he believes may offer substantially greater financial return and whose analyses are sure to offer substantially greater intellectual occupation.

The preceding example shows that the evaluation of CMOs can be quite challenging. If one attempted to carry out the tree methodology of that example, but on a monthly basis and for evaluation of the other classes, very large trees would be required. The main difficulty, of course, is that principal amounts are path dependent. It is for this reason that, in practice, CMO evaluation techniques are usually based on simulation (Monte Carlo) methods. However, it should also be clear from the example that the conceptual principles outlined in the past few chapters are appropriate for this area of finance.

14.10 MODELS OF INTEREST RATE DYNAMICS*

In previous sections the short rate was assigned directly by specifying it at every time and state. Although this is a good and practical method, an alternative is to specify the short rate as a process defined by an Ito equation, similar to the processes used to define stock behavior. This allows us to work in continuous time.

In this approach we specify that the (instantaneous) short rate $r(t)$ satisfies an equation of the Ito type,

$$dr = \mu(r, t)\, dt + \sigma(r, t)\, d\hat{z}. \tag{14.9}$$

where $\hat{z}(t)$ is a standardized Wiener process in the risk-neutral world. Given an initial condition $r(0)$, the equation defines a stochastic process $r(t)$.

Many such models have been proposed as being good approximations to actual interest rate processes. We list a few of the best-known models:

1. Rendleman and Bartter model

$$dr = mr\, dt + \sigma r\, d\hat{z}.$$

This model copies the standard geometric Brownian motion model used for stock dynamics. It leads to lognormal distributions of future short rates. It is now, however, rarely advocated as a realistic model of the short rate process.

2. Ho–Lee model

$$dr = \theta(t)\, dt + \sigma\, d\hat{z}.$$

This is the continuous-time limit of the Ho–Lee model. The function $\theta(t)$ is chosen so that the resulting forward rate curve matches the current term structure. A potential difficulty with the model is that $r(t)$ may be negative for some t.

3. Black–Derman–Toy model

$$d\ln r = \theta(t)\, dt + \sigma\, d\hat{z}.$$

This is virtually identical to the Ho–Lee model, except that the underlying variable is $\ln r$ rather than r. Using Ito's lemma, it can be transformed to the equivalent form

$$dr = [\theta(t) + \tfrac{1}{2}\sigma^2]r\, dt + \sigma r\, d\hat{z}.$$

4. Vasicek model

$$dr = a(b - r)\, dt + \sigma\, d\hat{z}.$$

The model has the feature of **mean reversion** in that it tends to be pulled to the value b. Again, it is possible for $r(t)$ to be negative, but this is less likely than in other models because of the mean-reversion effect. Indeed, if there were no stochastic term (that is, if $\sigma = 0$), then r would decrease if it were above b and it would increase if it were below b. This feature of mean reversion is considered to be quite important by many researchers and practitioners since it is felt that interest rates have a *natural* home (of about 6%) and that if rates differ widely from this home value, there is a strong tendency to move back to it.

5. Cox, Ingersoll, and Ross model

$$dr = a(b - r)\, dt + c\sqrt{r}\, d\hat{z}.$$

In this model not only does the drift have mean reversion, but the stochastic term is multiplied by $\sqrt{r}$, implying that the variance of the process increases as the rate r itself increases.

6. Hull and White model

$$dr = [\theta(t) - ar]\, dt + \sigma\, d\hat{z}.$$

This model is essentially the Ho–Lee model with a mean reversion term appended.

7. Black and Karasinski model

$$d\ln r = (\theta - a\ln r)\, dt + \sigma\, d\hat{z}.$$

This is the Black–Derman–Toy model with mean reversion.

All of these models are referred to as **single-factor models** because they each depend on a single Wiener process $\hat{z}$. There are other models that are **multifactor,** which depend on two or more underlying Wiener processes.

14.11 CONTINUOUS-TIME SOLUTIONS*

The three general methods of solution in discrete time each have a continuous-time analytic counterpart: (1) the method of backward recursion becomes a generalized Black–Scholes partial differential equation, (2) the method of discounted risk-neutral evaluation becomes evaluation of an integral, and (3) the forward recursion method becomes a forward partial differential equation that is dual to the Black–Scholes equation. We shall give some details on the first two of these methods.

The Backward Equation

The backward equation is perhaps the most useful. Suppose the short rate is governed by the Ito equation (14.9) in a risk-neutral world. And suppose $f(r, t)$ is a price function for an interest rate security with no payments except at the terminal time. Then it can be shown that f is governed by the generalized Black–Scholes equation

$$\frac{\partial f}{\partial t} + \frac{\partial f}{\partial r}\mu(r, t) + \frac{1}{2}\frac{\partial^2 f}{\partial r^2}\sigma(r, t)^2 - rf(r, t) = 0. \tag{14.10}$$

The boundary condition is defined at $t = T$ and depends on the final payoff structure. This equation is analogous to backward recursion.

For example, suppose we denote by $P(r, t, T)$ the price at time t of a zero-coupon bond maturing at time T when the current short rate (at t) is r. We define the function $f(r, t) = P(r, t, T)$, and the appropriate boundary condition is $f(r, T) = 1$.

In some cases the backward equation (14.10) can be solved analytically, and this leads to analytic formulas for valuing interest rate derivative securities. In practice, however, numerical solutions are usually required.

Example 14.10 (Constant interest rate)   The simplest case is when the short rate is governed by $dr = 0$, implying that the interest rate is constant. To find the price $P(r, t, T)$ of a zero-coupon bond, we set $f(r, t) = P(r, t, T)$. However, since r is constant, we may suppress the dependence on r and write $f(t)$. The backward equation reduces to

$$\frac{df(t)}{dt} - rf(t) = 0.$$

This can be written as

$$\frac{df(t)}{f(t)} = r\,dt$$

or, equivalently, as

$$d \ln f(t) = r \, dt.$$

This has solution

$$\ln f(t) = c + rt$$

where c is a constant. The boundary condition gives $f(T) = 1$ or, equivalently, $\ln f(T) = 0$. Hence we put $c = -rT$. The final solution is therefore

$$P(t, T) = e^{-r(T-t)}$$

which agrees with what we know about bond values when the interest rate is constant.

Example 14.11 (A Ho–Lee solution)   As a somewhat more complex example of an analytic solution consider the special case where the short rate is governed by

$$dr = a \, dt + \sigma \, d\hat{z}.$$

We will try to find the zero-coupon bond price $P(r, t, T)$. We set $f(r, t) = P(r, t, T)$ and solve (14.10). Motivated by the solution to the previous example, we try a solution of the form

$$f(r, t) = A(t, T)e^{-r(T-t)}.$$

Substituting this in the Black–Scholes equation, we find

$$\frac{dA(t, T)}{dt} - (T - t) A(t, T)a + \tfrac{1}{2}(T - t)^2 \sigma^2 A(t, T) = 0$$

where the common factor $e^{-r(T-t)}$ has been canceled from every term. This leads to the equation

$$d \ln A(t, T) = [(T - t)a - \tfrac{1}{2}(T - t)^2 \sigma^2] \, dt.$$

Accounting for the boundary condition $\ln A(T, T) = 0$, we find

$$\ln A(t, T) = -\tfrac{1}{2}(T - t)^2 a + \tfrac{1}{6}(T - t)^3 \sigma^2.$$

We thus have an explicit formula for $P(r, T, t)$.

Risk-Neutral Pricing Formula

The discounted risk-neutral pricing formula also works in the continuous-time case, and it can be used to define the value of any interest rate derivative security. Suppose the security pays a dividend of $Y(r, t)$ at t, and suppose that the short rate is governed by the risk-neutral process

$$dr = \mu(r, t) \, dt + \sigma(r, t) \, d\hat{z}.$$

Then the value of the security at time zero is

$$v(0) = \hat{E} \left\{ \int_0^T \exp \left[\int_0^t -r(s) \, ds \right] Y(r, t) \, dt \right\} \tag{14.11}$$

where $\hat{E}$ denotes expectation with respect to the risk-neutral probability defined by the process $\hat{z}$. Of course, this formula can rarely be evaluated directly. It does, however, provide a basis for simulation.

14.12 SUMMARY

Interest rate securities are extremely important because almost every investment entails interest rate risk. Interest rate derivatives, such as bond options, swaps, adjustable-rate mortgages, and mortgage-backed securities, can help control that risk. Analysis of interest rate securities requires a model of term structure variations. Simple models that merely add randomness to a term structure curve are not suitable because they may inadvertently allow arbitrage opportunities.

An elegant and workable approach is to define a short rate lattice spanning several time periods. The rate listed at each node is the interest rate that would apply at that node for loans of one period in length. Two sets of probabilities, are assigned to the arcs of the lattice. The first set defines the *real* probabilities, giving the likelihoods of various transitions. The second set defines the risk-neutral probabilities used for evaluation. Indeed, only the second set is needed for pricing interest rate derivatives.

Once the short rate lattice together with the risk-neutral probabilities is constructed, a security such as a bond can be valued by discounted risk-neutral pricing, working backward through the lattice. The short rate at a node defines the discount factor to be used as the process passes through that node.

Seemingly complex securities, such as options on bonds, options on bond futures, and adjustable-rate mortgages, can be evaluated with the discounted risk-neutral approach. In some cases the quantities necessary to determine the cash flow at a node are path dependent, in the sense that these quantities depend on the path to a node as well as on the node itself. In such cases a tree, rather than a lattice, can be used to accurately record the necessary information for the discounted risk-neutral valuation process. However, this can lead to a large increase in the number of nodes. There is a special method termed leveling that transforms an apparently path dependent situation into one that is not path dependent. This method is applicable when the cash flow at a node depends on the node itself and is a linear function of an underlying path-dependent variable. Adjustable-rate loans can be evaluated with this method.

An entire term structure can be extracted from the short rate lattice. One way to do this is to value zero-coupon bonds of all possible maturities. This method requires numerous separate valuation processes. A more efficient way to find the term structure is to construct a lattice of elementary prices. This can be done with a single forward sweep through the original short rate lattice.

The short rate lattice must be constructed carefully in order to give useful results. One common strategy is to construct the lattice so that the term structure that it implies matches the current term structure. Often some volatilities are matched as well. Two of the simplest methods are the Ho–Lee method and the Black–Derman–Toy method.

The short rate lattice also provides a new approach to bond portfolio immunization. In this approach, the portfolio is immunized against initial up and down movements in the short rate.

An important and challenging application of the methodology of interest rate derivative valuation is collateralized mortgage obligations (CMOs). These instruments can have very complex structures, which require careful analysis for proper evaluation. Usually some aspect of their mathematical representation is path dependent, and hence trees or Monte Carlo methods must be employed.

Continuous-time models of the term structure can be constructed by defining a short rate Ito process. This process is driven by a specified risk-neutral standardized Wiener process. Some models of this type lead to analytic expressions for their associated term structure.

EXERCISES

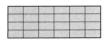

1. (A callable bond ⊕)   Construct a short rate lattice for periods (years) 0 through 9 with an initial rate of 6% and with successive rates determined by a multiplicative factor of either $u = 1.2$ or $d = .9$. Assign the risk-neutral probabilities to be .5.

   (a) Using this lattice, find the value of a 10-year 6% bond.
   (b) Suppose this bond can be called by the issuing party at any time after 5 years. (When the bond is called, the face value plus the currently due coupon are paid at that time and the bond is canceled.) What is the fair value of this bond?

2. (General adjustable formula)   Let V_{ks} be the value of an adjustable-rate loan initiated at period k and state s with initial principal of 100. The loan is to be fully paid at period n. The interest rate charged each period is the short rate of that period plus a premium p. The loan payment for a period is the amount that would be required to amortize the loan at the charged interest rate equally over the remaining periods. Write an explicit backward recursion formula for V_{ks} as a function of k and s.

3. (Bond futures option)   Explain how you would find the value of a bond futures option.

4. (Adjustable-rate CAP ⊕)   Suppose that the adjustable-rate auto loan of Example 14.5 is modified by the provision of a CAP that guarantees the borrower that the interest rate to be applied will never exceed 11%. What is the value of this loan to the bank?

5. (Forward construction ⊕)   Use the forward equation to find the spot rate curve for the lattice constructed in Exercise 1.

6. (Ho–Lee volatility)   Show that for the Ho–Lee model the (risk-neutral) standard deviation of the one-period rate is exactly $b_k/2$.

7. (Term match ⊕)   Use the Black–Derman–Toy model with $b = .01$ to match the term structure of Example 14.7.

8. (Swaps)   Consider a plain vanilla interest rate swap where party A agrees to make six yearly payments to party B of a fixed rate of interest on a notional principal of $10 million and in exchange party B will make six yearly payments to party A at the floating short

rate on the same notional principal. Assume that the short rate process is described by the lattice of Example 14.1.

(a) Set up a lattice that gives the value of the floating rate cash flow stream at every short rate node, and thereby determine the initial value of this stream.

(b) What fixed rate of interest would equalize both sides of the swap? (Compare with Exercise 11, Chapter 10.)

9. (Swaption pricing)   A swaption is an option to enter a swap arrangement in the future. Suppose that company B has a debt of $10 million financed over 6 years at a fixed rate of interest of 8.64%. Company A offers to sell company B a swaption to swap the fixed rate obligation for a floating rate obligation, with payments equal to the short rate, with the same principal and the same termination date. The swaption can be exercised at the beginning of year 2 (just after the payment for the previous year and when the short rate for the coming year is known). Assuming that the short rate process is that of Example 14.1, how much is this swaption worth?

10. (Change of variable ◇)   Suppose a short rate process in a risk-neutral world is defined by

$$dr = \mu(r, t)\, dt + \sigma(r, t)\, d\hat{z}$$

where $\hat{z}(t)$ is a standardized Wiener process. A standard way to approximate this equation at a point (r, t) over a small interval Δt is by the binomial tree shown in Figure 14.15. In this approximation,

$$r^+ = r + \sigma(r, t)\sqrt{\Delta t}$$
$$r^- = r - \sigma(r, t)\sqrt{\Delta t}$$
$$q = \frac{1}{2} + \frac{\mu(r, t)\sqrt{\Delta t}}{2\sigma(r, t)}.$$

(a) Show that in general this does not produce a recombining lattice. That is, show that an up move followed by a down move is not the same as a down move followed by an up move.

(b) Consider the change of variable

$$w(r, t) = \int_0^r \frac{dy}{\sigma(y, t)}.$$

Use Ito's lemma to write the process satisfied by $w(r, t)$, and show that its volatility term is constant. Conclude that the binomial approximation for $w(r, t)$ is recombining.

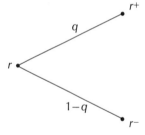

FIGURE 14.15   Approximation method. A short rate process can be approximated by a binomial lattice if an appropriate change of variable is used.

(*c*) Find the appropriate change of variable for the geometric process

$$dr = \mu r\, dt + \sigma r\, d\hat{z}.$$

11. (Ho–Lee term structure)   Refer to Example 14.11. Let $F(t)$ be the forward rate from 0 to t. By the basic definition of the forward rate, we have the identity

$$e^{-F(t)t} = P(r, 0, t).$$

Find an explicit formula for $F(t)$.

12. (Continuous zero $\diamond$)   Gavin wants to dig deep into pricing theory, so he decides to work out an application of Eq. (14.11). He suggests to himself that a simple model of interest rates in the risk-neutral world might be

$$dr = \sigma\, d\hat{z}$$

where $\hat{z}$ is standard Brownian motion, and where $r(0) = r_0$. He is working out a formula for the value of a zero-coupon bond that pays \$1 at time T, based on Equation (14.11), without using the Black–Scholes equation. Can you? Compare with Example 14.11.

REFERENCES

For general textbook presentations of interest rate derivatives see [1, 2]. The forward equation was presented in Jamshidian [3]. The Ho–Lee model was originally developed in [4] without the benefit of the short rate lattice concept. The short rate lattice was used in the presentation of the Black–Derman–Toy model in [5]. A more complex interest rate process, not describable as a single-factor model, is that of Heath, Jarrow, and Morton [6]. For an outline of CMOs and mortgage-backed securities, see [7]. For continuous-time models, see [8–13]. Exercise 10 is based on [14].

1. Hull, J. C. (1993), *Options, Futures and Other Derivative Securities*, 2nd ed., Prentice Hall, Englewood Cliffs, NJ.
2. Duffie, D. (1996), *Dynamic Asset Pricing,* 2nd ed., Princeton University Press, Princeton, NJ.
3. Jamshidian, F. (1991), "Forward Induction and Construction of Yield Curve Diffusion Models," *Journal of Fixed Income*, **1,** 62–74.
4. Ho, T. S. Y., and S.-B. Lee (1986), "Term Structure Movements and Pricing Interest Rate Contingent Claims," *Journal of Finance,* **41,** 1011–1029.
5. Black, F., E. Derman, and W. Toy (1990), "A One-Factor Model of Interest Rates and Its Application to Treasury Bond Options," *Financial Analysts Journal*, January-February, **46,** 33–39.
6. Heath, D., R. Jarrow, and A. Morton (1990), "Bond Pricing and the Term Structure of Interest Rates: A Discrete Time Approximation," *Journal of Financial and Quantitative Analysis*, **25,** 419–440.
7. Fabozzi, F. J., Ed. (1988), *The Handbook of Mortgage-Backed Securities*, rev. ed., Probus, Chicago, IL.
8. Brennan, M., and E. Schwartz (1979), "A Continuous Time Approach to the Pricing of Bonds," *Journal of Banking and Finance*, **3,** 133–155.
9. Vasicek, O. A. (1977), "An Equilibrium Characterization of the Term Structure," *Journal of Financial Economics*, **5,** 177–188.

10. Hull, J., and A. White (1990), "Pricing Interest Rate Derivative Securities," *Review of Financial Studies*, **3,** 573–592.
11. Black, F., and P. Karasinski (1991), "Bond and Option Pricing when Short Rates are Lognormal," *Financial Analysts Journal*, July-August, **47,** 52–59.
12. Rendleman, R., and B. Bartter (1980), "The Pricing of Options on Debt Securities," *Journal of Financial and Quantitative Analysis,* **15,** March, 11–24.
13. Cox, J. C., J. E. Ingersoll, and S. A. Ross (1985), "A Theory of the Term Structure of Interest Rates," *Econometrica*, **53,** 385–407.
14. Nelson, D., and K. Ramaswamy (1989), "Simple Binomial Processes as Diffusion Approximations in Financial Models," *Review of Financial Studies,* **3,** 393–430.

PART IV

GENERAL CASH
FLOW STREAMS

15 OPTIMAL PORTFOLIO GROWTH

Conclusions about multiperiod investment situations are not mere variations of single-period conclusions—rather they often *reverse* those earlier conclusions. This makes the subject exciting, both intellectually and in practice. Once the subtleties of multiperiod investment are understood, the reward in terms of enhanced investment performance can be substantial.

Fortunately the concepts and methods of analysis for multiperiod situations build on those of earlier chapters. Internal rate of return, present value, the comparison principle, portfolio design, and lattice and tree valuation all have natural extensions to general situations. But conclusions such as volatility is "bad" or diversification is "good" are no longer universal truths. The story is much more interesting.

This chapter begins the story by extending the elementary concept of internal rate of return, showing how to design portfolios that have maximal growth. The next chapter extends present value analysis.

15.1 THE INVESTMENT WHEEL

Understanding portfolio growth requires that one adopt a long-term viewpoint. To highlight the importance of such a viewpoint, consider the investment wheel shown in Figure 15.1. You are able to place a bet on any of the three sectors of the wheel. In fact, you may invest different amounts on each of the sectors independently. The numbers in the sectors denote the winnings for that sector after the wheel is spun. For example, if the wheel stops with the pointer at the top sector after a spin, you will receive $3 for every $1 you invested on that sector (which means a net profit of $2).

The top sector is very attractive, paying 3 to 1, even though the area of that sector is a full one-half of the entire wheel. A $1 bet (or investment) will return either $0 or $3, each with a probability of one-half. The expected gain is therefore $\frac{1}{2} \times \$3 + \frac{1}{2} \times \$0 - \$1 = \$.50$. This is quite favorable.

417

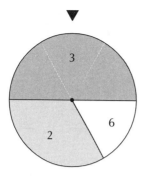

FIGURE 15.1   The investment wheel. The numbers shown are the payoffs for a one-unit investment on that sector. The wheel is favorable and can be expected to cause capital to grow if investments are properly managed.

The lower left sector, on the other hand, has unfavorable odds, since it pays only 2 to 1 for an area that is only one-third of the total. A bit better is the lower right segment, which pays even odds, since it pays 6 to 1 and is one-sixth of the area.

Suppose now that you start with $100 and have the opportunity to bet part or all of your money repeatedly, reinvesting your winnings on successive spins of the wheel. Because of the favorable top segment, you can make your capital grow over the long run through judicious investment. The question is, just what constitutes judicious investment?

Based on the odds we calculated, it seems appropriate to concentrate your attention (and your capital) on the top sector. One strategy would be to invest all of your money on that sector. Indeed, this strategy is the one that produces the highest single-period expected return. An investment of $100 is expected to gain an additional $50 on the very first spin. The problem is that you go broke half of the time and cannot continue with other spins. Even if you win and continue with this strategy, you will again face the risk of ruin at the next spin. Most people find this strategy too risky when given the opportunity to play repeatedly.

A second, more conservative, strategy would be to invest, say, one-half of your money on the top sector each spin, holding back the other half. That way if an unfavorable outcome occurs, you are not out of the game entirely.[1] But it is not clear that this is the best that can be done.

Analysis of the Wheel

To begin a systematic search for a good strategy, let us limit our investigation to **fixed-proportions** strategies. These are strategies that prescribe proportions to each sector of the wheel, these proportions being used to apportion current wealth among the sectors as bets at each spin. Let us number the sectors 1, 2, and 3, corresponding to top, left, and right, respectively. A general fixed-proportions strategy for the wheel is then described by a set of three numbers $(\alpha_1, \alpha_2, \alpha_3)$, where each $\alpha_i \geq 0$, $i = 1, 2, 3$, and where $\alpha_1 + \alpha_2 + \alpha_3 \leq 1$. The α_i's correspond to the proportions bet on the different

---

[1]This wheel investment problem actually makes a good game for a group, using play money or keeping records. Actual play forces people to think exactly how they wish to invest. The main point is that investment for the long run is not the same as investment for a single spin.

sectors. The remaining $1 - \alpha_1 - \alpha_2 - \alpha_3$ is held in reserve. As an example, the strategy mentioned earlier of investing one-half of your capital in the top segment each time is $(\frac{1}{2}, 0, 0)$.

Each fixed-proportions strategy leads to a series of multiplicative factors that govern the growth of capital. For example, suppose you bet $100 using the $(\frac{1}{2}, 0, 0)$ strategy. For one spin there are two possibilities: (1) with probability one-half you obtain a favorable outcome and end up with $50 + 3 \times \$50 = \$200$; and (2) with probability one-half you obtain an unfavorable outcome and end up with just $50. In general, with this strategy your money will be either doubled or halved at each spin, each possibility occurring with probability one-half. The multiplicative factors for one spin are thus 2 and $\frac{1}{2}$, each with probability one-half. After a long series of investments following this strategy, your initial $100 will be multiplied by an overall multiple that might be of the form $(\frac{1}{2})(\frac{1}{2})(2)(\frac{1}{2})(2)(2) \cdots (2)(\frac{1}{2})$, with about an equal number of 2's and $\frac{1}{2}$'s. Hence the overall factor is likely to be about 1. This means that during the course of many spins, your capital will tend to fluctuate up and down, but is unlikely to grow appreciably.

An alternative strategy is to bet one-fourth of your money on the top sector, corresponding to the strategy $(\frac{1}{4}, 0, 0)$. If that top sector is the outcome of a spin, your money will be multiplied by $1 - \frac{1}{4} + \frac{3}{4} = \frac{3}{2}$. If that sector is not the outcome, your money will be multiplied by $1 - \frac{1}{4} = \frac{3}{4}$. On average, two spins provides a factor of $(\frac{3}{2})(\frac{3}{4}) = \frac{9}{8}$. Hence each single spin provides, on average, a factor of $\sqrt{\frac{9}{8}} = 1.06066$. With this strategy your money will grow, on average, by over 6% each turn. (Exercise 1 shows that this strategy is, in a limited sense, optimal.)

15.2 THE LOG UTILITY APPROACH TO GROWTH

The investment wheel is representative of a large and important class of investment situations where a particular strategy leads to a random growth process. This class includes investment in common stocks, as shown later in this section. A general formulation is that if X_k represents capital after the kth trial, then

$$X_k = R_k X_{k-1} \tag{15.1}$$

for $k = 1, 2, \ldots$. In this equation R_k is a random return variable. We assume that it is a **stationary independent** process, where all R_k's have identical probability distributions and are mutually independent.

The investment wheel with the strategy of investing one-half of one's capital on the top segment corresponds to this model with R_k's that take on either of the two values 2.0 or .50, each with probability of one-half. The R_k variables all have the same probability density and are independent of one another (that is, other outcomes do not influence the present outcome).

In the general capital growth process, the capital at the end of n trials is

$$X_n = R_n R_{n-1} \cdots R_2 R_1 X_0.$$

Taking the logarithm of both sides gives

$$\ln X_n = \ln X_0 + \sum_{k=1}^{n} \ln R_k.$$

A little more manipulation produces

$$\ln \left(\frac{X_n}{X_0} \right)^{1/n} = \frac{1}{n} \sum_{k=1}^{n} \ln R_k. \tag{15.2}$$

Consider the right-hand side of (15.2) as $n \to \infty$. The variables $\ln R_k$ are each random variables that are independent and have identical probability distributions. The **law of large numbers**[2] therefore states that

$$\frac{1}{n} \sum_{k=1}^{n} \ln R_k \to \mathrm{E}(\ln R_1).$$

(We can use $\mathrm{E} \ln R_1$ in this expression since the expected value is the same for all k.) We define $m = \mathrm{E}(\ln R_1)$. Then we have from (15.2),

$$\ln \left(\frac{X_n}{X_0} \right)^{1/n} \to m.$$

This is the fundamental result that we now highlight:

Logarithmic performance   If $X_1, X_2, \ldots$ is the random sequence of capital values generated by the process

$$X_k = R_k X_{k-1}$$

then

$$\ln \left(\frac{X_n}{X_0} \right)^{1/n} \to m \tag{15.3}$$

as $n \to \infty$, where

$$m = \mathrm{E}(\ln R_1). \tag{15.4}$$

Taking the antilogarithm of both sides of (15.3) gives

$$\left(\frac{X_n}{X_0} \right)^{1/n} \to e^m.$$

Then, formally (although it is not quite legitimate to do so), we raise both sides to the power of n, and we find

$$X_n \to X_0 e^{mn}.$$

In other words, for large n the capital grows (roughly) exponentially with n at a rate m.

---

[2] The law of large numbers states that if $Y_1, Y_2, \ldots$ are independent random variables with identical distributions then $(1/n) \sum_{k=1}^{n} Y_k \to \mathrm{E}(Y_k)$. A simple example is that of flipping a coin and assigning $Y_k = +1$ if heads occurs on the kth trial and -1 if tails occurs. The average of the numbers tends to zero.

The foregoing analysis reveals the importance of the number m defined by (15.4). It governs the rate of growth of the investment over a long period of repeated trials. It seems appropriate therefore to select the strategy that leads to the largest value of m.

Log Utility Form

Note that if we add the constant $\ln X_0$ to (15.4) we find

$$m + \ln X_0 = E(\ln R_1) + \ln X_0 = E(\ln R_1 X_0) = E(\ln X_1).$$

Hence if we define the special utility function $U(X) = \ln X$, the problem of maximizing the growth rate m is equivalent to maximizing the expected utility $E[U(X_1)]$ and using this same strategy in every trial. In other words, by using the logarithm as a utility function, we can treat the problem as if it were a single-period problem. We find the optimal growth strategy by finding the best thing to do on the first trial, using the expected logarithm as our criterion. This single-step view guarantees the maximum growth rate in the long run.

Examples

Many important and interesting situations fit the framework presented in this section.

Example 15.1 (The Kelly rule of betting)   Suppose that you have the opportunity to invest in a prospect that will either double your investment or return nothing. The probability of the favorable outcome is p. Suppose that you have an initial capital of X_0 and you can repeat this investment many times. How much should you invest each time?

This situation closely resembles the game of blackjack, played by a player who mentally keeps track of the cards played. By adjusting the playing strategy to account for the composition of the remaining deck, such a player may have, on average, about a 50.75% chance of winning a hand; that is, $p = .5075$. The player must decide how much to bet in such a situation.

Let α be the proportion of capital invested (or bet) during one play. The player wishes to find the best value of α. If the player wins, his or her capital will grow by the factor $1 - \alpha + 2\alpha = 1 + \alpha$. If he or she loses, the factor is $1 - \alpha$. Hence to find the log-optimal value of α, we maximize

$$m = p \ln(1 + \alpha) + (1 - p) \ln(1 - \alpha).$$

Setting the derivative with respect to α equal to zero, we have

$$\frac{p}{1 + \alpha} - \frac{1 - p}{1 - \alpha} = 0.$$

This gives the equation

$$p(1 - \alpha) - (1 - p)(1 + \alpha) = 0$$

or $\alpha = 2p - 1$.[3] Hence in the blackjack example, a player should bet 1.5% of the total capital on each hand when $p = .5075$. Professional blackjack players actually do use this rule or a modification of it.

Blackjack may seem to offer an easy living! The growth rate of the Kelly rule strategy is

$$m = p \ln 2p + (1 - p) \ln(2 - 2p) = p \ln p + (1 - p) \ln(1 - p) + \ln 2.$$

For the case where $p = .5075$, this gives $e^m \approx 1.0001125$, which is a .01125% gain. To double your capital you must expect to play $72/.01125 = 6,440$ hands (remember the 72 rule of Chapter 2). This requires about 80 hours of play, which realistically requires about 1 month of activity. But there are many obstacles in the path of such a profession.

Example 15.2 (Volatility pumping)   Suppose there are two assets available for investment. One is a stock that in each period either doubles or reduces by one-half, each with a probability of 50%. The other just retains value—like putting money under the mattress. Neither of these investments is very exciting. An investment left in the stock will have a value that fluctuates a lot but has no overall growth rate. The other clearly has no growth rate. Nevertheless, by using these two investments in combination, growth can be achieved.

To see how, suppose that we invest one-half of our capital in each asset each period. Thus we **rebalance** at the beginning of each period by being sure that one-half of our capital is in each asset. Under a favorable performance, our capital will grow by the factor $\frac{1}{2} + \frac{1}{2} \times 2 = \frac{1}{2} + 1$. Under an unfavorable performance, the factor will be $\frac{1}{2} + \frac{1}{2} \times \frac{1}{2} = \frac{1}{2} + \frac{1}{4}$. Hence the expected growth rate of this strategy is

$$m = \frac{1}{2} \ln(\frac{1}{2} + 1) + \frac{1}{2} \ln(\frac{1}{2} + \frac{1}{4}) \approx .059.$$

Therefore $e^m = 1.0607$, and the gain on the portfolio is about 6% per period.

Figure 15.2 shows one simulation run of the performance of the 50–50 mix of the two assets versus the stock itself. The mixture portfolio outperforms the stock.

The gain is achieved by using the volatility of the stock in a **pumping** action. If the stock goes up in a certain period, some of the proceeds are put aside. If on the other hand the stock goes down, additional capital is invested in it. Capital is pumped back and forth between the two assets in order to achieve growth greater than can be achieved by either alone.

Note also that this strategy automatically, on average, follows the dictum of "buy low and sell high" by the process of rebalancing. In essence, that is why it produces growth.

Example 15.3 (Pumping two stocks)   Let us modify Example 15.2 by assuming that both assets have the property of either doubling or halving in value each period with probability one-half. Each asset moves independently of the other. Again we invest

---

[3]The answer implicitly assumes $p > .5$. If $p \leq .5$, the optimal α is $\alpha = 0$.

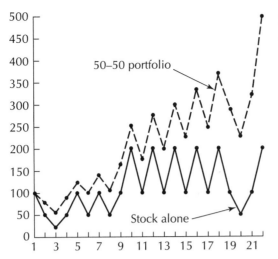

FIGURE 15.2 Mixture of two assets. Two mediocre stocks can be combined to give enhanced growth.

one-half of our capital in each asset, rebalancing at each period. We find immediately that

$$m = \tfrac{1}{4} \ln 2 + \tfrac{1}{2} \ln \tfrac{5}{4} + \tfrac{1}{4} \ln \tfrac{1}{2} = \tfrac{1}{2} \ln \tfrac{5}{4} = .1116 \,.$$

Hence $e^m = \sqrt{\tfrac{5}{4}} = 1.118$, which corresponds to an 11.8% growth rate each period. The pumping action is greatly enhanced over that of the previous example. Pumping between two volatile assets leads to large growth rates.

Example 15.4 (Large stock portfolios) Suppose that there are n stocks that have returns R_i, $i = 1, 2, 3, \ldots, n$, for any one period (of, say, a week). These returns are random, but they have the same probability distribution each period. The returns of different stocks may be correlated, but the returns of different periods are not correlated. We form a portfolio of these stocks by assigning weights $w_1, w_2, w_3, \ldots, w_n$ with $w_i \geq 0$ for each i and $\sum_{i=1}^{n} w_i = 1$. The overall return on the portfolio is $R = \sum_{i=1}^{n} w_i R_i$. To obtain the maximum possible growth of this portfolio, we select the weights so as to maximize $m = \mathrm{E}(\ln R)$. If we do this, the portfolio can be expected to grow roughly, on average, according to e^{mk}, where k is the number of periods.

   We shall study this example in greater detail later in this chapter.

Example 15.5 (The investment wheel) Let us compute the full optimal strategy for the investment wheel allowing for the possibility of investing on all sectors. For a strategy[4] $(\alpha_1, \alpha_2, \alpha_3)$ we find the results as follows:

1. If 1 occurs, $R = 1 + 2\alpha_1 - \alpha_2 - \alpha_3$.

---

[4]Recall that $1, 2, 3$ correspond to the top, left, and right, with payoffs 3, 2, and 6, respectively.

2. If 2 occurs, $R = 1 - \alpha_1 + \alpha_2 - \alpha_3$.

3. If 3 occurs, $R = 1 - \alpha_1 - \alpha_2 + 5\alpha_3$.

To maximize the expected logarithm of this return structure, we maximize

$$m = \tfrac{1}{2} \ln(1 + 2\alpha_1 - \alpha_2 - \alpha_3) + \tfrac{1}{3} \ln(1 - \alpha_1 + \alpha_2 - \alpha_3) + \tfrac{1}{6} \ln(1 - \alpha_1 - \alpha_2 + 5\alpha_3).$$

If we assume that the solution has $\alpha_i > 0$ for each $i = 1, 2, 3$, we can find the solution by setting the derivatives with respect to each α_i equal to zero. This gives the equations

$$\frac{2}{2(1 + 2\alpha_1 - \alpha_2 - \alpha_3)} - \frac{1}{3(1 - \alpha_1 + \alpha_2 - \alpha_3)} - \frac{1}{6(1 - \alpha_1 - \alpha_2 + 5\alpha_3)} = 0$$

$$-\frac{1}{2(1 + 2\alpha_1 - \alpha_2 - \alpha_3)} + \frac{1}{3(1 - \alpha_1 + \alpha_2 - \alpha_3)} - \frac{1}{6(1 - \alpha_1 - \alpha_2 + 5\alpha_3)} = 0$$

$$-\frac{1}{2(1 + 2\alpha_1 - \alpha_2 - \alpha_3)} - \frac{1}{3(1 - \alpha_1 + \alpha_2 - \alpha_3)} + \frac{5}{6(1 - \alpha_1 - \alpha_2 + 5\alpha_3)} = 0.$$

General equations of this form are difficult to solve analytically. However, in this case a solution is $\alpha_1 = \tfrac{1}{2}, \alpha_2 = \tfrac{1}{3}$, and $\alpha_3 = \tfrac{1}{6}$, which can be checked easily. (For a generalization of this problem and its solution see Exercise 4.) This means that one should invest in every sector of the wheel, and the proportions bet are equal to the probabilities of occurrence.

Substitution of this optimal strategy in the original objective of expected logarithm gives

$$m = \tfrac{1}{2} \ln \tfrac{3}{2} + \tfrac{1}{3} \ln \tfrac{2}{3} + \tfrac{1}{6} \ln 1 = \tfrac{1}{6} \ln \tfrac{3}{2}.$$

We then find that

$$e^m \approx 1.06991.$$

Hence the optimal solution achieves a growth rate of about 7%, which compares with the approximately 6% achieved by the strategy of investing one-fourth on the top segment and nothing on the other two.

The results of one simulation of 50 trials of the investment wheel are shown in Figure 15.3. The figure shows the results for three strategies: the optimal strategy, the simplified strategy of betting one-fourth on the top segment, and the poor strategy of investing one-half on the top segment. Also shown is a curve representing a 7% growth rate. The simulation has a great deal of volatility, and other runs may look quite different from this one. The long-term effect shows up when there are hundreds of trials, as there would be, for example, in the yearly result of daily stock market investments.

Notice that the optimal strategy requires an investment on the unfavorable sector 2, which pays only 2 to 1. This investment serves as a hedge for the other sectors—it wins precisely when the others do not.[5] It is like fire insurance on your home, paying when other things go wrong.

---

[5]The equations defining the optimal solution are actually degenerate for this problem. There is a whole family of optimal solutions, all giving the same value for m. An alternate solution is $\alpha_1 = \tfrac{5}{18}, \alpha_2 = 0$, $\alpha_3 = \tfrac{1}{18}$. In this solution nothing is invested on the unfavorable sector.

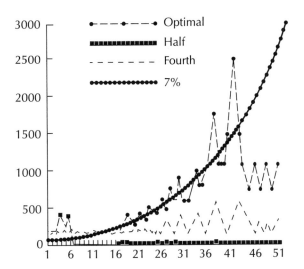

FIGURE 15.3 Wheel simulation. Under the optimal strategy, the wheel provides a growth rate of nearly 7%.

15.3 PROPERTIES OF THE LOG-OPTIMAL STRATEGY*

Although the log-optimal strategy maximizes the expected growth rate, the short run growth rate may differ. We can, however, make some definite statements about the log-optimal strategy that are quite impressive.

Suppose two people start with the same initial capital level X_0. Suppose further that person A invests using the log-optimal strategy and person B uses some other strategy (with a lower value of m). Denote the resulting capital streams by X_k^A and X_k^B, respectively, for the periods $k = 1, 2, \ldots$. Then it can be shown that

$$E\left(X_k^B / X_k^A\right) \leq 1, \qquad \text{for all } k.$$

This says that the ratio of the capital associated with alternative strategy B to the capital associated with the optimal strategy A is expected to be less than 1 at every stage. This property argues in favor of using the log-optimal strategy, and many people are indeed persuaded that this is the strategy they should adopt.

15.4 ALTERNATIVE APPROACHES*

The log-optimal strategy is not necessarily the best strategy to use in repetitive investment situations, but it is a good benchmark to keep in mind when considering alternatives. We mention some possible alternatives in this section.

Other Utility

One alternative is to use the standard framework of maximizing expected utility (as in the first part of Chapter 9). If there will be exactly K repetitions, we can define a utility function U for wealth at the end of period K and, accordingly, seek to maximize $E[U(X_K)]$.

The use of $U(X_K) = \ln X_K$ is one special case. In fact, because of a special recursive property, maximization of $E(\ln X_K)$ with respect to a fixed strategy is exactly equivalent to the log-optimal strategy of maximizing $E(\ln X_1)$. This follows from

$$E(\ln X_K) = E[\ln(R_K R_{K-1} \cdots R_1 X_0)] = \ln X_0 + E(\ln R_1) + \sum_{k=2}^{K} E(\ln R_k).$$

Maximization of the left side is equivalent to maximization of $E(\ln R_1)$ since all R_k's are identical random variables. This in turn is equivalent to maximization of $E(\ln X_1) = \ln X_0 + E(\ln R_1)$. Hence the choice of $U(X_K) = \ln X_K$ leads us once again to the log-optimal strategy.

One interesting class of utility functions is the class of power functions $U(X) = (1/\gamma)X^\gamma$ for $\gamma \le 1$. This class includes the logarithm [since $\lim_{\gamma \to 0}\{(1/\gamma)X^\gamma - 1/\gamma\} = \ln X$]; and it includes the linear utility $U(X) = X$.

This class of functions has the same recursive property as the log utility; that is, the structure is preserved from period to period. This is seen from

$$E[U(X_K)] = \frac{1}{\gamma}E[(R_K R_{K-1} \cdots R_1 X_0)^\gamma] = \frac{1}{\gamma}E(R_K^\gamma R_{K-1}^\gamma \cdots R_1^\gamma) X_0^\gamma$$

$$= \frac{1}{\gamma}E(R_K^\gamma) E(R_{K-1}^\gamma) \cdots E(R_1^\gamma) X_0^\gamma$$

where the last equality follows from the fact that the expected value of a product of independent random variables is equal to the product of the expected values. Hence to maximize $E[U(X_K)]$ with a fixed-proportions strategy it is only necessary to maximize $E[(R_1 X_0)^\gamma]$, so again to maximize $E[U(X_K)]$ one need only maximize $E[U(X_1)]$.

If $\gamma > 0$, the power utility function is quite aggressive. The extreme case of $\gamma = 1$, corresponding to $U(X) = X$ (leading to the expected-value criterion), was considered earlier when discussing the investment wheel. We found that the strategy that maximizes the expected value bets all capital on the most favorable sector—a strategy prone to early bankruptcy. Indeed, bankruptcy is likely for any γ with $1 \ge \gamma > 0$. For example, suppose $\gamma = \frac{1}{2}$. Consider two opportunities: (a) capital will double with a probability of .90 or it will go to zero with probability .10, and (b) capital will increase by 25% with certainty. Since $.9 \times \sqrt{2} > \sqrt{1.25}$, opportunity (a) is preferred to (b) with a square root utility. However, in a long sequence of repeated trials, an investor following opportunity (a) is virtually certain to go bankrupt. Most people prefer (b) when they understand that many trials will be played. A similar argument applies to any γ in the range $1 \ge \gamma > 0$.

It is more conservative to use $\gamma < 0$. However, many people find this to be *too* conservative. For example, suppose that $\gamma = -\frac{1}{2}$. Again consider two opportunities: (a) capital quadruples in value with certainty, and (b) with probability .5 capital remains constant and with probability .5 capital is multiplied by 10 million (or any finite number). Since $-4^{-1/2} > -.5 - .5(10,000,000)^{-1/2}$, an investor with the utility function $V(X) = -X^{-1/2}$ will prefer (a). This is quite conservative. Again, similar arguments apply for any $\gamma < 0$, although they become less compelling if γ is close to zero.

Based on the preceding discussion, we conclude that if an investor uses a power utility function, it is likely that it will be one with $\gamma < 0$, but γ close to zero. Such a utility function is close to the logarithm. We can argue that similar (although less precise) results hold for any broad class of possible utility functions; that is, only those close to the logarithm will seem appropriate when the long-term consequences are examined. Therefore, although in principle an investor may choose any utility function, supposedly reflecting individual risk tolerance, a repetitive situation tends to hammer the utility into one that is close to the logarithm.

Most long-term investors do consider the volatility of portfolio growth as well as the growth rate itself. This leads to consideration of the variance of the logarithm of return as well as the expected value of the logarithm of return. Indeed, if investors take a long-term view, it can be shown that (under certain assumptions) these two values are the only values of importance. We state this formally as follows:

 Growth efficiency proposition *An investor who considers only long-term performance will evaluate a portfolio on the basis of its logarithm of single-period return, using only the expected value and the variance of this quantity.*

This proposition interlaces well with the earlier discussion about power utility functions. We found that if the utility function $U(X_1) = (1/\gamma)X^\gamma$ were chosen, it is likely that $\gamma < 0$ and $\gamma \approx 0$. We can then use the approximation

$$\frac{1}{\gamma}(X^\gamma - 1) \approx \ln X + \frac{1}{2}\gamma(\ln X)^2.$$

This shows that use of this utility function is close to using a weighted combination of the expected logarithm of return and the variance of that logarithm. In other words, the expected logarithm and its variance are the two quantities of interest.

In view of the growth efficiency proposition, it is natural to trace out an efficient frontier of m versus σ similar to that for the ordinary mean–variance efficient frontier but where m and σ are, respectively, the mean and standard deviation of the logarithm of return. We shall do this for stocks whose prices are described by continuous-time equations in the next section.

15.5 CONTINUOUS-TIME GROWTH

Optimal portfolio growth can be applied with any rebalancing period—a year, a month, a week, or a day. In the limit of very short time periods we consider continuous rebalancing.

In fact, there is a compelling reason to consider the limiting situation: the resulting equations for optimal strategies turn out to be much simpler, and as a consequence it is much easier to compute optimal solutions. Hence even if rebalancing is to be carried out only, say, weekly, it is convenient to use the continuous-time formulation to do the calculations.

The continuous-time version also provides important insight. For example, it reveals very clearly how volatility pumping works.

Dynamics of Several Stocks

We first extend the continuous-time model of stock dynamics presented in Chapter 11 to the case of several correlated stocks. This model will then be used in our analysis of stock portfolios.

Suppose there are n assets. The price p_i of the ith asset, for $i = 1, 2, 3, \ldots, n$, is governed by a standard geometric Brownian motion equation

$$\frac{dp_i}{p_i} = \mu_i \, dt + dz_i$$

where z_i denotes a Wiener process, but with variance parameter σ_i^2 rather than 1. This is equivalent to the standard model for a single stock. The new element here is that the assets are correlated through the Wiener process components. In particular,

$$\text{cov}\,(dz_i, dz_j) = \text{E}(dz_i \, dz_j) = \sigma_{ij} \, dt.$$

We define the **covariance matrix S** as that with components σ_{ij}, and we use the convention $\sigma_i^2 = \sigma_{ii}$. We usually assume that $\mathbf{S}$ is nonsingular.

From Chapter 11, each asset i has a lognormal distribution, and at time t,

$$\text{E}\left[\ln\left(\frac{p_i(t)}{p_i(0)}\right)\right] = (\mu_i - \tfrac{1}{2}\sigma_i^2)t \equiv \nu_i t$$

and

$$\text{var}\left[\ln\left(\frac{p_i(t)}{p_i(0)}\right)\right] = \sigma_i^2 t.$$

Portfolio Dynamics

Now suppose that a portfolio of the n assets is constructed using the weights w_i, $i = 1, 2, \ldots, n$, with $\sum_{i=1}^{n} w_i = 1$. Let V be the value of the portfolio. Then because the instantaneous rate of return of the portfolio is equal to the weighted sum of the instantaneous rates of return of the individual assets, we have

$$\frac{dV}{V} = \sum_{i=1}^{n} w_i \frac{dp_i}{p_i}$$

$$= \sum_{i=1}^{n} w_i \mu_i \, dt + w_i \, dz_i.$$

The variance of the stochastic term is

$$\text{E}\left(\sum_{i=1}^{n} w_i \, dz_i\right)^2 = \text{E}\left(\sum_{i=1}^{n} w_i \, dz_i\right)\left(\sum_{j=1}^{n} w_j \, dz_j\right) = \sum_{i,j=1}^{n} w_i \sigma_{ij} w_j \, dt.$$

Hence the value $V(t)$ is lognormal with

$$\text{E}\left[\ln\left(\frac{V(t)}{V(0)}\right)\right] = \nu t = \sum_{i=1}^{n} w_i \mu_i t - \frac{1}{2} \sum_{i,j}^{n} w_i \sigma_{ij} w_j t. \tag{15.5}$$

The variance of $\ln[V(t)/V(0)]$ is

$$\sigma^2(t) = \sum_{i,j}^{n} w_i \sigma_{ij} w_j t.$$

Note that

$$\nu = \frac{1}{t} E \left[\frac{\ln V(t)}{V(0)} \right].$$

Hence ν gives the growth rate of the portfolio—analogous to m, used in previous sections. We can control this growth rate by the choice of the weighting coefficients $w_1, w_2, \ldots, w_n$.

Implications for Growth

Equation (15.5) explains how volatility can be pumped to obtain increased growth. As a specific example, suppose that the n assets are uncorrelated and all have the same mean and variance. A typical asset therefore has its price governed by the process

$$\frac{dp_i}{p_i} = \mu \, dt + dz_i$$

where now each dz_i has variance $\sigma^2 dt$. The expected growth rate of each stock individually is $\nu = \mu - \frac{1}{2}\sigma^2$. Suppose now that the n stocks are each included in a portfolio with a weight of $1/n$. Then from (15.5) the expected growth rate of the portfolio is

$$\nu_{\text{port}} = \mu - \frac{1}{2n}\sigma^2.$$

Pumping reduces the magnitude of the $-\frac{1}{2}\sigma^2$ correction term, thereby increasing the growth rate. In this example, the growth rate has increased over the ν of a single stock by

$$\nu_{\text{port}} - \nu = \frac{1}{2}\left(1 - \frac{1}{n}\right)\sigma^2 = \frac{1}{2}\left(\frac{n-1}{n}\right)\sigma^2.$$

The pumping effect is obviously most dramatic when the original variance is high. After being convinced of this, you will likely begin to *enjoy* volatility, seeking it out for your investments rather than shunning it, as you may have after studying the single-period theory of Chapters 6 and 7. Volatility is *not* the same as risk. Volatility is opportunity.

Example 15.6 (Volatility in action)   Suppose that a stock has an expected growth rate of 15% a year and a volatility (of its logarithm) of 20%. These are fairly typical values. This means that $\nu = \mu - \frac{1}{2}\sigma^2 = .15$ and $\sigma = .20$. Hence $\mu = .15 + .04/2 = .17$. By combining 10 such stocks in equal proportions (and assuming they are uncorrelated) we obtain an overall growth rate improvement of $(9/20) \times .04 = 1.8\%$—nice, but not dramatic.

If instead the individual volatilities were 40%, the improvement in growth rate would be 7.2%, which is substantial. At volatilities of 60% the improvement would be 16.2%, which is truly impressive. Unfortunately it is hard to find 10 uncorrelated stocks with this level of volatility, so in practice one must settle for more modest gains.[6]

The Portfolio of Maximum Growth Rate

We obtain the optimal growth portfolio by maximizing the growth rate ν. Referring to equation (15.5) we see that this is accomplished by finding the weights $w_1, w_2, \ldots, w_n$ that solve

$$\text{maximize} \sum_{i=1}^{n} w_i \mu_i - \tfrac{1}{2} \sum_{i,j=1}^{n} w_i \sigma_{ij} w_j$$

$$\text{subject to} \sum_{i=1}^{n} w_i = 1.$$

We solve this problem in the next section.

15.6 THE FEASIBLE REGION

Paralleling the familiar Markowitz concept, portfolios can be plotted on a two-dimensional diagram of ν versus σ. The region mapped out by all possible portfolios defines the **feasible region.** This is depicted in Figure 15.4.

There is, however, an important qualitative difference between the general shape of this region and the Markowitz region. The new region does not extend upward indefinitely, but instead there is a maximum value of ν, corresponding to the growth rate of the log-optimal portfolio. There is also, as in the Markowitz case, a point of minimum σ. These points are indicated on the figure.

The Efficient Frontier

Again, just as in the Markowitz framework, we define the **efficient frontier** of the feasible region to be the upper left-hand portion of the boundary. This frontier is efficient in the sense of growth as spelled out by the growth efficiency proposition of Section 15.4. In this case we can be quite specific and state that the efficient frontier is the portion of the boundary curve lying between the minimum-variance point and the log-optimal point.

---

[6]Of course we must temper our enthusiasm with an accounting of the commissions associated with frequent trading.

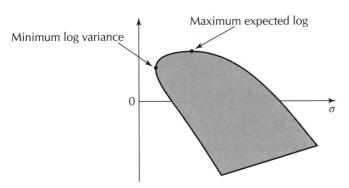

Minimum log variance

Maximum expected log

0

σ

FIGURE 15.4 Feasible region. The feasible region has a maximum expected log value and a minimum log variance value.

In fact, we obtain a strong version of the **two-fund theorem.** Any point on the efficient frontier can be achieved by a portfolio consisting of a mixture of the minimum-variance portfolio and the log-optimal portfolio. We now state this formally as a theorem. We also give a proof using vector–matrix notation. (The reader may safely skip the proof.)

The two-fund theorem   *Any point on the efficient frontier can be achieved as a mixture of any two points on that frontier. In particular the minimum-log-variance portfolio and the log-optimal portfolio can be used.*

Proof: Assume there are n securities. Let $\mathbf{u} = (\mu_1, \mu_2, \ldots, \mu_n)$, and let $\mathbf{w} = (w_1, w_2, \ldots, w_n)$ be portfolio weights. If $\mathbf{w}$ is efficient, it must solve the following problem for some s:

$$\text{maximize } \mathbf{w}^T\mathbf{u} - \tfrac{1}{2}\mathbf{w}^T\mathbf{S}\mathbf{w}$$

$$\text{subject to } \mathbf{w}^T\mathbf{1} = 1$$

$$\mathbf{w}^T\mathbf{S}\mathbf{w} = s.$$

By introducing Lagrange multipliers λ and $\gamma/2$, we form the Lagrangian

$$L = \mathbf{w}^T\mathbf{u} - \tfrac{1}{2}\mathbf{w}^T\mathbf{S}\mathbf{w} - \lambda(\mathbf{w}^T\mathbf{1} - 1) - \tfrac{1}{2}\gamma(\mathbf{w}^T\mathbf{S}\mathbf{w} - s).$$

The first-order conditions are

$$\mathbf{u} - \mathbf{S}\mathbf{w} - \lambda\mathbf{1} - \gamma\mathbf{S}\mathbf{w} = \mathbf{0}.$$

Hence the solution has the form

$$\mathbf{w} = \frac{1}{1+\gamma}\mathbf{S}^{-1}(\mathbf{u} - \lambda\mathbf{1}).$$

The constants λ and γ are determined so that the solution $\mathbf{w}$ satisfies the two constraints of the original problem.

Setting $\gamma = 0$ means that the second constraint is not active, and hence this solution corresponds to the log-optimal portfolio.

All solutions are linear combinations of the two vectors $\mathbf{S}^{-1}\mathbf{u}$ and $\mathbf{S}^{-1}\mathbf{1}$, so any two such solutions can be used to generate all others. In particular, the log-optimal and the minimum–variance solutions can be used. ∎

Inclusion of a Risk-Free Asset

Suppose that there is a risk-free asset with constant interest rate r_f. This asset can be considered to be a bond whose price $p_0(t)$ satisfies the equation

$$\frac{dp_0(t)}{p_0} = r_f\,dt.$$

Assuming that there is no other combination of assets that produces zero variance, the risk-free asset is on the efficient frontier. Indeed, it is the minimum-variance point. To find the entire efficient frontier it is therefore only necessary to find the log-optimal point, and we shall do that now.

The log-optimal portfolio is defined by a set of weights $w_1, w_2, \ldots, w_n$ for the risky assets and a weight $w_0 = 1 - \sum_{j=1}^{n} w_j$ for the risk-free asset. The weights for the risky assets are chosen to maximize the overall growth rate; that is, to solve the problem

$$\max\left[\left(1 - \sum_{j=1}^{n} w_j\right)r_f + \sum_{j=1}^{n}\left(\mu_i w_j - \tfrac{1}{2}\sum_{k=1}^{n} w_j \sigma_{jk} w_k\right)\right].$$

Setting the derivative with respect to w_k equal to zero, we obtain the equation for the log-optimal portfolio $\mu_i - r_f - \sum_{j=1}^{n} \sigma_{ij} w_j = 0$, which we highlight:

The log-optimal portfolio   *When there is a risk-free asset, the log-optimal portfolio has weights for the risky assets that satisfy*

$$\sum_{j=1}^{n} \sigma_{ij} w_j = \mu_i - r_f \tag{15.6}$$

for $i = 1, 2, \ldots, n$.

Equation (15.6) is a system of n linear equations that can be solved for the n weights.

The efficient frontier with a risk-free asset is shown in Figure 15.5. It should be clear from the figure that most investors will in fact *not* wish to design their strategies to correspond to the log-optimal point. This is because a first-order decrease in standard deviation can be attained with only a second-order sacrifice in expected (log) value by moving slightly leftward along the efficient frontier.

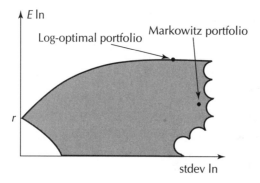

FIGURE 15.5   The feasible growth rate region. The Markowitz portfolio is not efficient in the sense of growth.

The Markowitz strategy can be defined by using the Markowitz portfolio weights and rebalancing regularly. This strategy will be inefficient with respect to the expected log-variance criterion.

Example 15.7 (A single risky asset) Suppose that there is a single stock with price S and a riskless bond with price B. These prices are governed by the equations

$$\frac{dS}{S} = \mu\,dt + \sigma\,dz$$

$$\frac{dB}{B} = r_f\,dt$$

where z is a standard Brownian motion process. The log-optimal strategy will have a weight for the stock given by (15.6). In this case that reduces to $w = (\mu - r_f)/\sigma^2$. The corresponding optimal growth rate is

$$\nu_{\mathrm{opt}} = r_f + \frac{(\mu - r_f)^2}{2\sigma^2}$$

and the corresponding variance is

$$\sigma_{\mathrm{opt}}^2 = \frac{(\mu - r_f)^2}{\sigma^2}.$$

Let us consider some numerical values. Suppose that the stock has an expected growth rate of 15% and a standard deviation of 20%. Suppose also that the risk-free rate is 10%. We know that $\sigma = .20$ and $\nu = \mu - \frac{1}{2}\sigma^2 = .15$. This means that $\mu = .17$. We find that $w = 1.75$, which means that we must borrow the risk-free asset to leverage the stock holding. We also find that the optimal value of ν is $\nu_{\mathrm{opt}} = .10 + (.07)^2/.08 = 16.125\%$. This is only a slight improvement over the 15% that is obtained by holding the stock alone. Furthermore, the new standard deviation is $.07/.20 = 35\%$, which is much worse than that of the stock. The situation is illustrated in Figure 15.6.

The log-optimal strategy does not give much improvement in the expected value, and it worsens the variance significantly. This shows that the log-optimal approach is

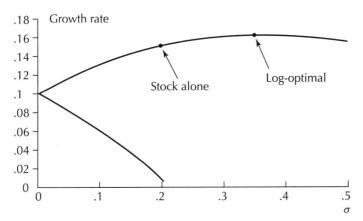

FIGURE 15.6 **Feasible region for one stock and a risk-free asset.** The log-optimal strategy gives only modest improvement in growth rate over holding the stock alone, at the expense of a greatly increased standard deviation.

not too helpful unless there is opportunity to pump between various stocks with high volatility, in which case there can be dramatic improvement.

Example 15.8 (Three stocks)   Suppose there are three risky stocks with prices governed by the equations

$$\frac{dS_1}{S_1} = .24\,dt + dz_1$$

$$\frac{dS_2}{S_2} = .20\,dt + dz_2$$

$$\frac{dS_3}{S_3} = .15\,dt + dz_3$$

with the covariance of dz being

$$\begin{bmatrix} .09 & .02 & .01 \\ .02 & .07 & -.01 \\ .01 & -.01 & .03 \end{bmatrix}.$$

The risk-free rate is 10%. We can calculate the corresponding growth rates: $v_1 = 19.5\%$, $v_2 = 16.5\%$, and $v_3 = 13.5\%$.

Referring to equation (15.6), the log-optimal portfolio weights satisfy the equations

$$.09w_1 + .02w_2 + .01w_3 = .14$$

$$.02w_1 + .07w_2 - .01w_3 = .10$$

$$.01w_1 - .01w_2 + .03w_3 = .05$$

which have solution

$$w_1 = 1.05$$

$$w_2 = 1.38$$

$$w_3 = 1.78.$$

It follows that μ_{opt} is the corresponding weighted sum of the individual μ's; that is,

$$\mu_{opt} = 1.05 \times .24 + 1.38 \times .20 + 1.78 \times .15 + (1 - 1.05 - 1.38 - 1.78) \times .10 = 0.4742$$

and

$$\sigma_{opt}^2 = \sum_{i,j=1}^{3} w_i w_j \sigma_{i,j}$$

$$= .09(1.05)^2 + .02(1.05)(1.38) + .01(1.05)(1.78) + .02(1.38)(1.05)$$

$$+.07(1.38)^2 - .01(1.38)(1.78) + .01(1.78)(1.05)$$

$$-.01(1.05)(1.38) + .03(1.78)^2$$

$$= 0.3742.$$

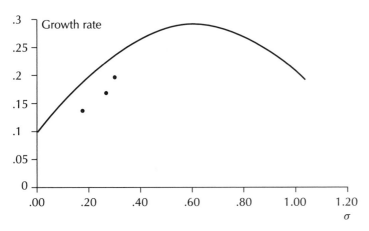

Hence $\sigma_{\text{opt}} = 61.17\%$. The growth rate is

$$\nu_{\text{opt}} = \mu_{\text{opt}} - \tfrac{1}{2}\sigma_{\text{opt}}^2 = 28.71\%.$$

Figure 15.7 shows the original three points and a portion of the boundary of the feasible region.

15.7 THE LOG-OPTIMAL PRICING FORMULA*

The log-optimal strategy has an important role as a universal pricing asset, and the pricing formula is remarkably easy to derive. As before, we assume that there are n risky assets with prices each governed by geometric Brownian motion as

$$\frac{\mathrm{d}p_i}{p_i} = \mu_i \, \mathrm{d}t + \mathrm{d}z_i, \qquad i = 1, 2, \ldots, n.$$

Since $\mathrm{E}(\mathrm{d}z_i) = 0$ for all i, the covariances σ_{ij} are defined by $\mathrm{E}(\mathrm{d}z_i \, \mathrm{d}z_j) = \sigma_{ij} \, \mathrm{d}t$. There is also a risk-free asset (asset number 0) with rate of return r_f. Any set of weights $w_0, w_1, w_2, \ldots, w_n$ with $\sum_{i=0}^{n} w_i = 1$ defines a portfolio in the usual way. The value of this portfolio will also be governed by geometric Brownian motion. We denote the corresponding covariances of this process with that of asset i by $\sigma_{i,\text{port}}$.

As a special case we denote the log-optimal portfolio by the subscript opt. This portfolio has variance denoted by σ_{opt}^2 and covariance with asset i denoted by $\sigma_{i,\text{opt}}$.

The μ of any asset can be recovered from the log-optimal portfolio by evaluating the covariance of the asset with that optimal portfolio. This is essentially a pricing formula because it shows the relation between drift and uncertainty. The pricing formula is stated here (in four different forms):

Log-optimal pricing formula (LOPF) *For any stock i there holds*

$$\mu_i - r_f = \sigma_{i,\text{opt}} \tag{15.7a}$$

$$\nu_i - r_f = \sigma_{i,\text{opt}} - \tfrac{1}{2}\sigma_i^2. \tag{15.7b}$$

Equivalently, we have

$$\mu_i - r_f = \beta_{i,\text{opt}} (\mu_{\text{opt}} - r_f) \tag{15.8a}$$

$$v_i - r_f = \beta_{i,\text{opt}} \sigma_{\text{opt}}^2 - \tfrac{1}{2}\sigma_i^2 \tag{15.8b}$$

where $\beta_{i,\text{opt}} = \sigma_{i,\text{opt}}/\sigma_{\text{opt}}^2$.

Proof: The result follows from the equation for the log-optimal strategy (15.6); namely,

$$\mu_i - r_f = \sum_{j=1}^n \sigma_{ij} w_j . \tag{15.9}$$

If V is the value of the log-optimal portfolio, we have

$$\frac{dV}{V} = \sum_{j=1}^n w_j(\mu_j \, dt + dz_j).$$

Hence $\sigma_{i,\text{opt}} = \mathrm{E}(dz_i \, dz_{\text{opt}}) = \sum_{j=1}^n \sigma_{ij} w_j = \mu_i - r_f$, where the last step is (15.9). This gives (15.7a). The version (15.7b) follows from $v_i = \mu_i - \tfrac{1}{2}\sigma_i^2$.

To obtain the alternative expressions we apply the first pricing formula [equation (15.7a)] to the log-optimal strategy itself, obtaining $\mu_{\text{opt}} - r_f = \sigma_{\text{opt}}^2$. Equation (15.8a) follows immediately. The version (15.8b) follows directly from the definition of $\beta_{i,\text{opt}}$. ∎

According to these formulas the covariance of an asset with the log-optimal portfolio completely determines the instantaneous expected excess return of that asset. Equations (15.7a) and (15.8a), in terms of $\mu - r_f$, are easy to remember because they mimic the CAPM equation. These equations express the excess expected instantaneous return as a single covariance or, in the alternate version, as a beta-type formula.

Example 15.9 (Three stocks again)   Consider the three stocks of Example 15.8. Let us determine μ_1 using (15.7a). The covariance of S_1 with the log-optimal portfolio is found from

$$\mathrm{E}\,[dz_1(w_1 \, dz_1 + w_2 \, dz_2 + w_3 \, dz_3)] = [1.05 \times .09 + 1.38 \times .02 + 1.78 \times .01]\, dt = .14\, dt.$$

Therefore,

$$\mu_1 = r_f + .14 = .24$$

which is correct since it coincides with the μ_1 originally assumed.

Equations (15.7b) and (15.8b), in terms of $v - r_f$, are perhaps the most relevant equations since v is the actual observed growth rate. Consider (15.8b), which is $v_i - r_f = \beta_{i,\text{opt}} \sigma_{\text{opt}}^2 - \tfrac{1}{2}\sigma_i^2$. For stocks with low volatility (that is, with σ_i^2 small) the excess

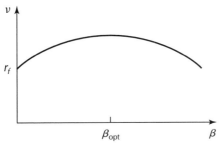

FIGURE 15.8   Log return versus beta.

growth rate is approximately proportional to $\beta_{i,\text{opt}}$. This parallels the CAPM result. Greater risk leads to greater growth. However, for large volatility the $-\frac{1}{2}\sigma_i^2$ term comes into play and decreases v.

Note in particular that if security i is uncorrelated with the log-optimal portfolio, its growth rate will be *less* than the risk-free rate. This is because its volatility provides opportunity that a risk-free asset does not.

The volatility term implies that the relation between risk and return is quadratic rather than linear as in the CAPM theory. To highlight this quadratic feature, suppose, as may on average be true, that the σ of any stock is proportional to its β; that is, $\sigma = \gamma\beta$, where γ is a constant. Then we find

$$v - r_f = \sigma_{\text{opt}}^2\,\beta - \frac{\gamma^2\beta^2}{2}.$$

A graph of this function is shown in Figure 15.8. Note that this curve has a different shape than the traditional beta diagram of the CAPM. It is a parabola having a maximum value at $\beta_{\text{opt}} = \sigma_{\text{opt}}^2/\gamma^2$.

Market Data

If we were to look at a family of many real stocks, we would not expect them to fall on a single curve like the one shown in Figure 15.8 since the true relationship has two degrees of freedom; namely, β and σ. However, according to the theory discussed, we would expect a scatter diagram of all stocks to fall roughly along such a parabolic curve. We can check this against the results of a famous comprehensive study of market returns which includes many decades of data.[7] The data shown in Figures 15.9 and 15.10 are taken from that study. The figures show annualized return, as computed on a monthly basis, over the period of 1963–1990. Of course the β used in the study is the normal β based on the market return, not on the log-optimal portfolio. This study has been used to argue that the traditional relation predicted by the CAPM does not hold, since the return is clearly not proportional to β. We have drawn a dashed parabola in each figure, which shows that the data *do* support the conclusion that the relation between return and β is roughly quadratic. To put this in perspective, we emphasize

---

[7]This is the Fama and French study cited at the end of the chapter. See table I of that reference.

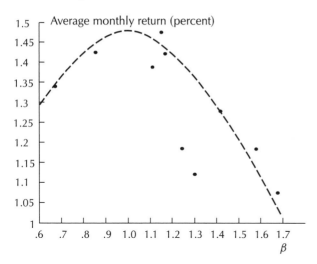

FIGURE 15.9   Observed return versus β for medium-sized companies. The data support the conclusion of the LOPF that return is approximately quadratic with respect to β with a peak at around $\beta = 1$.

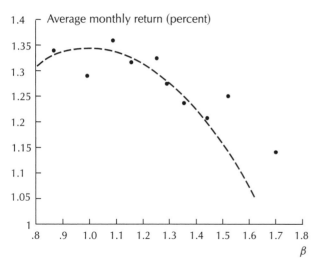

FIGURE 15.10   Observed return versus β for a cross section of all securities. The data support the conclusion of the LOPF that return is approximately quadratic with respect to β with a peak at $\beta = 1$.

that the LOPF is independent of how investors behave. It is a mathematical identity. All that a market study could test, therefore, is whether stock prices really are geometric Brownian motion processes as assumed by the model. Since returns are indeed close to being lognormal, the log-optimal pricing model must closely hold as well.

15.8 LOG-OPTIMAL PRICING AND THE BLACK–SCHOLES EQUATION*

The log-optimal pricing formula can be applied to derivative assets, and the resulting formula is precisely the Black–Scholes equation. Hence we obtain a new interpretation of the important Black–Scholes result and see the power of the LOPF. The log-optimal pricing equation is more general than the Black–Scholes equation, since log-optimal pricing applies more generally—not just to derivative assets.

As in the standard Black–Scholes framework, suppose that the price of an underlying asset is governed by the geometric Brownian motion process

$$dS = \mu S \, dt + \sigma S \, dz$$

where z is a normalized Wiener process. Assume also that there is a constant interest rate r. Finally, suppose that the price of an asset that is a derivative of the stock is $y = F(S, t)$ for some (unknown) function F.

The price y will fluctuate randomly according to its own Ito process. The equation of this process is given by Ito's lemma as

$$dy(t) = \left(\frac{\partial F}{\partial S} \mu S + \frac{\partial F}{\partial t} + \frac{1}{2} \frac{\partial^2 F}{\partial S^2} \sigma^2 S^2 \right) dt + \frac{\partial F}{\partial S} \sigma S \, dz. \tag{15.10}$$

If we divide the left side of 15.10 by $y(t)$ and the right side by $F(S, t)$, we will have an equation for the instantaneous rate of return of the derivative asset. The first term on the right is then the expected instantaneous rate of return. We can call this μ_{deriv} since it is the μ of the derivative asset. Then $\mu_{\text{deriv}} - r$ must be equal to the covariance of the instantaneous return of the derivative asset with the log-optimal portfolio. Writing this equation will give the final result. Before we carry this out, let us first find the log-optimal portfolio.

The log-optimal portfolio is a combination of the stock and the risk-free asset. The derivative asset cannot enhance the return achieved by these two assets, since it is by definition a derivative. Therefore the log-optimal portfolio is the combination found in Example 15.7. Specifically, it is the combination in which the weight of the stock is $w = (\mu - r)/\sigma^2$.

We can now write the log-optimal pricing formula directly as

$$\frac{1}{F} \left(\frac{\partial F}{\partial S} \mu S + \frac{\partial F}{\partial t} + \frac{1}{2} \frac{\partial^2 F}{\partial S^2} \sigma^2 S^2 \right) - r = \frac{1}{F} \left(\frac{\partial F}{\partial S} \sigma S \right) \left(\frac{\mu - r}{\sigma} \right).$$

The left-hand side is just $\mu_{\text{deriv}} - r$, where μ_{deriv} is the expected instantaneous return of the derivative asset. It is found by just copying the first part on the right of (15.10), dividing by F, and subtracting r. The right side is the covariance of this derivative asset with the log-optimal portfolio. Since both the derivative and the log-optimal portfolio have prices that are random only through the dz term, we simply multiply the corresponding coefficients of the instantaneous return equations to evaluate the covariance. The first part is just a copy of the dz coefficient in (15.10) divided by F and the second part is the standard deviation of the log-optimal portfolio, as found in Example 15.7.

The equation is simplified by multiplying through by F and canceling the two identical terms containing μ, yielding

$$\frac{\partial F}{\partial t} + \frac{\partial F}{\partial S} r S + \frac{1}{2} \frac{\partial^2 F}{\partial S^2} \sigma^2 S^2 = r F$$

which is the Black–Scholes equation.

We now have *three* different interpretations of the Black–Scholes equation. The first is a no-arbitrage interpretation, based on the observation that a combination of two risky assets can reproduce a risk-free asset and its rate of return must be identical to the risk-free rate. The second is a backward solution process of the risk-neutral pricing formula. The third is that the Black–Scholes equation is a special case of the log-optimal pricing formula.

15.9 SUMMARY

Given the opportunity to invest repeatedly in a series of similar prospects (such as repeated bets on an investment wheel or periodic rebalancing of a stock portfolio), it is wise to compare possible investment strategies relative to their long-term effects on capital. For this purpose, one useful measure is the expected rate of capital growth. If the opportunities have identical probabilistic properties, then this measure is equal to the expected logarithm of a single return. In other words, long-term expected capital growth can be maximized by selecting a strategy that maximizes the expected logarithm of return at each trial; this is the log-optimal strategy.

For bets that pay off either double or nothing, the log-optimal strategy is known as the Kelly rule. It states that you should bet a fraction $2p - 1$ of your wealth if the probability p of winning is greater than .5; otherwise, bet nothing.

For stocks, the log-optimal strategy pumps money between volatile stocks by keeping a fixed proportion of capital in each stock, rebalancing each period. This strategy automatically leads, on average, to following the maxim "buy low and sell high."

For stocks, the log-optimal approach is mathematically more tractable in a continuous-time framework than in a discrete-time framework, for in the continuous-time framework explicit formulas can be derived for the log-optimal strategy and the resulting expected growth rate—it is only necessary to solve a quadratic optimization problem. The resulting formula for the expected growth rate clearly shows the source of the pumping effect. Basically: growth rate is $v = \mu - \frac{1}{2}\sigma^2$. When assets are combined in proportions, the resulting μ is likewise a proportional combination of the individual μ's. However, the resulting σ^2 is reduced more than proportionally because it combines individual σ^2's with squares of the proportionality factors. Therefore the resulting v is greater than the proportional combination of individual v's. Hence v is pumped up by the reduction in the volatility term.

The growth efficiency proposition states that any long-term investor should evaluate a strategy only in terms of the mean and variance of the logarithm of return. This leads to the concept of an efficient frontier of points on a diagram that shows expected log-return versus standard deviation of log-return. Growth-efficient investors select points on this efficient frontier. This frontier has two extreme points: the log-optimal point and the minimum log-variance point. The two-fund theorem for this framework states that any efficient point is a combination of these two extreme-point portfolios. If there is a risk-free asset, it serves as the minimum log-variance point.

The log-optimal portfolio plays another special role as a pricing portfolio. Specifically, for any asset i, we find $\mu_i - r_f = \sigma_{i, \text{opt}}$. That is, the expected excess instantaneous return of an asset is equal to the covariance of that asset with the log-optimal portfolio. This formula, the log-optimal pricing formula (LOPF), can be transformed to $v_i - r_f = \beta_{i, \text{opt}} \sigma_{\text{opt}}^2 - \frac{1}{2}\sigma_i^2$. This shows that the growth rate v_i tends to increase with $\beta_{i,\text{opt}}$ as in the CAPM, but it decreases with σ_i^2. Roughly, this leads to security market lines that are quadratic rather than linear. Empirical evidence tends to support this conclusion.

The power of the log-optimal pricing formula (LOPF) is made clear by the fact that the Black–Scholes partial differential equation can be derived directly from the LOPF. However, the LOPF is not limited to the pricing of derivative securities—it is a general result.

EXERCISES

1. (Simple wheel strategy)   Consider a strategy of the form $(\gamma, 0, 0)$ for the investment wheel. Show that the overall factor multiplying your money after n steps is likely to be $(1 + 2\gamma)^{n/2}(1 - \gamma)^{n/2}$. Find the value of γ that maximizes this factor.

2. (How to play the state lottery)   In a certain state lottery, people select eight numbers in advance of a random drawing of six numbers. If someone's selections include the six drawn, they receive a large prize, but this prize is shared with other winners. Victor has discovered that some numbers are "unpopular" in that they are rarely chosen by lottery players. He has computed that by selecting these numbers he has one chance in a million of winning $10 million for a $1 lottery ticket. He has odds of 10 to 1 in his favor. Victor's current wealth is $100,000, and he wants to maximize the expected logarithm of wealth.

   (a) Should Victor buy a lottery ticket?
   (b) Victor knows that he can buy a fraction of a ticket by forming a pool with friends. What fraction of a ticket would be optimal?

3. (Easy policy)   Show that $(\frac{1}{2}, \frac{1}{2})$ is the optimal policy for Example 15.2.

4. (A general betting wheel ◇)   Consider a wheel with n sectors. If the wheel pointer lands on sector i, the payoff obtained is r_i for every unit bet on that sector. The chance of landing on sector i is p_i, $i = 1, 2, \ldots, n$. Let α_i be the fraction of one's capital bet on sector i. We require $\sum_{i=1}^{n} \alpha_i \leq 1$ and $\alpha_i \geq 0$ for $i = 1, 2, \ldots, n$.

   (a) Show that the optimal growth strategy is obtained by solving

   $$\max \sum_{j=1}^{n} p_j \ln \left(r_j \alpha_j + 1 - \sum_{i=1}^{n} \alpha_i \right).$$

   (b) Assuming that $\alpha_i > 0$ for all $i = 1, 2, \ldots, n$, show that the optimal values must satisfy

   $$\frac{p_k r_k}{r_k \alpha_k + 1 - \sum_{i=1}^{n} \alpha_i} - \sum_{j=1}^{n} \frac{p_j}{r_j \alpha_j + 1 - \sum_{i=1}^{n} \alpha_i} = 0$$

   for all $k = 1, 2, \ldots, n$.
   (c) Assume that $\sum_{i=1}^{n} 1/r_i = 1$. Show that in this case a solution is $\alpha_i = p_i$ for $i = 1, 2, \ldots, n$.
   (d) For the wheel given in Example 15.5, find the optimal solution and determine the corresponding optimal growth rate.

5. (More on the wheel ◇) Using the notation of Exercise 4, assume that $\sum_{i=1}^{n} 1/r_i = 1$, but try to find a solution where one of the α_k's is zero. In particular, suppose the segments are ordered in such a way that $p_n r_n < p_i r_i$ for all $i = 1, 2, \ldots, n$. Then segment n is the "worst" segment.

(a) Find a solution with $\alpha_n = 0$ and all other α_i's positive.
(b) Evaluate this solution for the wheel of Example 15.5.

6. (Volatility pumping) Suppose there are n stocks. Each of them has a price that is governed by geometric Brownian motion. Each has $v_i = 15\%$ and $\sigma_i = 40\%$. However, these stocks are correlated, and for simplicity we assume that $\sigma_{ij} = .08$ for all $i \neq j$. What is the value of v for a portfolio having equal portions invested in each of the stocks?

7. (The Dow Jones Average puzzle) The Dow Jones Industrial Average is an average of the prices of 30 industrial stocks with equal weights applied to all 30 stocks (but the sum of the weights is greater than 1). Occasionally (about twice per year) one of the 30 stocks splits (usually because its price has reached levels near $100 per share). When this happens, all weights are adjusted upward by adding an amount ε to each of them, where ε is chosen so that the computed Dow Jones Average is continuous.

Gavin Jones' father, Mr. D. Jones, uses the following investment strategy over a 10-year period. At the beginning of the 10 years, Mr. Jones buys one share of each of the 30 stocks in the Dow Jones average. He puts the stock certificates in a drawer and does no more trading. If dividends arrive, he spends them. If additional certificates arrive due to stock splits, he tosses them in the drawer along with the others. At the end of 10 years he cashes in all certificates. He then compares his overall return, based on the ratio of the final value to the original cost, with the hypothetical return defined as the ratio of the Dow Jones Average now to 10 years ago. He is surprised to see that there is a difference. Which return do you think will be larger? And why? (Ignore transactions costs, and assume that all 30 stocks remain in the average over the 10-year period.) [The difference, when actually measured, is close to 1% per year.]

8. (Power utility) A stock price is governed by

$$\frac{dS}{S} = \mu\, dt + \sigma\, dz$$

where z is a standardized Wiener process. Interest is constant at rate r. An investor wishes to construct a constantly rebalanced portfolio of these two assets that maximizes the expected value of his power utility $U(X) = (1/\gamma)X^\gamma$, $\gamma < 1$, at all times $t \geq 0$. Show that the proportion w of wealth invested in the risky asset is $w = (\mu - r)/[(1 - \gamma)\sigma^2]$. Use the following steps.

(a) Show that

$$X(t) = X(0)e^{\{rt + w(\mu-r)t - w^2\sigma^2 t/2 + wn\sigma\sqrt{t}\}}$$

where n is a normal random variable with mean 0 and variance 1.

(b) Use $E(e^{an}) = e^{a^2/2}$ to show that

$$E\big[U(X(t))\big] = \frac{1}{\gamma}e^{\gamma[rt + w(\mu-r)t - w^2\sigma^2 t/2] + \gamma^2 w^2\sigma^2 t/2} \ .$$

(c) Find w.

9. (Discrete-time, log-optimal pricing formula).   Suppose there are n assets. Asset i, $i = 1, 2, \ldots, n$, has rate of return r_i over a single period. There is also a risk-free asset with rate of return r_f. The log-optimal portfolio over one period has rate of return r_0, and we define $P_0 = 1/(1 + r_0)$.

(a) Derive the pricing formula

$$\bar{r}_i - r_f = -\frac{\text{cov}\,(r_i, P_0)}{\text{E}\,(P_0)}.$$

(b) Suppose that over a small period of length Δt the return of asset i is $1 + \mu_i\,\Delta t + n_i\sqrt{\Delta t}$, where n_i is a normal random variable with mean 0 and variance σ_i^2. Show that the discrete-time pricing formula in part (a) goes in the limit, as $\Delta t \to 0$, to the continuous-time log-optimal pricing formula given in Section 15.7.

REFERENCES

The special advantages of using a logarithmic utility function in situations of repeated investments was initially discovered by Kelly [1] and Latané [2]. The theory was developed more fully by Breiman [3]. See [4] for a good discussion of asymptotic properties. The idea that the expected logarithm and the variance of the logarithm are the only two quantities of importance in long-term behavior was presented in [5]. The fact that the log-optimal portfolio can be used for pricing was presented in [6]. The classic empirical study of security returns is [7].

1. Kelly, J. L., Jr. (1956), "A New Interpretation of Information Rate," *Bell System Technical Journal,* **35,** 917–926.
2. Latané, H. (1959), "Criteria for Choice among Risky Ventures," *Journal of Political Economy,* **67,** 144–155.
3. Breiman, L. (1961), "Optimal Gambling Systems for Favorable Games," Fourth Berkeley Symposium, vol. I, 65–78.
4. Algoet, P. H., and T. M. Cover (1988), "Asymptotic Optimality and Asymptotic Equipartition Properties of Log-Optimum Investment," *Annals of Probability,* **16,** 876–898.
5. Luenberger, D. G. (1993), "A Preference Foundation for Log Mean–Variance Criteria in Portfolio Choice Problems," *Journal of Economic Dynamics and Control,* **17,** 887–906.
6. Long, J. B., Jr. (1990), "The Numeraire Portfolio," *Journal of Financial Economics,* **26,** 29–69.
7. Fama, E. F., and K. R. French (1992), "The Cross-Section of Expected Stock Returns," *Journal of Finance,* **47,** no. 2, 427–465. (See especially Table I.)

GENERAL INVESTMENT EVALUATION

Analysis of an investment opportunity centers on the evaluation of its cash flow stream in present value terms. A proper evaluation, however, must account for the uncertainty of the stream and the relation of the stream to other assets. To structure a general evaluation procedure, therefore, we must have a framework for representing multiperiod stochastic cash flows of several assets. Given this framework, the familiar concepts of risk-neutral valuation and utility maximization can be extended to multiperiod situations.

16.1 MULTIPERIOD SECURITIES

We begin by building a framework for representing securities in a multiperiod setting with a finite number of states—a framework that generalizes the discussion of Chapter 9. (The reader should be familiar with Chapter 9 before reading this chapter.) The basic component of this multiperiod framework is a graph (usually a tree or a lattice) defining a random process of state transitions, as shown in Figure 16.1. The leftmost node represents the initial point of the process at time $t = 0$. The process can then move to any of its successor nodes at $t = 1$. A probability is assigned to each of the arcs. Each probability is greater than or equal to zero, and the sum of the probabilities for arcs emanating from any particular node must be 1.

The nodes of the graph can be thought of as representing various "states of the financial universe." They might be various weather conditions that would affect agriculture and hence the price of agricultural products. They might be conditions of unemployment that would affect wages and hence profits. Or they might be the various

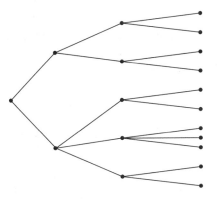

FIGURE 16.1 State graph. Each node represents a different state. The graph of this figure is a tree, but in general some nodes may combine.

possible prices of gold. The graph must have enough branches to fully represent the financial problems of interest. Particular security processes are defined by assigning numbers to the nodes, as discussed next.

Assets

An asset is defined by a cash flow process, which in turn is defined by assigning a cash flow (or dividend) to each node of the graph. Symbolically, such a cash flow or dividend process is represented by a series of the form $\delta = (\delta_0, \delta_1, \ldots, \delta_T)$, where each δ_t is the cash flow at time t. The flow δ_t is, however, random since it depends on which of the states at time t actually occurs, so really δ_t is a symbol for all possible values at time t.

Associated with each asset is another process, the price process, which is denoted by $S = (S_0, S_1, \ldots, S_T)$. The price S_t represents the price at which the asset would trade after receipt of the cash flow at t. Again, each S_t for $t > 0$ is random since it depends on which node is active at time t.

An example of an asset is a zero-coupon bond, which pays $1 at time T. This asset has a cash flow process that is zero at every node except those at time T, where the value is $1. The corresponding price process decreases as one moves backward through the graph, the actual values being representative of discount factors.

The state model can be used to represent several assets simultaneously. Different assets merely correspond to different cash flow and price processes.

The structure of an underlying graph requires some consideration. It is always safest to make this graph a full tree, with no combined nodes. This will assure that any derived quantities can also be accommodated. We prefer a simpler representation with a small number of nodes, such as a lattice; but a lattice representation that is adequate for an asset may not be adequate for a derived quantity because that quantity may be path dependent. (An example is the value of a lookback option whose price depends on the maximum price that a stock attains.) This phenomenon occurs in a graph representation of several assets as well, and hence we must watch for path dependencies (which require that nodes be separated). In general, it is easiest to assume merely that all assets are defined on a common state tree. Then we never need to worry about possible path dependencies. For computation, on the other hand, we aggressively seek opportunities to combine nodes—perhaps discovering a lattice representation. Then we struggle to keep the nodes from separating, so that we can devise a computationally efficient method of solution.

Portfolio Strategies

Assume that there are n assets. Asset i for $i = 1, 2, \ldots, n$ has (stochastic) cash flow process $\delta^i = (\delta^i_0, \delta^i_1, \ldots, \delta^i_T)$. Asset i also has the stochastic price process $S_i = (S^i_0, S^i_1, \ldots, S^i_T)$. A **trading strategy** is a portfolio of these assets whose composition may depend on time and on the particular nodes visited. Corresponding to a trading strategy, denoted by θ, there is an amount θ^i_t of asset i at time t, but θ^i_t also may depend on the particular state at time t. In other words, each $\theta^i = (\theta^i_0, \theta^i_1, \ldots, \theta^i_T)$ is itself a process defined on the underlying graph—the process of how much of asset i is held.

A trading strategy defines a new asset, with an associated cash flow process δ^θ. The cash flows are found from the equation

$$\delta^\theta_t = \sum_{i=1}^{n} \left[(\theta^i_{t-1} - \theta^i_t) S^i_t + \theta^i_{t-1} \delta^i_t \right]$$

where as a convention we put $\theta^i_{-1} = 0$ for all i. The first term inside the summation represents the amount of money received at time t due to changing the portfolio holdings at time t. The second term is the total dividend received at time t from the portfolio weights at time $t - 1$.

As a simple example, consider the trading policy of just buying an asset at time $t = 0$ for price S and holding it. This will generate the net cash flow stream $(-S, \delta_1, \delta_2, \ldots, \delta_T)$.

Arbitrage

It may be possible to find a strategy that is guaranteed to make money with no cost. Such a strategy is an **arbitrage.** Formally, a trading strategy θ is an arbitrage if $\delta^\theta \geq 0$ and δ^θ is not identically zero. In other words, θ is an arbitrage if it generates a dividend process that has at least one positive term and no negative terms. It is easy to imagine an arbitrage, since we have seen many examples in earlier chapters.

Short-Term Risk-Free Rates

An asset is **short-term risk free** at time t if its dividend at time $t + 1$ is $\delta_{t+1} = 1$ and zero everywhere else. Its price S_t at time t gives the discount factor $d_t = S_t$. Purchase of this security at time t yields the cash flow process $(0, 0, \ldots, -S_t, 1, 0, \ldots, 0)$. If there is no such underlying asset, it may be possible to construct one synthetically with a trading strategy. In either case, we say that short-term risk-free borrowing exists. We define the risk-free return as $R_{t,t+1} = 1/d_t$.

Suppose now that short-term risk-free borrowing exists for all t, $0 \le t \le T$. Then we define the forward return as

$$R_{ts} = \frac{1}{d_t d_{t+1} \cdots d_{s-1}}$$

for $s > t$.

The variable R_{ts} is the amount to which \$1 loaned at time t will grow at time s if it earns interest at the prevailing short rate each period from t to s. The quantity R_{ts} is, of course, random. If t is fixed, then at time s its specific value depends on the node at s. It is a conceptually attractive quantity, as we shall see, but it is computationally unattractive. It is unattractive because for $s - t > 1$ its description can require a full tree representation, even if the underlying short rate process is defined on a lattice, because the overall return between two periods is path dependent. (See Exercise 2.)

16.2 RISK-NEUTRAL PRICING

We now turn to one of the main themes emphasized throughout the book: risk-neutral pricing. We assume throughout this section that short-term risk-free borrowing exists for all periods, as described in the previous section. Hence there is a short rate defined for every node in the tree.

Assume again that there are n assets defined on the underlying state process graph. From these assets, new assets can be constructed by using trading strategies. We say that risk-neutral probabilities exist if a set of risk-neutral probabilities can be assigned to the arcs of the graph such that the price of any asset or any trading policy satisfies

$$S_t = \frac{1}{R_{t,t+1}} \hat{E}_t (S_{t+1} + \delta_{t+1}) \tag{16.1}$$

for every $t = 0, 1, 2, \ldots, T - 1$ and where $\hat{E}_t$ denotes expectation at time t with respect to the risk-neutral probabilities.

This definition applies only one period at a time, and it is expressed in a backward fashion. It gives S_t as a function of the reachable values of S_{t+1} and δ_{t+1}.

We cannot assume that risk-neutral probabilities exist for the particular set of assets in our collection. After all, the actual prices of the assets may not be related in a systematic fashion. However, as one might suspect, we can guarantee the existence of risk-neutral probabilities when the prices of the original assets are consistent in a way that makes arbitrage impossible. This is the content of the following theorem, which follows immediately from our earlier result in Chapter 9 on risk-neutral pricing because the risk-neutral pricing formula (16.1) is a single-period formula.

Existence of risk-neutral probabilities   *Suppose a set of n assets is defined on a state process. Suppose that from these assets, short-term risk-free borrowing is possible at every time t. Then there are risk-neutral probabilities such that the prices of trading strategies with respect to these assets are given by the risk-neutral pricing formula*

$$S_t = \frac{1}{R_{t,t+1}} \hat{E}_t(S_{t+1} + \delta_{t+1})$$

if and only if no arbitrage is possible.

> ***Proof:*** We already have all the elements. It is clear that risk-neutral pricing implies that no arbitrage is possible. This was shown in Section 14.3 for a short rate lattice, and the proof carries over almost exactly.
>
> It remains to be shown that if no arbitrage is possible, then there are risk-neutral probabilities. However, if no arbitrage is possible over the T periods, certainly no arbitrage is possible over the single period at t, starting at a given node. It was shown in Chapter 9 that this implies that risk-neutral probabilities exist for the arcs emanating from that node. Since this is true for all nodes at all times t, we obtain a full set of risk-neutral probabilities. ∎

The risk-neutral pricing formula (16.1) can be written in a nonrecursive form as

$$S_t = \hat{E}_t\left(\sum_{s=t+1}^{T} \frac{\delta_s}{R_{ts}} \right) \tag{16.2}$$

where now $\hat{E}_t$ denotes expectation of all future quantities starting at the known state at time t. This formula expresses S_t as a discounted risk-neutral evaluation of the entire remaining cash flow stream. It has the nice interpretation of generalizing the familiar present value formula used for deterministic cash flow streams. However, this form is not convenient for calculation because the quantity R_{ts} generally requires a full tree representation. (See Exercise 2.) There are cases where the result simplifies, of course, such as when interest rates are deterministic.

The preceding result is just a slight generalization of concepts developed in earlier chapters. We have already seen many examples of the application of the risk-neutral pricing equation. Binomial option pricing was the simplest and earliest example. More complex examples, involving interest rate derivatives, were discussed in Chapter 14. We will look at additional examples in this chapter that exploit the general formula, but first we need a bit more theory.

16.3 OPTIMAL PRICING

According to the definition, risk-neutral probabilities exist if there is no opportunity for arbitrage among the available assets. The theorem does not say that these probabilities are unique, and, in general, they are not.

If the assets span the degrees of freedom in the underlying graph, as is the case of two assets on a binomial lattice, then the risk-neutral prices *are* unique. If they do not span, as in the case of two assets on a trinomial lattice, there will be additional degrees of freedom, and the risk-neutral probabilities are not unique.

When there are extra degrees of freedom, a specific set of risk-neutral probabilities can be defined by introducing a utility function U, measuring the utility of the final wealth level, and finding the trading policy that maximizes the expected value of $U(X_T)$. This optimal trading policy will imply a set of risk-neutral prices in a manner similar to that for the single-period case discussed in Chapter 9.

We shall limit our consideration to utility functions that have a separation property (as was done in Chapter 15). To review, suppose that we begin with a wealth level X_0. After the first period, our wealth will be $X_1 = \alpha_0^{\theta_0} \times X_0$, where $\alpha_0^{\theta_0}$ is a random return factor that depends on the trading policy variables at period zero. Continuing in this fashion we see that $X_T = \alpha_0^{\theta_0} \times \alpha_1^{\theta_1} \times \cdots \times \alpha_{T-1}^{\theta_{T-1}} \times X_0$. If we select $U(X_T) = \ln X_T$, then $U(X_T) = \ln \alpha_0^{\theta_0} + \ln \alpha_1^{\theta_1} + \cdots + \ln \alpha_{T-1}^{\theta_{T-1}} + \ln X_0$. Hence we maximize $E_0[U(X_T)]$ by maximizing $E_t[\ln(\alpha_t^{\theta_t})]$ for each t, where E_t denotes expected value as seen at time t. This maximization is equivalent to maximization of $E_t[\ln(\alpha_t^{\theta_t} X_t)] = E_t[U(X_{t+1})]$ with respect to θ_t. This is the separation property. Maximization of the expected final utility is obtained by maximizing the same utility function at each step of the process.

The separation property holds for the logarithm, and it also holds for the power utility function $U(X_T) = (1/\gamma)X_T^\gamma$. When the separation property holds, the multi-period case reduces to a series of single-period problems, all having the same form of utility function. This greatly simplifies the necessary calculations (although most of the general conclusions hold for other utility functions).

The Single-Period Problem

Recall that there are n assets. The single-period problem at time t, and at a specific node at that time, is to select amounts θ_t^i for $i = 1, 2, \ldots, n$ of the n assets, forming a portfolio. We wish to maximize the expected utility of the value of this portfolio at $t + 1$ subject to the condition that the total cost of the portfolio at time t is 1. Hence we seek θ_t^i's to solve

$$\underset{\theta_t}{\text{maximize}} \quad E_t[U(X_{t+1})] \tag{16.3}$$

$$\text{subject to} \quad \sum_{i=1}^n \theta_t^i S_t^i = 1 \tag{16.4}$$

$$\sum_{i=1}^n \theta_t^i (S_{t+1}^i + \delta_{t+1}^i) = X_{t+1}. \tag{16.5}$$

The expectation is taken with respect to the actual probabilities of successor nodes. If there are K such nodes, we denote these probabilities by $p_1, p_2, \ldots, p_K$. Given amounts θ_t^i, $i = 1, 2, \ldots, n$, the value of next-period wealth X_{t+1} depends on the particular successor node k that occurs. The objective function can be written as $\sum_{k=1}^{K} p_k U(X_{t+1})_k$, where $U(X_{t+1})_k$ denotes the value of $U(X_{t+1})$ at node k.

Using the results of Chapter 9, a set of risk-neutral probabilities can be found from the solution. Specifically, the risk-neutral probabilities are

$$q_k = \frac{p_k U'(X_{t+1}^*)_k}{\sum_{k=1}^{K} p_k U'(X_{t+1}^*)_k} \tag{16.6}$$

where X_{t+1}^* is the optimal (random) value of next-period wealth. If the utility function U is increasing, $U'(X_{t+1}^*)_k$ will be positive, and hence all the q_k's will be positive.

These risk-neutral probabilities can be used to price any asset using the general formula

$$S_t = \frac{\hat{E}_t(S_{t+1} + \delta_{t+1})}{R_{t,t+1}}$$

which takes the specific form

$$S_t = \frac{\sum_{k=1}^{K} q_k (S_{t+1} + \delta_{t+1})_k}{R_{t,t+1}}.$$

Applications

If this method is used to find a set of risk-neutral probabilities when there are more states than basic assets, the risk-neutral probabilities will depend on the choice of utility function. The variations in the risk-neutral probabilities will not affect the prices of the original assets, but will lead to variations in the prices assigned to other (new) assets. The price assigned to a new asset this way is such that an individual with the given utility function will not choose to include that asset in the optimal portfolio (either long or short).

Example 16.1 (Log-optimal pricing of an option)   The optimal pricing method provides the foundation for a new lattice procedure for pricing a call option. Suppose that we plan to use moderately large period lengths in our lattice, but to maintain accuracy we decide to use a multinomial (rather than binomial) lattice. We assign (real) probabilities to the arcs of this lattice to closely match the actual characteristics of the stock.

In this situation, risk-neutral probabilities are not uniquely specified, but we can infer one set of such probabilities by using a utility function, say, the logarithmic utility function $U(X) = \ln X$. Once the risk-neutral probabilities are found, we can price the call option by the usual backward computational process.

What does the resulting price assigned to the call option represent? It is the price of the call that would cause someone with a logarithmic utility to be indifferent about including it in his or her portfolio. Specifically, this person could first form a log-optimal portfolio (rebalanced every period) of the stock and the risk-free asset. Then if the call were offered at the derived price, this person would find that inclusion of the call, either short or long, would not increase utility. Hence it would not be added to the portfolio. In other words, the utility-based price is the price that leads to a zero level of demand.

Example 16.2 (A 5-month call) As a specific example let us consider the 5-month call option studied in Example 12.3. The underlying stock had $S(0) = \$62$, $\mu = .12$, and $\sigma = .20$. The risk-free rate is $r = 10\%$ per annum, and the strike price of the option is $K = \$60$.

We use a trinomial lattice with 1-month periods. To match the parameters of the stock, we decide on the trinomial parameters $u = 1.1$, $d = 1/u$, and the middle branch has a multiplicative factor of 1. To find the real probabilities we must solve the equations that correspond to: (1) having the probabilities sum to 1, (2) matching the mean, and (3) matching the variance. These equations, first given in Section 13.7, are

$$
\begin{aligned}
p_1 + p_2 + \quad p_3 &= 1 \\
u p_1 + p_2 + \quad d p_3 &= 1 + \mu \, \Delta t \\
u^2 p_1 + p_2 + d^2 p_3 &= \sigma^2 \Delta t + (1 + \mu \, \Delta t)^2.
\end{aligned}
$$

They have solution $p_1 = .228$, $p_2 = .632$, and $p_3 = .140$.

Now that the lattice parameters are fixed, we must solve one step of the log-optimal portfolio problem. Hence we solve the problem

$$
\max_{\alpha} \; E\{\ln[\alpha R + (1 - \alpha) R_0]\}
$$

where R is the random return of the stock over one period and R_0 is the risk-free return. Written out in detail this is

$$
\max \left\{ p_1 \ln[\alpha u + (1 - \alpha) R_0] + p_2 \ln[\alpha + (1 - \alpha) R_0] + p_3 \ln[\alpha d + (1 - \alpha) R_0] \right\}.
$$

This has optimal solution $\alpha = .505$. The corresponding risk-neutral probabilities are then readily found from (16.6) to be

$$
q_1 = \frac{p_1}{\alpha u + (1 - \alpha) R_0} c \tag{16.7}
$$

$$
q_2 = \frac{p_2}{\alpha + (1 - \alpha) R_0} c \tag{16.8}
$$

$$
q_3 = \frac{p_3}{\alpha d + (1 - \alpha) R_0} c \tag{16.9}
$$

where c is the normalizing constant. When normalized the values are $q_1 = .218$, $q_2 = .635$, and $q_3 = .148$.

With these values in hand it is possible to proceed through the lattice in the normal backward solution method. The results are shown in Figure 16.2. The price obtained is $\$5.8059$, which is very close to the the Black–Scholes value of $\$5.80$.

Stock price lattice					99.85
				90.77	90.77
			82.52	82.52	82.52
		75.02	75.02	75.02	75.02
	68.20	68.20	68.20	68.20	68.20
62.00	62.00	62.00	62.00	62.00	62.00
	56.36	56.36	56.36	56.36	56.36
		51.24	51.24	51.24	51.24
			46.58	46.58	46.58
				42.35	42.35
					38.50

FIGURE 16.2 Log-optimal pricing of a 5-month call option using a trinomial lattice. The upper lattice contains the possible stock prices. The lower lattice is found by risk-neutral valuation using inferred probabilities.

Log pricing lattice					39.85
				31.27	30.77
			23.51	23.02	22.52
		16.51	16.01	15.52	15.02
	10.43	9.85	9.27	8.70	8.20
5.8059	5.20	4.56	3.85	3.03	2.00
	1.92	1.43	.92	.43	.00
		.26	.09	.00	.00
			.00	.00	.00
				.00	.00
					.00

16.4 THE DOUBLE LATTICE

The starting point for general investment analysis as presented in this chapter is a graph that represents a family of asset processes. How can we construct such a graph to embody the characteristics of each asset and the relations between assets? Clearly, this construction may be quite complex.

This section shows how a graph for two risky assets can be constructed by combining the separate representations for each asset. Specifically, two binomial lattices are combined to produce a double lattice that faithfully represents both assets.

Suppose that we have two assets A and B, each represented by a binomial lattice. Each has up and down factors and probabilities, but movements in the two may be correlated. A representation of one time period is shown in Figure 16.3.

The combination of these two lattices is really a lattice with *four* branches at each time step. It is most convenient to use double indexing for this new combined lattice; call the nodes 11, 12, 21, and 22. The first index refers to the first lattice and the second

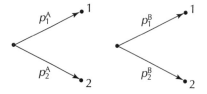

FIGURE 16.3   One step of two separate lattices. Their movements may be correlated.

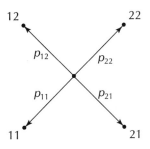

12   22   **FIGURE 16.4   Nodes of the combination.** There are four possible successor nodes from the central node.

p_{12} p_{22}

p_{11} p_{21}

11   21

to the second. We define the transition probabilities as p_{11}, p_{12}, p_{21}, and p_{22}, respectively. A picture of the combined lattice is shown in Figure 16.4. Here the center node is the node at an initial time, and the four outer nodes are the four possible successors.

Suppose the lattice for stock A has node factors u^A and d^A with probabilities p_1^A and p_2^A, respectively; and the lattice for stock B has node factors u^B and d^B with probabilities p_1^B and p_2^B. If the covariance of the logarithm of the two return factors σ_{AB} is known, we may select the probabilities of the double lattice to satisfy[1]

$$p_{11} + p_{12} = p_1^A$$

$$p_{21} + p_{22} = p_2^A$$

$$p_{11} + p_{21} = p_1^B$$

$$\left(p_{11} - p_1^A p_1^B\right) U^A U^B + \left(p_{12} - p_1^A p_2^B\right) U^A D^B$$

$$+ \left(p_{21} - p_2^A p_1^B\right) D^A U^B + \left(p_{22} - p_2^A p_2^B\right) D^A D^B = \sigma_{AB}$$

where $U^A = \ln u^A$, $D^A = \ln d^A$, $U^B = \ln u^B$, and $D^B = \ln d^B$.

A special case is when the covariance is zero, corresponding to independence of the two asset returns. In that case it follows that the appropriate lattice probabilities are $p_{11} = p_1^A p_1^B$, $p_{12} = p_1^A p_2^B$, $p_{21} = p_2^A p_1^B$, and $p_{22} = p_2^A p_2^B$.

Example 16.3 (Two nice stocks)   Consider two stocks with identical binomial lattice representations of $u = 1.3$, $d = .9$, and $p_u = .6$, $p_d = .4$. Assume also that they have a correlation coefficient of $\rho = .3$. Let us find the double lattice representation.

Let S_A and S_B be the random values of the two stocks after one period when initiated at unity. We have

$$E(\ln S_A) = E(\ln S_B) = .6 \times \ln 1.3 + .4 \times \ln .9 = .11527$$

$$\sigma^2 = \text{var}(\ln S_A) = \text{var}(\ln S_B) = .6(\ln 1.3)^2 + .4(\ln .9)^2 - .11527^2 = .03245$$

$$\text{cov}_{AB} = .3\sigma^2 = .009736.$$

---

[1]Summing the first two equations gives $p_{11} + p_{12} + p_{21} + p_{22} = p_1^A + p_2^A = 1$, so the probabilities sum to 1. Also, subtracting the third equation from this above equation gives $p_{12} + p_{22} = 1 - p_1^B = p_2^B$. Note also that the last equation can be written $p_{11} U^A U^B + p_{12} U^A D^B + p_{21} D^A U^B + p_{22} D^A D^B = \sigma_{AB} + (p_1^A U^A + p_2^A D^A)(p_1^B U^B + p_2^B D^B)$.

Therefore we must solve

$$p_{11} + p_{12} = .6$$

$$p_{21} + p_{22} = .4$$

$$p_{11} + p_{21} = .6$$

$$p_{11}(\ln 1.3)^2 + p_{12}(\ln 1.3)(\ln .9) + p_{21}(\ln 1.3)(\ln .9) + p_{22}(\ln .9)^2$$
$$= .009736 + (.11527)^2 = .023023 .$$

This has solution

$$p_{11} = .432$$

$$p_{12} = .168$$

$$p_{21} = .168$$

$$p_{22} = .232 .$$

16.5 PRICING IN A DOUBLE LATTICE

The double lattice construction does provide a valid representation of the two assets, but there is a problem. When a risk-free asset is adjoined, we have four nodes, but only *three* assets: the two risky assets and the risk-free asset. There is an extra degree of freedom. Therefore the risk-neutral probabilities are not completely specified as they are in the two original small lattices. We must find a way to pin down that extra degree of freedom in the definition of the risk-neutral probabilities.

One way to specify risk-neutral probabilities is to introduce a utility function, as in the previous section. Different utility functions may lead to different risk-neutral probabilities, but it turns out that under certain conditions a fourth relation holds independently of the particular utility function.

Let us introduce a utility function U. We determine the risk-neutral probabilities by maximizing expected utility. Denote the optimal value of wealth at the next time point, at node ij, by X_{ij}^*; and, correspondingly, define $U_{ij}' = U'(X_{ij}^*)$. Then the risk-neutral probabilities are, from (16.6),

$$q_{ij} = \frac{p_{ij} U_{ij}'}{\sum_{k,l=1}^2 p_{kl} U_{kl}'} \tag{16.10}$$

for $i, j = 1, 2$. If the utility function U is strictly increasing, then the risk-neutral probabilities are strictly positive.

In certain special cases there will be a relation among the q_{ij}'s that will supply the additional relation needed to make them unique. Two of those cases are spelled out in the following theorem:

Ratio theorem   *Suppose the q_{ij}'s are determined by (16.10). Then the relation*

$$\frac{q_{11}q_{22}}{q_{12}q_{21}} = \frac{p_{11}p_{22}}{p_{12}p_{21}}$$

holds if either of the following two conditions is satisfied:

(a) One of the original assets appears at zero level in the optimal portfolio.

(b) The time Δt between periods is vanishingly small.

Proof: We shall prove that under either condition $U'_{11}U'_{22} = U'_{12}U'_{21}$. This fact will then lead to the final conclusion.

(a) Suppose that asset A has zero level in the optimal portfolio. Then changes in asset A do not influence U'. Hence $U'_{11} = U'_{21}$ and $U'_{12} = U'_{22}$. Therefore $U'_{11}U'_{22} = U'_{12}U'_{21}$. Clearly, the same result holds if asset B has zero level in the optimal portfolio.

(b) Now, as a second case, assume that Δt is small. At the optimal portfolio we may write $X_{ij} = (\tilde{R}_i^A + \tilde{R}_j^B + \tilde{R}^0)X_t$, where the terms $\tilde{R}_i^A$, $\tilde{R}_j^B$, and $\tilde{R}^0$ are the returns in the portfolio that correspond to the risky asset A, the risky asset B, and the risk-free asset, respectively. For small Δt the return over one period must be close to 1. Hence,

$$\tilde{R}_i^A + \tilde{R}_j^B + \tilde{R}^0 = 1 + r_i^A + r_j^B + r^0$$
$$\approx (1 + r_i^A)(1 + r_j^B)(1 + r^0).$$

where r_i^A, r_j^B, and r^0 are small. This approximation carries over to U' as well, giving

$$U'_{ij} = U'[(1 + r_i^A + r_j^B + r^0)X_t]$$
$$\approx U'(X_t) + U''(X_t)(r_i^A + r_j^B + r^0)X_t$$
$$\approx U'(X_t)(1 + \gamma r_i^A)(1 + \gamma r_j^B)(1 + \gamma r_0)$$

where

$$\gamma = \frac{U''(X_t)X_t}{U'(X_t)}.$$

This product form for U'_{ij} implies that

$$U'_{11}U'_{22} = U'_{12}U'_{21}.$$

Under condition (a) or (b) we have $U'_{11}U'_{22} = U'_{12}U'_{21}$. We then compute

$$\frac{q_{11}q_{22}}{q_{12}q_{21}} = \frac{p_{11}U'_{11}p_{22}U'_{22}}{p_{12}U'_{12}p_{21}U'_{21}} = \frac{p_{11}p_{22}}{p_{12}p_{21}}. \quad \blacksquare$$

An important special case of the two lattice construction is where the two original lattices are independent. In that case $p_{11} = p_1^A p_1^B$, $p_{12} = p_1^A p_2^B$, $p_{21} = p_2^A p_1^B$, and

$p_{22} = p_2^A p_2^B$. It follows by direct substitution that

$$\frac{p_{11}p_{22}}{p_{12}p_{21}} = 1.$$

Then if either of the conditions of the ratio theorem is satisfied,

$$\frac{q_{11}q_{22}}{q_{12}q_{21}} = 1$$

and from this it can be shown that the original two lattices are independent with respect to the risk-neutral probabilities as well as with respect to the original probabilities. That is, independence with respect to original probabilities implies independence with respect to risk-neutral probabilities.[2]

Now let us return to our original problem. In the double lattice we have four successor nodes but only three assets. For small Δt, the ratio formula gives the fourth relation required to determine a set of four risk-neutral probabilities.

An important special case of the two-lattice situation is that where one of the lattices is a short rate lattice for interest rates. This case can be treated by the same technique, as illustrated by the Simplico gold mine example that follows.

Example 16.4 (Double stochastic Simplico gold mine)   Consider a 10-year lease on the Simplico mine. In evaluating this lease we recognize that the price of gold and the interest rate are *both* stochastic, but we will assume that they are independent.

Recall that up to 10,000 ounces of gold can be extracted from this mine each year at a cost of $200 per ounce. The price of gold is initially $400 per ounce and fluctuates according to a binomial lattice that has an up factor of $u = 1.2$ and a down factor of $d = .9$. The price obtained for sale of the gold produced in a year is assumed to be the gold price at the beginning of the year, but the cash flow occurs at the end of the year.

In this version of the problem we assume that the term structure of interest rates is governed by a short rate lattice. The initial short rate is 4%, and the lattice is a simple up–down model with $u' = 1.1$ and $d' = .9$. The risk-neutral probabilities are given as .5. We shall use the small Δt approximation to assert that the result of the ratio theorem applies. Then since the gold price fluctuations and the short rate fluctuations are independent of each other, we conclude that the risk-neutral probabilities are also independent. Hence the actual probabilities are irrelevant for pricing purposes.

We solve this problem by constructing a double lattice. Each node of this lattice represents a combination (g, r) of gold price g and short rate r. Each of these nodes is connected to four neighbor nodes with values $(ug, u'r)$, $(ug, d'r)$, $(dg, u'r)$, and $(dg, d'r)$. The risk-neutral probabilities of these arcs are just the product of the risk-

---

[2]Briefly: Let $\mathbf{Q}$ be the 2×2 matrix with components $[q_{ij}]$. Then the invariance condition says that $\mathbf{Q}$ is singular, which means $\mathbf{Q} = \mathbf{a}\mathbf{b}^T$ for some 2×1 vectors $\mathbf{a}$, $\mathbf{b}$. Normalization makes both of these vectors have components that sum to 1; and these define the individual probabilities.

neutral probabilities for movement in the two elementary lattices. For interest rates, these are each .5. For gold, the probability of an up move is $q_u = (1 + r - d)/(u - d)$, where r is the (current) short rate. Hence the four probabilities for the double lattice, corresponding to arcs leading to the nodes listed, are $q_{11} = .5q_u$, $q_{12} = .5q_u$, $q_{21} = .5(1 - q_u)$, and $q_{22} = .5(1 - q_u)$.

The double lattice can be set up as a series of 10 two-dimensional arrays. Each array contains the possible (g, r) pairs for that period. The arrays are then linked by the risk-neutral pricing formula. This formula simply multiplies the values at each of the four successor nodes by their risk-neutral probabilities, adds those plus the cash flow for the end of the year, and discounts the sum using the current short rate. The values at time 10 are all zero. Figure 16.5 shows the values at the nodes for time periods 9 and 8.

The first column shows the possible g values and the first row shows the possible r values. The entries in the main arrays are the corresponding values (in millions of dollars) of the lease. A node in the period 8 array is found from four nodes in the period 9 array, as illustrated in the figure.

Working backward this way we find an array with just one node at period zero, having a value of $22.2551 million dollars.

Period 9

g	0.0155	0.0189	0.0231	0.0283	0.0346	0.0423	0.0517	0.0631	0.0772	0.0943	r
2063.91	18.355	18.293	18.217	18.126	18.016	17.883	17.724	17.532	17.304	17.033	
1547.93	13.274	13.229	13.174	13.108	13.029	12.933	12.817	12.679	12.514	12.318	
1160.95	9.463	9.431	9.392	9.345	9.288	9.220	9.137	9.039	8.921	8.781	
870.71	66.048	6.582	6.555	6.523	6.483	6.435	6.378	6.309	6.227	6.129	
653.03	4.461	4.446	4.428	4.406	4.379	4.347	4.308	4.261	4.206	4.140	
489.78	28.535	2.844	2.832	2.818	2.801	2.780	2.755	2.726	2.690	2.648	
367.33	1.648	1.642	**1.635**	**1.627**	1.617	1.605	1.591	1.574	1.553	1.529	
275.50	7.435	0.741	**0.738**	**0.734**	0.730	0.724	0.718	0.710	0.701	0.690	
206.62	0.065	0.065	0.065	0.064	0.064	0.064	0.063	0.062	0.061	0.061	
154.97	0	0	0	0	0	0	0	0	0	0	

Period 8

g	0.0172	0.0210	0.0257	0.0314	0.0384	0.0470	0.0574	0.0702	0.0857	r
1719.93	29.917	29.812	29.685	29.531	29.345	29.121	28.852	28.529	28.144	
1289.95	21.463	21.390	21.301	21.194	21.064	20.907	20.719	20.493	20.224	
967.46	32.925	15.073	15.013	14.941	14.853	14.747	14.619	14.466	14.283	
725.59	21.784	10.336	10.297	10.251	10.194	10.126	10.044	9.946	9.828	
544.20	14.492	6.782	6.760	6.733	6.701	6.661	6.613	6.555	6.486	
408.15	9.058	4.118	4.107	4.095	4.080	4.062	4.040	4.013	3.980	
306.11	4.123	2.119	**2.118**	2.117	2.115	2.113	2.110	2.106	2.100	
229.58	1.900	0.620	0.626	0.633	0.641	0.651	0.662	0.675	0.690	
172.19	0.025	0.026	0.026	0.027	0.028	0.030	0.031	0.033	0.035	

FIGURE 16.5   Arrays for two periods of the Simplico gold mine. Each node at period k has four successor nodes at period $k + 1$, as indicated by the corresponding shaded areas. Values are in millions of dollars.

16.6 INVESTMENTS WITH PRIVATE UNCERTAINTY

Suppose a project requires an initial cash outlay and will produce an uncertain cash flow at the end of one year. Suppose also that the uncertainty consists of both **private** uncertainty and **market** uncertainty. Basically, market uncertainty can be replicated with market participation, whereas private uncertainty cannot. For example, the cash flow of a gold mine lease depends both on the market uncertainty of gold prices and on the private uncertainty of how much gold is in the yet unexplored veins.

One way to assign a value to such a project is to make believe that the project value is a price, and then set the price so that you would be indifferent between either purchasing a small portion of the project or not. This is termed **zero-level pricing** since you will purchase the project at zero level. Of course, it is assumed that you have the option to purchase other assets, including at least a risk-free security with total return R.

If there is only private uncertainty the zero-level price is just the discounted expected value of the project (using actual probabilities). It cannot be priced any lower, for then you would want to purchase a small amount of it. Likewise, it cannot be priced any higher, or you would want to sell (short) some of it. The value is therefore

$$V = c_0 + \frac{1}{R}E(c_1)$$

where c_0 and c_1 are the initial and final cash flows, respectively.

Notice that this is somewhat different than the formula for the price of market assets. Market assets already have prices, and you will likely want to include them in your portfolio at a nonzero level (either long or short).

Example 16.5 (When to cut a tree)   Suppose that we can grow trees (for lumber). The trees grow randomly, and the cash flows associated with harvest after 1 year or after 2 years are shown by the (diagram) tree on the left side of Figure 16.6. Each arc of the tree has a probability of .5. The uncertainty is private because the tree growth depends only on local weather conditions and is not related to market variables.

The initial cash flow of -1 must be paid to carry out the project. The cash flow figures shown at the end of the period are those that will be received if the trees are cut after 1 year. Likewise, the final values shown are the cash flows that will be received

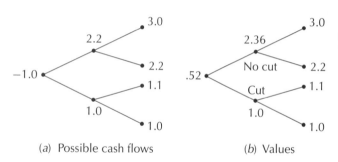

(a) Possible cash flows   (b) Values

FIGURE 16.6   **When to cut a tree.** (a) Cash flow generated at a node if the trees are cut at that point. (b) Value at a node and best policy.

if the trees are not cut until after 2 years. We wish to evaluate this project, assuming that the interest rate is constant at 10%. To do so we will need to determine the best strategy for cutting the trees.

We use the zero-level pricing method, and since there is more than one period, we work backward in the usual fashion. The expected value of the top two nodes at the last time period is 2.6. Discounted by 10% this is a value of 2.36. Since this is higher than 2.2, this is the best value that can be attained if we arrive at the upper node after 1 year. We record this optimal value on the values diagram in Figure 16.6(*b*). We also place a notation near that node that we should not cut the trees if we arrive there. Likewise, the expected value of the bottom two nodes at the last time period is 1.05. Discounted, this is .95, which is less than 1.0, so we would assign 1.0 at the next backward node in the values diagram, and place a notation there that we should cut the trees if we arrive at that node. The expected value of these two optimal one-period values is .5(2.36 + 1.0) = 1.68, which discounted is 1.52. Hence the overall value is .52.

General Approach

The preceding result concerning zero-level pricing of projects with private uncertainty can be generalized to projects that are characterized as having both private uncertainty and market uncertainty. The private uncertainties include such things as unknown production efficiency (due to new production processes), uncertainty in resources (such as the amount of oil in an oil field), uncertainty of outcome (as in a research and development project), and a component of the price uncertainty of commodities for which there is no liquid market (such as the future price of an isolated piece of land). Market uncertainties are those associated with prices of traded commodities and other assets.

Formally, suppose that the states of the world are factored into two parts: a market component and a nonmarket (private) component. A general state (or node in the state graph) therefore can be written as (s_t^m, s_t^n) corresponding to the market and nonmarket components at time t. For simplicity (although it is not necessary) we assume that these two components are statistically independent.

From a given state there are various successor states. In the lattice framework we index the successor market states (which are nodes in the lattice) by i and the nonmarket nodes by j. The probability of the ith market node is p_i^m and the probability of the jth nonmarket node is p_j^n. Since the two components are independent, the probability of i and j together is $p_{ij} = p_i^m p_j^n$. We are now in the situation of a double tree or double lattice.

We also assume that the market portion of the system is complete in the sense that there is a set of securities that spans all market states. In this case we know that there are unique risk-neutral probabilities q_i for the market states.

If the prices are such that the project itself enters the optimal portfolio at zero level, U'_{ij} is independent of the index j, and by the ratio theorem of the previous section, the risk-neutral probabilities q_{ij} are independent. Hence q_{ij} has the form $q_{ij} = q_i^m p_j^n$, where q_i^m is the risk-neutral probability for the market state, and p_j^n is

TABLE 16.1
Oil Production Possibilities for the Initial
5 Years of Operation (in Thousands of
Barrels per 5-Year Period).

Oil produced	0	20	40	60	100
Probability	.3	.1	.2	.3	.1

the probability for the nonmarket state[3] (which is also the risk-neutral probability for that state).

Note that if there is no market component to a project, the project price (or value) is determined by its ordinary probabilities; that is, as the discounted expected value of its cash flows. At the other extreme, if the project has no private component, its price is determined by the risk-neutral market probabilities; that is, as the discounted risk-neutral expected value of its cash flows.

Here is a comprehensive example illustrating how these ideas can be used to evaluate a complex project. This example incorporates many of the concepts of this book and is worthy of careful study as an integrated review.

Example 16.6 (Rapido: a rapidly declining oil well)   You are considering the possibility of investing in an oil well venture. If successful, the well life is likely to be about 25 years. The geological formations and other data indicate that this might be a favorable site. Before any initial drilling, the best estimate of the initial flow from the well if it is drilled is expressed as a list of possibilities and their probabilities, as shown in Table 16.1. We shall take a period length of 5 years in our analysis (to keep the problem size small enough to fit across a page). There are five possible levels of oil flows for the first 5 years of operation, which are shown in the table.

The initial drilling cost is $220,000. After drilling, the initial flow can be estimated quite accurately, and a decision is then made as to whether to complete the well, making it ready for production. The completion cost is $500,000. If the well is completed, the oil flow will decline as the reservoir is depleted. This decline can be expressed as a random chance that at the end of each 5-year period the flow will fall to the next lower category with a probability of 30%. This is a very rapid rate of decline for an oil well, and hence the name "Rapido."

If the well is operated, the 5-year operating cost is $400,000 of fixed cost plus $5 per barrel in variable cost. All oil pumped from the well can be sold at the market price for crude oil, which is currently $16 per barrel. We wish to find a fair price for this oil well venture, which has market risk associated with the future price of oil and technical (private) risk associated with the uncertainty of oil production.

The technical uncertainty regarding production possibilities is summarized by the lattice shown in Figure 16.7.

Next we must specify the market structure. For simplicity, we assume that the interest rate is constant at 7% per year or, equivalently, 40% for each 5-year period. It

---

[3]The independence argument applies even if there are more than two states in each part of the double tree.

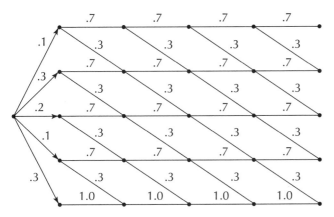

FIGURE 16.7 Technology of an oil well. There are five possible levels of initial flow, which correspond to the five nodes that are successors to the initial node. The specific successor will be determined by the results of drilling. Then after each subsequent 5-year period, the oil flow either remains the same (with probability .7) or decreases one level (with probability .3).

remains to specify the relevant aspects of the oil market. For this purpose we would first like an estimate of the volatility of oil prices. Such an estimate can be derived from a history of oil spot prices, but it is also possible to estimate the volatility directly from a single day's record of option prices. There are no options for spot oil, but we can use options on oil futures as a good substitute. A listing of these options is shown in the left table of Figure 16.8.

If we study the call options for August with strike prices of 1600 and 1700, we can use the Black–Scholes formula to solve for the implied volatility and the implied current futures price. This leads to an estimate of $\sigma = 21\%$ (see Exercise 7), and we may assume that this is also the volatility of spot oil. If we use the standard binomial lattice approximation, we then set the up factor for oil at $u = e^{\sigma \sqrt{\Delta t}} = e^{.21\sqrt{5}} = 1.60$ and the down factor $d = 1/1.60 = .625$. (It is a great stretch of imagination to

OIL

CRUDE OIL (NYM)

1,000 BBLS.; $ PER BBL.

Strike	Calls-Settle			Puts-Settle		
Price	Jun	Jly	Aug	Jun	Jly	Aug
1600	1.33	1.21	1.29	0.04	0.21	0.42
1650	0.86	0.86	0.97	0.10	0.36	0.59
1700	0.51	0.58	0.70	0.22	0.60	0.82
1750	0.25	0.40	0.50	0.46	0.90	....
1800	0.11	0.25	0.34	0.82	1.25	....
1850	0.04	0.16	0.24	....	....	....

Est vol 3,794 Wed 18,173 calls 8,785 puts

Op int Wed   211,586 calls 170,881 puts

METALS AND PETROLEUM

	Open	High	Low	Settle	Chg	Lifetime High	Low	Open Interest
CRUDE OIL, Light Sweet (NYM) 1,000 bbls.; $ per bbl.								
Jun	16.84	17.30	16.78	17.29	+ .43	21.35	14.02	124,032
July	na	17.02	16.60	17.00	+ .35	20.78	14.15	73,360
Aug	na	16.90	16.56	16.88	+ .30	20.78	14.35	34,123
Sept	na	16.81	16.57	16.83	+ .27	20.78	14.50	28,809
Dec	16.57	16.80	16.55	16.80	+ .23	21.25	14.93	28,690
Jun	16.90	16.87	16.87	16.96	+ .18	21.21	15.73	17,396
Dec	....	....	....	17.18	+ .16	20.80	16.50	10,793
Jun	17.40	17.58	17.40	17.43	+ .14	20.26	17.22	14,698
Dec	....	....	....	17.73	+ .13	20.40	17.53	19,072

FIGURE 16.8 Quotes of oil future options and oil futures, May 6, 1994. Volatility can be estimated from option prices. Risk-neutral probabilities can be determined directly from futures market prices. Source: *Wall Street Journal*, May 6, 1994.

consider $\Delta t = 5$ as "small"; however, we are treating this as a prototype model. A more complete model would use a smaller Δt.)

Now, usually, the next step would be to calculate the risk-neutral probabilities for this lattice using the formula $q_u = (R-d)/(u-d)$, giving $q_u = .80$, but this is *not* appropriate here. Oil has a significant storage cost; hence replication using oil would require paying storage costs. This will change the formula for risk-neutral probabilities. (See Section 13.9.) In fact, oil is generally not held as an investment, even though oil storage is possible, because the expected rate of return for doing so is not high enough to overcome the high storage costs. This tightness of the oil market is verified by the right side of Figure 16.8, which shows that the prices of oil futures contracts do not increase even as fast as the compounding of interest, as they would if markets were not tight. (See Section 10.3.) Indeed, we note that increasing the settlement date by $2\frac{1}{2}$ years only increases the futures price by a factor of $17.73/17.29 = 1.025$. This is equivalent to about 1% per year.

We can, however, use the futures price information to determine appropriate risk-neutral probabilities. Given a spot price of S, next period the price will be either Su or Sd according to our model. The current futures price for a contract that expires in 5 years will be about $F = 1.05S$. Since the current value of a futures contract is zero, and the payoff in 5 years will be either $Su - F$ or $Sd - F$, we must have

$$0 = q_u S(1.6 - 1.05) + q_d S(.62 - 1.05).$$

This yields

$$q_u = .44, \qquad q_d = .56.$$

These are the values that we can use for the risk-neutral probabilities for oil price states.

We are now ready to carry out the backward recursion to determine the zero-level price of the oil venture. At the final period, from $t = 20$ to $t = 25$, there are 25 possible states, corresponding to five oil flow components and five oil price components at that time. We think of these as being laid out in a 5 by 5 array. At the previous period there are the same five oil flow components and four oil price components, forming a 5 by 4 rectangle. This pattern progresses backward to period zero, just after completion of the well, where there is a 5 by 1 rectangle of states. Then, also at year 0, but before initial drilling, there is only a single node.

All of this is shown in Figure 16.9. To construct this figure the possible oil prices were first generated with a binomial lattice in the usual fashion, and these prices were laid out across the top row of the array according to the year in which they may occur. The possible flows were laid out down the last column of the array.

The backward calculation is a straightforward discounted expectation of cash flow and value. We assume for simplicity that all cash flow in a 5-year period occurs at the beginning of that period. Note that the final array consists only of profits from production in the last period. Earlier periods add current profit to a discounted risk-neutral expected value of the next period's value. For example, the top right-hand

	t = 0	t = 5		t = 10			t = 15				t = 20					
Price	16	10	25.6	6.25	16	41	3.91	10	25.6	65.5	2.44	6.25	16	41	105	Flow
	1,938	517	3,994	67	1,523	6,713	0	279	2,756	9,395	0	0	700	3,196	9,586	100
	860	167	2,061	14.2	651	3,735	0	61	1,398	5,418	0	0	260	1,758	5,591	60
	288	46.9	1,000	1.94	203	2,085	0	8.8	694	3,292	0	0	40	1,038	3,594	40
Total	34.8	3.98	153	0	18.1	618	0	0	82.2	1,251	0	0	0	319	1,597	20
31.7	0	0	0	0	0	0	0	0	0	0	0	0	0	0	0	0

FIGURE 16.9 Rapido oil well evaluation. The possible oil prices shown in the second row were generated by a binomial lattice, so the number of entries increases by one each period. There are five oil-flow possibilities each period. Backward evaluation is straightforward, once the proper risk-neutral probabilities are determined.

corner element in the array at $t = 15$ is

$$v = \text{flow} \times \text{oil price} - \text{cost} + \frac{1}{R} \text{ (risk-neutral value of next period)}$$

$$= 100 \times 65.5 - 400 - 5 \times 100 + \tfrac{1}{1.4}(.44 \times .7 \times 9586 + .44 \times .3 \times 5591$$

$$+.56 \times .7 \times 3196 + .56 \times .3 \times 1758)$$

$$= 9395 \text{ (accounting for rounding errors)}.$$

The overall zero-level price accounts for the option to either complete the well or not. The zero-level price is $31,700. Note how this rather complex problem is solved by a simple spreadsheet analysis—an analysis which, however, embodies a good deal of theory.

16.7 BUYING PRICE ANALYSIS

Frequently project opportunities arise in which investment must be either at a fixed positive level or at zero level, with nothing in between. An example is the opportunity to participate in a joint venture where each participant must subscribe to a fixed fraction of the project. Another is the prospect of taking on a project alone, such as the purchase of investment real estate. In such situations the zero-level price may not be the appropriate value, since the cash outlay required may represent a significant portion of one's investment capital.

A better concept of value in such situations is the **buying price.** The buying price is defined as the price that the investor would be willing to pay for participation in the project at the specified level. This price v_0 is best understood in terms of expected utility. We first calculate the expected utility that would be achieved without participation in the project. Then we calculate the expected utility that would be achieved with participation, including an additional initial payment of an amount v_0. The value of v_0 that makes these two expected utility values equal is the buying price. In other words, if v_0 is the price to be paid for the project, the investor is indifferent between having the project or not. This price is different than the zero-level price, which makes the investor indifferent between no participation and participation at a very small level.

Certainty Equivalent and Exponential Utility

The buying price of a project can be computed easily if it is assumed that the investor's utility function is of exponential form, $U(x) = -e^{-ax}$ for some $a > 0$. The computing procedure uses certainty equivalents rather than expected values.

Let us briefly review the certainty equivalent concept. Suppose that an investor has a utility function U. Suppose that X is a random variable describing the investor's wealth at the terminal point. Then the expected utility of this wealth is $E[U(X)]$. The certainty equivalent is the (nonrandom) amount $\bar{x}$ such that $U(\bar{x}) = E[U(X)]$. We often write $CE(X)$ for the certainty equivalent of X.

As a specific case suppose that $U(X) = -e^{-aX}$ and suppose that the random variable X has two possible outcomes X_1 and X_2 occurring with probabilities p_1 and p_2, respectively. The expected utility is

$$E\big[U(X)\big] = p_1 U(X_1) + p_2 U(X_2) = -p_1 e^{-aX_1} - p_2 e^{-aX_2}.$$

To find the certainty equivalent $\bar{x}$ we solve

$$e^{-a\bar{x}} = p_1 e^{-aX_1} + p_2 e^{-aX_2}.$$

Taking the logarithm of both sides, we obtain

$$CE(X) = \bar{x} = -\frac{1}{a}\ln\{p_1 e^{-aX_1} + p_2 e^{-aX_2}\}. \tag{16.11}$$

This may look complicated, but it has a very special and important property.

The special property of this form is that if a constant, say Δ, is added to a random variable, the certainty equivalent increases by this same constant. This property is often referred to as the **delta property.** Formally,

$$CE(X + \Delta) = CE(X) + \Delta$$

for any random variable X and any constant Δ. This property can be checked easily for the two-outcome case by referencing (16.11).

Here is a general proof for exponential utility. We have

$$E\left(e^{-aX}\right) = e^{-aCE(X)}.$$

Therefore,

$$E\left[e^{-a(X+\Delta)}\right] = e^{-a\Delta}\,E\left(e^{-aX}\right) = e^{-a\Delta}e^{-aCE(X)} = e^{-a[CE(X)+\Delta]}.$$

This says that

$$CE(X + \Delta) = CE(X) + \Delta.$$

This delta property only holds for utility functions that are exponential or linear.

 Delta property   *A utility function is linear or exponential if and only if for all random variables X and all constants Δ, the certainty equivalent satisfies*

$$CE(X + \Delta) = CE(X) + \Delta.$$

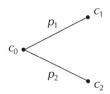

FIGURE 16.10 Simple project. This project has initial cash flow c_0, followed at the end of the period by a cash flow of value either c_1 or c_2.

Sequential Calculation of CE

Consider a one-period project having an initial known cash flow c_0 followed at the end of the period by a random cash flow that takes one of the values c_1 or c_2 with probabilities p_1 and p_2, respectively. There is also a risk-free asset with return R. This project is illustrated in Figure 16.10.

Assume that the investor has initial wealth X_0 and uses an exponential utility on final wealth. Risk-free borrowing or lending is used to transfer any cash flow at the initial time to a cash flow at the final time. If the project is not taken, then the final utility value will be $U(RX_0)$ since the initial wealth is transformed by the risk-free return.

If the project is taken at a price v_0, the expected utility of final wealth will be

$$p_1 U\{[c_1 + R(X_0 + c_0 - v_0)]\} + p_2 U\{[c_2 + R(X_0 + c_0 - v_0)]\}.$$

When the price v_0 is set correctly, the expected utility with the project will equal the value without the project; namely, $U(RX_0)$. Setting the certainty equivalents of these two equal to each other, we obtain[4]

$$\text{CE}[c_1 + R(x_0 + c_0 - v_0), c_2 + R(x_0 + c_0 - v_0)] = RX_0.$$

Note that both terms on the left contain $R(X_0 + c_0 - v_0)$. This is a constant, and by the delta property it can be taken out of the CE expression. We therefore obtain

$$\text{CE}[c_1, c_2] + R(X_0 + c_0 - v_0) = RX_0.$$

Solving for v_0, we obtain an expression for the buying price,

$$v_0 = c_0 + \frac{1}{R}\text{CE}[c_1, c_2]. \tag{16.12}$$

Note that this equation looks just like a net present value formula. The certainty equivalent is used to summarize the cash flow at the end of the period.

Multiperiod Case

The preceding technique extends to cash flow processes defined over several periods, but the risk aversion coefficient of the utility function must be adjusted each period.

---

[4] As a shorthand notation, if c_1 and c_2 are cash flows in two final states, we write $\text{CE}[c_1, c_2]$ for the corresponding certainty equivalent.

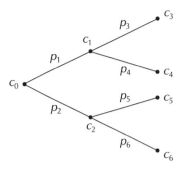

FIGURE 16.11   **Two-period project.** The buying price can be found by evaluating the certainty equivalent by a backward process.

Specifically, the risk aversion coefficient used to evaluate the certainty equivalent at time t must be aR^{T-t} instead of the original a. This reflects the fact that the effective utility function for money X received at time t is $U(R^{T-t}X)$ rather than $U(X)$ because X will be transformed to $R^{T-t}X$ at time T.

As an example of the full calculation, consider the two-period project shown in Figure 16.11. To evaluate this project we work backward in the usual fashion. First we calculate v_1 at the node where c_1 occurs by using the formula for the one-period case; namely, $v_1 = c_1 + (1/R)\text{CE}_2[c_3, c_4]$, where the subscript on CE denotes that the appropriate risk aversion coefficient at $t = 2$ (which is a) is used. Next v_2 is computed at the c_2 node in an analogous fashion as $v_2 = c_2 + (1/R)\text{CE}_2[c_5, c_6]$. Finally, we find

$$v_0 = c_0 + \frac{1}{R}\text{CE}_1[v_1, v_2]. \qquad (16.13)$$

This final certainty equivalent is computed with the risk aversion coefficient magnified by one period of interest, and with the probabilities p_1 and p_2 for v_1 and v_2, respectively.

Example 16.7 (When to cut a tree)   Consider again the tree-cutting example treated in the last section, but this time suppose that we are planning to purchase this project ourselves. We must buy the full project or none of it. The project cash flow possibilities are shown in Figure 16.12(a). Recall that the figures at the intermediate nodes are the cash flows that would be attained if the trees were cut there and the process terminated. Also, all arcs have probability .5.

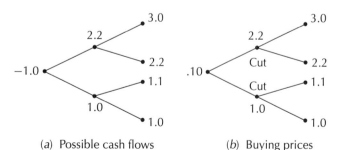

(a) Possible cash flows   (b) Buying prices

FIGURE 16.12   **Buying price for tree farm.** (a) Cash flow generated at a node if the trees are cut at that point. (b) Certainty equivalent at a node and best policy.

Assume that our utility function is $U(x) = -e^{-3x}$ and the interest rate is 10% per year, as in the earlier example. The first step is to calculate the certainty equivalent of the last two upper nodes. This certainty equivalent is

$$-\frac{1}{3}\ln[.5e^{-3\times3.0} + .5e^{-3\times2.2}] = 2.4.$$

When discounted one period, this becomes 2.18. Since this is less than the 2.2 value that would be achieved by cutting the trees at that point, we decide to cut, and we assign the buying price of 2.2 to that node. The node below that also retains the value of 1.0, since it is clear that the discounted certainty equivalent of the lower last phase is less than 1.

Finally, we calculate the buying price at the first node. To calculate the certainty equivalent, we must change the risk aversion coefficient from a to aR, or in this case from 3 to 3.3. Accordingly, the proper utility function for this period is $U(x) = -e^{-3.3x}$. Hence the certainty equivalent of the middle two nodes is

$$-\frac{1}{3.3}\ln[.5e^{-3.3\times2.2} + .5e^{-3.3\times1.0}] = 1.21.$$

Discounting this and accounting for the original cash flow, we find $v_0 = .10$. This is quite a bit lower than the zero-level price of .52 found in the last section. The price must be lower to induce us to purchase the entire project rather than just a small fraction of it.

General Approach

Suppose now that states of the world can be factored into independent market and nonmarket components. A general state at time t is written as in the last section as (s_t^m, s_t^n), corresponding to the market and nonmarket components. We also assume that the market portion of the system is complete; that is, there is a complete set of assets that span all dimensions of the market. In that case we know that there are unique risk-neutral probabilities q_i for the market states.

We assume that the investor has an exponential utility function for final wealth. The project has cash flows specified at each node.

To find the buying price, we proceed recursively, starting at the final time. At the final time the buying price at any node is equal to the cash flow at that node. At any other (previous) node (s_t^m, s_t^n) of the backward process, two calculation steps are required. First, for each fixed market successor i, we compute the certainty equivalent with respect to the nonmarket components j. That is, we find the certainty equivalent CE_i such that $U(R^{T-t}CE_i) = \sum_j p_j^n U(R^{T-t}v_{ij})$, where v_{ij} is the buying price of the successor node ij. Then we find the new buying price from

$$v_t^{m,n} = c_t^{m,n} + \frac{1}{R}\sum_i q_i\, CE_i.$$

In other words, we use certainty equivalent calculation on the nonmarket component and risk-neutral pricing on the market component.

Example 16.8 (Rapido oil well)   We can analyze the Rapido oil well using a certainty equivalent analysis. Only a few modifications to the earlier zero-level price analysis are required. We assume that a single investor is planning to finance the entire project. This investor has a utility function $U(X) = -e^{-X/10,000}$, where X is in thousands of dollars. This is realistic for an investor having a net worth of about $10 million (20 years from now).

In order to find the buying price, we simply change the risk-neutral discounting formula to one that is a mixture of risk-neutral pricing of the market state (the oil price) and a certainty equivalent of the technical factors (the flow level). We must remember to update the effective utility function by the factor of $R = 1.4$ in the exponent each period. The results are shown in Figure 16.13.

The final array, at $t = 20$, is identical to that of the earlier example, since that array contains final cash flows. The upper right-hand corner element of the array at $t = 15$ is evaluated as

$$v = \text{flow} \times \text{oil price} - \text{cost}$$

$$+ \frac{1}{R}\left[q_u\text{CE}(9586, 5591) + q_d\text{CE}(3196, 1758)\right].$$

We have

$$\text{CE}(9586, 5591) = -10,000 \times \ln\left[.7e^{-.9586} + .3e^{-.5591}\right] = 8211$$

$$\text{CE}(3196, 1758) = -10,000 \times \ln\left[.7e^{-.3196} + .3e^{-.1758}\right] = 2742.$$

Then using $q_u = .44$, and $q_d = .56$ from the earlier example, we obtain

$$v = 100 \times 65.5 - 400 - 5.100 + \frac{.44 \times 8211 + .56 \times 2742}{1.4}$$

$$= 9331.$$

Note that the initial buying price is negative, which indicates that the project is too big for this investor to take on alone. It is a good project, as shown by the zero-level analysis, but only when a smaller share is taken or a smaller risk aversion coefficient is used.

	$t = 0$	$t = 5$		$t = 10$			$t = 15$			$t = 20$					
Price	16	10	25.6	6.25	16	41	3.91	10	25.6	65.5	2.44	6.25	16	41	105	Flow
	1,900	512	3,926	66.8	1,514	6,624	0	278	2,748	9,331	0	0	700	3,196	9,586	100
	849	165	2,041	14.2	649	3,710	0	60.8	1,396	5,402	0	0	260	1,758	5,591	60
	281	46.7	985	1.94	201	2,063	0	8.79	692	3,276	0	0	40	1,038	3,594	40
Total	34.5	3.98	150	0	18.1	610	0	0	81.9	1,242	0	0	0	319	1,597	20
−5	0	0	0	0	0	0	0	0	0	0	0	0	0	0	0	0

FIGURE 16.13   Certainty equivalent analysis of Rapido oil well. A complex problem is treated by a single spreadsheet model. Vertical pairs are combined by certainty equivalents, and horizontal pairs of these are combined by risk-neutral probabilities.

16.8 CONTINUOUS-TIME EVALUATION*

The principles of evaluation discussed in this chapter can be applied to problems formulated in continuous time as well as in discrete time. The evaluation equations are more compact and the results are neater in continuous time. However, implementation in a form for actual computation is likely to involve approximation. The underlying framework is analogous to the description of an underlying state graph used in discrete time, as described in Section 16.1, but involves rather advanced probability theory. With only a slight loss of rigor we can present the main results.

The Risk-Neutral World

As a simple case consider a single stock whose price is governed by the Ito equation

$$dS = \mu(S, t)\, dt + \sigma(S, t)\, dz$$

where z is a standardized Wiener process. Suppose also that there is a constant interest rate r. To price a security that is a derivative of the stock price it is useful to have the risk-neutral probability structure. This is given by

$$dS = rS\, dt + \sigma(S, t)\, d\hat{z}$$

where $\hat{z}$ is again a standardized Wiener process. In other words, we just change the factor $\mu(S, t)$ to rS. This result was proved for the case $\sigma(S, t) = \sigma S$ in Section 13.4.

This single-asset result extends nicely to the case of several asset price processes. For notational simplicity we state the result for just two underlying assets.

General risk-neutral world result   *Suppose two assets have prices S_1 and S_2 governed by*

$$dS_1 = \mu_1(S_1, S_2, t)\, dt + \sigma_{11}(S_1, S_2, t)\, dz_1 + \sigma_{12}(S_1, S_2, t)\, dz_2 \quad (16.14)$$

$$dS_2 = \mu_2(S_1, S_2, t)\, dt + \sigma_{21}(S_1, S_2, t)\, dz_1 + \sigma_{22}(S_1, S_2, t)\, dz_2 \quad (16.15)$$

where z_1 and z_2 are independent standardized Wiener processes. Suppose the risk-free rate is r. Then the risk-neutral world generated by these assets is defined by

$$dS_1 = rS_1\, dt + \sigma_{11}(S_1, S_2, t)\, d\hat{z}_1 + \sigma_{12}(S_1, S_2, t)\, d\hat{z}_2 \quad (16.16)$$

$$dS_2 = rS_2\, dt + \sigma_{21}(S_1, S_2, t)\, d\hat{z}_1 + \sigma_{22}(S_1, S_2, t)\, d\hat{z}_2, \quad (16.17)$$

where again $\hat{z}_1$ and $\hat{z}_2$ are independent standardized Wiener processes.

Suppose that S is the price of any derivative of the two assets; and suppose that this derivative has cash flow process $\delta(S_1, S_2, t)$ and final value $S(S_1, S_2, T)$. Then the price of the derivative asset at any time $t < T$ is

$$S(t) = \hat{E}_t \left[\int_t^T e^{-ru} \delta(S_1, S_2, u)\, du + e^{-r(T-t)} S(S_1, S_2, T) \right]$$

where $\hat{E}_t$ denotes expectation with respect to the risk-neutral world as seen at time t.

Proof: In essence, this result says that $S(t)$ is equal to the discounted risk-neutral expected value of all future cash flows. It is a powerful result because (in its generalization to n underlying assets) it applies broadly to any set of underlying securities. It is a general pricing result in the continuous-time framework.

The result can be inferred directly from the results concerning double lattices. Roughly, the proof is this: If σ_{12} and σ_{21} are both zero, the two original processes are independent. Then we know (by taking $\Delta t \to 0$ in a double lattice) that the resulting risk-neutral processes are also independent. Hence we just apply the result for a single process twice. If $\sigma_{12} = \sigma_{21}$ are not zero, then a linear change of variables can be found so that the two new processes, say S_1' and S_2', are independent. We apply the result to these two independent processes. The drift coefficient for both of these will be r in the risk-neutral world. Then we transform back to the original variables. These original variables will also have drift coefficient r because both of the transformed variables have this coefficient. ∎

In other words, as in the case of a single security, we just change the drift terms from $\mu_i(S_1, S_2, t)$ to rS_i. The result generalizes in the obvious way to many assets.

Interest Rate Processes

The preceding result can be extended to the case where interest rates are themselves stochastic. Suppose, in particular, that pricing of interest rate derivatives is based on the risk-neutral short rate process

$$dr = \mu(r, t)\, dt + \sigma(r, t)\, d\hat{z}_0 \tag{16.18}$$

where $\hat{z}_0$ is a standardized Wiener process, which is independent of the processes in (16.14). Then the risk-neutral world is found by simply appending (16.18) to the system (16.16) using the process r as the interest rate in the security price equations.

For a security that is derivative to S_1, S_2, and r the pricing equation is as follows:

General pricing equation *A derivative security with cash flow process δ and final value $S(T)$ has a value determined by the risk-neutral pricing equation*

$$S(t) = \hat{E}_t \left\{ \int_t^T \exp\left[\int_t^s -r(u)\, du \right] \delta \, ds + \exp\left[\int_t^T -r(u)\, du \right] S(S_1, S_2, T) \right\}.$$

Example 16.9 (The Continuco gold mine) The Continuco gold mine is operated continuously. It can extract gold at a rate of up to 10,000 ounces per year with an operating cost of \$200 per ounce. The price of gold is governed by the standard geometric Brownian motion process

$$dg = .14g\, dt + .25g\, dz$$

with initial value $g_0 = \$400$. Interest rates are determined by a risk-neutral process for the short rate, which has the Ho–Lee form

$$dr = .005\, dt + .01\, d\hat{z}_0$$

with initial value $r_0 = .04$. Interest rate fluctuations are independent of gold price fluctuations. What is the value of a 10-year lease of the Continuco mine?

One way to solve this problem is by simulation, using the processes of the risk-neutral world. We would simulate the equations

$$dg = rg\, dt + .25g\, d\hat{z}$$

$$dr = .005\, dt + .01\, d\hat{z}_0$$

with $g_0 = 400$ and $r_0 = .04$, using two independent random number generators for $\Delta\hat{z}$ and $\Delta\hat{z}_0$.

After a forward run of a particular simulation, the corresponding cash flow stream is evaluated by a *backward* simulation (which, however, is not stochastic). The appropriate backward simulation is

$$dS = rS\, dt - c\, dt \tag{16.19}$$

with $S(T) = 0$. The cash flow c is

$$c = \max(g - 200, 0) \times 10{,}000.$$

The differential equation (16.19) is solved backward using the time paths of g and r found in the forward simulation run. The value of $S(0)$ obtained is one estimate of the value of the mine. A good overall estimate of the value is obtained by averaging many particular values found on different runs.

Note that the simulation equation (16.19) is equivalent to

$$S(t) = \int_t^T \exp\left(\int_t^s -r_u\, du\right) c\, ds.$$

Another way to solve the problem is to set up a lattice and use backward risk-neutral valuation. (See Exercise 10.)

16.9 SUMMARY

Evaluation of an investment opportunity reduces to the evaluation of its cash flow stream, but account must be made of the impact of this stream on an overall optimal portfolio. As a first step of analysis, a model of the cash flow process of the investment and its relation to other relevant assets must be developed. One general model is a graph with a number of states (or nodes) at each time point. There must be enough nodes to represent all important states.

Once this graph is established, it is possible to determine an optimal portfolio, which maximizes the expected utility of final wealth. This optimal portfolio implies a set of risk-neutral probabilities that can be used to value a new asset whose cash flow stream can be represented within the same graph. The price obtained this way is the price at which an investor with the given utility function would be indifferent between including the asset or not. It is a zero-level price.

The construction of a graph to represent a group of assets can be a challenge. One approach is to start with binomial lattice representations of each asset separately, and combine them into a double, triple, or multilattice in such a way as to capture the covariance structure of the assets. This method is straightforward and has some useful theoretical properties, but it can lead to high-dimensional structures. At every period, the combined lattice will have more states than there are securities, so risk-neutral probabilities are generally not unique. Those probabilities are unique, however, if Δt is small. Once the risk-neutral probabilities are determined, the price of a security can be found by the backward process of discounted risk-neutral valuation.

Private uncertainty is treated differently from market uncertainty because there are no associated market prices. Usually this means that the actual private probabilities should be used just like risk-neutral probabilities to determine the zero-level price of an asset.

The buying price of a project or asset is the price that an investor would pay to accept the project or asset in full (or a specified portion of it). This price depends on the investor's utility function and is usually lower than the zero-level price. If the utility function for final wealth is exponential, a backward evaluation process can be used to find the buying price. This procedure uses certainty equivalents to evaluate private uncertainty and risk-neutral prices to evaluate market uncertainties. This is because the private uncertainty cannot be hedged, but the market uncertainty can.

Almost all of these valuation ideas can be applied to continuous-time models, and the formulation is more compact. However, computational techniques usually involve approximation by discrete-time models.

EXERCISES

1. **(A state tree)**   A certain underlying state graph is a tree where each node has three successor nodes, indexed a, b, c. There are two assets defined on this tree which pay no dividends except at the terminal time T. At a certain period it is known that the prices of the two assets are multiplied by factors, depending on the successor node. These factors are shown in Table 16.2.

TABLE 16.2

		a	b	c
Security	1	1.2	1.0	0.8
	2	1.2	1.3	1.4

(a) Is there a short-term riskless asset for this period?
(b) Is it possible to construct an arbitrage?

2. (Node separation) Consider a short rate binomial lattice where the risk-free rate at $t = 0$ is 10%. At $t = 1$ the rate is either 10% (for the upper node) or 0% (for the lower node). Trace out the growth of $1 invested risk free at $t = 0$ and rolled over at $t = 1$ for one more period. The values obtained at $t = 1$ and $t = 2$ correspond to R_{01} and R_{02}. Show that these factors cannot be represented on a binomial lattice, but rather a full tree is required. Draw the tree.

3. (Bond valuation) Assuming the short rate process of Exercise 2 and risk-neutral probabilities of .5, consider a zero-coupon bond that pays $1 at time $t = 2$. Find the value at time $t = 0$ of this bond in two ways:

(a) Using the short rate lattice and equation (16.1).
(b) Using the tree for R_{0s} and equation (16.2).

4. (Optimal option valuation ⊕) Find the values of the 5-month call option of Example 16.2 using the same trinomial lattice used in that example but employing the utility function $U(x) = \sqrt{x}$. What is α?

5. (Gold correlation) Suppose that in the double stochastic Simplico gold mine example the real probability of an up move in gold is .6 and the real probability of an up move in the short rate is .7. Suppose also that gold price and short rate fluctuations have a correlation coefficient of $-.4$. Find the appropriate q_{ij}'s.

6. (Complexico mine ⊕) Use the information about the Complexico mine of Example 12.8, Chapter 12, but assume that gold prices and interest rates are governed by the models of Example 16.4. Find the value of the Complexico lease.

7. (Simultaneous solution) Calculate the volatility and the current price of oil futures implied by the call 1600 August and the call 1700 August of Figure 16.8 by using the Black–Scholes formula with $T = .25$.

8. (Default risk ⊕) A company issues a 10% coupon bond that matures in 5 years. However, this company is in trouble, and it is estimated that each year there is a probability of .1 that it will default that year. (Once it defaults, no further coupons or principal are paid.) What is the value of the bond?

(a) Assume the term structure of interest is flat at 10%.
(b) Assume that the short rate is currently 10% and the the short rate is multiplied by either 1.2 or .9 each year with risk-neutral probabilities of .5. Default risk is independent of the interest rate.

9. (Automobile choice) Mr. Smith wants to buy a car and is deciding between brands A and B. Car A costs $20,000, and Mr. Smith estimates that at the rate he drives he will sell it after 2 years and buy another of the same type for the same price. The resale price will be either $10,000 or $5,000, each with probability .5, at the end of each 2-year period. Car B costs $35,000 and will be sold after 4 years with an estimated resale price of either $12,000 or $8,000, each with probability .5. The yearly maintenance costs of the two cars are constant each year and identical for the two cars. Mr. Smith has an exponential utility function with risk aversion coefficient of about $a = 1/\$1,000$ now. Real interest is constant at 5%. Which car should he decide is better from an economic perspective over a 4-year period, and what is the certainty equivalent of the difference?

10. (Continuco mine simulation ⊕)   Evaluate the Continuco gold mine lease by simulation, using $\Delta t = .25$.

11. (Gavin's final)   Mr. Jones was considering a new grapefruit venture that would generate a random sequence of yearly cash flows. He asked his son, Gavin, "People tell me I should use a cost of capital figure to discount the stream. They say it's based on the CAPM. Have you given up on that? I haven't heard you talk about it for awhile."

Gavin replied, "Special conditions are required to justify it for more than one period. We had a complicated final exam question on it."

Consider a two year model. The risk-free rate for each is r. The (random) rates of return for the Markowitz portfolio in the two years are r_1 and r_2, respectively, and they are independent. There is a single random cash flow x_2 at the end of the second year. Denote by $x_{2|0}$ and $x_{2|1}$ the random variable x_2 given the information at times zero and one, respectively, and let E_0 and E_1 denote expectation at times zero and one. Likewise let V_0 and V_1 denote the value at time zero and one, respectively, of receiving x_2 at time 2. Assume that $E_0\{E_1[x_{2|1}]\} = E_0[x_{2|0}]$ and that $\mathrm{cov}[x_{2|1}/V_1, r_2]$ is independent of the information received at time one. Show that the value at time zero of receiving x_2 at time 2 is

$$V_0 = \frac{E_0[x_{2|0}]}{[1 + r + \beta_1(\bar{r}_1 - r)][1 + r + \beta_2(\bar{r}_2 - r)]}$$

where

$$\beta_1 = \mathrm{cov}[V_1/V_0, r_1]/\sigma_{r_1}^2.$$

Find V_1 and β_2.

REFERENCES

Much of the material in this chapter is relatively new. The overall structure of multiperiod investments is presented comprehensively in Duffie [1]. Construction of multivariable lattices has been approached in several ways. See for example [2–3]. The theory here was presented in [4]. The buying price analysis is adapted from Smith and Nau [5].

1. Duffie, D. (1996), *Dynamic Asset Pricing Theory,* 2nd ed., Princeton University Press, NJ.
2. Boyle, P. P., J. Evnine, and S. Gibbs (1989), "Numerical Evaluation of Multivariate Contingent Claims," *Review of Financial Studies,* **2,** 241–250.
3. He, H. (1990), "Convergence from Discrete- to Continuous-Time Contingent Claims Prices," *Review of Financial Studies,* **3,** 523–546.
4. Luenberger, D. G. (1996), "Double Trees for Investment Analysis," presented at the Conference on Computational Economics and Finance, Geneva, June.
5. Smith, J. E., and R. F. Nau (1995), "Valuing Risky Projects: Option Pricing Theory and Decision Analysis," *Management Science,* **41,** no. 5, 795–816.

Appendix A

BASIC PROBABILITY THEORY

A.1 GENERAL CONCEPTS

As discussed in Chapter 6, a random variable x is described by its **probability density function.** If x can take on only a finite number of values, say, $x_1, x_2, \ldots, x_m$, then the density function gives the probability of each of those outcome values. We may express the probability density function as $p(\xi)$, and it has nonzero values only at values of ξ equal to $x_1, x_2, \ldots, x_m$. Specifically,

$$p(x_i) = \text{prob}(x_i);$$

that is, $p(x_i)$ is the probability that x takes on the value x_i. We always have $p(\xi) \geq 0$ for all x. Also, $\sum_i p(x_i) = 1$.

If the random variable x can take on a continuum of values, such as all real numbers, then the probability density function $p(\xi)$ is also defined for all these values. The interpretation in this case is, roughly, that

$$p(\xi)\,d\xi = \text{prob}(\xi \leq x \leq \xi + d\xi).$$

The **probability distribution** of the random variable x is the function $F(\xi)$ defined as

$$F(\xi) = \text{prob}(x \leq \xi).$$

It follows that $F(-\infty) = 0$ and $F(\infty) = 1$. In the case of a continuum of values, if F is differentiable at ξ, then $dF(\xi)/d\xi = p(\xi)$.

Two random variables x and y are described by their **joint probability density** or **joint probability distribution.** The joint distribution is the function F defined as

$$F(\xi, \eta) = \text{prob}(x \leq \xi, y \leq \eta).$$

The joint density is defined in terms of derivatives, or if there are only a finite number of possible outcomes, the joint density at a pair x_i, y_j is $p(x_i, y_j)$ equal to the probability of that pair occurring. In general, n random variables are defined by their joint probability distribution defined with respect to n variables.

From a joint distribution the distribution of any one of the random variables can be easily recovered. For example, given the distribution $F(\xi, \eta)$ of x and y, the distribution of x is

$$F_x(\xi) = F(\xi, \infty).$$

The random variables x and y are **independent** if the density function factors into the form

$$p(\xi, \eta) = p_x(\xi) p_y(\eta).$$

This is the case for the pair of random variables defined as the outcomes on two fair tosses of a die. For example, the probability of obtaining the pair (3, 5) is $\frac{1}{6} \times \frac{1}{6}$.

The **expected value** of a random variable x with density function p is

$$E(x) = \int_{-\infty}^{\infty} \xi \, p(\xi) \, d\xi.$$

If $E(x)$ is denoted by $\bar{x}$, the **variance** of x is

$$\text{var}(x) = \int_{-\infty}^{\infty} (\xi - \bar{x})^2 p(\xi) \, d\xi.$$

Likewise the **covariance** of x and y is

$$\text{cov}(x, y) = \int_{-\infty}^{\infty} \int_{-\infty}^{\infty} (\xi - \bar{x})(\eta - \bar{y}) p(\xi, \eta) \, d\xi \, d\eta.$$

It is easy to show that if x and y are independent, then they have zero covariance.

A.2 NORMAL RANDOM VARIABLES

A random variable x is said to be **normal** or **Gaussian** if its probability density function is of the form

$$p(\xi) = \frac{1}{\sqrt{2\pi}\sigma} e^{-\frac{1}{2\sigma^2}(\xi - \mu)^2}.$$

In this case the expected value of x is $\bar{x} = \mu$ and the variance of x is σ^2. This density function is the characteristic "bell-shaped" curve, illustrated in Figure A.1.

A normal random variable is **normalized** or **standard** if $\bar{x} = 0$ and $\sigma^2 = 1$. Thus a standard normal random variable has the density function (written in terms of the variable x)

$$p(x) = \frac{1}{\sqrt{2\pi}} e^{-\frac{1}{2}x^2}.$$

The corresponding standard distribution is denoted by N and given by the expression

$$N(x) = \frac{1}{\sqrt{2\pi}} \int_{-\infty}^{x} e^{-\frac{1}{2}\xi^2} \, d\xi.$$

There is no analytic expression for $N(x)$, but because of its importance, tables of its values and analytic approximations are available.

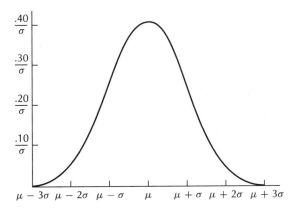

FIGURE A.1   Normal distribution. The expected value is μ and the variance is σ^2.

To work with more than one normal random variable it is convenient to use matrix notation. We let $\mathbf{x} = (x_1, x_2, \ldots, x_n)$ be a vector of n random variables. The expected value of this vector is the vector $\bar{\mathbf{x}}$, whose components are the expected values of the components of $\mathbf{x}$. The **covariance matrix** associated with $\mathbf{x}$ is the $n \times n$ matrix $\mathbf{Q}$ with components $[\mathbf{Q}]_{ij} = \mathrm{cov}(x_i, x_j)$. If $\mathbf{x}$ is regarded as a column vector and $\mathbf{x}^T$ is the corresponding row vector, then $\mathbf{Q}$ can be expressed as

$$\mathbf{Q} = \mathrm{E}[(\mathbf{x} - \bar{\mathbf{x}})(\mathbf{x} - \bar{\mathbf{x}})^T].$$

If the n variables are jointly normal, the distribution of $\mathbf{x}$ is

$$p(\mathbf{x}) = \frac{1}{(2\pi)^{n/2}|\mathbf{Q}|^{1/2}} e^{-\frac{1}{2}(\mathbf{x}-\bar{\mathbf{x}})^T \mathbf{Q}^{-1}(\mathbf{x}-\bar{\mathbf{x}})}.$$

If two jointly normal random variables are uncorrelated, then it is easy to see that the joint density function factors into a product of densities for the two separate variables. Hence if two jointly normal random variables are uncorrelated, they are independent.

A most important property of jointly normal random variables is the summation property. Specifically, if x and y are jointly normal, then all random variables of the form $\alpha x + \beta y$, where α and β are constants, are also normal. This result is easily extended to higher order sums. In fact if $\mathbf{x}$ is a column vector of jointly normal random variables and $\mathbf{T}$ is an $m \times n$ matrix, then the vector $\mathbf{Tx}$ is an m-dimensional vector of jointly normal random variables.

A.3 LOGNORMAL RANDOM VARIABLES

A random variable z is lognormal if the random variable $\ln z$ is normal. Equivalently, if x is normal, then $z = e^x$ is lognormal. In concrete terms this means that the density function for z has the form

$$p(\zeta) = \frac{1}{\sqrt{2\pi}\sigma\zeta} e^{-\frac{1}{2\sigma^2}(\ln \zeta - \nu)^2}.$$

We have the following values:

$$E(z) = e^{(v+\sigma^2/2)} \tag{A.1}$$

$$E(\ln z) = v \tag{A.2}$$

$$\mathrm{var}(z) = e^{(2v+\sigma^2)}(e^{\sigma^2} - 1) \tag{A.3}$$

$$\mathrm{var}(\ln z) = \sigma^2. \tag{A.4}$$

It follows from the summation result for jointly normal random variables that products and powers of jointly lognormal variables are again lognormal. For example, if u and v are lognormal, then $z = u^\alpha v^\beta$ is also lognormal.

Appendix B

CALCULUS AND OPTIMIZATION

This appendix reviews the essential elements of calculus and optimization mathematics used in the text.

B.1 FUNCTIONS

A function assigns a value that depends on its independent variables. Usually a function is denoted by a single letter, such as f. If the value of f depends on a single variable x, the corresponding function value is denoted by $f(x)$. An example is the function $f(x) = x^2 - 3x$. We can evaluate this function at $x = 2$ as $f(2) = 2^2 - 3 \times 2 = -2$. Although a function is most properly called by its name, such as f, it is sometimes convenient, and quite common, to refer to $f(x)$ as a function, even though $f(x)$ really is the value of f at x.

A function may be defined only for certain numerical values. In many cases, for example, a function is defined only for integer values, in which case the independent variable is usually denoted by i, j, k, m, or n. An example is the function $d(n) = 1/(1 + r)^n$, which is the discount function.

Functions of several variables are also important. For example, a function g may depend on two variables x and y, in which case the value of g at x and y is $g(x, y)$. An example is $g(x, y) = x^2 + 3xy - y^2$.

Certain types of functions are commonly used in investment science. These include:

1. **Exponential functions** An exponential function is a function of a single variable of the form

$$f(t) = ac^{bt}$$

where a, b, and c are constants. Very often the constant c is $e = 2.7182818\ldots$, the base of the natural logarithm.

The exponential function also arises when the variable is restricted to be an integer, such as the function $k(n) = (1+r)^n$, which shows how capital grows under compound interest. In this case the function is said to exhibit geometric growth, or to be a geometric growth function.

2. **Logarithmic functions**   The natural logarithm is the function denoted by ln, which satisfies the relation

$$e^{\ln(x)} = x.$$

Some important values are $\ln(1) = 0$, $\ln(e) = 1$, and $\ln(0) = -\infty$.

3. **Linear functions**   A linear function of a single variable x has the form $f(x) = ax$, where a is a constant. A function f of several variables $x_1, x_2, \ldots, x_n$ is linear if it has the form

$$f(x_1, x_2, \ldots, x_n) = a_1 x_1 + a_2 x_2 + \cdots + a_n x_n$$

for some constants $a_1, a_2, \ldots, a_n$.

4. **Inverse functions**   A function f has an inverse function g if for every x there holds $g(f(x)) = x$. Often the inverse function is denoted by f^{-1}.

   As an example consider the function $f(x) = x^2$. This function has the inverse $f^{-1}(y) = \sqrt{y}$. Clearly $f^{-1}(f(x)) = \sqrt{x^2} = x$. As another example, if f is the logarithmic function $f(x) = \ln(x)$, then the inverse function is $f^{-1}(y) = e^y$ because $e^{\ln(x)} = x$. It is also true that if g is the inverse of f, then f is the inverse of g. For example, we know that $\ln(e^x) = x$.

5. **Vector notation**   When working with several variables it is convenient to regard them as a vector and write, for example, $\mathbf{x} = (x_1, x_2, \ldots, x_n)$. We then write the value of a function of these variables as $f(\mathbf{x})$.

B.2 DIFFERENTIAL CALCULUS

It is assumed that the reader is familiar with differential calculus. We shall review a certain number of concepts that are used in the text.

1. **Limits**   Differential calculus is based on the notion of a limit of a function. If the function value $f(x)$ approaches the value L as x approaches x_0, we write

$$L = \lim_{x \to x_0} f(x).$$

An example is $\lim_{x \to \infty} 1/x = 0$.

2. **Derivatives**   Given a function f, the derivative of f at x is

$$\frac{df(x)}{dx} = \lim_{\Delta x \to 0} \frac{f(x + \Delta x) - f(x)}{\Delta x}.$$

Sometimes we write $f'(x)$ for the derivative of f at x. It is important to know these common derivatives:

(a) If $f(x) = x^n$, then $f'(x) = nx^{n-1}$.
(b) If $f(x) = e^{ax}$, then $f'(x) = ae^{ax}$.
(c) If $f(x) = \ln(x)$, then $f'(x) = 1/x$.

3. **Higher order derivatives**   Higher order derivatives are formed by taking derivatives of derivatives. For example, the second derivative of f is the derivative of the function f'. We denote the nth derivative of f by $d^n f/dx^n$. In the special case of the second derivative we often use the alternative notation f''.

   As an example, consider the function $f(x) = \ln(x)$. The first derivative is $f'(x) = 1/x$; the second derivative is $f''(x) = -1/x^2$.

4. **Partial derivatives**   A function of several variables can be differentiated partially with respect to each of its arguments. We define

$$\frac{\partial f(x_1, x_2, \ldots, x_n)}{\partial x_i} = \lim_{\Delta x \to 0} \frac{f(x_1, x_2, \ldots, x_i + \Delta x, x_{i+1}, \ldots, x_n) - f(x_1, x_2, \ldots, x_n)}{\Delta x}.$$

   For example, suppose $f(x, y) = x^2 + 3xy - y^2$. Then $\partial f(x, y)/\partial x = 2x + 3y$ and $\partial f(x, y)/\partial y = 3x - 2y$.

   We write the total differential of f as

$$df = \frac{\partial f}{\partial x_1} dx_1 + \frac{\partial f}{\partial x_2} dx_2 + \cdots + \frac{\partial f}{\partial x_n} dx_n.$$

5. **Approximation**   A function f can be approximated in a region near a given point x_0 by using its derivatives. The following two approximations are especially useful:

   (a) $f(x_0 + \Delta x) = f'(x_0)\Delta x + O(\Delta x)^2$
   (b) $f(x_0 + \Delta x) = f(x_0)\Delta x + \frac{1}{2}f''(x_0)(\Delta x)^2 + O(\Delta x)^3$

   where $O(\Delta x)^2$ and $O(\Delta x)^3$ denote terms of order $(\Delta x)^2$ and $(\Delta x)^3$, respectively. These approximations apply only to ordinary functions with well-defined derivatives. They do not apply to functions that contain Wiener processes. (See Chapter 11.)

B.3 OPTIMIZATION

Optimization is a very useful tool for investment problems. This section reviews only the barest essentials; but these are sufficient for most of the work in the text.

1. **Necessary conditions**   A function f of a single variable x is said to have a maximum at a point x_0 if $f(x_0) \geq f(x)$ for all x. If the point x_0 is not at a boundary point of an interval over which f is defined, then if x_0 is a maximum point, it is necessary that the derivative of f be zero at x_0; that is,

$$f'(x_0) = 0.$$

   This equation can be used to find the maximum point x_0.

   For example, consider the function $f(x) = -x^2 + 12x$. To find the maximum, we set the derivative equal to zero to obtain the equation $-2x + 12 = 0$. This has solution $x = 6$, which is the maximum point.

   A similar result holds when the function f depends on several variables. At a maximum point (with none of the variables at a boundary point) each of the partial derivatives of f must be zero. In other words, at the maximum point,

$$\frac{\partial f(x_1, x_2, \ldots, x_n)}{\partial x_1} = 0$$

$$\frac{\partial f(x_1, x_2, \ldots, x_n)}{\partial x_2} = 0$$

$$\vdots$$

$$\frac{\partial f(x_1, x_2, \ldots, x_n)}{\partial x_2} = 0.$$

This is a system of n equations for the n unknowns $x_1, x_2, \ldots, x_n$.

2. **Lagrange multipliers**   Consider the problem of maximizing the function f of several variables when there is a constraint that the point x must satisfy the auxiliary condition $g(x_1, x_2, \ldots, x_n) = 0$. We say that we are looking for a solution to the following maximization problem:

$$\underset{\mathbf{x}}{\text{maximize}} \, f(x_1, x_2, \ldots, x_n)$$

$$\text{subject to } g(x_1, x_2, \ldots, x_n) = 0.$$

The condition for a maximum can be found by introducing a Lagrange multiplier λ. We form the Lagrangian

$$L = f(x_1, x_2, \ldots, x_n) - \lambda g(x_1, x_2, \ldots, x_n).$$

We can then treat this Lagrangian function as if it were unconstrained to find the necessary conditions for a maximum. Specifically, we set the partial derivatives of L with respect to each of the variables equal to zero. This gives a system of n equations, but there are now $n+1$ unknowns, consisting of $x_1, x_2, \ldots, x_n$ and λ. We obtain an additional equation from the original constraint $g(x_1, x_2, \ldots, x_n) = 0$. Therefore we have a system of $n + 1$ equations and $n + 1$ unknowns.

   If there are additional constraints, we define additional Lagrange multipliers—one for each constraint. For example, the problem

$$\underset{\mathbf{x}}{\text{maximize}} \, f(x_1, x_2, \ldots, x_n)$$

$$\text{subject to } g(x_1, x_2, \ldots, x_n) = 0$$

$$h(x_1, x_2, \ldots, x_n) = 0$$

can be solved by introducing the two Lagrange multipliers λ and μ. The Lagrangian is

$$L = f(x_1, x_2, \ldots, x_n) - \lambda g(x_1, x_2, \ldots, x_n) - \mu h(x_1, x_2, \ldots, x_n).$$

The partial derivatives of this Lagrangian are all set equal to zero, giving n equations. Two additional equations are obtained from the original constraints. Therefore there are $n + 2$ equations and $n + 2$ unknowns.

Some problems have inequality constraints of the form $g(x_1, x_2, \ldots, x_n) \leq 0$. If it is known that they are satisfied by strict inequality at the solution [with $g(x_1, x_2, \ldots, x_n) < 0$], then the constraint is not active and can be dropped from consideration; no Lagrange multiplier is needed. If it is known that the constraint is satisfied with equality at the solution, then a Lagrange multiplier can be introduced, as before. In this case the Lagrange multiplier is nonnegative (that is, $\lambda \geq 0$).

ANSWERS TO EXERCISES

T he answers to all odd-numbered exercises are given here.[1] If the exercise in-volves a proof, a very brief outline or hint is given.

CHAPTER 2

1. (*a*) $1,000; (*b*) $1,000,000.

3. (*a*) 3.04%; (*b*) 19.56%; (*c*) 19.25%.

5. PV = $4,682,460.

7. $x < 3.3$.

9. $6,948.

11. $NPV_1 = 29.88$ and $NPV_2 = 31.84$; hence recommend 2.
    $IRR_1 = 15.2\%$ and $IRR_2 = 12.4\%$; hence recommend 1.

13. (*b*) $c = .940$, $r = 6.4\%$.

15. No inflation applied: NPV = $-$435,000$; inflation applied: NPV = $89,000.

CHAPTER 3

1. $4,638.83.

3. (*a*) 95.13 years; (*b*) $40,746; (*c*) $38,387.

5. YTM < 9.366%.

7. The annual worths are $A_A = $6,449$ and $A_B = $7,845$.

9. 91.17.

11. $D = \dfrac{1+r}{r}$, $D_M = 1/r$.

13. $dP/d\lambda = -DP$.

15. $C = T^2$.

---

[1]Compilation of these answers was the result of a massive project by a number of devoted individuals. We do not guarantee that they are free from errors. Please report errors to the author.

CHAPTER 4

1. 7.5%.

3. $P = 65.9$.

5. (a) $f_{t_1, t_2} = [s(t_2)t_2 - s(t_1)t_1]/(t_2 - t_1)$; (c) $x(t) = x(0)e^{s(t)t}$.

7. $P = 37.64$.

9. $(1 + r)^i (1 + f_{i,j})^{j-i} = (1 + r)^j$ implies $(1 + f_{i,j})^{j-i} = (1 + r)^{j-i}$, which implies $f_{i,j} = r$.

11. PV $= 9.497$.

13. $x_1 \approx -13.835$, $x_2 \approx 30.995$.

15. $a_k = 1/(1 + r_{k-1})^2$, $b_k = 1/(1 + r_{k-1})$.

CHAPTER 5

1. Approximate: projects 1, 2, 5; optimal: projects 1, 2, 3.

3. NPV $= \$610,000$ achieved by projects 4, 5, 6, 7 or 1, 4, 5, 7.

5. 16 in lattice, 40 in tree.

7. Critical $d^* = \frac{1}{2}(\sqrt{5} - 1) \approx .618$. Values $r = .33$ and $r = .25$ give $d = .75$ and $d = .8$, so solutions are the same.

9. (b) PV $= \$366,740$; enhance 2 years, then normal.

11. Use hint and solve for S.

CHAPTER 6

1. $R = (2X_0 - X_1)/X_0$.

3. (a) $\alpha = 19/23$; (b) 13.7%; (c) 11.4%.

5. (a) $(1.5 \times 10^6 + .5u)/(10^6 + .5u)$; (b) 3 million units, 0 variance, 20% return.

7. (a) $\mathbf{w} = (.5, 0, .5)$; (b) $\mathbf{w} = \left(\frac{1}{3}, \frac{1}{6}, \frac{1}{2}\right)$; (c) $\mathbf{w} = (0, .5, .5)$.

9. $r = \left[\sum_{i=1}^{n}(1/A_i)\right]^{-1} - 1$.

CHAPTER 7

1. (a) $\bar{r} = .07 + .5\sigma$; (b) $\sigma = .64$, borrow \$1,000 and invest \$2,000; (c) \$1,182.

3. (a) $.1 \leq \bar{r}_M \leq .16$; (b) $.12 \leq \bar{r}_M \leq .16$.

5. $\beta_i = x_i \sigma_i^2 \left(\sum_{j=1}^{n} x_j \sigma_j^2\right)^{-1}$.

7. (a) $A = 1$; (b) $\alpha = \sigma_0^2/(\sigma_0^2 - \sigma_i^2)$; (c) zero-beta point is efficient but below MVP; (d) $\bar{r}_i = 10\%$.

9. The identities require simple algebra.

CHAPTER 8

1. (a) 11.44%; (b) $\sigma = 16.7\%$.

3. Normalized $\mathbf{v} = (.217, .263, .360, .153)$; eigenvalue $= 311.16$; principal component follows market well.

5. (a) $\sigma(\hat{\bar{r}}) = \sigma$; (b) $\sigma(\hat{\sigma}^2) = \sqrt{2}\sigma^2/\sqrt{n-1}$.

7. *Method:* Index half-monthly points by i. Let r_i and ρ_i be returns for full month and half month starting at i. Assume ρ_i's uncorrelated. Then $r_i = \rho_i + \rho_{i+1}$. Show that $\mathrm{cov}(r_i, r_{i+1}) = \frac{1}{2}\sigma^2$. Find error in $\hat{\bar{r}} = \frac{1}{24}\sum_{i=1}^{24} r_i$. Ignoring missing half-month terms at the ends of the year, the method gives same result as the ordinary method.

CHAPTER 9

1. $108,610.

3. $a(x)$.

5. $a = (A' - B')/[U(A') - U(B')]$, $b = [B'U(A') - A'U(B')]/[U(A') - U(B')]$.

7. $C = (3 + e)^2/16$, $e = 4\sqrt{C} - 3$.

9. $b' = b/W$.

11. $1,500.

13. From hint: $\bar{R}_i - R = cW[E(R_M, R_i) - \bar{R}_M R] = cW[\mathrm{cov}(R_M, R_i) + \bar{R}_M(\bar{R}_i - R)]$. This implies $\bar{R}_i - R = \gamma\, \mathrm{cov}(R_M, R_i)$ for some γ. Apply to R_M to solve for γ.

15. $P = E\left(\dfrac{d}{R^*}\right) = E\left(\dfrac{Rd}{RR^*}\right) = \dfrac{1}{R}E\left(\dfrac{Rd}{R^*}\right) = \dfrac{\hat{E}(d)}{R}$.

CHAPTER 10

1. $442.02.

3. 5%.

5. There is no cash flow at $t = 0$. At T the flow is $S/d(0, M) + \sum_{k=0}^{M-1} c(k)/d(k, M) - F$, which must be zero.

7. $-$100.34.

9. (a) $V_{i-1}(r_i) = 1 - d(i-1, i)$; (b) $V_0(r_i) = d(0, i-1) - d(0, i)$; (c) $1 - d(0, M)$.

11. (a) $3.971 million; (b) 8.64%.

13. $-131,250$ lb orange juice; $\sigma_{\mathrm{new}} = .714\sigma_{\mathrm{old}}$.

15. Short $163,200 Treasury futures.

17. Proof based on $\text{cov}(x, y^2) = E(xy^2) - E(xy)E(y) = 0$. Both $E(xy^2)$ and $E(y)$ are zero by symmetry.

CHAPTER 11

1. Assuming Δt small, $p = .65$, $u = 1.106$, $d = .905$; without small Δt approximation, $p = .64367$, $u = 1.11005$, $d = .90086$. Probabilities of nodes (from the top with small approximation) are .179, .384, .311, .111, .015.

3. (a) Use $(v_1 - v_2)^2 \geq 0$; (b) 15% and 9.54%; (c) arithmetic for simple interest, geometric for compound. Usually geometric is best.

5. $\text{var}(u) = e^{2\overline{w}+\sigma^2}(e^{\sigma^2} - 1)$.

7. $dG = (\frac{1}{2}a - \frac{1}{8}b^2)G\,dt + \frac{1}{2}bG\,dz$.

9. To first order both have expected value $S(t_{k+1}) = (1 + \mu\Delta t)S(t_k)$.

CHAPTER 12

1. Cost is nonnegative.

3. $Q = (S - K) - 0 + K = S$ if $S \geq K$. Likewise $Q = 0 - (K - S) + K = S$ if $S \leq K$.

5. $2.83 American, $2.51 European.

7. $C(S, T) \geq \max[0, S - KB(T)] \to S$ as $T \to \infty$. Clearly $C(S, T) \leq S$. Hence in the limit $C = S$.

9. $7.

11. Offer is close: low by about .3%.

13. Almost identical! One-month interval: $4.801; half-month: $4.796.

15. $6.73.

CHAPTER 13

1. $2.57.

3. $\sigma = .251$.

5. $C(63) = \$6.557$, $\Delta = .759$, $\Theta = 6.02$.

7. $\Gamma = \dfrac{\partial\Delta}{\partial S} = \dfrac{\partial N(d_1)}{\partial S} = N'(d_1)\dfrac{\partial d_1}{\partial S} = \dfrac{N'(d_1)}{S\sigma\sqrt{T}}$. For Θ use Γ and Exercise 6.

9. $a = -\text{cov}(x, y)/\text{var}(y)$.

11. (a) $.53; (b) $2.04.

13. $42.42 million.

CHAPTER 14

1. (a) 91.72; (b) 90.95.

3. Do backward evaluation on futures price lattice.

5. 6.00, 6.15, 6.29, 6.44, 6.59, 6.74, 6.89, 7.05, 7.19, 7.35 percent.

7. 7.67, 8.829, 9.799, 10.66, 11.3, 11.93 are a_0 through a_5.

9. $162,800.

11. $F(t) = r - \frac{1}{2}at + \frac{1}{6}\sigma^2 t^2$.

CHAPTER 15

1. $\gamma = \frac{1}{4}$.

3. $\max\left\{\frac{1}{2}\ln[2\alpha + (1 - \alpha)] + \frac{1}{2}\ln[\alpha/2 + (1 - \alpha)]\right\}$ gives $\alpha = \frac{1}{2}$.

5. (a) $\alpha_k = p_k - p_n r_n/r_k$ for $k < n$; (b) $\alpha_1 = \frac{5}{18}, \alpha_2 = 0, \alpha_3 = \frac{1}{18}$.

7. Dow Jones average outperforms Mr. Jones.

9. (a) Conditions are

$$E\left(\frac{r_i - r_f}{1 + r_0}\right) = 0, \text{ or } E(r_i P_0) - r_f E(P_0) = 0,$$

$$\text{or} \quad \text{cov}(r_i, P_0) + \bar{r}_i E(P_0) = 0,$$

$$\text{or} \quad \bar{r}_i - r_f = -\frac{\text{cov}(r_i, P_0)}{E(P_0)}.$$

(b) We have

$$(\mu_i - r_f)\Delta t = -\frac{\text{cov}\left[n_i\sqrt{\Delta t}, 1/(1 + \mu_0\Delta t + n_0\sqrt{\Delta t})\right]}{E[1/(1 + \mu_0\Delta t + n_0\sqrt{\Delta t})]}.$$

To first order $(\mu_i - r_f)\Delta t = \sigma_{i,0}\Delta t$.

CHAPTER 16

1. (a) Yes, use portfolio weights $\frac{1}{3}, \frac{2}{3}$ to get 1.2 risk free; (b) yes, use weights $-\frac{1}{2}, \frac{1}{2}$.

3. (a) and (b) $.8678.

5. $q_{11} = .1$, $q_{12} = .36$, $q_{21} = .4$, $q_{22} = .14$.

7. $S = 16.81, $\sigma = 20.6\%$.

9. Car B preferred by certainty equivalent difference of $370.74.

11. $V_1 = \dfrac{E(x_{2|1})}{1 + r + \beta_2(\bar{r}_2 - r)}$, $\beta_2 = \dfrac{\text{cov}(x_{2|1}/V_1, r_2)}{\sigma_{r_2}^2}$

INDEX